INSTRUMENTAL METHODS OF CHEMICAL ANALYSIS

Fifth Edition

Galen W. Ewing

Formerly Professor of Analytical Chemistry
Seton Hall University

McGraw-Hill Book Company

New York   St. Louis   San Francisco   Auckland   Bogota   Hamburg
London   Madrid   Mexico   Montreal   New Delhi
Panama   Paris   São Paulo   Singapore   Sydney   Tokyo   Toronto

INSTRUMENTAL METHODS OF CHEMICAL ANALYSIS
INTERNATIONAL EDITION

2 3 4 5 6 7 8 9 20 SEP 9 8 7

This book was set in Times Roman.
The editor was Stephen Zlotnick;
The production supervisor was Leroy A. Young.

Library of Congress Cataloging in Publication Data

Ewing, Galen Wood, date
    Instrumental methods of chemical analysis.

    Includes bibliographies and index.
    1. Instrumental analysis. I. Title.
QD79.15E95   1985   543'.08   84-12209
ISBN 0-07-019857-8

When ordering this title use ISBN 0-07-066277-0

CONTENTS

PREFACE

As in previous editions, the general objective of this book is to survey the theory and practice of modern analytical instrumentation. Emphasis is placed on the possibilities and limitations inherent in the various methods.

The text is planned for use in upper-level undergraduate or first-year graduate classes. To be most effective, this course should follow work in elementary quantitative analysis and a year of physics; it may follow or run concurrently with physical chemistry. The treatment is not highly mathematical, but elementary calculus is employed where needed.

It is always difficult to decide what to include and what to omit. The words "analytical" and "instrumental" are not amenable to objective definition. With respect to the former, H. A. Laitinen has written: "The vital point here is that if the research is aimed at methods of solution of a measurement problem, it is properly classified as analytical chemistry, whereas the interpretation of the results of the measurements infringes upon other fields of chemistry." [Editorial, *Anal. Chem.*, **1966**, *38*, 1441.] I have attempted to include just enough interpretive material to suggest the areas in which a method can be useful.

With respect to detailed coverage, I have tried to be led primarily by usefulness to chemistry students, with due consideration to their expected background. Thus it is assumed that the principles of the analytical balance have been treated in prior courses.

A treatment of photoacoustic spectroscopy has been added as a separate chapter, since its applications cannot be restricted to either the infrared or ultraviolet–visible spectral regions.

The chapter on electronic circuitry has been expanded to include material on analog-to-digital conversion and related techniques leading toward computer interfacing. The treatment of computers in analytical chemistry has been expanded considerably, with emphasis on the significance of the monumental increase in the incorporation of microprocessors in commercial instruments. Enough material is presented to give a picture of how these devices function, and their limitations.

As in previous editions, the electronics chapter is placed at the end of the book, and is cross-referenced in the text as needed. The instructor can easily introduce this material at the start of the course if desired.

The SI system of units is used throughout. Other conventional units that are still frequently encountered in the literature are defined and used occasionally in problems to give students practice in interconversion.

Mention of the products of individual manufacturers does not necessarily imply that I consider them superior to competing items. The aim is to describe instruments typical of their class or possessing some special features of interest, not to write a complete catalog of analytical apparatus.

I wish to express my sincere appreciation to my colleagues and students over the years, who have offered advice and pointed out shortcomings. Particular thanks go to the following individuals who have read the manuscript with care and provided most helpful critiques: Professors Richard J. Cook, Frank A. Guthrie, Arno Heyn, Joseph Jordan, and Edward H. Piepmeier. I am greatly indebted also to the personnel of instrument companies and distributors, too numerous to list, without whose cooperation the book could not be a success.

Some of the work on this edition was performed while I was visiting professor at Carleton College, and I wish to acknowledge the use of library and other facilities at Carleton during my very pleasant stay there.

Galen W. Ewing

INSTRUMENTAL METHODS
OF CHEMICAL ANALYSIS

INTRODUCTION

Analytical chemistry may be defined as the science and art of determining the composition of materials in terms of the elements or compounds contained in them. Historically, the development of analytical methods has followed closely the introduction of new measuring instruments. The first quantitative analyses were gravimetric, made possible by the invention of a precise balance. In the closing decades of the nineteenth century, the invention of the spectroscope brought with it an analytical approach that proved to be extremely fruitful. At first it could be applied only qualitatively, gravimetric and volumetric methods remaining for many years the only quantitative procedures available. Gradually a few colorimetric and turbidimetric methods were introduced. Then it was found that electrical measurements could be used to advantage to detect end points in titrations. Since about 1930, the rapid development of electronics has resulted in a major revolution in analytical instrumentation. Today the chemist, whether he calls himself an analytical specialist or not, must have a working knowledge of a dozen or so instrumental methods virtually unknown a generation ago.

Nearly any physical property characteristic of a particular element or compound can be made the basis of a method for its analytical determination. A quick summary of the topics included in this book will indicate the great variety of such methods. In successive chapters we will consider first a whole series of spectroscopic techniques involving the absorption or emission of radiant energy in all regions of the electromagnetic spectrum. Then we will turn to a survey of electrochemical methods, followed by a treatment of chromatography as applied to both gas and liquid phases. Chapters on thermometric and nuclear methods conclude the treatment of analytical disciplines.

In recent years, several techniques have evolved that combine two or more methods into one. These "hyphenated" techniques are described arbitrarily under one of the methods involved and cross-referenced under the others. One of the earliest of these hybrid areas to be developed involved the marriage of a mass spectrometer (MS) with a gas chromatograph (GC), hence is referred to as "GC/MS"; it is treated in Chap. 20.

Many features of analytical methods are similar or identical from one to another. To avoid excessive duplication, some of these are treated together in Chap. 26. Here will be found, for example, a discussion of the method of standard additions, which is a technique for the calibration of an analytical procedure that is used in several of the subject areas of earlier chapters.

Before proceeding to these substantive topics, some general remarks concerning the objectives of instrumentation and the means of attaining them are in order.

The fundamental task to be performed by an instrument is the translation of chemical information into a form that is directly observable by an operator. It does this by means of a *transducer*. This is a component whereby the information is caused to control or "modulate" an electric current. The succeeding electronic circuitry must then extract the information from the carrier current, amplify it if necessary, and display it on a readout device.

ELECTRONICS

Analytical instruments are usually designed to be as sensitive as practicable, so that they are able to measure precisely the smallest signal that can be produced by the transducer. Provision for logical or arithmetic processes, such as the automatic subtraction of a background, are frequently included in the electronics package.

In many methods it is necessary to apply some sort of stimulus to the system (a beam of radiation, for example), and this stimulus is often produced, measured, and regulated with the aid of additional electronic circuitry.

Because of these close relations with chemical instruments, the fundamentals of electronics form an integral part of any treatment of instrumentation. Fortunately, modern electronics has developed in the direction of modularization. A variety of amplifiers and logic elements are available as low-cost plug-in units that can be used as building blocks for the construction of most of the electronic circuitry described in this book.

A short summary of those aspects of electronics pertinent to our main subject is given in Chap. 27. This may be studied separately if desired, or used as resource material to aid in a better understanding of the various instruments as they are treated.

DEDICATED MICROCOMPUTERS

The most significant development in instrumentation during the last few years has been the introduction of the *microprocessor* as a versatile, general-purpose, electronic component. The term "microprocessor" designates a single integrated circuit, usually fabricated in a plastic package about 1 by 5 cm in size, with 40 contact pins. This forms the heart of an assembly of related smaller components that together constitute a *microcomputer*. The cost of these components has dropped to the point where the designer of any but the simplest instruments can include microcomputer control features for about the same cost as conventional electronics. The result is that the newer generation of instruments provide considerably greater flexibility and ease of operation than their predecessors, through automatic or semiautomatic control of instrumental parameters.

Through most of this book, little mention will be made of the computer features, not because they are unimportant, but rather because they are so similar from one type of instrument to another.

Many tasks that are given to the computer could also be done without it, given sufficient time, but there are some areas where the computer permits achieving results that would be practically impossible without its aid. For example, to follow the course of a fast chemical process, many hundreds of data points may be required in a few seconds of elapsed time, and for this a computer is essential. Several techniques require the mathematical transformation of data between time and frequency domains, a process that uses Fourier transforms. This can be done easily by a computer, but would be completely out of reach as an analytical tool without it.

In any case computer control is a great convenience, in that it relieves the operator from much of the tedium formerly associated with repetitious analytical procedures. It must always be kept in mind, however, that the computer cannot prevent errors in technique. The ease of reading the data put out by the computer can sometimes lead an inexperienced operator to a false confidence in his results, even though he may not have carried out the needed calibration checks and taken due care of other aspects of the analysis.

At the close of this book, a brief introduction will be given to the principles of interfacing analytical instruments to computers.

COMMERCIAL INSTRUMENTS

Typically, over the years, new principles of measurement have been developed in academic laboratories, and not necessarily by chemists. Only after working instruments have been constructed and their utility demonstrated, have instrument manufacturers stepped in. The manufacturer supplies much valuable engineering know-how, and may produce several models based on the same principle.

For an inclusive study of instrumentation, one must look not only at established instruments that are commercially available, but also at those that

Table 1-1 Selected SI units

The units listed below are abstracted from the complete tabulation in the Bureau of Standards Special Publication 330. Included are those that are likely to be of use to readers of this book, omitting those that are obvious extensions of some listed.

Quantity	Name	Symbol

Base units

Quantity	Name	Symbol
Length	meter	m
Mass	kilogram	kg
Time	second	s
Electric current	ampere	A
Temperature	kelvin	K
Amount of substance	mole	mol

Derived units

Quantity	Name	Symbol
Wave number	1 per meter	m^{-1}
Concentration	mole per cubic meter	mol/m^3
Frequency	hertz	$1/s$
Force	newton	$N = m \cdot kg \cdot s^{-2}$
Pressure	pascal	$Pa = N/m^2$
Energy	joule	$J = N \cdot m$
Power	watt	$W = J/s$
Electric charge	coulomb	$C = A \cdot s$
Electric potential	volt	$V = W/A$
Capacitance	farad	$F = C/V$
Resistance	ohm	$\Omega = V/A$
Conductance	siemens	$S = A/V$
Magnetic flux density	tesla	$T = V \cdot s/m^2$
Inductance	henry	$H = V \cdot s/A$

Optional units

Quantity	Name	Symbol
Volume	liter	$10^{-3} m^3$
Energy	electronvolt	eV (Note a)
Mass (atomic)	atomic mass unit	u (amu) (Note b)

Units permitted reluctantly or not at all

Quantity	Name	Symbol
Length	ångström	$Å = 10^{-10}$ m
Length	micron	$\mu = 10^{-6}$ m
Mass	gamma	$\gamma = 10^{-9}$ kg
Pressure	bar	$bar = 10^5$ Pa
Pressure	torr	$(101,325/760)$ Pa
Pressure	atmosphere	760 torr
Radioactivity	curie	Ci
Energy	erg	$erg = 10^{-7}$ J
Energy	calorie	4.184 J
Force	dyne	$dyne = 10^{-5}$ N
Magnetic field strength	gauss	10^{-4} T (Note c)
Volume	lambda	$\lambda = 10^{-9} m^3$

Notes: (a) An experimental unit; $1\ eV = 1.60219 \times 10^{-19}$ J, approximately. (b) An experimental unit; $1\ amu = 1.66057 \times 10^{-27}$ kg, approximately. (c) The gauss and tesla do not measure precisely the same quantity.

4

have yet to achieve this status. The latter are accessible only through reports published in the scientific literature. Both classes of instruments are treated in this book.

NOTE ON UNITS

Worldwide agreement on units and their symbols is of prime importance to science. A determined effort in this direction has been mounted by a number of international conferences with the cooperation of the National Bureau of Standards (NBS) in the United States and corresponding offices in other countries. This effort has resulted in the *Système International d'Unités* (International System of Units, abbreviated SI). The system is described in a booklet published by the NBS.†

In this book, SI units are used throughout. Where other units are still widely employed, this fact will be pointed out. The chief difference is the abandonment of such well-known units as the angstrom, micron, gauss, and torr. Table 1-1 lists those units of importance in our context. The standard prefixes for multiples and submultiples of units are listed in Appendix B.

BIBLIOGRAPHY

The student who wishes to pursue in greater depth any of the topics mentioned in this book has many avenues to which to turn. In addition to the references at the ends of chapters, and the general reference sources, such as *Chemical Abstracts*, many journals devoted to analytical chemistry are available.

General coverage of the analytical field is offered by *Analytical Chemistry*, *Analytica Chimica Acta*, *Talanta*, *The Analyst* (including *Analytical Abstracts*), the *Zeitschrift für analytische Chemie*, *CRC Critical Reviews in Analytical Chemistry*, and *Analytical Letters*, among others. In specific fields, one finds such journals as *Applied Spectroscopy*, *Analytical Biochemistry*, the *Journal of Electroanalytical Chemistry*, and the *Journal of Gas Chromatography*, to name only a few. With emphasis on instruments per se, one should consult the *Review of Scientific Instruments* and the *Journal of Scientific Instruments*.

On the theoretical side, the *Treatise on Analytical Chemistry*, edited by I. M. Kolthoff and P. J. Elving (Wiley-Interscience, New York) is invaluable, especially Part I, both first and second editions. Many of the volumes in the series *Physical Methods of Chemistry*, edited by A. Weissberger and B. W. Rossiter (Wiley-Interscience) present a wealth of information on analytical instrumentation.

† *The International System of Units (SI) 1981.* Available from the Superintendent of Documents, U.S. Government Printing Office, Washington, DC 20402; SD Catalog No. C 13.10:330/4; price $4.75.

The *Annual Reviews* issue of *Analytical Chemistry*, published each April, contains critical reviews in all fields of analysis; in even years the reviews are classed by the analytical principles involved, and in odd years by field of application.

An immense amount of useful information, with succinct reviews of theoretical principles, has been collected under the editorship of L. Meites in the *Handbook of Analytical Chemistry*, published by McGraw-Hill, New York, in 1963. In spite of its age, this remains one of the most useful sources of information to the analytical chemist.

TWO

INTRODUCTION TO OPTICAL METHODS

A major class of analytical methods is based on the interaction of electromagnetic radiant energy with matter. In the present chapter we shall review some of the pertinent properties, both of radiation and of matter, and then discuss those features of optical instrumentation that apply to all or several spectral regions. In subsequent chapters each major spectral region (visible, ultraviolet, infrared, x-ray, microwave) will be considered separately, with respect to theory, instrumentation, and chemical applications.

THE NATURE OF RADIANT ENERGY

An investigation into the properties of electromagnetic energy reveals an essential duality in our understanding of its nature. In some respects its properties are those of a wave, while in others it appears to consist of a series of discrete packets of energy, called *photons*. The photon concept is almost always required in the rigorous treatment of the interactions of radiation with matter, although the wave picture may be used to give approximately correct results when large numbers of photons are involved.

Radiant energy can be described in terms of a number of properties or parameters. The *frequency* v is the number of oscillations per unit time described by the electromagnetic wave; the usual unit of frequency is the *hertz* (1 Hz = 1 cycle per second). The *velocity* c of propagation is just over 2.9979×10^8 m·s^{-1} for radiation traveling through a vacuum, and somewhat less for passage through a transparent medium.

7

The wavelength λ is the distance between adjacent crests of the wave in a beam of radiation. It is given by the ratio of the velocity to the frequency. The units of wavelength are the *micrometer* (1 μm = 10^{-6} m; formerly called the *micron*, μ), and the *nanometer* (1 nm = 10^{-9}; formerly called the *millimicron*, mμ). The *angstrom* (1 Å = 10^{-10} m), although not sanctioned by the SI system, is widely used in spectroscopy. Another quantity which is often convenient is the *wave number* $\tilde{v}$, the number of waves per unit distance.† The unit most commonly used for wave number is the reciprocal centimeter (cm^{-1}), sometimes called the kaiser. Both wavelength and wave number are dependent on the refractive index of the medium through which the radiation is passing, whereas the frequency is independent of this property. We shall return to consideration of the refractive index in a later paragraph.

The velocity, wavelength, and wave number, *in vacuo*, are related to the frequency by the expression

$$v = \frac{c}{\lambda} = \tilde{v}c \tag{2-1}$$

The energy content E of a photon is directly proportional to the frequency

$$E = hv = \frac{hc}{\lambda} = hc\tilde{v} \tag{2-2}$$

where h is Planck's constant, approximately 6.6262×10^{-34} J·s. Thus there is an inverse relationship between energy content and wavelength, but a direct relation between energy and frequency or wave number. For this reason, many spectroscopists prefer to present spectra in terms of wave number rather than wavelength.

It is convenient, particularly with nuclear radiations and x-rays, to characterize the radiation by the energy content of its photons in *electronvolts* (eV); 1 eV = 1.6022×10^{-19} J, corresponding to a frequency of 2.4180×10^{14} Hz, or the (in vacuo) wavelength $\lambda = 1.2395 \times 10^{-6}$ m. The multiples kiloelectron volt (keV) and megaelectron volt (MeV) are often encountered.

In a representative spectroscopic instrument, a beam of radiation carries energy from its source through a medium or series of media to a receptor where it is absorbed. On its way from source to ultimate absorber, the beam may undergo partial absorption by the media through which it passes, and it may be changed in direction by reflection, refraction, or diffraction.

Since energy per unit time is power, one is often interested in the *radiant power* carried by the beam, a quantity often loosely referred to as "intensity." *Intensity* more correctly refers to the power emitted by the source per unit solid angle in a specified direction. A photoelectric cell gives a response related to the rate of

---

† It is unfortunate that the symbol $\tilde{v}$ has been chosen to represent the wave number, because of its likely confusion with v for frequency; indeed, in certain areas of physics it is customary to use these symbols in exactly the opposite sense. An expression such as "a frequency of 1600 wave numbers" though often found in the literature, is not strictly correct. Frequency may be *proportional* to wave number, but cannot be its equivalent, as the dimensions are unlike. Furthermore, a wave number is not a unit, so "1600 wave numbers" is no more correct than describing this page as "6 distances wide." It is correct to speak of a wave number of 1600 inverse centimeters, or 1600 reciprocal centimeters.

reception of photons, i.e., the incident power. A photographic plate, on the other hand, integrates the power over the time of exposure, and its response (silver deposit) is a function of the total number of photons received per unit area. In both photoelectric cells and photographic plates, as well as in the human eye, the sensitivity is a more or less complicated function of the wavelength.

SPECTRAL REGIONS

The spectrum of radiant energy is conveniently broken down into several regions, as shown in Table 2-1. The limits of these regions are determined by the practical limitations of appropriate experimental methods of production and detection of radiation. The figures in the table are not in themselves especially significant, and should be considered only as rough boundaries.

The differentiation of spectral regions has additional significance for the chemist in that the interactions of the radiations with chemical systems follow different mechanisms and provide different kinds of information. The most important atomic or molecular transitions pertinent to the successive regions are:

X-ray	K- and L-shell electrons
Far ultraviolet	Middle-shell electrons
Near ultraviolet	Valence electrons
Visible	Valence electrons
Near and mid infrared	Molecular vibrations
Far infrared	Molecular rotations and low-lying vibrations
Microwave	Molecular rotations
Radio waves	Nuclear magnetic resonance

The ultraviolet and infrared regions are often referred to by their abbreviations: UV and IR.

Table 2-1 Regions of the electromagnetic spectrum†

Designation	Wavelength limits		Frequency limits, Hz	Wave number limits, cm^{-1}
	Usual units	Meters		
X-rays	$10^{-2}-10^{2}$ Å	$10^{-12}-10^{-8}$	$10^{20}-10^{16}$	
Far ultraviolet	10–200 nm	$10^{-8}-2 \times 10^{-7}$	$10^{16}-10^{15}$	
Near ultraviolet	200–400 nm	$2 \times 10^{-7}-4.0 \times 10^{-7}$	$10^{15}-7.5 \times 10^{14}$	
Visible	400–750 nm	$4.0 \times 10^{-7}-7.5 \times 10^{-7}$	$7.5 \times 10^{14}-4.0 \times 10^{14}$	25,000–13,000
Near infrared‡	0.75–2.5 μm	$7.5 \times 10^{-7}-2.5 \times 10^{-6}$	$4.0 \times 10^{14}-1.2 \times 10^{14}$	13,000–4,000
Mid infrared‡	2.5–50 μm	$2.5 \times 10^{-6}-5.0 \times 10^{-5}$	$1.2 \times 10^{14}-6.0 \times 10^{12}$	4,000–200
Far infrared‡	50–1000 μm	$5.0 \times 10^{-5}-1 \times 10^{-3}$	$6 \times 10^{12}-10^{11}$	200–10
Microwaves	0.1–100 cm	$1 \times 10^{-3}-1$	$10^{11}-10^{8}$	$10-10^{-2}$
Radio waves	1–1000 m	$1-10^{3}$	$10^{8}-10^{5}$	

† Where a numerical factor is omitted, it is because the precision of delineation of the region does not warrant a greater number of significant figures.

‡ The limits for the subdivisions of the infrared follow the recommendations of the Triple Commission for Spectroscopy; *J. Opt. Soc. Am.*, **1962**, *52*, 476.

INTERACTIONS WITH MATTER

Electromagnetic radiation originates in the deceleration of electrically charged particles, primarily electrons, and can be absorbed by the reverse process, contributing its energy to accelerate particles. Hence an understanding of the interaction between matter and radiation must be built upon a knowledge of the electronic structure of atoms and molecules.

ATOMIC SPECTRA

Figure 2-1 shows a few of the energy levels of the outer electrons of the neutral sodium atom, in accordance with current theories. Under ordinary conditions, essentially all the atoms in a body of sodium vapor are in the ground state, that is, their valence electrons lie in the $3s$ level. If irradiated with a beam of energy including the wavelengths 589.00 and 589.59 nm, the outer electrons of many of the atoms will absorb photons and be accelerated to the $3p$ levels. (The two very close $3p$ levels differ only in their spin characteristics.) The excited electron has a

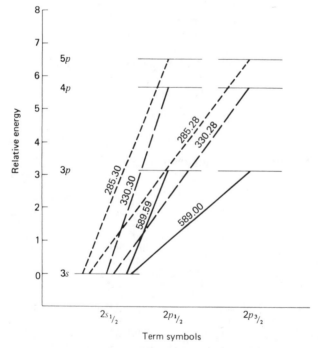

Figure 2-1 Partial energy-level diagram for the valence electron in the sodium atom. The "term symbols" are the quantum designations of the several energy levels. The numbers on the lines are the corresponding wavelengths, in nanometers.

strong tendency to return to its normal (3s) state, and in so doing emits a photon. This emitted photon possesses a definite amount of energy, dictated by the spacing of the energy levels. In the present example, the emitted radiation constitutes the familiar yellow light of the sodium flame or lamp. The radiation produced in this simple case, in which the outer electron is raised to an excited state and then returns to its previous level, is known as *resonance radiation*, or *resonance fluorescence*.

If the electron is given more energy, it may be raised to some higher level than 3p, such as 4p or 5p. In such a case it may not drop back to 3s by a single process, but may pause at intermediate levels, like a ball rolling down steps. This situation can be quite complex. For one thing, not all conceivable transitions are actually possible—some are "forbidden" by the selection rules of quantum mechanics.

With a highly energetic source of excitation, many electrons (not only the outermost) in any element can be excited to varying degrees, and the resulting emitted radiation may contain up to several thousand discrete and reproducible wavelengths, mostly in the UV and visible regions. This is the basis of the analytical method of *emission spectroscopy.*

If even more energy is available for excitation, an inner electron can be torn entirely away from its atom. An electron from some higher level will then drop in to fill the vacancy. The energy change corresponding to this inner orbital transition is much greater than in the case of excited outer electrons, and so the photons emitted will be of much greater frequency and correspondingly shorter wavelength. This describes the emission of x-rays from atoms subjected to bombardment by a beam of fast-moving electrons.

MOLECULAR SPECTRA

In a typical covalent molecule, as contrasted with an atom, the first few energy levels for outer electrons might show relations such as those of Fig. 2-2. The molecule to which this diagram applies has a singlet ground state designated S_0, which represents its normal, unexcited, condition. Also shown are two higher levels, S_1 and T_1, belonging respectively to the singlet and triplet series. (There are many other states in both series, not shown.) Each of these *electronic energy levels* has associated with it a subseries of levels $(v_1, v_2, \ldots)$ corresponding to quantized *vibrational energy states.*

When the molecule is irradiated with electromagnetic radiation, energy absorption can cause a transition to one of the higher levels. This can only occur if the incident photons contain the exact amount of energy associated with a transition from S_0 to a higher level or sublevel in the singlet series, designated in Fig. 2-2 as process I. If the transition terminates on an excited vibrational level, such, for example, as the v_3 sublevel within the S_1 electronic level, then the molecule immediately degrades to the parent S_1 level, the excess energy appearing as heat in the sample. This is shown in the figure as process II.

The excited molecule at level S_1 can lose its remaining excitation energy by any of three mechanisms. It can transfer its energy to some other chemical species

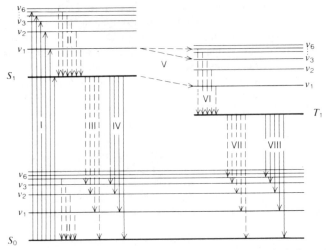

Figure 2-2 Energy-level diagram of a typical organic molecule, including only ground singlet, first excited singlet, and first excited triplet states. Solid vertical lines indicate the absorption or emission of radiation; dashed lines indicate nonradiative transitions. Process I: absorption. Process II: vibrational deactivation. Process III: quenching of excited singlet state. Process IV: fluorescence. Process V: intersystem crossing to the triplet state. Process VI: vibrational deactivation in the triplet system. Process VII: quenching of the triplet state. Process VIII: phosphorescence.

by collision (process III, called *collisional quenching*), or it can radiate the energy by process IV (*fluorescence*). Under certain conditions, it can cross over to a triplet sublevel that has nearly equal energy (process V, *intersystem crossing*), following which, processes VI, VII, and VIII, the counterparts of II, III, and IV, can occur. Process VIII is called *phosphorescence*.

MOLECULAR ABSORPTION SPECTRA

Transitions within molecular species can be studied by observation of the selective absorption of radiation passed through them, or by emission processes such as fluorescence and phosphorescence. A related method, not readily illustrated in a diagram such as Fig. 2-2, is *Raman spectroscopy*, which is given treatment paralleling fluorescence and phosphorescence in Chap. 6.

Transitions between electronic levels are found in the UV and visible regions; those between vibrational levels, but within the same electronic level, lie in the near and mid-IR and can also be observed with Raman techniques. Selective absorption in the far IR and microwave regions correspond to low-energy transitions involving the rotation of molecules or of portions of molecules.

Electronic transitions involve jumps to and from the various vibrational sublevels, so that UV-visible absorption spectra are in effect the sum total of absorptions taking place at many closely spaced frequency intervals. The contributions of the individual transitions are too close together to be resolved by most laboratory instruments, and hence such spectra appear as wide bands, though often showing some residual structure. Spectra taken in the gas phase or at low temperature (cooled with liquid nitrogen, for example), show fine structure much sharpened and with more detail, as compared with spectra of solutions at room temperature.

Absorption spectra are readily measured in each spectral region, and are of great utility in analytical studies, as will be made evident in subsequent chapters.

PHOTOACOUSTIC AND PHOTOTHERMAL SPECTROSCOPY

Nonradiative transitions following excitation by a beam of radiation (process II in Fig. 2-2) can sometimes be observed by measurement of the heat produced in the sample. Direct measurement (*photothermal*) is seldom sufficiently sensitive, but an indirect determination through pressure changes in a gas in contact with the sample (*photoacoustic*) is an important technique, usable in the UV, visible, and IR regions. This is the subject of Chap. 7.

FLUORESCENCE

The emission represented by process IV in Fig. 2-2 is of considerable importance in solution chemistry. As seen from the lengths of the arrows in the figure, the emitted radiation will usually have less energy per photon, and hence a longer wavelength, than the exciting radiation. (Exceptions to this generality include the case of resonance, where the emitted photons are identical to those absorbed, and the case in which the electron is initially in an excited vibrational state.) Many organic and some inorganic compounds, when irradiated with UV radiation, fluoresce in the visible region. Fluorescence also occurs in atomic spectra, in the UV, IR, and x-ray regions.

PHOSPHORESCENCE

In some molecules a nonradiative transition from an excited singlet state to the corresponding triplet level (process V of Fig. 2-2) can occur. The excess energy can then be radiated (processes VI and VIII) as the molecule reverts to its ground state. The transition from the triplet to the ground state has a low probability, as it involves a change in electronic spin. Hence its half-life is considerable, and the radiation may continue to be visible for a measurable time interval after the excitation is removed. An energy level from which the transition to the ground state has a low probability is called *metastable*. This persistent radiation is *phosphorescence*. It contrasts with fluorescence, which has a half-life of well below one microsecond.

RAMAN SPECTROSCOPY

A phenomenon related to fluorescence is the *Raman effect*. Here also radiation is emitted from the sample with wavelength changed from that of the incident exciting radiation. But, whereas to excite fluorescence the primary radiation must be absorbed by the sample, the incident radiation in order to produce the Raman effect need not be appreciably absorbed. The shift in wavelength in the Raman effect is caused by the extraction of energy from the incident photons to raise the molecule to a higher vibrational state. The emergent photons can thus be thought of as being the same ones that entered, but with less energy.

REFRACTION

We turn now from atomic and molecular phenomena to "bulk" phenomena concerning matter in its interaction with radiation.

The *index of refraction* (n) of an optical medium is an important bulk property, defined as the ratio of the velocity of radiation of a particular frequency in a vacuum (c) to that in a medium (c_m)

$$n = c/c_m \qquad (2\text{-}3)$$

The variation of refractive index of a substance with wavelength is called its *refractive dispersion* or simply its *dispersion*. The dispersion of a substance throughout the electromagnetic spectrum is intimately related to the degree to which radiation is absorbed. In regions of high transparency, the refractive index decreases (not linearly) with increasing wavelength; in regions of high absorbance, the index rises abruptly with wavelength, but in these areas is difficult to measure precisely.

The refractive index is an important property of transparent materials. Its variation with wavelength is responsible for chromatic aberration in lenses and the characteristic dispersion of radiation by prisms, both of significance in the design of optical instruments. These and other applications will be treated elsewhere in this text.

POLARIZATION AND OPTICAL ACTIVITY

Another property sometimes shown by matter is the ability to polarize radiation or to rotate the plane of already plane-polarized radiation. A beam of nonpolarized radiation can be thought of as a bundle of waves with their sinusoidal motions distributed over a family of planes, all of which include the line of propagation. Figure 2-3a shows diagrammatically the cross section of such a ray which is proceeding in a direction perpendicular to the plane of the paper. If this beam is passed through a *polarizer*, each separate wave in the bundle, for example that vibrating along the vector **AOA'** (Fig. 2-3b), is resolved into its orthogonal com-

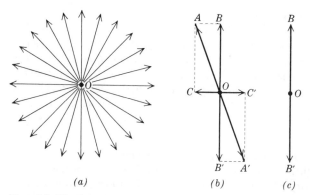

(a)   (b)   (c)

Figure 2-3 Vibration vectors in ordinary and plane-polarized electromagnetic radiation.

ponents **BOB′** and **COC′** in the directions of the x and y axes characteristic of the polarizer. The polarizing material has the property of absorbing one of these component vibrations (say **COC′**) and passing the other (**BOB′**). Thus, provided that the polarizer is 100 percent efficient, the emerging beam will consist of vibrations in one plane only (Fig. 2-3c), and is said to be *plane-polarized*. Most real polarizers are less than perfect, and produce partial polarization only.

A second polarizer, called the *analyzer*, placed in the beam will similarly pass only that component of the radiation vibrating parallel to its axis. Since the beam is already polarized, there will be one angular position of the analyzer at which essentially all the radiation will come through, but turning the analyzer through a 90° angle will reduce the power to zero. This is illustrated in Fig. 2-4; radiation from a lamp, rendered parallel by a lens, passes through polarizer A, which has its axis oriented vertically. The analyzer B, also with a vertical axis, has no further effect on the beam, but C, with its axis horizontal, cuts the radiation to zero. If C is rotated in its own plane, the power of the transmitted radiation will vary as the sine of the angle. Two polarizers placed in series are said to be *crossed* if their axes are mutually perpendicular. A beam of radiation may possess any degree of plane polarization from 0 (complete symmetry) to 100 percent (complete polarization).

Polarization is important in chemistry because of the ability of some crystals and liquids to rotate the plane of polarized radiation passed through them. This is the property known as *optical activity*. Further details about the applications of polarized radiation, including circular and elliptical polarization, will be found in Chap. 10.

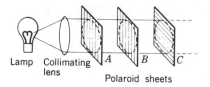

Lamp   Collimating
       lens
            Polaroid sheets   **Figure 2-4** Plane polarization of radiation.

PRACTICAL SOURCES OF RADIATION

For many spectroscopic applications, it would be desirable to have a source that would provide monochromatic (i.e., single-wavelength) radiation that could be swept over the entire wavelength region of interest. Unfortunately no such source is available at present. Hence, for such applications, it is necessary to utilize a source with a *monochromator*, an instrument that can be tuned to pass a narrow band of wavelengths, an approximation of monochromaticity.

Incandescent sources Any substance at a temperature above absolute zero emits radiation due to the thermal motion of its electrons. The theory of this thermal radiation has been thoroughly worked out in terms of an ideal emitter called a *blackbody*. Figure 2-5 shows the manner in which blackbody radiation is distributed as a function of wavelength for various temperatures.[1] The wavelength λ_{max} corresponding to maximum energy at temperature T is given by the *Wien displacement law*

$$\lambda_{max} \cdot T = 2.8978 \times 10^6 \qquad (2\text{-}4)$$

(The numerical constant is valid if the wavelength is expressed in nanometers and the temperature in kelvins.) It is because of this reciprocal dependence on temperature that incandescent sources are practical only in the visible and infrared,

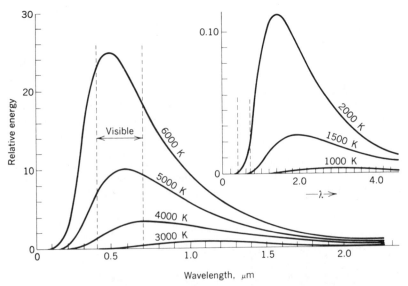

Figure 2-5 Blackbody radiation as a function of temperature. The vertical dashed lines in both plots demark the limits of the visible spectrum. (*McGraw-Hill Book Co.*[1])

but must be operated at inconveniently high temperature for UV coverage. The shape of the blackbody curve is given by *Planck's law*, which states that the total radiant power emitted per unit area of the source is

$$M_e = \frac{2\pi hc^2}{\lambda^5 \exp{(hc/\lambda kT)} - 1} \tag{2-5}$$

where h is Planck's constant, c is the velocity of light in vacuo, and k is the Boltzmann constant. Actual materials may give considerably less emission at some wavelengths than indicated by the blackbody curve; these are sometimes called *gray bodies*.

Gaseous discharge sources A discharge through a gas typically produces a *line spectrum*. At low pressures, each line approaches a single wavelength, but as the pressure is increased, the lines broaden in proportion, due to collisional perturbations, until at sufficiently high pressures, neighboring lines coalesce and a continuous spectrum results.

Low-pressure discharges are useful as radiation sources in special cases. In analysis by *atomic absorption*, for example, to determine a metal such as chromium in the vapor state, it is desirable to use as a source of radiation a low-pressure discharge in which chromium is present; the resonance emission from the source is selectively absorbed by the same element in the sample. A lamp with a cup-shaped cathode made of or plated with the desired metal (a *hollow-cathode lamp*) is often used for this purpose (see Chap. 5).

Another use for a low-pressure discharge lamp is in a UV detector for a chromatograph. The emission line of mercury at 253.7 nm, which is much more intense than any other emissions from a mercury lamp, is absorbed by a great many organic compounds, hence can be used to indicate when such samples are being eluted from the chromatograph. This will be detailed in Chaps. 20 and 21.

Continuous spectra can be obtained from discharges in various gases, e.g., in xenon at several atmospheres pressure and in mercury vapor at pressures that may go higher than 100 atmospheres. The very useful continuous discharge in hydrogen or deuterium at about 1 or 2 kPa† arises through a different mechanism. Molecules of H_2 or D_2 are raised to excited states (usually designated by an asterisk) and their excess energy is released through a process such as: $D_2^* \rightarrow D + D + h\nu$. Since the excited molecules can have varying amounts of energy, and the dissociated atoms can occupy various vibrational levels, the resulting radiation covers a continuous spectrum, with superimposed fine structure.[2]

The useful ranges of representative silica-window lamps are (in nanometers): xenon, 250 to 1000; high-pressure mercury, 280 to 1400; hydrogen or deuterium, 160 to 365.

---

† One kPa (kilopascal) = 7.5 torr (7.5 mm of mercury).

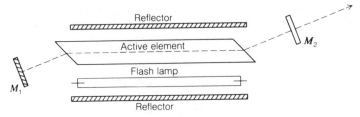

Figure 2-6 A typical laser. Mirrors M_1 and M_2 define the laser cavity; M_1 is totally reflecting, M_2 only partially reflecting. The active element can be a solid, as ruby, a gas, as mixed helium–neon, or a liquid solution of a dye. The active element is terminated with windows slanted at Brewster's angle. The output beam extends to the right from the semitransparent mirror. Excitation is from a xenon flash lamp.

LASERS†

A laser is a source of monochromatic radiation available in the UV, visible, and IR regions. The earliest example, reported in 1960, consists of a carefully ground rod of ruby (Al_2O_3 with Cr_2O_3 as a minor constituent) with parallel ends. A mirror is placed at one end so that all radiation approaching from the interior of the crystal is reflected back. A mirror at the other end is coated with a thin layer of silver so that only a fraction (typically 80 to 90 percent) of the incident radiation is reflected, the remainder escaping to form the output beam. When the rod is subject to an intense flash of light, as from a xenon discharge lamp (Fig. 2-6), nearly all the chromium atoms become excited, and most of them immediately drop into a metastable level. The first electrons to return from there to the ground state radiate photons of the corresponding wavelength, 694.3 nm. Some of this radiation is directed parallel to the axis of the rod and is reflected back and forth many times, with some escaping at every pass. Laser action results because the presence of this radiant energy at exactly the required frequency *stimulates* emission from the remainder of the metastable chromium atoms, so that the radiant flux builds up rapidly. The action is so efficient that a large pulse of monochromatic radiation is emitted within a period of perhaps 0.5 ms. The power in each pulse may reach into the megawatts.

Lasers can be made with a variety of other active materials. Among solids, a glass matrix containing a few percent of neodymium or other lanthanide element is useful, as is yttrium aluminum garnet (YAG). A number of gases can be made to undergo laser action by passing an electric discharge directly through the gas. Notable in this area are helium–neon, argon, nitrogen, and carbon dioxide lasers. Gas lasers can give continuous as well as pulsed outputs.

† "Laser" is an acronym for Light Amplification by Stimulated Emission of Radiation. A symposium on lasers and their applications in chemistry was held in New York in 1981. The papers presented have been published in the June 1982 issue of the *Journal of Chemical Education*; this collection is recommended reading.

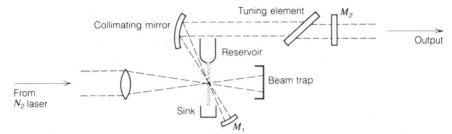

Figure 2-7 A dye laser using a freely falling stream of dye solution. The laser cavity is defined by the concave, fully reflecting mirror M_1, and the partially reflecting M_2. Excitation is from a nitrogen laser, not shown. The dye laser can be tuned by means of an element which might be an interference filter at an adjustable angle. The dye solution can be recirculated by a pump.

Each of the lasers mentioned above produces only certain discrete wavelengths that can only be varied to a very limited extent. There is another type capable of being tuned over a wider range of wavelengths, the *dye laser*.[3,4] The active substance is a fluorescent organic dye, such as Rhodamine 6G or fluorescein, in aqueous or alcoholic solution. Intense radiation at any wavelength within the absorption band of the dye can send large numbers of molecules into the excited (S_1) level, from which they can drop back to the ground state by laser action. The emitted radiation can be tuned over a range of perhaps 40 nm by means of a dispersive element (see next section) included in the space between the laser mirrors (the laser cavity). Dye lasers are usually energized by radiation from another laser, such as a nitrogen laser. Figure 2-7 shows a typical dye laser assembly. This type of laser is finding extensive use in analytical research.

The radiation from a laser has several unique properties.[5] It can be made highly monochromatic, and it is coherent. This means that the waves originating from all the atoms or molecules of the active substance are in phase with each other (not true of conventional sources). Partly as a consequence of the coherence, the collimated beam of laser radiation has very little tendency to spread out (lose collimation) as it propagates. This permits a large amount of energy to be concentrated on a small target, even though at a considerable distance. The radiation from some lasers is partially or completely polarized.

The importance of lasers for analytical purposes lies in the high degree of monochromaticity and the high-power levels that can be achieved. Among their applications may be mentioned their use as sources of localized heating, and as excitation sources in Raman and fluorescence spectroscopy.

WAVELENGTH SELECTION

In the study of absorption spectra it is usually desirable to employ as narrow a band of wavelengths as possible. As mentioned previously, this can be done with the aid of a device called a monochromator. In some instances a line source can be used, but even then a monochromator is often needed to isolate a single line.

There are two basic methods of wavelength selection: (1) the use of filters, and (2) geometrical dispersion by means of a prism or diffraction grating.

A *filter* is a device that will transmit radiation of some wavelengths but wholly or partially absorb others. Filters for the visible region are usually of colored glass. A great selection of such filters are available, more or less evenly spaced throughout the visible spectrum.

Filters are also made which function on the principle of interference. Figure 2-8 represents a section through such an *interference filter*. This device is made by depositing a semitransparent film of a reflective metal such as silver on a transparent plate. The reflective film is then overlaid with a very thin layer of a transparent material such as magnesium fluoride and then another film of silver. Each silver film reflects about half of any radiation that strikes it, and transmits the rest. Part of the incident beam is reflected repeatedly by the silver layers, but at each reflection some is transmitted outward. The several emergent rays to the right reinforce each other for radiation such that the distance between the silver films is an exact multiple of half the wavelength ($k\lambda/2$, where λ is the wavelength and $k = 1, 2, 3, \ldots$). For all other wavelengths, the beams interfere destructively in the MgF_2 layer, so that essentially no energy passes through. In commercial interference filters the thin layers are covered with another transparent plate for protection. The wavelength band isolated by this filter is much narrower and the peak transmittance much greater than in the corresponding glass filter. Interference filters transmit radiation of multiple *orders*, i.e., values of k. The unwanted orders can be removed by an appropriate absorbing layer. For the visible range, the second and higher orders lie in the UV, hence are easily eliminated merely by using glass plates for the substrate.

Filters of one type or another are available which, alone or in combination, permit selection of wavelength bands in almost any region of the spectrum from x-rays through the IR.

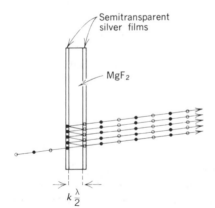

Figure 2-8 An interference filter, schematic. The open circles represent crests and the filled circles troughs in the wave of radiation; shown for $k = 1$.

MONOCHROMATORS

A monochromator is an instrument that can isolate a selected narrow band of wavelengths anywhere within a comparatively wide spectral range. It can be adjusted by an automatic or manual control to any desired wavelength.

The *monochromator* consists of a dispersing element (a prism or diffraction grating) together with two narrow slits to serve as entrance and exit ports for the radiation. The entrance slit defines a narrow beam which falls on the dispersing device. This component deflects the beam through an angle depending on the wavelength, and thus "fans out" the beam, as shown for the visible region in Fig. 2-9. An exit slit can be positioned so as to pass a narrow band of wavelengths at any point in the spectrum. (A practical monochromator may also require lenses or mirrors, incidental to its major function.)

A *polychromator* is similar, but equipped with two or more exit slits, so that a number of wavelengths can be examined simultaneously.

A *spectrograph* is an instrument similar to a monochromator, but with the exit slit omitted. A photographic film or plate is mounted so that successive wavelengths are focused at adjacent points.

A *spectrophotometer* is an instrument combining a monochromator, a source of radiation, and a photoelectric detector. It is the standard instrument for measuring absorption and fluorescence spectra.

Except for the source and detector, instrumental features are essentially the same for these several classes of instruments, so it is convenient to discuss them together.

DISPERSION BY PRISMS

Prisms are suitable dispersing elements from the UV through the mid-IR regions, but are not generally applicable elsewhere. In principle, any transparent medium can be used to fashion a prism if it has high enough dispersion. In the UV, the

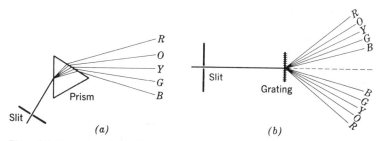

Figure 2-9 Dispersion of white light (*a*) by a prism, and (*b*) by a transmission grating.

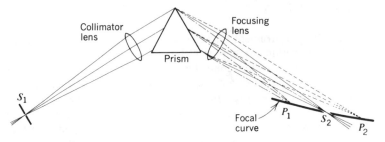

Figure 2-10 A 60° prism spectrograph or monochromator. As a spectrograph, a photographic film or plate holder is located along the focal curve, from P_1 to P_2. As a monochromator, an exit slit is provided at the point marked S_2.

only generally useful solid materials are silica and alumina.† *Silica* can be used either as quartz or in the vitreous form, sometimes called "fused quartz." *Alumina*, in the form of artificial sapphire, is more expensive than silica and offers little advantage as a prism material. These media transmit freely from somewhat below 200 nm in the UV up to about 4 μm in the IR.

In the visible region the dispersion of silica falls off, so that it is inferior to optical glass. For the IR, prisms may be constructed of salts such as NaCl, KBr, or CsBr, all of which must be protected from atmospheric moisture. These and other IR-transmitting materials will be considered further in Chap. 4.

The simplest prism monochromator is based on a 60° prism and two lenses, as in Fig. 2-10. Radiation enters through slit S_1, is rendered parallel by a collimating lens, and falls at an oblique angle on one face of the prism. The dispersed radiation is brought to a focus by a second lens, so that the image of the entrance slit corresponding to the desired wavelength is centered on the exit slit, S_2.

This instrument can be made more compact and economical by folding around its center line, resulting in the *Littrow* design, as in Fig. 2-11. The 60° prism is replaced by one with a 30° angle (for the same dispersive power), with its back surface mirrored. Now a single element can serve to collimate the incoming radiation and to focus the dispersed beam.

For many applications it is desirable to substitute a concave mirror for the lens (Fig. 2-11*b*). This has the advantage that a single mirror will serve equally well over the whole optical range (from UV to IR) that can be reflected by a metallic surface. This is because the radiation need not pass through any medium that would limit the range; furthermore, a mirror focuses all wavelengths at the same point, which a lens does not.

Various other types of prisms are employed occasionally for special purposes.

† Several ionic crystals, such as NaCl and MgF_2, are transparent in the UV and visible, but are seldom used in these regions. One disadvantage is that intense UV radiation tends to produce color centers in the crystals, thereby reducing the transparency.

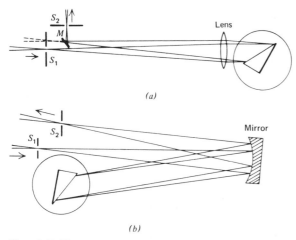

(b)

Figure 2-11 Littrow-mounted prism monochromators: (a) with field lens, the exit slit offset by a diagonal mirror M, (b) with a concave mirror in place of the lens. The 30° dispersing prism, with mirrored back, is mounted on a table that can be turned to select wavelengths.

DISPERSION BY GRATINGS

The most common form of dispersing element in modern instruments is the diffraction grating. Consider first a beam of monochromatic radiation passing through a transparent plate that has a large number of very fine parallel lines ruled on it. It is observed that the beam is split into a number of beams. One of these proceeds straight through, as though the plate were unruled. The other beams are deviated from this forward direction, as shown in Fig. 2-9b, through angles that depend on the spacing of the ruled lines and on the wavelength of the radiation. This can be explained by the assumption that each clear portion between the lines, when illuminated from behind, acts as though it were itself a source of the radiation which emanates from it in all forward directions (Huygens' principle). However, the rays coming from these numerous secondary sources will be destroyed by interference in most directions. Only at those angles where the geometry is just right will the beams reinforce each other. Figure 2-12 shows one of the possible deviated beams. The angle of deviation is θ, the difference in the lengths of the paths taken by beamlets from successive transparent areas is a, and the distance between centers of adjacent lines (the grating space) is d. Thus $a = d \sin \theta$. This gives the fundamental relation called the *grating equation*

$$m\lambda = d \sin \theta \qquad (2\text{-}6)$$

where m is any integer, 0, 1, 2, 3, ..., called the *order*,† and λ is the wavelength.

---

† The order is commonly designated by n, but in this book m will be used to avoid confusion with the index of refraction.

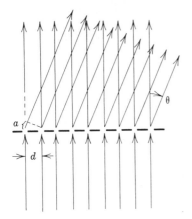

Figure 2-12 Diffraction at a plane transmission grating.

It follows from Eq. (2-6) that, if a beam of polychromatic radiation is passed through the grating, it will be fanned out into a series of spectra located symmetrically on each side of the normal. On each side there will be a spectrum corresponding to each of the first few values of m. The equation further shows that for a particular angle θ there will be several wavelengths for which the value of $m\lambda$ will be the same. For example, a grating with 2000 lines per centimeter (grating space $d = 1/2000 = 5 \times 10^{-4}$ cm) will deflect through an angle $\theta = 6.89°$ radiation of those wavelengths given by

$$\lambda = \frac{d \sin \theta}{m} = \frac{(5 \times 10^{-4})(\sin 6.89°)}{m}$$

$$= \frac{(5 \times 10^{-4})(0.1200)}{m} = \frac{6.00 \times 10^{-5}}{m} \quad \text{cm}$$

$$= \frac{600}{m} \quad \text{nm}$$

The actual wavelengths corresponding to successive orders at this angle will be:

Order, m	1	2	3	4
Wavelength, λ, nm	600	300	200	150

This relation is shown diagrammatically in Fig. 2-13, which gives selected wavelengths on one side of the normal.

Equation (2-6) can be expanded to provide greater generality. If the incident radiation makes an angle ϕ with the grating surface, then the grating equation becomes

$$m\lambda = d(\sin \theta + \sin \phi) \tag{2-7}$$

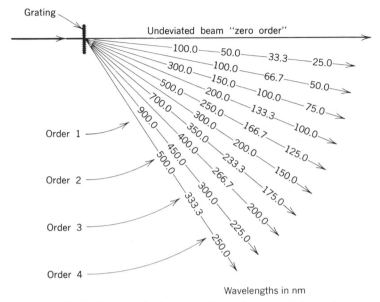

Figure 2-13 Overlapping orders in the spectrum formed by a transmission grating.

The fact that successive orders of spectra overlap might seem to be a great drawback, but in practice it gives little trouble. If only the visible spectrum is to be observed, the question will not arise, since the visible region (400 to 750 nm) of the various orders do not overlap. If the spectrum is to be recorded photographically, the spectral sensitivity of the plate or film will at least partially limit the degree of overlap. Overlapping can be reduced or eliminated by placing ahead of the grating an auxiliary prism of small deviation, called a *foreprism* or *Order-Sorter*, or by the use of absorbing filters to remove one region of the spectrum while allowing another region to pass.

The grating discussed above is of the type known as a plane *transmission grating*. In practical instruments, other than small, hand-held ones, *reflection gratings* are more common. In these the lines are engraved on the surface of a mirror, which may be either a polished metal slab or a glass plate on which a metallic film has been deposited.

It is possible to rule a reflection grating in such a way as to throw a maximum fraction of the radiant energy into those wavelengths that are diffracted at a selected angle. This is accomplished by ruling with a specially shaped diamond point held at a specified angle. The resulting grating is called an *echelette*, and is said to have been given a *blaze* at a particular angle. Figure 2-14 shows the geometry of a portion of an echelette reflection grating. The wider faces of the grooves make an angle ϕ with the surface of the grating. A ray incident at angle α will be reflected from the groove face at an angle β such that $\alpha + \phi = \beta - \phi$. The rays reflected from

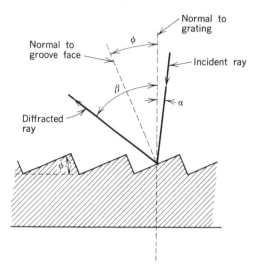

Figure 2-14 The geometry of a blazed reflection grating (echelette).

successive grooves then undergo interference as already described. Because of the efficiency of specular reflection at the metal surface, much more energy will be diffracted at this angle (β) than at any other, for a given value of α. The energy will be only slightly less at angles close to β, so the grating can be used to advantage for a considerable wavelength span in a given order. A grating blazed for a particular wavelength in the first order will also be blazed for half that wavelength in the second order, one-third of it in the third order, and so on. Very little energy will be found at the symmetric position on the other side of normal to the grating.

In general, best results are obtained if the grating space is of the same order of magnitude as the wavelength region to be dispersed. For special purposes, other grating spaces may be found useful. An *echelle*, for example, is a grating with step-shaped rulings a few hundred times wider than the average wavelength to be studied. It must be used at an order m of 100 or more, which produces difficult problems of overlapping orders, but it is capable of tremendous dispersion.

The manufacture of precision diffraction gratings is very exacting work. It is performed with an extremely precise and delicate machine, called a *ruling engine*, that scribes the fine parallel lines with a diamond point. Most spectrographs and spectrophotometers use *replica gratings*, made by casting a plastic material on an original grating, then stripping it off and mounting it on a rigid support. The art of replication has reached the point where gratings made this way are of nearly as good quality as the originals.

Some of the highest-quality gratings are made by the use of laser radiation, in a process known as *holography*. A glass plate coated with a photographic emulsion is illuminated simultaneously by two beams coming from the same laser, under such conditions that a pattern of parallel interference fringes is established in the emulsion. Photographic development produces an array of parallel lines that constitute an excellent diffraction grating.

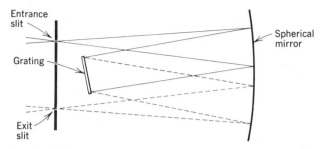

Figure 2-15 Ebert mounting for a plane reflection grating. The wavelength is selected by turning the grating about a vertical axis at its center.

There are several ways in which a plane reflection grating can be mounted in a monochromator or spectrograph. One of these is the Littrow mounting mentioned previously. It is analogous in plan to Fig. 2-11a or b, with the grating replacing the prism on the rotatable table. An example may be found in Fig. 4-5.

The other common mounting for a plane grating was invented by Ebert in 1889, but was little used until it was resurrected and improved by Fastie[6] in 1952. In this design (Fig. 2-15) a single, large, spherical mirror serves for both collimation and focusing, with symmetrically placed slits. Wavelength selection is effected by rotating the grating. Czerny and Turner[7] suggested using two smaller spherical mirrors mounted symmetrically, to save the expense of the large Ebert mirror, much of which was unused, and most current instruments with this geometry incorporate the best features of the Czerny–Turner and Ebert designs. Figure 2-16 shows two commercial examples.

The Littrow mounting is slightly more compact than the Ebert, and saves one mirror, but the two slits must be close together, which tends to cramp the design. The Ebert is somewhat freer of aberrations, because of the symmetry.

Another class of instruments make use of a reflection grating in which the lines are ruled on a concave spherical surface. Rowland, in 1882, discovered the following principle of design which bears his name: If a circle (the *Rowland circle*) is drawn tangent to the concave grating at its center, but with a diameter equal to the radius of curvature of the grating, then the diffracted images of the entrance slit will lie on the circle if the slit itself is on the circle. This will apply to all wavelengths in all orders of diffraction, and is illustrated in Fig. 2-17. Several mechanical designs have been devised to make use of this principle, ranging from very large spectrographs with high resolution to small portable spectrophotometers.

Instruments making use of concave gratings suffer from the inherent defect of *astigmatism*. This means that, although the image of the entrance slit is very sharply focused along the circle, so that its wavelength can be measured with precision, its height is not sharply defined. This must be taken into consideration in making quantitative measurements, as some radiation is masked off by the top and bottom of the exit slit.

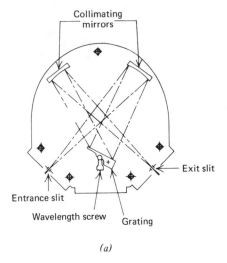

(a)

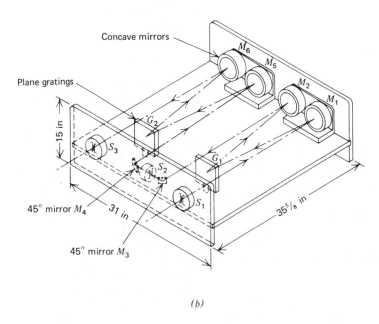

(b)

Figure 2-16 Czerny–Turner monochromators: (a) modified to provide a 90° angle between input and output beams of radiation (*Farrand Optical Company*), (b) double monochromator with an intermediate slit, S_2 (*Spex Industries*).

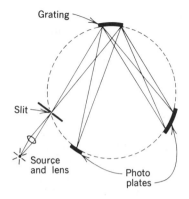

Figure 2-17 Plan of a concave grating spectrograph, showing the principle of the Rowland circle.

DISPERSION

The dispersion of a spectrograph or spectrometer is defined in terms of the derivative $d\lambda/dx$, where x is the distance measured along the focal plane, e.g., on the surface of a developed photoplate. It is called the *reciprocal linear dispersion*, and may be specified in nanometers per millimeter. In a monochromator or spectrophotometer, the corresponding quantity is the *effective bandpass*. This is a measure of the band of wavelengths allowed to pass through the instrument for a given width of the exit slit. The bandpass is given by the product of the slit width and the reciprocal linear dispersion.

The entrance and exit slits of most monochromators are of equal width; if they are variable, a single control operates both, maintaining their equality. The band of wavelengths emerging from the exit slit includes contributions from both sides of the central or nominal wavelength (Fig. 2-18). The band $\Delta\lambda$ between the half-height points is the effective bandpass of the system.

A grating instrument produces a *normal* spectrum, i.e., one that is spread out nearly uniformly on a wavelength scale. The dispersion and the bandpass are then essentially uniform over the entire spectrum. A prism, on the other hand, gives an unequally spaced spectrum with the longer wavelengths crowded together as

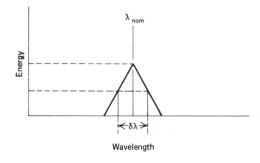

Figure 2-18 Band of wavelengths emerging from the exit slit of a monochromator illuminated from a broad-band source.

compared to the shorter. The bandpass in a prism instrument is not constant but differs from one wavelength to another, and from one instrument design to another.

RESOLVING POWER

A very narrow slit produces an interference pattern (Fig. 2-19) consisting of a large central maximum flanked by a series of lesser maxima (usually negligible), symmetrically located on both sides. The width of the central maximum (measured between adjacent minima) is $2f\lambda/d$, where d is the slit width, f the focal length of the focusing lens or mirror, and λ is the wavelength. As the entrance slit is opened up, the spot of light appearing on the focal plane, initially diffuse and of very low intensity, becomes narrower, until it eventually passes through a minimum width; it then broadens, the intensity steadily increasing as more energy enters the slit. The minimum position will give the best possible spectral resolution. The corresponding slit width is given by

$$d_{\text{opt}} = 2f\lambda/w \tag{2-8}$$

where w is the diameter of the lens or mirror. For a typical case, where $w = 8$ cm, $f = 40$ cm, and $\lambda = 500$ nm, the optimum slit width is 5 μm.

This optimum slit width gives the instrument the greatest *resolving power* (ability to separate adjacent wavelengths) of which it is capable. This parameter is arbitrarily defined by the criterion proposed many years ago by Lord Rayleigh: Two wavelengths differing by $\Delta\lambda$ are said to be resolved when the central diffraction maximum of one coincides with the first minimum of the other. The resolving power is then

$$R = \lambda/\Delta\lambda \tag{2-9}$$

where λ is the mean of the two wavelengths. For a grating, this resolving power is given by the product Nm, where N is the number of lines illuminated and m is

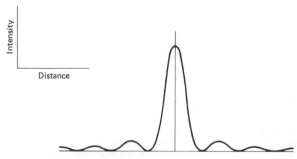

Figure 2-19 Diffraction pattern from a single slit.

the spectral order. For a prism instrument, the corresponding quantity is

$$R = b\left(\frac{dn}{d\lambda}\right) \tag{2-10}$$

where b is the width of the prism at its base, and n is the refractive index.

A monochromator is often operated with wider slits than that suggested by Eqs. (2-9) or (2-10), if the source is of low intensity, in order to gather enough energy to measure precisely; the resolution suffers, however.

Most monochromators are provided with entrance and exit slits of equal width; if they are variable, one control operates both, maintaining their equality. The wavelength of the radiation emerging from the exit slit includes contributions from both sides of the central or nominal wavelength (Fig. 2-19). The band $\Delta\lambda$ between the half-height points is the *effective bandpass* of the system.

PROBLEMS

2-1 In Fig. 2-1, determine the wave number in inverse centimeters and the energy in electronvolts for each of the transitions shown.

2-2 The legal definition of the meter in the United States[8] is 1,650,763.73 wavelengths in vacuo of the $2p_{10}$ to $5d_5$ transition in isotopically pure ^{86}Kr. Compute the wave number in inverse centimeters; the wavelength in angstroms, nanometers, and micrometers; the frequency in hertz; and the energy per photon in electronvolts for this radiation. Take the velocity of propagation in vacuo as

$$(2.99792458 \pm 1.2) \times 10^8 \text{ m} \cdot \text{s}^{-1}$$

and Planck's constant as $(6.626176 \pm 36) \times 10^{-34}$ J·s, where the uncertainties quoted are standard deviations in the last digits. Give each of your answers with the appropriate uncertainty limits. (If you do not have access to a calculator that can handle enough digits, round off the numbers as necessary, and explain the extent to which this degrades your calculations.)

2-3 Calculate figures for two more columns in Table 2-1, giving the energy content of photons in the respective ranges in (a) electronvolts, and (b) calories per mole.

2-4 A source of radiation for use as a laboratory standard closely approximates a blackbody. It has an active area of 1 cm^2, and is operated at a temperature of 5500 K. Calculate (a) the wavelength of maximum energy, and (b) the radiant power at that wavelength.

REFERENCES

1. F. A. Jenkins and H. E. White, "Fundamentals of Optics," McGraw-Hill, New York, **1962**.
2. S. S. Penner, "Quantitative Molecular Spectroscopy and Gas Emissivities," Addison-Wesley, Reading, Mass., **1959**; chap. 3.
3. B. A. Lengyel, "Introduction to Laser Physics," Wiley, New York, **1966**.
4. J. P. Webb, *Anal. Chem.*, **1972**, *44*(6), 31A.
5. R. B. Green, *J. Chem. Educ.*, **1977**, *54*, A365, A407.
6. W. G. Fastie, *J. Opt. Soc. Am.*, **1952**, *42*, 641.
7. M. Czerny and A. F. Turner, *Z. Phys.*, **1930**, *61*, 792.
8. Natl. Bur. Stand. Tech. News Bull., **1963**, *February and October*.

THREE

THE ABSORPTION OF RADIATION: ULTRAVIOLET AND VISIBLE

If a beam of white light passes through a glass container (cuvet) filled with liquid, the emergent radiation is always less powerful than that entering. The diminution of power is generally of different extent for different wavelengths. The loss is due in part to reflections at the surfaces and to scattering by any suspended particles present, but in the absence of such particles, it is primarily accounted for by the *absorption* of radiant energy by the liquid.

If the energy absorbed is greater for some visible wavelengths than for others, the emergent beam will appear colored. Table 3-1 gives the wavelength bands designated by familiar color names, along with their complements. These wavelengths are taken from a study originating at the National Bureau of Standards,[1] and are inherently somewhat arbitrary. The apparent color of the solution is always the *complement* of the color absorbed. Thus a solution absorbing in the blue region will appear yellow, one that absorbs green will appear purple, etc.

In referring to color, we are for the moment restricting the discussion to the visible region of the spectrum, but most of the concepts and analytical methods to be discussed will apply with no change in principle both to the ultraviolet and infrared ranges.

To the analytical chemist, the importance of colored solutions lies in the fact that the radiation absorbed is characteristic of the material doing the absorbing. A solution containing the hydrated copper (II) ion absorbs yellow and is transparent to blue, so copper may be determined by measuring the degree of absorption of yellow light under standardized conditions. Any soluble colored material may be determined quantitatively in this way. In addition, a substance that is colorless

Table 3-1 Colors of visible radiation[1]

Approximate wavelength range, nm	Color	Complement
400–465	Violet	Yellow-green
465–482	Blue	Yellow
482–487	Greenish blue	Orange
487–493	Blue-green	Red-orange
493–498	Bluish green	Red
498–530	Green	Red-purple
530–559	Yellowish green	Reddish purple
559–571	Yellow-green	Purple
571–576	Greenish yellow	Violet
576–580	Yellow	Blue
580–587	Yellowish orange	Blue
587–597	Orange	Greenish blue
597–617	Reddish orange	Blue-green
617–780	Red	Blue-green

or only faintly colored may often be determined by adding a reagent that will convert it to an intensely colored compound. Thus the addition of ammonia to a copper solution produces a much more intense color than that of the hydrated ion itself, and therefore provides a more sensitive analytical test.

The general term for chemical analysis through the measurement of absorption of radiation is *absorptiometry*. The term *colorimetry* applies only in relation to the visible region. *Spectrophotometry* is a division of absorptiometry that refers specifically to the use of a spectrophotometer.

MATHEMATICAL THEORY

The absorption of radiant energy by matter can be described quantitatively through the general principle known as *Beer's law*. Consider a glass cuvet with plane parallel faces traversed by monochromatic radiation. Losses by reflection at the surfaces and absorption by the glass will be neglected for the moment. Suppose that the cuvet is filled with an absorbing species dissolved in a nonabsorbing solvent. The radiation diminishes in power the further it penetrates into the solution, and the greater the concentration of solute. More generally stated, the diminution in power is proportional to the number of absorbing molecules in the path of the beam. The quantitative statement of this relation is Beer's law:† *Successive increments in the number of identical absorbing molecules*

---

† This relation is sometimes known as the Beer–Lambert or the Beer–Bouguer law, as contributions to its development were made by Lambert and by Bouguer (as well as by others). It is frequently stated in terms of intensities *I* rather than power *P*.

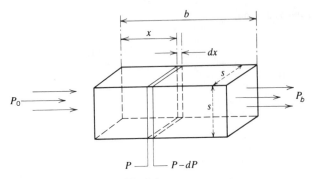

Figure 3-1 The derivation of Beer's law.

in the path of a beam of monochromatic radiation absorb equal fractions of the radiant power traversing them.

The number of absorbing molecules in the volume element $s^2\, dx$ (defined in Fig. 3-1) is given by $Ncs^2\, dx$, where c is the concentration in moles per liter, and N is Avogadro's number. Hence Beer's statement can be expressed as

$$\frac{dP}{Ncs^2\, dx} = -kP \tag{3-1}$$

in which k is a constant representing the fraction of the power P that is absorbed in the distance element dx. Avogadro's number can be merged into the constant factor. For unit cross section, we can write

$$\frac{dP}{P} = -kc\, dx \tag{3-2}$$

Integration of this expression over the path length b gives

$$\int_0^{P_b} \frac{dP}{P} = -kc \int_0^b dx \tag{3-3}$$

$$\ln \frac{P_b}{P_0} = -kcb \tag{3-4}$$

For convenience we can write this in terms of common logarithms, replacing k by a new constant a that includes the logarithm conversion factor, and dropping the subscript b, as

$$\log \frac{P_0}{P} = abc \equiv A \tag{3-5}$$

Note that the ratio P_0/P has been inverted to remove the negative sign. The quantity $\log (P_0/P)$ is so important that it has been given a special symbol, A, and is called the *absorbance*. The shortest statement of Beer's law is thus $A = abc$.

Since the transmitted power P can vary between the limits zero and P_0, the logarithm of the ratio can, in theory, vary from 0 to infinity. In practice, however, absorbances greater than 2 or 3 are seldom usable (because of the influence of stray radiation). The range that will give adequate analytical precision is even more limited, the exact permissible values being determined in part by the type of measuring instrument employed.

ABSORPTIVITY

The constant a of Eq. (3-5) is called the *absorptivity*. It is characteristic of a particular combination of solute and solvent for a given wavelength. Its units are dependent on those chosen for b and c (b is customarily in centimeters), and the symbol varies accordingly, as indicated in Table 3-2. Other symbols and names that have been widely used in the past are included for reference.

It must be noted carefully that absorptivity is a property of a substance (an intensive property), whereas absorbance is a property of a particular sample (an extensive property) and will therefore vary with the concentration and the length of the light path through the container.

Percent transmittance (percent T, defined as $100P/P_0$) is a convenient quantity if the transmitted radiation is of more interest than the chemical nature of the absorbing material. Filters for colorimetry and photography are commonly rated in terms of percent transmittance. In most spectrophotometers the actual quantities measured are P and P_0, and the absorbance is calculated from them.

Either the absorbance A or the absorptivity a is a measure of the degree of absorption of radiation. The symbol a, with the units of liters per gram·cm, is appropriate for absorptivity if the nature of the absorbing material, hence its molecular weight, is not known. The molar absorptivity, ϵ (units: liters per

Table 3-2 Units and symbols for use with Beer's law

Accepted symbol	Definition†	Accepted name	Obsolete or alternate Symbol	Obsolete or alternate Name
T	P/P_0	Transmittance	. . . . . .	Transmission
A	$\log P_0/P$	Absorbance	D, E	Optical density, extinction
a	A/bc	Absorptivity	k	Extinction coefficient, absorbancy index
ϵ	AM/bc	Molar absorptivity	a_M	Molar (molecular) extinction coefficient, molar absorbancy index
b	. . . .	Length of path	l, d	

† The definitions of P and P_0 are given in the text. The units of c are grams per liter; of b, centimeters; M is the molecular weight. A symbol formerly much used is $E_{1\ cm}^{1\%}$, which may be defined as A/bc', where c' is the concentration in percent by weight and $b = 1$ cm.

mol·cm) is preferable if it is desired to compare quantitatively the absorption of various substances of known molecular weight.

Beer's law indicates that the absorptivity is a constant, independent of concentration, length of path, and intensity of incident radiation. The law provides no hint of the effect of temperature, the nature of the solvent, or the wavelength. In practice, the temperature is found to have only secondary effects unless it is varied over an unusually wide range. The concentration will vary slightly with a change in temperature, because of the volume change. Also, if the absorbing solute is in a state of equilibrium with other species, more or less variation with temperature is to be expected. On the other hand, some substances show quite different absorption if cooled to liquid nitrogen temperature. For much practical analytical work, temperature effects may be disregarded, especially if the absorption of an unknown is to be compared directly with a standard at the same temperature.

The effect on the absorptivity of a given solute brought about by a change of solvent cannot be predicted in any general way. The analyst is frequently limited to a particular solvent or class of solvents in which the material is soluble, so the question may not arise. A further restriction applies particularly to work in the UV, where many common solvents are no longer transparent. Water, alcohol, ether, and saturated hydrocarbons are satisfactory, but aromatic compounds, chloroform, carbon tetrachloride, carbon disulfide, acetone, and many others absorb too strongly to be useful except in the very near UV. Table 3-3 gives the appropriate limits of UV transmission for a number of common solvents.

Even at constant temperature and in a specified solvent, it is sometimes found that the absorptivity may not be truly constant. If the absorbance A is plotted against concentration, a straight line through the origin is predicted by Beer's law (curve 1 of Fig. 3-2). However, in some systems some degree of curvature is found. Such deviations from the law may be more apparent than real, as will be

Table 3-3 Ultraviolet transmission limits of common solvents†

180–195 nm	210–220 nm	265–275 nm
Sulfuric acid (96%)	n-Butyl alcohol	Carbon tetrachloride
Water	Isopropyl alcohol	Dimethyl sulfoxide
Acetonitrile	Cyclohexane	Dimethyl formamide
200–210 nm	Ethyl ether	Acetic acid
Cyclopentane	245–260 nm	280–290 nm
n-Hexane	Chloroform	Benzene
Glycerol	Ethyl acetate	Toluene
2,2,4-Trimethylpentane	Methyl formate	m-Xylene
Methanol		Above 300 nm
Ethanol		Pyridine
		Acetone
		Carbon disulfide

† Transmission limits taken arbitrarily at the point where $A = 0.50$ for $b = 10$ mm; within each group, solvents are arranged in approximate order of increasing wavelength limit. Data supplied by Matheson Coleman & Bell, Cincinnati, Ohio.

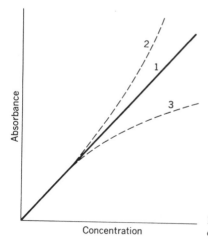

Figure 3-2 Beer's law plots: (1) obeyed; (2) positive deviation; (3) negative deviation.

discussed in the next section. Deviations are designated as positive or negative according to whether the observed curve is concave upward or downward, respectively.

It must be realized that conformity to Beer's law is not necessary for the absorbing system to be useful for quantitative analysis. Once a curve corresponding to Fig. 3-2 is established for material under specified conditions, it may be used as a calibration curve. The concentration of an unknown can then be read from the curve as soon as its absorbance is found by observation.

APPARENT DEVIATIONS FROM BEER'S LAW

In general, Beer's law may be expected to hold rather closely for radiation of any given wavelength, but the absorptivity and therefore the absorbance will in general be different for different wavelengths. The width of the band of wavelengths employed may also effect the apparent value of absorptivity. Figure 3-3 shows the absorption spectrum of the permanganate ion in water solution. Reference to Table 3-1 shows that a substance absorbing as this does in the range 480 to 570 nm should appear red-purple, which of course we know to be true. If an absorption measurement were made on this solution, using radiation passed by a filter of green glass with transmission limits approximately at the wavelengths marked A and F, the effects of the detailed peaks and valleys of the absorption curve would be smoothed out, so that the value of the molar absorptivity so determined might be about 1700 to 1800. However, if by some means the wavelength range were limited to the region B to E, the value found would be roughly the average of the true values within this range, perhaps 2300. Reducing the width of the band still further to the region C to D, the molar absorptivity would approach its true maximum value at this wavelength, 2500.

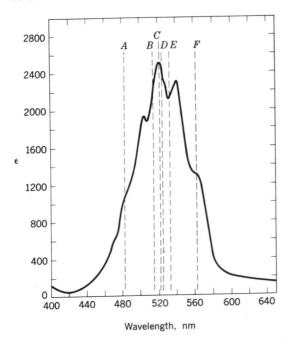

Figure 3-3 Absorption spectrum of aqueous potassium permanganate.

That the absorptivity will vary from linearity if determined with nonmonochromatic radiation can be shown from the following considerations: Suppose that a solution is examined at two wavelengths, λ_1 and λ_2, and that Beer's law is obeyed exactly at each of these wavelengths individually. The absorbance at λ_1 is given by

$$A_1 = \log \frac{P_{0,1}}{P_1} = a_1 bc \qquad (3\text{-}6)$$

or

$$\frac{P_{0,1}}{P_1} = 10^{a_1 cd} \qquad (3\text{-}7)$$

Similar equations can be written for λ_2, using subscript 2 rather than 1. If now we measure a pair of values for P_0 and P, using both wavelengths simultaneously, we get an apparent absorbance, A_{app}

$$A_{app} = -\log \frac{P_1 + P_2}{P_{0,1} + P_{0,2}} \qquad (3\text{-}8)$$

Substitution from Eq. (3-7) gives

$$A_{app} = \log \left(\frac{P_{0,1} + P_{0,2}}{P_{0,1}10^{-a_1 bc} + P_{0,2}10^{-a_2 bc}} \right)$$

$$= \log (P_{0,1} + P_{0,2}) - \log (P_{0,1}10^{-a_1 bc} + P_{0,2}10^{-a_2 bc}) \qquad (3-9)$$

Clearly, if $a_1 = a_2$, this equation will become equivalent to Beer's law, but if they are not equal, the relation between A_{app} and c cannot be linear, and a deviation will be observed, in either sense, depending on the relative values of a_1 and a_2.

It is interesting to compare monochromatic radiation from a laser with that from a narrow-slit monochromator. A research report[2] describes the absorbance of a dye with a sharp maximum at 635 nm, as examined against a water reference, and also differentially against a standard solution. To obtain a large enough signal-to-noise ratio the spectrophotometer required a slit width of 1.48 mm for a differential analysis with a tungsten lamp, as compared with 0.08 mm with a laser. Absorbance-concentration curves were found to be linear as far as they could be followed (to about 1.4 absorbance) with the laser, but marked negative deviation was observed with the tungsten lamp. This was caused in part by the wider wavelength band passed, and in part by excessive stray light effects.

The shape of an absorption curve may sometimes change with changes in concentration of the solution, causing an apparent failure of Beer's law. This phenomenon may be due to interaction of the solute molecules with each other or with the solvent.

A striking example is methylene blue.[3] This compound shows an intense absorption at 664 nm in dilute solution, but with an increase of 200 times in concentration, only a shoulder remains at this wavelength, the major absorption appearing at 600 nm. This is ascribed to the formation of dimers at the higher concentration. A plot of absorbance against concentration would be expected to show a negative deviation from Beer's law at 664, and positive deviation at 600 nm.

An example of chemically caused apparent deviation is the change in color of a solution of $K_2Cr_2O_7$ from orange to yellow on dilution with water. The absorption curves for $K_2Cr_2O_7$ and K_2CrO_4 [equal concentrations in terms of the Cr(VI) content] are shown in Fig. 3-4. The pertinent equilibrium is

$$Cr_2O_7^{2-} + H_2O \rightleftharpoons 2H^+ + 2CrO_4^{2-}$$
(Orange) (Yellow)

As the dichromate solution is diluted, the absorbance gradually changes from curve 2 to curve 1, with respect to shape, though diminished in actual absorbance values.

All the "deviations" from Beer's law discussed to this point are considered "apparent" deviations. They are caused by deviation from the conditions for which the law was derived, and disappear if the *actual* rather than stoichiometric concentrations are used.

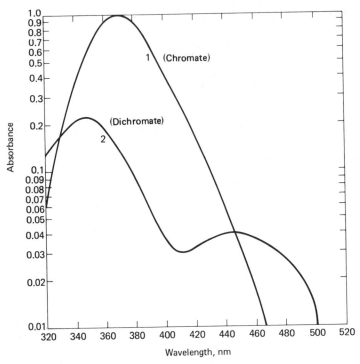

Figure 3-4 Absorption spectra of (1) K_2CrO_4 in 0.05 M KOH, and (2) $K_2Cr_2O_7$ in 1.75 M H_2SO_4. Both correspond to 0.01071 mg of Cr per ml; path length, 10.0 mm. The absorbance is plotted on a logarithmic scale for convenience only.

There exists also a possible source of deviation that is more fundamental, depending on the index of refraction n of the solution under study. Actually, dispersion theory indicates that the absorptivity should be multiplied by the factor $n/(n^2 + 2)^2$ to give a quantity that is truly independent of concentration.[4] However, as most absorption measurements for analytical purposes are made on dilute solutions, for which the refractive index is essentially that of the solvent, this restriction is not likely to be felt in practice.

INSTRUMENTATION

Instruments for the measurement of the selective absorption of radiation by solutions are called *spectrophotometers*. Simple photoelectric devices using a filter for wavelength selection are best considered to be abridged spectrophotometers, though sometimes called by the older, inexact, designation of "colorimeters." One occasionally hears the term "absorptiometer" used in a generic sense to cover all of these.

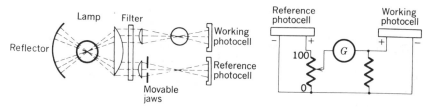

Figure 3-5 Schematic representation of the Klett–Summerson Photoelectric Colorimeter. (*Klett Manufacturing Company.*)

Filter Photometers

An example of an abridged spectrophotometer is shown in Fig. 3-5. Two beams from an incandescent lamp are passed through a glass filter to a pair of matched photocells, one beam traversing the sample, the other bypassing it. Two photovoltaic cells (described in more detail in Chap. 27), produce currents proportional to the power in the radiation striking them. Each of the photocells is shunted by a low-value resistor, the one across the reference cell being provided with a sliding contact (a potentiometer). In use, the contact is first set at the upper end of its resistor, marked 100 on the scale. With solvent in the cuvet, the movable jaws are adjusted to zero the galvanometer, thus ensuring equal illumination on the two photocells. The solvent is then replaced by the colored test solution. Since the sample must absorb more radiation than does the solvent, the current generated by the working cell is decreased, producing a smaller voltage drop across its resistor. The potentiometer must then be adjusted downward to pick off an equal voltage from the reference photocell to return the galvanometer to zero. The scale of the potentiometer reads directly in percent transmittance. Comparable instruments have been produced by many manufacturers and have proved very useful. The best precision to be expected is within 3 or 4 percent.

Another example of an abridged spectrophotometer is the Du Pont 400, shown in Fig. 3-6. This instrument consists of a series of modular building blocks that can be assembled in various configurations, of which two are shown in the figure. In (*a*) the radiation passes through the sample and then is split into two beams. These beams are filtered separately so that the indicator will give the ratio of radiant powers in two wavelength bands. The measuring and reference beams are set, respectively, at wavelengths that are absorbed and that are transmitted by the substance sought. In the configuration shown in (*b*), the radiation is passed through a single filter before splitting into two beams. One beam then traverses a reference solution, the other the sample to be analyzed, so that the readout gives the ratio of the absorbing species in the unknown to that in the standard.

The Du Pont photometer is intended primarily for continuous monitoring of flowing streams, either liquid or gaseous. An example of its application is the determination of oxides of sulfur and nitrogen in gaseous combustion products. The configuration of Fig. 3-6*a* is used, with a mercury-vapor lamp as source.

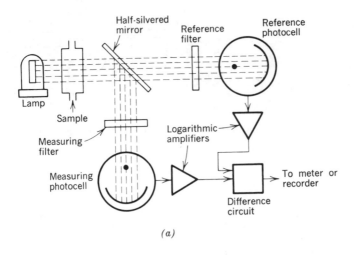

(a)

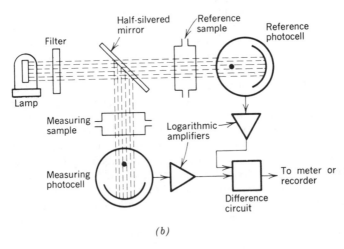

(b)

Figure 3-6 Schematic representation of the DuPont 400 Photometric Analyzer, shown in two configurations. (*E. I. Du Pont de Nemours & Co.*)

Figure 3-7 shows the absorption spectra of SO_2 and NO_2, and indicates the mercury wavelengths utilized. The reference beam only uses the yellow doublet at 578 nm, where the desired oxides do not absorb. For SO_2 determinations, the measuring beam is so filtered that only the complex of mercury lines near 280 nm is observed, and for NO_2 the blue line at 436 nm. Provision is made for the in situ oxidation of NO to NO_2, so that before-and-after measurements at 436 nm will give information on both of these oxides.

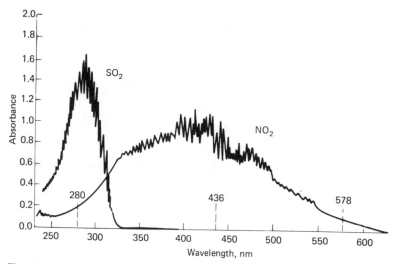

Figure 3-7 Absorption spectra of SO_2 and NO_2, showing the wavelengths used for their determination (280, 436, and 578 nm). (*E. I. Du Pont de Nemours & Co.*)

DOUBLE-BEAM SPECTROPHOTOMETERS FOR THE UV AND VISIBLE

The range covered by UV-visible spectrophotometers generally extends at its lower end down to between 165 and 210 nm. The upper limit is never less than about 650 nm and may reach 1000 nm or even further.

The most flexible, general-purpose spectrophotometers are double-beam, automatically recording types. The double-beam design provides two equivalent paths for radiation, both originating with the same source. One of these beams traverses the sample, while the other passes through an identical cuvet containing reference material. The two beams are measured separately, either by duplicate detectors or by the rapidly alternating use of the same detector.

The relation of this double-beam arrangement to Beer's law can be clarified by the following argument: Consider the radiant powers related to each of a pair of identical cuvets (Fig. 3-8). Let P'_0 denote the power of the beam coming from

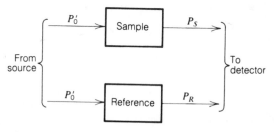

Figure 3-8 Power relations in a double-beam photometer. P'_0, the power from the source, is assumed equal on the two cells; P_R is passed by the reference, and P_S by the sample solution.

the source (equal for the two cuvets). Let P_S and P_R represent the powers transmitted through the sample and reference, both necessarily smaller than P'_0. The respective absorbances are, by Beer's law,

$$A_S = \log \frac{P'_0}{P_S} \quad \text{and} \quad A_R = \log \frac{P'_0}{P_R}$$

Combining these gives

$$A_S - A_R = \log \frac{P'_0}{P_S} - \log \frac{P'_0}{P_R} = \log \frac{P_R}{P_S} \qquad (3\text{-}10)$$

If the reference material is identical to the sample except for the absorbing solute, it is permissible to replace P_R and P_S by P_0 and P, respectively, in the Beer's law statement, to give

$$A = \log \frac{P_0}{P} \qquad (3\text{-}11)$$

where A is now the true absorbance value, corrected for absorption in the reference material. Note that P_0 is no longer the power of the incident beam, but rather represents that power diminished by all losses that are duplicated in the two cuvets. Specifically, since P'_0 does not appear in the final equation, reasonable variations in the intensity of the lamp will not effect the measured absorbance. The contents of the reference cuvet should be as nearly as possible identical to the sample with respect to absorbing impurities and refractive index.

If the spectrophotometer is designed to use a single detector, then some device is required that will alternate the radiation between the two equivalent paths. This component often takes the form of a rotating disk, usually called a *chopper*, half of which is a mirrored surface, the other half cut away, as in Fig. 3-9a. As the disk turns, driven by a constant-speed motor, the radiation is either reflected by the mirror, taking the path that traverses the reference cuvet (see Fig. 3-9b), or allowed to pass through along the path including the sample cuvet. The signal produced by the detector then has the form shown in Fig. 3-10. The heights of the

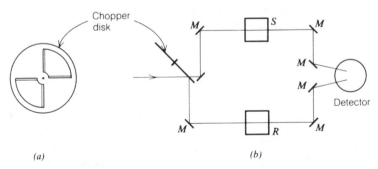

(a)   *(b)*

Figure 3-9 Double-beam photometric system using a single chopping wheel.

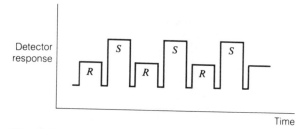

Figure 3-10 The response of the detector in the photometer of Fig. 3-9, as displayed against time. R and S refer to the reference and sample beams, respectively.

segments marked R are proportional to the quantity P_R, and those marked S to P_S. The zero line is established by the valleys between the S and R segments, corresponding to the opaque portions of the disk. It is not difficult to design electronic circuitry that will sort out these signals and compute the corrected absorbance. There are many possible variations on the double-beam optical design; two are shown in Fig. 3-11.

The linearity of the Beer's law plot is likely to be limited at higher concentrations by the presence of *stray radiation*.[5] In a spectrophotometer, this refers to any spurious radiation finding its way to the detector. Some of it may be higher-order diffraction from a grating, and some may be the result of reflections from optical surfaces of lenses and prisms. It can be reduced by careful placement of opaque baffles, but not eliminated entirely. The effects of stray radiation are most pronounced near the ends of the wavelength range of the monochromator, where it is necessary to open up the slits to obtain enough sensitivity. The residual stray radiation of a well-made single monochromator may be of the order of a few tenths of one percent of the total radiation through most of its range.

The stray radiation can be cut drastically by means of a *double monochromator*. If a single monochromator gives, say, 0.1 percent stray radiation, then passing its output through another equivalent stage should reduce it to 0.1 percent of this, or about 1 ppm.

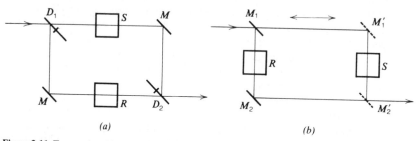

(a)   *(b)*

Figure 3-11 Two optional layouts for a double-beam photometer. In (a), two synchronized chopping disks, D_1 and D_2, are used. In (b), a carriage bearing two small mirrors moves back and forth between locations M_1, M_2, and M_1', M_2', as used in the Beckman Models DB and DBG spectrophotometers.

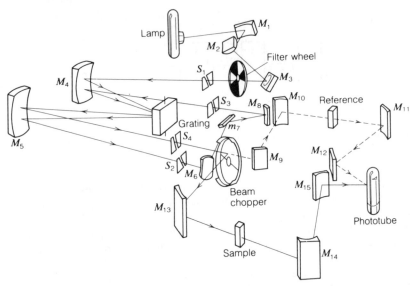

Figure 3-12 Optical schematic of the Varian–Cary Model 219 spectrophotometer. The filter wheel automatically introduces suitable filters, as needed, to eliminate overlapping spectral orders. Slits S_1 and S_4 are located physically above S_3 and S_2, respectively. All slits are curved, as shown, since this results in the best resolution in this Czerny–Turner monochromator. This diagram is somewhat simplified for clarity. (*Instrument Division of Varian Associates.*)

As an example of a high-performance, UV-visible, spectrophotometer with double monochromation, we will describe the Varian-Cary Model 219. This instrument makes double use of its one monochromator, sending the beam of radiation through it twice. Figure 3-12 shows the optical diagram. Radiation from a deuterium lamp (or, for the visible, a tungsten-halogen lamp, not shown) is focused by the combination of curved mirrors M_1, M_2, and M_3 onto the entrance slit, S_1. The upper part of the concave mirror M_4 collimates the beam and directs it onto the plane grating. The dispersed radiation is focused by the lower portion of M_5 onto slit S_2. A selected narrow band of wavelengths passes through the slit to be transferred by mirrors M_6, M_7, and M_8 to slit S_3. It now passes through the monochromator again, this time utilizing the lower part of M_4 and the upper part of M_5, finally leaving the monochromator by the exit slit S_4.

The beam next encounters the rotating semicircular mirror of the chopping wheel, and passes alternately via mirrors M_9 to M_{12}, through the reference cuvet, or mirrors M_{13} to M_{15} and the sample cuvet, to the single photomultiplier tube.

The outer rim of the chopping wheel is so shaped that it intercepts the beam between the mirrors M_6 and M_7 twice per revolution, double the frequency of the alternation from sample to reference beam. The electronic amplifier is tuned to accept only signals that are interrupted at this double frequency. Since the stray radiation originating in the first pass through the monochromator will not have been subjected to this higher frequency chopping, this is equivalent to the use of two separate monochromators. The manufacturer's specifications give 0.002 percent as the maximum stray radiation to be expected, but they show data for a particular instrument that were better than this by at least a factor of 10 for wavelengths above 220 nm.

SINGLE-BEAM SPECTROPHOTOMETERS

The earliest ultraviolet photoelectric spectrophotometer on the American market was the Beckman Model DU, introduced in 1941.[6] This was a single-beam instrument using a prism of natural quartz in a Littrow mounting. It has contributed greatly over the years to our knowledge of the UV region, both for theoretical and analytical purposes. The DU has been modernized, so that the most recent model, the DU-8, shows little external resemblance to its original ancestor. It is still, however, a single-beam spectrophotometer, but the quartz prism has been replaced by a holographic grating. The entire instrument is under microcomputer control, so that the absorbance of the sample can be corrected for that of the solvent blank, and compared to a standard, all through information stored in computer memory.

For routine analytical purposes a measurement of absorbance at a single wavelength may be all that is required. For such applications, an expensive double-beam instrument may not be justified, since a simpler, single-beam version may be quite satisfactory.

A widely used instrument, primarily for the visible range (340 to 625 nm, capable of extension to 950 nm by change of phototube and insertion of a filter) is the Bausch & Lomb Spectronic-20 (Fig. 3-13). A plane reflection grating (600 lines per mm) is mounted on a rotatable table. This resembles a Littrow mounting, but the lens is not traversed twice as in a Littrow. The fact that the incident radiation is slightly convergent rather than collimated means that the band width of radiation isolated at the exit slit (stated to be 20 nm) is somewhat broader than the best that could be obtained from the same grating, and represents a compromise between precision and expense.

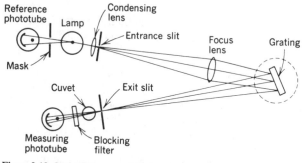

Figure 3-13 Optical diagram of the Bausch & Lomb Spectronic-20 spectrophotometer. The grating is turned from a panel knob through a cam-and-bar linkage. The blocking filter is used only with the infrared phototube, to eliminate overlapping orders. (*Bausch & Lomb, Inc.*)

The detector is a gas-filled phototube coupled to a linear amplifier. Both transmittance and absorbance are indicated on a large panel meter. There are three manual controls: wavelength selection and zero and sensitivity adjustments. An electronic voltage regulator suppresses any variation in line voltage that might give spurious signals.

DUAL-WAVELENGTH SPECTROPHOTOMETERS

An instrument can be designed so that two beams of radiation of different wavelengths pass through a single cuvet simultaneously. This can be useful in several distinct ways. (1) It can be utilized, without scanning, to monitor two components, recording their variation with time. (2) One wavelength can be set at a fixed point where the absorbance is negligible, while the other is scanned, thus permitting correction for variations in lamp intensity as in dual-beam operation but with a single cuvet. (3) It can be operated in the same configuration as (2) to give valid absorption spectra in the presence of turbidity[7]; the effective path length is inherently uncertain in this case, because of the effect of multiple reflections from suspended particles, and this arrangement guarantees that both beams follow the same path, whatever it may be. Finally (4), the two wavelengths can be scanned simultaneously, but with an offset of a few tens of nanometers, so that the resulting spectrogram will display the difference ΔA between the absorbances at the two wavelengths, against the mean wavelength, a *derivative* curve.

The original design of a dual-wavelength spectrophotometer was described by Chance in 1951.[8] Figure 3-14 shows a recent version.[9] The radiation from the source is divided into two parts by a mask. The two parts trace their paths through the same Czerny–Turner monochromator, but are dispersed by separate gratings. The chopping disk allows the two to pass sequentially through the sample to a single photomultiplier. There are two optional positions for sample cuvets. The *primary* position, almost in contact with the photomultiplier, is used whenever two wavelengths are to pass through a single cuvet; for turbid samples it is essential that the cuvet be close to the detector so that as much as possible of the scattered radiation will be collected. The *secondary* sample position is used for double-beam configurations with two cuvets.

A recent detailed discussion of sources of error in dual-wavelength spectrophotometry[10] should be studied carefully by anyone entering this field.

DERIVATIVE SPECTROSCOPY

A derivative spectrum can be obtained by other means than a dual-wavelength spectrophotometer. A derivative of any continuous function can be taken conveniently by a suitable electronic circuit, and this principle can easily be applied to absorption spectra.

Still another method is by use of an oscillating refractor plate mounted just within one of the slits of a monochromator. As shown in Fig. 3-15, the action of this

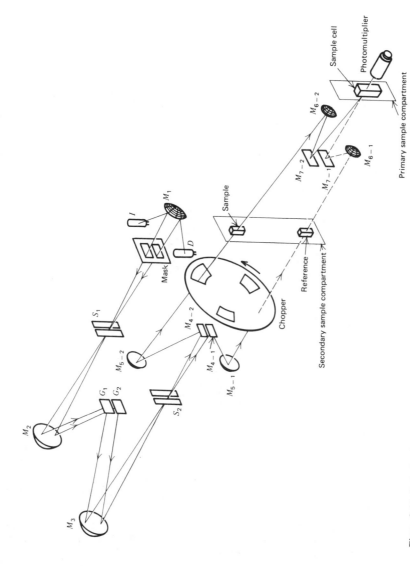

Figure 3-14 Optical schematic, dual-wavelength spectrophotometer, Perkin–Elmer Model 356, simplified. (*Perkin–Elmer Corporation.*)

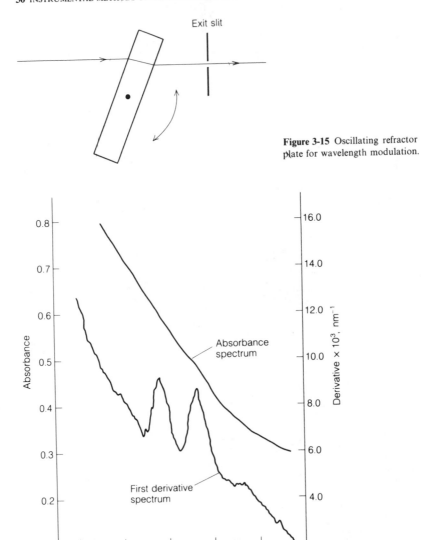

Figure 3-15 Oscillating refractor plate for wavelength modulation.

Figure 3-16 The normal and first-derivative absorption spectra of a diluted nickel-plating solution containing 12 mg/l of saccharin. (*Analytical Chemistry*.[12])

silica plate is to offset the beam of radiation, which remains parallel to its original path. As the plate swings back and forth by a few angular degrees, the wavelength of the exiting beam will vary by a few nanometers, sinusoidally, about its central value, an example of *wavelength modulation*.[11] The electronic amplifier is tuned to the frequency of oscillation, which leads to a derivative spectrum.

A derivative spectrogram shows a peak or valley corresponding to every inflection point in the normal spectrum, giving greatly enhanced resolution. Figure 3-16 compares the normal and derivative spectra of a nickel plating solution containing a small percentage of saccharin.[12] (Saccharin, *o*-benzoic sulfimide, causes an improvement in the physical properties of the electroplated nickel.) Two slight perturbations can be seen in the normal spectrum, that might well be overlooked, whereas the derivative curve has converted these into easily measured maxima.

Figure 3-17 shows the normal and derivative absorption spectra of two closely related steroids.[13] These two compounds can be distinguished much more readily from the derivative than the normal spectra.

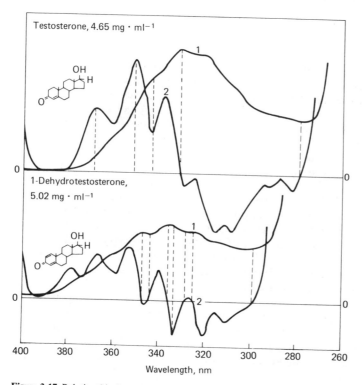

Figure 3-17 Relationship between normal UV absorption spectra (1) and their first derivatives (2). (*Analytical Chemistry*.[13])

SOURCES OF RADIATION

The tungsten filament incandescent lamp is unexcelled as a spectrophotometric source through the visible region and adjacent portions of the UV and IR, approximately 320 nm to 3.5 μm. Its lifetime at high temperature can be extended significantly by the inclusion of a small pressure of iodine vapor. This is the *tungsten-halogen* lamp (sometimes called *quartz-iodine* because it is enclosed in a silica, rather than glass, envelope to permit higher temperature operation). The iodine reacts with vaporized or sputtered tungsten atoms to form a volatile compound; this pyrolyzes when it comes in contact with the hot filament, redepositing the metal atoms on the filament rather than allowing them to accumulate on the cooler walls of the bulb.

For the UV region, hydrogen or deuterium discharge lamps are widely employed. They are useful from about 160 to 360 nm. The deuterium lamp gives somewhat greater intensity than its hydrogen counterpart, has a longer life expectancy, and costs more. A xenon arc lamp gives good coverage, but its powerful output is seldom required in absorption spectroscopy.

DETECTORS

The most widely used detector in the UV is the *photomultiplier* (PMT).[14] This device utilizes a photosensitive cathode composed of a thin layer of selected semiconductive material containing an alkali metal, such as Cs_3Sb, K_2CsSb, Na_2KSb with a trace of Cs, or successively deposited Ag, O, and Cs. The active layer can be supported by a metallic surface, or held on the inner surface of a silica or glass envelope. Different cathode materials show different spectral response curves. Some tubes, such as the popular type 1P28, respond through the range 200 to 650 nm. Special tubes extend to as low as 150 nm or as high as 1.18 μm. Figure 3-18 shows some representative spectral sensitivity curves.

The action of a PMT depends upon the emission of secondary electrons as the result of the impact of primary electrons on a sensitive surface. This can be followed with Fig. 3-19. The radiant energy incident on the photocathode liberates electrons that become accelerated by an electrostatic field, and focused on the first of a series of *dynodes*. Each electron impacting on a dynode causes the ejection of n secondary electrons, where the factor n is of the order of 3 to 5, depending on the applied voltage. The electrons ejected from the first dynode are in turn focused on the second, and so on down the string of 10 to 15 dynodes. The amplification is given by the factor n raised to a power given by the number of dynodes. Thus for 12 dynodes and $n = 4$, the amplification would be 4^{12}, or nearly 17×10^6. These 17 million electrons, resulting from a single primary photoelectron, constitute a pulse that typically lasts for about 5 ns, corresponding to an average anode current of about 0.5 mA.

Figure 3-20 shows a basic electronic circuit for a PMT. The anode current is fed into an *operational amplifier* (abbreviated "op amp," and symbolized by a

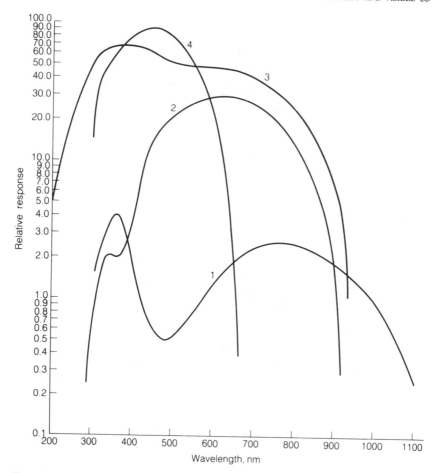

Figure 3-18 Spectral sensitivity curves for representative photomultiplier tubes. Curve (1): cathode material is Ag—O—Cs, envelope is borosilicate glass. Curve (2): cathode is multialkali, envelope is borosilicate glass. Curve (3): cathode is GaAs(Cs), envelope is UV glass. Curve (4): cathode is bialkali, envelope is borosilicate glass. (*From literature of Hamamatsu Corporation.*)

triangle). The op amp is an extremely valuable and versatile circuit component that will be enountered many times in this book, and discussed thoroughly in Chap. 27. For present purposes, the following three principles will suffice to understand its function in the PMT circuit: (1) An op amp must be provided with a feedback path from its output to the input marked with a negative sign (here the resistor R provides this path); (2) no current can enter either of the inputs to the op amp; (3) a properly connected op amp will generate whatever voltage is needed at its output to maintain (through the feedback loop) its two inputs at virtually equal potentials. In the present application, the current from the PMT anode,

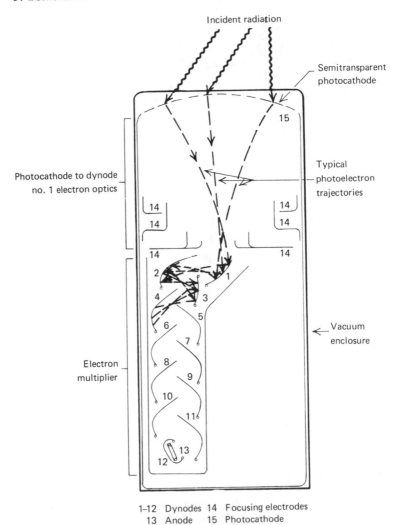

Incident radiation

Semitransparent photocathode

Photocathode to dynode no. 1 electron optics

Typical photoelectron trajectories

Electron multiplier

Vacuum enclosure

1–12 Dynodes   14 Focusing electrodes
13 Anode   15 Photocathode

Figure 3-19 Schematic of a typical end-window photomultiplier, showing a few of the electron trajectories. (*RCA Corporation.*)

I_a, since it cannot enter the amplifier, must be exactly equalled by a current from the amplifier output through resistor R, so that the $(-)$ input will be maintained at virtual ground [since the $(+)$ input is grounded]. Therefore the output voltage will be given by $E_{out} = I_a R$. This is an efficient and convenient method of measuring the small current. Many modifications of the circuit of Fig. 3-20 have been devised, each with some special advantage. Several of these are described in Ref. 15.

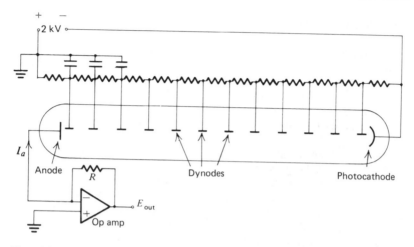

Figure 3-20 Typical connections for a photomultiplier. The resistors in the voltage divider chain are all equal, perhaps 50 kΩ each. The capacitors are needed only if fluctuating or pulsed radiation is being measured. The operational amplifier is discussed in the text.

If less sensitivity is required, a nonmultiplying phototube is often used for its relative simplicity and economy. This consists of a photocathode similar to that of a PMT, together with an anode, enclosed in a glass or silica envelope. As shown in Fig. 3-21, an op amp can be used in exactly the same way here as with the PMT. The resistor R is typically 1 to 10 MΩ, which (by Ohm's law) makes E_{out} 1 to 10 V for a photocurrent of 1 μA. The spectral range of these tubes is determined by the nature of the cathode material, the same as for PMTs. Tubes filled with a low pressure of argon have a sensitivity 10 to 20 times greater than their vacuum counterparts, but are considered somewhat less stable and reliable for precision photometry.

A variety of solid-state photocells are available for applications in the visible and near-IR regions. These include photovoltaic cells, photoconductive diodes, and phototransistors. A photoconductive diode of PbS is the detector of choice for the near IR, and is included in some UV-visible spectrophotometers to allow them to be used in this region. Details of semiconductor devices are given in Chap. 27.

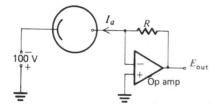

Figure 3-21 Connections for a vacuum or gas-filled phototube.

PHOTOMETRIC ACCURACY

The concentration range over which photometric analyses are useful is limited at both high and low values. At high concentrations of absorbing material, so little radiant energy can penetrate, that the sensitivity of the photometer becomes inadequate. At low concentrations, on the other hand, the error inherent in reading the output device becomes large compared to the quantity being measured. Therefore it follows that there must be some intermediate concentration where the precision is greatest.

This point at which the relative concentration error is a minimum can be located mathematically, provided only that the system obeys Beer's law. Two cases can be distinguished, depending on the noise characteristics of the detector employed. Any detector of radiation is limited in sensitivity by the noise it generates. By "noise" is meant the random fluctuations unavoidably present in all electrical circuitry.[16] Of interest in the present discussion are two types of noise that may prevail in photodetectors.

Vacuum phototubes and photomultipliers are limited by the so-called *shot noise*, caused by the statistical fluctuations in the rate at which individual electrons are emitted from the cathode. It can be shown that shot noise varies in magnitude as the square-root of the power of the incident radiation. On the other hand, most other detectors are limited by *resistance noise* (also called *Johnson noise*), due to the random thermal motion of electrons in any resistive component. This kind of noise is constant, not related to the power of the radiation being measured.

For greatest accuracy in the measurement of the absorbance, the quantity ΔA, the smallest measurable increment of absorbance, must be as small a fraction as possible of the actual absorbance A; that is, $\Delta A/A$ must be minimized. To determine the value of A for which $\Delta A/A$ is a minimum, it is necessary to differentiate twice the expression $A = \log(P_0/P)$, and to set the second derivative equal to zero. It is convenient to rewrite this expression in the form

$$A = \log P_0 - \log P \tag{3-12}$$

Then

$$dA = 0 - (\log e)\,\frac{1}{P}\,dP = 0 - 0.434\,\frac{1}{P}\,dP \tag{3-13}$$

Dividing both sides by A, and substituting for P its equal $P_0 \cdot 10^{-A}$ gives

$$\frac{1}{A}\,dA = -\frac{0.434}{AP_0 10^{-A}}\,dP \tag{3-14}$$

Replacing differentials by finite increments gives us

$$\frac{\Delta A}{A} = -\frac{0.434\,\Delta P}{P_0}\left(\frac{1}{A 10^{-A}}\right) \tag{3-15}$$

in which ΔP is the increment of power corresponding to ΔA.

For the case where ΔP is constant (i.e., resistance-limited noise), a second differentiation gives

$$\frac{d(\Delta A/A)}{dA} = - \frac{0.434\,\Delta P}{P_0}\left(\frac{10^A \ln 10}{A} - \frac{10^A}{A^2}\right) \tag{3-16}$$

The condition for the minimum value of $\Delta A/A$ is that the right-hand member of this equation be zero, and thus that the factor within the parentheses must be zero

$$\frac{10^A \ln 10}{A} = \frac{10^A}{A^2} \tag{3-17}$$

from which we can write

$$A_{opt} = \frac{1}{\ln 10} = 0.434 \tag{3-18}$$

On the other hand, if the detector is shot-noise limited, so that $\Delta P \propto \sqrt{P}$, a similar derivation gives

$$A_{opt} = \frac{2}{\ln 10} = 0.868 \tag{3-19}$$

Thus the optimum absorbance is twice as great for photomultiplier detectors as for photoconductive or other types. The curves corresponding to these two cases are plotted in Fig. 3-22. The minimum for shot-noise limited detectors is much broader than for the resistance-noise case, so that valid measurements can be made up to absorbances considerably greater than 2, whereas for a resistive detector the practical limit is about $A = 0.8$. The lower limits are about the same in the two cases, around $A = 0.25$.

The conventional method of plotting a calibration graph for a photometric analysis is the straight line of Fig. 3-2. This shows the region over which Beer's

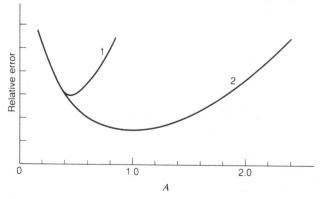

Figure 3-22 Relative photometric error plotted as a function of absorbance: (1) resistance-noise limited, (2) shot-noise limited.

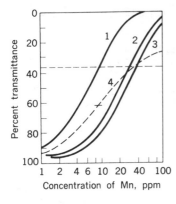

Figure 3-23 Standard curves for permanganate. The solid curves are determined with a spectrophotometer at wavelengths (1) 526, (2) 480, and (3) 590 nm. The dashed curve (4) is from data taken with a filter photometer, using a filter centering at 430 nm. Compare this with Fig. 3-3. (*Analytical Chemistry.*[18])

law is followed, but it fails to give any indication of the relative precision at various levels of absorbance. Another method of plotting has been suggested,[17,18] that permits some added conclusions to be drawn. Figure 3-23 shows the curve obtained by plotting percent transmittance against the logarithm of the concentration. If a sufficient range has been included, an S-shaped curve, known as a *Ringbom plot*, always results. If the system follows Beer's law, the point of inflection (for a resistance-noise limited detector) occurs at 37 percent transmittance; if not, the inflection is at some other value, but the form of the curve is the same. The curve generally has a considerable region which is nearly straight. The extent of this straight portion indicates directly the optimum range of concentration for the analysis.

The range of concentrations suitable for analysis with adequate precision may be too short for application to the range of unknowns likely to be encountered. The useful range can often be extended to higher concentrations by using a cuvet of shorter path length or by a different choice of wavelength. As Fig. 3-23 shows, the useful range for permanganate is about 6 to 60 ppm of manganese at 580 nm, as compared with 2 to 20 ppm at 526 nm.

PHOTON COUNTING

As the power incident on a detector is diminished, it becomes more and more difficult to distinguish between the signal and random noise. In such conditions, the response can be greatly improved by observing incident photons individually. If the arrival rate of the photons is low enough to resolve single events, a separate pulse can be observed for each photon, and these pulses can be counted electronically with greater accuracy than can be attained by averaging them out and measuring a steady current.

The random noise present in the circuit also consists of pulses, mostly smaller in amplitude than those produced by photons. An electronic circuit called a *discriminator* can suppress all pulses smaller than some selected cutoff level,

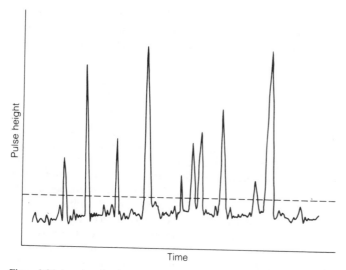

Figure 3-24 A series of pulses rising above random noise. Only those pulses extending above some cutoff level (dashed line) are counted.

allowing only the larger pulses to be counted (Fig. 3-24). If the measurement were carried out by current-measuring techniques, then the noise and signal would be additive, both contributing to the output. The conventional method is preferable when the signal is large compared to the noise, but photon counting gives better accuracy when they are of the same order of magnitude.[19] The technique is useful in absorption spectrophotometry of highly absorbing solutions, and is of great value in such areas as fluorimetry, where only very low levels of radiation are to be observed.

SPECTROPHOTOMETER OPERATION

There are a number of controls that must be provided in any spectrophotometer. A listing of these will promote full understanding of such instruments.

Manual spectrophotometers require (1) a wavelength (or wave number) control, usually involving a mechanical linkage to rotate the grating or prism; (2) a slit-width adjustment; (3) a zero-adjustment, sometimes called a dark-current compensator; and (4) a gain control. In addition recording spectrophotometers require scanning and recording controls.

Some of these adjustments are omitted in less expensive instruments, at the cost of reduced flexibility. On the other hand, more elaborate models may have additional controls, e.g., one to permit using a double-beam instrument in a single-beam mode. In the majority of recent spectrophotometers, all of these features are under microprocessor control.

A variety of attachments or accessories are available for most spectrophotometers, for example, adaptors to enable one to obtain reflectance or fluorescence spectra, and special holders to accept unusually long-path absorption cells, among others.

HIGH-PRECISION TECHNIQUES

In older spectrophotometers, the limit of precision was dictated by the precision with which the reading of the output meter or of the recorder trace could be made. In such instruments it is possible to increase the overall precision by means of scale expansion. This requires the preparation of one or more standard solutions with nearly the same concentration as the unknown. The high-transmittance end of the scale is then set with the most dilute standard rather than with pure solvent, while the low-transmittance end is set with a more concentrated standard. Such procedures are seldom used today, largely because the digital output display, so commonly in use, gives greatly reduced reading errors. At high absorbances, photon counting likewise increases the precision. Nevertheless, scale-expansion methods should be kept in mind as possible alternatives; their advantages and limitations have been delineated by Ingle.[20]

CHEMICAL APPLICATIONS

The absorption of radiant energy in the UV and visible spectral regions depends primarily on the number and arrangement of the electrons in the absorbing molecules or ions. Among inorganic substances, selective absorption may be expected whenever an unfilled electronic energy level is covered or protected by a completed level, usually formed by coordinate covalences with other atoms.

Consider copper as an example. The simple Cu^{2+} ion is never found in aqueous solution (though often written as such), because it has a great tendency to form coordinate bonds with any available molecules or ions that carry unshared pairs of electrons. Such unshared pairs are present in water, ammonia, cyanide ion, chloride ion, and many other entities. The structure of the copper (II) ion coordinated with any of these Lewis bases has only 17 electrons in the third (M) major energy level, whereas the fourth (N) level contains a stable octet. The several ions do not have identical colors, as the nature of the ligand has an effect on the energy of the electrons.

Selective absorption among organic molecules is again related to the deployment of electrons in the molecule. Completely saturated compounds show no selective absorption throughout the visible and the accessible UV regions. Compounds that contain a double bond absorb strongly in the far UV (195 nm for ethylene). Conjugated double bonds produce absorption at longer wavelengths. The more extensive the conjugated system, the longer will be the wavelengths at which absorption is observed. If the system extends far enough, the absorption enters the visible region, and color results. Thus β-carotene, with 11 conjugated double bonds, absorbs strongly in the region 420 to 480 nm, and hence is yellow-green in appearance. The complete conjugated system in a compound is called its *chromophore*.

The wavelengths of the absorption maxima of a compound provide a means for identifying the chromophore it contains. The spectra are in general modified by the presence of various atomic groups when these are substituted for the hydrogen atoms on the carbons of the chromophore. Such substituents usually have the effect of shifting the absorption bands toward longer wavelengths, and changing their absorbance values. Substituents that produce these effects are known loosely as *auxochromes*.

In Table 3-4 are listed a number of organic compounds containing representative chromophores, together with their wavelengths of maximum absorption and approximate molar absorptivity values. Many of these illustrative compounds, especially those with larger chromophores, also have many lesser maxima in their spectra. This table cannot be used in the precise identification of absorbing groups, the way the corresponding IR table can.

Table 3-4 Representative chromophores†

Compound	Chromophore	Solvent	λ_{max}, nm	$\log \epsilon$
Octene-3	C=C	Hexane	185	3.9
			230	0.3
Acetylene	C≡C	(Vapor)	173	3.8
Acetone	C=O	Hexane	188	2.9
			279	1.2
Diazoethyl acetate	N=N	Ethanol	252	3.9
			371	1.1
Butadiene	C=C—C=C	Hexane	217	4.3
Crotonaldehyde	C=C—C=O	Ethanol	217	4.2
			321	1.3
Dimethylglyoxime	N=C—C=N	Ethanol	226	4.2
Octatrienol	C=C—C=C—C=C	Ethanol	265	4.7
Decatetraenol	[—C=C—]₄	Ethanol	300	4.8
Vitamin A	[—C=C—]₅	Ethanol	328	3.7
Benzene	(benzene ring structure)	Hexane	198	3.9
			255	2.4
1,4-Benzoquinone	O=(ring)=O	Hexane	245	5.2
			285	2.7
			435	1.2
Naphthalene	(naphthalene ring structure)	Ethanol	220	5.0
			275	3.7
			314	2.5
Diphenyl	(diphenyl ring structure)	Hexane	246	4.3

† Data collected from various sources; to be taken as illustrative only.

Table 3-5 Effect of auxochromes on the benzene chromophore[21]

Compound	Solvent	Ethylenic band		Benzenoid band	
		λ_{max}, nm	ϵ_{max}	λ_{max}, nm	ϵ_{max}
Benzene	Hexane	204	7900	256	200
Anilinium cation	Aq. acid	203	7500	254	160
Chlorobenzene	Ethanol	210	7600	265	240
Phenol	Water	210.5	6200	270	1450
o-Catechol	Water, pH 3	214	6300	276	2300
Anisole	2% Methanol	217	6400	269	1480
Aniline	Water	230	8600	280	1430
Phenolate anion	Aq. alkali	235	9400	289	2600
Thiophenol	Hexane	236	10000	269	700
o-Catechol anion	Water, pH 11	236.5	6800	292	3500
Diphenyl ether	Cyclohexane	255	11000	272	2000
				278	1800

In aromatic compounds, the benzene ring is the simplest chromophore. Two or more rings in conjugation, as in either naphthalene or diphenyl, again increase the absorption and shift it toward the visible. Table 3-5 shows the effect of some auxochromes on the absorption of benzene.[21]

The quinoid ring is much more effective as a chromophore than is the benzene ring. An example contrasting the two types is found in phenolphthalein, which has the following structures in acidic and basic solutions, respectively:

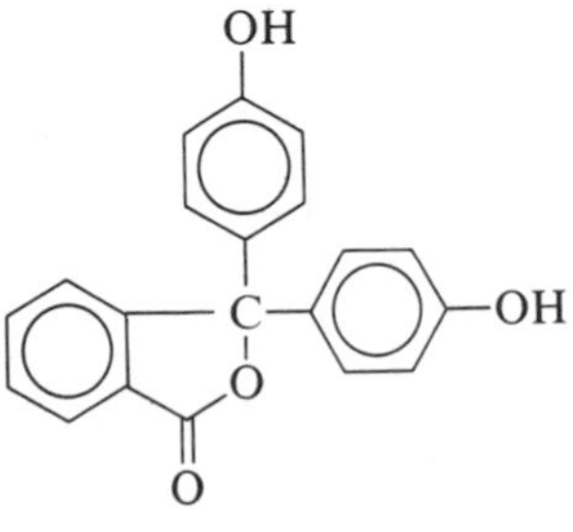

Colorless molecule
(in acid solution)

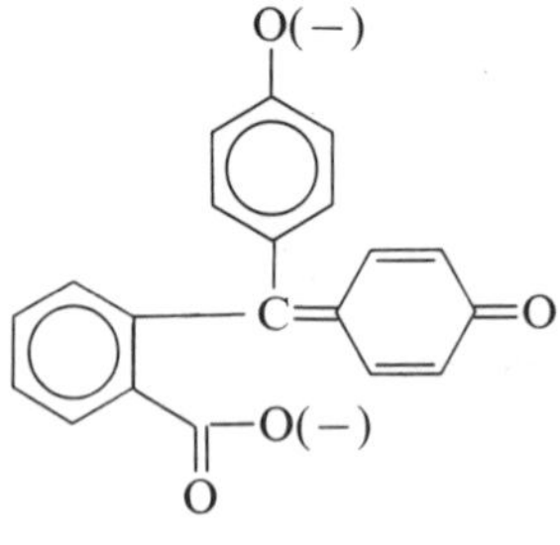

Red anion (in basic
solution)

In the colorless form, conjugation does not extend outside the individual rings (except that one ring is conjugated with a carbonyl group). In the red form, however, one ring has been converted to the corresponding quinone, which results in extending the conjugation to include the central carbon and, through it, the other two rings. So we must conclude that the entire anion constitutes a chromophore, whereas in acid solution, the molecule contains three separate and nearly identical lesser chromophores, the benzene rings. Figure 3-25 shows the corresponding absorption spectra.

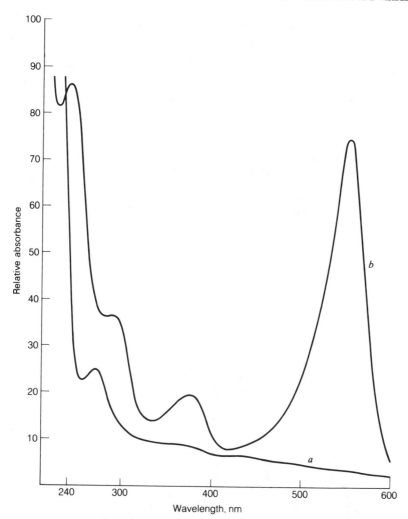

Figure 3-25 Absorption spectra of phenolphthalein: (*a*) in acid solution, (*b*) in basic solution. The vertical scale is relative absorbance.

QUALITATIVE ANALYSIS

Ultraviolet and visible absorption spectra provide a useful source of supporting evidence in the elucidation of organic structures. Selective absorption in itself is seldom sufficiently unique to serve as an identifying fingerprint for a particular structure, but it may serve to rule out certain alternatives. If there is no absorption from about 210 nm to the visible, it is certain that the compound contains no conjugated unsaturation. If the transparency extends down to 180 nm, then even isolated double bonds must be absent.

A number of empirical correlations between wavelengths of absorption maxima and structure have been worked out. One of these, due to Woodward,[22,23] concerns α,β-unsaturated carbonyl compounds. A basic absorption can be assigned at 215 nm; additional conjugated double bonds will add 30 nm each; a saturated substituent on C-2 will add 10, on C-3, 12, and on C-4 or higher, 18; a 2-bromo substituent adds 23; etc. The measured absorption maximum can be compared with values calculated for various possible structures.

The variation of the absorption spectrum of an acid-base indicator as a function of pH provides a method for determining the pertinent pK value. In Fig. 3-26a are plotted the absorption curves for phenol red at a series of pH values. It is seen that with increasing pH the absorption at 550 nm increases, while the lesser absorption at 425 nm decreases. Note that the several curves cross very

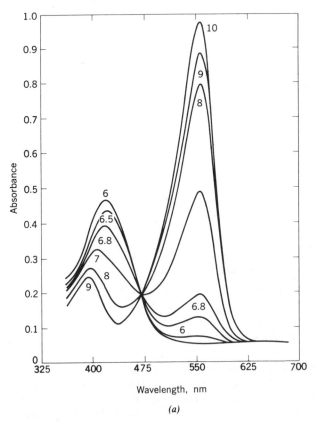

Wavelength, nm

(a)

Figure 3-26 Phenol red: (a) absorbance curves at various pH values.

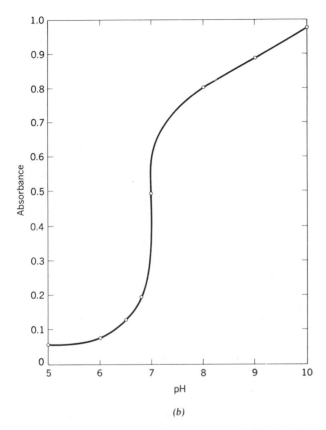

(b)

Figure 3-26 Phenol red: (*b*) absorbance at 550 nm as a function of pH. The pK of the indicator is seen to be very nearly 7.0.

nearly at a common point at 475 nm; this is called an *isosbestic point*. Such a point is indicative of a system containing two chromophores which are interconvertible, so that the total quantity is constant: the two chromophores have the same absorptivities at the isosbestic point.

If the absorbance at one of the maxima (550 nm in the case of phenol red) is plotted against pH, an S-shaped curve is obtained (Fig. 3-26*b*). The horizontal portion to the left corresponds to the acidic form of the indicator, while the upper portion to the right corresponds to nearly complete conversion to the basic form. Since the pK is defined as the pH value for which one-half of the indicator is in each form, this is determined by a point midway between the two horizontal segments, pH 7.0 in the example.

The dissociation constants of compounds with absorption in the UV rather than the visible can often be determined by a similar procedure. Examples

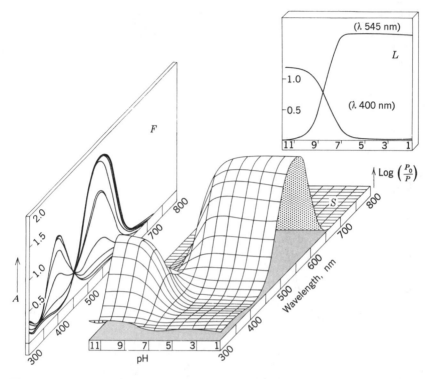

Figure 3-27 A three-dimensional plot of the absorption spectra of benzeneazodiphenylamine. In part S, the vertical axis measures absorbance as a function of pH (left-right axis) and wavelength (oblique axis). F and L are two-dimensional modes of representing the same data, corresponding to Figs. 3-26, a and b, respectively. (*Chemical and Engineering News.*[26])

are theobromine[24] (240 nm), theophylline[24] (240 nm), and benzotriazole[25] (274 nm). It is instructive to plot the data in three dimensions, as reported for benzeneazodiphenylamine in Fig. 3-27.[26] In this presentation, the three axes refer to wavelength, pH, and absorbance, respectively. The isosbestic point on graph F corresponds to a straight line parallel to the pH axis on the three-dimensional plot.

The existence of an isosbestic point is evidence that a chemical equilibrium exists between two absorbing species. If instead of one absorption peak disappearing as another appears (the condition for an isosbestic point), the wavelength of a maximum shifts gradually on change of pH, concentration, or other variable, then one can assume that the change is due to a physical interaction between the absorbing substance and its environment, or to the existence of a series of complexes of about the same stability.

DETERMINATION OF THE
LIGAND/METAL RATIO IN A COMPLEX

Since organometallic complexes generally show selective absorption in the UV or visible, this property is widely employed to determine their composition and stability constants. The stoichiometry of a stable complex can be determined by either of two related techniques: the *mole-ratio* method introduced by Yoe and Jones[27] and the method of *continuous variations* attributable to Job and modified by Vosburgh and Cooper.[28]

In the mole-ratio method, the absorbances are measured for a series of solutions which contain varying amounts of one constituent with a constant amount of the other. A plot is prepared of absorbance as a function of the ratio of moles of ligand to moles of metal ion. This is expected to give a straight line from the origin to the point where equivalent amounts of the constituents are present. The curve will then become horizontal, since all of one component is used up, and the addition of more of the other component can produce no more of the absorbing complex. If the constituent in excess itself absorbs at the same wavelength, the curve after the equivalence point will show a slope that is positive, but less than that prior to equivalence. Figure 3-28 shows the result of such an experiment using the complex of diphenylcarbazone with Hg(II) ions.[29]

The method of continuous variations requires a series of solutions of varying concentration of the two constituents wherein their *sum* is kept constant. The difference between the measured absorbance and the absorbance calculated for the mixed constituents on the assumption of no reaction between them is plotted against the mole fraction. The resulting curve will show a maximum (or less often a minimum) at the mole fraction corresponding to that in the complex (Fig. 3-29).

It will be noted that the Yoe–Jones method is essentially a titration of a known amount of metal ion by a solution of ligand, where the end point (the

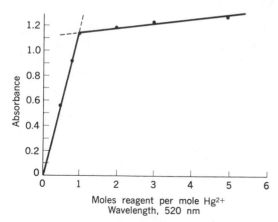

Figure 3-28 Yoe–Jones plot for the mercury–diphenylcarbazone complex. (*Analytical Chemistry.*[29])

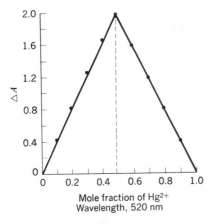

Mole fraction of Hg^{2+}
Wavelength, 520 nm

Figure 3-29 Job plot (continuous variations) for the mercury–diphenylcarbazone complex. The vertical coordinate represents the difference between the absorbance of the mixed solution and the sum of the absorbances that the reagents would have shown had they not reacted. (*Analytical Chemistry.*[29])

intersection of two lines) gives information about the stoichiometry of the complex. It has been pointed out by McCarthy[30] that if the two solutions (metal ion and ligand) are of the same molar concentration, then at any point in the titration, the total concentration of ion-plus-ligand is necessarily constant. Hence the Yoe–Jones plot contains all the information needed to construct a Job plot. The Job treatment thus amounts to a graphical procedure for accentuating the end point in the titration.

The breaks in the curves of either of these methods are often less sharp than one might wish. Curvature in the vicinity of the equivalence point depends on the magnitude of the stability constant of the complex, and indeed often provides a convenient means of measuring this constant.[31–33]

QUANTITATIVE ANALYSIS

The determination of an absorbing substance can be carried out directly through Beer's law if no other absorbing material is present to interfere, or if the interfering material can be removed or corrected for. A good example of this approach, reported recently, is the measurement of ozone concentration in urban smog.[34] A high-pressure mercury arc lamp was set up on the roof of a building, and its radiation received by a simplified prism spectrophotometer located on another building about 100 m distant. Since a double-beam system was impractical, zero calibration was made at night, when atmospheric ozone was known to drop to negligible values. The ozone measurements were interfered with by other oxidants such as NO_2, but this effect was eliminated by determining the ratio of absorbances at the ozone maxima of 313 and 265 nm. Ozone was found to rise to about 22 parts in 10^8 at noon, as the average of 50 days.

Substances that do not show useful absorption can in many instances be determined spectrophotometrically following the addition of a reagent to produce an absorbing complex or other chromophore. One of the more important reagents is *dithizone* (diphenylthiocarbazone). This green compound, soluble in chloroform, reacts with cations of most of the transition metals to give red or violet complexes. The reagent can be made specific by adjustment of the pH. Details of the dithizone method are readily available[35,36] and will not be repeated here. Another example of developed absorption is the determination of trace amounts of Hg(II) with the dye 4,4'-bis(dimethylamino)diphenylamine, known as Bindschedler's Green, in citrate buffer.[37] The complex, extracted into 1,2-dichloroethane, follows Beer's law from 8×10^{-7} to 4×10^{-6} M Hg(II). Only tin, out of 21 metals checked, interferes with the determination. Reference 35 lists hundreds of comparable analytical procedures.

ADDITIVITY OF ABSORBANCES

In our discussion of Beer's law it was pointed out that the absorbance is proportional to the number of particles that are effective in absorbing radiation at the specified wavelength. This is easily extended to cover the presence in the same solution of more than one absorbing species. Each species absorbs as though the others were not present. We can write

$$A = \sum_i A_i = b \sum_i a_i c_i \qquad (3\text{-}20)$$

which states formally that the absorbance is an additive property. This relation presumes, of course, that there is no chemical interaction between solutes.

This additivity can be useful in a number of ways. It validates the familiar use of a blank to subtract from the observed absorbance that due to the solvent and reagent impurities. It also permits one to subtract from the spectrum of an unknown the absorbance due to a chromophore known to be present, in order to identify or measure quantitatively a second chromophore. For example, consider Fig. 3-30.[38] It was desired to determine with precision the UV absorption spectrum of 7-dehydrocholesterol, a material difficult to purify because of air-oxidation. Esters, however, can be purified readily. Curve (*a*) is the spectrum of a pure sample of the 4-nitrobenzoyl ester of the sterol. From this was subtracted the spectrum of cyclohexyl 4-nitrobenzoate, curve (*b*). The result was curve (*c*), which is identical in shape with a spectrum of authentic 7-dehydrocholesterol, but with a molar absorptivity unaffected by lack of purity.

The additivity of absorbance is also essential in *multiple analysis*, the simultaneous determination of two or more absorbing substances in the same solution. The requirement for multiple analyses is merely that the absorption curves for the individual components do not approach too close to coincidence. Some partial overlapping is permissible, but the greater the overlap, the less precise the analysis. The relation can be understood by reference to Fig. 3-31. Curves 1 and 2 are the absorption spectra of the pure components, and curve 3 that of the mixture. It is assumed that no other substances present absorb in this region.

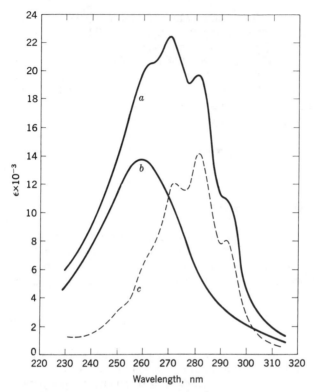

Figure 3-30 Ultraviolet absorption spectra of (*a*) 7-dehydrocholesterol 4-nitrobenzoate, (*b*) cyclohexyl 4-nitrobenzoate, and (*c*) 7-dehydrocholesterol, determined by subtraction. Solvent: hexane. (*Journal of the American Chemical Society.*[38])

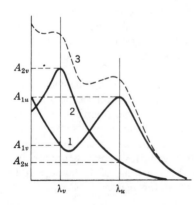

Figure 3-31 Two-component analysis with a spectrophotometer, a hypothetical example.

Note that the maxima of curve 3 are displaced slightly from the wavelengths of the maxima of curves 1 and 2. Clearly, both substances contribute to the absorption at both wavelengths λ_u and λ_v. Let c_1 and c_2 represent the concentrations of the two components in the mixture, and let A_{1u} represent the absorbance of substance 1 at wavelength λ_u, etc., as indicated in the figure. Then the absorbance of curve 3 at λ_v will be given by

$$A_v = A_{1v} + A_{2v} = a_{1v}bc_1 + a_{2v}bc_2$$

and at λ_u by

$$A_u = A_{1u} + A_{2u} = a_{1u}bc_1 + a_{2u}bc_2$$

Since A_v and A_u are determined by experimental observation on the mixture, and the a's by observation on the pure substances, the above equations can be solved simultaneously for c_1 and c_2. For best precision, a_{1v} and a_{2u} should be as low as possible, while a_{1u} and a_{2v} should be high.

The simultaneous equations are readily solved with a computer, or the solution can be arrived at by a graphical procedure.[39]

An example that shows the possibilities of the method is the simultaneous determination of Mo, Ti, and V by means of their colored complexes with H_2O_2.[40] The standard curves are reproduced in Fig. 3-32.

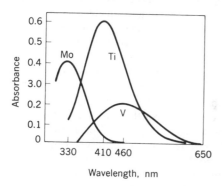

Metal	Absorbances, A		
	330 nm	410 nm	460 nm
Mo	0.416	0.048	0.002
Ti	0.130	0.608	0.410
V	0.000	0.148	0.200

Figure 3-32 Comparison spectra of the products of reaction of hydrogen peroxide with Mo, Ti, and V. Concentration: 4 mg of metal per 100 ml. (*Analytical Chemistry*.[40])

PHOTOMETRIC TITRATIONS

In classical visual titrimetry, the equivalence point in a reaction is detected by observing a change in color, either inherent in one of the reactants (e.g., permanganate), or produced by an indicator. Under favorable conditions, precision within a few parts per thousand is easily attainable by operators with normal vision. Good results are difficult or impossible to obtain, however, if the color change is gradual, or if the colors of the two forms do not contrast sharply.

Such difficulties can be overcome by carrying out the titration in a cuvet in a spectrophotometer or filter photometer. An optimum wavelength (or filter) is selected and the zero adjustments made in advance. Then a photometric reading is taken following each incremental addition from a buret. Conventional spectrophotometers may require some structural modifications to permit the insertion of a titration vessel of convenient size, as well as a buret tip and some kind of stirrer.

Numerous automatic or semiautomatic titrators are available. These can carry out all the steps of a titration with a minimum of operator attention. In some the results are plotted out on a pen recorder, while in others the buret stopcock is closed electrically at the end point. Here again, computer control is the rule in modern instruments.

The usual photometric titration curve is a plot of absorbance against the volume of added reagent. If the absorbing substances (titrant, substance titrated, or both) follow Beer's law, then the titration curve, corrected for dilution, will consist of two straight lines intersecting at the equivalence point. The intersection is likely to show some degree of curvature as a result of incompleteness of reaction at the equivalence point. This is usually of little consequence, as the more remote segments of the curve are nearly straight and can be extrapolated to an intersection.

Figure 3-33 shows the titration curve of a mixture of m- and p-nitrophenols titrated by NaOH.[41] The absorbance was measured at 545 nm, a wavelength where the anions of both isomers absorb, but where the corresponding acids do not. The absorptivity of the m-isomer is greater than that of the p-isomer. The latter is neutralized first, because it is the stronger of the two weak acids. The end points corresponding to the two straight-line intersections were in error by slightly over 1 percent in this particular experiment. It would be impossible to determine these two acids in the presence of each other by visual observation, with or without an indicator, as the color change corresponding to the first equivalence point would be very gradual. For a similar reason, the analysis would also be impractical by potentiometric (pH-meter) techniques.

Satisfactory results can be obtained in the titration of a weak acid if CK_a, the product of the molar concentration and the acid ionization constant, is greater than about 10^{-12}.[42] Strong acids cannot be titrated in this way, as they are in the ionized state at all times. They may, however, be monitored photometrically by following the absorbance of an added indicator. The indicator is, as usual, a weak acid such that the free acid and its anion absorb at different wavelengths.

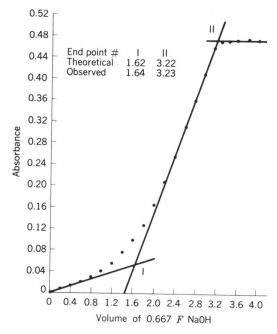

End point #	I	II
Theoretical	1.62	3.22
Observed	1.64	3.23

Volume of 0.667 F NaOH

Figure 3-33 Photometric titration of a mixture of 50 ml of 0.0219 M 4-nitrophenol and 50 ml of 0.0213 M 3-nitrophenol with 0.667 M NaOH. Wavelength: 545 nm. (*Analytical Chemistry*.[41])

The indicator is not selected on the same basis as for visual titrations, however. For visual work, it is desirable to have the pK_a of the indicator coincide with the pH of the titration reaction at its equivalence point. For a photometric system, on the other hand, when measurements are made in the region of absorption of the indicator anion, an indicator should be chosen that has a small enough pK_a value that it does not start to be neutralized until the stronger acid has essentially completely reacted. The equivalence point can then be found by the intersection of two straight-line segments, as at a in Fig. 3-34. Intersection b corresponds to complete titration of the indicator, so this system can be considered to be the titration of a mixture of a strong and a weak acid.

The titration of various metals by EDTA and similar complexogens is one of the most fruitful applications of photometric titration. Figure 3-35 shows an

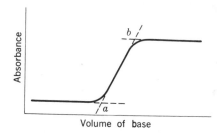

Volume of base

Figure 3-34 Photometric titration curve of acid titrated by base with an added indicator.

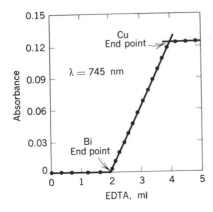

Figure 3-35 Photometric titration of a bismuth–copper mixture with a 0.1 M solution of EDTA. (*Analytical Chemistry.*[43])

example in which Bi and Cu are determined successively in a single titration.[43] Measurements were made at 745 nm, where the Cu-EDTA complex absorbs strongly, but the Bi-EDTA complex does not.

Precipitation titrations represent another important application of photometric end-point detection, but discussion of them is postponed to Chap. 8.

PROBLEMS

3-1 A particular sample of a solution of a colored substance, known to follow Beer's law, shows 80.0 percent transmittance when measured in a cuvet 1.00 cm in length. (*a*) Calculate the percent transmittance for a solution of twice the concentration in the same cuvet. (*b*) What must be the path length in the cuvet to give the same transmittance (80.0 percent) for a solution of twice the original concentration? (*c*) Calculate the percent transmittance of the original solution contained in a cuvet with 0.50 cm path length. (*d*) If the original concentration was 0.0050 percent (weight/volume), what is the value of the absorptivity a?

3-2 In the preparation of a reference curve for an analysis with a photoelectric filter photometer, the following values were obtained:

Concentration (mg/liter)	P_0	P
0.00	98.0	98.0
1.00	97.0	77.2
2.00	100.0	63.5
3.00	99.5	50.0
4.00	100.0	41.3
5.00	100.0	33.5
6.00	100.0	27.9
7.00	99.0	23.4
8.00	98.2	20.3
9.00	100.0	18.1
10.00	100.0	16.4

(a) Calculate absorbances, and plot them against concentration. Do these data indicate any deviation from Beer's law, and if so, what sign? (b) Plot these data according to Ringbom's method, and state the approximate range of concentrations that should give adequate analytical precision.

3-3 Vitamin D_2 (calciferol, mol wt $= 397$), shows an absorption maximum at 264 nm, with a molar absorptivity (in alcohol) of 18,200. Beer's law is followed over a wide range. (a) What is the absorptivity a? (b) What range of concentrations, expressed in grams per liter, can be used for analysis if it is desired to keep the absorbance between the limits 0.4 to 0.9? Assume $b = 1.00$ cm.

3-4 On the basis of Fig. 3-4, predict the sign of any apparent deviation from Beer's law in aqueous K_2CrO_4 solutions, at the following wavelengths, as absorbance is plotted against total Cr(VI) in solution: 350 nm, 370 nm, 445 nm, 480 nm.

3-5 For each of the following situations, predict whether Beer's law would show an apparent negative deviation, positive deviation, or practically none at all. (a) The absorbing substance is the undissociated form of a weak acid. (b) The absorbing entity is the cation in equilibrium with the weak acid. (c) A metal is being determined by means of a color-forming reagent, measured with a photoelectric photometer with the appropriate glass filter.

3-6 A silicate rock is to be analyzed for its chromium content. A sample is ground to a fine powder, and a 0.5000-g portion is weighed out for analysis. By suitable treatment, the material is decomposed, the chromium being converted to Na_2CrO_4. The filtered solution is made up to 50.00 ml with 0.1 M H_2SO_4, following the addition of 2 ml of 0.25 percent diphenylcarbazide, a reagent that gives a red-violet color with Cr(VI). A standard solution is available that contains 15.00 mg of pure $K_2Cr_2O_7$ per liter. A 5.00-ml aliquot of the standard is treated with 2 ml of the diphenylcarbazide solution and diluted to 50.00 ml with 0.1 M H_2SO_4. The absorbances of the two final solutions are determined in a spectrophotometer and found to be $A_{std} = 0.354$; $A_{unkn} = 0.272$. What is the amount of chromium in the rock, expressed in terms of percent Cr_2O_3?

3-7 Set up simultaneous equations for the determination of Mo, Ti, and V mixtures by the peroxide method, using the data of Fig. 3-32 and the associated table. In one experiment, a test solution was treated with excess hydrogen peroxide and perchloric acid, and diluted to 50.00 ml. The following absorbances were obtained:

Wavelength, nm	330	410	460
Absorbance A	0.284	0.857	0.718

Calculate the quantities of the three elements in milligrams present in the sample. Assume equal path length in all measurements.

3-8 Caffeine, $C_8H_{10}O_2N_4 \cdot H_2O$ (formula weight $= 212.1$), has been shown to have an average absorbance $A = 0.510$ for a concentration of 1.000 mg per 100 ml at 272 nm. A sample of 2.500 g of a soluble coffee product was mixed with water to a volume of 500 ml, and a 25-ml aliquot was transferred to a flask containing 25 ml of 0.1 M H_2SO_4. This was subjected to the prescribed clarification treatment and made up to 500 ml. A portion of this treated solution showed an absorbance of 0.415 at 272 nm. (a) Calculate the molar absorptivity. (b) Calculate the number of grams of caffeine per pound (453.6 g) of soluble coffee. Assume $b = 1.00$ cm.

3-9 According to Wetters and Uglam[44] the molar absorptivity of the nitrite ion is 23.3 at 355 nm, and the ratio of the absorptivity at 355 to that at 302 nm is 2.50. The molar absorptivity for the nitrate ion is negligible at 355 nm, and 7.24 at 302 nm. A particular mixture gave $A_{302} = 1.010$ and $A_{355} = 0.730$. Calculate the molarities of both ions in the mixture. Assume $b = 1.00$ cm.

3-10 The following facts are abstracted from a published article.[45] (a) Both As and Sb can be oxidized from the trivalent to the pentavalent state by Br_2, As more readily than Sb. (b) Sb(III) forms a complex with Cl^- ion (in 6 M HCl) which absorbs in the UV at 326 nm, whereas Sb(V), As(III), and As(V) do not. (c) $KBrO_3$ and KBr dissolved together in water form a stable solution that will liberate Br_2 quantitatively upon being added to an acid solution, according to the equation $BrO_3^- + 5Br^- + 6H^+ = 3Br_2 + 3H_2O$. (d) Free Br_2, in the presence of excess Br^- ion, absorbs strongly in the UV, including the vicinity of 326 nm, though its maximum is at a shorter wavelength. Bromide alone shows no such absorption. On the basis of the above statements, show how trivalent As and Sb can be determined in mixed solution in HCl, by titration with standard $KBrO_3$-KBr reagent.

Hint: The absorbance of the solution is to be determined at 326 nm after each addition of reagent. A curve will result with two breaks corresponding to the two elements sought.

3-11 Water has been determined by spectrophotometric titration in a solvent consisting of anhydrous acetic and sulfuric acids.[46] The reagent is acetic anhydride, $(AcO)_2O$. The titration is followed by the absorption of radiation at 257 nm by the reagent. Sketch a titration curve and explain its features.

3-12 A method has been reported[47] for the spectrophotometric determination of chlorate impurity in ammonium perchlorate for use in rocketry. This is based on the reduction of chlorate to free chlorine: $ClO_3^- + 5Cl^- + 6H^+ = 3Cl_2 + 3H_2O$. The chlorine then reacts with benzidine (I) to give a colored product (II) with a maximum absorption at 438 nm.

$$H_2N-\text{⬡}-\text{⬡}-NH_2 + Cl_2 \longrightarrow \left[H_2N=\text{⬡}-\text{⬡}=NH_2 \right]^{2+} + 2Cl^-$$

$$(I) \qquad\qquad\qquad (II)$$

Experiments with standard $KClO_3$ solutions showed the following straight-line relation to hold under prescribed experimental conditions (in 10.0-mm cuvets):

$$A = (1.17 \times 10^3)C - 0.186$$

where C is the molar concentration of $KClO_3$. (a) Explain why (II) gives a colored solution while (I) does not. (b) What color is the solution of (II), and what color of filter would be suitable for its determination? (c) Does this system obey Beer's law? (d) The term "-0.186" was ascribed to a reducing impurity in the reagents. Explain why this would be expected to give a subtractive term. (e) A sample of 6.000 g of commercial NH_4ClO_4 was suitably treated with reagent and diluted to 100.0 ml. A portion of this showed an absorbance of 0.450 in a 10.0-mm cuvet at 438 nm. Calculate the concentration of NH_4ClO_3 in the NH_4ClO_4 in terms of mole percent.

3-13 The maximum absorbance of an aqueous solution of phenol shifts from 269 to 286 nm when the solution is made alkaline with NaOH. The absorptivity also increases. It has been reported[48] that this shift can be used for the determination of phenols in natural waters, down to tens of parts per billion (ppb). (a) Explain, in terms of molecular structure, why the shift to longer wavelengths and greater absorptivity occurs. (b) After studying the referenced paper, explain the method by which the ratio of absorbances at two wavelengths is obtained. (c) How did the authors take into account the spectral differences between various phenols?

3-14 A 12-dynode photomultiplier is found to deliver an average anode current of 0.92 mA over a period of 4.2 ns, as a pulse resulting from a single ejected photoelectron. Calculate the multiplication factor per dynode.

REFERENCES

1. D. B. Judd, in *Analytical Absorption Spectroscopy* (M. G. Mellon, ed.), Wiley, New York, **1950**; Chap. 9.
2. M. J. Houle and K. Grossaint, *Anal. Chem.*, **1966**, *38*, 768.
3. S. Malkin and D. Cahen, *Anal., Chem.*, **1981**, *53*, 1426.
4. G. Kortüm and M. Seiler, *Angew. Chem.*, **1939**, 52, 687.
5. R. B. Cook and R. Jankow, *J. Chem. Educ.*, **1972**, 49, 405.
6. A. O. Beckman, W. S. Gallaway, W. Kaye, and W. F. Ulrich, *Anal. Chem.*, **1977**, *49*, 280A.
7. J. C. Cowles, *J. Opt. Soc. Am.*, **1965**, 55, 690.
8. B. Chance, *Rev. Sci. Instrum.*, **1951**, 22, 634; *Science*, **1954**, *120*, 767.
9. T. J. Porro, *Anal. Chem.*, **1972**, 44(4), 93A.

10. K. L. Ratzlaff and D. F. S. Natusch, *Anal. Chem.*, **1979**, *51*, 1209.
11. T. C. O'Haver, *Anal. Chem.*, **1979**, *51*, 91A.
12. G. L. Fix and J. D. Pollack, *Anal. Chem.*, **1980**, *52*, 1589.
13. E. C. Olson and C. D. Alway, *Anal. Chem.*, **1960**, *32*, 370.
14. *RCA Photomultiplier Handbook*, RCA Corporation, Lancaster, PA., **1980**.
15. G. W. Ewing, "Transducers," in *Treatise on Analytical Chemistry*, 2d ed., I. M. Kolthoff and P. J. Elving (eds.), Wiley-Interscience, New York, part I, vol. 4, chap. 5 (in press).
16. B. H. Vassos and G. W. Ewing, *Analog and Digital Electronics for Scientists*, 2d ed., Wiley-Interscience, New York, **1980**, pp. 19 ff.
17. A. Ringbom, *Z. anal. Chem.*, **1939**, *115*, 332.
18. G. H. Ayres, *Anal. Chem.*, **1949**, *21*, 652.
19. J. D. Ingle, Jr., and S. R. Crouch, *Anal. Chem.*, **1972**, *44*, 785.
20. J. D. Ingle, Jr., *Anal. Chem.*, **1973**, *45*, 861.
21. R. M. Silverstein, G. C. Bassler and T. C. Morrill, *Spectrometric Identification of Organic Compounds*, 4th ed., Wiley, New York, **1981**, p. 322.
22. R. B. Woodward, *J. Am. Chem. Soc.*, **1941**, *63*, 1123; **1942**, *64*, 72, 76.
23. L. F. Fieser and M. Fieser, *Steroids*, Reinhold, New York, **1959**, pp. 17 ff.
24. A. Turner, Jr., and A. Osol, *J. Am. Pharm. Assoc., Sci. Ed.*, **1949**, *38*, 158.
25. J. E. Fagel, Jr., and G. W. Ewing, *J. Am. Chem. Soc.*, **1951**, *73*, 4360.
26. R. M. Archibald, *Chem. Eng. News*, **1952**, *30*, 4474.
27. J. H. Yoe and A. L. Jones, *Ind. Eng. Chem., Anal. Ed.*, **1944**, *16*, 111.
28. W. C. Vosburgh and G. R. Cooper, *J. Am. Chem. Soc.*, **1941**, *63*, 437.
29. J. L. Gerlach and R. G. Frazier, *Anal. Chem.*, **1958**, *30*, 1142.
30. P. McCarthy, *Anal. Chem.*, **1978**, *50*, 2165.
31. K. Momoki, J. Sekino, H. Sato and N. Yamaguchi, *Anal. Chem.*, **1969**, *41*, 1286.
32. W. Likussar and D. F. Boltz, *Anal. Chem.*, **1971**, *43*, 1265, 1273.
33. P. J. Lingane and Z. Z. Hugus, Jr., *Inorg. Chem.*, **1970**, *9*, 757.
34. N. A. Renzetti, *Anal. Chem.*, **1957**, *29*, 869.
35. E. B. Sandell, *Colorimetric Determination of Traces of Metals*, 3d ed., Wiley-Interscience, New York, **1959**, pp. 87 ff.
36. I. M. Kolthoff, E. B. Sandell, E. J. Meehan, and S. Bruckenstein, *Quantitative Chemical Analysis*, 4th ed., Macmillan, New York, **1969**, pp. 351, 1064.
37. M. Tsubouchi, *Anal. Chem.*, **1970**, *42*, 1087.
38. W. Huber, G. W. Ewing and J. Kriger, *J. Am. Chem. Soc.*, **1945**, *67*, 609.
39. K. A. Connors and C. J. Eboka, *Anal. Chem.*, **1979**, *51*, 1262.
40. A. Weissler, *Ind. End. Chem., Anal. Ed.*, **1945**, *17*, 695.
41. R. F. Goddu and D. N. Hume, *Anal. Chem.*, **1954**, *26*, 1679, 1740.
42. A. L. Underwood, in *Advances in Analytical Chemistry and Instrumentation*, C. N. Reilley (ed.), Wiley-Interscience, New York, **1964**, vol. 3, pp. 31 ff.
43. A. L. Underwood, *Anal. Chem.*, **1954**, *26*, 1322.
44. J. H. Wetters and K. L. Uglam, *Anal. Chem.*, **1970**, *42*, 335.
45. P. B. Sweetser and C. E. Bricker, *Anal. Chem.*, **1952**, *24*, 1107.
46. S. Bruckenstein, *Anal. Chem.*, **1959**, *31*, 1757.
47. E. A. Burns, *Anal. Chem.*, **1960**, *32*, 1800.
48. J. E. Fountaine, P. B. Joshipura, P. N. Keliher and J. D. Johnson, *Anal. Chem.*, **1974**, *46*, 62.

FOUR

THE ABSORPTION OF RADIATION: INFRARED

Whereas the absorption of ultraviolet and visible radiation is conveniently considered as a unit, the infrared region is better treated separately. There are two important reasons for this: first, the optical techniques are sufficiently divergent that no spectrophotometers are available to cover both the IR and UV-visible regions without modification; second, the physical mechanism on which IR absorption is based differs from that of the shorter wavelengths.

It was pointed out in Chap. 2 that the absorption of IR radiation depends on increasing the energy of vibration or rotation associated with a covalent bond, provided that such an increase results in a change in the dipole moment of the molecule. This means that nearly all molecules containing covalent bonds will show some degree of selective absorption in the IR. The only exceptions are diatomic elements such as H_2, N_2, and O_2, because only in these can no mode of vibration or rotation be found that will produce a dipole moment. Even these simple species show slight IR absorption at high pressures, apparently as the result of distortions during collisions.

Infrared spectra of polyatomic covalent compounds are often quite complex, consisting of numerous narrow absorption bands (see, for example, the spectrum of a film of polystyrene, Fig. 4-1). This contrasts strongly with the usual UV and visible spectra. The difference arises in the nature of the interaction between the absorbing molecules and their environment. This interaction (in condensed phases) has a great effect on electronic transitions occurring within a chromophore, broadening the absorption lines so that they tend to coalesce into wide regions of absorption. In the IR, on the other hand, the frequency and absorptivity due to a

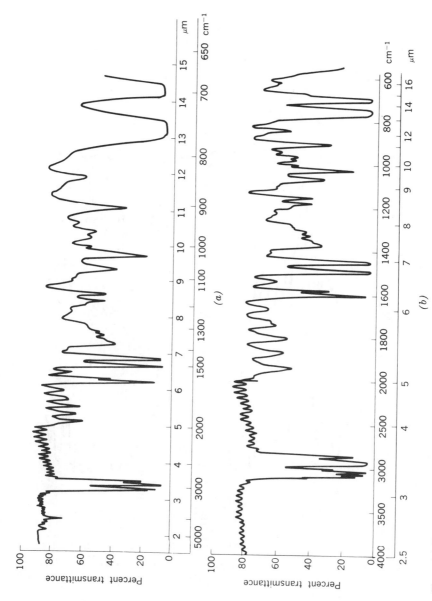

Figure 4-1 The infrared spectrum of a polystyrene film: (*a*) on a linear wavelength scale, and (*b*) linear in wave number.

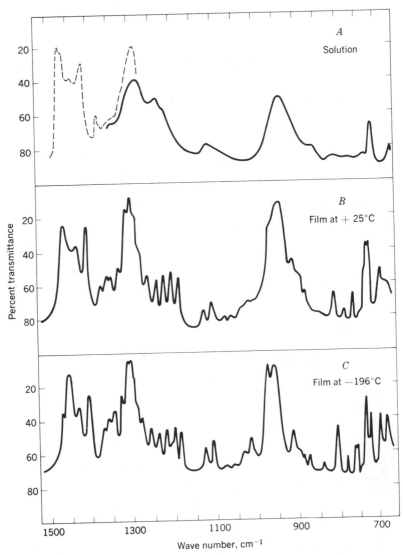

Figure 4-2 Infrared spectra of stearic acid in different physical states: (*A*) in CCl_4 solution (dashed curve) and in CS_2 solution (solid curve); (*B*) film of the beta polymorph at room temperature; (*C*) same, at $-196°C$. (*Wiley-Interscience*.[1])

particular bond usually show only minor alterations with changes in its environment (which includes the rest of the molecule). The lines are not likely to be broadened so as to coalesce.

Exceptions to this generalization sometimes occur. For example, a long-chain molecule in the liquid phase is free to assume a limitless number of configurations, because of free rotation around the many C—C bonds. The spectra of these many forms will be nearly but not quite identical, so that a broadening of the bands will appear. Hence it is preferable to examine compounds of this type in the solid phase. Figure 4-2 shows the change in appearance of such a compound, stearic acid, as it appears under various conditions. Notice that by comparison with the room-temperature solid, the solution shows considerable broadening of peaks and loss of detail, while a drastic reduction of temperature has the opposite effect.

Infrared spectra are usually plotted as percent transmittance, as in Fig. 4-1, rather than as absorbance.† This convention makes absorption bands appear as dips in the curve rather than as the maxima familiar in the UV. This method of plotting is not universally followed, however, and Fig. 4-2 shows an inverted format. The independent variable in IR spectra is sometimes given as the wavelength in micrometers (formerly called "microns"), and sometimes as the wave number in inverse centimeters. Many workers strongly favor the wave-number treatment, as being more easily correlated with the vibrations within the molecule. On the other hand, some prefer linear wavelength presentation because the highly detailed "fingerprint" region (about 5 to 15 μm) is spread out conveniently rather than compressed at the short wavelength end. The two presentations are compared in Fig. 4-1.

INSTRUMENTATION

The majority of IR spectrophotometers follow the same basic design as those used at shorter wavelengths, modified to allow for the differences in optical materials. There is in addition another type, not widely used in the UV-visible range, based on principles of interferometry.

Optical Materials

Lenses are almost never used in IR spectrophotometers, but are replaced by front-surface concave mirrors. Mirrors have many advantages, for which they are often used in the UV and visible, as well as the IR. They have no chromatic aberration, which means that they focus all wavelengths at the same point; they can be made of sturdy materials such as metal or aluminized glass, without regard to optical transmission, and they are easier to mount.

---

† This is because of the instrumental limitations of the early IR spectrophotometers which were used to build up extensive libraries of spectra.

Table 4-1 Infrared-transmitting solid materials

Material	Limiting wavelengths,† μm
Optical glass	0.4–2.6
Vitreous silica	0.16–4.0
LiF	0.12–9.0
CaF_2	0.13–12.0
Si‡	1.2–15
Ge	1.8–23
NaCl	0.2–25
KBr	0.25–40
CsBr	0.2–55
KRS-5§	0.55–40

† Taken from more extensive tabulations given by Barker.[2] Figures indicate regions where transmission is greater than 10 percent for a 2-mm thickness.
‡ Shows a transmission dip near 9 μm, due to Si—O bonds on the surface.
§ Mixed crystal of thallium bromide and iodide.

Any objects through which radiation must pass, such as the windows of sample containers,† must be made of solid materials that transmit freely in the wavelength band of interest. Several materials with their useful transmission limits are listed in Table 4-1. It will be noted that several of the entries in the table are water-soluble salts. This means that parts made of these materials must be carefully protected from moisture. Clearly, aqueous solutions cannot be handled in cells with salt windows, but this is no great restriction in practice, as water absorbs IR too strongly to be of much use as a solvent. Salt cells should be stored in a desiccator.

Many older spectrophotometers used prisms made of NaCl or KBr for dispersion. In these instruments the monochromator was generally sealed against the entry of possibly moist air, and a heater was provided in the vicinity of the prism to prevent any condensation on its surfaces.

Sources

Incandescent sources are well suited for spectrophotometry in the portions of the IR of primary interest in analytical chemistry. A tungsten lamp with a glass or silica envelope is useful for the near IR, but the glass absorbs too strongly beyond about 3.5 μm. Probably the best emitter to cover the range from 1 to about 30 μm is the *Nernst glower*. This consists of a rod or hollow tube about 2 cm long and 1 mm in diameter, made by sintering together oxides of such elements as cerium,

† In the IR region, a container for liquid or gaseous samples is generally called an "absorption cell" rather than a "cuvet."

zirconium, thorium, and yttrium. It is maintained at a high temperature by electrical heating, and can be operated in air, since it is not subject to oxidation. The glower has a negative temperature coefficient of resistance, and must be preheated before it will draw enough current to maintain its own temperature, following which the current must be limited to prevent burnout.

Another source, the *Globar*, is a rod of silicon carbide of somewhat larger dimensions than the Nernst glower. It is operated at a lower temperature, to avoid oxidation, and its terminals must be cooled by forced ventilation. It has greater emissivity than the glower at wavelengths beyond about 30 μm.

A simple coil of nichrome wire can be used as an IR source, though rather limited in range and intensity. It is often the source of choice for less expensive spectrophotometers.

Detectors

Infrared detectors suitable for absorption spectroscopy,[3] can be classified in two broad groups: (1) those designated as *thermal detectors*, which depend on the integrated energy of a large number of incident photons to produce a measurable response via their heating effects; and (2) *photon detectors*, semiconductor devices in which an electron can absorb the energy of a single quantum of IR radiation to be promoted from the valence band to the conduction band, where they can contribute to electrical conductivity. In general, photon detectors are faster and more sensitive, but are severely restricted in wavelength range, and must be cooled to liquid-nitrogen temperature or below. Thermal detectors, on the other hand, are usable over a wide range of wavelengths and do not require cooling, but have relatively low sensitivity and slow response. Except for the PbS photoconductive detector, which is widely used at room temperature in the near-IR, photon detectors are seldom seen in laboratory spectrophotometers, and will not be discussed further.

Thermal detectors give nearly equal response, on an energy basis, throughout the near-UV, the visible, and the IR, out nearly to millimeter wavelengths. They are not usually used in the UV and visible, because photomultipliers are more sensitive.

Most types are usually fabricated with a tiny bit of blackened gold foil as the actual absorber of radiation. In one common structure (Fig. 4-3), two bits of foil, identical, except that only one is blackened, are mounted in an evacuated space in such a way that only the blackened one is subject to the radiation to be measured. In this way, the two foils will be affected equally by changes in ambient temperature, but only one of them by the radiation. The measuring device must consist of two identical transducers, in thermal contact with the two foils, and connected electrically to respond to the difference between the two.

The *thermocouple* is one of the most commonly used of the thermal IR detectors. Identical junctions between two unlike metal wires are welded onto the back surfaces of the two foils, as shown in Fig. 4-3. Thermocouples are low-impedance devices, and are usually coupled to a preamplifier through a transformer with a

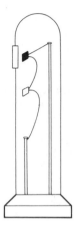

Figure 4-3 A differential thermocouple IR detector.

high ratio of turns (1000 to 1), to respond to the low-frequency ac signal generated by the chopped beam of radiation.

Another type of thermal detector is the *bolometer*, a miniature resistance thermometer with a tiny bit of platinum wire or a thermistor as sensing element. The *thermistor* is a resistor made by sintering a mixture of several metallic oxides; it has a larger temperature coefficient than platinum by a factor of about 5, and can respond faster to chopped radiation, but it is likely to be somewhat less reproducible. Identical Pt wires or thermistors are cemented to the back surfaces of the two gold foils previously described.

The resistance of a bolometer can be measured by conventional circuits, for example, the Wheatstone bridge shown in Fig. 4-4. The output voltage is proportional to the ratio of the resistances of the two identical elements, the effect of changes in ambient temperature being essentially eliminated.

Pyroelectric detectors[4] are unique in that they respond to the time-derivative of the temperature, rather than to the temperature itself, hence do not require a

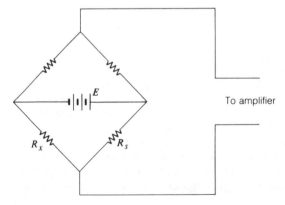

To amplifier   Figure 4-4 Wheatstone bridge circuit for a bolometer. R_x is the irradiated element, and R_s is an identical one, shielded from radiation, but at the same ambient temperature. The other two resistors are adjustable, for setting the zero point.

duplicate unit shielded from the radiation to be measured. The detector consists of a tiny slab of a crystalline material whose molecules have a permanent dipole moment. Absorption of heat causes a change in the lattice spacing, hence in the dipole moment, and produces a change in the electric charges sensed by metal foil electrodes on opposite faces of the crystal.[5,6] Useful crystals include triglycine sulfate (TGS), barium titanate, lead zirconate, and lithium tantalate. These detectors have a much greater speed of response than other thermal detectors, and can be used with radiation chopped at frequencies of the order of 10^5 Hz, contrasted with 15 or 20 Hz maximum chopping frequency for thermocouples or bolometers.

SPECTROPHOTOMETERS

Automatic scanning spectrophotometers for the mid-IR region can be divided into two main classes: low-cost models for routine identification work, and flexible research instruments. The latter can be equipped with various refinements which permit higher precision, higher resolution, and more versatility with respect to mode of presentation of the spectrum. All of these utilize the double-beam principle.

A surprising number of IR spectrophotometers of various manufacturers and in all price classes have nearly identical optical layouts. The differences arise in the precision tolerances of the many optical and mechanical components, and are reflected primarily in the specifications of wavelength and photometric accuracy and of resolution. (For a thorough discussion of resolution in the IR, its significance, and how to measure it, refer to the treatise by Stewart.[7])

A typical IR optical system is diagrammed in Fig. 4-5a. Radiation from the source N is reflected by two sets of mirrors to form two symmetrical beams, one of which passes through the sample cell, the other through a blank or reference cell. The two beams are reflected by a further array of mirrors, so that both are focused on the slit S_1. C is a motor-driven circular chopping disk, half reflecting and half cut away (Fig. 4-5b), which permits the two beams to reach the slit during alternate time periods. Slit S_1 is the entrance slit to a Littrow monochromator equipped with a pair of back-to-back diffraction gratings to cover different portions of the range. The selected wavelength band passes out through the exit slit S_2, and is brought to a focus on the detector D.

· The detector sees a square wave corresponding in amplitude to the difference in powers of the two beams. This AC signal, after amplification, drives a servo motor to control the position of a comb attenuator (Fig. 4-5c), which adjusts the power of the reference beam to equal that of the sample beam, an *optical null*. The motor simultaneously positions the pen on the built-in stripchart recorder.

Two gratings are required to give the desired resolution over the whole range. The first grating, typically, has 300 lines per millimeter, blazed at 3 μm, and is in the operating position, rotating slowly, while the spectrophotometer scans from about 2 to 5 μm. When 5 μm is reached, the grating table abruptly turns to bring

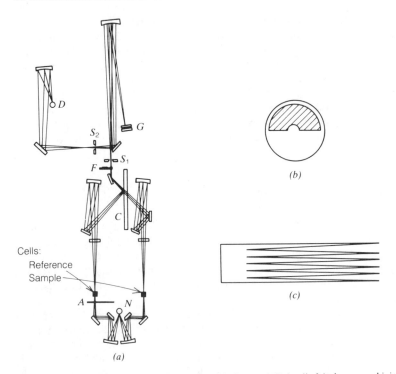

Figure 4-5 A typical IR spectrophotometer: (a) optical system; (b) detail of the beam-combining mirror (C in the diagram); (c) detail of the optical attenuator (A). (*Beckman Instruments, Inc.*)

the second grating (100 lines per millimeter, blazed at 7.5 μm) into position and the scan resumes, covering the range from 5 to 16 μm. Both gratings are operated in the first order. Four filters *F* are required to eliminate higher orders; they are positioned sequentially by the drive mechanism at the required wavelengths.

Either prism or grating spectra can be linear in either wavelength or wave number, according to the design of the cams and bars making up the mechanical linkage between the scanning motor and the prism or grating table. The case of linear wavelength with grating dispersion is simplest to design, but from the standpoint of the operator, one is as convenient to use as another.

Rapid-Scan Spectrophotometers

One of the limitations of conventional IR spectrophotometers with thermocouple or bolometer detectors is their inherently slow response. High-speed instruments are needed for kinetic studies and for on-line identification of the constituents of a flowing stream, such as the effluent from a gas chromatograph. This objective can be achieved through the use of a pyroelectric detector. A wavelength-scanning instrument can be designed so that the effluent flows directly through the sample cell, while pure carrier flows through the reference cell. The entire spectrum can be plotted in a few seconds, less than the time usually required to elute a component. The details of this application will be discussed in Chap. 20, and comparable adaptation to liquid chromatography in Chap. 21.

INTERFEROMETRIC (FOURIER-TRANSFORM) SPECTROPHOTOMETERS

Since radiant energy consists of trains of electromagnetic waves, generally of many frequencies superimposed, the instantaneous electrical and magnetic fields at any point will be the resultant of those due to the individual frequencies. Therefore it should be possible, in principle, to retrieve *all* the information carried by a beam simply by letting it fall on a radiation detector and plotting the response as a function of time. The trouble with such a direct approach is that the alternating fields, with frequencies of the order of 10^{14} Hz, are many orders of magnitude too fast to follow with any known detector.

The speed difficulty can be overcome through the use of the Michelson interferometer diagrammed in Fig. 4-6. Radiation from the source is collimated by lens L and then divided into two equal parts by the beam splitter BS. The beams are reflected back by plane mirrors M_1 and M_2. Portions of both beams are finally incident on the detector. If the two mirrors are equidistant from BS, the detector will see the same time-varying electromagnetic fields that it would have seen without the interferometer, but they will be only half as intense. If mirror M_2 is then moved to the right along the optical axis, the phases of the two beams reaching the detector will differ, and interference will result. The retardation of the phase for a given increase in path length depends on the wavelength of the radiation, and is observed by the detector as a series of successive maxima and minima of intensity.

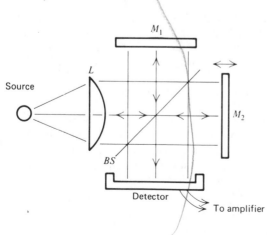

Figure 4-6 Michelson interferometer, as used in a Fourier-transform IR spectrometer.

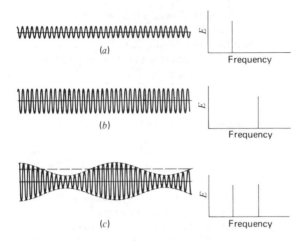

Figure 4-7 Comparison of information in the time domain (left) and frequency domain (right): (a) cosine wave of frequency ν_1; (b) cosine wave, ν_2; (c) both frequencies present together.

To be used as a spectrophotometer, mirror M_2 is forced to move at a constant speed for a distance of a few millimeters, many times longer than the longest wavelength to be encountered. This causes the response of the detector to fluctuate at a rate dependent on the speed of motion and the wavelength of the radiation. The action of the interferometer can be thought of as equivalent to chopping the radiation at a frequency given by $2v\bar{\nu}$ where v is the velocity of the moving mirror (in cm·s^{-1}), and $\bar{\nu}$ is the wave number of the radiation (in cm^{-1}). In a typical instrument, this is equivalent to chopping simultaneously at a frequency continuously variable from about 1250 Hz at the high wave-number end of the spectrum (~ 4000 cm^{-1}) to 125 Hz at the low end (~ 400 cm^{-1}). The pyroelectric detector can easily follow these frequencies.

Ideally, monochromatic radiation should produce a cosine wave as the two optical paths deviate from equality (cosine rather than sine because the amplitude is maximal at zero deviation). Figure 4-7a and b shows this for two monochromatic frequencies. If both frequencies enter into the interferometer together, curve c will result. Carrying this synthetic approach further will produce great complications in the spectra (see Fig. 4-8). However, it follows that any combination of frequencies with corresponding amplitudes will produce a unique *interferogram* containing all the spectral information of the original radiation.

Figure 4-9 gives the complete optical diagram of a typical Fourier-transform spectrophotometer. Radiation from the IR source (upper left) is collimated by a concave mirror and passed into the interferometer. The pulsating beam leaving the interferometer is directed into an oscillating mirror that is positioned alternately to send the beam through the sample cell (as shown) or through a reference (dashed lines). A second oscillating mirror, synchronized with the first, sends the beams to be focused on the detector.

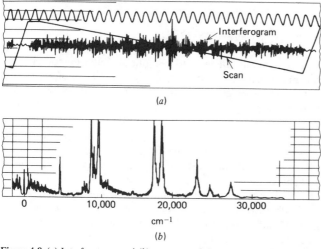

(a)

(b)

Figure 4-8 (a) Interferogram and (b) spectrum of the same organic compound. The sine wave at the top of (a) is a reference curve for use in calibration; the sloping line marked "scan" tracks the movement of the mirror. (Spex Industries.)

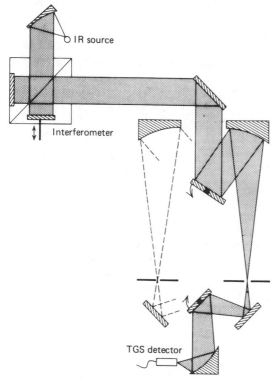

Figure 4-9 Optical diagram of a Fourier-transform IR spectrophotometer. (Digilab, Inc.)

Interferograms are not readily interpreted without a digital computer. The interferogram, from a mathematical standpoint, is the *Fourier transform* of the spectrum, so the task of the computer is to apply the inverse Fourier transform. The derivation and application of the pertinent equations can be found in Refs. 8 and 9.

Interferometric or Fourier-transform spectroscopy (FTS), as here described, has two great advantages over conventional techniques: (1) It makes use of all frequencies from the source simultaneously, rather than sequentially as in a scanning instrument. (This is called the *Fellgett advantage*, after the scientist who first described it.) The Fellgett advantage amounts to an improvement in the S/N ratio equal to $M^{1/2}$, where M is the number of resolution elements desired in a particular spectrum.[8,9] (2) In addition to the Fellgett advantage, the sensitivity of the FT method is greater than that of the dispersive technique because more radiation enters the slitless system; this is called the *Jacquinot advantage*.

Many chemical applications in which the FT instrumentation is distinctly superior to the conventional dispersive methods have been described.[8,10] These applications for the most part require the increase in sensitivity made possible by the Fellgett and Jacquinot advantages, namely applications to situations where there is only a small flux of radiation to be measured, such as the kinetic study of fast processes, where a spectrum must be recorded quickly or not at all. Other examples of low-energy spectrometry include absorption measurements in the far IR, where the available sources are weak, and the field of IR emission spectroscopy. Spectra of faint remote sources, such as hot gases emerging from a smokestack have been recorded by FT-IR techniques.[11] The method has been applied in various astronomical measurements.

Abridged Spectrophotometers

Low-resolution instruments It is possible to make useful measurements with a manual, single-beam, IR photometer, much like the photoelectric filter photometer in the visible range. A series of such instruments, manufactured under the trade-name Miran,† uses a variable interference filter for wavelength selection; this provides considerably less resolution than a grating, but is still adequate for many uses. The sensitivity is high, because a larger cone of radiation can be accepted than with a conventional spectrophotometer (a Jacquinot advantage). These instruments are characterized by lower cost, ruggedness, and portability. Photometers of this type are appropriate for the estimation of a compound or class of compounds when it is not necessary to distinguish between closely related species.

Nondispersive photometers that depend on selective filtering for specificity are widely used to monitor gas streams and in air pollution studies. Consider as an example the determination of CO in the presence of other gases. Since CO

---

† Foxboro Analytical, South Norwalk, Connecticut.

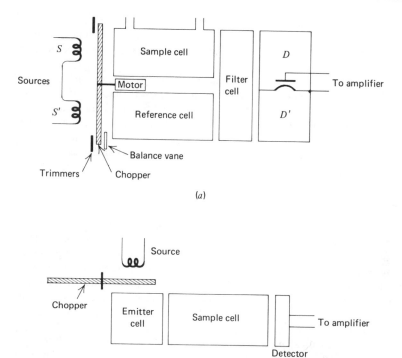

Figure 4-10 Nondispersive IR analyzers: (*a*) with differential detector; (*b*) with an IR fluorescent source.

only absorbs certain characteristic frequencies, it is only these frequencies that are of interest in its measurement. Effective elimination of all other frequencies can be achieved in either of two ways, as shown in Fig. 4-10. In Fig. 4-10*a* beams of radiation from a pair of identical sources traverse the sample and reference cells and impinge on a differential detector that contains CO (usually diluted with argon to reduce the heat capacity).[12] Any difference in power between the two beams results in a temperature differential between the two sides of the detector. It is highly selective, because the only radiation that will produce heating in the detector is precisely that absorbed by CO in the sample. An added filter cell is provided to desensitize the instrument to other possible components of the gas stream for which absorption bands overlap those of CO. The two chambers of the detector are separated by a metallized flexible diaphragm which, together with a fixed plate, forms a variable capacitor.

A chopping wheel to interrupt the two beams simultaneously is required because the differential detector is a dynamic device; i.e., it responds to rapid changes more effectively than to gradual drifts. The sensing capacitor is incorporated into a high-frequency electronic circuit that energizes a small servomotor to drive a balancing vane across the reference beam thereby achieving an optical null. The amount of such compensation is indicated on a meter or recorded on a chart.

The single-beam instrument diagrammed in Fig. 4-10b makes use of a cell containing CO as the *source* of radiation rather than the detector.[13] The CO is heated by infrared from an incandescent source, and then emits radiation at the characteristic CO frequencies, which passes through the sample to a nonselective detector. This instrument is less liable to interference from vibration and ambient temperature changes than the previous model. Either type can be sensitized to any polyatomic gas desired.

Far-Infrared Spectrophotometers

Dispersive instruments for the region beyond about 50 μm are much less common than those for shorter wavelengths. A convenient source in the far-IR consists of a high-pressure mercury arc with a quartz envelope. The quartz is opaque to wavelengths below about 60 μm, but the useful range, nevertheless, extends below this, the radiation being emitted by the hot quartz itself, rather than the arc. A pyroelectric detector is applicable. Atmospheric absorption is a problem in the far-IR, and it is necessary to evacuate the spectrophotometer or to purge it with dry nitrogen.

Several gratings must be interchanged at successive wavelength intervals; for the longest wavelengths a grating may have as few as 2 or 3 lines per millimeter. Filters must be present to cut background radiation and unwanted orders. There are two types of filters suited for far-IR applications, both depending on selective reflection rather than transmission. One of these utilizes the phenomenon of *Reststrahlen*,† the narrow bands of high reflection in crystalline substances which correspond to the refractive index maxima associated with areas of high absorption.[14,15] The other type consists of a *scatter plate*, which may be a metallic film deposited on a rough-ground glass plate, or a grating with its rulings horizontal rather than parallel to the vertical slits. The scattering is very effective in reducing the amount of higher frequency radiation passing through the optical system, but does not degrade the long waves of interest.

It is particularly important in the far-IR to chop the radiation *prior* to its passage through the sample and monochromator, because spontaneous thermal radiation from the optical elements may be far from negligible. Chopping, together with the use of a tuned amplifier, ensures that the detector can only respond to radiation from the source itself.

Fourier-transform spectrometers are particularly valuable in the far-IR. The expense of their manufacture is less in this region, because the mechanical requirements are less severe.

† From the German, meaning "residual rays."

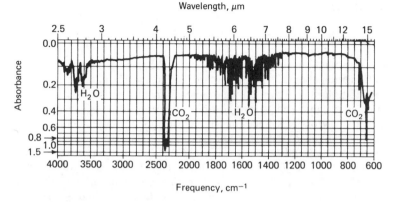

Figure 4-11 Single-beam IR trace with no sample, showing the absorption bands due to atmospheric water and carbon dioxide. (*Plenum Press.*[22])

CALIBRATION AND STANDARDIZATION

The calibration of an IR spectrophotometer with respect to both wavelength and transmittance may change gradually with continued use, as the result of mechanical wear, fogging of optical surfaces, or aging of components, so that periodic checks are highly advisable.

The wavelength (or wave number) scale can in theory be calibrated by the dispersion geometry of a grating of known spacing, but this is not practicable as a routine procedure. The most common check is to run the spectrum of a thin sheet of polystyrene as a secondary standard. Manufacturers of IR instruments usually supply mounted samples for this purpose, along with a standard spectrum for comparison. The spectrum (see Fig. 4-1) shows easily recognizable, sharp absorption bands distributed throughout the mid-IR.

Another convenient wavelength check can be performed by switching to single-beam operation and scanning the spectrum with no sample present. Under this condition, the absorption by atmospheric water vapor and carbon dioxide will be clearly seen (Fig. 4-11), and as their wavelengths are known with precision, the scale can readily be checked at a number of points. (This spectrum makes evident one of the major advantages of a dual-beam spectrophotometer—the cancellation of atmospheric absorption.)

If the spectrophotometer is to be used for quantitative measurements, the linearity of its photometric scale must also be verified occasionally. This can be done roughly by measurements on the polystyrene spectrum, and more precisely by measuring the transmittance of a series of thicknesses of a liquid such as benzene.

CHEMICAL APPLICATIONS

Quantitative Analysis

Since IR absorption is related to covalent bonds, the spectra can provide much detailed information about the structure of molecular compounds.

It is possible, through a painstaking examination of a large number of spectra of known materials, to correlate specific vibrational absorption maxima with the responsible atomic groupings. Such empirical correlations provide a powerful tool for the identification of covalent compounds.

Some sweeping generalizations can be made. It is useful to distinguish such types of vibrations as *stretching, distortion, bending,* etc. The shorter IR wavelengths, from about 0.7 to 4.0 μm, include mostly stretching vibrations of bonds between hydrogen and heavier atoms; this includes the near-IR region, and is especially useful in the identification of functional groups that contain hydrogen. The 4.0- to 6.5-μm region contains vibrations of double and triple bonds. Above this wavelength are found the "skeletal" distortion and bending modes, including —C—H bending.

The absorptions in the far-IR region, beyond about 25 μm, correspond to vibrational modes involving heavy atoms and groups of atoms, including bonds between carbon and phosphorus, silicon, and heavy metals, and also between heavy metals and oxygen, and other similar bondings. Also found in this region are some low-lying distortional frequencies, such as the ring-puckering mode in four-membered rings, as well as *torsional* vibrations of methyl and other groups, and the majority of purely rotational bands.

Table 4-2 gives an indication of the regions corresponding to frequently occurring bond types. Much more extensive and detailed correlations, taking into account the intramolecular environment of each bond, are available. These have been prepared in convenient chart form by Goddu[16] for the 1.0- to 3.1-μm region, and by Colthup[17] for 2.5 to 25 μm. Bentley[18] has compiled a chart that extends out to 33 μm. All of these charts are reproduced in Meites' *Handbook of Analytical Chemistry*. Many of the major manufacturers of IR spectrophotometers publish charts corresponding to the ranges and formats of their own instruments. Detailed discussion of such correlations can be found in numerous texts and monographs intended to assist in the determination of organic structures.[16.19-22]

There are many situations in which the IR absorption of a compound is altered more or less extensively by the conditions under which it is observed. Because of such variations in the location of absorption bands, empirical tables and charts must be used with great caution when attempting to deduce the structure of an unknown compound. The causes of these variations may be either instrumental or chemical in origin. Figure 4-12[22] illustrates the effects of changes in slit widths and scanning rates; gross changes in either could interfere with an identification.

Another type of interaction is exemplified by the effect of hydrogen bonding on the absorption frequency of a carbonyl group. The frequency corresponding to the stretching mode of the C=O bond in a compound dissolved in a nonpolar

Table 4-2 Infrared positions of various bond vibrations†

Bond	Mode‡§	Relative strength¶	Wavelength, μm	Wave number, cm^{-1}
C—H	Stretch	s	3.0–3.7	2700–3300
C—H	Stretch (2v)	m	1.6–1.8	5600–6300
C—H	Stretch (3v)	w	1.1–1.2	8300–9000
C—H	Stretch (C)	m	2.0–2.4	4200–5000
C—H	Bend, in-plane	m–s	6.8–7.7	1300–1500
C—H	Bend, out-of-plane	w	12.0–12.5	800–830
C—H	Rocking	w	11.1–16.7	600–900
O—H	Stretch	s	2.7–3.3	3000–3700
O—H	Stretch (2v)	s	1.4–1.5	6700–7100
O—H	Bending	m–w	6.9–8.3	1200–1500
N—H	Stretch	m	2.7–3.3	3000–3700
N—H	Stretch (2v)	s	1.4–1.6	6300–7100
N—H	Stretch (3v)	w	1.0–1.1	9000–10000
N—H	Stretch (C)	m	1.9–2.1	4800–5300
N—H	Bending	s–m	6.1–6.7	1500–1700
N—H	Rocking	s–m	11.1–14.3	700–900
C—C	Stretch	m–w	8.3–12.5	800–1200
C—O	Stretch	m–s	7.7–11.1	900–1300
C—N	Stretch	m–s	7.7–11.1	900–1300
C=C	Stretch	m	5.9–6.3	1600–1700
C=O	Stretch	s	5.4–6.1	1600–1900
C=O	Stretch (2v)	m	2.8–3.0	3300–3600
C=O	Stretch (3v)	w	1.9–2.0	5000–5300
C=N	Stretch	m–s	5.9–6.3	1600–1700
C≡C	Stretch	m–w	4.2–4.8	2100–2400
C≡N	Stretch	m	4.2–4.8	2100–2400
C—F		s	7.4–10	1000–1350
C—Cl		s	13–14	710–770
C—Br		s	15–20	500–670
C—I		s	17–21	480–600
Carbonates		s	6.9–7.1	1400–1450
Carbonates		m	11.4–11.6	860–880
Sulfates		s	8.9–9.3	1080–1120
Sulfates		m	14.7–16.4	610–680
Nitrates		s	7.2–7.4	1350–1390
Nitrates		m	11.9–12.3	820–840
Phosphates		w	9.0–10.0	1000–1100
Silicates		. . .	9.0–11.1	900–1100

† Approximate only; fundamentals unless noted; collected from various literature sources.

‡ (2v) means second harmonic or first overtone, etc.

§ (C) means combination frequency.

¶ s = strong, m = medium, w = weak.

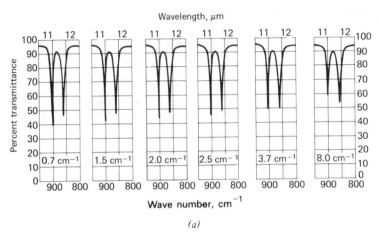

(a)

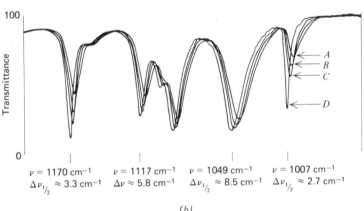

$\nu = 1170\ cm^{-1}$ $\nu = 1117\ cm^{-1}$ $\nu = 1049\ cm^{-1}$ $\nu = 1007\ cm^{-1}$
$\Delta\nu_{1/2} \approx 3.3\ cm^{-1}$ $\Delta\nu \approx 5.8\ cm^{-1}$ $\Delta\nu_{1/2} \approx 8.5\ cm^{-1}$ $\Delta\nu_{1/2} \approx 2.7\ cm^{-1}$

(b)

Figure 4-12 The effects of instrumental variables on IR spectra: (a) the 861 and 903 cm^{-1} bands of cyclohexane at various spectral slit widths, as marked; (b) a spectrum recorded at several scanning speeds; effective times for full scans: A, 8 min; B, 11 min; C, 16 min; D, 3 h. (*Plenum Press.*[22])

solvent is lowered considerably by the formation of hydrogen bonds with an added hydroxylic substance, or by changing to a hydroxylic solvent. The carbonyl absorption is also altered by its environment within its own molecule: the absorption of the C=O bond is significantly different in a carboxylic acid, in which an intermolecular hydrogen bond (formation of a dimer) can occur, as compared with an ester in which such a bond cannot form. The anion is affected by resonance which renders the two oxygen atoms equivalent to each other, so that the double-bond character of the carbonyl is even more profoundly changed. Table 4-3 shows representative values for the carbonyl stretching vibrations of a few aliphatic compounds.[20] This discussion of the carbonyl absorption is presented as an

Table 4-3 Carbonyl stretching vibrations

Ketone	5.81–5.85 μm	1720–1710 cm^{-1}
Carboxylic acid monomer	5.67–5.71	1765–1750
Carboxylic acid dimer	5.81–5.85	1720–1710
Ester	5.73–5.80	1745–1725
Salt, asymmetric stretch	6.21–6.45	1610–1550
Salt, symmetric stretch	~7.14	~1400

abbreviated example of the kind of structural considerations that can be of great value to the organic chemist as well as to the analyst.

One result of the complexity of IR spectra is that no two different compounds will have identical curves. Hence the spectrum of a pure compound presents a sure method of "fingerprint" identification, provided that a compilation or atlas of spectra of known compounds is available. Several such atlases have been published.†[23–25]

Inorganic Applications

Infrared absorption can also be a useful technique for the examination of inorganic entities that contain covalent bonds. This includes not only organometallic compounds, but also polyatomic anions. IR absorption is not often used in inorganic analysis, simply because there are so many competing techniques that may be more convenient. A good summary of the field is given in Ref. 20.

PREPARATION OF SAMPLES

Gaseous samples can be examined in an IR spectrophotometer with no prior preparation other than the removal of water vapor. Many manufacturers provide gas cells equipped with mirrors to allow the radiation to traverse the sample many times. Path lengths up to 40 m have been attained in commercial equipment.

Solvents present difficulties because no liquids are available that are entirely free of absorption on their own account. Carbon tetrachloride is satisfactory over a considerable range, but dissolves only a limited number of substances. Chloroform, cyclohexane, and other liquids can be used in restricted wavelength ranges and in very thin layers. Figure 4-13 shows in chart form the spectral regions where various solvents can be used. The degree of absorption by the solvent that can be tolerated depends on the sensitivity of the spectrophotometer. It can be canceled out to some degree by the usual means of placing a blank cell in the reference beam, but this reduces the amount of energy reaching the detector, and so is of only limited applicability.

† A series of reference spectra of particularly high reliability is compiled by the Coblentz Society. Their requirements and necessary precautions make interesting reading.[26] The Coblentz spectra are commercially available.[25]

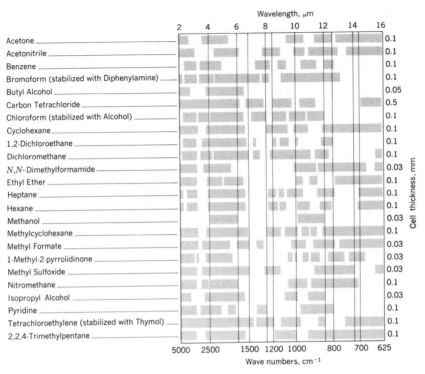

Figure 4-13 The IR transmission regions for a number of solvents. The shaded rectangles designate the areas of transmission. (*Eastman Kodak Company.*)

It is sometimes possible to select two solvents with complementary absorption regions, so that two successive spectra will cover the entire wavelength span of interest. CCl_4 (4000 to 1335 cm^{-1}) and CS_2 (1350 to 400 cm^{-1}) form such a pair, and are useful where solubilities permit. An example is seen in Fig. 4-2a.

A variety of absorption cells for liquids are available, ranging from inexpensive disposable types to cells that can be disassembled for cleaning. Some cells are provided with screw threads to allow adjustment of thickness. The *cavity cell* is a convenient form made by machining a parallel-sided hole in a salt block.

A *demountable cell* is shown in Fig. 4-14. It consists of a pair of salt plates separated by a shim or gasket made of metal or Teflon, the whole held together as a sandwich by metal clamps. Two holes are drilled through the metal frame and one of the salt plates for filling and flushing. Such cells are usually filled, emptied, and rinsed with the aid of a hypodermic syringe (without needle), the nib of which fits the orifice in the cell. A cell can often be used many times before it becomes necessary to take it apart for cleaning and for repolishing the salt plates.

Liquids of high viscosity are often simply sandwiched as a layer between two salt plates, since it is not easy to introduce viscous liquids into preassembled cells.

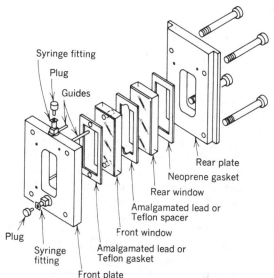

Syringe fitting

Plug

Guides

Rear plate
Neoprene gasket
Rear window
Amalgamated lead or
Teflon spacer
Plug   Front window
Syringe   Amalgamated lead or
fitting   Teflon gasket
Front plate

Figure 4-14 Demountable cell for holding a liquid sample in an IR spectrophotometer. (*Beckman Instruments, Inc.*)

Solid samples can be prepared for analysis by incorporating them into a pressed plate or pellet of potassium bromide (or less commonly potassium iodide or cesium bromide). A weighed portion of the powdered sample is thoroughly mixed in a small ball mill with a weighed quantity of highly purified and desiccated KBr powder. The mixture is placed in an evacuable die and subjected to a pressure of 10 to 20 MPa (megapascals; this is the equivalent of several tons weight per square inch). This produces a highly transparent plate or disk that can be inserted into a special holder for the spectrophotometer. The disk is typically about 1 cm in diameter and perhaps 0.5 mm thick. If the exact thickness is required for quantitative purposes, it can either be determined from the dimensions of the die, or measured with a caliper.

There are potential difficulties with the KBr pellet technique. If the particle size is not small enough, excessive scattering results. Some heat-sensitive materials (steroids, for example) may show signs of partial decomposition, presumably arising from the heat generated in crushing crystals of salt. The technique has been reviewed with critical detail in a paper by Hannah.[27]

Another frequently used procedure is called *mulling*. The powdered sample is mixed to form a paste with a little heavy paraffin oil (medicinal grade Nujol is often used). The oil has only a few isolated absorption bands, specifically at about 3.5, 6.9, and 7.2 μm. If these bands interfere, the mull may be made with Fluorolube, a fluorocarbon material that has no absorption at wavelengths shorter than about 7.7 μm. The mull is sandwiched between salt plates for measurement.

Solid samples can also be examined in the form of a thin layer deposited by sublimation or solvent evaporation on the surface of a salt plate. This simple procedure may, however, give trouble from excessive scattering of radiation.

QUANTITATIVE ANALYSIS

Beer's law, as presented in Chap. 3, applies equally in the infrared region

$$A = \log \frac{P_0}{P} = abc \tag{4-1}$$

In the near-IR, 10-mm cuvets and dilute solutions are the rule, and so no special difficulties arise in the use of this relation. Beyond this region, however, the path length b is usually much less and the concentration greater, because of the lack of suitably transparent solvents for use in the IR. The greater concentration is apt to cause deviations from the law, as a result of molecular interactions. Furthermore, it is often difficult to make an accurate photometric measurement because of the overlap of absorption bands, and because many IR spectrophotometers have a bandpass that is wider than the absorption bands that are to be measured.

The path length can be measured by a number of methods. In a cell that has plane parallel walls, interference fringes resulting from multiple internal reflections can be recorded by running the spectrophotometer so as to indicate apparent transmission through the empty cell, with nothing other than air in the reference path.[20] The resulting trace will resemble Fig. 4-15. The value of b can then be computed from the equation

$$b = \frac{n}{2(\tilde{v}_1 - \tilde{v}_2)} \tag{4-2}$$

where n is the number of fringes between wave numbers $\tilde{v}_1$ and $\tilde{v}_2$.

Some cells do not have walls sufficiently flat to give sharp interference fringes. The effective or average path length can then be determined by measuring the absorbance at 850 cm^{-1} with benzene in the cell. Experiment has shown that 0.1 mm of cell thickness corresponds to 0.22 in absorbance units.

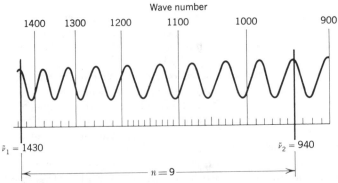

Figure 4-15 Typical fringes used in the calculation of path lengths. (*Allyn and Bacon.*[20])

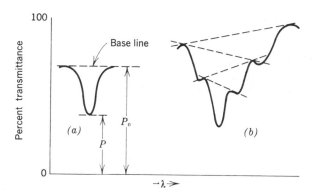

Figure 4-16 Hypothetical IR absorption spectra, illustrating: (a) the base-line measuring technique; (b) uncertainty as to where to draw the base line.

The path length in demountable cells can be determined simply by measuring the thickness of the spacer, using a micrometer caliper.

Deviations from Beer's law due to high concentration can be handled only by careful calibration with a series of solutions of known concentrations. The experimental determination of absorbance often requires the use of a *base-line* technique to overcome difficulties due to overlapping absorption bands. Suppose it is desired to find the absorbance corresponding to the band shown in Fig. 4-16a. A base line is drawn across the shoulders of the band; the quantities P_0 and P can then be measured as shown, and the absorbance calculated. However, with an absorption such as b in the same figure, the proper location of the base line is open to much doubt; a few possibilities are suggested. In this situation, which frequently occurs, the only procedure is to standardize on one particular way to draw the line. The certainty of one's results could be improved by measuring several absorption bands in the same spectrum; consistent results would go far to prove the adequacy of the method.

INTERNAL REFLECTION SPECTROSCOPY[28]

When a beam of radiation encounters an interface between two media, approaching it from the side of higher refractive index, total reflection occurs if the angle of incidence is greater than some critical angle, the value of which is given by

$$\alpha_c = \sin^{-1} \frac{n_2}{n_1} \qquad (4\text{-}3)$$

where n_1 and n_2 are the two indices of refraction, with $n_1 > n_2$. Not so generally realized, though predicted by electromagnetic theory[28,29] is the fact that, in total

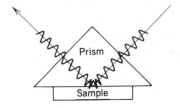

Figure 4-17 Schematic representation of the total internal reflection of a beam of radiation, showing some degree of penetration into the substrate. The prism must have a larger refractive index than the sample. (*Foxboro Analytical.*)

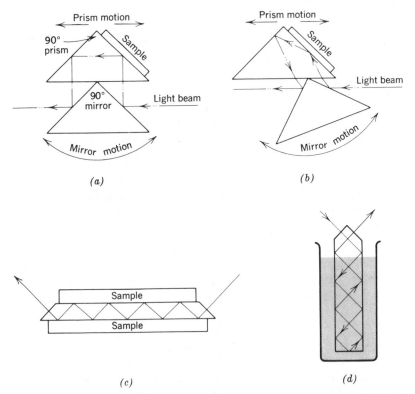

Figure 4-18 ATR apparatus: (*a*) and (*b*) an arrangement whereby the entering and leaving beams are in the same straight line (the lower prism and the left face of the upper must be silvered; motion of the parts as indicated will permit the angle of reflection at the sample to be varied), (*c*) a device for multiple reflections, (*d*) an immersible plunger to permit multiple reflections with a bulk liquid sample. (*a to c, Foxboro Analytical; d, Harrick Scientific Corporation.*)

reflection, some portion of the energy of the radiation actually crosses the boundary and returns (Fig. 4-17). If the less dense medium absorbs at the wavelength of the radiation, the reflected beam will contain less energy than the incident, and a wavelength scan will produce an absorption spectrum.

In principle, this will apply to any spectral region, but it has been found most useful in the IR. The distance to which the radiation appears to penetrate in internal reflection depends on the wavelength, but is of the order of 5 μm or less in the mid-IR region. The phenomenon is generally known as *attenuated total reflection* (ATR).

Special sample holders have been devised to make use of ATR for analytical purposes, mostly designed to fit the sample compartment of conventional spectrophotometers; a few are shown in Fig. 4-18. In (*a*) is an arrangement for a single reflection at the sample surface, at a variable angle. By moving the lower prism (*b*), which has silvered surfaces and hence reflects at any angle, the angle of incidence at the sample can be varied, still maintaining the entering and exit beams on the same straight line. The drawing at (*c*) shows a linear device for multiple reflections[28] that is especially convenient for solid samples; it consists of a slab of a transparent solid of high index that may be several centimeters long. Figure 4-18*d* represents an elongated prism with plane parallel sides, so arranged that the radiation enters and leaves at the same end[28]; this type can be surrounded by a liquid sample, as shown, or can be clamped between solids.

The Miran line of abridged spectrophotometers, previously mentioned, are provided with a convenient accessory for ATR measurements. This makes use of a slab of crystalline zinc selenide ($n = 2.89$) with a horizontal surface of several square centimeters mounted flush with the top surface of the instrument. A sample, either liquid or solid, can be placed directly on this surface for spectral measurement, then removed and the surface cleaned with solvent if necessary.

ATR spectra are not identical to those obtained conventionally, but are quite similar. The distortion becomes greater as the angle of incidence approaches the critical angle. The further from the critical angle, however, the less the absorption, and so a greater number of reflections must be introduced to obtain sufficient sensitivity. ATR has been found most useful with opaque materials that must be observed in the solid state. Applications include studies of rubber and other polymeric materials, adsorbed surface films, and paints and other coatings.

MICROWAVE ABSORPTION

Absorption in the microwave region[30,31] can be considered an extension of the far-infrared, as the phenomena giving rise to the absorption are primarily rotational transitions in molecules possessing a permanent dipole moment. Absorptions can also be observed under appropriate conditions in molecules possessing magnetic moments, such as O_2, NO, NO_2, ClO_2, and in free radicals. The spectral region most fruitful for chemical spectroscopy lies between approximately 8 and 40 GHz. As we will see in a later chapter, this includes the frequencies useful in electron spin magnetic resonance (ESR), so these two methods share some features in common, though based on different molecular mechanisms.

There are no microwave absorptions that are characteristic of specific bond types or functional groups, such as we find at lower frequencies. Qualitative analysis can be applied only by means of comparison with known spectra. The microwave region complements the IR in the identification of relatively small compounds by the fingerprint approach. This is partly due to the very great number of frequencies available. If absorption bands can be resolved at a separation of 200 kHz, a reasonable figure, this gives a total of 160,000 spaces or channels in the 8- to 40-GHz span. By comparison, if an average resolution of 1 cm^{-1} is attainable over the IR region from the visible up to 200 cm^{-1} (50 μm), only 10,000 channels are available. Of course there are many frequencies that do not appear in any known spectra, so these figures may be somewhat misleading. Nevertheless, an extremely large number of compounds can in principle be examined in a microwave spectrometer with very little probability of overlap. Only gaseous samples can be studied, but the vapor pressure need not be higher than 0.1 to 10 Pa (approximately 10^{-3} to 10^{-1} torr).

The chief limitation arises from interactions between the rotational energy levels associated with various bonds within the molecule. If there are more than three or four rotors present, so many interactions will appear that the spectrum will become a mass of lines, few of which will be sufficiently intense to be useful. Hence large molecules cannot be studied unless cyclic structures prevent rotation around some of the bonds.

In the mathematical treatment of microwave absorption, it is more appropriate to use Lambert's law, which relates the logarithm of the transmittance to path length in a homogeneous medium, rather than Beer's law, which concerns concentrations. The law can be stated as

$$P = P_0 \times 10^{-\alpha b} \quad \text{or} \quad \log \frac{P_0}{P} = \alpha b \tag{4-4}$$

where P_0 and P represent, respectively, the radiant microwave power incident on and passing through the absorption cell, which has an effective length b. The absorption coefficient α corresponds to the absorbance A as employed in the optical region, taken per unit length of the absorption cell. Ideally it is a function only of the number of absorbing molecules per unit path length, and hence should be related to the partial pressure of the substance in a mixture of gases.

The degree to which such a relation is valid depends largely on the way in which the absorption coefficient is measured and utilized. At low pressures and power levels, where saturation effects are not evident, the pressure of the absorbing species is proportional to α_{max}, the height of the absorption maximum. At higher pressures, the value of α_{max} becomes constant, and an increase in pressure results in the broadening of the line as measured at half-height. Above this point it can be shown that the partial pressure is very nearly proportional to the integrated absorbance

$$Kp = \int \alpha(v) \, dv \tag{4-5}$$

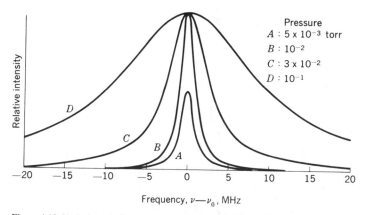

Figure 4-19 Variation of microwave absorption with change of pressure. The peak intensity remains constant over a wide pressure range. (*John Wiley & Sons, Inc.*[37])

where v = frequency, p = partial pressure, and K is a proportionality constant. Figure 4-19 shows the absorption curves of a typical band at a series of partial pressures.

In spite of pressure broadening, the absorption maxima are narrow enough that overlap with maxima of other compounds is extremely unlikely. This means that the partial pressure as determined from Eq. (4-5) can be taken directly as an analytical result, without the need of correction for impurities. Armstrong[32] has reported that SO_2 produces a linear response from 100 percent concentration down to 20 ppb in free air, a truly remarkable dynamic range.

As an example of a straightforward analytical application, see Ref. 33, which describes the estimation of trace methanol in commercial wines. The sample was injected by syringe directly into the sample cell, where it was completely vaporized before measurement of the absorption line at 31.2267 GHz.

Molecular conformations can be studied by microwave absorption, as trans and gauche forms of a compound have different spectra and can be identified thereby. Barriers to intramolecular rotation can also be measured.[31] If isotopic substitution alters the dipole moment of a compound, this will show up in the spectra. Figure 4-20 shows an example of this effect, which will also serve to illustrate the general appearance of a microwave spectrogram.

Microwave Instrumentation

The details of theory and construction of apparatus cannot be discussed here for lack of space. Spectrophotometers have been constructed that are comparable to both single- and double-beam instruments in the more familiar spectral ranges. The source is either a specialized vacuum tube (a klystron, for example) or a solid-state oscillator based on a tunnel diode or a Gunn diode. These oscillators can

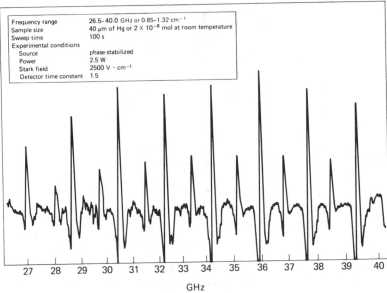

Frequency range	26.5–40.0 GHz or 0.85–1.32 cm^{-1}
Sample size	40 μm of Hg or 2×10^{-8} mol at room temperature
Sweep time	100 s
Experimental conditions	
Source	phase-stabilized
Power	2.5 W
Stark field	2500 V · cm^{-1}
Detector time constant	1.5

Figure 4-20 Microwave absorption spectrum of 4-chlorotoluene. Each peak appears as a doublet, corresponding to the two chlorine isotopes. (*Hewlett–Packard Company.*)

be swept through a considerable frequency range, generating essentially mono-chromatic radiation at each point. The beam chopper is replaced by an electronic modulation system based on the Stark effect. A crystal rectifier serves as detector of the radiation. The majority of microwave spectrometers are home-built from modular components.

PROBLEMS

4-1 A sample of ethyl bromide suspected of containing trace amounts of water, ethanol, and benzene was examined in an IR spectrophotometer. The following relative absorbances were obtained by a base-line method: at 2.65 μm, $A = 0.110$; at 2.75 μm, $A = 0.220$; and at 14.7 μm, $A = 0.008$. The instrument, cells, etc., exactly duplicated those for which reference data have been reported.[34,35] Calculate the amounts of the three impurities present.

4-2 It has been reported[36] that hexacyanoferrates (II) and (III) can be determined in the presence of each other in aqueous solutions by their IR absorptions. The following observations were made:

Anion	$Fe(CN)_6^{4-}$	$Fe(CN)_6^{3-}$
Molar absorptivity ϵ (l·mol^{-1}·cm^{-1})	4.23×10^3	1.18×10^3
Linear range (mol·l^{-1})	0.00031–0.04	0.0012–0.1
Wave number at maximum (cm^{-1})	2040	2115

The cells used were of 50-μm path length between windows of Irtran-1 (a proprietary form of MgF$_2$). In a particular photographic bleach solution, the following data were read from the spectrogram: base line, flat at $A = 0.043$; $A = 0.258$ at 2040 cm^{-1} and 0.515 at 2115 cm^{-1}. What are the concentrations of the two species in moles per liter?

4-3 The following observations have been reported[20] for the apparent absorbance of cyclohexanone in cyclohexane solution at 5.83 μm. The cell thickness was 0.096 mm.

Concentration, $g \cdot l^{-1}$	Absorbance
5	0.190
10	0.244
15	0.293
20	0.345
25	0.390
30	0.444
35	0.487
40	0.532
45	0.562
50	0.585

Plot these data. (*a*) Over what range is Beer's law followed, after the necessary background corrections have been made? (*b*) Compute the value of the molar absorptivity.

4-4 Gasohol should contain 10 percent by volume of ethanol in unleaded gasoline. Other alcohols that may sometimes be present are methanol, isopropanol, *n*-butanol, and *t*-butanol. Gasoline can be assumed to consist of *n*-alkanes, C_4 to C_{12}. In an atlas, find the spectra for these compounds, and select the best wave numbers to use in an IR determination of ethanol in gasoline. Outline a procedure, including allowance for possible impurities in the gasoline.

4-5 Determine the path length (in millimeters) of the cell that produced the interference fringes shown in Fig. 4-15. At what wave number is the cell thickness just equal to 10 wavelengths?

4-6 A high-temperature gas stream in a plant manufacturing "water gas" contains as major constituents H_2, CO, CO_2, and H_2O, with a possible small quantity (less than 0.5 percent by volume) of CH_4. It is desired to sensitize a nondispersive IR analyzer to monitor the CH_4 content. The gas is cooled prior to introduction into the analyzer, so that excess H_2O condenses out and is removed. Find the pertinent spectra in an atlas, and describe in detail what should be placed in each compartment of the analyzer of Fig. 4-10*a*.

4-7 Calculate the approximate number of photons, at wavelength 10 μm, needed to be just detectable with a thermistor having the following specifications: Receptor: gold, $1.0 \times 0.1 \times 0.005$ mm; thermistor: 10 kΩ (at 25°C), coefficient of resistance, $-500 \, \Omega \cdot K^{-1}$. The least measurable resistance change is $\Delta R = 1 \, \Omega$. The heat capacity of gold is $0.0308 \, cal \cdot g^{-1} \cdot K^{-1}$, and its density is $19.32 \, g \cdot cm^{-3}$. (Note that, because of heat loss to the surroundings, the actual number of photons may have to be considerably greater than this calculation will predict.)

4-8 An alcohol shows a faint absorption peak at 0.952 μm in the near-IR. This must be an overtone (multiple) of a fundamental vibration that might be a C—O or O—H stretch. Consult Table 4-2 and decide which, if either, of these is probable.

4-9 A KBr pellet, measuring 7.50 mm diameter by 1.5 mm thickness, shows absorbance $A = 0.722$ at wavelength 6.02 μm. The solute is known to have an absorptivity $a = 43.2 \, l/g \cdot cm$ at this wavelength. Calculate the amount of solute contained in the pellet, in milligrams.

4-10 The path length of a demountable cell was measured by two techniques: (*a*) The thickness of the Teflon spacer was measured directly with a machinist's micrometer, giving a reading of 22.0 mil (1 mil = 0.001 inch); (*b*) The cell was filled with benzene and its absorbance as measured at 850 cm^{-1} was found to be 0.125. How closely do these measurements agree? Comment on which you would consider more reliable, and why.

4-11 In the ATR apparatus of Fig. 4-18*d*, the angle of incidence of the beam of radiation at each reflection is exactly 45°. If the absorption of samples with refractive index as great as 1.8 are to be measured, what must be the refractive index of the solid plunger?

REFERENCES

1. R. N. Jones and C. Sandorfy, in *Chemical Applications of Spectroscopy*, W. West (ed.), Wiley-Interscience, New York, **1956**, p. 308.
2. J. D. Barker, *Electro-Opt. Syst. Des.*, October **1970**, p. 32.
3. G. W. Ewing, *J. Chem. Educ.*, **1971**, *48*, A521.
4. E. H. Putley, "The Pyroelectric Detector," in *Semiconductors and Semimetals*, R. K. Willardson and A. C. Beer (eds.), vol. 5, Academic Press, New York, **1970**, chap. 6.
5. W. M. Doyle, *Electro-Opt. Syst. Des.*, November **1978**, p. 12.
6. E. J. McLellan and S. C. Stotlar, *Opt. Spectra*, March **1981**, p. 55.
7. J. E. Stewart, *Infrared Spectroscopy, Experimental Methods and Techniques*, Dekker, New York, **1970**, pp. 276 ff.
8. P. R. Griffiths (ed.), *Transform Techniques in Chemistry*, Plenum Press, New York, **1978**.
9. R. J. Bell, *Introductory Fourier Transform Spectroscopy*, Academic Press, New York, **1972**.
10. J. L. Koenig, *Appl. Spectrosc.*, **1975**, *29*, 293.
11. D. H. Chenery and N. Sheppard, *Appl. Spectrosc.*, **1978**, *32*, 79.
12. S. H. Walters, in *Process and Controls Handbook*, D. M. Considine (ed.), McGraw-Hill, New York, **1957**, pp. 6–73.
13. W. T. Link, E. A. McClatchie, D. A. Watson, and A. B. Compher, "AIAA Paper No. 71-1047, Joint Conference on Sensing of Environmental Pollutants," American Institute of Aeronautics and Astronautics, New York, **1971**.
14. M. F. Kimmitt, *Far-Infrared Techniques*, Pion, London, **1970**.
15. Ref. 7, p. 165.
16. R. F. Goddu and D. A. Delker, *Anal. Chem.*, **1960**, *32*, 140.
17. N. B. Colthup, *J. Opt. Soc. Am.*, **1950**, *40*, 397.
18. F. F. Bentley and E. E. Wolfarth, *Spectrochim. Acta*, **1959**, *15*, 165.
19. L. J. Bellamy, *The Infrared Spectra of Complex Molecules*, 3d ed., Chapman & Hall, London, **1975**.
20. R. T. Conley, *Infrared Spectroscopy*, 2d ed., Allyn and Bacon, Boston, **1972**.
21. R. M. Silverstein, G. C. Bassler, and T. C. Morrill, *Spectrometric Identification of Organic Compounds*, 4th ed., Wiley, New York, **1981**.
22. N. L. Alpert, W. E. Keiser, and H. A. Szymanski, *IR: Theory and Practice of Infrared Spectroscopy*, 2d ed., Plenum Press, New York, **1970**.
23. American Petroleum Institute, "Catalog of Infrared Spectrograms," API Research Project 44, Texas A & M University, College Station, Texas.
24. C. J. Pouchert, "The Aldrich Library of Infrared Spectra," Aldrich Chemical Company, Milwaukee, **1970**.
25. Sadtler Research Laboratories, "Sadtler Standard Spectra," Philadelphia (a continually updated subscription service).
26. The Coblentz Society, *Anal. Chem.*, **1975**, *47*, 945A.
27. R. W. Hannah, *Instrum. News.* **1963**, *14(3,4)*, 7; (Perkin-Elmer Corporation).
28. N. J. Harrick, *Internal Reflection Spectroscopy*, 2d ed., Harrick Scientific Corp., Ossining, New York, **1979**.
29. M. V. Klein, *Optics*, Wiley, New York, **1970**, p. 579.
30. G. W. Chantry (ed.), *Modern Aspects of Microwave Spectroscopy*, Academic Press, New York, **1979**.
31. R. Varma and L. W. Hrubesh, *Chemical Analysis by Microwave Rotational Spectroscopy*, Wiley, New York, **1979**.
32. S. Armstrong, *Appl. Spectrosc.*, **1969**, *23*, 575.
33. R. W. Kitchin, R. E. Willis, and R. L. Cook, *Anal. Chem.*, **1981**, *53*, 1190.
34. G. A. McCrory and R. T. Scheddel, *Anal. Chem.*, **1958**, *30*, 1162.
35. V. Z. Williams, *Anal. Chem.*, **1957**, *29*, 1551.
36. D. M. Drew, *Anal. Chem.*, **1973**, *45*, 2423.
37. W. Gordy, W. V. Smith, and R. F. Trambarulo, *Microwave Spectroscopy*, Wiley, New York, **1953**, reprinted by Dover, New York, **1966**.

FIVE

ATOMIC ABSORPTION

In this chapter we shall consider absorption by atomic rather than molecular species. In order to observe the optical properties of free atoms, the sample must be in the gaseous state, and this generally requires volatilization of liquids or solids, followed by the dissociation of molecules to give free atoms.

Atomic absorption (AA) obeys the same general laws as the absorption by molecules studied in previous chapters. Hence an AA spectrophotometer must have the same sequence of components, altered where necessary to meet different requirements. The most striking departure is in the sample itself, so we will start there in our discussion.

Atomic fluorescence (AF), often classed with AA, will be treated in Chap. 9 together with other types of atomic emission.

ATOMIZATION

There are a number of techniques by which metallic elements can be atomized, in most cases by heat energy, either electrically produced or from a flame. Careful control of the temperature is needed for optimum conversion to the atomic vapor. Too high a temperature can be just as unfavorable as too low, as it will cause a fraction of the atoms to become ionized, and hence not to absorb at the expected wavelengths. On the other hand, a high temperature tends to reduce matrix effects, and so is desirable. A compromise must be reached between these two extremes.

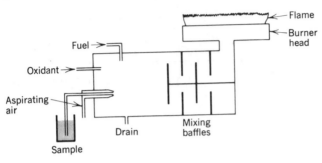

Figure 5-1 Laminar flow, premix burner for AA.

Flame Atomization

A typical burner for flame AA is shown in Fig. 5-1. The fuel and oxidant gases are fed into a mixing chamber, where they proceed through a series of baffles to ensure complete mixing, to the burner head. The flame orifice is in the form of a long, narrow slot, so that a ribbon flame is produced. The sample, in solution, is aspirated into the mixing chamber by a small air jet. This kind of aspirator produces droplets of a wide range of sizes, which could lead to poor reproducibility. This is overcome by contact with the mixing baffles which tend to intercept the larger drops, so that those reaching the flame are smaller and more nearly uniform.

Such a burner using premixed gases presents a safety hazard, for if the flame should strike back into the mixing chamber, a violent explosion would ensue. The likelihood of a flashback is minimized by making the burner slot as narrow as possible, so that the gases will blow through at a high velocity, and by making the metal parts around the slot rather massive so that heat will be conducted away readily. Even then, explosion can occur if the gas flow is not adjusted properly. Commercial burners are made to come apart harmlessly in case of flashback. A heavy safety shield should always be in place when the burner is operating.

Compressed air and acetylene are most commonly chosen as oxidant and fuel for AA. The maximum temperature attainable is about 2200°C. When higher temperature is needed, nitrous oxide (N_2O) can be substituted for the air. This gas decomposes to give a 2:1 mixture of nitrogen and oxygen, compared to the 4:1 ratio in air; the highest temperature it can reach when burning acetylene is almost 3000°C. Pure oxygen cannot be used with acetylene in a premix burner, because the flame propagates so rapidly that flashback cannot be avoided.

Although the flame is a convenient and reproducible source of heat, it is less than ideal as a sampling device for AA, in that the two sequential endothermic processes (solvent evaporation followed by atomization), must take place within the very short time interval that it takes for a particle to shoot through the flame. In addition, the flame introduces significant random fluctuations in the effective optical path length, because of turbulence, and this causes excessive noise in the signal.

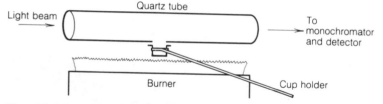

Figure 5-2 Delves cup sampling system. The cup is held beneath an orifice in a horizontal silica tube, open at both ends, through which the beam of radiation passes.

An improvement can be achieved by using the flame only as a source of heat. In one technique, the dissolved sample is placed in a small metal boat or cup, called a *Delves cup*,[1] and dried on a hot plate. The cup is then held in the flame to vaporize the sample. The vapor enters through a central hole into a horizontal quartz tube (Fig. 5-2) heated by the ribbon flame, where it is measured. The quartz tube serves as a holding tank, appreciably lengthening the time that the atoms can be observed. This technique has been found particularly useful for determining traces of lead. Nickel cups are used except for acidic samples, in which case tantalum or other inert material is substituted.

Graphite Furnace Atomizers

During the last decade, electrical heating as an alternative to the flame has become more and more widely used. Several types of heaters have been proposed, of which the most successful consists of a small tube of graphite,[2] heated by passing through it a large current (up to perhaps 500 A) at low voltage. The graphite tube (in the Varian model) is a few millimeters in inside diameter, and about a centimeter in length. It has a small orifice in its upper surface, through which the dissolved sample can be inserted, as seen in Fig. 5-3. The internal surface is coated with an impervious form of carbon called pyrolytic graphite. Comparable tubes from other manufacturers differ in detail. The tube, often called a *graphite furnace*, must be surrounded with an atmosphere of an inert gas, such as argon, to prevent oxidation of both the sample and the hot carbon.

The temperature of the graphite atomizer, as used with liquid samples, is generally programmed in three steps. It is first raised to about 300°C, and held there for perhaps a minute, to evaporate the solvent. Any organic matter is next removed by charring at about 1700°C for another minute or so. Only after this is the temperature increased to the point needed to dissociate inorganic compounds into atoms; this may require as high as 3000°C.

Each of these time intervals and temperatures can, in most models, be varied by the operator, to meet the requirements of different samples. The trace on a time-based recorder will often show an extraneous absorption peak during the drying period, due to the solvent vapor. A peak may also appear during the charring step if much organic matter is present. Analytical information is obtained

Figure 5-3 The Varian carbon-rod atomizer, Model CRA-90. The graphite tube is the small transverse cylinder clamped between a pair of graphite rods that hold it mechanically and conduct the current. The hose to the left connects to a source of inert gas. The photo shows an operator inserting a sample from a pipet. (*Varian Techtron.*)

from a measurement of the peak height as observed at the final temperature. The height of the peak is influenced by the *rate* of heating and by the furnace dimensions,[3] so these and any other variables must be reproduced with care when unknown samples are to be related to standards.

Volatile Hydrides

Another sample-handling technique is available for those elements that form volatile hydrides, particularly As, Bi, Ge, Sb, Se, and Te.[4] The hydrides are prepared by reaction of the salts of these elements with alkaline sodium boro-hydride. The effluents can then be swept out from the solution with a stream of air, directly into the atomization device of the AA spectrophotometer. A hydrogen–air flame is often used, but an externally heated quartz furnace permits going to some-what lower concentrations, because of the longer residence time. Tin and lead have also been determined this way, but with less satisfactory results.

In a similar manner, mercury can be reduced to the elemental state (if it is not already so), and swept out in an air current into a quartz tube cuvet, which need not be heated.[4]

SOURCES OF RADIATION

Nearly all commercial AA spectrometers use special lamps that generate line spectra characteristic of specific elements. These are much more effective, when used in conjunction with the usual medium-resolution monochromators, than are continuous sources such as the lamps described in Chap. 3. The purpose of the monochromator is to select the emission line desired, rather than to narrow the spectral band width. The difficulty with a continuous source is caused by the extreme narrowness of the absorption lines of neutral atoms in the flame or furnace. This is of the order 0.001 nm, compared to the bandwidth of a few tenths of a nanometer produced by a conventional monochromator. Figure 5-4 shows this relation. The area beneath curve a, the output of the source, is only very slightly diminished by the narrow atomic absorption line at b.

The most successful line source for AA is the *hollow-cathode lamp*. This consists of a glass or quartz envelope containing two electrodes, one of which (the cathode) is cup-shaped and made of the specified element (Fig. 5-5). The material of which the anode is made is not critical. The lamp is filled with a low pressure of a noble gas. Application of 100 to 200 V will produce, after a short warm-up period, a glow discharge with most of the emission coming from within the hollow cathode. Positive ions from the inert gas bombard the cathode, removing metal atoms by a

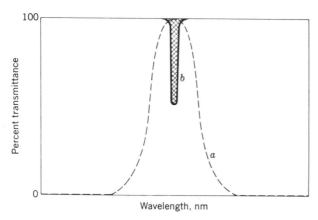

Figure 5-4 Radiation from a continuous source, showing the relative absorption by an atomic vapor. Curve (a) represents the band of wavelengths passed by the monochromator, and curve (b) the absorption by an atomic species in the flame. Curve (b) should be many times narrower in comparison to curve (a). (*Unicam Instruments, Ltd.*)

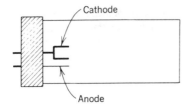

Figure 5-5 A hollow-cathode lamp.

process known as *sputtering*. These atoms can then accept energy of excitation and emit their characteristic radiation. The emissions consist of discrete lines of the metal, plus those of the fill gas. The gas is selected by the manufacturer to give the least spectral interference with the metal concerned.

The spectrum of a typical hollow-cathode lamp is shown in Fig. 5-6. Note that the sensitive 232-nm line is surrounded by numerous other nickel lines that will not be absorbed by nickel vapor. The desired line can be isolated by a narrow bandpass monochromator. Figure 5-7 shows schematically the relation between the emission spectrum of a hollow-cathode lamp (*a*), the same, seen through a monochromator (*b*), and the effect of absorption by the metal vapor (*c*). The absorption band is always broader than the emission line, though narrower than the bandpass of the monochromator. Hence the diminution in power of the beam of radiation reaching the detector is directly dependent on the number of atoms of the metal encountered in the sampling area.

It is possible to fabricate hollow-cathode lamps with a mixture of several metals lining the cathode cup, as long as they do not interfere spectrally with each other, and provided that they require about the same amount of energy for vaporization.

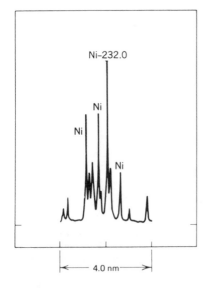

Figure 5-6 Emission from a lamp with a hollow cathode made of nickel. Only the line at 232.0 nm is appreciably absorbed by Ni atoms in the flame. (*Westinghouse Electric Corporation.*)

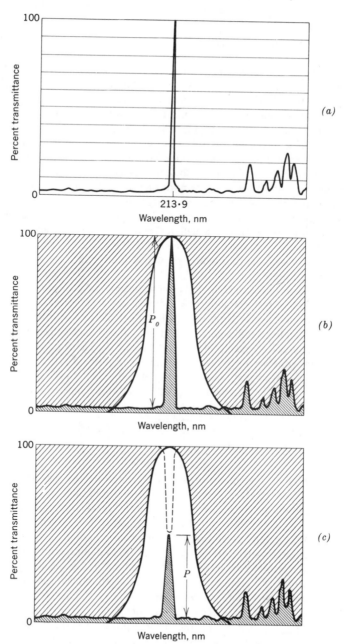

(a)

(b)

(c)

Figure 5-7 Atomic absorption: (a) the spectrum of a zinc cathode lamp (the width of the 213.9-nm line has been exaggerated for clarity), (b) extraneous zinc lines are eliminated by a monochromator centered at 213.9 nm, (c) the power of the 213.9-nm line is sharply reduced by the absorption due to zinc atoms. (*Unicam Instruments, Ltd.*)

This makes it possible to determine these several elements without the necessity of changing lamps. Examples are lamps that contain Ca, Mg, and Al; Fe, Cu, and Mn; Cu, Zn, Pb, and Sn; and Cr, Co, Cu, Fe, Mn, and Ni.

As with many sources of radiation, hollow-cathode lamps take some time after turn-on to reach a steady output. This is particularly annoying with single-element lamps if several elements are to be determined on the same sample. One way to overcome this difficulty is to provide a turret assembly that will hold several lamps, maintaining them at standby, so that any one of them can be rotated into position for use. A double-beam system to correct for varying lamp brilliance will also serve to shorten the delay when changing lamps.

Another type of lamp that can be used as a source in AA is the *electrodeless discharge lamp*. This consists of a sealed quartz tube containing a small amount of the pure metal and a low pressure of an inert gas. It is excited by an intense microwave field in a waveguide cavity, and emits essentially the same spectrum as its hollow-cathode counterpart.

It is also possible to use a lamp that gives a continuous spectrum, together with a high-resolution monochromator. O'Haver and coworkers[5,6] have shown that the high power of a xenon lamp used with an echelle monochromator permits narrowing the bandpass sufficiently to yield valid absorbance measurements. This has the advantage of easy change of wavelength from one element to another. They described an instrument equipped with 16 photomultiplier tubes that would permit the simultaneous determination of as many elements, but with somewhat lower sensitivity than could be obtained with hollow-cathode lamps. No commercially available AA spectrometers utilize continuum sources.

BACKGROUND CORRECTION

Correction for backgound effects cannot be accomplished by the simple double-beam approach that is so effective with solution spectrophotometry. Such a method would require duplicate flames or graphite furnaces, one with the sample, one without, and it would be extremely difficult to make them optically equivalent. Nevertheless, background correction is essential for quantitative work.

The background signal arises in part from the radiation emitted by the hot sample itself. This source of background is unique to AA, resulting from the inevitable electronic excitation of analyte atoms that spontaneously emit photons at the same wavelengths being studied in absorption. As indicated schematically in Fig. 5-8a, if no precautions are taken, the observed radiant power, P_{obs}, will be given by $P_0 T + P_e$, where P_0 is the incident power, T is the transmittance of the sample, and P_e is that portion of the power emitted by the sample that reaches the monochromator. Since the radiation relating to P_0 and P_e are at the same wavelength, both pass through the monochromator to the detector, and are indistinguishable from each other. This effect can be eliminated by chopping the radiation from the hollow-cathode lamp, as shown at *b*, leaving untouched the radiation originating in the sample. The electronic amplifier can be synchronized

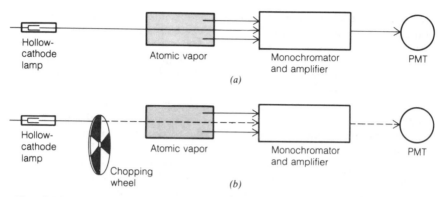

Figure 5-8 Basic structure of an AA spectrophotometer: (a) continuous operation without chopping; emission from the hot sample adds to the radiation from the hollow-cathode lamp, leading to ambiguity, (b) with chopping; only the radiation from the lamp is observed by the detector with its selective electronics.

with the chopper so that that component of the signal which is generated by emission from the sample is subtracted from the total signal. Some manufacturers achieve the same end by exciting the hollow-cathode lamp with electrical pulses, thereby producing pulsed radiation, instead of interrupting the steady radiation with a chopping wheel.

Considerable background remains even after implementing the chopping feature. Part of this is noise, caused largely by scattering of radiation by particles of smoke from the sample matrix, and, with flame excitation, by turbulence.

The background may also contain contributions due to absorption by other components of the sample. Several methods have been described for minimizing this type of interference. The first of these involves the use of a continuous source, such as a hydrogen or deuterium lamp, simultaneously with the line source,[7,8] as in Fig. 5-9. Radiation from the auxiliary lamp passes through the sample along with the resonance radiation from the hollow-cathode lamp. The electronic system sorts out the signals from the two sources and takes their ratio. One manufacturer (Perkin–Elmer) alternates the two by means of a rotating sector mirror; another

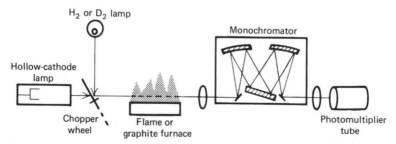

Figure 5-9 An AA spectrophotometer with H_2 (or D_2) lamp for background correction.

(Instrumentation Laboratories) sends both beams through the optical system at once, but chops them at different rates. The two beams are attenuated equally by background absorption or scattering, but only the resonance radiation is appreciably absorbed by the sample. The relative alignment of the two lamps is critical, as both beams of radiation must pass through exactly the same path in order that the correction be valid.

A second method for eliminating the background signal depends on an application of the *Zeeman effect*. Since both emission and absorption of UV and visible radiation depend on the properties of electrons circulating within atoms, it is not surprising that these phenomena are strongly affected by the presence of a magnetic field. Theory predicts[9] and experiment verifies that if either the source of radiation (the hollow-cathode lamp), or the absorbing sample, is placed within a transverse magnetic field, each line of the emitted radiation will, in the simplest case, be split into three lines, one slightly longer, one slightly shorter, and one unchanged in wavelength. The shifted and unshifted lines are polarized perpendicularly to each other, and hence a polarizer in the optical path can distinguish between them.

In Fig. 5-10 is shown the optical system of an AA spectrophotometer (manufactured by Hitachi) that uses the Zeeman principle for background correction. A permanent magnet is placed around the atomizer (which can be either a graphite furnace, as shown, or a flame). Between it and the hollow-cathode source is placed a polarizer that can be turned so that the plane of polarization of the beam is either parallel to or perpendicular to the orientation of the magnetic field. When the radiation is polarized at right angles to the field, it is not absorbed by the atomic vapor, but when parallel, absorption takes place as it would if the field were not present. However, the absorption due to the background is no different in the two situations, and so subtraction of one (perpendicular) from the other (parallel) gives an absorption spectrum free from background. This has the advantage over

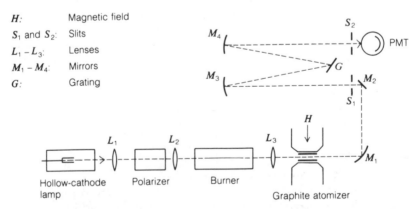

H: Magnetic field
S_1 and S_2:   Slits
$L_1 - L_3$:   Lenses
$M_1 - M_4$:   Mirrors
G: Grating

Figure 5-10 Optical diagram of the Hitachi Model 180/70 AA Spectrophotometer, showing the Zeeman magnetic field surrounding the graphite furnace atomizer. (*Hitachi, Ltd.*)

the deuterium lamp method that, since only one lamp is used, no special alignment problems exist. Other alternative arrangements of the components in a Zeeman-corrected spectrophotometer are possible.[10,11] Their relative merits have been discussed in a recent review.[12]

The third method of background correction to be described is based on the technique of wavelength modulation mentioned in Chap. 3. Harnly and O'Haver[13] have derived an expression for the absorbance of the sample which requires electronic isolation of the dc and ac components of the photomultiplier current. The ac component results from the sinusoidal wavelength shift produced by an oscillating quartz refracting plate placed just inside the exit slit. The expression is

$$A = \log\left(\frac{P_0}{P}\right) = \log\left[\frac{DC + 0.38AC}{DC - 0.62AC}\right] \qquad (5\text{-}1)$$

where AC and DC represent, respectively, the peak-to-peak ac component and the dc component. The authors have demonstrated that this method is about twice as effective as are the deuterium lamp and Zeeman methods.

Yet another method for background correction has recently been announced,[14] that has much to recommend it. In this method, the hollow-cathode lamp serves as its own corrector. A low-current pulse (12 mA) is applied to the lamp to measure the absorbance of the desired element plus background. Then a brief high-current pulse (250 mA) is applied to broaden the emission line from the lamp. The relative absorption by the sample element is greatly reduced, whereas the background absorbs a constant proportion of the radiation. The difference between the two signals gives the corrected analytical information.

Detection Limits

The sensitivities of AA methods depend in a complicated way on the optical properties of the atomic vapor, the temperature, the relative line widths of lamp and absorber, and the geometry of the optical system. Relative detection limits for many elements as determined by flame and furnace AA are compared in Fig. 9-11, which includes also comparative data for certain atomic emission methods that are discussed in Chap. 9. It will be observed that, in general, furnace AA is capable of lower detection limits than flame AA by a factor of 100 or more, though there are exceptions such as K, Fe, and Sn, which are about the same in both. Tabulated detection limits like these must be taken with some reservations, as other workers with different equipment may find quite different values.

INTERFERENCES

The chemical reactions taking place in flames can give rise to interferences in AA using a flame as sample medium. The chief difficulty is due to incomplete dissociation or to the formation of refractory compounds. Some elements, like Ti, Al,

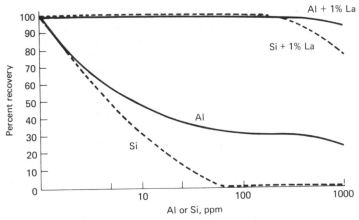

Figure 5-11 An example of the chemical removal of interferences in AA. The addition of lanthanum protects strontium from interference due to aluminum and silicon.

and V, are oxidized in the flame, forming compounds that withstand the temperature of the air–acetylene flame; most such compounds yield to the N_2O–acetylene flame. In other cases the element being sought forms stable compounds with some other constituent of the sample. For example,[15] consider the determination of Sr in the presence of Al or Si. Figure 5-11 shows how greatly the analysis is interfered with. This interference can be nearly eliminated by the addition to the sample of a small quantity of an La salt. Lanthanum preferentially binds the Al or Si, leaving the Sr free.

Interference may also be found in the examination of Ca salts. Calcium compounds are completely dissociated in the N_2O–acetylene flame, but the temperature is so high that an appreciable fraction of the Ca atoms are ionized and hence lost to the analysis. This effect can be controlled by the addition of a more easily ionized element such as Na, to keep the Ca in its neutral state.

Another source of interference arises from differences in viscosity or other bulk property of the solution, altering the ease with which it is aspirated and transported through the flame. Thus two solutions with the same concentration of metal but varying amounts of other extraneous materials may give different instrument readings.

With graphite furnace atomizers, the problems are similar. Here it is carbon rather than oxygen that is likely to form refractory compounds. The carbides of aluminum and silicon can be dissociated thermally, but not those of tungsten and boron.

Applications of Atomic Absorption

Atomic absorption is useful in the determination of a large number of metals, especially at trace levels. It is widely used in such fields as water and pharmaceutical analysis and in metallurgy. The exact conditions required for any given determination are quite critical, and unless one is prepared to undertake a lengthy methods research, it is essential to obtain specific directions and to follow them carefully. The major instrument manufacturers provide extensive manuals including procedures for all common metals in a variety of matrices. The book by Van Loon[4] is an excellent source of procedures and general discussion of the principles of AA analysis.

PROBLEMS

5-1 Sodium can be measured in the 0.5 to 2 percent range by AA using the 330.259- and 330.294-nm nonresonant radiation from a zinc hollow-cathode lamp. This is about one-fiftieth as sensitive as the sodium secondary resonances at 330.232 and 330.299 nm from a sodium lamp, and the brightness at this wavelength is about half as great for the zinc lamp as for the sodium lamp. The presence of zinc in the absorption flame gives no interference in the determination of sodium. (*a*) Account for the seeming contradiction that, although the lamp is half as bright, the sensitivity is only one-fiftieth with the zinc lamp as compared to the sodium lamp. (*b*) Why does not zinc interfere?

5-2 To compare quantitatively the effectiveness of continuous and line sources in AA, the following data were taken. A xenon lamp with a conventional monochromator gave a band of which the full width at half-maximum height (FWHM) was 5 nm, whereas the radiation from a hollow-cathode lamp showed FWHM = 0.01 nm. The absorption curve of the corresponding element in a flame showed an absorbance FWHM = 0.02 nm (see Fig. 5-12). In a particular pair of experiments, one with the hollow-cathode, and another with the xenon lamp, the concentration was such that the peak height of the radiation within the absorption band was diminished by absorption to one-half its value at zero concentration. How does the integrated area beneath the power–wavelength curve compare for radiation from the two sources after passage through the flame? Assume triangular line shapes and neglect stray light effects.

5-3 To monitor the presence of mercury vapor in the atmosphere in a metallurgical laboratory, a mercury-vapor lamp with its principal output at 253.7 nm, the resonance line, was set up as shown in Fig. 5-13 with a suitable photodetector at a total distance of 4 m. For calibration, the same lamp and photocell were placed close to each other, so that the radiation passed through a silica cuvet with a 2-cm path. With the calibration cuvet at 100°C, a drop of mercury produces a vapor pressure of 36.4 Pa ($= 0.273$ torr). If the observed absorbance in the long-path experiment is just 1.0 percent of that with the cuvet, what is the indicated partial pressure of mercury vapor in the room?

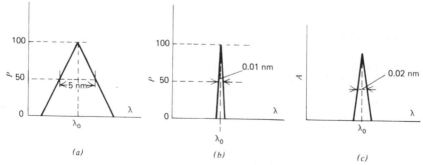

Figure 5-12 (*a*) Emission band from a continuous source with a monochromator; (*b*) emission from a hollow-cathode lamp; (*c*) the corresponding absorption line.

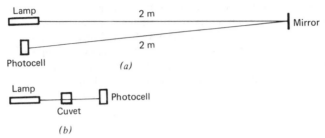

Figure 5-13 Mercury lamp and photocell: (a) deployed at a distance; (b) oriented for calibration.

5-4 Aldehydes can be determined by an indirect AA procedure,[16] whereby the aldehyde is oxidized by Ag^+ ion (Tollen's reagent), resulting in the formation of 2 moles of elementary silver for each mole of aldehyde. The silver is subsequently dissolved in nitric acid and determined by AA at 328.1 nm. The linear range for the silver determination is stated to be 2 to 20 $\mu g/ml$. What range of quantities of aldehyde would this correspond to (in micromoles) if the samples were diluted to 10 ml?

5-5 Suppose that the chopping wheel in an AA spectrophotometer like that of Fig. 5-8b is moved to a position *between* the sample and monochromator. Would the PMT current be increased or decreased? Explain.

5-6 The nickel content of a river water is to be determined by flame AA. A preliminary experiment shows that the nickel concentration is too low to be measured directly, so a preconcentration procedure must be used. An ion-exchange column is set up, containing a cation exchanger in its sodium form. A 10-liter portion of water is run through the column, all the nickel (and other cations) being retained, displacing sodium ions. The column is subsequently eluted with $HClO_4$, thus washing out all the nickel. The eluate is diluted to 50.00 ml. Successive 10-ml aliquots of this solution are "spiked" with known quantities of a standard solution of $Ni(ClO_4)_2$ containing 0.0700 μg of Ni per ml, and aspirated into the flame. The following results are obtained (at 232.0 nm), in terms of deflection of the recorder pen:

10 ml unknown	20 mm
10 ml unknown + 5 ml std	48 mm
10 ml unknown + 10 ml std	76 mm
10 ml unknown + 15 ml std	104 mm

What is the concentration of nickel in the river water, in parts per 10^9? (For the method of standard additions, see Chap. 26.)

REFERENCES

1. H. T. Delves, *Analyst (London)*, **1970**, *95*, 431.
2. R. Woodriff, *Appl. Spectrosc.*, **1974**, *28*, 413.
3. R. E. Sturgeon, *Anal. Chem.*, **1977**, *49*, 1255A.
4. J. C. Van Loon, *Analytical Atomic Absorption Spectroscopy: Selected Methods*, Academic Press, New York, **1980**, pp. 31, 60.
5. T. C. O'Haver, J. M. Harnly, and A. T. Zander, *Anal. Chem.*, **1978**, *50*, 1218.
6. J. M. Harnly, T. C. O'Haver, B. Golden, and W. R. Wolf, *Anal. Chem.*, **1979**, *51*, 2007.
7. S. R. Koirtyohann and E. E. Pickett, *Anal. Chem.*, **1965**, *37*, 601.
8. H. L. Kahn, *At. Abs. Newsletter*, **1968**, *7(2)*, 40.
9. F. A. Jenkins and H. E. White, *Fundamentals of Optics*, 4th ed., McGraw-Hill, New York, **1976**, pp. 679–686.

10. K. G. Brodie and P. R. Liddell, *Anal. Chem.*, **1980**, *52*, 1059.
11. P. R. Liddell and K. G. Brodie, *Anal. Chem.*, **1980**, *52*, 1256.
12. S. D. Brown, *Anal. Chem.*, **1977**, *49*, 1269A.
13. J. M. Harnly and T. C. O'Haver, *Anal. Chem.*, **1977**, *49*, 2187.
14. J. J. Sotera and H. L. Kahn, *Am. Lab.*, **1982**, *14(11)*, 100.
15. H. L. Kahn, *J. Chem. Educ.*, **1966**, *43*, A7, A103.
16. P. J. Oles and S. Siggia, *Anal. Chem.*, **1974**, *46*, 911.

SIX

MOLECULAR LUMINESCENCE: FLUORIMETRY, PHOSPHORIMETRY, AND RAMAN SPECTROSCOPY

In this chapter we will examine several methods in which radiation is absorbed by molecular species and reemitted with a change in wavelength. Raman spectroscopy is included because the mechanism on which it is based is fundamentally similar, though actual absorption is not involved.

Figure 6-1 is a recapitulation of Fig. 2-2 with emphasis on those processes that result in the emission of radiation from the sample. The process numbered IX has not been introduced before; it involves a hypothetical, nonstable level that we can designate as R, responsible for Raman spectra.

It is instructive to compare these several phenomena with respect to the time delay between the initial absorption event and the ultimate emission of a photon. The most easily observed difference is between fluorescence and phosphorescence. The latter may sometimes persist for many seconds after the excitation is removed, whereas the time delay in fluorescence is of the order of 10^{-9} to 10^{-7} s. These times are actually half-lives of an excited species, the time required for half of the molecules to emit photons and thus return to their ground states. To put it another way, the excited state of a fluorescing molecule may last on the average of 10^{-8} s, whereas that of a phosphorescent substance, being metastable, lasts much longer. On the other hand, the Raman-active molecule, finding no available level at R, can only return immediately to the ground electronic level S_0. Clearly these three phenomena follow different mechanisms.

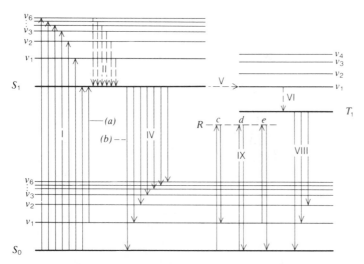

Figure 6-1 Transitions involved in molecular fluorescence and phosphorescence. This is a detailed view of a portion of Fig. 2-2, with consistent labels. The transition marked (*a*) is responsible for the overlap of excitation and fluorescence spectra, as it is less energetic than transition (*b*). Transition IX is concerned with Raman spectroscopy.

FLUORIMETRY

During the process of excitation (process I), most of the affected molecules acquire vibrational as well as electronic energy, terminating in some vibrational sublevel of an excited electronic state. The tendency is for the majority of such excited molecules to drop to the lowest vibrational level, losing energy through collisions (process II). This radiationless process stops at the S_1 excited singlet electronic level, from which the molecules are able to return directly to the ground state by radiation of a photon (fluorescence, process IV). Less commonly, they may shift to a metastable triplet level before emitting radiation (phosphorescence, processes V, VI, and VIII). In either case the molecule may end up in any of the vibrational states of the ground level. This is why both fluorescence and phosphorescence spectra generally consist of many closely spaced lines, mostly in the visible region. In the presence of a solvent, the lines are broadened and fuse together to give a less structured spectrum of the same general appearance as a UV or visible absorption spectrum.

Since molecules that are excited to vibrational sublevels of the S_1 electronic state drop back to its base level S_1 *before* producing fluorescence, it follows that for the most part the transitions that result in fluorescence (process IV) are less energetic than the absorption transitions of process I. However, at room temperature there will always be some molecules in the lower one or two vibrational sublevels of the ground state. Hence there can be excitation (shown as transition *a*

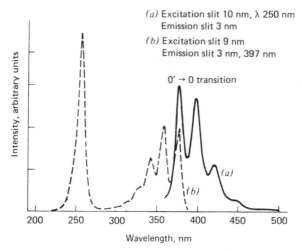

Figure 6-2 Spectra of anthracene: (a) fluorescence emission; (b) excitation. Note that the mirror-image relationship does not extend to the absorption maximum at 250 nm. (*Research and Development.*[1])

in the figure) from such a level to the S_1 state, that involves less energy than the transition marked *b*. The result is that while most of the fluorescence emission is at a longer wavelength (less energy per photon) than the excitation, there will usually be some degree of overlap, and some small fraction of the emitted radiation will appear at a shorter wavelength than the longest waves of the excitation spectrum. Furthermore, since the spacing of vibrational levels is nearly the same in the S_0 and S_1 electronic levels, the spectrum of the fluorescence radiation will resemble roughly the *mirror-image* of the excitation spectrum.

Figure 6-2 shows a comparison of the excitation and fluorescence spectra of anthracene, in which the mirror-image effect is evident.[1] The S_0 to S_1 transition at 378 nm is seen in both spectra. The intense absorption at 250 nm is due to a transition from S_0 to S_2; any molecules that find themselves in the S_2 (or higher) electronic levels drop to S_1 by nonradiative transitions, hence no counterpart appears in the emission spectrum.

Since fluorescence originates in the sample, it is emitted equally in all directions, and so can in principle be observed from any angle. In practice, three different geometries are used (Fig. 6-3). A 90° angle (*a*) is the most convenient from a design standpoint, and is selected for all less expensive fluorimeters. Observation at a small angle (*b*) is advantageous if the solution is so concentrated that most of the absorption, and hence most fluorescence generation, takes place close to the irradiated surface. The configuration is also desirable if the solution absorbs appreciably at the wavelengths of the fluorescence, because the emitted radiation need traverse only a minimal thickness of solution. The in-line construction of (*c*) has advantages if theoretical deductions (the quantum yield, for example) are to be drawn from the observations, as the equations involve fewer approximations.[2]

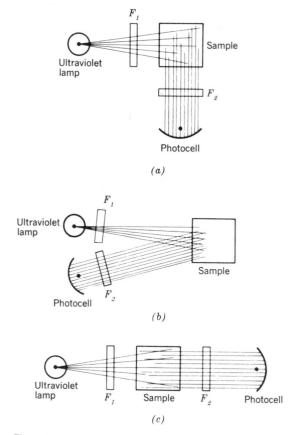

Figure 6-3 Alternative fluorimeter configurations, observed at: (a) 90°, (b) a small angle, (c) 180°. F_1 and F_2 are the primary and secondary filters, either or both of which may be replaced by monochromators.

The mathematical treatment of fluorescence is more complex than the mathematics of simple absorption leading to Beer's law. For one thing, the amount of primary radiation absorbed varies exponentially throughout the body of the solution, in accordance with the absorption law. For another, the fluorescence radiation is always subject to at least slight absorption in the solution, and the thickness of solution through which it passes is not constant, since the radiation does not originate at a single point. The complete equations are too lengthy to include in the present discussion, but may be found in the literature.[2,3]

The simplest case is that in which only a single absorbing and fluorescing species is present in a dilute solution. The governing equation for this case is

$$F = P_0 K (1 - 10^{-A})$$ (6-1)

where F is the power of fluorescence radiation reaching the detector, and P_0 is the power of the incident UV radiation. K, a constant for a given system and instrument, is the factor for converting absorbed power to the fraction of unabsorbed fluorescence reaching the detector, and A is the absorbance of the solution at the primary wavelength.

This expression can be transformed to a more useful form by application of Taylor's series expansion for 10^{-A}

$$F = P_0 K \left[2.30A - \frac{(2.30A)^2}{2!} + \frac{(2.30A)^3}{3!} - \cdots \right] \tag{6-2}$$

This means that to a first approximation for solutions of low absorbance, the squared and higher terms can be neglected, giving a direct proportionality between the fluorescence power F and the absorbance, which in turn is proportional to the concentration. However, inclusion of the term in A^2 decreases the mathematically introduced error[4] by a factor of about 8. Clearly the number of terms to be retained should be selected so that the error from this source will be less than that from the experimental procedure.

For routine analytical purposes, errors can best be minimized by the use of a calibration curve prepared from known solutions. Figure 6-4 shows the

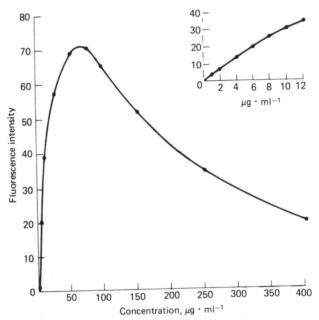

Figure 6-4 The fluorescence of phenol in water as a function of concentration. The inset is an enlargement of the portion of the main graph near the origin. Excitation, 296 nm; fluorescence observed at 330 nm; pH = 6.5. (*Journal of Clinical Pathology.*[5])

fluorescence of phenol in aqueous solution as a function of concentration[5]; it is seen to be nearly linear only to about 10 $\mu g/ml$, and single-valued to about 70 $\mu g/ml$. Beyond this point, the curve falls off because of excessive absorption of the emitted radiation by the solution.

Fluorescence is thus a useful analytical tool only for very low concentrations, much lower than suitable for absorbance measurements. In observing the fluorescence of a dilute solution, the photocell sees a faint light against a dark background, whereas in observing the absorbance of the same solution, the quantity to be determined is the attenuation of the incident radiation by a very small fraction, which amounts to the precision determination of the ratio of two nearly equal large numbers, a highly unfavorable situation. Thus the concentration region that gives proportionality according to Fig. 6-4 matches exactly these favorable instrumental conditions, resulting in an extraordinarily sensitive analytical method.

Quenching

This is the name given to any reduction in the intensity of fluorescence (or phosphorescence) due to specific effects of constituents of the solution itself. Quenching may occur as the result of excessive absorption of either primary or emitted radiation by the solution; this is called *concentration quenching* or the *inner-filter effect*. If the effect is produced by the fluorescent substance itself, it is known as *self-quenching*; the decline in fluorescence of phenol with increasing concentration, shown in Fig. 6-4, is an example.

Quenching can also be caused by nonradiative loss of energy from the excited molecules. The quenching agent may facilitate conversion of the molecules from the excited singlet to a triplet level from which emission cannot occur. The quenching of many aromatic compounds by dissolved oxygen is thought to follow this mechanism. Electron transfer from or to the excited molecule can cause quenching in some systems, such as the fluorescence of methylene blue, quenched by ferrous ion.

Chemical quenching is a term sometimes applied to the reduction in emission due to actual changes in the chemical nature of the fluorescent substance. A common observation is pH sensitivity. Aniline, for example, shows blue fluorescence in the range pH 5 to 13, when excited at 290 nm. At lower pH, aniline exists as the anilinium cation, and in highly alkaline media as the anion; neither ion is fluorescent.

The amount of fluorescence of many compounds is dependent on the temperature to a greater degree than one might expect from experience with absorption spectroscopy. A frequent source of difficulty in fluorimetry is the ease of contamination with fluorescent substances in amounts undetectable by most other means. Indeed, water and aqueous solutions can extract fluorescent substances from rubber and plastic laboratory ware, even from Bakelite bottle caps.[6] Significant amounts of quenchers can sometimes be picked up from similar sources; traces of chromium from chromic acid cleaning mixtures may offer a case in point.

SPECTROFLUORIMETERS

The fundamental requirement for a fluorimeter calls for two optical systems, one for excitation, the other for the fluorescence radiation. Either or both systems may include a monochromator, or may substitute a filter.

An instrument with monochromators in both positions is a *spectrofluorimeter*; an example is the Perkin–Elmer Model MPF-44B, diagrammed in Fig. 6-5. Chopped radiation from a 150-W xenon lamp is passed through a Czerny–Turner monochromator and focused onto a silica cuvet, where it is partially absorbed by the sample. A portion of the fluorescent emission is analyzed by a second monochromator. A fixed fraction of the primary beam is split away from the main path and monitored by an auxiliary detector which provides a means of correcting the output of the principal photomultiplier for changes in the luminance of the xenon lamp as the wavelength is scanned.

The operation of a spectrofluorimeter usually follows some such procedure as this: By rough preliminary observations, a suitable wavelength in the emission spectrum is chosen, and the second monochromator set at this point. An excitation spectrum is then plotted by scanning the first monochromator. Similarly an emission spectrum is obtained by scanning the second monochromator with the first set at a suitable value. With most substances neither spectrum is found to vary

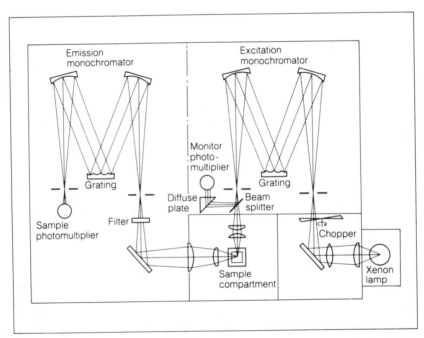

Figure 6-5 Design of the Perkin–Elmer Model MPF-44B Spectrofluorimeter. (*Perkin–Elmer Corporation.*)

greatly as the result of a change in wavelength selected for the *other* monochromator, as long as it is at a point of fairly high signal.

Spectrofluorimeters are useful for establishing conditions for analysis and for studying interferences, as well as for carrying out actual analyses. For the best precision in the latter function, results should be compared with standards run on the same instrument. It is frequently found that comparable spectra measured on different instruments give varying results, primarily as a result of the variations with wavelength of the output of the sources of radiation, the absolute sensitivities of the detectors, and the efficiencies of the monochromators. The observed spectra represent some combination of the spectral properties of the substance itself with artifacts generated by the instrument. Such variations are particularly disturbing in measurements of the quantum efficiency of the fluorescence process.

It is possible to calibrate a spectrofluorimeter by painstaking comparisons involving a standard source and thermocouple detector or precalibrated photomultiplier tube. The corrections so derived may be rather large—a factor varying from less than unity to as high as 50 or more[7] (see Fig. 6-6).

Much of the tedium of such methods can be eliminated by the use of a fluorescent material as a standard of comparison. The aluminum chelate of the azo dye Pontachrome blue-black R has been recommended.[8] A solution of Rhodamine G is known to have a uniform response to excitation over a wide wavelength

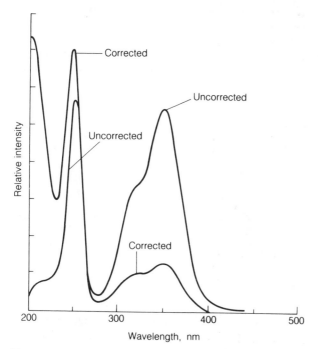

Figure 6-6 Corrected and uncorrected excitation spectra of quinine (0.1 ppm) in 0.05 M H_2SO_4. (*Wiley-Interscience.*[7])

range (220 to 600 nm), and hence can be used as a *quantum counter*, facilitating the calibration of the measuring photomultiplier.[9] Application of the calibration techniques described in these references should go far toward eliminating the reporting of "uncorrected" fluorescence spectra.

It will be seen that the spectrofluorimeter of Fig. 6-5 is not truly a double-beam instrument in the sense that this term is used in absorption spectrophotometry. The second photomultiplier serves only to correct for changes in the output of the lamp. Any background due to fluorescence of the solvent and reagents or to scattering by dust particles or the like must be determined by running a blank and subtracting, an operation easily performed with those modern instruments that are equipped with microprocessor controls.

FILTER FLUORIMETERS

For analytical applications, it is often not necessary to resolve fluorescence peaks. This would be true, for example, in the case where a solution is treated with a reagent that selectively converts the species of interest to a fluorescing derivative. There is then no need for expensive monochromators, and filters can be used instead. Figure 6-7 shows the simplified instrument that can be substituted. Two filters are required: F_1 to pass the UV but remove visible radiation, and F_2 to absorb any UV that may have been scattered toward the detector, while passing the visible emission. This abridged fluorimeter may well show greater sensitivity than a spectrofluorimeter because of the greater amount of radiation that can pass through a filter compared to a monochromator. The power supplies feeding both lamp and photomultiplier should be carefully stabilized in both types of instrument.

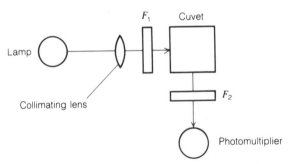

Figure 6-7 A simple filter fluorimeter with 90° geometry.

APPLICATIONS

Fluorimetry is noted for its great sensitivity, often 10^2 to 10^4 times greater than comparable absorption techniques. It is also more selective, since fewer compounds fluoresce efficiently than merely absorb radiation.

Visible fluorescence occurs mainly in two classes of substances: (1) a large variety of minerals and inorganic solid-state "phosphors," and (2) organic and organometallic compounds with extensive ultraviolet absorption.

In the first of these classes, we will mention only a method for the determination of traces of uranium, as found in rocks and natural waters.[10] The sample, in solution, is treated with $Ca(NO_3)_2$ followed by slow addition of NH_4F. The precipitate of CaF_2 so formed brings down with it any uranium as the fluoride. This material is filtered out, dried, calcined at 800°C, then crushed. The resulting powder is pressed into pellets for examination in a fluorimeter. As described in the reference, excitation was by the 488-nm radiation from an argon–ion laser. The limit of detection reported was 0.01 pg/ml (10^{-5} ppb).

An example of a fluorimetric analysis in inorganic chemistry is the determination of trace amounts of cadmium by reaction with calcein, a carboxymethyl derivative of bis(dimethylaminomethyl)fluorescein.[11] The cadmium must first be separated from various interfering ions by an ion-exchange procedure. The fluorescence at 520 nm was measured in 0.5 M KOH with excitation at 490 nm. The detection limit was 2.2 ng/ml.

Most organic applications are in the determination of polycyclic molecules, including a great many substances of biochemical and pharmacological significance. The following paragraphs outline two such analytical methods.

Thiamine (vitamin B_1) can be assayed by the blue fluorescence of its oxidation product, thiochrome.[12] The sample is treated with phosphatase, an enzyme that causes hydrolysis of the phosphate esters of thiamine, frequently present in foodstuffs. The phosphatase and other insoluble matter is filtered off, and the filtrate diluted to a known volume. Two aliquots are taken, one for analysis, one for a blank. To the first is added an oxidizing agent (ferricyanide), and to both, NaOH and isobutyl alcohol. After shaking and removal of the aqueous layer, the alcoholic solution is examined in the fluorimeter.

Riboflavin can also be determined fluorimetrically.[12] The fluorescent power is dependent to a large degree on the exact conditions and on the nature and amount of impurities present. In order to make certain that any impurities have the same effect on standard and unknown, the method of standard additions is adopted. The fluorescence of a portion of the standard is measured in the same solution with the unknown. The procedure also takes advantage of the fact that riboflavin can readily be oxidized to a nonfluorescing substance that in turn can easily be reduced to regenerate riboflavin quantitatively.

A different sort of application of spectrofluorimetry lies in the determination of UV absorption spectra in very small or very dilute samples. This takes advantage of the virtual identity of corrected fluorescence excitation spectra and conventional absorption spectra. The excitation spectrum is likely to show less fine structure, but on the other hand, the method is more selective than absorption spectroscopy, as many contaminants do not fluoresce. If only uncorrected fluorescence spectra can be obtained, this method must be used with caution because of possible drastic alteration of the spectrum caused by quenching. Duplicate spectra should be obtained at several concentration levels; if these are identical, concentration

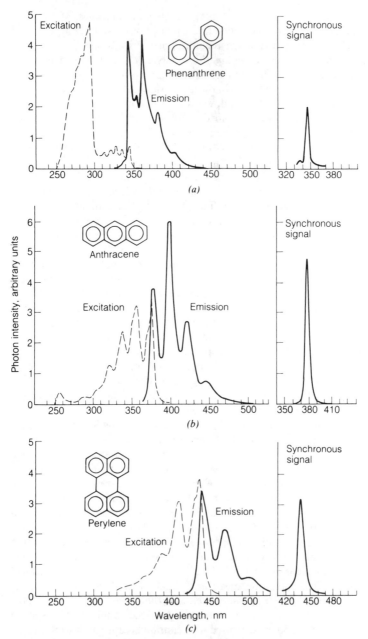

Figure 6-8 Fluorescence excitation, emission, and synchronous spectra of (a) phenanthrene, (b) anthracene, and (c) perylene. (*Analytical Chemistry.*[13])

quenching is probably absent. In favorable cases, absorption spectra can be obtained on nanogram to microgram quantities of fluorescent compounds.

Synchronous Fluorimetry

It is possible to obtain a sharply peaked fluorescence response by scanning both monochromators of a spectrofluorimeter simultaneously.[13,14] The peak will appear only in the region where the excitation and emission spectra overlap. The shortest wavelength peak in the emission spectrum is often slightly offset toward longer wavelengths with respect to the longest wavelength peak of the excitation spectrum. Hence optimum results will be obtained if a small constant wavelength (or frequency[15]) difference is maintained between the two monochromators.

Figure 6-8 shows the kind of response obtained from three aromatic hydrocarbons by this method. The wavelength offset was 3 nm. The advantage of this mode of operation lies in the greatly enhanced resolution when dealing with mixtures of fluorescent compounds (Fig. 6-9).

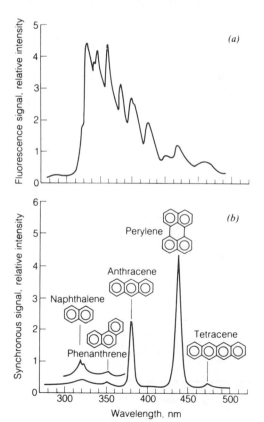

Figure 6-9 Fluorescence spectra of a mixture of naphthalene, phenanthrene, anthracene, perylene, and tetracene: (a) conventional; (b) synchronous. (*Analytical Chemistry*.[13])

PHOSPHORIMETRY

Phosphorescence is distinguished operationally from fluorescence, first by its longer decay time (half-life 10^{-1} to 10 s, contrasted with 10^{-7} to 10^{-9} s for fluorescence), and second, by a shift to longer wavelengths. Both these features can be explained by reference to Fig. 6-10. Transitions that involve a change in multiplicity ($S \to T$ or $T \to S$) are "forbidden," which means that the probability of their occurrence is small. However, an intersystem crossing can take place readily from S_1 to one of the vibrational levels of the T_1 state that has very nearly the same energy (process V in the figure). This is followed immediately by non-radiative decay (process VI) to the T_1 base level.

The triplet state T_1 is metastable, and molecules populating it have excess energy to dispose of. This energy can be lost by any of several competing mechanisms, including phosphorescence radiation (process VIII). Of the other possible decay paths, two are particularly important. One is oxygen quenching: energy is transferred to molecular oxygen, which can easily undergo a transition since it has a triplet ground state. For this reason, oxygen must be scrupulously excluded from the cuvet of a phosphorimeter.

The second path for energy loss is by collisions, a process that is of greater significance in phosphorescence than in fluorescence because of the longer times involved. Collisional deactivation can be diminished or eliminated by any procedure that makes the sample rigid, so that its molecules are immobilized. This has conventionally been accomplished by increasing the viscosity of a suitable solvent by cooling it to the point where a rigid glass is obtained. An often used solvent is

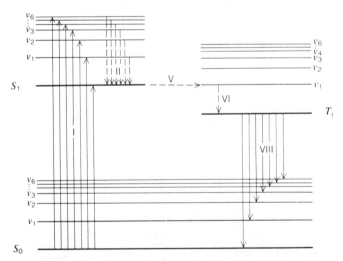

Figure 6-10 Transitions involved in molecular phosphorescence, a detailed view of the pertinent portions of Fig. 6-1.

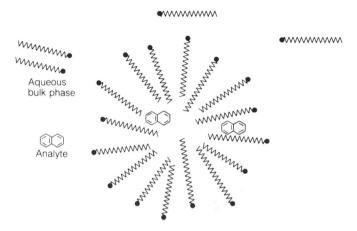

Figure 6-11 A schematic representation of an anionic micelle with its environment. Molecules of analyte (naphthalene) are entrapped within the micelle. (*American Laboratory*,[18] *redrawn*.)

"EPA," a mixture of ethyl ether, isopentane, and ethanol in the volume ratio of 5:5:2, used at liquid nitrogen temperature (77 K). This mixture does not crystallize, an advantage, as crystallization might tend to segregate the solute undesirably.

More recently, it has been found possible to dispense with the awkward requirement of a liquid nitrogen cryostat by using instead other methods for immobilizing the sample.[16] Room-temperature phosphorescence can be observed in samples that are adsorbed on filter paper or other solid substrate. This is easily done, but suffers from the high background due to phosphorescence of the substrate itself.

Another possibility is to use a surface-active agent, such as sodium lauryl sulfate that forms micelles in aqueous suspension.[17,18] A micelle is a tiny globule of some 40–100 detergent molecules oriented so that the outer surface consists of the hydrophilic sulfate groups, while the interior is filled with the hydrophobic hydrocarbon (lauryl) moieties. Figure 6-11 is a two-dimensional representation of such a micelle.[18] The interior of the cluster forms an environment that is receptive to nonpolar molecules. These molecules become entrapped in the tangle of hydrocarbon chains, so that they are protected from collisions, and also to a large extent from chemical quenching agents. This permits examination of their phosphorescence spectra using standard fluorimetric techniques and instruments.

The rates of intersystem crossing (both $S_1 \rightarrow T_1$ and $T_1 \rightarrow S_0$) can be increased significantly by the incorporation of an atom of high atomic weight into the environment surrounding the analyte, the *heavy-atom effect*.[19] Both of these rate increases serve to enhance the phosphorescence spectrum. In cooled EPA solutions this may be accomplished by the addition of methyl iodide to the solvent. In micelle preparations, a fraction (50–60 percent) of the sodium in the surface-active agent can be replaced by thallium.[18] A typical example is shown in Fig. 6-12.

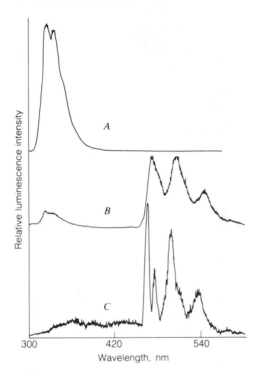

Figure 6-12 Phosphorescence spectra of 6×10^{-5} M naphthalene: (a) in aqueous micelles; (b) in micelles containing Tl substituted for 30 percent of the Na atoms; recorded at ten times the sensitivity used for (a); (c) ethanol solution at 77 K; recorded at 25 times the sensitivity used in (a). (*American Laboratory*.[18])

PHOSPHORIMETERS

Compounds that phosphoresce invariably fluoresce as well, and a phosphorimeter must be able to distinguish between the two. One way to do this is by means of a rotating shutter, called a *phosphoroscope* (Fig. 6-13). This device introduces a definite delay between the time intervals during which the sample is irradiated and observed. Several commercial instruments work on this principle. Theoretical aspects of optimum shutter design have been discussed in an interesting paper by O'Haver and Winefordner.[20]

Pulse techniques can be used in place of the rotating shutter.[21] A flash tube is used as the source of primary radiation. An electronic timing circuit first triggers the flash, and then at a selected time interval later, activates the photomultiplier. With this system, decay times as short as 10^{-5} s can be measured, a speed not easily attainable with a mechanical shutter.

Many organic compounds with conjugated ring systems phosphoresce intensely, and phosphorimetry provides excellent opportunities for their trace analysis. The subject has been discussed in some detail by Winefordner and Latz.[22] They developed a simple, fast procedure for the determination of aspirin in blood serum and plasma, in which the presence of free salicyclic acid does not interfere.

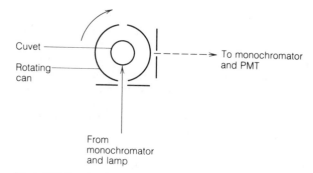

Figure 6-13 Plan drawing of a rotating can phosphoroscope. The delay in observation of the spectrum corresponds to the time required for the can to turn through 90°.

An additional technique possible with phosphorimetry is time resolution.[23] This permits multicomponent analysis, provided the components have sufficiently different decay times. The time resolution can be achieved merely by changing the delay between activation and observation, or more powerfully by logarithmic subtraction.[21] For two components A and B the emitted power is

$$P_{ph} = P_A + P_B = P_{0,A} \exp\left(-\frac{t}{\tau_A} \right) + P_{0,B} \exp\left(-\frac{t}{\tau_B} \right) \qquad (6\text{-}3)$$

where τ is the decay time, the time required for the phosphorescence of a substance to decrease to $1/e = 36.8$ percent of its initial value. If the values of P_{ph} are recorded as a function of time until both emissions have disappeared, the amount of the species with the longer decay time can be determined from the data taken after the radiation from the other component has died away. Then its contribution can be subtracted out, leaving a record of the emission of the shorter-lived species.

It is possible to adapt synchronous scanning to phosphorescence.[24] The offset in wavelength between the excitation and emission monochromators must correspond to the energy difference between the S_1 and T_1 levels, which makes the method less simple than synchronous scanning in fluorescence, but the advantage of good resolution of mixed analytes still holds.

RAMAN SPECTROSCOPY[25,26]

Process IX in Fig. 6-1 suggests that under suitable circumstances a photon can transfer its energy temporarily to a molecule regardless of its energy content, elevating the molecule to a "virtual" level R. This energy level, however, does not in general correspond to a stable position and the molecule must immediately drop back to its ground state. In falling back the molecule may end up in an excited vibrational state (transition c in the diagram), in which case the emitted photon will have *less* energy than the excitation by the amount characteristic of the particular vibrational level. On the other hand, (e), some molecules may already be excited vibrationally, and the photon emitted will then have slightly *greater* energy. If the molecule returns to the same level it started from (*d*), then there will be no energy or wavelength change.

As we shall see, actual Raman spectra do in fact show a symmetrical series of frequencies ("lines") on each side of a central frequency. Those on the long-wavelength side are called *Stokes lines*, and those of shorter wavelength, *anti-Stokes*. The central line that shows no frequency shift corresponds to a simple scattering process that will be treated in Chap. 8. (Because of this, the entire Raman phenomenon is frequently thought of as a type of scattering.)

Since the exciting radiation can, in principle, be at any frequency, the instrument designer has considerable latitude in selecting a source. The requirements are that the radiation be as nearly monochromatic as possible and at the same time quite powerful. A laser is by far the best source for Raman spectroscopy, and has completely displaced the mercury lamps formerly used. A laser operating in the visible region is usually chosen, most commonly either a helium–neon laser (632.8 nm) or an argon–ion laser (488.8 or 514.6 nm).

Raman spectra are usually displayed as a plot of the "Raman shift" $\Delta \tilde{v}$ given by the relation

$$\Delta \tilde{v} = \pm(\tilde{v}_i - \tilde{v}_R) \tag{6-4}$$

where $\tilde{v}_1$ and $\tilde{v}_R$ are the wavenumbers of the incident and Raman radiations (see Fig. 6-14). The Stokes lines correspond to the positive sign. The vertical scale is the

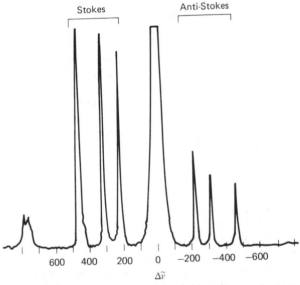

Figure 6-14 Raman spectrum of liquid CCl_4 scanned at 500 cm^{-1}/min using a 3-μl sample with helium–neon 632.8 nm excitation. The strong signal at $\Delta \tilde{v} = 0$ is due to Rayleigh scattering of laser radiation. (*Journal of Chemical Education.*[34])

relative output of a photomultiplier. Stokes lines are always more intense than anti-Stokes, and the line due to scattered laser light ($\Delta\bar{\nu} = 0$) is much more powerful than either.

Raman spectra are observed in molecular compounds for which the *polarizability* is altered by vibrations corresponding to the wave number transition $\Delta\bar{\nu}$. Polarizability is a measure of the ease of inducing a dipole as a result of the electromagnetic field of the incoming photon. Since this is not restricted to those molecules that have no dipoles, whereas infrared absorption does require a permanent dipole, it follows that frequencies observed in the IR may not be active in the Raman spectrum, and vice versa. There may be some vibrational modes that affect *both* the polarizability and the dipole moment, and these will be evidenced in both techniques. Comparison spectra of 1,4-dioxane in the two modes (Fig. 6-15) illustrate these features.

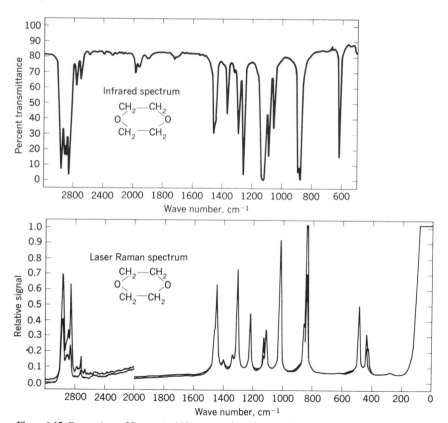

Figure 6-15 Comparison of Raman and IR spectra of 1,4-dioxane. The spectra are printed with wave-number scales in register, showing many points of similarity. Note the band at 1220 cm^{-1} which is strong in the Raman and almost invisible in the IR. Conversely, the band at 620 cm^{-1} is active in the IR but not in the Raman. (*Courtesy of Cary Instruments Division of Varian Associates.*)

Ordinarily, Raman spectra are observed in a spectral region where the sample does not absorb appreciably. This is because the faint Raman radiation would otherwise never reach the detector. However, if a sufficiently powerful, tunable, dye laser be used, and the frequency is brought nearly but not quite to coincidence with an absorption maximum, it is found that the sensitivity is increased manyfold. This is known as the *resonance Raman* technique[27]; it has not yet found many analytical applications, but shows promise for the future.

A source of interference in Raman work that may often be a limiting factor is fluorescence. Since fluorescence radiation is usually much more intense than Raman radiation, a small amount of a fluorescent impurity, or slight fluorescence generated by the solvent, can easily swamp out the signal that one is looking for. This can sometimes be avoided by selecting a laser that produces its radiation at a wavelength outside the band that excites the fluorescence.

There are a number of rather exotic techniques that are modifications of the basic Raman phenomenon, the most important being *coherent anti-Stokes Raman spectroscopy (CARS)*. These require the simultaneous use of two highly powerful lasers. Details can be found in the literature.[27,28]

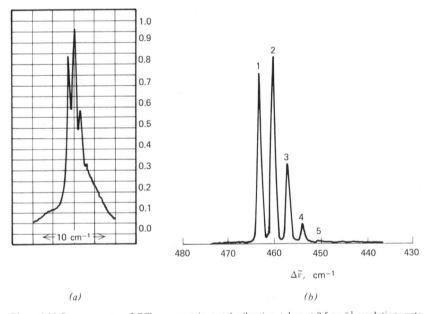

(a)   *(b)*

Figure 6-16 Raman spectra of CCl_4, symmetric stretch vibration, taken at 0.5 cm⁻¹ resolution; note that this resolves one of the peaks shown in Fig. 6-14. (*a*) At room temperature, and (*b*) at 77 K, deposited on a cooled copper block. The complex structure arises from the five possible combinations of chlorine isotopes. The spectrum is clearly resolved at the low temperature, as the bands are narrower. (*Applied Spectroscopy.*[30])

Applications of Raman Spectroscopy

As evident from Fig. 6-15, a Raman spectrum can be just as useful in fingerprint identification as the IR spectrum. Atlases of Raman spectra are available.[29] In this application, and in structure elucidation, Raman and infrared supplement rather than duplicate each other.[30] Both can also be useful in quantitative analysis.

Sample preparation for liquids requires careful filtration to remove all traces of suspended matter that would increase scattering. Fluorescent impurities must be rigidly excluded. Filtered gases can be examined in multipass cells. Solids, or thin films deposited on solid supports, can be studied by reflecting the laser beam from the surface. Temperature control is not usually required, but the spectra of cooled samples may give interesting fine structure (Fig. 6-16).

PROBLEMS

6-1 A 2-g sample of pork is to be analyzed for its vitamin B_1 (thiamine) content by the thiachrome method. It is extracted with HCl, treated with phosphatase, and diluted to 100 ml. An aliquot of 15 ml is purified by adsorption and elution, during which process it is diluted to 25 ml. Of this, two 5-ml portions are taken, one of them (A) is treated with $K_3Fe(CN)_6$, and both (A and B) made up to 10 ml for fluorimetric examination. A standard solution of thiamine containing 0.2 μg/ml is subjected to similar treatment, except that the portion introduced into the adsorption column is made up to its original volume after elution (i.e., not diluted). Two 5-ml aliquots are taken, one (C) is oxidized, and both (C and D) are made up to a final volume of 10 ml for the measurement of fluorescence. The following observations are recorded:

Solution	Relative fluorescent power
A (std, oxidized)	62.4
B (std, blank)	7.0
C (sample, oxidized)	52.0
D (sample, blank)	8.0

Calculate the vitamin B_1 content of the pork in terms of micrograms per gram.

6-2 It has been shown[31] that the Hantzch reaction can be used in a very sensitive analysis for either aldehydes or primary amines, including ammonia. In the presence of 2,4-pentanedione (acetylacetone) a cyclic adduct is formed at pH 6 that is strongly fluorescent. The reaction is

(*a*) If ammonia is in excess, the fluorescent power, after subtraction of a blank value, is nearly linear with concentration of formaldehyde in the range 0.005 to 1.0 μg/ml. What is the approximate linear range for the determination of traces of aniline with excess formaldehyde present? (*b*) The absorption spectrum of the fluorescent compound shows a fairly intense maximum at 410 nm (ϵ = 8000), too great to be accounted for by two unrelated 2,3-unsaturated ketone chromophores. Can you offer a possible explanation?

6-3 In the fluorimetric determination of 7H-benz(*de*)anthracene-7-one (BO) as an air pollutant, considerable interference is encountered from fluorescent polynuclear hydrocarbons.[32] The latter fluorescence is more readily quenched by 1,3-dinitrobenzene (DNB), a fact that makes the analysis possible.

(*a*) Addition of 15 percent DNB to the solution reduces the fluorescence power F of 5 × 10^{-6} M BO from 0.7 to 0.4 (relative units), with the use of a filter fluorimeter. If this amount of DNB diminishes the fluorescence of interfering materials to 0.005 of its original value, how great an improvement in sensitivity would result from the use of the quenching agent? (*b*) Would you expect that the quencher could be dispensed with if the measurement were made with a spectrofluorimeter?

6-4 The absorption spectrum of a fluorescent substance determined with a conventional spectrophotometer is likely to be in error because of the fluorescence. Suppose a compound has an absorption maximum (hence an excitation maximum) at 290 nm and a fluorescence maximum at 350 nm. At what wavelength would you expect the greatest error? Would the observed absorbance be too large or too small at this point? Would your answers be different for a spectrophotometer in which the radiation from the lamp passes through the cuvet *before* dispersion in the monochromator? Explain.

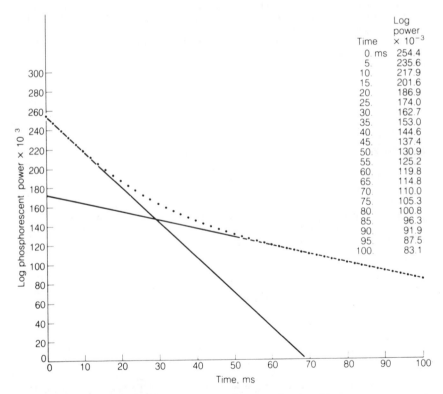

Figure 6-17 Phosphorescence of a two-component mixture as a function of time.

MOLECULAR LUMINESCENCE **145**

6-5 A Raman spectrum of a pure compound is observed, using the 488.8-nm radiation from an argon-ion laser for excitation. Raman lines are found at wavelengths 496.6, 498.5, 506.5, and 522.0 nm. (*a*) Compute the values of the Raman shifts for these lines in terms of wavenumber. (*b*) What is the wavelength of the anti-Stokes line corresponding to the Stokes line at 522.0 nm?

6-6 Raman spectrometry can be applied to the quantitative analysis of gas mixtures. A pilot study[33] dealt with ternary mixtures of methane, isobutane, and nitrogen. The following Raman shifts were utilized (in cm^{-1}): methane, 2917; isobutane, two shifts, at 800 and 2917; nitrogen, 2331. What measurements would you make on pure standards or known mixtures to establish a routine procedure for analyzing mixtures of these three gases?

6-7 It has been reported that Raman lines can be observed as close as 2 cm^{-1} from the exciting radiation in favorable cases, using the helium–neon laser for illumination. What are the wavelength and frequency for the corresponding transitions observed in IR absorption?

6-8 Explain qualitatively the shape of the phenol fluorescence curve of Fig. 6-4. Assume that the geometry of Fig. 6-3*a* is applicable.

6-9 Search the literature for information about the use of Rhodamine G and related compounds as "quantum counters," and explain how they function.

6-10 Figure 6-17 shows computer-generated data that simulate the phosphorescence emitted by a solution containing two active substances *A* and *B*. The vertical axis is the logarithm (to the base 10) of the phosphorescent power P_{ph} [Eq. (6-3)] that would be observed by a PMT. (The table inset in Fig. 6-17 gives a few of the actual points.) Calculate the two decay constants, τ_A and τ_B, and the relative concentrations of *A* and *B*. Assume that the two have equal sensitivities [i.e., that the constant *K* in Eq. (6-1) is the same for both] and that one wavelength is suitable for both.

REFERENCES

1. H. F. Smith, *Res. and Dev.*, July **1968**, p. 20.
2. M. H. Fletcher, *Anal. Chem.*, **1963**, *35*, 278, 288; R. G. Milkey and M. H. Fletcher, *J. Am. Chem. Soc.*, **1957**, *79*, 5425.
3. J. F. Holland, R. E. Teets, P. M. Kelly, and A. Timnick, *Anal. Chem.*, **1977**, *49*, 706.
4. R. B. Lam and J. J. Leary, *Appl. Spectrosc.*, **1979**, *33*, 17.
5. R. T. Williams and J. W. Bridges, *J. Clin. Pathol.*, **1964**, *17*, 371.
6. H. A. Kordan, *Science*, **1965**, *149*, 1382.
7. P. A. St. John, "Fluorometric Methods for Traces of Elements," in *Trace Analysis: Spectroscopic Methods for Elements*, J. D. Winefordner (ed.), Wiley-Interscience, New York, **1976**, p. 248.
8. R. J. Argauer and C. E. White, *Anal. Chem.*, **1964**, *36*, 368; (correction, p. 1022).
9. J. N. Demas and G. A. Crosby, *J. Phys. Chem.*, **1971**, *75*, 991.
10. D. L. Perry, S. M. Klainer, H. R. Bowman, F. P. Milanovich, T. Hirschfeld, and S. Miller, *Anal. Chem.*, **1981**, *53*, 1048.
11. A. J. Hefley and B. Jaselskis, *Anal. Chem.*, **1974**, *46*, 2036.
12. Association of Vitamin Chemists, Inc., *Methods of Vitamin Assay*, 3d ed., Wiley-Interscience, New York, **1966**.
13. T. Vo-Dinh, *Anal. Chem.*, **1978**, *50*, 396.
14. T. Vo-Dinh, *Appl. Spectrosc.*, **1982**, *36*, 576.
15. E. L. Inman, Jr., and J. D. Winefordner, *Anal. Chem.*, **1982**, *54*, 2018.
16. J. N. Miller, *Trends in Anal. Chem.*, **1981**, *1*, 31.
17. L. J. Cline Love, M. Skrilec, and J. G. Habarta, *Anal. Chem.*, **1980**, *52*, 754.
18. L. J. Cline Love and M. Skrilec, *Am. Lab.*, **1981**, *13(3)*, 103.
19. W. J. McCarthy, "Phosphorescence Spectrometry," in *Spectrochemical Methods of Analysis*, J. D. Winefordner (ed.), Wiley-Interscience, New York, **1971**, p. 467.
20. T. C. O'Haver and J. D. Winefordner, *Anal. Chem.*, **1966**, *38*, 602.
21. R. P. Fisher and J. D. Winefordner, *Anal. Chem.*, **1972**, *44*, 948.

22. J. D. Winefordner and H. W. Latz, *Anal. Chem.*, **1963**, *35*, 1517.
23. J. D. Winefordner, *Acc. Chem. Res.*, **1969**, *2*, 361.
24. T. Vo-Dinh and R. B. Gammage, *Anal. Chem.*, **1978**, *50*, 2054.
25. D. A. Long, *Raman Spectroscopy*, McGraw-Hill, New York, **1977**.
26. W. Demtröder, in *Analytical Laser Spectroscopy*, N. Omenetto (ed.), Wiley, New York, **1979**, pp. 276 ff.
27. A. J. Melveger (ed.), *Resonance Raman Spectroscopy as an Analytical Tool*, Franklin Inst. Press, Philadelphia, **1978**.
28. S. A. Borman, *Anal. Chem.*, **1982**, *54*, 1021A.
29. Sadtler Research Laboratory, Inc., Philadelphia.
30. H. J. Sloane, *Appl. Spectrosc.*, **1971**, *25*, 430.
31. S. Belman, *Anal. Chim. Acta*, **1963**, *29*, 120.
32. E. Sawicky, H. Johnson, and M. Morgan, *Mikrochim. Acta*, **1967**, 297.
33. D. E. Diller and R. F. Chang, *Appl. Spectrosc.*, **1980**, *34*, 411.
34. B. J. Bulkin, *J. Chem. Educ.*, **1969**, *46*, A781, A859.

SEVEN

PHOTOACOUSTIC SPECTROSCOPY

The excitation of a molecule by the absorption of radiation initiates a series of events by which the excess energy is dissipated, allowing the molecule to return to its ground state. These events we have classified as radiative (fluorescence or phosphorescence) on the one hand, and nonradiative on the other. The latter category has not interested us greatly in the context of previous chapters, but will now be treated more fully.

As seen in Fig. 2-2, nonradiative transitions can occur from higher vibrational sublevels to the base levels (S_0, S_1, T_1, etc.). If the substance under study is a liquid or gas, the énergy corresponding to these transitions simply goes to increasing the thermal agitation of all the molecules of the sample. If the substance is a solid, the energy is first converted to increased lattice vibrations (sometimes specified in terms of the *phonon*, the quantum of lattice vibrational energy), and may then be transferred to any gas or liquid that may be in contact with the sample.

Since this energy is directly or indirectly converted to heat, it should be possible to obtain useful information by measurement of the temperature rise. This has been done by direct measurement with a thermistor,[1] but more successfully by the technique known as *photoacoustic spectroscopy* (PAS), also called *optoacoustic spectroscopy.*

In PAS, a pulsating (chopped) beam of radiation is utilized, so that the heat effect produced in the absorbing sample fluctuates at the same frequency. The periodic increase and decrease in vibrational energy propagates through the medium as a sound wave. Any wave motion is characterized by three parameters: an amplitude, a velocity, and a frequency. In the present case, the frequency is that at which the radiation is chopped, the velocity is the speed of sound in the medium, and the amplitude corresponds to the amount of energy absorbed and converted to heat.

The sonic signal can be measured in either of two ways: by a microphone, or by a piezoelectric transducer. If the absorbing sample is a gas, the sound wave can be picked up directly by a microphone. If the sample is a solid, the most convenient (though not the most sensitive) arrangement is to couple the sonic wave in the solid to the microphone by immersing both in an enclosed space filled with a gas (usually air).[2,3] There is substantial loss of energy as the wave crosses the solid-gas boundary, and this must be recovered by electronic amplification.

Another alternative is to attach the solid sample to a piezoelectric transducer (PZT) by means of an adhesive.[4] This makes more efficient use of the available energy, but is hardly suitable for routine use because of the inconvenience of sample manipulation. Liquid samples can be handled either by the air-coupled microphone or by contact with a PZT in a closed system.

Since the microphone method is used in commercial instruments, we will emphasize it in our treatment.

A block diagram of a basic PAS spectrometer is shown in Fig. 7-1, and a typical cell in Fig. 7-2. The pulsed radiation enters through a transparent window, and then encounters the sample, which is either the gas within the cell or the solid (or liquid) material designated in the figure by cross-hatching. The microphone is often placed in a side-arm, as shown, to protect it from direct radiation. The sensitivity will be increased by selecting a cell of such dimensions that it will resonate at the frequency of the chopped radiation; a larger sample is required, however.

The chief limitation of PAS is due to a saturation phenomenon. This is the result of the limited rate of diffusion of heat through the sample from the point

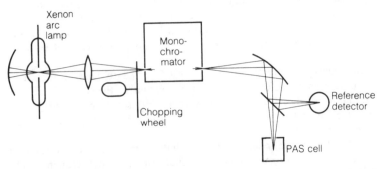

Figure 7-1 A single-beam photoacoustic spectrometer. The signals from the PAS cell and the reference detector are processed by separate lock-in amplifiers synchronized with the rotation of the chopping wheel.

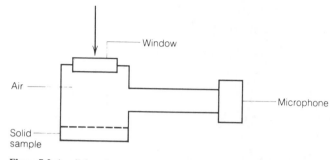

Figure 7-2 A cell for photoacoustic measurements. Radiation enters from above. The microphone is placed at the end of a side-arm, but in contact with the air space of the detector body.

where a photon is absorbed to the surface where the heat can be transferred to the surrounding gas. Both the process of optical absorption and that of thermal diffusion are characterized by constants with the units of cm^{-1}: β, the absorption coefficient, defined by the relation

$$\frac{P}{P_0} = e^{-\beta l} \tag{7-1}$$

where l is the path length within the absorbing material, and a_s, the coefficient of thermal diffusion, given by

$$a_s = \left(\frac{\pi v}{\alpha_s}\right)^{1/2} \tag{7-2}$$

where v is the frequency in hertz, and α_s is the thermal diffusivity in cm^2/s. If $\beta < a_s$, a photoacoustic signal will result that is proportional to β, as is desired, but when β increases to equal or exceed a_s, the signal becomes constant ("saturates"). Figure 7-3 shows this effect for a hypothetical sample.[3] If one were to determine this substance by means of the PAS spectrum, measurements should be made at a or b, not at c. Saturation effects can be minimized by grinding the solid sample together with a transparent diluent, such as powdered Al_2O_3 or KBr.[5]

It will be noted that the spectrometer diagrammed in Fig. 7-1 is a single-beam instrument provided with a reference detector that monitors the beam of radiation emerging from the monochromator. This reference detector (usually pyroelectric) provides a signal against which the signal from the microphone can be ratioed so as to compensate for variations in the output of the lamp. In some designs a second PAS cell in a dual-beam arrangement contains carbon black as a reference material. Carbon black absorbs essentially all the radiation that hits it, and thus gives a saturated response that is uniform at all wavelengths. Hence any variation in the signal from the reference cell must be due to variations in the lamp, and can be compensated as such.

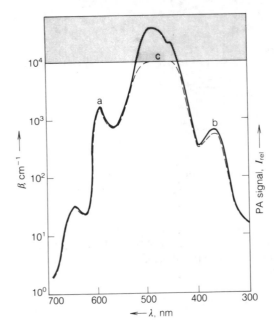

Figure 7-3 Comparison of optical absorption (solid line) and PAS (dashed line) spectra of a hypothetical sample. Saturation occurs in the shaded zone, corresponding (arbitrarily) to $\beta = 10^4$ cm^{-1}. (*Angewandte Chemie*.[3])

The signal from a PAS cell is proportional to the power of the exciting radiation, in the absence of saturation, and therefore it is advantageous to use as powerful a lamp as possible. For work in the UV and visible, a xenon arc lamp is commonly employed, operating sometimes as high as 1000 W.

There is no sufficiently powerful source of continuum radiation in the IR to operate a PAS spectrometer like that of Fig. 7-1. For PAS studies in this region, it is necessary to use an interferometric (Fourier-transform) spectrometer in order to take advantage of the Fellgett and Jacquinot advantages described in Chap. 4.[6,7] This adaptation, denoted by the abbreviation FT-PAS, has found applications in studying high polymers[8] and coal.[9] PAS measurements can be made at isolated frequencies in the IR by using a laser as the source of radiation. This has been found particularly useful in the detection and measurement of noxious gases as air pollutants.[10]

APPLICATIONS

For samples that do not fluoresce or phosphoresce, PAS spectra can be expected to be essentially identical with conventional absorption spectra. Figure 7-4 shows the close correspondence between the PAS spectrum of powdered Cr_2O_3[2] and the absorption spectrum of a thin section of a crystal.[11] (The latter depends on the orientation of the specimen, as the crystal is not isotropic.)

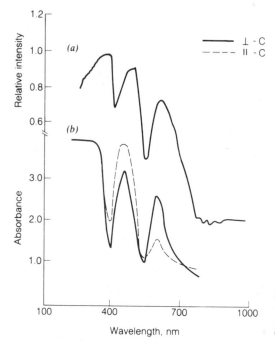

Figure 7-4 Absorption spectra of crystalline Cr_2O_3: (*a*) PAS, (*b*) conventional method. (*Analytical Chemistry*[2]; curve *b* from *Journal of Chemical Physics*,[11])

PAS has several major advantages over conventional absorption spectroscopy. First, it provides the only accurate method of determining the spectra of opaque solids; second, because of its high sensitivity, it can be used to measure the absorption of radiation by highly transparent media; and third, since only the radiation that is actually absorbed is detectable, interferences from scattered light are minimal.

One of the most significant areas of application of PAS is in biological and biochemical systems, which are often subject to excessive scattering by particulate matter. Figure 7-5 shows the inherent possibilities; a PAS spectrum of whole blood shows the absorption that is responsible for the red color just as clearly as do the spectra of red cells alone after plasma removal, and of extracted hemoglobin itself.[2]

PAS can be adapted to use in monitoring flowing liquid streams, as in a detector for liquid chromatography. Oda and Sawada[12] have devised a cell for this purpose, making use of a PZT protected from the liquid by a thin platinum foil. The volume of such a cell must be as small as possible to prevent mixing of components of the flowing stream; that described was only 0.02 ml. A 500-mW argon–ion laser operating at 488 nm gave excellent resolution between isomers of chloro-4-(dimethylamino)azobenzene, at concentrations of 3×10^{-7} M each, far below the limits for a conventional spectrophotometer.

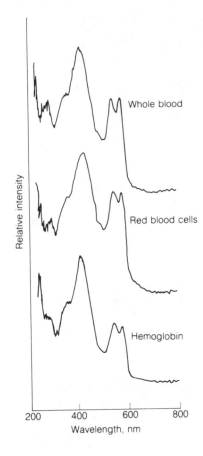

Figure 7-5 PAS spectra of (top) whole blood, (middle) purified red cells, and (bottom) hemoglobin extracted from red blood cells. (*Analytical Chemistry.*[2])

PROBLEM

7-1 Locate a description of the Golay IR detector (see, for example. Refs. 3, 7, and 14 of Chap. 4). Compare this with the photoacoustic detectors described in this chapter. Comment on their relative advantages and disadvantages.

REFERENCES

1. G. H. Brilmyer, A. Fujishima, K. S. V. Santhanum, and A. J. Bard. *Anal. Chem.*, **1977**, *49*, 2057.
2. A. Rosencwaig, *Anal. Chem.*, **1975**, *47*, 592A.
3. R. B. Somoano, *Angew. Chem.*, *Int. Ed.* (English), **1978**, *17*, 238.
4. M. M. Farrow, R. K. Burnham, M. Auzanneau, S. L. Olsen, N. Purdie, and E. M. Eyring, *Appl. Optics*, **1978**, *17*, 1093.
5. W. H. Fuchsman and A. J. Silversmith, *Anal. Chem.*, **1979**, *51*, 589.
6. L. B. Lloyd, S. M. Riseman, R. K. Burnham, E. M. Eyring, and M. M. Farrow, *Rev. Sci. Instrum.*, **1980**, *51*, 1488.

7. L. B. Lloyd, R. K. Burnham, W. L. Chandler, E. M. Eyring, and M. M. Farrow, *Anal. Chem.*, **1980**, *52*, 1595.
8. S. M. Riseman, S. I. Yaniger, E. M. Eyring, D. Macinnes, A. G. Macdiarmid, and A. J. Heeger, *Appl. Spectrosc.*, **1981**, *35*, 557.
9. M. G. Rockley and J. P. Devlin, *Appl. Spectrosc.*, **1980**, *34*, 407.
10. P. C. Claspy, in *Optoacoustic Spectroscopy and Detection*, Y.-H. Pao (ed.), Academic Press, New York, **1977**, chap. 6.
11. D. S. McClure, *J. Chem. Phys.*, **1963**, *38*, 2289.
12. S. Oda and T. Sawada, *Anal. Chem.*, **1981**, *53*, 471.

General references

13. A. Rosencwaig, *Photoacoustics and Photoacoustic Spectroscopy*, Wiley-Interscience, New York, **1980**.
14. J. F. McClelland, *Anal. Chem.*, **1983**, *55*, 89A.

EIGHT

THE SCATTERING OF RADIATION

The term *scattering* as applied to the interaction of radiant energy with matter, covers a variety of phenomena. The word always implies a more-or-less random change in the direction of propagation. The mechanism involved depends on the wavelength of the radiation, the size and shape of the particles responsible for the scattering, and sometimes on their spatial arrangement.

The detailed electromagnetic theory of scattering has been developed by Mie,[1-4] but is too complex to utilize directly. Simplifications can be achieved in restricted areas of application, so it is convenient to distinguish *Rayleigh scattering* (in which the particles are small compared to the wavelength), and *Tyndall scattering* (for larger particles). Raman spectroscopy is often thought of as a scattering phenomenon in which the wavelength is shifted.

RAYLEIGH SCATTERING

It was shown by Lord Rayleigh in 1871 that radiation falling on a small transparent particle induces in the particle an electric dipole oscillating at the frequency of the radiation. The oscillating dipole then acts as a source, radiating energy in all directions at the same frequency (but not with uniform power in all directions).

The Rayleigh-Mies theory predicts that scattering from small particles will be proportional to the inverse fourth power of the wavelength; this neatly accounts for the blue of the sky and the redness of the setting sun, where scattering is predominantly due to particles of molecular dimensions. In chemical systems the

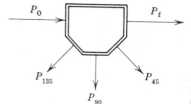

Figure 8-1 Power relations in light scattering. P_0 is the power of the incident beam, and P_t that of the transmitted beam; P_{45}, P_{90}, P_{135} are the powers scattered at the corresponding angles.

exponent of the wavelengths may vary from -4 to -2, principally because of larger particles. This variation indicates a gradual transition from Rayleigh to Tyndall scattering.

Measurements are nearly always carried out with radiation in the visible region. The sample is illuminated by an intense beam of power P_0 (Fig. 8-1). The transmitted power P_t can then be measured just as in absorption spectroscopy, or the power scattered at a specific angle (such as P_{90} at 90°) may be determined. The ratio P_t/P_0 decreases with increasing number of particles in suspension, while ratios such as P_{90}/P_0 will increase, at least up to moderate concentrations. For very dilute suspensions, measurement at an angle is much more sensitive than in-line measurements, as it permits observation of the faint scattered light against a dark background.

In-line measurement is called *turbidimetry*, whereas measurement at an angle of 90° (or other) is called *nephelometry*.

The rigorous mathematical treatment of these techniques is not a simple matter, but fortunately is not necessary for the usual analytical applications. For in-line measurements, a quantity called *turbidance*, corresponding to absorbance, can be defined that follows a relation analogous to Beer's law

$$S = \log \frac{P_0}{P} = kbN \tag{8-1}$$

where S represents turbidance, k is a proportionality factor called the *turbidity coefficient*, b is the path length, and N is the number of scattering particles per milliliter. (The turbidity function τ, sometimes reported, is equal to 2.303 k.) The theoretical treatment shows that

$$k = 0.4343 \left[\frac{2}{3} \pi^5 d^6 \lambda^{-4} \left(\frac{m^2 - 1}{m^2 + 2} \right)^2 \right] \tag{8-2}$$

where d is the particle diameter, λ is the wavelength, and m is the ratio of the refractive index of the particles to that of the solvent. This relation holds for dilute suspensions in which the particle size is uniform and small compared to the wavelength.

Any filter photometer or spectrophotometer can be utilized for turbidimetric measurements. If the solvent and dispersed particles are both colorless, then a wavelength in the blue or near-UV should be selected for maximum sensitivity. If colored, the optimum wavelength had best be determined by trial.

A theoretical equation has yet to be derived for use in nephelometry, relating the radiation scattered at a specific angle of observation to the concentration and other variables. The best we can do is to write, as a working relation,

$$P = K_\alpha c P_0 \qquad (8\text{-}3)$$

where K is an empirical constant for the system, the subscript α defines the angle of measurement, and c is the concentration.

The 90° angle of observation is not necessarily the optimum. In some instances a large increase in sensitivity has been found at angles as small as physically possible, just a few degrees from "straight through." However, there are instrumental problems involved that make precision measurements difficult to achieve. If a cylindrical cuvet is employed, the curved surfaces will act like a lens to decollimate the primary beam and to gather into the photocell rays originating from a considerable region in the cuvet, so that the angle of scattering is uncertain, and dependent on the refractive indices of both solvent and dispersed particles. On the other hand, prismatic cuvets, either square or multifaceted (like that in Fig. 8-1), permit only specified angles to be observed.

Instruments

A turbidimeter with unusual properties is the DuPont Model 430 (Fig. 8-2). This is a double-beam instrument that depends for its operation on the relative degree of polarization of the transmitted and scattered radiation. If a suspension is illuminated with plane-polarized radiation, the transmitted beam will be found to be depolarized in proportion to the concentration of particles in suspension. In the DuPont instrument, the beam first passes through a polarizer and then the sample. The transmitted radiation is split into two beams by a half-silvered mirror. One of these beams passes through another polarizer with its axis parallel to that of the primary polarizer, and the other through a similar polarizer that has its axis crossed with the primary. The response of photocell no. 1 is *decreased* by the scattering, while that of no. 2 is *increased*. The electronics automatically determines the ratio between the two signals, and this is directly proportional to the concentration of suspended matter. The instrument is insensitive to the color of solvent or particles or to lamp fluctuations, but cannot be used with solutions that contain optically active constituents.

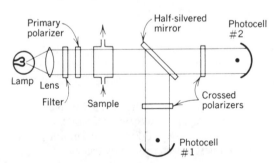

Figure 8-2 Schematic diagram of the DuPont Model 430 Turbidimeter. (*E. I. Du Pont de Nemours & Co.*)

Kaye[5] has described a low-angle light-scattering photometer using a helium–neon laser as a light source. The laser radiation forms a narrow beam with very little divergence, and the detector can measure scattering as close as 2° to the primary beam. Another advantage of the laser technique is a great reduction in required sample size; 2×10^{-5} ml is enough, compared with approximately 0.5 ml as the smallest amount that can be handled in a conventional instrument.

The geometry of an instrument for nephelometry is identical with that for fluorimetry, and so any fluorimeter can be used as a nephelometer. As there is no change in wavelength, there is no reason to have a secondary monochromator or filter, but if these are present they should be set at the primary wavelength. Many manufacturers of fluorimeters specify appropriate adjustments for use in nephelometry.

ANALYTICAL APPLICATIONS

Light scattering is so highly dependent on the size of the particles that conditions must be rigidly standardized to permit valid comparisons between standards and unknowns. If such precautions are taken, a considerable variety of analytical procedures of great sensitivity and adequate precision become available. Phosphate, for example, can be detected at a concentration of 1 part in more than 300 million parts of water as a precipitate with a strychnine–molybdenum reagent. One part of ammonia in 160 million parts of water can be detected by a mercuric chloride complex (Nessler's reagent). Sulfur can be determined by conversion to sulfate and precipitation as the barium salt under conditions that lead to a stable colloidal suspension; the method is valid to a few parts per million.

Molecular Weights and Particle Sizes

Debye has shown that scattering can be used to advantage in the determination of the weight-average molecular weight of a polymer in solution. The Debye equation calls for knowledge of the turbidity, concentration, refractive index, wavelength, the derivative of the index with respect to concentration, and the second virial coefficient, which is a measure of the nonideality of the solution. It is subject to the restriction that the molecules must be small compared to the wavelength; the details are beyond our present scope.[6]

Several companies manufacture light-scattering photometers for work with high molecular weight polymers. These provide a high degree of versatility, with a wide choice of cuvets, several angles of observation, and polarization-measuring devices that give information about the shape of the particles.

Scattering in Gases

Smoke and fog are visible largely because of light-scattering, so it is not surprising that instruments for measuring these effects are useful tools in monitoring atmospheric pollution. The diminution in the power of a laser beam over a long path, as from one building to another, correlates with the amount of particulate matter present. A sensitive smoke detector can be assembled from a small laser and photocell combination, that will easily detect a few micrograms of particles 0.1 to 1 μm in diameter, per cubic meter.

TURBIDIMETRIC AND NEPHELOMETRIC TITRATIONS[7]

Ever since the work of Gay-Lussac on silver chloride precipitation (1832), titration to a turbidimetric end point has been extensively employed. Such titrations can be carried out visually or in an absorption photometer.

Titrations of the form $A + B \rightarrow C$, where C is insoluble, might be expected to give a curve of either turbidance or scattered intensity consisting of two intersecting straight lines (curve 1 of Fig. 8-3), as the amount of precipitate must increase to a maximum and then stay constant. Meehan and Chiu,[8] however, have pointed out that this can be true only if the *number* of particles increases linearly to the equivalence point, while all remain the same size. This is not likely to be the case; more probably, added reagent will simultaneously form some new particles and increase the size of those nuclei previously formed. In this situation, titration curves cannot be predicted in detail. If the particles become too large, a poorly defined end point or none at all (curves 2 and 3 of Fig. 8-3) will result. A complicating factor is that, unless the suspension is very dilute, the particles will continue to grow between added increments of titrant, so that excessively long times (several minutes) must be allowed between additions.

Meehan and Yamaguchi[9] have shown that addition of uniformly dispersed seed crystals prior to the start of a titration increases markedly the precision of nephelometric titrations of dilute solutions. In one series of experiments they titrated KBr in aqueous isopropyl alcohol with $AgNO_3$, having added as seed a colloidal suspension of AgBr amounting to about 10 percent of the amount expected to be formed during the titration. They obtained easily observed end points for bromide concentrations of the order of 10^{-6} M, with a relative standard deviation of 1.3 percent.

Bobtelsky and his coworkers[10,11] have been successful in carrying out many hundreds of turbidimetric titrations at somewhat higher concentrations, usually

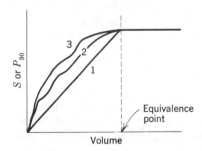

Figure 8-3 Turbidimetric titration curves. Curve 1 is idealized; curves 2 and 3 might result from precipitates with mixed particle sizes, poor stirring, etc.

10^{-3} to 10^{-4} M. They made no attempt to control the particle size, and ran the titrations at normal speed. The curves give reproducible and useful results, but cannot be interpreted in terms of true turbidance, as Eq. (8-1) cannot be expected to hold. In view of this, Bobtelsky is careful not to use the term turbidimetry, but calls his method *heterometry*, and his simplified photometer a *heterometer*.

PROBLEMS

8-1 The sulfur content of organic sulfonates and sulfonamides can be determined turbidimetrically by means of a $BaSO_4$ precipitate following digestion to destroy the organic matter.[12] A 25-mg sample of a particular preparation of p-toluenesulfonic acid monohydrate ($C_7H_7SO_3H \cdot H_2O$; formula weight, 190.2), was subjected to the digestion, and exactly one-tenth of it made up to a volume of 10.00 ml with a conditioning solution. Then 5.00 ml of 1.34 M $BaCl_2$ was added with controlled shaking. After 25 min the turbidity at 355 nm as measured in a Spectronic-20 was found to be 0.295. A standard $(NH_4)_2SO_4$ solution containing 0.200 mg of sulfur, similarly treated, gave a turbidance of 0.322 and showed a linear relation on dilution prior to treatment. Calculate the percent purity of the original preparation.

8-2 As the number of particles in a suspension increases, eventually a point will be reached where the sample has become effectively opaque, and both P_t and P_{90} (Fig. 8-1) become zero. This would imply that S becomes infinite. How would Eq. (8-3) be affected?

8-3 A technique that is sometimes used[13] is to measure the ratio R of scattered to transmitted radiation, that is, $R = P_{90}/P_t$. Derive an expression for R as a function of concentration. Is this valid over the entire concentration range, or just the linear portion? Do you see any advantages to this method? Explain.

8-4 A suspension of AgCl in water consists of uniform particles 0.040 μm in diameter, density 5.56 g/cm^3, and refractive index 2.07. Calculate the percent transmittance in a cell 10 cm in width, when measured at 500 nm.

REFERENCES

1. F. W. Billmeyer, Jr., in *Treatise on Analytical Chemistry*, I. M. Kolthoff and P. J. Elving (eds.), pt. I, vol. 5, chap. 56, Wiley-Interscience, New York, **1964**.
2. G. Mie, *Ann. Physik.*, **1908**, *25*, 377.
3. H. C. Van de Hulst, *Light Scattering by Small Particles*, Wiley, New York, **1957**.
4. C. C. Gravatt, Jr., *Appl. Spectrosc.*, **1971**, *25*, 509.
5. W. Kaye, *Anal. Chem.*, **1973**, *45*, 221A.
6. B. Vollmert, *Polymer Chemistry*, Springer-Verlag, New York, **1973**, pp. 348 ff.
7. A. L. Underwood, in *Advances in Analytical Chemistry and Instrumentation*, Wiley-Interscience, New York, **1964**, vol. 3, p. 31.
8. E. J. Meehan and G. Chiu, *Anal. Chem.*, **1964**, *36*, 536.
9. E. J. Meehan and S. Yamaguchi, *Anal. Chem.*, **1977**, *49*, 2268.
10. M. Bobtelsky, *Anal. Chim. Acta*, **1955**, *13*, 172.
11. M. Bobtelsky, *Heterometry*, American Elsevier, New York, **1960**.
12. G. Zdybek, D. S. McCann, and A. J. Boyle, *Anal. Chem.*, **1960**, *32*, 558.
13. R. D. Vanous, *Am. Lab.*, **1978**, *10(7)*, 67.

NINE

ATOMIC EMISSION SPECTROSCOPY

Ever since the work of Bunsen and Kirchhoff (1860), it has been known that many elements under suitable excitation emit radiations of characteristic wavelengths. This fact is utilized in the familiar qualitative flame tests for the alkali and alkaline earth elements. By employing more powerful electrical excitation in place of the flame, the method can be extended to all metallic and many nonmetallic elements. With some, such as sodium and potassium, the spectra are simple, consisting of only a few wavelengths, while in others, including iron and uranium, thousands of distinct reproducible wavelengths are present.

Quantitative analysis with the spectrograph is based on an empirical relation between the power of the emitted radiation of some particular wavelength and the quantity of the corresponding element in the sample. The radiant power is influenced in a complicated way by many variables, some of which cannot be controlled by the operator. Hence procedures must be rigidly standardized, and the spectra of unknowns must be compared with those of standard samples prepared with the same apparatus under identical conditions.

Emission spectroscopy saw extensive development during the period between the two world wars, with the construction of large spectrographs using photographic detection. Since the introduction of electronics to laboratory instrumentation in the 1950s and 60s, the photographic instruments have diminished in importance, many of their applications having been taken over by similar emission spectrometers using photomultiplier detection and by the newly developed AA spectrophotometers and x-ray fluorescence spectrometers. A significant resurgence in interest in atomic emission methods has occurred starting in the mid-1970s with the invention of reliable plasma sources.

EXCITATION OF SAMPLES

As we have seen in Chap. 2, a free atom can accept energy from an external source to become *excited*, meaning that one of its electrons has been raised to an energy level above the ground state. In falling back to its normal condition the atom can emit a photon of radiation containing energy corresponding to a particular frequency and wavelength.

In practical emission spectroscopy, there are several alternative methods of providing excitation energy, the most important of which include an electric arc or spark, a flame, and an electrically generated plasma in a carrier gas. We will treat each of these, along with descriptions of appropriate instruments.

The Arc Discharge as a Source

In the dc arc, a powerful electric discharge is passed between two portions of the sample or between the sample and a *counter electrode* that is free of the elements being sought. Graphite is particularly advantageous as a counter electrode, in that it is highly refractory (that is, it does not melt or sublime at the temperature of the arc), it is a sufficiently good electrical conductor, and it introduces few spectral lines of its own. A drawback, however, is that the hot carbon reacts slowly with the nitrogen of the air to form cyanogen gas, which becomes excited and gives emission bands of luminosity in the region of 360 to 420 nm that can interfere with the desired observations. This can be avoided if necessary by enclosing the discharge in a mantle containing steam or an inert gas.

The dc arc provides a highly sensitive method of excitation that is particularly useful for the qualitative analysis of metals. A current of 5 to 15 A at 100 to 300 V is caused to flow through the arc in series with a variable resistor, often called a *ballast* (10 to 40 Ω). The chief disadvantage of the dc arc is that it is less reproducible than might be desired. The discharge tends to become localized in "hot spots" on the surface of the electrode, and this results in uneven sampling.

This defect is less noticeable in the *ac arc*, wherein the discharge is interrupted 120 times a second. A source of 2000 to 5000 V at 1 to 5 A is required. The ballast can be either a resistor or a variable inductor in the circuit. The ac arc is especially useful for analyzing the residues from solutions that have been evaporated onto the surface of an electrode.

The Spark Source

A spark differs from an arc in several ways: it uses very high voltage (15 to 40 kV) and it delivers its power in short bursts (milliseconds). The discharge itself acts as a high-frequency generator, and 10 to 20 oscillations at 10^4 to 10^5 Hz occur within each burst. As used in spectroscopy, these bursts are repeated 120 times a second. The high voltage is obtained from a step-up transformer or Tesla coil, with a capacitor connected across its secondary winding. An electronic circuit, including a thyratron, monitors the power line and triggers the spark at the optimum point in the ac cycle, at which time the energy stored in the capacitor is discharged through the spark gap. The spark is better suited than the arc for precise timing of exposures, and in addition it does not destroy the sample, as only minute amounts are vaporized.

Preparation of Electrodes and Samples

Bulk metallic samples, if in a shape that can be handled easily, need no special preparation, but are merely clamped into position before the light-gathering lens of the spectrograph. The counter electrode can be another piece of the same sample; it can be graphite, or it can be made of the major constituent of the sample. For example, in the qualitative analysis of a steel for alloyed elements, the counter electrode could be a simple steel, shown spectrographically to be free of the elements sought.

Samples other than free metals are deposited on a graphite electrode. By one method the sample is brought into solution, with acid or other reagent if necessary, a few drops are placed in a cup drilled in the end of a graphite electrode (Fig. 9-1e), and the solvent evaporated by preheating in a small oven. The electrode is then positioned in the lower electrode holder, with a plain carbon counter electrode (Fig. 9-1c) above it, for arcing. In another procedure, the sample, in powder form, is mixed with pure graphite powder and poured dry into the cup of the electrode. The added graphite, because of its electrical conductivity, tends to stabilize the arc. Many modified procedures have been published that show advantages with particular kinds of samples.

The spectroscopist using the hot arc source must always keep in mind possible differences in the volatility of components of the sample. In some cases, one or

Figure 9-1 Representative types of graphite electrodes. Forms *a* and *c* are counter electrodes. Forms *b*, *d*, and *e* are provided with cups into which the sample is inserted. Types *b* and *d* have a central post to which the arc is struck. The narrow neck is to reduce thermal conductance. (*Ultra Carbon Corporation.*)

more components may volatilize rapidly and be completely burned within half a minute or so after the arc is started, before other substances present have been heated sufficiently to appear in the arc. It is sometimes possible to take advantage of differences in volatility, so that the spectra of volatile constituents can be recorded without interference from the less volatile. An example is the determination of lithium, aluminum, and other oxides as impurities in uranium oxide[1]; uranium is especially rich in spectral lines, and hence determination of trace impurities is difficult. In this method, the uranium is first converted to the nonvolatile U_3O_8, and 2 percent of its weight of Ga_2O_3, a comparatively volatile oxide, is added. The Ga_2O_3 acts as a carrier to sweep out even minute quantities of the impurities into the arc. This results in high sensitivity and accuracy, even for impurities present only to the extent of a few parts per million.

INSTRUMENTATION

At this point we will describe some of the basic spectroscopic instruments, then return to a discussion of other forms of excitation. Instruments for observing and measuring emission spectra range from hand-held direct-vision spectroscopes to giant photographic or photoelectric spectrographs of high resolution and great sensitivity.

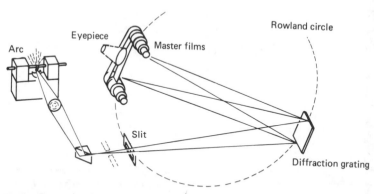

Figure 9-2 Optical diagram of the Vreeland spectroscope. The sample is held on a small hearth beneath the horizontal electrodes. The grating and slit are mounted on a Rowland circle in a vertical plane. (*Spectrex Company.*)

Representative of the smaller spectrometers for qualitative and semiquantitative analysis of solid samples in the visible region is the Vreeland Spectroscope.† This is a bench-top instrument provided with ac arc excitation and a concave grating of 42.5 cm focal length, 600 lines per mm. The spectrum is focused on a translucent plastic screen fitted to the Rowland circle (Fig. 9-2). Reference spectra

† Spectrex Company, Palo Alto, California.

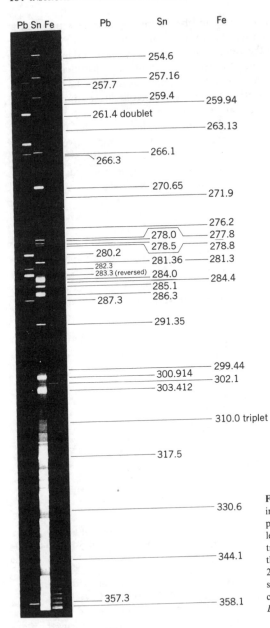

Figure 9-3 Spectra of lead, tin, and iron, photographed on a large Littrow prism spectrograph. Some of the brighter lead lines are just visible in the tin spectrum on the original plate, showing that the sample contained a trace of lead. The 283.3-nm line of lead is so intense that it shows photographic reversal (dark center) on the original plate. (*Bausch & Lomb, Inc.*)

are supplied as positive films that can be placed adjacent to the spectrum on each side for direct line-by-line comparison.

Much of the classical work in emission spectrography has been accomplished with large spectrographs using either quartz prisms or concave reflection gratings, and photographic detection. Many of these instruments are still in constant use, though few are currently manufactured. Figure 9-3 shows typical spectra taken on a Littrow prism spectrograph.

The iron spectrum is routinely used as a wavelength calibration standard, chosen because it contains thousands of lines fairly evenly spaced throughout the UV and visible regions. All of these iron lines have been measured repeatedly with great care, on both prism and grating spectrographs of high dispersion, and the resulting data can serve as a precise measuring scale for other spectra. Elements are identified on the photoplate either by direct comparison with spectra of authentic samples, or by determining the wavelengths of several lines by reference to the iron spectra and consultation of published wavelength tables.

QUANTITATIVE ANALYSIS

In the absence of a complete mathematical theory giving a relation between the amount or concentration of a constituent of the sample and the optical density† of a silver deposit on a photoplate, calibration must be on an empirical basis. The comparison of standards and unknowns can best be carried out by the method of *internal standards*. This depends on measuring the ratio of the radiant power of a given line of the unknown to that of a selected line of another constituent of the sample that is present in known (or at least constant) amount. This standard may be an element already present in the specimen, such as the iron in a steel sample, or it may be an extraneous element added in known quantity to all samples, This procedure goes far toward eliminating errors due to inequalities of plate characteristics and photographic development. The line to be used as a standard should be as close as possible to the unknown both in wavelength and in power, so that any nonlinearity of the photographic emulsion with respect to these factors will not be a serious source of error. Two lines selected as appropriate for this purpose are known as a *homologous pair*.

Measurement of the optical density of a line on the photographic plate requires the use of a *densitometer*, a special-purpose photometer for measuring transmittance. It consists of a light source with lenses to focus a beam of light onto a very small area of the plate, and a photomultiplier or equivalent beneath the

---

† *Optical density* is the equivalent of absorbance as defined in Beer's law. Although this term is obsolete in connection with absorption spectroscopy, it continues to be used to evaluate the amount of silver on a photographic film or plate.

plate. A motor drive is provided to move the photoplate slowly across the light spot. A strip-chart recorder then provides a trace of optical density against position on the plate. The height of a peak above the base line is a nearly linear measure of the energy incident on the plate at that particular wavelength.

A typical analytical procedure will be presented in some detail as an illustration of the internal standard technique. The example selected is the determination of traces of magnesium in solution, with molybdenum as internal standard. The reader is referred to Nachtrieb[2] for further details and many other similar procedures.

A spark discharge between copper electrodes has been found convenient for analyses of this type where copper is not itself to be determined. The electrodes are rods about 5 mm in diameter. The tips must be machined smooth in a lathe to ensure uniformity and to remove surface contamination. After machining they must be protected from dust and not handled with the fingers. A series of standard solutions are prepared from pure $MgCl_2$ at concentrations from 0.1 ng to 10 μg of Mg per ml. Ammonium molybdate is added to each solution to the extent of 20 μg of Mo per ml. (The distilled water must be shown spectroscopically to be free of Mg.) For each solution, two electrodes are placed upright in a small heating coil, and a 50-μl portion pipetted on to the tip of each. The solution is then carefully evaporated to dryness, the electrodes are clamped in position with an accurately measured spacing of 2.0 mm, and a 25-kV spark is struck across them. The spectra of all the standards can usually be recorded on a single photoplate.

The spectrum contains lines from both Mg and Mo, as well as Cu and any other metals that may be present. Several homologous pairs are available and are about equally well suited to the analysis. The lines at 279.81 nm (Mg) and 281.62 nm

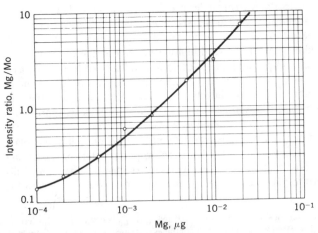

Figure 9-4 Working curve for the determination of magnesium by the copper spark method, with molybdenum as internal standard. (*McGraw-Hill*.[3])

(Mo) are one such pair. The difference between the optical densities produced by these two lines (i.e., the ratio of the powers of the emissions at these two wavelengths) is plotted on log-log paper against the amount of Mg in the sample (Fig. 9-4). To analyze an unknown, a sample is treated according to the same procedure, including the addition of ammonium molybdate. The optical densities of the two lines on the photoplate are measured and ratioed, permitting the quantity of Mg in the 50-μl aliquot to be read from the graph. This method is relatively fast and convenient, and at the same time highly sensitive. It is possible to identify 1 ng of Mg in a volume of 1 ml, with a precision of about 5 to 10 percent; quite satisfactory, in view of the small quantities involved.

The photographic plate is inherently an integrating detector, as the amount of silver deposit relates to the product of radiant power P and exposure time Δt

$$\text{Optical density} = kP \, \Delta t \qquad (9\text{-}1)$$

Ideally the proportionality factor k should be constant, but actually this is only true over a limited range. This is the reason why the two lines of the homologous pair should be selected to have similar densities.

DIRECT READING SPECTROMETERS

The inconvenience of photographic processing can be avoided by substituting a series of photomultiplier tubes for the photoplate. Wavelength scanning, as practiced in solution spectrophotometry, is not readily applicable with arc or spark excitation, because the source is not sufficiently stable over the time required for a scan, particularly in view of the variation in volatility previously mentioned. This difficulty can be solved by placing a number of exit slits along the focal curve, each positioned to receive a suitable line emitted by a particular element. Thus 12 slits with 12 photomultipliers can measure simultaneously the emissions from 12 elements in the same sample. The corresponding amplifiers can be provided with integrators so that the power at each wavelength can be integrated over a selected time interval, to give the corresponding energy. One channel is reserved for the internal standard, and the controlling computer can provide the data-processing steps needed to reference each analytical signal to it. The resulting information can be made available as a computer printout. Figure 9-5 shows the construction of such a multiple-slit spectrometer.

It must be emphasized that the data produced by a large and complex instrument like this, though it may have high precision (reproducibility), cannot be assumed to be accurate. Accuracy is often affected by the matrix in which the analyte is present, and by sample-handling techniques, as well as by the accuracy with which the standards have been prepared. Any quantitative analytical procedure, whether spectroscopic or other, must be proved to be valid, generally by analyzing known samples, such as those obtainable in the United States from the National Bureau of Standards.

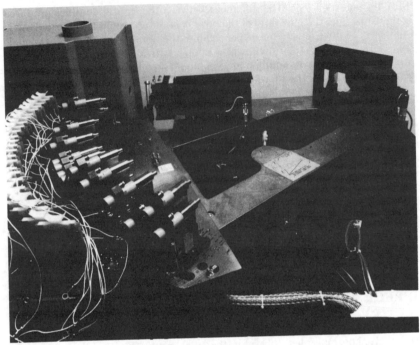

Figure 9-5 Internal layout of the Jarrell–Ash Plasma AtomComp spectrometer. The ICP torch is enclosed in the housing at left rear. The metal box at the far right holds the concave grating. In the left foreground can be seen about 15 photomultiplier tubes, each with its own exit slit, located along the focal curve. (*Jarrell–Ash Division of Fisher Scientific Company.*)

PLASMA EXCITATION

The second major excitation mechanism operates through a plasma produced electrically in a carrier gas such as nitrogen or argon. A *plasma* can be defined as a neutral gas containing significant numbers of both positive and negative ions or free electrons. A plasma can only be created and maintained by the continued injection of enough energy to ensure that new ions are created fast enough to compensate for those that are continually recombining to form neutral atoms. (A combustion flame is one example of a plasma, wherein energy is obtained from the chemical reaction.) The energy levels of argon make this element especially well suited for plasma production, and argon has the added advantage of chemical inertness.

Two types of argon plasma sources are in use. One is energized by radio-frequency ac coupled to the gas through electromagnetic induction (called ICP, for *inductively coupled plasma*), whereas the other uses dc excitation (DCP). ICP

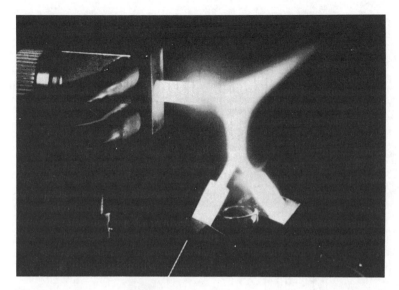

Figure 9-6 A dc plasma arc. The cathode is at the upper left, the two anodes at the lower right, with the sample jet between them. (*Spectra Metrics, Inc.*)

is the more sensitive of the two types, but dc plasma sources are considerably less expensive.

Figure 9-6 is a photograph of a dc plasma source, a model that uses three electrodes. The two lower are both anodes, connected in parallel, and the upper is the cathode. Argon is supplied through channels drilled axially through the electrodes. The temperature at the junction of the three plasma plumes may reach as high as 5000 K. The sample is aspirated with additional argon through a jet pointing upward just beneath this hot spot. Radiation is emitted from the central part of the plasma column and is focused onto the slit of a spectrograph for observation.

A typical ICP source is diagrammed in Fig. 9-7. It consists of three concentric silica tubes through which argon flows, and a two- or three-turn copper coil surrounding the tubes near the upper end. Alternating current at a frequency of 27.14 MHz† and power levels up to several kilowatts is passed through the copper coil. Once some ions have been produced by means of an auxiliary spark circuit, a heavy current is caused to flow in a circular path in the ionized gas, powered by magnetic induction. This raises the temperature of the resulting plasma to some 10,000 K. This is far above the softening point of vitreous silica, so clearly some way must be found to protect the torch from destroying itself. This is done by using the flow of argon itself as coolant. The bulk of the argon enters the outer tube (Fig. 9-7) at a tangential angle, so that it swirls through the annular space, as shown,

_____
† This frequency is set aside by federal regulations in the United States for industrial use.

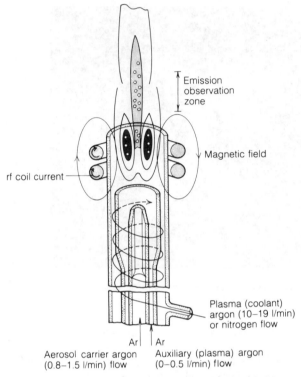

Figure 9-7 Schematic diagram of an ICP torch. (*McGraw-Hill.*[5])

at high speed, thus moderating the temperature. The hot plasma tends to stabilize in the form of a toroid at some little distance from the walls, and this also serves to prevent overheating. The sample is aspirated in a nebulizer (not shown) and is carried by a slower stream of argon directed centrally toward the "hole in the doughnut." Here the sample is heated by conduction and radiation, and may reach 7000 K, where it is completely atomized and excited. Loss of analyte atoms by ionization, a source of difficulty in flame AA, does not occur significantly in ICP spectroscopy, presumably because of the presence of the more easily ionized argon atoms.

Spectrometers for use with plasma sources are not inherently different from those described earlier. Some models operate in a sequential mode, wherein the wavelengths for all desired elements are scanned in order, others act in a simultaneous mode, in which many elements are detected at the same time, either photographically or with multiple phototubes.

Plasma emission spectroscopy, though a newcomer to the market, is rapidly becoming one of the most popular techniques for the quantitative determination of metals, replacing atomic absorption in many applications.

FLAME EXCITATION

The use of a gas flame as a source of excitation for atomic emission has been exploited extensively in the past, under the designation *flame photometry*. It is now used principally for the determination of alkali and alkaline earth metals. Many atomic absorption spectrophotometers can be operated in the emission mode, making use of the same flame and nebulizer system. The flame must usually be hotter than required for AA, since in AA the atoms must be in their ground states for resonance absorption to occur, whereas in emission, they must also be raised to an excited state.

The power of the radiation from the flame at a wavelength characteristic of a particular element is closely proportional to the concentration of the metal, provided suitable background correction is made. Interferences due to the presence of other metals (the matrix effect) is sometimes observed, either enhancing or repressing the normal luminescence. This difficulty can be overcome, though possibly with some loss of sensitivity, by intentionally adding a large excess of any likely contaminating elements. In the analysis of natural waters, for example,[3] where the determination of Na, K, Ca, and Mg is required, interference in the determination of each element by the other three can be avoided by the use of *radiation buffers*. For instance, in the determination of Na, to a 25-ml sample is added 1 ml of a solution that is saturated with respect to the chlorides of K, Ca, and Mg. Any slight variation in the amounts of these elements in the sample is negligible compared to the amount added. The response of the photometer to the mixed solution at the sodium wavelength must be compared to a calibration curve prepared from standards. Concentration differences of 1 or 2 ppm can easily be detected for Na or K, and 3 or 4 ppm for Ca; the method is less sensitive for Mg.

Another procedure for the elimination of interferences is the method of standard additions, discussed in the general case in Chap. 26. After measurement of the emission from the sample, a known amount of the desired element is added to a second aliquot of the unknown and the measurement repeated. The added standard will be subject to the same interferences as the constituent of the sample, and analysis by direct comparison is possible.

Simplified flame emission photometers using interference filters to isolate lines from desired elements are useful in clinical laboratories for determining Na, K, and Ca in blood. Lithium is often added as an internal standard. Such an instrument is convenient to use and is highly sensitive.

ATOMIC FLUORESCENCE (AF)[5]

Yet another mode of atomic excitation depends upon irradiation with UV at the same resonant frequency employed in atomic absorption, causing the emission of radiation at this or a lower frequency. The emitted radiation is also at this frequency. This method is generally known as *atomic fluorescence*. The power in the radiation depends on the number of fluorescing atoms, hence on the concentration.

The atomized sample must be held in a plasma, which can be a flame or an ICP. The fluorescence emission is observed at an angle (usually 45 or 90°) from the exciting radiation. Just as in molecular fluorescence, this faint radiation is observed against a dark background. The source of the exciting radiation is usually a hollow-cathode lamp, specially designed to give a more powerful output than the lamps used for AA. Xenon arc lamps, giving a continuous spectrum in the UV, can also be used successfully.

With a hollow-cathode lamp as the source, no monochromator is required, and the optical design of the instrument can be quite simple. Figure 9-8 shows a combination of hollow-cathode lamp and photomultiplier that will detect one species in an ICP plasma. An interference filter is mounted in front of the photomultiplier to improve the signal-to-noise ratio by excluding wavelengths remote from that desired. An instrument incorporating this arrangement is manufactured by the Baird Corporation; as many as 10 such assemblies can be operated simultaneously, all looking at the same ICP. The handling of samples and operation of the ICP are essentially the same described earlier.

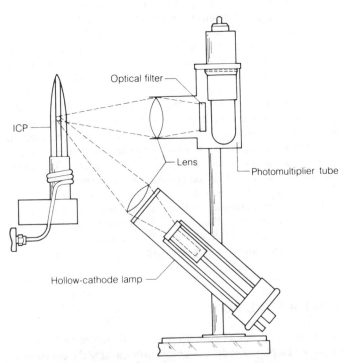

Figure 9-8 Schematic diagram of an ICP and associated photomultiplier, monitoring an ICP. (*Baird Corporation.*)

Atomic fluorescence has been little used in practical analytical work in the past, due to lack of a commercial instrument, but its inherent simplicity and sensitivity predict considerable expansion in the future.

Laser Excitation

A powerful laser beam, focused on a small spot, can provide enough local heating to vaporize a significant amount of material, even refractory compounds.[6] The vapor may have received enough excitation thermally to produce radiant emission, or an electric discharge may be superimposed. The localization of the effect can be an advantage, permitting examination of areas as small as 50 μm in diameter, or it can be a disadvantage, rendering more difficult the representative analysis of a larger sample. An advantage of laser excitation is that the sample need not be electrically conducting.

COMPARISON OF PLASMA AND RELATED METHODS

It is instructive to summarize the properties of those spectroscopic methods that depend on hot gases or plasmas for excitation. We can include here ICP and DCP emission, flame emission and absorption, graphite furnace absorption, atomic fluorescence, and arc and spark methods.

Sensitivity

Figure 9-9 shows in chart form the detection limits for many elements for flame and furnace AA, flame fluorescence, flame and ICP emission, as extracted from the literature by Winefordner et al.[7] The reference should be consulted for actual numerical values for these and other elements and for the original references. Such comparisons can only be taken as general guides, since exact values depend on the conditions of analysis and on the working definition of "detection limits," which often varies from one literature report to another. It can readily be seen from this chart that ICP emission is generally a more sensitive method than flame AA or flame emission, but less sensitive than furnace AA. ICP fluorescence is stated[8] to have about the same detection limits as flame fluorescence.

Data for arc and spark methods are not included in Fig. 9-9, because sensitivities for components of solid samples cannot readily be converted to concentration units. Tables of relative sensitivities can be found in specialized texts, such as that of Nachtrieb.[2]

Chemical Interferences

Generally ICP is much less prone to interferences that are chemical in origin than are flame and furnace methods. This is partly because of freedom from oxygen, but primarily because of the much higher temperature and the longer time of

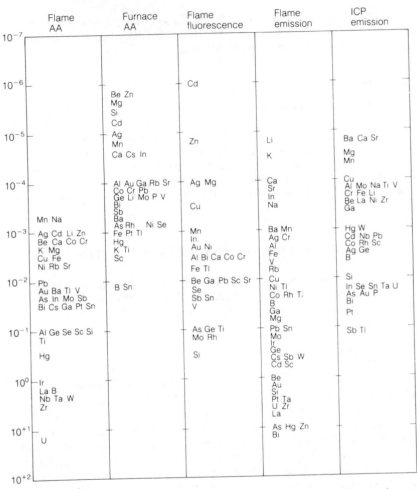

Figure 9-9 Detection limits for selected elements in aqueous solution, as determined by several spectroscopic techniques, expressed in μg/ml. (*Applied Spectroscopy*.[7])

contact with the heated region where dissociation takes place. Note in Fig. 9-9 the greatly increased sensitivity of ICP to W, Zr, and U, elements that form refractory oxides in a flame.

Spectral Interferences

ICP emission is more likely to show interferences from overlapping spectral lines than is AA. This is because emission spectra are very rich in lines. McLaren et al.[10] have given this matter rather detailed attention; they analyzed marine sediments for trace elements, and since such samples invariably contain much iron and aluminum, interference from these elements was severe. They developed a computer-controlled procedure whereby readings are taken at slightly longer and slightly shorter wavelengths than the desired peak, to provide background correction. For example, in the determination of copper, the line at 324.754 nm was selected; they took readings at 324.719, 324.754, and 324.789 nm, and used the first and third to calculate a correction to apply to the reading taken at the copper line itself. The copper line suffers from interference from the iron line at 324.739 nm; if this were severe enough, a correction factor could be calculated following the determination of iron at another wavelength (such as 259.940 nm).

AA and AF are seldom troubled by spectral overlap problems, since the absorption spectrum shows so few lines that resonate with the emission from the hollow-cathode lamp.

Concentration Range

The physical characteristics of the plasma plume in ICP lead to minimal self-absorption, one of the causes of nonlinearity in flame emission and dc-arc spectrography, as also in DCP. Hence the range of concentrations observable in ICP emission is unusually large, from 10 ng to 1 mg per ml for iron. This makes it possible, in a multielement spectrometer, to determine major, minor, and trace constituents of a sample at the same time.

Convenience

ICP has the major advantage as compared to conventional AA of being able to determine many elements without changing any parameters other than wavelength and perhaps a slight adjustment of the height of the observation port above the ICP torch. In AA, of course, the hollow-cathode lamp must be changed when proceeding from one element to another.

A convenient feature in both ICP and furnace AA is the need for only one gas (argon), rather than two or more as in flame AA or flame emission. The present (1984) cost of ICP spectrometers is considerably greater than their AA counterparts.

PROBLEMS

9-1 A shipment of "chemically pure" aluminum metal is to be analyzed for its magnesium content. A 1.000-g sample is dissolved in acid and enough ammonium molybdate added to contain 2.000 mg of Mo. The solution is diluted to 100.0 ml, and 50 μl is evaporated onto the tips of two copper electrodes and sparked before the spectrograph slit. The resulting plate, examined with a densitometer, shows an optical density of 1.83 for the 279.81-nm line and 0.732 for the 281.62-nm line. With the aid of Fig. 9-4, compute the percent Mg in the sample.

9-2 The sketch in Fig. 9-10 shows a portion of a spectrograph plate as seen through a magnifier with a built-in scale of millimeters. The field of view includes portions of the spectra produced by arcing first

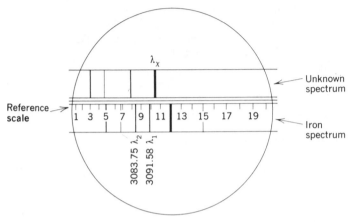

Figure 9-10 Magnified region of a spectrum plate, with scale for interpolation. Wavelengths are in angstroms.

iron electrodes, then electrodes fashioned from an unknown thought to be an aluminum alloy. The iron lines marked λ_1 and λ_2, have been identified by comparison with a standard iron spectrum. Line x of the unknown is to be identified. The scale readings are as follows: $\lambda_1 = 9.990$ mm, $\lambda_2 = 8.37$ mm, and $\lambda_x = 10.25$ mm. (*a*) Calculate the dispersion of the spectrograph in this region in terms of nanometers per millimeter. (*b*) Determine the wavelength of the unknown line. (*c*) Refer to a table of wavelengths and make a tentative identification of this line, with due regard for the elements likely to be found in this type of alloy. In what region of the spectrum would you search for strong lines to confirm your identification?

9-3 Plot the dispersion curve for the spectrograph on which the spectra of Fig. 9-3 were taken.

9-4 The indirect determination of micromolar quantities of primary amides by atomic emission has been reported.[11] The weighed sample is treated with barium hypobromite, $Ba(OBr)_2$, prepared from $Ba(OH)_2$ and Br_2. The overall reaction is

$$RCONH_2 + 2\,Ba(OH)_2 + Br_2 \longrightarrow RNH_2 + BaCO_3 + BaBr_2 + H_2O$$

The insoluble $BaCO_3$ is filtered off, redissolved in HNO_3, and the resulting solution analyzed for its barium content with an atomic emission spectrometer, either flame or ICP. In a particular experiment the following data were obtained. Calculate the amount of amide in the unknown, in micromoles per milliliter.

Sample: 2.00 ml of solution
Volume after reaction: 100 ml

Sample	Instrument reading
0 (blank)	0.002
5 μmol Ba/ml	0.117
10	0.229
15	0.342
Unknown	0.157

9-5 In the determination of traces of copper in marine sediments by the method of McLaren,[10] measurements are taken on the ICP emission at the copper wavelength, 324.754 nm, and also at 324.719 and 324.789 nm, where no emission is seen, to provide data for background correction. In addition, if iron is present, a measurement must be taken at the Fe emission wavelength, 324.739 nm.

In a particular experiment, three spectra are recorded, with the following results (the numbers are μA photomultiplier current):

	Wavelengths (nm)			
	324.719	324.739	324.754	324.789
Cu calibration	23.1	$\cdots$	63.71	8.1
Fe calibration	$\cdots$	8.75×10^5	10.5	
Cu analysis	27.5	2.94×10^4	27.49	9.2

The Cu standard for the first spectrum contained 50.0 $\mu g/g$ Cu, no Fe. Calculate (a) the background correction, (b) the correction factor to eliminate the effect of spectral overlap between Fe and Cu, and (c) the amount of Cu in the sample. All data should be expressed in terms of $\mu g/g$.

REFERENCES

1. B. F. Scribner and H. R. Mullin, *J. Res. Nat. Bur. Standards*, **1946**, *37*, 379.
2. N. H. Nachtrieb, *Principles and Practice of Spectrochemical Analysis*, McGraw-Hill, New York, **1950**.
3. P. W. West, P. Folse, and D. Montgomery, *Anal. Chem.*, **1950**, *22*, 667.
4. R. M. Barnes, in *McGraw-Hill Yearbook of Science and Technology*, McGraw-Hill, New York, **1978**, p. 342.
5. J. D. Winefordner, *J. Chem. Educ.*, **1978**, *55*, 72.
6. T. Ishizuka, *Anal. Chem.*, **1973**, *45*, 538.
7. J. D. Winefordner, J. J. Fitzgerald, and N. Omenetto, *Appl. Spectrosc.*, **1975**, *29*, 369.
8. D. R. Demers, D. A. Busch, and C. D. Allemand, *Am. Lab.*, **1982**, *14(3)*, 167.
9. D. R. Demers and C. D. Allemand, *Anal. Chem.*, **1981**, *53*, 1915.
10. J. W. McLaren, S. S. Berman, V. J. Boyko, and D. S. Russell, *Anal. Chem.*, **1981**, *53*, 1802.
11. R. P. D'Alonzo and S. Siggia, *Anal. Chem.*, **1977**, *49*, 262.
12. J. C. Van Loon, *Anal. Chem.*, **1981**, *53*, 332A.

TEN

POLARIMETRY, OPTICAL ROTATORY DISPERSION, AND CIRCULAR DICHROISM

In preceding chapters we have been concerned with radiant energy principally from the standpoint of its absorption, its emission, and its spectral distribution. Its wave nature has only interested us in connection with diffraction effects. We will now discuss phenomena concerned with polarized radiation.

Many transparent substances that are characterized by a lack of symmetry in their molecular or crystalline structure have the ability to rotate the plane of polarized radiation. (Refer to Chap. 2 for a brief introduction to the nature of plane-polarized radiation.) Materials possessing this property are said to be *optically active*. Probably the most familiar examples are crystalline quartz and the sugars, but many other organic and inorganic compounds act similarly.† The angle through which the plane is rotated varies widely from one active compound to another. The rotation is said to be *dextro* (+) if it is clockwise to an observer looking toward the light source, and *levo* (−) if counterclockwise. For any given compound, the extent of rotation depends on the number of molecules in the path of the radiation, or in the case of solutions, on the concentration and the length of the containing vessel. It is also dependent on the wavelength of the radiation and on the temperature. The *specific rotation*, represented by the symbol $[\alpha]^t$, is defined by the formula

$$[\alpha]^t_\lambda = \frac{\alpha}{dc} \tag{10-1}$$

† The interpretation of optical activity and stereoisomerism is well covered in textbooks on organic chemistry, and will not be treated here.

Table 10-1 Specific rotations of solutions (at 20°C)

Active substance	Solvent	$[\alpha]_D^{20}$
Camphor	Alcohol	+ 43.8°
Calciferol (vitamin D_2)	Chloroform	+ 52.0
Calciferol (vitamin D_2)	Acetone	+ 82.6
Cholesterol	Chloroform	− 39.5
Quinine	0.5 M HCl	−220.0
l-Tartaric acid	Water	+ 14.1
Sodium potassium tartrate (Rochelle salt)	Water	+ 29.8
Sucrose	Water	+ 66.5
β-d-Glucose	Water	+ 52.7
β-d-Fructose	Water	− 92.4
β-Lactose	Water	+ 55.4
β-Maltose	Water	+130.4

where α is the angle (measured in degrees) through which the plane is rotated by a solution of concentration c grams of solute per milliliter of solution, contained in a cell d decimeters in length; t designates the temperature and λ the wavelength. The latter is commonly specified as 589.3 nm, the "D-line" of a sodium vapor lamp. $[\alpha]^t$ then becomes $[\alpha]_D^t$. Some representative values are given in Table 10-1.

POLARIMETERS

The most general instrument in this field is the *polarimeter* (Fig. 10-1). A typical manual instrument is shown schematically in Fig. 10-2. Monochromatic radiation from a sodium lamp is made parallel by a collimator and polarized by a calcite

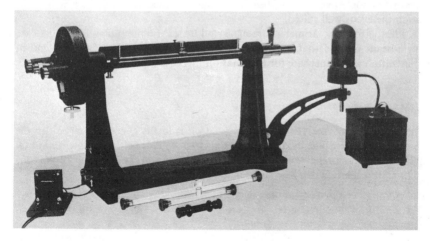

Figure 10-1 A precision polarimeter, equipped with a sodium lamp. (*O. C. Rudolph and Sons.*)

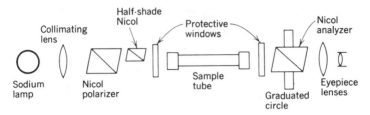

Figure 10-2 Diagram of a conventional polarimeter.

(Nicol) prism. Following the polarizer is placed a small auxiliary Nicol arranged to intercept half the beam (to be explained below). The radiation then passes through the sample, which is contained in a glass tube of known length, closed at both ends by glass plates, and an analyzer, to the eyepiece for visual observation.

In principle the polarimeter could function without the small auxiliary prism. The two polarizers would initially be crossed without any sample in the beam, and then again with the sample present. The angle through which the analyzer had to be turned between these two points would be the quantity sought. However, this simple arrangement is unsatisfactory because it requires the observer to identify the position where the transmitted light is zero, which cannot be done with precision. The added prism in half the beam makes it possible to avoid this difficulty. It is permanently oriented at an angle of a few degrees from that of the polarizer. There is then a particular position of the analyzer at which the radiations passed in the two halves of the beam are just equal in power. This provides a satisfactory reference point, since the visual observation consists of matching exactly the powers of two half-beams at some intermediate level, for which application the eye is well suited.

Photoelectric polarimeters are marketed by several manufacturers. These are single-beam devices that include a servomechanism for rotating the plane of polarization to compensate for the rotation by the sample.

Applications

The widest use of analysis by optical rotation is in the sugar industry.[1] In the absence of other optically active material, sucrose can be determined quantitatively by a direct application of Eq. (10-1). For sucrose in the customary 2-dm tube at 20°C, this relation can be written in the form

$$c = \frac{\alpha}{d[\alpha]_D^{20}} = \frac{\alpha}{(2)(66.5)} = \frac{\alpha}{130} \qquad (10\text{-}2)$$

If other active substances are present, a more elaborate treatment is needed. Sucrose, alone among common sugars, can be made to undergo a hydrolysis reaction in the presence of acid, according to the equation

$$C_{12}H_{22}O_{11} \longrightarrow C_6H_{12}O_6 + C_6H_{12}O_6$$

Sucrose	Glucose	Fructose
$[\alpha]_D^{20} = +66.5°$	$+52.7°$	$-92.4°$

The resulting mixture of glucose and fructose is called *invert sugar*, and the reaction *inversion*. During the inversion process, the specific rotation changes from $+66.5$ to $-19.8°$, corresponding to an equimolar mixture of the products. By measuring the rotation before and after inversion, it is possible to calculate the amount of sucrose present. The usual procedure is to start with a 100-ml sample, measure its rotation, and then add 10 ml of concentrated HCl. The acidified solution must stand at least 10 min at 70°C, to ensure complete reaction, after which the rotation is redetermined. Under these conditions the weight of sucrose in the sample is

$$w_s = -1.17\Delta\alpha - 0.00105[\alpha]_{D(X)}^{20}w_x \qquad (10\text{-}3)$$

where $\Delta\alpha$ is the observed change in angle of rotation, $[\alpha]_{D(X)}^{20}$ is the specific rotation of any other active material that may be present, and w_x is the weight of this active impurity. If nearly all the active material is sucrose, the second term becomes negligible. On the other hand, if sucrose is to be determined as a minor constituent in a large portion of another active substance of known specific rotation, the second term can be evaluated and the weight of sucrose calculated from the observed $\Delta\alpha$.

Another example of an analytical procedure based on optical rotation is the simultaneous determination of penicillin and the enzyme penicillinase.[2] Penicillin is destroyed quantitatively by the enzyme at a rate that is directly dependent on the amount of enzyme present, but independent of the penicillin concentration. A graph of rotation against time gives a straight line which terminates when the penicillin is all used up. The slope of the line is a measure of the enzyme. Figure 10-3 shows such a graph for several values of enzyme concentration. It will be seen that the curves tail off, an effect due to secondary reactions. The true time of disappearance of penicillin is found by the intersection of the extrapolated straight portions. The concentration can be determined with a precision of about ± 1 percent for the penicillin and about ± 10 percent for the enzyme.

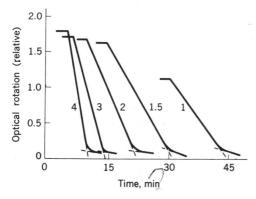

Figure 10-3 The enzymatic destruction of penicillin with varying concentrations of penicillinase in a phosphate buffer at pH 7. The figures indicate relative concentrations of enzyme. (*Analytical Chemistry.*[2])

OPTICAL ROTATORY DISPERSION
AND CIRCULAR DICHROISM

The wavelength dependence of optical activity, known as *optical rotatory dispersion* (ORD), is a more fruitful source of structural information about asymmetric compounds than is the specific rotation at a single wavelength.[3] It is closely related to the phenomenon called *circular dichroism* (CD).[4]

In Chap. 2 it was shown that an ordinary beam of light can be resolved into two plane-polarized beams. We now carry that line of thought forward another step. Plane-polarized radiation can be further resolved into two beams said to be circularly polarized in opposite senses (Fig. 10-4a). The indices of refraction of an optical medium for the left- and right-hand circularly polarized components may not be the same, and will be designated n_L and n_R, respectively. The corresponding absorptivities a_L and a_R can also differ. For an isotropic medium such as glass or water, $n_L = n_R$ and $a_L = a_R$, and we say that the index and the absorptivity are

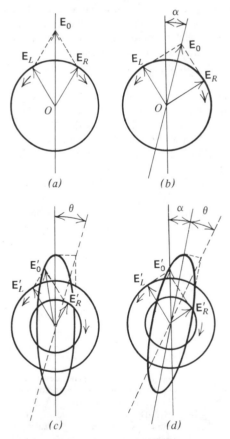

(a) *(b)*

(c) *(d)*

Figure 10-4 (*a*) resolution of plane-polarized radiation into left- and right-hand circularly polarized components. The two radius vectors E_L and E_R, rotating in opposite directions, are the equivalent of vector E_0 vibrating in a vertical plane. The beam of radiation propagates perpendicularly into the plane of the paper at the center of the circle. (The vectors referred to are the *electric* vectors of the respective beams of radiation.) (*b*) corresponding vector diagram of the beam of radiation in (*a*) after passing through an optically active material. A phase difference has appeared, corresponding to a rotation of the plane of polarization by angle α. (*c*) vector diagram for the radiation in (*a*) after traversing a sample for which the right-circularly polarized component is absorbed more than the left. The resultant vector E_0' now describes an ellipse with its major radius equal to $E_L' + E_R'$ and its minor radius equal to $E_L' - E_R'$. This is a hypothetical case of CD not accompanied by optical rotation. The ellipticity is the angle θ. (*d*) corresponding vector diagram for the radiation after passing through a sample that shows both optical activity and CD.

independent of the state of polarization. If $n_L \neq n_R$, a phase difference appears between the two components, which is tantamount to saying that the plane of polarization has been rotated, i.e., that the angle $\alpha \neq 0$ (Fig. 10-4b). If $\alpha_L \neq \alpha_R$, then one component is absorbed more strongly than the other; the vector diagram representing the polarization then turns out to be elliptical, with the eccentricity θ a measure of $a_L - a_R$ (Fig. 10-4c and d). The electric vector **E** of an electromagnetic wave is proportional to the square root of the power of the beam, hence the vectors in Fig. 10-4c and d are, respectively, $\mathbf{E}'_L = \mathbf{E}_L \sqrt{T_L}$ and $\mathbf{E}'_R = \mathbf{E}_R \sqrt{T_R}$, where T_L and T_R are the transmittances.[5]

It can be shown[3] that the angle of rotation, as used in Eq. (10-1), expressed in radians, is given by

$$\alpha = \frac{\pi}{\lambda}(n_L - n_R)d \tag{10-4}$$

in which d is the optical path length in the sample.

The *ellipticity*, defined as the angle whose tangent is the ratio of major to minor axes of the ellipse, is given (in radians) by

$$\theta = \tfrac{1}{4}(k_L - k_R)d \tag{10-5}$$

where k is the absorption coefficient in the absorption law expressed in the form

$$P = P_0 e^{-kd} \tag{10-6}$$

Equation (10-5) can be expressed in a more convenient form as

$$[\theta] = \theta \cdot \frac{180}{\pi} \cdot \frac{M}{C}$$
$$\cong 3300(\epsilon_L - \epsilon_R)d \tag{10-7}$$

where $[\theta]$ is the *molecular ellipticity* in degree $\cdot$ cm^2/mol, and where ϵ_L and ϵ_R are the molar absorptivities for left- and right-circularly polarized radiation. The relation between these quantities can be seen in Fig. 10-5.

The quantity $(n_L - n_R)$ is called the *circular birefringence*, and $(k_L - k_R)$ is the *circular dichroism* (CD). Both are very small quantities compared to the mean values, $(n_L + n_R)/2$ and $(k_L + k_R)/2$, respectively. The value of α can be measured directly with a suitable instrument, but θ can only be determined indirectly from the CD.

The combined phenomena of nonzero circular birefringence and dichroism is known as the *Cotton effect*, named for its discoverer. This effect appears in connection with chromophoric absorptions in optically active compounds. An example is shown in Fig. 10-6. The maxima of CD and of absorption and the inflection of the ORD curve theoretically coincide in wavelength, but the superimposed effects of other chromophores may cause shifts in the observed maximum in absorbance (as is the case in Fig. 10-6). CD curves will often pinpoint "hidden"

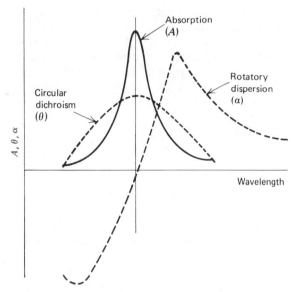

Figure 10-5 The UV absorption, CD, and ORD spectra of a compound for which the CD is positive.

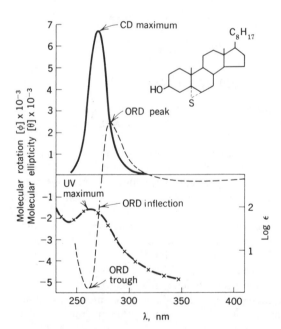

Figure 10-6 The ORD, CD, and UV absorption spectra of the weak transition due to the episulfide group in 3β-hydroxycholestane-5α, 6α-episulfide. (*Talanta.*[6])

absorption maxima, with less ambiguity than will the corresponding ORD curves. On the other hand, ORD curves are affected to a considerable degree by more distant chromophoric bands, and hence are more characteristic of specific compounds than CD. Both ORD and CD can give essential information about stereochemical features of optically active materials. In practice the relation between the several curves for the same substance may be more complex than the example in Fig. 10-6; as the theory is not within the scope of this book, the reader is referred to the literature for further details.[4]

ORD Photometers

There are several recording spectropolarimeters in present manufacture. They can be considered to be modified single-beam spectrophotometers, as shown schematically in Fig. 10-7. In this instrument the beam of light from a conventional monochromator passes sequentially through a polarizer, the sample, and an analyzer, to the photomultiplier tube. The beam is modulated with respect to its state of polarization at 12 Hz by a motor-driven device that causes the polarizer to rock back and forth through an angle of 1 or 2 degrees. The servoamplifier responds only to the 12-Hz frequency, and causes the servomotor to adjust the analyzer continuously to the point where the 12-Hz signal is symmetrically disposed about the null point. The servomotor also positions the pen of a strip-chart recorder.

Other forms of modulators can be used in place of the oscillating polarizer. One such is a *Faraday cell*,[7] which consists of a glass or silica rod surrounded by a coil carrying 60-Hz alternating current. This device rotates the plane of polarization through a few degrees, alternating in sign at the applied frequency.

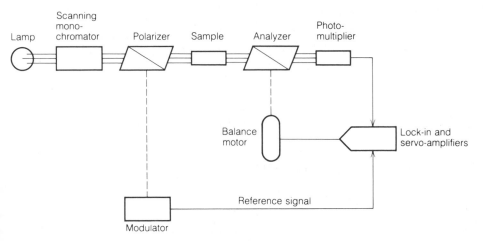

Figure 10-7 Block diagram of a typical spectropolarimeter.

CD Apparatus

Since conventional spectrophotometers are designed to determine the difference between the absorbances of a sample and a standard, they can easily be adapted to measure CD, which is likewise the difference between two absorbances.

Circular polarization is accomplished in two steps. First the beam of radiation must be plane-polarized and, second, the polarized beam must be passed through a device that will resolve it into its right- and left-circularly polarized components. One component must then be *retarded* by exactly one-quarter wavelength. The most important circular resolvers are of three types: the *Fresnel rhomb*; the *Pockels electrooptic modulator*, and the *photoelastic stress modulator*.

An example of the first type is shown in Fig. 10-8. This depends on total internal reflection of the light beam from two glass–air surfaces, wherein one of the orthogonal plane-polarized components is changed in phase while the other is not. If the angles are correctly chosen, the emerging beam will be circularly polarized.[7] This device has a somewhat limited wavelength range.

In the Pockels modulator, a high potential (kilovolts) is applied across a plate of crystalline KH_2PO_4 or similar material, in which the electric field induces birefringence, so that the initially plane-polarized radiation becomes circularly polarized.[8] The retardation can be altered by choice of potential, and thus can be programmed to give continuously correct output as the wavelength is changed. The range is only limited by the region of transparency of the crystal.

The photoelectric modulator depends on the birefringence induced in isotropic optical elements as a result of mechanical stress.[9] Such modulators are available made of vitreous silica, calcium fluoride, and zinc sulfide, the latter two permitting work through the UV and visible and well into the IR.

A detailed discussion of the calibration procedures necessary for quantitative CD spectrometers has been presented by Schippers and Dekkers.[10]

Applications of CD

Quantitative analysis by means of CD is possible, though apparently not widely used. Bowen, Purdie, and coworkers have reported determinations of heroin,[11]

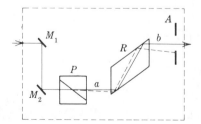

Figure 10-8 An optical assembly for measurement of CD. Radiation enters at the left, is displaced downward by mirrors M_1 and M_2, is plane-polarized by the compound prism P, and is passed through the Fresnel rhomb R, where it undergoes two internal reflections, introducing a phase retardation of one-quarter wavelength thus producing circular polarization. The mask A eliminates the unwanted ray while permitting the desired one to pass. The entire unit fits into the sample chamber of a standard spectrophotometer. A second unit, oppositely oriented, is required for the reference path. The sample is placed at point b for CD measurements, or at a to study plane-polarized transmission. (*Cary Instruments Division of Varian Associates.*)

cocaine, and other drugs.[12] In principle, any optically active compound can be determined if no other compounds are present that show CD curves in the same region. In the case of illicit cocaine preparations, for example, the usual diluents and additives are lactose, lidocaine, and benzocaine. Lactose is optically active, but being saturated, does not show selective UV absorption in the same wavelengths that cocaine does. The other compounds mentioned do absorb in the same region (due to the benzenoid chromophere), but are not optically active, hence do not interfere.

The majority of CD measurements are for the purpose of structure determinations in the area of stereochemistry and conformation.

PROBLEMS

10-1 A 10.00-g sample of impure Rochelle salt is dissolved in enough water to make 100.0 ml of solution. A 20-cm polarimeter tube is first filled with distilled water (to establish the true zero of the scale), and then with a portion of the solution. The following observations are made at 20°C:

Scale setting for water $+2.020°$
Scale setting for solution $+5.750°$

What is the percent by weight of Rochelle salt in the sample?

10-2 Compute the percent error introduced into the determination of sucrose by Eq. (10-3) with the second term omitted, in each of the following samples: (a) 30 g sucrose plus 2 g lactose, (b) 16 g sucrose plus 16 g lactose, and (c) 2 g sucrose plus 30 g lactose. The variation of the specific rotation of lactose between 15 and 20°C may be neglected.

10-3 A certain compound, in aqueous solution, measured in 1-dm cuvets at 500 nm, shows an angle of rotation of plane-polarized light of 10.0°. Compute its circular birefringence.

REFERENCES

1. F. J. Bates, et al., "Polarimetry, Saccharimetry, and the Sugars," *Nat. Bur. Standards Circ.* C440, **1942**.
2. G. B. Levy, *Anal. Chem.*, **1951**, *23*, 1089.
3. C. Djerassi, *Optical Rotatory Dispersion: Applications to Organic Chemistry*, McGraw-Hill, New York, **1960**.
4. L. Velluz, M. Legrand, and M. Grosjean, *Optical Circular Dichroism*, Academic Press, New York, **1965**.
5. J. J. Duffield, A. Abu-Shumays, and A. Robinson, *Chem. Instrum.*, **1968**, *1*, 59.
6. C. Djerassi, H. Wolf, D. A. Lightner, E. Bunnenberg, K. Takeda, T. Komeno, and K. Kuriyama, *Tetrahedron*, **1963**, *19*, 1547.
7. J. M. Bennett and N. E. Bennett, "Polarization," in *Handbook of Optics*, W. G. Driscoll and W. Vaughan (eds.), McGraw-Hill, New York, **1978**, p. 10-120.
8. E. Hartfield and B. J. Thompson, "Optical Modulators," in *Handbook of Optics*, W. G. Driscoll and W. Vaughan (eds.), McGraw-Hill, New York, **1978**; sec. 17.
9. M. E. Koehler and F. L. Urbach, *Appl. Spectrosc.*, **1979**, *33*, 563.
10. P. H. Schippers and H. P. J. M. Dekkers, *Anal. Chem.*, **1981**, *53*, 778.
11. J. M. Bowen, T. A. Crone, R. K. Kennedy, and N. Purdie, *Anal. Chem.*, **1982**, *54*, 66.
12. J. M. Bowen and N. Purdie, *Anal. Chem.*, **1981**, *53*, 2237, 2239.

ELEVEN

X-RAY METHODS

When a beam of energetic electrons impinges on a target material, the electrons are, in general, slowed down by multiple interactions with the electrons of the target. The energy lost is converted into a continuum of x-radiation, called *Bremsstrahlung*.† This continuum shows a sharp minimum wavelength λ_{min} (maximum frequency) corresponding to the maximum energy of the electrons, which cannot be exceeded. This cutoff wavelength (in nanometers) is given by

$$\lambda_{min} = \frac{hc}{Ve} = \frac{1240}{V} \tag{11-1}$$

where h = Planck's constant, c = the velocity of the electromagnetic radiation in vacuo, e = the electronic charge, and V = the accelerating potential across the x-ray tube, in volts.

As the potential is increased, a point is reached where the energy is sufficient to knock a planetary electron completely out of the target atom. Then as another electron falls back into the vacancy, a photon of x-radiation is emitted, with a wavelength dependent on the energy levels, and hence characteristic of the element. The high energies involved affect principally the electrons closest to the nucleus. Thus a K electron may be ejected and its place taken by an electron from the L shell. Since these inner electrons are not appreciably concerned with the state of chemical combination of the atoms (except for the lighter elements), it follows that the x-ray properties of the atoms are independent of chemical combination or physical state, to a close degree of approximation. (Chapter 12 discusses some

† From the German, meaning "braking radiation."

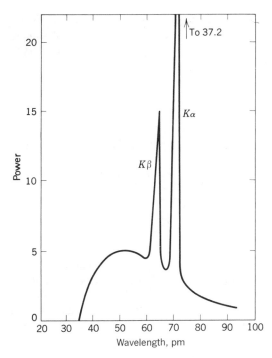

Figure 11-1 Emission spectrum of x-rays from a tube with a molybdenum target, operated at 35 kV. The continuous background is due to Bremsstrahlung radiation; the peaks are the $K\alpha$ and $K\beta$ transitions. (*Wiley.*[1])

exceptions to this generalization.) The wavelengths corresponding to such high energies are small, of the order of 1 to 1000 pm.† The range of 70 to 200 pm includes the wavelengths most useful for analytical purposes.

The x-ray emission spectrum of a given target material irradiated by high-energy electrons resembles that shown in Fig. 11-1, a continuum with superimposed discrete lines. The lines due to transitions from the L to the K shell are designated as $K\alpha$ x-rays, $K\alpha_1$ and $K\alpha_2$ corresponding to electrons originating in different sublevels of the L shell; x-rays due to transitions from the M to the K shell are called $K\beta$, and so on. Heavy elements show other groups of lines corresponding to transitions to the L, M, and higher levels.

Excitation can also be brought about by incident x-rays, an example of fluorescence; in this case the continuum does not appear, and only the characteristic lines are present. This is a favorable situation for x-ray emission analysis, greatly increasing the signal-to-noise ratio.

For analytical purposes, x-radiation can be utilized in several distinct ways. (1) The absorption of x-rays will give information about the absorbing material, just as in other spectral regions. (2) The diffraction of x-rays permits identification

---

† X-ray wavelengths are usually given in angstroms (Å). In furtherance of the SI unitary system, this book uses nanometers (nm) or picometers (pm); 1 nm = 10 Å = 1000 pm.

of crystalline materials with a high degree of specificity and accuracy. (3) Wavelength or energy measurements will identify elements in the excited sample. (4) Measurement of radiant power at selected wavelengths can be a quantitative indicator of the composition of the sample.

THE ABSORPTION OF X-RAYS

In common with other regions of the electromagnetic spectrum, x-rays can be absorbed by matter, and the degree of absorption is controlled by the nature and amount of the absorbing material.

When the thickness of an absorbing material is of primary interest, it is convenient to write Beer's law in the form:

$$P_x = P_0 e^{-\mu x} \tag{11-2}$$

or

$$\ln (P_0/P) = \mu x \tag{11-3}$$

for monochromatic x-rays, where P_0 is the initial power of the radiation and P_x is the power after passage through an absorbing sample x cm in length. The *linear absorption coefficient*, μ represents the fraction of energy absorbed per centimeter for a given element. Notice that, for historical reasons, the natural log function is used in Eq. (11-3) rather than logs to the base 10. Often more convenient is a *mass absorption coefficient*, defined as

$$\mu_M = \frac{\mu}{\rho} \tag{11-4}$$

where ρ is the density of the absorbing material. When the absorbing material is an element, the coefficient is found empirically to be related to the wavelength and atomic properties of the absorber by the formula

$$\mu_m = CNZ^4 \lambda^n / A \tag{11-5}$$

where N is Avogadro's number, Z is the atomic number of the absorbing element and A is its atomic weight, λ is the wavelength, n is an exponent between 2.5 and

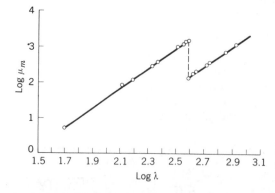

Figure 11-2 The x-ray absorption of argon in the region 50 to 1000 pm. Note the K absorption edge at $\log \lambda = 2.59$. (*From data of Compton and Allison.*[2])

3.0, and C is a constant that is the same for all elements within limited regions, as will appear.

The variation of μ_m with wavelength follows an exponential law, so that if the logarithms are plotted, a straight line should result, with its slope equal to the exponent of λ. Figure 11-2 shows such a plot for the absorption coefficient of argon. The most striking feature of this graph is the discontinuity at

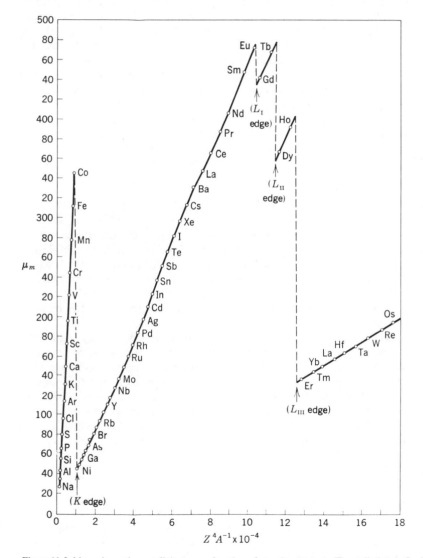

Figure 11-3 Mass absorption coefficients as a function of atomic constants. The radiation is Cu $K\alpha$, 154.18 pm. (*From data of Compton and Allison.*[2])

$\log \lambda = 2.59$ ($\lambda = 387.1$ pm). This is known as the *K critical absorption edge* for argon. Radiation of longer wavelength has insufficient energy to eject the K electrons of argon, and hence it is not absorbed as strongly as is radiation of slightly shorter wavelength. Heavier atoms than argon show similar discontinuities at longer wavelengths corresponding to the photoelectric ejection of L and M electrons.

It is instructive to plot μ_m against the ratio Z^4/A for x-rays of a particular wavelength, as in Fig. 11-3, which shows the values for Cu $K\alpha$ radiation for the elements from sodium to osmium. The critical absorption edges also appear in this plot, since as the atomic nucleus increases in charge, the electrons of a specified shell are bound more and more tightly to it, and there is a point in the size parameter where the energy of the Cu $K\alpha$ x-ray is insufficient to eject the electrons. The "constant" C of Eq. (11-5) changes value abruptly at the edge discontinuities, and is not perfectly constant between them, as shown by the slight curvature most easily visible between the K and L_I edges. This curvature can alternatively be ascribed to variation in the exponent n. Equation (11-5) will need refinement as our knowledge of the underlying phenomena improves. Empirical absorption data for most elements are to be found in the literature.[1,2]

MONOCHROMATIC X-RAY SOURCES

It is a relatively simple matter to obtain narrow bands of wavelengths at various discrete points in the x-ray region, but not so simple to construct a monochromator that can be varied at will. Narrow bands can be obtained by three methods: (1) by choosing characteristic emission lines that are much stronger than the background, and isolating them with the aid of filters; (2) by means of a monochromator in which a crystal of known spacing acts as a diffraction grating; and (3) by using certain radioactive sources.

A nearly monochromatic beam can sometimes be obtained by means of a filter made of an element (or its compound) that has a critical absorption edge at just the right wavelength to isolate a characteristic line from a source target. For example, Fig. 11-4 shows the absorption spectrum (dashed line) of zirconium superimposed on the emission spectrum of molybdenum (cf. Fig. 11-1). The Mo $K\beta$ and most of the Bremsstrahlung will be absorbed by the Zr filter, whereas the Mo $K\alpha$, situated on the low-energy side of the Zr critical edge, is essentially unattenuated. Isolation of the $K\alpha$ line is not complete, but is nevertheless acceptable for many purposes. Table 11-1 lists filters suitable for $K\alpha$ isolation from several targets.

Crystal Monochromators

If more nearly monochromatic radiation is required than can be obtained with filters, a grating monochromator can be employed. Design of this instrument will be detailed later, in connection with x-ray diffraction.

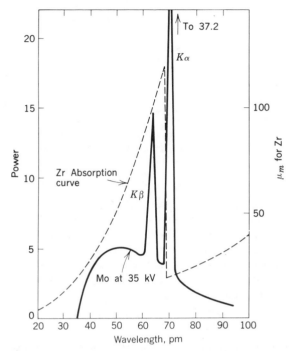

Figure 11-4 The zirconium absorption curve superimposed on the 35-kV molybdenum emission spectrum results in the nearly monochromatic radiation of Mo $K\alpha$. (*Wiley.*[1])

Table 11-1 Characteristic wavelengths and filters for x-ray tubes with commonly available targets

| Target | Wavelengths | | Filter | | Foil thickness, μm | Percent $K\beta_1$ absorbed |
	$K\alpha_1$, pm	$K\beta_2$, pm	Element	K-edge, pm		
Cr	228.9	208.5	V	226.9	15.3	99.0
Fe	193.6	175.7	Mn	189.6	12.1	98.7
Co	178.9	162.1	Fe	174.3	14.7	98.9
Ni	165.8	150.0	Co	160.8	14.3	98.4
Cu	154.1	139.3	Ni	148.8	15.8	97.9
Mo	70.9	63.2	Zr	68.9	63.0	96.3
Ag	55.9	49.7	Pd	50.9	41.3	94.6
W†	20.9	18.5				

† No suitable filter material is available for tungsten radiation.

Table 11-2 Isotopes useful as sources of x-rays or gamma rays†

Isotope	Half-life	Radiations‡
^{55}Fe	2.60 years	EC: Mn K, 210.3 pm
^{57}Co	270 days	EC: Fe
		Gamma: 86.1, 10.17 pm
^{60}Co	5.26 years	Gamma: 1.06, 0.931 pm
^{241}Am	458 years	EC: Np L, 88.9 pm, Np L, 69.8 pm, Np L, 59.7 pm
		Gamma: 20.87, 47.0 pm

† The data are taken from Refs. 3, 4, and 5, recalculated to consistent units as necessary.

‡ EC, electron-capture.

Such a monochromator could produce a narrow band of wavelengths at any point in the spectrum if a continuous source of x-rays were available. However, the continuous radiation produced at reasonable tube voltages is not powerful enough to be of much use, so for practical purposes, we are still restricted to the various characteristic wavelengths. The advantage of the monochromator over the filter lies in its great reduction of background, which results in an improved signal-to-noise ratio in spite of a considerably attenuated signal.

Radioactive Sources

Radiations in the x-ray region are emitted from radioactive elements by either of two mechanisms.[3] The first of these, correctly called *gamma radiation*, involves intranuclear energy levels, and so is not truly x-radiation. The other is known as *electron capture* (EC) or *K capture*. Since an electron in a K orbital has a finite probability of spending some of its time very close to the nucleus, there is, in many atoms, a finite probability of the capture of a K electron by the nucleus. The process lowers the atomic number by one unit and leaves a vacancy in the K shell. Hence true x-rays of the next lower element result, unaccompanied by any significant continuous radiation. Table 11-2 lists a few isotopes that have proved useful as x- or gamma-ray sources. Filters may still be needed to separate individual lines.

Radioactive sources have the advantage of not requiring an elaborate high-voltage supply and an evacuated tube with limited lifetime. On the other hand, they have the disadvantage that they cannot be turned off; potential radiation hazard is present at all times, whether an experiment is in progress or not.

X-RAY DETECTORS

X-rays were first detected by the latent image they produce in photographic materials. Photography is no longer widely used for quantitative purposes, but it is convenient for certain diffraction techniques in which a two-dimensional pattern is produced and its geometry must be precisely established. Film for this purpose is coated with layers of emulsion on both sides, to increase absorption of the penetrating x-radiation. Other detectors are based on the ability of x-rays to produce flashes of light (scintillations) in certain materials, or to cause ionization in others.

Scintillation Detectors

Certain materials have the property of emitting a tiny flash of light when an x-ray photon is absorbed, a case of fluorescence. A prominent example is crystalline NaI into which a small amount (1 or 2 percent) of TlI has been incorporated. These flashes can be observed with a photomultiplier tube to give a reliable measure of the number of photons incident on the crystal. The duration of each flash is very short (of the order of 10^{-8} s), but the resulting electrical pulse may be somewhat longer due to the limitations of the electronic circuitry. Separate scintillations can be distinguished and counted up to at least 10^6 per second. Although the random spacing of the pulses causes overlapping pulses at high count rates, separate scintillations can be distinguished and counted at average rates at least as high as 10^6 counts per second. The basic circuitry for use with a photomultiplier has been mentioned in Chap. 3.

Gas-Ionization Detectors

Since x-rays ionize gases through which they pass, their presence can be detected by the conductivity of the gas. This can be done with an *ionization chamber*, a simple metallic container with an insulated central electrode, filled with dry gas. The electrode is charged to a potential of 100 V or more, and the resulting current measured with an electrometer. The signals from individual photons are not resolved, and the observed current represents an averaged or steady state condition.

Much improved response can be obtained by increasing the voltage to the point where electrons liberated in the initial ionizing event are accelerated sufficiently to ionize additional molecules by collision. The number of ions so produced depends on the energy of the incident x-ray photon, so the current is proportional to the photon energy. When used in this mode, the device is called a *gas proportional counter*. Its action is fast enough to permit electronic counting of individual photons. If the voltage is raised still higher, a saturation effect becomes evident and all pulses are of equal magnitude, regardless of the energy of the incident photon. In this mode, the detector is called a *Geiger-Müller* (or *Geiger*) *counter*. Chapter 24 includes a more detailed treatment of gas-ionization detectors.

Solid-state Ionization Detectors

Germanium and silicon, as free elements, can be sensitized to x-ray and other ionizing radiations by the addition of lithium. The lithium is allowed to diffuse into the crystalline material (*drifting* is the technical term), scavenging impurities as it

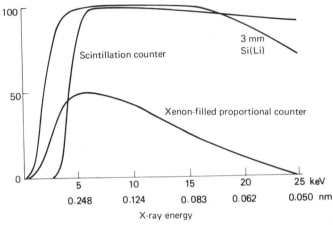

Figure 11-5 Relative spectral response of gas-proportional, scintillation, and Si(Li) detectors. (*EDAX*.)

penetrates. An x-ray photon entering the crystal dislodges electrons from the lattice, leaving vacancies commonly called *holes*, equivalent in effect to mobile positive charges. The number of such charge-separation events is directly related to the energy content of the photon, and hence the signal obtained (the conductivity) is also proportional. Detectors of this type must be cooled to liquid-nitrogen temperatures even when not in use, to prevent further diffusion of the lithium, which would greatly reduce the sensitivity and eventually destroy the detector.

The electrical output from one of these solid-state detectors is much smaller than the signal from a gaseous or scintillation detector, so that high-gain electronic amplification is necessary.

Figure 11-5 shows the relative spectral response of typical detectors of these several kinds. Note that the abscissa scale is given in energy units, proportional to the reciprocal of the wavelength. Each detector gives a somewhat broadened peak for nominally monochromatic radiation, as shown in Fig. 11-6. The Fe $K\alpha$ and Fe $K\beta$ lines at 193.7 and 175.7 pm (6.40 and 7.05 keV) are reproduced by a Si(Li) solid-state detector, but not by either gas proportional or scintillation detectors.

Analysis by X-ray Absorption

As an analytical tool, x-ray absorption is of most value where the element to be determined is the sole heavy component in a matrix of low atomic weight. A number of important analyses fall in this category and make the method a significant one for industrial control purposes. Lead in gasoline can be determined this way,[6] as can chlorine in organic compounds,[7] and uranium in solutions of its salts.[8] X-ray and gamma-ray gauges are used to monitor the thickness of household aluminum foil in the rolling process.

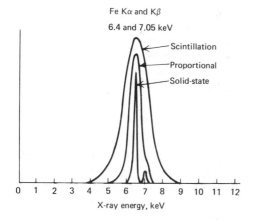

Fe Kα and Kβ

6.4 and 7.05 keV

Scintillation

Proportional

Solid-state

0 1 2 3 4 5 6 7 8 9 10 11 12

X-ray energy, keV

Figure 11-6 Comparison of the resolution obtainable from scintillation, gas-proportional, and Si(Li) detectors. (*EDAX.*)

Analysis by direct x-ray absorption has largely been displaced by the x-ray fluorescence methods to be described in a later section. The latter give qualitative as well as quantitative information, with comparable apparatus.

Absorption Edge Analysis

Another method of applying x-ray absorption makes use of critical absorption edges as means of identification and quantitative analysis. Since the absorption by an element in a sample is markedly greater at a wavelength just below one of its absorption edges than just above it, and since the location of such edges on the wavelength scale is characteristic of the absorbing element, a pair of measurements bracketing the wavelength of the edge will serve to determine both the presence and the amount of the element sought.

If the power of an x-ray beam is plotted against wavelength in the vicinity of the K edge of an element, a curve like that of Fig. 11-7 will typically be obtained. The jump at λ_E, the wavelength of the absorption edge, is somewhat curved as

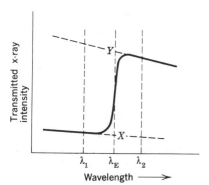

Transmitted x-ray intensity

Y

X

λ_1 λ_E λ_2

Wavelength ⟶

Figure 11-7 Absorption at a critical edge. (*Analytical Chemistry.*[9])

shown, rather than vertical, because of the necessity of using slits of finite width. The quantity desired is the vertical distance between the intersections X and Y obtained by extrapolation. This height can be estimated with good precision from measurements taken at two equally spaced wavelengths, λ_1 and λ_2. Mathematical details and justification for this short-cut procedure are given by Dunn,[9] who found that a relative error as low as 1 percent can be obtained at concentrations down to 0.1 percent for many elements.

Absorption Apparatus

Laboratory analyses by x-ray absorption are usually carried out with general-purpose equipment. For industrial control purposes, apparatus is commonly designed specifically for each installation. A portable x-ray absorption analyzer for S and Pb in petroleum products, made by Columbia Scientific Industries, uses a radioactive source.

X-RAY MONOCHROMATORS

Since x-rays are electromagnetic waves, they can be diffracted in a manner similar to radiations in other spectral regions (Fig. 11-8). The equation given in Chap. 2 for diffraction by a grating

$$m\lambda = d \sin \theta \tag{11-6}$$

can also be applied to x-rays. In this case, however, the wavelength is smaller by a factor of 1000 or more, so that to obtain reasonable values of θ, the grating space d must also be made smaller by about the same factor. It is impracticable to rule a grating finely enough to meet this requirement, but fortunately it happens that the spacing between adjacent planes of the atoms in many crystals is of just the required order of magnitude. A variety of crystals are suited for x-ray gratings; the most widely used include lithium fluoride, sodium chloride, calcite, gypsum, topaz, ethylenediamine d-tartrate (EDDT or EDT), and ammonium dihydrogen phosphate (ADP). In the simplest arrangement, the x-ray beam is reflected from a plane crystal (Fig. 11-8), and the wavelength selected by varying the angle. Since the waves reflected at successive crystal planes must pass twice across the space between the planes, Eq. (11-6) becomes the Bragg equation

$$m\lambda = 2d \sin \theta \tag{11-7}$$

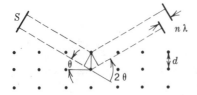

Figure 11-8 Diffraction of x-rays by successive layers of atoms in a crystal. S represents an incoming plane wave front.

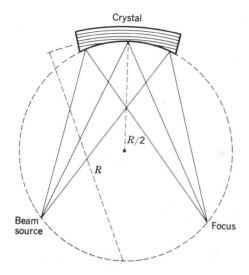

Crystal

$R/2$

R

Beam
source

Focus

Figure 11-9 An x-ray monochromator based on the Rowland circle. The crystal is bent and ground for accurate focus. (*Wiley.*[1])

where d is now the distance between adjacent planes in the crystal. This equation can easily be derived with the aid of Fig. 11-8. The angles of incidence and of diffraction must be equal in this case, a restriction that does not apply in optical diffraction.

It is also possible to use concave gratings with Rowland-circle focusing.[10] For this purpose a crystal must be curved to conform to the geometric requirements. For improved focus, a crystal must first be bent so that its diffracting planes are curved with a radius equal to twice that of the Rowland circle, and then ground so that the surface is given a curvature with radius equal to that of the circle (Fig. 11-9). The focusing monochromator is more expensive, largely because of the difficult hand work required in shaping the crystal, but it can give monochromatic intensity perhaps 10 times that of a plane crystal.

X-RAY DIFFRACTION

The diffraction of x-rays is of great analytical interest as applied to the study of the crystalline material producing the diffraction. No two chemical substances would be expected to form crystals in which the spacing of the planes is identical in all analogous directions, and so a complete study in which the sample assumes all possible angular positions in the path of the x-rays should give a unique result for each substance.

Equipment for x-ray diffraction is essentially comparable to an optical grating spectrometer, but since lenses and mirrors cannot be used with x-rays, the instrument is quite different in appearance from its optical analog. A reasonably

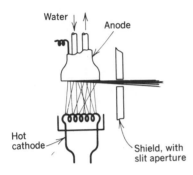

Figure 11-10 The electrodes of a typical x-ray tube, showing the beam taken at a glancing angle.

collimated beam can be obtained from the output of an x-ray source with an extended target by passage through a bundle of metal tubes, or if collimation in one plane only is required, through the spaces between a stack of parallel metal sheets. In some designs the emitting surface of the target is observed at a glancing angle (Fig. 11-10), which gives a close approximation to a line source with maximum intensity. Such a tube can be mounted vertically, anode up, and beams can be taken through each of several ports in different horizontal directions, permitting two, three, or even four independent experiments to be conducted simultaneously.

X-ray diffraction leads primarily to the identification of *crystalline* compounds. For example, each of the oxides of iron gives its own particular pattern, and the appearance of a certain pattern proves the presence of that particular compound. Elements as such will be observed only if in the free crystalline state. This contrasts sharply with x-ray absorption and emission, in which the response is to the elements present, without much concern about their states of chemical combination.

The power of a diffracted beam is dependent on the quantity of the corresponding crystalline material in the sample. It is accordingly possible to obtain a quantitative determination of the relative amounts of the constituents of a mixture of solids.

Diffraction Apparatus

The diffracted beam of x-rays can be detected photographically or by one of the detectors previously described. The photographic method is typified by an apparatus known as a *Debye–Scherrer powder camera* (Figs. 11-11 and 11-12). The sample is prepared in the form of a fine homogeneous powder, and a thin layer of it is inserted in the path of the x-rays. The powder can be mounted on any noncrystalline material, such as paper, with an organic mucilage or glue as adhesive. The powdered sample contains so many particles that some are oriented in every possible direction relative to the beam of radiation. There will therefore be diffracted rays corresponding to all sets of planes in the crystals. A strip of x-ray

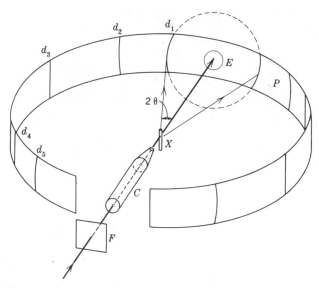

Figure 11-11 Geometry of the Debye–Scherrer powder camera. Radiation enters through filter F and collimator C to strike the sample X. The undeviated central beam is caught in a trap at E (not shown, but visible in Fig. 11-12) to prevent its fogging the film. Diffracted beams impinge on the film at points d_1, d_2, etc. (*Wiley*.[1])

Figure 11-12 Debye–Scherrer x-ray powder camera. (*General Electric Company.*)

Figure 11-13 X-ray diffraction patterns from films exposed in a powder camera. The radiation was Cu K; a nickel filter 15 μm thick was in place for films a to d and the upper portion of e. The specimen in each case was mounted on a fine glass fiber, except in e, where it was packed in a glass capillary. (a) Pb(NO$_3$)$_2$, (b) W metal, (c) NaCl, (d) and (e) quartz. (Science.[11])

film is held in a circular position around the sample, as shown. Upon development, this film will show a series of arcs symmetrically arranged on each side of the central spot produced by the undeviated beam. The distance on the film from the central spot to a given arc, together with the radius of the camera, will determine the diffraction angle θ. Then if the wavelength and order are known, the spacing d can be calculated from the Bragg equation. Several examples of films from a powder camera are reproduced in Fig. 11-13.

Diffraction studies on single crystals are best observed with ionization or scintillation detectors. The detector is most conveniently mounted in a housing that can move in a circular path around the sample, an apparatus called a *goniometer* (Figs. 11-14 and 11-15). In the model illustrated, the target of the x-ray tube provides a high-intensity line source 0.06 by 10 mm in cross section. The angular aperture of the beam is indicated by the divergent lines in Fig. 11-15. It is defined by a single mask, called a divergence slit, that also limits the primary beam to the specimen area. An aperture of 1° is commonly used. Flat specimens up to 10 by 20 mm can be accommodated, or a suitable sample can be rotated by a small motor. The receiving slit defines the width of the reflected beam going to the detector. A set of equally spaced thin metal foils (parallel slit assembly) limit the divergence of the beam in any plane parallel to the line source; two sets are used, as shown, permitting high resolution to be achieved. The scatter slit serves to reduce the background response caused by stray radiation. The output from the detector is amplified and fed into a pen recorder. As both the recording paper and the arm bearing the detector are driven by synchronous motors, the recorded graph may be interpreted as intensity of the diffracted beam plotted as a function of the angle of diffraction, usually denoted by 2θ.

Figure 11-14 Philips goniometer. The sample is mounted on the needle projecting to the left, and is rotated by the motor that is visible to the right. The x-ray beam enters from the slit beyond the sample; the x-ray source is not shown. The detector is located in the tubular housing at the top, and can be turned in an arc around the sample, either manually or by a motor drive. (*Philips Electronic Instruments, Inc.*)

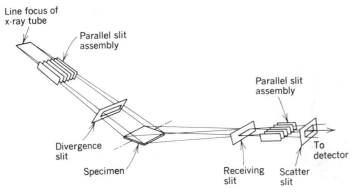

Line focus of
x-ray tube

Figure 11-15 Optical system of the Philips goniometer. (*Philips Electronic Instruments, Inc.*)

X-RAY FLUORESCENCE

The fluorescent emission of x-rays provides one of the most potent tools available to the analyst for the identification and measurement of heavy elements in the presence of each other and in nearly any matrix. The method fails with elements lighter than sodium and is only marginal below calcium.

The sample is irradiated by a primary beam of x-rays, which have the same effect as a beam of energetic electrons, i.e., the ejection of electrons from inner orbital shells. The primary beam must consist of photons with greater energy than the most energetic of the expected secondary x-rays to be emitted by the sample. The high-energy radiation from a tungsten target tube is most commonly selected. The primary radiation need not be monochromatic.

Each heavy element in the sample is caused to emit radiation of the same frequencies it would if it were made the target of a separate x-ray tube, but essentially free from the Bremsstrahlung continuum. The radiation from the sample is analyzed with the aid of a goniometer and detector, as diagrammed in Fig. 11-16. Several analyzing crystals may be needed to cover different ranges, and provision must be made for their interchange. The resolution attainable with each crystal is given by a *dispersion curve*, a plot of the angle 2θ read from the goniometer as a function of the atomic number Z of the fluorescing elements (Fig. 11-17).

X-ray fluorescence provides a convenient means of analysis for high-alloy steels such as those of the Cr-Ni-Co type. The determination of elements present at low concentrations is limited by a matrix effect: the emitted radiation is too greatly absorbed by the other elements of the specimen. Samples in which the main constituents are elements of high atomic weight will absorb a higher percentage of the radiation than would be absorbed by light elements. Thus Ni can be determined in an Al alloy with greater sensitivity than Ni in steel or in a Pb alloy, where the absorption of the Ni $K\alpha$ is high. In favorable circumstances, accuracy of the order of 0.5 percent of the element present can be achieved. The limit of detectability may be as low as a few parts per million.

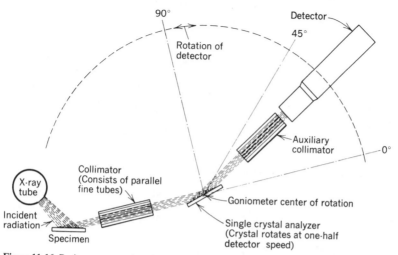

Figure 11-16 Basic geometry of an x-ray fluorescence spectrometer. (*Philips Electronic Instruments, Inc.*)

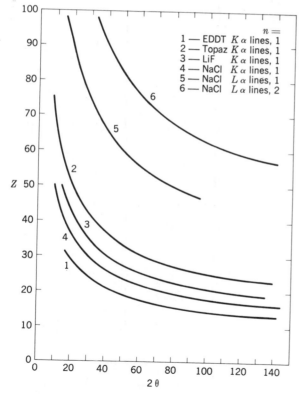

Figure 11-17 X-ray dispersion curves for a number of crystals.

Figure 11-18 shows a fluorescence spectrum of a Cr–Ni plating on a Cu–Ag base. Notice that the $K\alpha$ lines of Cr and Ni are much stronger than those of Ag and Cu, even though they arise from a thin plating, due to the partial attenuation of both the primary and the secondary radiation in passing through the plated layer.

X-ray fluorescence has been applied successfully in the determination of Hf in Zr, and of Ta in Nb.[12] It was possible, for example, to determine 1 percent

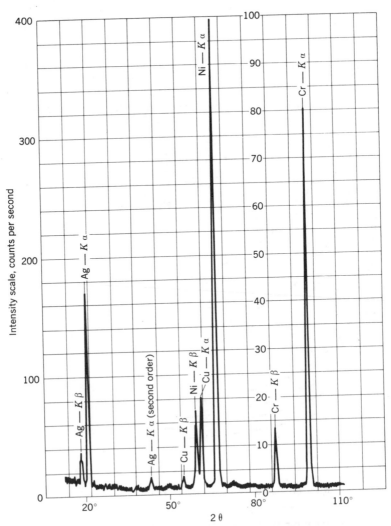

Figure 11-18 X-ray fluorescence spectrum of a silver–copper alloy plated with nickel and chromium. (*Philips Electronic Instruments, Inc.*)

Ta with a precision of ± 0.04 percent (that is, ± 4 percent of the amount present) in a sample of Nb.

Fluorescence methods have also been applied in trace analysis following a preconcentration step. In one report,[13] a 90-min electrolysis onto a cathode of pyrolytic graphite, with subsequent x-ray examination of the cathode surface, permitted determination of various metals in concentrations of a fraction of 1 μg/ml. Pyrolytic graphite is particularly advantageous, because it can be cleaved into thin layers convenient to mount in the x-ray apparatus, and in addition, carbon is of low enough atomic number to contribute almost no background.

ENERGY DISPERSIVE X-RAY SPECTROMETERS[14-16]

The energy E contained in a photon is related to the wavelength λ of the radiation by the equation

$$E\lambda = hc \tag{11-8}$$

in which both h and c are natural constants [cf. Eq. (2-2)]. This formulation stresses the mathematical symmetry of energy and wavelength, and suggests the possibility that spectral dispersion may be based on energy as well as on wavelength.

Energy dispersion depends on the availability of a detector that responds linearly to the energy content of the individual photons incident upon it. This requirement must be carefully distinguished from the response to the total average energy or power, which depends on both the energy per photon and the number of photons received per unit time. Those detectors that we have designated as *proportional*, namely scintillation counters, gas counters operated at an intermediate range of voltages, and lithium-drifted silicon or germanium detectors, are capable of measuring photon energies. These types vary in their ability to resolve close x-ray lines, as shown in Fig. 11-6. It was the development of practical solid-state detectors that made possible energy-dispersive spectrometers in a useful form.

Wavelength instruments, using a diffraction crystal, are capable of greater resolution than their energy-dispersive counterparts, but the latter show a gain of 100 times or more in efficiency and hence in sensitivity.[17] This is because they detect all frequencies simultaneously, another instance of the Fellgett advantage mentioned in Chap. 4 in connection with interferometric spectrophotometers. The spectra produced by the two classes of x-ray spectrometers are identical except for the difference in resolving power. This fact is emphasized in Fig. 11-5 by the inclusion of two abscissa scales. The graph can be made linear in either variable.

A basic energy-dispersive spectrometer with a radioactive source is shown schematically in Fig. 11-19[5] An x-ray tube could have been used as a source, but would have contributed more background. The background can be reduced, no

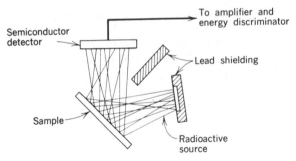

Figure 11-19 An energy-dispersive x-ray analyzer with a radioactive source.

matter which radiation source is selected, by installing a fluorescent plate between the primary source and the sample. Figure 11-20 shows two configurations in which a radioactive source can be utilized, with and without an intermediate fluorescent plate.

The signal from the solid-state detector is analyzed by a series of electronic energy discriminators that permit separate counting of signal pulses of successive energy brackets. How this operates is suggested for a six-channel analyzer in Fig. 11-21. The pulses correspond to photons arriving at random times. The figures indicate two "peaks," corresponding approximately to channels 2 and 5. Obviously many more channels and data points would be needed to make a valid experiment. Multichannel pulse-height analyzers are available from a number of manufacturers. A favorite size has 1024 channels. They are used for a variety of applications besides that described here.

Figure 11-22 shows a spectrum taken with an energy-dispersive spectrometer. Many applications for instruments of this type have been reported.[15,16] Hanson,[18] in a 25-page article, has described a comprehensive program for determining the elemental composition of any object made of metal, glass, or ceramic: he includes the necessary data for 71 elements. Rasberry[19] has reported comparative data for four types of portable energy-dispersive x-ray fluorescence analyzers for the in situ detection of Pb in wall paint; he found a lower limit of detectability of less than 1 mg of Pb per cm^2 of painted surface.

Surkov et al. have described a most interesting x-ray fluorescence spectrometer with which they have carried out elemental analyses of rocks on the surface of Venus.[20] The instrument contained both ^{55}Fe and ^{238}Pu sources. The alpha radiation from the plutonium excites x-rays from the light elements Mg, Al, and Si, whereas the iron source is much more effective with the heavier elements such as K, Ca, and Ti. Still heavier elements, particularly Mn and Fe, are excited by the x-rays emitted by the plutonium. The spectrometer contained four gas-proportional counters and a dual 128-channel pulse-height analyzer. Various modifications to conventional instruments were made to take account of the severe ambient conditions on the Venusian surface (500°C, 90 atm pressure).

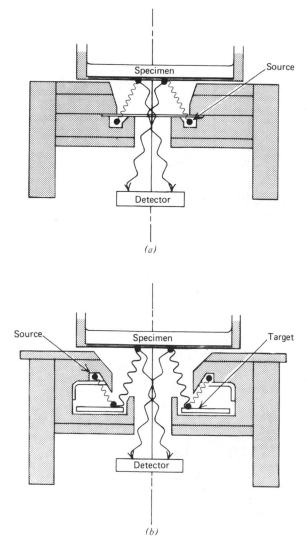

Figure 11-20 Energy-dispersive x-ray emission analyzers: (*a*) the specimen is irradiated directly by the gamma rays from the radioactive source. (*b*) radiation reaches the specimen only as x-rays generated in a fluorescent target excited by the primary gamma radiation. (*EXAX*.)

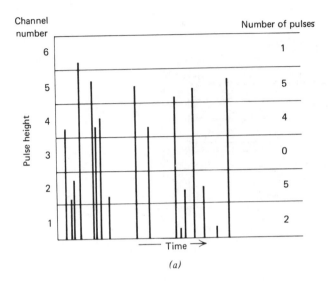

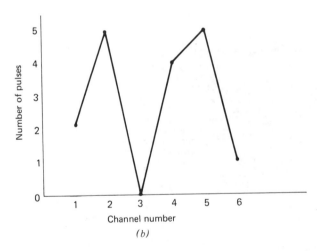

Figure 11-21 (*a*) Hypothetical distribution of 17 pulses over 6 energy channels in a multichannel analyzer, and (*b*) the resulting channel profile.

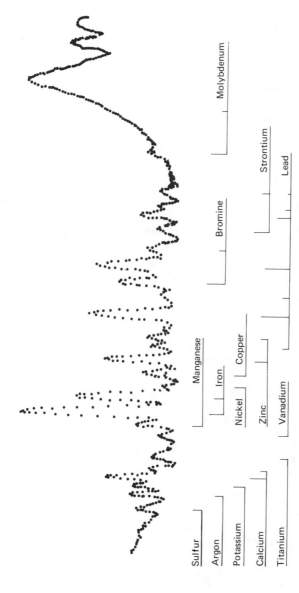

Figure 11-22 A study of particulates in an urban air sample. Air was pumped through a filter, and the filter paper examined in an energy-dispersive x-ray spectrometer. The source is the gamma-emitting isotope ^{109}Cd. Each dot represents the signal stored in one channel of a multichannel analyzer. (*Kevex Corporation.*[15])

ELECTRON MICROPROBE ANALYSIS[3,21]

In the past several decades the methods of focusing electron beams (*electron optics*) have been developed to a high degree. It is possible to focus a beam finely enough to excite x-rays in a solid sample as small as 1 μm^3 (10^{-18} m^3). A schematic diagram of a typical apparatus is shown in Fig. 11-23. The electron beam originates at the electron gun at the top of the diagram, and is focused by specially shaped electromagnets (magnetic lenses) onto the sample. (This section of the instrument is very similar to an electron microscope.) The radiation produced in the sample is analyzed in an x-ray spectrometer, either wavelength- or energy-dispersive. An optical microscope must be incorporated, so that the operator can locate precisely the desired spot on the sample.

The details of the instrument are more complex than shown in the figure; it is not an easy design problem to dovetail the electron system, the optical system, and the x-ray system, so that they do not interfere with each other, and yet so that each can operate at its maximum efficiency. The electron beam must, of course, be enclosed in a highly evacuated chamber, which provides further complications. The associated electronics must include controls for the electron lenses, the electron gun, the x-ray detector, and the vacuum pumps and gauges. The complete instrument is therefore large, complex, and expensive. In spite of this, it provides such a

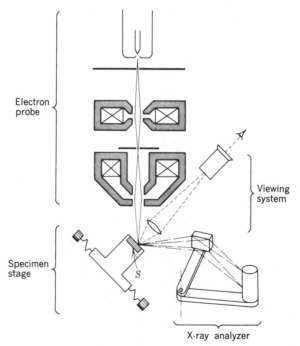

Electron probe

Viewing system

Specimen stage

S

X-ray analyzer

Figure 11-23 Schematic view of an electron-probe microanalyzer. (*Wiley.*[20])

wealth of information that a number of firms make such equipment. It is useful for phase studies in metallurgy and ceramics, for following the process of diffusion in the frabrication of semiconductor devices, for establishing the identity of impurities and inclusions, and for many other purposes.

PROBLEMS

11-1 What are the dimensions of the "constant" C in Eq. (11-5)?

11-2 A metallic sample is irradiated in an x-ray spectrometer with radiation from a tungsten target tube. The spectrometer is equipped with a calcite crystal for which the grating space is 302.9 pm. A strong line is observed at an angle $2\theta = 34°23'$. Calculate the wavelength of the observed x-ray and, from a handbook listing, determine what element must be present. (The spectrum is in the first order.)

11-3 The μ_m values for cobalt at several wavelengths are given as:

λ, pm	50.0	100.0	150.0	200.0	250.0	300.0
μ_m	15.5	110.0	345.0	87.0	177.0	270.0

The Ni $K\alpha$ radiation occurs at 150.0 pm. The density of cobalt is 8.9 g/cm³. The power of the Ni $K\alpha$ is approximately three times that of Ni $K\beta$ as emitted from the target. By plotting the absorption coefficient for cobalt, determine its value at the wavelengths of the Ni $K\alpha$ and Ni $K\beta$ radiations. With the data given above, and that in Table 11-1, determine the ratio of the two nickel radiations that will penetrate a cobalt foil of 0.005 mm thickness.

11-4 The wavelength of Ni $K\alpha$ radiation is 165.8 pm. (a) What is the energy content of each photon in kiloelectron volts? (b) Suppose that an ideal detector (i.e., one with 100 percent efficiency) shows 100 counts per second, corrected for background, in a particular instrument, when measuring Ni $K\alpha$ x-rays. Calculate the power delivered to the detector, in microwatts.

11-5 Steel wires for use in radial tires are customarily plated with brass to improve the adhesion of the rubber.[22] The manufacturer must monitor closely both the thickness of the brass layer and its copper content. Devise a procedure, based on x-ray fluorescence, for making both of these determinations.

11-6 Demonstrate the validity of the numerical factor 1240 in Eq. (11-1). Is Fig. 11-1 consistent with this value?

11-7 List some advantages and disadvantages of energy-dispersive and wavelength-dispersive x-ray spectrometers.

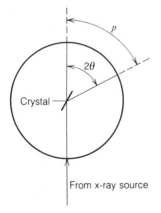

From x-ray source

Figure 11-24 Geometry of a Debye–Scherrer camera.

11-8 (*a*) The most precise way to measure the effective radius of a Debye–Scherrer camera is by calculation from the arc resulting from a crystal with known spacing and radiation of known wavelength. In a particular experiment, using Mo $K\alpha$ radiation ($\lambda = 70.90$ pm), the camera radius was determined from the x-ray diffracted by a sodium chloride crystal, with a spacing d given by handbook tables as 2.821 Å. The distance p measured on the film (see Fig. 11-24) was 1.50 cm. Calculate the camera radius.

Hint: Note that p bears the same relation to the circumference of the circle in the figure that the angle 2θ does to 360°.

(*b*) The same camera was used to measure the interplanar spacing in metallic aluminum. The angle 2θ observed was 20.32°. Calculate d, and compare with tabular values.

REFERENCES

1. H. P. Klug and L. E. Alexander, *X-Ray Diffraction Procedures*, Wiley, New York, **1954**.
2. A. H. Compton and S. K. Allison, *X-Rays in Theory and Experiment*, Van Nostrand, New York, **1935**.
3. G. Friedlander, J. W. Kennedy, E. S. Marcias, and J. M. Miller, *Nuclear and Radiochemistry*, 3d ed., Wiley-Interscience, New York, **1981**.
4. H. A. Liebhafsky, H. G. Pfeiffer, E. H. Winslow, and P. D. Zemany, *X-Rays, Electrons, and Analytical Chemistry*, Wiley-Interscience, New York, **1972**.
5. H. R. Bowman, E. K. Hyde, S. G. Thompson, and R. C. Jared, *Science*, **1966**, *151*, 562; T. Hall, *Science*, **1960**, *153*, 320; H. R. Bowman and E. K. Hyde, *Science*, **1966**, *153*, 321.
6. R. C. Vollmar, E. E. Petterson, and P. A. Petruzzelli, *Anal. Chem.*, **1949**, *21*, 1491.
7. L. H. Griffin, *Anal. Chem.*, **1962**, *34*, 606.
8. T. W. Bartlett, *Anal. Chem.*, **1951**, *23*, 705.
9. H. W. Dunn, *Anal. Chem.*, **1962**, *34*, 116.
10. R. Rudman, "X-Ray Diffraction Analysis," in *Topics in Chemical Instrumentation*, G. W. Ewing (ed.), Chem. Education Pub. Co., Easton, Pa., **1971**, p. 75.
11. W. Parrish, *Science*, **1949**, *110*, 368.
12. L. S. Birks and E. J. Brooks, *Anal. Chem.*, **1950**, *22*, 1017.
13. B. H. Vassos, R. F. Hirsch, and H. Letterman, *Anal. Chem.*, **1973**, *45*, 792.
14. D. E. Porter and R. Woldseth, *Anal. Chem.*, **1973**, *45*, 604A.
15. R. Woldseth, *X-Ray Energy Spectrometry*, Kevex Corp., Burlingame, Calif., **1973**.
16. K. F. J. Heinrich, D. E. Newbury, and R. L. Myklebust (eds.), *Energy Dispersive X-Ray Spectrometry*, NBS Special Publication 604, National Bureau of Standards, Washington, D.C., **1981**.
17. K. F. J. Heinrich, p. 1 of ref. 16.
18. V. F. Hanson, *Appl. Spectrosc.*, **1973**, *27*, 309.
19. S. D. Rasberry, *Appl. Spectrosc.*, **1973**, *27*, 102.
20. Yu. A. Surkov, O. P. Shcheglov, L. P. Moskalyeva, V. S. Kirichenko, A. D. Dudin, V. L. Gimadov, S. S. Kurochkin, and V. N. Rasputny, *Anal. Chem.*, **1982**, *54*, 957A.
21. D. B. Wittry, in *Treatise on Analytical Chemistry*, I. M. Kolthoff and P. J. Elving (eds.), pt. I, vol. 5, chap. 61; Wiley-Interscience, New York, **1964**.
22. R. L. M. van Lingen, H. E. C. Schuurs, G. J. Veenstra, J. M. B. Roes, and E. C. J. Loef, *Talanta*, **1980**, *27*, 641.

TWELVE

ELECTRON AND ION SPECTROSCOPY

Several different phenomena can result from the bombardment of a substance by energetic particles or photons. The primary process is the ejection of electrons from target atoms, which leaves vacancies. Following this, relaxation (i.e., return to the normal configuration) may follow either of two competing paths: characteristic x-rays may be emitted, or secondary (Auger†) electrons may be ejected. In the preceding chapter, the analytical significance of x-ray emission was explored; this chapter will demonstrate the importance of electron emissions.

Another useful technique arises from the bombardment of a target material by such positive ions as He^+ or Ar^+. In this case, the energy content of ions rebounding after elastic collisions gives a clue as to the nature of the target atoms. These various methods are summarized in Table 12-1.

Figure 12-1 is a generalized diagram of a heavy atom showing a series of electronic energy levels.[1] The outer segment consists of a continuous band containing valence electrons in molecular orbitals. Below this band are discrete levels occupied by the core electrons, those not directly involved in chemical bonding.

In the upper right portion of the diagram some radiation sources are listed that are capable of ejecting electrons at successive levels. The far-UV radiations from singly and doubly ionized helium can only remove valence electrons to produce ions. The soft Y $M\zeta$ x-ray‡ can cause ejection of outer core electrons, but more energetic radiation such as Al $K\alpha$ or Cr $K\alpha$ is required to reach the inner shells.

---

† Pronounced as in French: "oh-zhay."
‡ Yttrium M-zeta.

Table 12-1 Types of electron and ion spectroscopy

Excitation	Detection	Techniques†
X-ray	Electrons	AES, ESCA, IEE, PESIS, XPS
Far-UV	Electrons	PES, PESOS, UPS
Electrons	Electrons	AES, EIS, LEED, LEES
Ions	Scattered ions	ISS, SIMS

† Abbreviations:

AES: Auger electron spectroscopy
EIS: electron impact spectroscopy
ESCA: electron spectroscopy for chemical analysis
IEE: induced electron emission
ISS: ion scattering spectroscopy
LEED: low-energy electron diffraction
LEES: low-energy electron spectroscopy
PES: photoelectron spectroscopy

PESIS: photoelectron spectroscopy of inner shells
PESOS: photoelectron spectroscopy of outer shells
SIMS: secondary ionization mass spectroscopy
UPS: ultraviolet photoelectron spectroscopy
XPS: x-ray photoelectron spectroscopy

(Note that some of these designations are synonymous; SIMS is discussed in Chap. 22.)

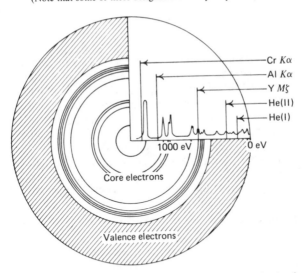

Figure 12-1 Schematic representation of electronic energy levels of an atom. The inset shows the regions that can be excited by several sources of radiation, having the following wavelengths and energies:

Cr $K\alpha$	0.2294 nm	5406.0 eV
Al $K\alpha$	0.8342 nm	1487.0 eV
Y $M\zeta$	9.34 nm	132.8 eV
He$_{II}$	30.38 nm	41.0 eV
He$_I$	58.44 nm	21.0 eV

(*Endeavour.*[1])

216

X-RAY PHOTOELECTRON SPECTROSCOPY (XPS)

This is the area commonly referred to as ESCA, though that designation should be of wider applicability. The energy relation in the ejection of a photoelectron by an x-ray can be expressed as

$$E_b = h\nu - (E_k + C) \tag{12-1}$$

E_b, called the *binding energy*, is defined as the energy of attraction between the electron and the atomic nucleus. This is the energy that must be overcome if the

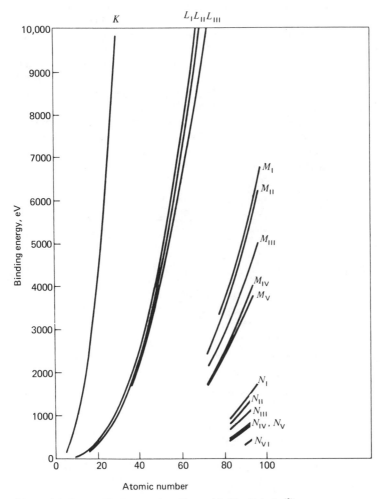

Figure 12-2 Electron binding energies. (*Chemical Rubber Pub. Co.*[3])

electron is to be ejected from the atom. Equation (12-1) shows the relation between the energy $h\nu$ of the x-ray photon and the measurable kinetic energy of the emerging electron. The quantity C is a corrective term depending on the properties of the particular spectrometer system.[2] The binding energy is specific for a given electron in a given element, and can serve for the identification of that element. Figure 12-2 shows a plot of binding energies that have been determined by XPS.[3] For light elements ($Z < 60$), two well-separated energy peaks are observed, corresponding to the K and L electrons. Above about 70 a more complex pattern of M and N electrons becomes evident.

Even though the electrons come from the inner core shells, their binding energies are measurably affected by the state of chemical combination (e.g., the oxidation state), as this changes the effective force field of the nucleus. Hence E_b exhibits a sensitivity to the molecular environment of the emitting atom, a *chemical shift*, amounting to a spread of up to about 10 eV for many elements. Thus sulfur ($Z = 16$), whose $2p$ electrons have a normal binding energy of 165 eV, can yield photoelectrons corresponding to binding energies from about 160 to 168 eV. Some of these chemical shifts are summarized in Fig. 12-3, taken from Hercules.[4] Similar correlation charts have been published for carbon and nitrogen.[4,5]

Two examples of photoelectron spectra, showing the variation in binding energy of electrons in different atoms of the same compound, are depicted in Fig. 12-4. The abscissas can be specified either as the binding energy itself, or as the chemical shifts relative to a convenient peak taken as a reference point. The relative

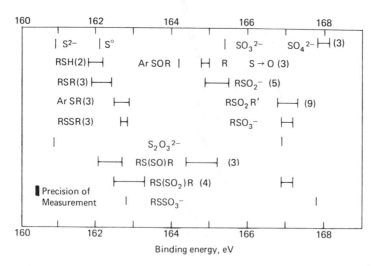

Figure 12-3 Correlation chart for sulfur $2p$ electron binding energies and functional groups. The bars indicate ranges of observed energies; the number of compounds used in the correlation is given in parentheses. (*Analytical Chemistry.*[4])

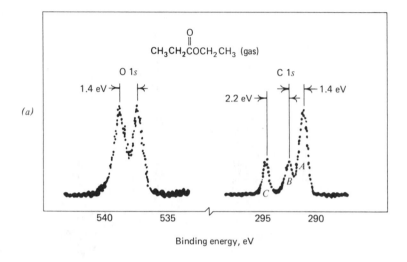

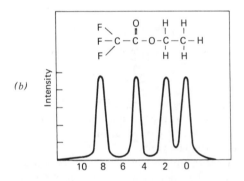

Figure 12-4 (*a*) Photoelectron spectrum of ethyl propionate; note the splitting of the oxygen and carbon 1*s* lines due to chemical shifts. (*b*) Carbon 1*s* electron spectrum of ethyl trifluoroacetate. Excitation is by monochromatic x-rays; the peaks correspond to the carbon atoms written above them. (*Endeavour.*[1])

areas beneath successive peaks give an approximate measure of the numbers of atoms in the molecule with the same chemical environment. The binding energies of 1*s* electrons in methyl and methylene carbons bound only to hydrogen and other carbon atoms is very nearly identical,[5] so the *A* peak in Fig. 12-4*a* can be identified as due to the first, second, and fifth carbon atoms in the formula. The other two peaks correspond to the two remaining carbons, both of which are bound to

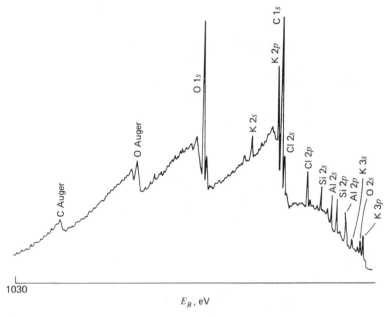

E_B, eV

Figure 12-5 XPS spectrum of elements in a lunar soil sample. Excitation is by Mg $K\alpha$ x-rays. (*American Laboratory.*[6])

oxygen. The atom responsible for a given peak can be decided only by correlations with other compounds, facilitated by the use of a chart of carbon chemical shifts. The two oxygen peaks in the figure are of equal size, as would be expected. The four peaks of Fig. 12-4b are all equal in area.

XPS, in common with other branches of electron spectroscopy, is essentially a *surface* tool, as the electrons have little chance of escape if they originate more than perhaps 5 nm below the surface of the sample. This makes it particularly valuable for a variety of applications involving surface properties. On the other hand, it can be applied to bulk samples only if the surface is representative of the bulk composition. In many materials, the surface can be etched away gradually by bombardment with such projectiles as ions of argon, so sources of such ions are sometimes built in to ESCA instruments. This allows the operator to examine the chemical species present at successive depths within a sample by running an electron spectrum after each short treatment with ions. We will return to this feature later.

XPS can be applied to many problems of structure determination or to the identification of compounds in either solid or gas phase. Two representative examples are shown in Figs. 12-5 and 12-6.[6] Details of other examples can be found in the literature.[2,4–6]

Quantitative analysis by means of XPS cannot be expected to give high precision, simply because there are so many variables that cannot readily be

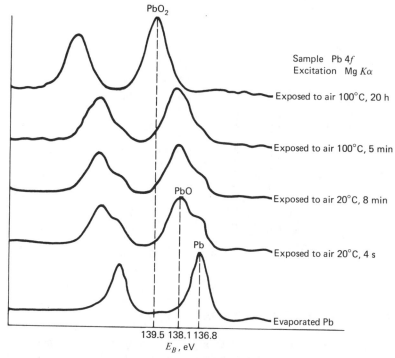

Figure 12-6 Chemical shifts in binding energy of the 4f electrons in lead, as oxide layers are formed on a clean sample. Excitation is Mg $K\alpha$ x-rays. (*American Laboratory*.[6])

controlled. Wagner[7] has published a detailed study, in which he has given separate consideration to each identifiable potential source of error. He concluded that the best that can be done at the present state of the art is about ± 10 percent standard deviation.

ULTRAVIOLET PHOTOELECTRON SPECTROSCOPY (UPS)

The major difference between spectroscopy of electrons ejected by far-UV radiation and by x-rays is the restriction indicated in Fig. 12-1: Only valence electrons can be observed by UPS. This provides an opportunity to obtain direct information about bonding, oxidation states, and molecular ionization potentials. However, association of spectral peaks with individual atoms may not be possible, because of delocalization of electrons in molecular orbitals. Simple molecules can be identified using UPS as a fingerprint technique. Figure 12-7 shows a UPS spectrum of air with its major constituents identified.[8] UPS does not seem to present an analytical tool comparable in versatility with XPS.[8,9]

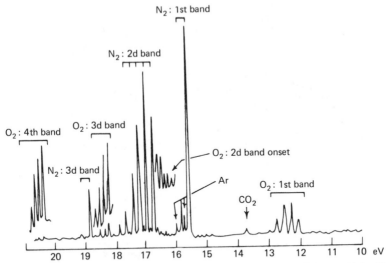

Figure 12-7 Photoelectron spectrum of air. Portions are shown rerun at higher sensitivity. (*Analytical Chemistry.*[8])

ELECTRON IMPACT SPECTROSCOPY (EIS)

A diagram similar to Fig. 12-1 representing excitation by electron bombardment would show that, just as with electromagnetic irradiation, the energy of the primary beam determines the depth of penetration into the target atoms. Low-energy incident electrons generally result in the promotion of valence electrons from ground to excited states (contrasted with UPS, where ions are usually produced). This phenomenon is the basis of *electron-impact spectroscopy*. High-energy electrons induce the Auger effect to be discussed in the next section.

In EIS, the energy required to promote a valence electron is conveniently measured by observing the *decrease* in kinetic energy of the incident electrons as they are scattered by the molecules. Only gaseous samples can be handled in presently available equipment, and only forward-scattered electrons can be detected. The resulting information concerns the energy differences between ground and excited states, particularly with respect to vibrational and rotational energy levels. The method thus complements both IR and Raman spectroscopy. At least in theory, all levels can be observed up to the availably energy; there are no selection rules to forbid some transitions. A considerable potential for analytical usefulness is indicated; the determination of CO in air down to about 50 ppm has been reported,[10] but the ultimate limit of detection is undoubtedly much lower.

AUGER ELECTRON SPECTROSCOPY (AES)

When a core electron is ejected, whether it be by action of an incident x-ray or an energetic electron, an electron from a higher level will drop in to fill the vacancy.

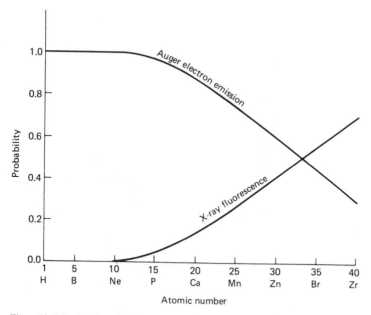

Figure 12-8 Probability of emission of Auger electrons and of fluorescence x-rays, as a function of atomic number. (*Analytical Chemistry.*[4])

The energy released by this transition is sufficient to remove another electron from the same shell in the atom. Thus if a K electron is ejected in the primary event, one L electron may take its place in the K shell, while at the same time a second L electron is ejected from the atom. This is the *Auger effect*. In Fig. 12-8 the probabilities of this process and of x-ray fluorescence taking place are plotted against the atomic number.[4] This shows that Auger spectroscopy is of most value for the light elements, just the area where we have seen that x-ray fluorescence breaks down.

The kinetic energy E_A of an Auger electron from the L shell is given by

$$E_A = (E_K - E_L) - E_L \qquad (12\text{-}2)$$

where E_K and E_L are the binding energies of electrons in the K and L shells. The quantity $(E_K - E_L)$ is the energy released by the electron as it falls from the L to the K shell; the second E_L is the energy required to remove the Auger electron from the L level. Since these terms all describe properties of the atom itself, the Auger energy is independent of the energy of the primary radiation, whereas by Eq. (12-1), the kinetic energy of photoelectrons changes if the source of the primary beam is altered. Figure 12-9 shows this effect for a sample irradiated with x-rays from two different targets.[6] The *derivative* of the signal rather than the signal itself is often recorded, in order to discriminate against the considerable background due to random scattering of electrons.

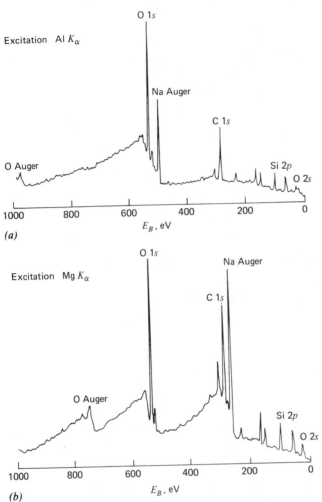

Figure 12-9 X-ray induced photoelectron spectra of a sample of glass with two different sources of radiation. Auger peaks are readily identified by their changed locations on the binding energy scale. (*American Laboratory.*[6])

As Fig. 12-9 demonstrates, Auger peaks are seen in XPS as well as in electron-generated spectra. The latter, however, are more satisfactory if Auger spectra alone are desired. Figure 12-10 indicates that the energy of Auger lines can be used to identify low atomic-weight elements.[11]

Differentiation between compounds depends on a chemical shift that is quite different from that seen in XPS. Wagner et al.[12] have pointed out that a judicious combination of information from XPS and Auger studies can greatly enhance the

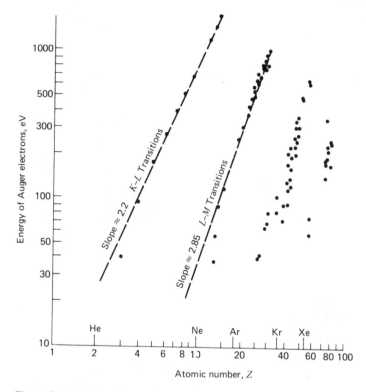

Figure 12-10 Energies of Auger electrons as a function of the atomic number. (*Journal of Applied Physics.*[11])

sensitivity of either alone with respect to the state of chemical combination. They have defined a parameter (designated by α') that is the sum of the kinetic energy of the Auger electron and the binding energy of the photoelectron. This parameter is independent of the energy of the exciting photon. Figure 12-11 is an example of the many plots presented in their paper. The binding energy is plotted (decreasing) on the abscissa, the Auger energy on the ordinate axis. Diagonal lines are constant in α'. Each rectangle corresponds to a particular compound, the dimensions of the rectangle approximating the precision of measurement.

Figure 12-12 gives an example of surface analysis by Auger spectroscopy.[13] (Note the derivative nature of the curves.) The sample is a silicon plate on which a film of nichrome has been deposited. Before treatment with an ion beam to etch away the surface, the largest concentration of atoms was oxygen. After removal of a 10-nm layer, oxygen had nearly disappeared, and chromium and nickel were evident, while at 20 nm these also were nearly gone, and only silicon could be seen. It is apparent that some CO_2 had been adsorbed on the nichrome surface.

Auger studies on gases have also been reported.[14]

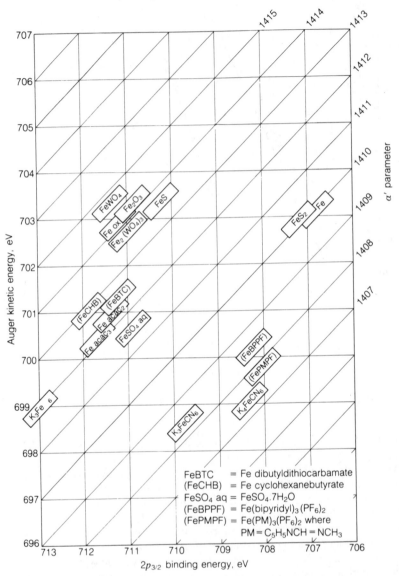

Figure 12-11 Correlation chart between Auger energy and photoelectron binding energy, showing the α′ parameter of Wagner et al. Note the grouping together of various compounds that have a similar type of bonding to the iron atom. The compound FeS_2 is electrically conductive and hardly distinguishable spectroscopically from metallic iron. (*Analytical Chemistry*.[12])

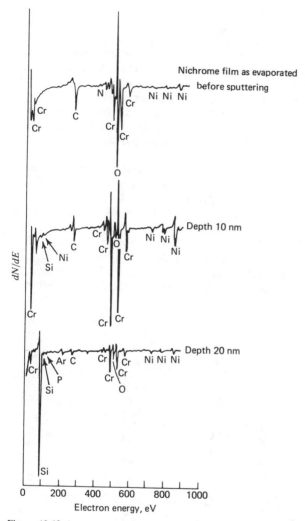

Figure 12-12 Auger spectra taken at various depths into a 15-nm film of nichrome on a substrate of silicon. (*Journal of Vacuum Science and Technology.*[13])

INSTRUMENTATION

An electron spectrometer must contain the following components: (1) a source of radiation with which to excite the sample; (2) an energy analyzer; (3) an electron detector; and (4) a high-vacuum system. The entire apparatus must also be shielded from the earth's magnetic field. In addition, many instruments are provided with an ion-bombardment gun and other accessories.

Radiation Sources

The source of radiation is either an x-ray tube, an electron gun, or a helium discharge lamp. It is important that the radiation be energetically homogeneous. As x-ray sources, aluminum- or magnesium-targeted tubes can often be used without a monochromator, because of the high intensity and narrow wavelength bands of the $K\alpha$ lines of these light elements. An aluminum window on a tube with an aluminum target acts as a filter to remove the $K\beta$ line and much of the background.[15] One commercial instrument (Hewlett–Packard) includes a Rowland-circle crystal monochromator, even though it reduces the available intensity.

Likewise, electron-beam excitation can be used either with or without a monochromator. Electrons from a heated cathode, accelerated by an electric field, are fairly homogeneous, but have some spread owing to the fact that they are emitted from the cathode with a range of kinetic energies. If it is desirable to obtain a greater degree of homogeneity, an energy filter may be employed, several forms of which are shown in Fig. 12-13. In the system in (a), the electrons are subjected to a retarding field between the two grids; only those with sufficient energy to overcome the field can escape to the right. This is essentially a high-pass filter, in that there is a lower but not an upper limit to the energy of the emerging electrons.

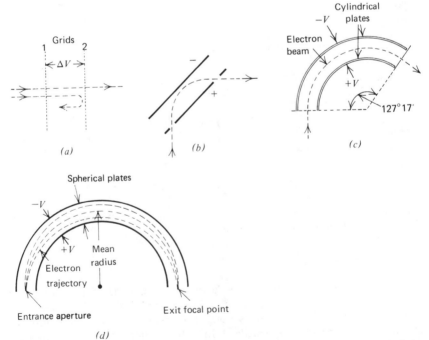

Figure 12-13 Energy filters: (a) retarding field, (b) parallel plates, (c) cylindrical, and (d) spherical.

In form (*b*), the electron beam enters at a 45° angle into the space between two parallel plane conductors; only those within a specified narrow energy band will emerge through the second slit. The energy band is determined by the distance between the plates and by the impressed potential.

If the electrodes are made cylindrical instead of planar, as in (*c*), not only will good energy discrimination be obtained, but in addition electrons entering the filter at a slightly divergent angle will be focused on an exit slit. The angle 127.28° ($=\pi/\sqrt{2}$ radians) is required to obtain this double-focusing effect.[9] The modification in (*d*) uses 180° hemispherical, rather than 127° cylindrical, segments as electrodes. The focusing properties are nearly as good, and a larger fraction of the electron beam can be accepted.

The special discharge tubes to give He_I and He_{II} resonance radiation for UPS studies are described by Brundle.[9]

Energy Analyzers

The energy analyzer (monochromator) between sample and detector has a more stringent efficiency requirement than the filters described above (Fig. 12-13), since the electron beam is orders of magnitude less intense.

Retarding field analyzers (Fig. 12-13*a*) have been used, but geometric restrictions are needed to ensure that all electrons are moving normal to the grid. Magnetic deflection analyzers (Fig. 12-14*a*) are effective, but less convenient to design and use than the electrostatic types.[4] The nonuniform magnetic field employed provides double focusing at 254.93° ($=\pi\sqrt{2}$ radians).

The most widely used monochromators utilize either cylindrical or spherical electrostatic fields. The cylindrical type is an extension of the filter of Fig. 12-13*b* (not *c*), as though the plane electrodes were bent into a cylinder about the line joining input and output slits. This is shown in Fig. 12-14*b*. From the theory of this analyzer,[16] it appears that optimum focus will be obtained with the angle between the electron beam and the axis of symmetry within a few degrees of 42.3°. Practical designs accept electrons in an annular cone of several degrees spread around this value. The spherical analyzer (Fig. 12-15) is an extension of the filter of Fig. 12-13*d*, making use of a nearly complete sphere.

Detectors

Though not the only possible detection device, the electron multiplier is almost universally employed because of its sensitivity and convenience. There are several varieties of electron multipliers; one is similar to the photomultiplier described in Chap. 3, but constructed to receive electrons directly instead of from a photocathode. Just as with photomultipliers, the system of dynodes can be arranged in many different patterns. Another widely used form, the *channel electron multiplier* (Fig. 12-16) is constructed from a small, curved, glass tube. The inner surface is coated with a high-resistance conducting material, connected to a source of 2 to 3 kV, that acts as a combination of a continuous dynode and a resistive voltage divider. This device accepts electrons at one end and emits more electrons at the

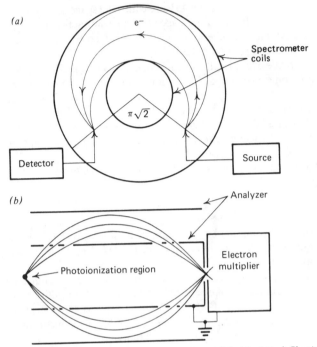

Figure 12-14 Electron energy analyzers: (*a*) magnetic (*Analytical Chemistry*,[4]) and (*b*) cylindrical electrostatic.

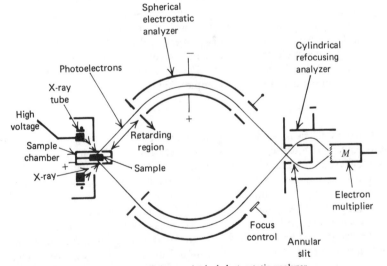

Figure 12-15 An instrument containing a spherical electrostatic analyzer.

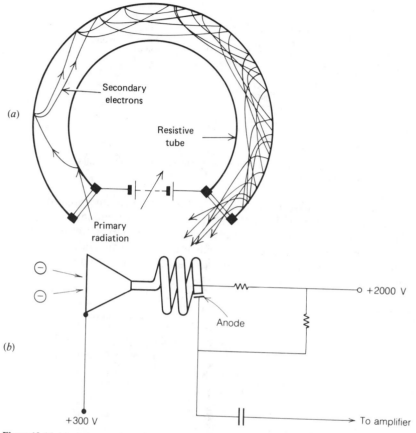

Figure 12-16 (*a*) electron trajectories in a channel multiplier. (*b*) a channel electron multiplier, with electrical connections for pulse counting (*Galileo Electro-Optics Corporation.*)

other, acting as a current amplifier. It has a gain up to 10^8, and very fast response, so that it can count individual electrons.

The associated electronics can be designed either to take data from the multiplier in conventional analog form, or to count pulses with digital circuitry. In the latter option, repetitive scans can be made and the data stored in a multichannel analyzer (see Chap. 11).

Auxiliary Systems

The trajectories of electrons are easily distorted by stray magnetic fields, including that of the earth, so that electron spectrometers must be magnetically isolated. One way to do this is to enclose the sensitive regions in a shield of high-permeability ferromagnetic material. Another way is through the use of *Helmholtz*

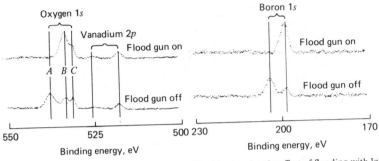

Figure 12-17 Electron spectrum of vanadium diboride, showing the effect of flooding with low-energy electrons. (*Hewlett-Packard.*[17])

coils, which are adjusted to produce a field exactly equal and opposite to the naturally occurring field. The latter system can be made automatic. A magnetometer probe is placed in the vicinity of the spectrometer and connected electrically to modify the current in the Helmholtz coils as needed to maintain a zero net field. Thus even transient magnetic events, such as caused by the operation of an elevator motor, can be rendered harmless.

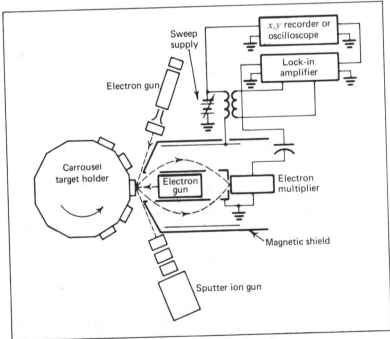

Figure 12-18 Schematic layout of the electron optics and electronics for an Auger electron spectrometer. (*Physical Electronics Div., Perkin–Elmer Corporation.*)

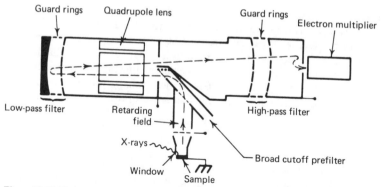

Figure 12-19 Electron optics of an ESCA spectrometer. (*E. I. Du Pont de Nemours & Co.*)

A source of difficulty in XPS and UPS is the *sample charging* effect. As electrons are expelled from the sample, a positive charge remains. If the sample is electrically conducting and in contact with the metal parts of the spectrometer, the positive charge cannot accumulate, but if the sample is an insulator, the charge will quickly build up to the point where electrons are prevented from leaving. In this event the observed signal is diminished, and scattered electrons, which are always present to a greater or lesser extent, are attracted to the sample, until an equilibrium is attained. This charging effect can be very serious. It is overcome by including in the instrument a source of low-energy electrons to flood the sample. This can actually result in additional useful information. Figure 12-17 shows two portions of a spectrum of vanadium diboride that has been exposed to air.[17] The $1s$ electrons of boron show two peaks when the flood gun is turned off, but only one (the area equalling the sum of the other two) with the gun on. This is interpreted to mean that there is only one kind of boron present, but that about two-thirds of its atoms are electrically insulated from the bulk of the sample. The vanadium peaks ($2p$) show no change with the gun on or off, but the changes in the $1s$ peaks of oxygen are taken to show that the peak marked C is due to atoms linked to vanadium, while the A and B oxygens are bound to boron.

The high-vacuum system is conventional, with either an oil-diffusion pump or an ion pump backed up by a mechanical forepump. In some instruments, particularly those for gaseous samples, two sets of pumps are required, so that the pressure in the analyzer can be held as low as possible (1 μPa $\cong 10^{-8}$ torr is typical), while that in the sample area can be perhaps 100 times greater.

Figures 12-15, 12-18, and 12-19 show diagrammatically three commercial electron spectrometers, with energy analyzers of contrasting designs.

ION-SCATTERING SPECTROSCOPY (ISS)

In the bombardment of a solid sample by a beam of positive ions, elastic collisions with target atoms occur, from which the ions rebound in random directions, the recoil energy being absorbed by the bulk of the sample. If the kinetic energy of the incident ions is sufficient, atoms of the target will be driven away from the solid surface. Removal of surface atoms in this manner is known as *sputtering*, and is the mechanism for producing a clean surface for ESCA studies, as already noted.

It is possible to collect the sputtered atoms and determine their masses in a small, dedicated, mass spectrometer, but of greater interest in the present discussion, because of its similarity to ESCA, is the examination of the scattered ions. The energy E of a scattered ion is given in terms of the energy E_0 of the ion before impact by the relation

$$E = E_0 \frac{M_s - M_0}{M_s + M_0} \tag{12-3}$$

where M_s and M_0 are, respectively, the masses of the surface atom and the incident ion. This is valid only if $M_0 < M_s$. The energy E is most sensitive to small differences in M_s if M_0 is only slightly smaller than M_s, so it is advantageous to be able to select ions from a variety of gases. The noble gases, He and Ar especially, are most frequently chosen in the interests of avoiding side reactions.

The diagram for an ISS instrument is shown in Fig. 12-20. Ions are formed by bombarding gas atoms with electrons. The positive ions are accelerated and focused on the sample at an angle of 45°. Ions are scattered in all directions, but only those in a selected small angle are admitted to the 127° electrostatic analyzer. The detector can be a solid-state (Si) device. A channel electron multiplier can be used, since energetic ions will cause release of electrons within the channel. Detailed descriptions of two instruments can be found in Refs. (18) and (19).

A representative scattered-ion spectrum is shown in Fig. 12-21.[19] The sample was crystalline silicon coated with a thin gold film. Note that with H^+ ions the several peaks are crowded together toward the high-energy end of the spectrum

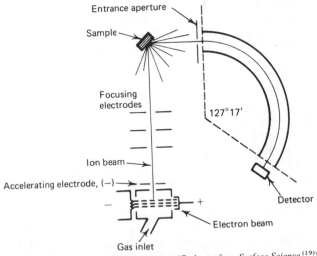

Figure 12-20 Ion-scattering spectrometer. (*Redrawn from Surface Science.*[19])

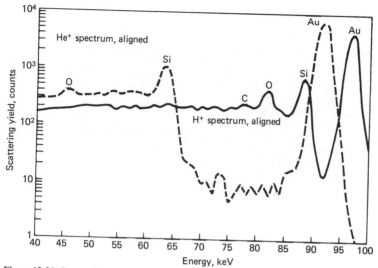

Figure 12-21 Comparison of back-scattering spectra for 100-keV He$^+$ and H$^+$ ions on a silicon surface coated with gold; —— H$^+$, - - - He$^+$. (*Surface Science*.[19])

relative to the analogous peaks with He$^+$ ions, as would be predicted qualitatively by Eq. (12-3). The designation "aligned" refers to the fact that, with these small ions, the sample can be oriented so that the ion beam penetrates a significant distance through aligned channels in the crystal structure. [The actual energies recorded in Fig. 12-21 are slightly lower than Eq. (12-3) predicts, because ions were collected at an angle of 120° from the forward direction, rather than 90°.]

PROBLEMS

12-1 Cr $K\alpha$, the most energetic source listed in Fig. 12-1, is also the *least* energetic of the x-rays included in Table 11-1. Can you suggest why shorter wavelength x-rays (such as Co $K\alpha$ or Mo $K\alpha$) are not often utilized in ESCA?

12-2 Reconcile the statement that the energy of Auger electrons is independent of the primary radiation with the change in positions of the Auger lines in Fig. 12-9. The wavelengths are Al $K\alpha = 832.0$ pm and Mg $K\alpha = 987.0$ pm.

12-3 In an ESCA experiment, Cr $K\alpha$ x-rays (wavelength 2.294 Å) caused the ejection of electrons from a calcium compound. The measured kinetic energy, E_k, was 1.201 keV. The constant C of Eq. (12-1) can be taken as 4.5 eV. Calculate the value of the binding energy, E_b, for these electrons in the calcium atom.

REFERENCES

1. K. Siegbahn, *Endeavour*, **1973**, *32*, 51.
2. T. L. James, *J. Chem. Educ.*, **1971**, *48*, 712.
3. J. A. Bearden and A. F. Burr, in *CRC Handbook of Chemistry and Physics*, 50th ed., p. E-185, Chemical Rubber Publishing Co., **1967–1970**; quoted from *Rev. Mod. Phys.*, **1967**, *39*, 125.

4. D. M. Hercules, *Anal. Chem.*, **1970**, *42(1)*, 20A.
5. W. E. Swartz, Jr., *Anal. Chem.*, **1973**, *45*, 788A.
6. J. F. Rendina, *Am. Lab.*, **1972**, *4(2)*, 17.
7. C. D. Wagner, *Anal. Chem.*, **1977**, *49*, 1282.
8. D. Betteridge and A. D. Baker, *Anal. Chem.*, **1970**, *42(1)*, 43A.
9. C. R. Brundle, *Appl. Spectrosc.*, **1971**, *25*, 8.
10. R. E. Grojean and J. F. Rendina, *Anal. Chem.*, **1971**, *43*, 162.
11. L. A. Harris, *J. Appl. Phys.*, **1968**, *39*, 1419.
12. C. D. Wagner, L. H. Gale, and R. H. Raymond, *Anal. Chem.*, **1979**, *51*, 466.
13. P. W. Palmberg, *J. Vac. Sci. Technol.*, **1972**, *9*, 160.
14. M. Thompson, P. A. Hewitt, and D. S. Wooliscroft, *Anal. Chem.*, **1976**, *48*, 1336.
15. C. A. Lucchesi and J. E. Lester, *J. Chem. Educ.*, **1973**, *50*, A205, A269.
16. H. Z. Sar-el, *Rev. Sci. Instrum.*, **1967**, *38*, 1210.
17. M. A. Kelly and C. E. Tyler, *Hewlett-Packard J.*, **1973**, *24(11)*, 2.
18. R. F. Goff and D. P. Smith, *J. Vac. Sci. Technol.*, **1970**, *7*, 72.
19. T. M. Buck and G. H. Wheatley, *Surf. Sci.*, **1972**, *33*, 35.

THIRTEEN
MAGNETIC RESONANCE SPECTROSCOPY

A radically different type of interaction between matter and electromagnetic forces can be observed by subjecting a sample simultaneously to two magnetic fields, one stationary, and the other varying at some radiofrequency (RF). At particular combinations of fields, energy is absorbed by the sample, and the absorption can be observed as a change in the signal developed by an RF amplifier and detector.

The energy absorption can be related to the magnetic dipole nature of spinning nuclei. Quantum theory tells us that nuclei are characterized by a spin quantum number I which can have positive values of $n/2$ (in units of $\hbar$),† where n can take the values 0, 1, 2, ... If $I = 0$, the nucleus does not spin, and hence cannot be observed by the method considered here; this applies to ^{12}C, ^{16}O, and ^{32}S, among others. Maximum resolution in the spectra is obtained with nuclides for which $I = 1/2$, including ^1H, ^{19}F, ^{31}P, ^{13}C, ^{29}Si, and others. The first three of these are easily observed because they constitute substantially 100 percent in natural abundance, whereas the others contribute less than 5 percent to their elements.

The spinning nuclei simulate tiny magnets, and so interact with the externally impressed magnetic field H. It might be supposed that they would all line up with the field like so many compass needles, but instead their rotary motion causes them to precess, like a gyroscope in a gravitational field. According to quantum mechanics, there are $2I + 1$ possible orientations, and hence energy levels, which

† $\hbar = h/2\pi$, where h is Planck's constant.

means that the proton, for example, has two such levels. The energy difference between them is given by

$$\Delta E = \frac{\mu H}{I} \qquad (13\text{-}1)$$

where μ is the magnetic moment of the spinning nucleus. Energy will be absorbed from an RF field of frequency v if the condition $hv = \Delta E$ is fulfilled. This characteristic frequency is the precession frequency of the dipoles, and is called the *Larmor frequency*. It is convenient to introduce ω, the angular frequency of precession, which is equal to $2\pi v$. The above relations can be combined to give the expression

$$\frac{\omega}{H} = \frac{2\pi\mu}{hI} = \frac{\mu}{\hbar I} = \gamma \qquad (13\text{-}2)$$

The ratio ω/H is a fundamental constant characteristic of any nuclear species that has a nonzero value of I. This is called the *magnetogyric ratio* (or sometimes the *gyromagnetic ratio*), and is given the symbol γ.

At a frequency of 100 MHz (one of the commonly used values), the energy difference ΔE is about 10^{-2} cal·mol^{-1}, which means that the RF oscillator need not be very powerful, though the detector must be quite sensitive.

Another effect of the imposed RF field at the Larmor frequency is to cause all the spinning nuclei to precess *in phase*. Thus we have a multitude of nuclear oscillators which, according to electromagnetic theory, must radiate energy, and since they are all in phase with each other they will act as a *coherent* source. Their radiation can be picked up by another coil in the neighborhood of the sample, if it is positioned with its axis mutually perpendicular to the oscillator coil and the fixed field.

There are two major types of spectrometer for the observation and measurement of nuclear magnetic resonance (NMR). In the simpler of these, either the absorption of energy or the emission of resonant radiation is measured while the magnetic field is swept through the point of resonance. The second type of instrument makes use of Fourier-transform techniques to obtain a much greater signal-to-noise ratio. We will consider these types in turn.

SCANNING NMR SPECTROMETERS

Introductory Experiment

Let us consider the single-coil NMR spectrometer of Fig. 13-1, containing a borosilicate glass tube filled with distilled water. The RF oscillator is set at 5 MHz, and the magnetic field varied at a constant rate from 0 to about 1 T,† while the output of the detector is monitored. The resulting recorder trace will resemble

---

† The SI unit of magnetic flux density (field strength) is the *tesla* (T), which corresponds to 10^4 gauss.

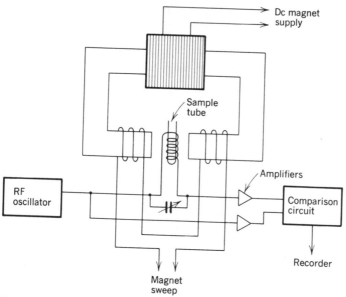

Figure 13-1 A single-coil scanning NMR spectrometer.

Fig. 13-2, with resonance maxima corresponding to each isotope present for which $I > 0$. The indicated field values correspond to the gyromagnetic ratios at $v = 5$ MHz. The copper peaks result from the wire of the RF coil, and the others from the various elements present in the water and glass. Clearly this provides the possibility of effective qualitative analysis. Quantitative measurements are also possible, through integration of the areas beneath the peaks.

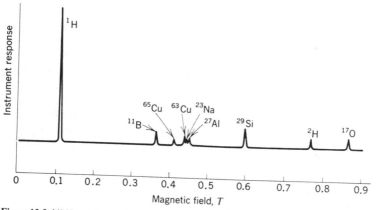

Figure 13-2 NMR spectrum of a sample of water in a borosilicate glass tube, taken on a low-dispersion spectrometer at a frequency of 5 MHz. (*Varian Associates.*)

An instrument capable of performing an experiment of this type is called a *wide-line* or *low-resolution* NMR spectrometer. Its potential as an analytical tool has not been widely exploited, partly, no doubt, because of its inability to sense. nuclei for which $I = 0$. It has found some use in investigations of the physical environment of nuclei, including certain crystal parameters in solids.

HIGH-RESOLUTION NMR

In analytical practice, NMR finds its greatest utility if restricted to the study of the fine structure in the resonance of a single nuclear species; an instrument for this purpose is a *high-resolution* NMR spectrometer. Some instruments are designed only for the study of hydrogen nuclei (protons), whereas others are capable of observing fluorine or phosphorus as well.

In the preceding discussion it was assumed that the nucleus under consideration is actually subjected to the full measured intensity of the applied magnetic field. If this were strictly true, then only a single peak would be seen, resulting from resonance with all the atoms of the selected isotope in the sample, as in a wide-line instrument. This is only a rough approximation to the truth, however. Observations with a high-resolution spectrometer show that the resonance of a particular isotope can be resolved into a series of closely spaced peaks. Two types of fine structure can be observed, known respectively as the chemical shift and spin-spin coupling.

For convenience, we will first discuss proton resonances, as they are the most widely known and utilized, then we will see what modifications to both theory and instrumentation are needed to study other nuclei, particularly ^{13}C.

THE CHEMICAL SHIFT

Every nucleus in a compound is surrounded by a cloud of electrons which are in constant motion. Under the influence of the applied magnetic force these electrons are caused to circulate in such a sense as to oppose the field. This has the effect of partially shielding the nucleus from feeling the full value of the external field. Therefore, either the frequency or the field will have to be changed slightly to bring the shielded nucleus into resonance. In most instruments this is accomplished by an adjustment of the magnetic field by means of direct current passed through an auxiliary winding. This auxiliary current is varied linearly to sweep the field over a narrow span (less than 100 μT per tesla of field, i.e., 100 ppm). The electronic circuitry converts the value of the added field to its frequency equivalent for presentation to the recorder.

This *chemical shift*, usually designated by δ, is the ratio of the change of field necessary to achieve resonance to the field strength that resonates with a standard:

$$\delta = \frac{H_{sample} - H_{ref}}{H_{ref}} \tag{13-3}$$

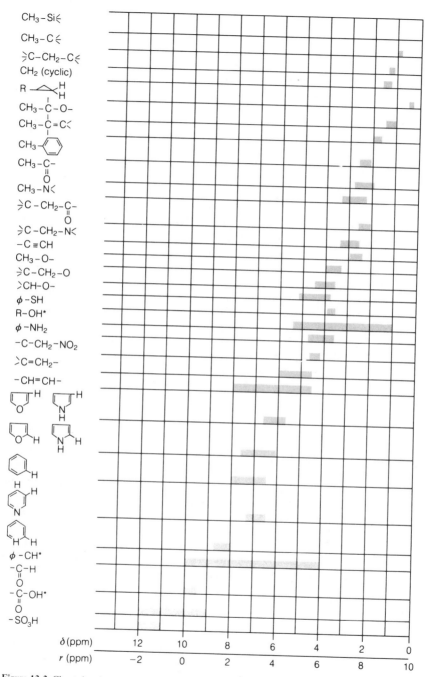

Figure 13-3 Chart showing ranges of proton chemical shifts for various molecular environments.

The chemical shift is thus a dimensionless quantity, usually expressed in ppm. The magnitude of the shift required to bring a proton into resonance depends upon its immediate chemical environment, since this determines the shielding by electrons.

Since we cannot observe the resonance of a test-tube full of protons without any shielding electrons, there is no absolute standard with which to compare shifts, and an arbitrary comparison standard must be adopted. For this purpose a small amount of tetramethylsilane (TMS), $(CH_3)_4Si$, is commonly added as an internal standard. This compound has two favorable features that account for its selection: all its 12 hydrogen atoms are in an identical environment, and they are more strongly shielded than the protons in most purely organic compounds. The position of TMS on the scale of chemical shifts is arbitrarily assigned the value of 0. Some authors prefer to give TMS the value 10 and to denote the shift by τ, where $\tau = 10 - \delta$. Greater shielding corresponds to an "upfield" chemical shift; that is, the field must be increased to compensate for the shielding. Hence δ decreases with increased shielding, whereas τ increases.

Figure 13-3 shows the approximate ranges of both δ and τ for protons in various chemical environments.[1] The exact values depend to a large degree on substituent effects, solvent, concentration, hydrogen bonding, etc., but are reproducible for any given set of conditions.

Samples for NMR spectra are usually examined in solution. Choice of solvents is limited to those that do not have protons that would complicate the spectra. For organic materials, solvents completely lacking in protons are selected wherever possible. Suitable choices are CCl_4 or CS_2 or perdeuterated solvents such as $CDCl_3$ (deuterochloroform), C_6D_6 (perdeuterobenzene), or D_2O (heavy water).

SPIN-SPIN COUPLING

The second type of structure frequently observed in NMR spectra is due to the interaction of the spin of a proton with that of another proton or protons attached to an adjacent carbon. The interaction involves the spins of the bonding electrons of all three bonds (H—C, C—C, and C—H), but we need not be concerned with the detailed mechanism. If the protons are in equivalent environments, the interaction will not be observed, but otherwise the maxima at each chemical shift position will be split into a close multiplet.

As an example, consider the spectrum of ethyl iodide dissolved in $CDCl_3$ with added TMS (Fig. 13-4). The high-resolution spectrum is shown by the solid curve. The dashed line is an auxiliary trace plotted by a built-in integrator; the height of each step is a measure of the area beneath the corresponding portion of the main curve. The multiplet at $\delta = 3.2$ is produced by the two methylene protons, that at 1.8 by the three protons of the methyl group. The areas beneath the curve, integrated over each complete multiplet, are determined by the number of identical protons; in this case they are in the ratio of 2:3, as would be predicted. The peak at $\delta = 0$ is due to the added TMS. The small pip at $\delta = 7.25$ is caused by a residual impurity of $CHCl_3$ in the solvent.

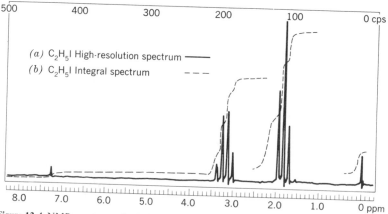

Figure 13-4 NMR spectrum of ethyl iodide dissolved in deuterochloroform (CDCl₃): (a) normal spectrum, (b) integral spectrum. (*Courtesy of R. F. Hirsch.*)

The methylene resonance is split into a quadruplet in the approximate ratio of 1:3:3:1. These magnitudes are the result of the possible orientations of the spins of the three *methyl* protons: there is an equal probability of their all being lined up *with* the field, which we may denote by ⇄, or *against* it, ⇆, but it is three times as probable that two will face one way and one the other ⇌ ⇌ ⇄, and similarly ⇄ ⇄ ⇄. Thus there are two possible alignments with the field, and two opposed to the field. This results in four peaks, in a 1:3:3:1 ratio, straddling the position that would have been occupied by an unsplit peak. By analogous reasoning, it can be shown that the two methylene protons should cause the splitting of the methyl resonance in a 1:2:1 ratio. It can be seen from the figure that the predicted intensity ratios are not exactly followed. The multiplets that are related to each other can often be identified by noting that they are unsymmetrical; the peaks of each set that are closer to the other are larger than those that are farther away, as can be seen in Fig. 13-4. The closer together the chemical shifts, the more marked is this effect.

The spacings between the components of both multiplets are all equal and designated by a *coupling constant J* with units of frequency. *J* is typically between 1 and 20 Hz.

INSTRUMENTATION FOR NMR

The requirements for the design of high-resolution NMR spectrometers are quite severe. If the closest peaks to be resolved are separated by unit *J* value, the magnetic field must be homogeneous to 1 part in 10⁸ for a 100-MHz spectrometer. In order to assure a sufficiently uniform magnetic field, the pole pieces must be much larger than the area actually occupied by the sample probe. Even the most carefully machined magnet cannot equal these requirements, so specially shaped

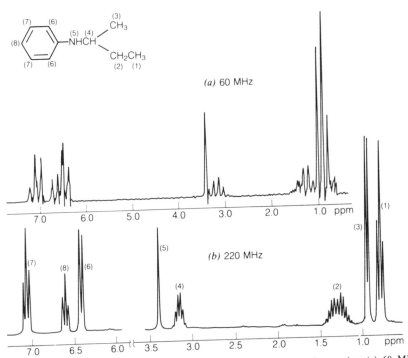

Figure 13-5 Proton NMR spectra of N-*sec*-butylaniline taken at two frequencies: (*a*) 60 MHz ($H = 1.4$ T); (*b*) 220 MHz (5.2 T). (*Science*.[2])

auxiliary windings called *shimming coils* are powered with adjustable dc to counter-act any residual inhomogeneity. The field felt by the nuclei of the sample may still have some lack of uniformity originating in the sample itself; the effect of this can largely be eliminated by spinning the sample probe by means of a small air turbine.

The RF excitation is derived from a stable, crystal-controlled oscillator and fed to the probe coils and the receiver through coaxial cables.

The resolution obtainable increases with increase in the magnetic field and hence the RF frequency. The least expensive high-resolution spectrometers commonly manufactured operate at 60 MHz ($H = 1.409$ T for protons), the next higher class at 100 MHz ($H = 2.350$ T). Premium instruments may go as high as 600 MHz (14.4 T).† Figure 13-5 illustrates the significantly improved resolution of a 220-MHz instrument compared to one operating at 60 MHz. In many spectrom-eter models, provision is made for operation at lower frequencies to match the magnetic field to the resonances of other nuclei. Table 13-1 gives the frequencies for a number of nuclei for which $I = \frac{1}{2}$, together with other pertinent data.

† Magnets above about 2.5 T are constructed of superconducting materials and operated at liquid helium temperature.

Table 13-1 NMR data for selected isotopes for which $I = \frac{1}{2}$

Isotope	Natural abundance	γ rad$\cdot$T$^{-1}\cdot$s^{-1}	ν (MHz) $H = 1.409$ T	ν (MHz) $H = 2.350$ T
^{1}H	99.98	2.68	60.0	100.0
^{13}C	1.11	0.675	15.1	25.2
^{19}F	100.0	2.520	56.5	94.2
^{29}Si	4.70	0.531	11.9	19.9
^{31}P	100.0	1.086	24.3	40.5

Frequency Lock

An automatic circuit to maintain a constant field-to-frequency ratio is essential in a high-resolution NMR spectrometer. It uses a frequency-controlling feedback circuit that locks onto some specific nuclear resonance and continually adjusts the RF oscillator to keep the reference signal maximized. Without this automatic control, the performance of the instrument would be adversely affected by extraneous magnetic events in the vicinity, such as operation of electrical machinery.

In most instruments the reference signal is taken from a nucleus in the sample itself (*internal lock*), often TMS, which then serves a dual role, being a standard for both chemical shifts and frequency locking. Some instruments provide for an *external lock*, in which the reference material is located in a separate probe, mounted close to that of the analytical sample. The external lock has the advantage that control is not interrupted during change of samples, and the disadvantage that the reference and analytical samples may not sense exactly equal magnetic fields; it provides greater convenience at the expense of precision. Another choice, especially for work with nuclei other than ^{1}H, is between a *homonuclear* and a *heteronuclear* lock. In the latter, the lock is established on a different nuclear species than the one being examined. In ^{13}C NMR, for example, the lock can be taken on the deuterium nuclei in a solvent such as CDCl$_3$. The ^{2}H nucleus, with $I = 1$, gives a peak without noticeable chemical shifts, hence is suitable for a reference frequency.

DOUBLE RESONANCE

Spin-spin coupling is sometimes of considerable help in identifying resonances, but in relatively complex molecules it may complicate the spectrum to the point where the structure cannot be elucidated. A *spin decoupler* is of great assistance in such cases. This is an auxiliary oscillator that can produce a signal at a selectable frequency and can impose this field on the sample with considerable intensity. If this added frequency is tuned to resonate with one set of coupled protons while the contribution of the other set is under observation, the multiplet caused by the coupling will collapse to a sharp singlet. In Fig. 13-4, for example, if the auxiliary

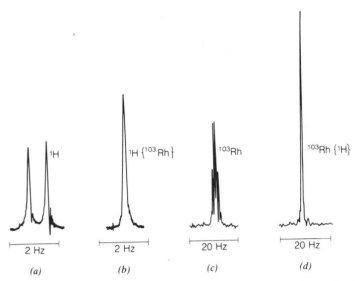

Figure 13-6 Partial NMR spectra of cyclopentadienyl-dicarbonylrhodium(I), showing the effects of spin-spin decoupling: (a) proton resonance, showing splitting due to coupling with ^{103}Rh; (b) proton resonance with decoupling oscillator at the ^{103}Rh frequency; (c) ^{103}Rh resonance showing splitting resulting from coupling with the protons of the cyclopentadienyl moiety; (d) ^{103}Rh decoupled from the protons. (*Reviews of Scientific Instruments.*[3])

frequency is set at 110 Hz downfield from TMS (that is, $\delta = 1.83$), the quadruplet at $\delta = 3.20$ will change to a singlet at the same location and with the same integrated area. Likewise, if the decoupling field is adjusted to 190 Hz ($\delta = 3.20$), the triplet at $\delta = 1.83$ will collapse to a singlet. Another example is given in Fig. 13-6.[3]

This decoupling is caused by the rapid equilibration of the irradiated protons between their two energy states, so that the protons being observed cannot distinguish the separate states, and hence cannot be split.

Another type of double resonance, called the *nuclear Overhauser effect* (NOE), depends on disruption of the normal relaxation mechanisms.[4] *Relaxation* refers to the process by which a nucleus, having absorbed energy, returns to its normal state. The most important of such processes involves dipole-dipole interaction between spinning nuclei. This interaction is strongly dependent on the distance separating the nuclei concerned, an inverse sixth-power relation. If one of these nuclei is saturated by radiation from an auxiliary oscillator, it becomes more difficult for the other nucleus to lose its excess energy, and this results in a larger NMR signal. If the nuclei are both protons, the enhancement can be as much as 1.5 times, whereas if a ^{13}C resonance is observed while a nearby proton is irradiated, the signal can be increased by nearly 3 times. This effect increases the signal-to-noise ratio to a useful degree, but more important, it can help pinpoint which peaks are due to nuclei in close proximity to each other in the molecule. Thus it can often distinguish between conformational or other stereoisomers. As an example, consider[5] the compound

Irradiation at the frequency of the methyl group protons produced an enhancement of the signal from the two protons in position 4, but not that at 2, thereby showing that the methyl is much closer to the number 4 carbon, and therefore is *trans* with respect to the carboxyl.

APPLICATIONS OF PROTON NMR

Qualitative Analysis

The theory presented above is sufficient indication of the great utility of NMR in the identification of pure substances. Atlases of spectra are available (Aldrich, Sadtler, Varian, for example), comparable to those of UV and IR absorption spectra. For substances of unknown structure, NMR provides a valuable diagnostic tool. Chemical shifts as well as spin coupling and decoupling observations are all useful in this connection.

In the first place, one can establish how many different environments for hydrogen atoms exist in the molecule, and with the aid of the integrator, the relative numbers of atoms located in each. Then, through study of fine structure (multiplicity) of peaks, it is possible to determine which hydrogen types are closest to each other. Spin decoupling and NOE observations are invaluable in this phase of the study.

Quantitative Analysis

As a quantitative tool, NMR has the advantage that a pure sample of the substance sought is not necessary. This contrasts with most optical spectra and with such methods as gas chromatography, in which an authentic pure sample is required. In NMR, a pure reference compound is still needed as an internal standard, but it can be any compound that has an easily identifiable spectrum not overlapping that of the sample. An example[6] is the determination of the degree of esterification of pentaerythratol, $C(CH_2OH)_4$, by a complex mixture of acids represented by $R-COOH$. A weighed portion of the mixed esters was combined with a weighed

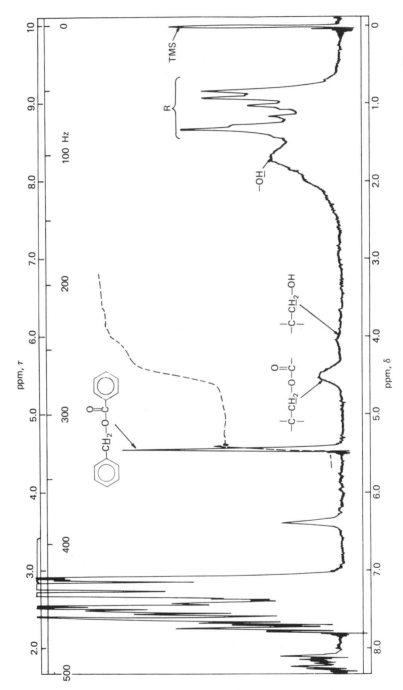

Figure 13-7 Proton NMR spectrum of pentaerythritol esterification products. The dashed line is the integral trace. (*American Laboratory*.[6])

amount of benzyl benzoate, giving the NMR spectrum depicted in Fig. 13-7. The sharp peak at $\delta = 5.43$ is due to the single $-CH_2-$ group of benzyl benzoate, and its integral serves to calibrate the spectrum in terms of area per proton. The three broad peaks at $\delta = 1.70, 4.06,$ and 4.52 correspond to $-OH, -CH_2-OH,$ and $-CH_2-OCOR$ (italicized hydrogens), respectively. The $-OH$ resonance cannot be used because of the overlap of several sharp peaks originating in the protons of the R-groups, but the other two peaks are usable. Since the relation between integrated area and number of protons has already been established, it is a simple matter to compute the concentrations of the $-CH_2-OH$ and $-CH_2-OCOR$ functional groups in terms of milliequivalents per gram of sample.

It should be noted that the analytical peaks in Fig. 13-7 are broad because of the contributions to each from a considerable number of molecular species with differing R-groups, so that the chemical shifts are only approximately the same. Note also that the relatively large noise evident in these peaks does not show up in the integrator traces. This is characteristic of integrators; noise is equally probable in positive and negative senses, so that contributions to the area tend to cancel. The experimental results quoted in the reference showed relative standard deviations of the order of 2 to 10 percent, which are considered quite acceptable.

Suitable mixtures of compounds can be analyzed with excellent precision, as illustrated in Fig. 13-8. A mixture similar to certain types of petroleum was prepared from 1,2,3,4-tetrahydronaphthalene (tetralin), naphthalene, and n-hexane.

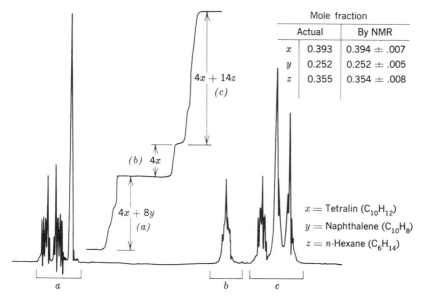

		Mole fraction	
		Actual	By NMR
x		0.393	0.394 ± .007
y		0.252	0.252 ± .005
z		0.355	0.354 ± .008

x = Tetralin ($C_{10}H_{12}$)
y = Naphthalene ($C_{10}H_8$)
z = n-Hexane (C_6H_{14})

Figure 13-8 Analysis of a hydrocarbon mixture by NMR. (*Varian Associates.*)

The aromatic hydrogens showed overlapping multiple resonances in the region marked (a) in the figure. The hydrogens on carbon atoms adjoining an aromatic ring (alpha to the ring) appeared at (b), and the purely aliphatic hydrogens at (c). Tetralin has 4 aromatic protons, while naphthalene has 8. Tetralin has 4 alpha-protons plus 4 that are essentially aliphatic, while all 14 protons of hexane are aliphatic. A set of three simultaneous equations can be solved for the mole fractions of the three compounds, leading to the data inset into the figure. These are in good agreement with the composition of the mixture as calculated from the weights taken.

NMR SHIFT REAGENTS

The chemical shifts due to protons located near an atom with a lone pair of electrons (Lewis base) can be markedly altered by coordinating the electron pair with an ion of one of the lanthanide elements, using an organic complex of the lanthanide as reagent. Figure 13-9 shows the structures of several of these reagents. Those denoted by THD and FOD can be used in nonaqueous solvents such as $CDCl_3$, while DOTA is water-soluble, hence can be used in D_2O solutions. Figure 13-10 shows an application of $Eu(THD)_3$ in increasing the resolution of the spectrum of 6-methylquinoline in $CDCl_3$. The effect of the paramagnetic Eu(III) atom is to shift downfield the resonances of nearby protons with only slight effect on those that are more distant. It can be seen that the protons nearest the nitrogen atom (2 and 8) are most greatly affected.

To use shift reagents to best advantage, one must have a number of them available, as their application can be quite specific.[7, 8] Those most widely used contain europium (Eu), holmium (Ho), praseodymium (Pr), and thulium (Tm).

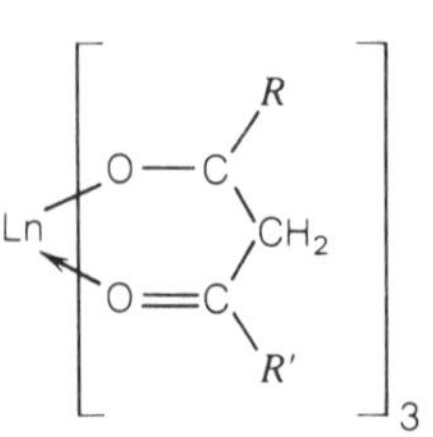

Designation	R	R'
THD	$-C(CH_3)_3$	$-C(CH_3)_3$
FOD	$-C(CH_3)_3$	$-C_3H_7$
	Ref. 6	

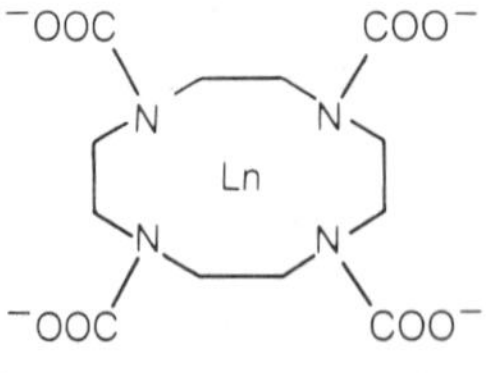

DOTA (The Ln atom is coordinated with four N's and four O's.)
Ref. 7

Figure 13-9 Structures of a few NMR shift reagents.

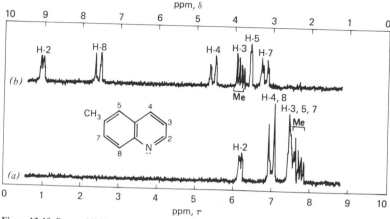

Figure 13-10 Proton NMR spectra of 6-methylquinoline over the range $\delta = 1 - 10$, in $CDCl_3$: (*a*) without shift reagent, (*b*) with 0.3 mmol Eu(THD)$_3$ added. Proton assignments are marked. (*Perkin–Elmer Corporation.*)

NMR OF OTHER ELEMENTS

Of the 18 elements other than hydrogen that have natural isotopes with spin $I = 1/2$, the only ones with great enough sensitivities for practical utility at the present state of the art are the following:

$$^{19}F \ (83.3)$$
$$^{203}Tl \text{ and } ^{205}Tl \ (13.5)$$
$$^{31}P \ (6.63)$$
$$^{129}Xe \ (0.55)$$
$$^{115}Sn \text{ and } ^{119}Sn \ (0.45)$$
$$^{195}Pt \ (0.34)$$
$$^{123}Te \text{ and } ^{125}Te \ (0.22)$$
$$^{207}Pb \ (0.139)$$
$$^{111}Cd \text{ and } ^{113}Cd \ (0.134)$$
$$^{77}Se \ (0.062)$$
$$^{29}Si \ (0.037)$$
$$^{13}C \ (0.018)$$

The figures are percentages of the proton sensitivity for equal field strengths, and take into account the natural abundances of the magnetic isotopes.† Of these only ^{19}F, ^{31}P, and ^{13}C are utilized to any great extent. The principles are, of course, the same as for protons. The chemical shifts in general increase with atomic number, covering a span of about 600 ppm for ^{19}F and ^{13}C, 1000 for ^{31}P, and up to about

---

† These sensitivities can be rationalized as follows (for ^{13}C): The intrinsic sensitivity of a nucleus can be shown theoretically to be proportional to γ^3. Given $\gamma_{1H} = 2.68$, $\gamma_{13C} = 0.675$, and the natural abundance of $^{13}C = 1.11$ percent, the sensitivity for ^{13}C is $(0.675/2.68)^3(1.11) = 0.0177$ percent.

25,000 (i.e., 2.5 percent) for ^{207}Pb. This means that useful information can be obtained with instruments of lower resolution than required for protons.[9]

Fluorine-19

NMR of ^{19}F offers no particular difficulties, and can be carried out by the same techniques as proton spectroscopy at the appropriate field-frequency combinations (see Table 13-1).[10] An interesting possibility is the preparation of fluorine-containing derivatives of organic compounds as a means of avoiding solvent and other interferences present in proton-NMR. For example, Leader[11] has used hexafluoroacetone as a reagent to form easily identified derivatives with alcohols and amines. He quotes chemical shifts for adducts with 125 compounds.

Phosphorus-31

Except for its lower sensitivity, ^{31}P shows magnetic properties similar to those of ^{1}H and ^{19}F.[12] Representative applications[13,14] are the quantitative analysis of condensed phosphates, hydroxymethylphosphines, and thiophosphates. The method is in excellent agreement with prior methods of analysis and is much faster.

CARBON-13

The sensitivity for this important isotope is so low that conventional scanning NMR spectrometers are not adequate for its study. Repetitive scans with signals stored in an electronic memory and automatically averaged (a multichannel analyzer) can be used to advantage, as can chemical enrichment with ^{13}C. The method of choice, however, involves Fourier-transform instrumentation, described in the next section. This gives 100 or more times the sensitivity of a standard instrument with a signal averager.

^{13}C spectra show chemical shifts that are more sensitive to details of structure than are proton shifts. Differences between structural and stereoisomers can easily be seen. Since most carbon atoms in organic compounds have hydrogen atoms attached to them, ^{13}C—^{1}H spin-spin interactions are pronounced, whereas they are not significant in proton spectroscopy because of the low abundance of ^{13}C. Therefore, ^{13}C—^{1}H spin decoupling is essential.

Decoupling can be accomplished with a wide-band oscillator that will saturate *all* protons simultaneously, allowing all ^{13}C multiplets to collapse to singlets. Other double-resonance methods permit retention of coupling information concerning directly attached protons but elimination of that due to more remote protons. With this technique, called *off-resonance decoupling*, a nonprotonated ^{13}C gives a singlet, ^{13}CH a doublet, ^{13}CH$_2$ a triplet, and ^{13}CH$_3$ a quartet. More details and a wealth of examples can be found in the literature.[15–17]

FOURIER-TRANSFORM (FT) NMR[18–21]

The efficiency of NMR spectroscopy, just as in IR, can be greatly improved by exciting all possible resonances simultaneously rather than scanning them sequentially. In the IR, this means irradiating the sample with undispersed (white) radiation, changing the effective time scale with an interferometer, and then converting information from time to frequency domain. In NMR, the sample is likewise flooded with radiation of all possible frequencies in the range of interest, followed by Fourier time-to-frequency conversion. An interferometer is not needed, since the signals are already on a time scale that can be handled directly.

The most convenient way of obtaining a wide range of frequencies is by means of a short burst or pulse of RF energy. A pulse of this type is the equivalent of a band of frequencies centered around the oscillator (carrier) frequency, the bandwidth depending on the duration of the pulse. A 10-μs pulse covers a frequency range of about 10^5 Hz.

Following each pulse the excited nuclei, which are precessing in the magnetic field, continue to emit signals at their characteristic Larmor frequencies as they relax back to their ground states. This emission, following the excitation pulse, is known as *free-induction decay* (FID). These emissions can be picked up by a probe coil. Each pulse contains the information of one complete spectrum, collected in the 1- or 2-s interval between pulses. These data are digitized at a high rate by a sampling technique, and stored in computer memory for subsequent averaging over many pulses.

The FID of a single resonance takes the form of an exponentially decaying sine wave of frequency $v = |v_L - v_C|$, where v_L is the Larmor frequency, and v_C is the carrier frequency. With multiple resonances, the FID patterns, called *interferograms*, become more complicated. As an example to show the relations between the scanning and FT spectra, consider Fig. 13-11. Part (a) is the conventional spectrum of $^{13}CH_3I$, showing the 1:3:3:1 quartet of the ^{13}C coupled to the 3 protons, with a separation $J = 135$ Hz (for a 2.35-T field). The corresponding FID is shown at (b); here the reciprocal of the coupling constant marks the separation of well-defined interference beats. When this time-domain signal is subjected to Fourier transformation, the spectrum of part (c) is obtained, which has the same appearance as (a), but with greatly increased signal and decreased background noise.

Figure 13-12 shows how complicated an interferogram can be, even for a rather simple molecule such as 3-ethylpyridine.

Fourier-transform spectrometers are manufactured by several companies, who place their emphasis on ^{13}C spectroscopy, though many models can be used for protons and other isotopes as well. They invariably have a built-in computer ·facility.

Solid State NMR[22,23]

In recent years theory and practice have been developed for the NMR study of solids, a field that is likely to become important in analysis. Factors connected with the orientation of molecules in the crystal lattice provide a wealth of structural information in addition to that obtained from solution spectroscopy. As an example,[22] a ^{13}C nucleus in a carbonyl group is shielded more strongly if the magnetic field is perpendicular to the C=O bond than if parallel, an example of

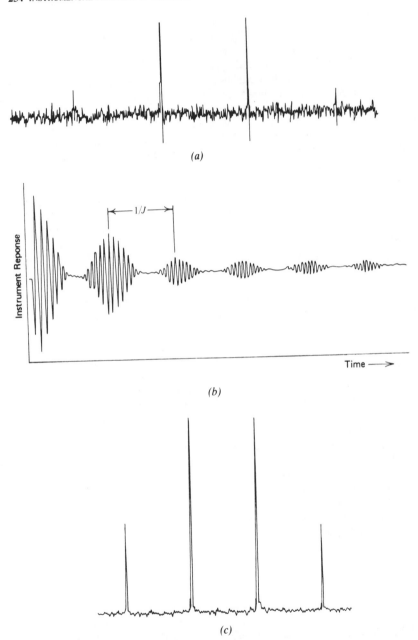

Figure 13-11 ^{13}C NMR spectra of ^{13}CH$_3$I: (*a*) taken on a scanning instrument with a multichannel analyzer; (*b*) FID pattern; (*c*) Fourier transform of the FID. [*JEOL (USA), Inc.*]

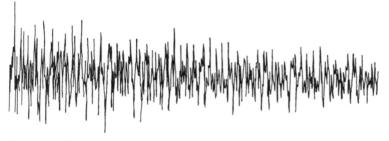

Figure 13-12 FID of 3-ethylpyridine [*JEOL (USA), Inc.*]

shielding anisotropy. In a powdered crystalline material, all orientations are present, and the signal observed is a distribution of resonances, hence a relatively wide peak is seen, whereas the fluidity of a liquid solution ensures that only a single sharp peak is observable.

Chemical anisotropy can be eliminated by spinning the sample at an angle of 54.74° to the direction of the external field. Spinning at this "magic angle" causes the broad maxima mentioned above to collapse to sharp peaks.

NMR spectra of solids are more affected by dipole-dipole interactions resulting from near-neighbor magnetic dipoles than is true in liquids, an effect that is likely to obscure the chemical shift. This also mandates much higher RF power for decoupling than is needed in solution spectroscopy.

These factors mean that an NMR spectrometer designed for liquids is not adequate for solid work, though the reverse is not true.

Solid-state NMR has many potential applications in the characterization of solids that are largely intractable by other means. Such complex solids as bio-polymers and fossil fuels, for example, can be examined by this technique.

ELECTRON SPIN RESONANCE (ESR)†

Since electrons always possess a spin, they also have a magnetic moment, and hence the basic magnetic resonance theory applies to electrons as well as to spinning nuclei. The gyromagnetic ratio for an electron is 1760 rad·T^{-1}·s^{-1} (as compared to 2.68 for the proton). It is customary in ESR theory to rewrite Eq. (13-1) in the form

$$\Delta E = \frac{\mu H}{I} = g\beta H \tag{13-4}$$

where β represents the Bohr magneton, a universal constant with the value 9.2732×10^{-24} J·T^{-1}, and g is a dimensionless constant called the *splitting factor*. The quantum number I has the value 1/2, so that the electron has just two energy

† This subject is also known as *electron magnetic resonance* (EMR).

states, as does the proton. The value of g is 2.0023 for free electrons, and varies from this by a few percent for free radicals, transition-metal ions, and other species containing unpaired electrons. If electrons are paired, their magnetic moments effectively cancel, and they are not observable.

Unpaired electrons have a great tendency to show fine structure in their resonances due to coupling with spinning nuclei in their vicinity. The principles are similar to those involved in the spin coupling of protons, but are often much more complex, frequently to the point where the source of each component of the spectrum cannot be identified. The ethyl free radical, for instance, produces an array of four triplets. Spin decoupling can sometimes help.

ESR Instrumentation

Most of the work in ESR is carried out at a constant frequency in the neighborhood of 9.5 GHz with the corresponding field of about 340 mT. Other instruments operate at frequencies as high as 35 GHz. The most obvious difference between the instrumentation for ESR and NMR is that at such high frequencies, RF power is more effectively conducted from one point to another by rigid waveguides than by flexible coaxial cables. The sample cell is inserted through an orifice in a waveguide at a point where the magnetic (rather than electric) vector of the electromagnetic wave is a maximum. The efficiency of transfer of energy to the sample is generally less than about 30 percent, but even so, the method is quite sensitive. Typically as little as 10^{-10} to 10^{-8} mole percent of free radicals in a 1-g sample can be detected.

It is customary to record ESR spectra in derivative form, to obtain better resolution. Quantitative measurements must then be made on the second time-integral of the recorded curve.

Applications of ESR

Just as in NMR, a standard reference substance is convenient in ESR. One such is the 1,1-diphenyl-2-picrylhydrazyl free radical (DPPH)

which is a chemically stable material with a splitting factor $g = 2.0036$. It cannot be used as an *internal* standard with other free radicals, since the g values show only slight variation, so that the standard cannot be distinguished from the substance studied. They can be recorded consecutively, however, with all parameters kept constant. A tiny chip of ruby crystal cemented permanently to the sample cell

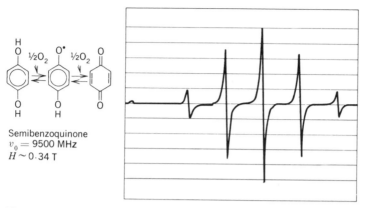

Figure 13-13 ESR spectrum of the semiquinone intermediate in the oxidation of hydroquinone. (*Varian Associates.*)

has been recommended as a standard; ruby contains a trace of Cr(III) entrapped in its crystal lattice, and shows a strong resonance at $g = 1.40$.

The chief application of ESR is in the study of free radicals at very low concentrations. Figure 13-13 shows the ESR spectrum of a quinone-hydroquinone redox system. It has been taken to prove conclusively that a semiquinone free radical exists as an intermediate. The five-line pattern is a consequence of the magnetic spin interaction between the odd electron and the four hydrogens on the ring; statistics show that the intensities should stand in the ratios $1:4:6:4:1$. Figure 13-14 gives the results of a kinetic study of the formation and decay of the semiquinone. The ESR instrument was tuned to the point of maximum signal and observed over a period of time. The sample cell was designed to permit two solutions (hydroquinone and oxygen) to flow through the observation area. The flow rate was faster than the rate of production of the radical, but as soon as the flow was stopped, its production and further reaction could be monitored easily. The half-time of the formation reaction under one set of conditions was 0.15 s.

Cells have been devised that permit the formation of free radicals in situ by irradiation with UV, gamma- or x-rays, or by electrolytic redox reactions. The great sensitivity of the method permits observation of transient species that could

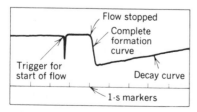

Figure 13-14 Kinetic study of the formation and decay of the semiquinone of Fig. 13-13. (*Varian Associates.*)

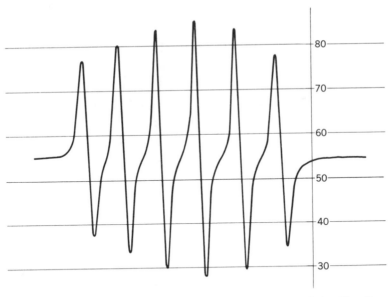

Figure 13-15 ESR spectrum of the Mn^{2+} ion in 10^{-4} M aqueous solution. (*Perkin–Elmer Corporation.*)

be detected in no other way. For example, the fivefold resonance of the ethyl radical becomes visible when ethanol is subjected to x-radiation.

Another important field of application of ESR is in the estimation of trace amounts of paramagnetic ions, particularly in biological work. Figure 13-15 shows the six resonances of the Mn^{2+} ion as observed in aqueous solution. The multiplicity is given by $2I + 1$; for Mn, $I = \frac{5}{2}$, which accounts for the six peaks. This ion can be measured at concentrations as low as 10^{-6} M before becoming lost in the background noise.

Many other applications can be found in the literature.[24]

PROBLEMS

13-1 Justify the (*a*), (*b*), and (*c*) assignments of Fig. 13-8 by comparison with Fig. 13-3. Measure as accurately as you can the heights of the three steps in the integral curve, and calculate the amounts of the three components.

13-2 Figure 13-16 shows the NMR spectrogram of a mixture of cyclohexane, toluene, and water. By comparison with Fig. 13-3, identify the four peaks, and from the integral curve, estimate the composition of the mixture.

13-3 Corsini et al.[25] used ESR evidence to determine which of the following two formulas is correct for the complex obtained between copper ion and 8-quinolinethiol (C_9H_7NS):

    (*a*) $Cu(I)(C_9H_7NS)(C_9H_6NS^-)$

    (*b*) $Cu(II)(C_9H_6NS^-)_2$

Show that the ESR approach is appropriate for this determination.

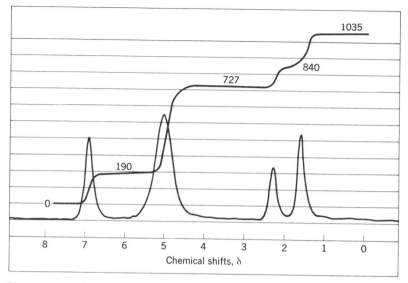

Figure 13-16 Proton NMR spectrum at moderate resolution, of an emulsion of cyclohexane, toluene, and water. (*Varian Associates.*)

13-4 The molecular weight of a compound is to be determined by proton NMR. A preliminary study of the spectrum shows a particular peak to correspond to 6 hydrogen atoms. A solution is prepared that contains 1.50 g of the unknown and 1.45 g of 1,3,5-trinitrobenzene as a reference compound. The integrator trace in the spectrum of the mixture showed 421 units for the reference peak and 1240 units for the unknown. Calculate the molecular weight of the unknown.[26]

13-5 (*a*) What magnetic field strength is needed to observe ^{19}F nuclei at a frequency of 220 MHz? (*b*) Calculate the γ-value for a nuclide that gives a resonance of 2.35 T and 19.7 MHz. Identify it from handbook tables.

13-6 Reconcile Eqs. (13-2) and (13-3) for the electron, using the values given in the text for γ and g.

13-7 What is the relative sensitivity for the NMR detection of ^{15}N, given the following properties. $I = \frac{1}{2}$, natural abundance = 0.37 percent, resonant frequency at 1 T, 4.314 MHz.

REFERENCES

1. E. D. Becker, *High Resolution NMR*, 2d ed., Academic Press, New York, **1980**.
2. R. C. Ferguson and W. D. Phillips, *Science*, **1967**, *157*, 257.
3. R. W. Dykstra, A. M. Harrison, and B. D. Dombek, *Rev. Sci. Instrum.*, **1981**, *52*, 1690.
4. P. D. Kennewell, *J. Chem. Educ.*, **1970**, *47*, 278.
5. K. Isono, K. Asahi, and S. Suzuki, *J. Am. Chem. Soc.*, **1969**, *91*, 7490.
6. G. A. Ward, *Am. Lab.*, **1970**, *2(3)*, 12.
7. R. E. Rondeau and R. E. Sievers, *Anal. Chem.*, **1973**, *45*, 2145.
8. C. C. Bryden, C. N. Reilley, and J. F. Desreux, *Anal. Chem.*, **1981**, *53*, 1418.
9. R. R. Sharp, in *Applications of the Newer Techniques of Analysis*, I. L. Simmons and G. W. Ewing (eds.), Plenum Press, New York, **1973**, pp. 123, ff.
10. W. W. Paudler, *Nuclear Magnetic Resonance*, Allyn and Bacon, Boston, **1971**, p. 22.

11. G. R. Leader, *Anal. Chem.*, **1973**, *45*, 1700.
12. Ref. 10, p. 24.
13. J. G. Colson and D. H. Marr, *Anal. Chem.*, **1973**, *45*, 370.
14. D. A. Stanislawski and J. R. Van Wazer, *Anal. Chem.*, **1980**, *52*, 96.
15. G. C. Levy and G. L. Nelson, *Carbon-13 Nuclear Magnetic Resonance for Organic Chemists*, Wiley-Interscience, New York, **1972**.
16. J. R. Wasson, *Anal. Chem.*, **1982**, *54*, 125R.
17. F. A. L. Anet and G. C. Levy, *Science*, **1973**, *180*, 141.
18. E. D. Becker, *Appl. Spectrosc.*, **1972**, *26*, 421.
19. D. A. Netzel, *Appl. Spectrosc.*, **1972**, *26*, 430.
20. T. C. Farrar, in *Transform Techniques in Chemistry*, P. R. Griffiths (ed.), Plenum Press, New York, **1978**, chap. 8.
21. E. D. Becker, J. A. Ferretti and P. N. Gambhir, *Anal. Chem.*, **1979**, *51*, 1413.
22. M. Reinhold, *Am. Lab.*, **1982**, *14(2)*, 164.
23. B. C. Gerstein, *Anal. Chem.*, **1983**, *55*, 781A, 899A.
24. A series of eight papers in *Appl. Spectrosc.*, **1980**, *34*, 268–310.
25. A. Corsini, Q. Fernando, and H. Freiser, *Talanta*, **1964**, *11*, 63.
26. W. R. Rahman, A. R. Gennaro, and M. Zanger, *Am. Lab.*, **1981**, *13(11)*, 42.

FOURTEEN

INTRODUCTION TO ELECTROCHEMICAL METHODS

A number of important analytical methods are based on the electrochemical properties of solutions. Consider a solution of an electrolyte contained in a glass vessel and in contact with two metallic conductors. Connection of this cell to an outside source of a few volts of electricity will cause a current to flow through the solution. On the other hand, the cell itself may act as a source of electrical energy and produce a current through the external circuit.

In general, such electrical effects will depend on the composition of the solution and on the nature of the electrodes, and hence can have analytical importance. The distinctions between the various electroanalytical methods are determined largely by the nature of the electrodes and by the external instrumentation. We shall consider first the properties of aqueous redox reactions that enable them to interact with a system of electrodes.

THE CELL REACTION

Whenever a direct current passes through an electrolytic cell, an oxidation-reduction (redox) reaction must take place. Oxidation (loss of electrons) occurs at the electrode known as the *anode*, and simultaneously reduction (gain of electrons) at the *cathode*. The primary function of the external circuit is to convey the electrons from the anode to the cathode. The electrical circuit is completed by ionic conduction through the solution.

A generalized redox reaction can be written as

$$rA_{red} + sB_{ox} + \cdots \quad \rightleftharpoons \quad pA_{ox} + qB_{red} + \cdots$$

where the subscripts "ox" and "red" refer to the oxidized and reduced forms of substances A and B. For simplicity, we shall restrict the discussion to the case in which A and B are the only substances oxidized or reduced (i.e., we will eliminate the " $+ \cdots$ ").

The equilibrium constant K is defined as

$$K = \frac{(A_{ox})_{eq}^p (B_{red})_{eq}^q}{(A_{red})_{eq}^r (B_{ox})_{eq}^s} \tag{14-1}$$

in which the parentheses denote molar activities† and the subscripts "eq" denote equilibrium quantities. We can also define a quantity Q, the activity quotient, as

$$Q = \frac{(A_{ox})^p (B_{red})^q}{(A_{red})^r (B_{ox})^s} \tag{14-2}$$

where the activities are the actual values in an experiment, not necessarily the equilibrium values. It can be shown from thermodynamic considerations that the change in free energy (the maximum available work at constant temperature and pressure) is given by

$$\Delta G = RT \ln Q - RT \ln K \tag{14-3}$$

where R is the universal gas constant ($8.316 \, \text{J} \cdot \text{mol}^{-1} \cdot \text{K}^{-1}$) and T is the kelvin temperature. In electrochemical reactions, the free energy is related to electrical quantities through the expression

$$\Delta G = -nFE_{cell} \tag{14-4}$$

in which E_{cell} is the potential of the cell in volts, F is the Faraday constant, approximately 96,487 coulombs per equivalent, and n is the number of electrons transferred for each formula unit of the reaction. Thus

$$E_{cell} = -\frac{\Delta G}{nF} = -\frac{RT}{nF} \ln Q + \frac{RT}{nF} \ln K \tag{14-5}$$

By substitution of the defined values of K and Q, followed by rearrangement of the logarithmic terms, we can show that

$$E_{cell} = \left[\frac{RT}{nF} \ln \frac{(A_{ox})_{eq}^p}{(A_{red})_{eq}^r} - \frac{RT}{nF} \ln \frac{(A_{ox})^p}{(A_{red})^r} \right]$$

$$- \left[\frac{RT}{nF} \ln \frac{(B_{ox})_{eq}^s}{(B_{red})_{eq}^q} - \frac{RT}{nF} \ln \frac{(B_{ox})^s}{(R_{red})^q} \right] \tag{14-6}$$

---

† We will consistently use parentheses for activities and brackets for concentrations.

Now let us define

$$E_A^\circ = \frac{RT}{nF} \ln \frac{(A_{red})_{eq}^r}{(A_{ox})_{eq}^p} \tag{14-7}$$

and a similar expression for E_B°, which gives

$$E_{cell} = \left[E_B^\circ - \frac{RT}{nF} \ln \frac{(B_{red})^q}{(B_{ox})^s} \right]$$

$$- \left[E_A^\circ - \frac{RT}{nF} \ln \frac{(A_{red})^r}{(A_{ox})^p} \right] \tag{14-8}$$

By this procedure, we have separated into two terms the effects of the two substances A and B on the potential of the cell. This can be carried a step farther by defining what we will call *half-cell potentials*

$$E_A = E_A^\circ - \frac{RT}{nF} \ln \frac{(A_{red})^r}{(A_{ox})^p} \tag{14-9}$$

$$E_B = E_B^\circ - \frac{RT}{nF} \ln \frac{(B_{red})^q}{(B_{ox})^s} \tag{14-10}$$

Then, from Eq. (14-8), it follows that

$$E_{cell} = E_B - E_A \tag{14-11}$$

Equations such as (14-9) and (14-10) were first introduced by Walther Nernst, and are frequently referred to as *Nernst equations*.

Just as the expression for the potential of the cell has been broken down into two portions, so the chemical equation for the cell reaction can be separated into two portions, called *half-reactions*

$$rA_{red} \; \rightleftharpoons \; pA_{ox} + ne^-$$

and

$$sB_{ox} + ne^- \; \rightleftharpoons \; qB_{red}$$

where e^-, as usual, symbolizes an electron.

It is convenient, particularly for purposes of tabulation, to write all half-reactions with the electrons on the same side. Following recent practice, we will write them as *reductions*

$$pA_{ox} + ne^- \; \rightleftharpoons \; rA_{red} \tag{14-12}$$

$$qB_{ox} + ne^- \; \rightleftharpoons \; sB_{red} \tag{14-13}$$

To obtain the complete cell reaction, the two half-reactions must be multiplied by suitable numerical factors to make the number of electrons equal. The oxidation half-reaction is then *subtracted* algebraically from the reduction half-reaction.

The potentials E_A and E_B are associated with the respective half-reactions. The corresponding quantities E_A° and E_B° are called the *standard reduction potentials* for the half-reactions. The cell potential [E_{cell} of Eq. (14-11)], can be measured easily, as we shall see presently, but no valid method has been discovered for determining the *absolute* potential of a single electrode and half-reaction. Hence it is necessary to choose some specific electrode and its half-reaction to be assigned arbitrarily to the zero position on the scale of potentials. The *standard hydrogen electrode* (SHE) has been selected for this purpose. This is an electrode system in which hydrogen gas at a partial pressure of one atmosphere is bubbled over a platinum foil immersed in an aqueous solution in which the activity of hydrogen ion is unity. The potential of the SHE has been defined by international agreement to be zero at all temperatures.

A graphical display of the Nernst equation for a number of elements is presented in Fig. 14-1. The potentials are referred for convenience to both the SHE and the saturated calomel electrode (SCE), which will be described later. The abscissas must be on a logarithmic basis, and are conveniently plotted as the negative logarithms of the concentration or activity. If the scale is based on *activities*, then the straight (dashed) lines give true potentials; if on the other hand the scale is taken as *concentrations*, the solid curves will give values more nearly in agreement with experiment. The deviations between straight and curved portions represent the effect of the activity coefficients, and indeed potential measurements provide one of the most useful methods of determining these coefficients. It will be noted that activities and concentrations become indistinguishable below about 10^{-3} or 10^{-4} M.

The particular elements included in Fig. 14-1 are some of those that most closely follow the Nernst equation. Others tend to show considerable deviation due to complexation and other effects. For transition metals, particularly, standard potentials are less useful because the determination of activities usually requires data that are not available. For this reason it is often convenient to use instead a quantity called the *formal potential*, $E^{\circ\prime}$, defined by the relation

$$E^{\circ\prime} = E^\circ - \frac{RT}{nF} \ln \frac{\gamma_{red}^r}{\gamma_{ox}^p} \tag{14-14}$$

where γ's denote the respective activity coefficients. Let us rewrite Eq. (14-9) showing the activity coefficients

$$E_A = E_A^\circ - \frac{RT}{nF} \ln \frac{[A_{red}]^r \gamma_{A(red)}^r}{[A_{ox}]^p \gamma_{A(ox)}^p}$$

$$= E_a^{\circ\prime} - \frac{RT}{nF} \ln \frac{[A_{red}]^r}{[A_{ox}]^p} \tag{14-15}$$

The composition of the medium in which the measurements were made must be specified carefully whenever formal potentials are used. The values in Table

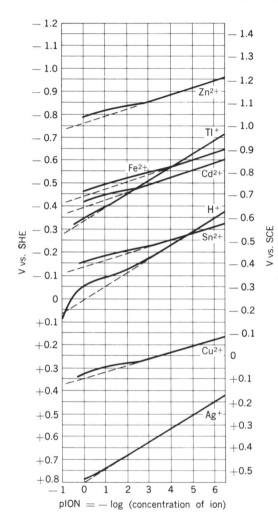

Figure 14-1 Electrode potentials of various elements as functions of the ionic activities. For the significance of the dashed lines, see text.

14-1, taken from the compilation by Meites,[1] show how greatly the formal potentials of a system can vary with the nature of the medium. Figure 14-2 shows graphically the formal potentials of a number of redox systems, plotted as a function of acid concentration. Note that the sequence of potentials of various systems may change with the acidity. For example, Fe(III) will oxidize As(III) in 2 M HCl, but in 8 M HCl, Fe(II) will be oxidized by As(V). It must be remembered that relative potentials are *thermodynamic* data, and have nothing to say about reaction rates. For example, although Ce(IV) has a much higher reduction potential than As(V), it will not oxidize As(III) unless a suitable catalyst is present.

Table 14-1 Formal potentials of the system: Fe(III)/Fe(II)[1]

Medium	$E^{o'}$, V vs. SHE
Standard potential	+0.771
1 M HClO$_4$	0.735
0.5 M HCl	0.71
1 M H$_2$SO$_4$	0.68
5 M HCl	0.64
10 M HCl	0.53
2 M H$_3$PO$_4$	0.46
0.5 M Na tartrate (pH 5-6)	0.07
1 M K$_2$C$_2$O$_4$ (pH 5)	0.01
10 M NaOH	−0.68

The standard and formal potentials for half-cells are of such importance that a great many of them have been determined with precision and made available in handbook tables. See App. A for a selection of standard potentials.

It is often convenient or even mandatory to place the two electrodes in separate compartments of a cell, always maintaining electrolytic contact between them. This contact may be made with a porous porcelain or fritted glass barrier, or it may be through the medium of a salt bridge. Such a separation of the electrodes is necessary if the electrolytes of the two half-cells are incompatible, or if the redox reaction would occur directly should the two electrolytes mix with each other.

The boundary between the two solutions constitutes an additional source of potential, the *liquid-junction potential*, arising from unequal migration of cations in one direction and anions in the other. There is no way in which this extraneous potential can be entirely eliminated, but it can be minimized by the use of a salt bridge containing a concentrated solution of KCl, NH$_4$NO$_3$, or other salt, the two ions of which have about the same mobilities.

Thus it happens that we frequently employ half-cells that not only have their own half-reactions and half-cell potentials, but also have independent physical existence. It must always be remembered, however, that *one* half-cell is of no use; any application must involve at least two.

There are several types of half-cells of particular importance. A few examples follow.

1 A metal in equilibrium with its ions (class I electrodes)

$$Zn^{2+} + 2e^- \longrightarrow Zn \quad E^\circ = -0.763 \text{ V}$$

$$Cu^{2+} + 2e^- \longrightarrow Cu \quad E^\circ = +0.337 \text{ V}$$

$$Ag^+ + e^- \longrightarrow Ag \quad E^\circ = +0.799 \text{ V}$$

The oxidized form [A_{ox} in Eq. (14-12)] is the cation, and the reduced form A_{red} is the free metal. The E° values are given in volts relative to the SCE at 25°C. The

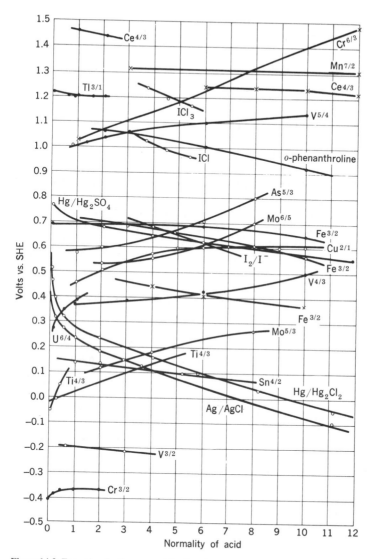

Figure 14-2 Formal reduction potentials of various systems relative to the SHE. The notation $M^{4/3}$ denotes the potentials pertaining to the equilibrium $M(IV) + e^- \rightleftharpoons M(III)$. Open circles (○) denote chloride solutions, closed circles (●) sulfates, and crosses (×) phosphates. The scale of abscissas is given in terms of molarity of HCl or the equivalent in H_2SO_4 or H_3PO_4. (*After Furman,*[2] *John Wiley & Sons., Inc., with the addition of curves for* $Cr^{6/3}$, $Mn^{7/2}$, *and* $Ce^{4/3}$ *phosphates, after Rao and Rao,*[3] *Talanta.*)

electrolyte for these half-cells is ordinarily a solution of a salt of the metal with the anion of a strong mineral acid, its selection often dictated by solubilities and complexing tendencies. Sulfates, nitrates, and perchlorates are often appropriate. Equation (14-9) takes the form

$$E_A = E_A^\circ + \frac{RT}{nF} \ln (A_{ox}) \tag{14-16}$$

because the activity of a pure solid element is always taken as unity. The quantity (A_{ox}) refers to the activity of the simple hydrated cationic species; in the presence of a complex-forming substance this will be less, often much less, than the total amount of the metal in solution.

The simplicity of this type of electrode can be misleading, and actually only a few examples are useful in practice. The more active metals cannot be used this way, as they are not sufficiently stable in an aqueous environment. Even the less active metals, such as silver, may not give the desired response in dilute solutions, as the potential may be determined by substances other than silver ion. Furthermore, the physical condition of the electrode surface is often important and difficult to control.

2 A metal in equilibrium with a saturated solution of a slightly soluble salt (class II electrodes)

$$AgCl_{(s)} + e^- \longrightarrow Ag + Cl^-_{(a=1)} \qquad E^\circ = +0.222 \text{ V}$$

$$Hg_2Cl_{2(s)} + 2e^- \longrightarrow 2Hg + 2Cl^-_{(a=1)} \qquad E^\circ = +0.268 \text{ V}$$

Half-cells of this type are widely used as *reference electrodes*, which in effect constitute secondary standards to replace the inconvenient SHE. For such service, the activity (or concentration) of the anion is established at a known value by the addition of a solution of soluble salt with the same anion; in the examples cited, a solution of KCl is usually chosen. The properties required of a practical reference electrode include ease of fabrication, reproducibility of potential, and low temperature coefficient. A few common reference electrodes are:

(*a*) Saturated calomel electrode (SCE)

$$Hg_2Cl_{2(s)} + 2e^- \longrightarrow 2Hg + 2Cl^-_{(sat'd\ KCl)} \qquad E = +0.246 \text{ V}$$

(*b*) Molar calomel electrode (MCE)

$$Hg_2Cl_{2(s)} + 2e^- \longrightarrow 2Hg + 2Cl^-_{(1\ M\ KCl)} \qquad E = +0.280 \text{ V}$$

(*c*) Molar silver/silver chloride electrode

$$AgCl_{(s)} + e^- \longrightarrow Ag + Cl^-_{(1\ M\ KCl)} \qquad E = +0.237 \text{ V}$$

The Nernst equation for class II electrodes must be modified to take account of the solubility product of the sparingly soluble salt involved. For the case of the silver/silver chloride electrode, $K_{sp} = (Ag^+)(Cl^-)$, so we can write

$$E = E^\circ + \frac{RT}{nF} \ln (Ag^+)$$

$$= E^\circ + \frac{RT}{nF} \ln \frac{K_{sp}}{(Cl^-)}$$

$$= E^\circ - \frac{RT}{nF} \ln (Cl^-) + \frac{RT}{nF} \ln K_{sp} \qquad (14\text{-}17)$$

The last term is a constant (at a given temperature).

3 A metal in equilibrium with two slightly soluble salts with a common anion (class III electrodes)

$$\begin{cases} Ag_2S_{(s)} \longrightarrow 2Ag^+ + S^{2-} \\ CdS_{(s)} \longrightarrow Cd^{2+} + S^{2-} \end{cases}$$

This half-cell can serve as a measure of the activity of Cd^{2+} ion. It is a requirement that the second salt (CdS) be slightly more soluble than the first (Ag_2S). One widely applicable electrode that can be placed in this class is that involving the equilibria between EDTA, Hg^{2+} ions, and the ions of a di-, tri-, or tetravalent metal; the slightly dissociated complexes play the same roles as the slightly soluble sulfide salts in the above example.

4 Two soluble species in equilibrium at an inert electrode

$$Ce^{4+} + e^- \longrightarrow Ce^{3+} \qquad E^\circ = +1.61 \text{ V}$$

$$2Hg^{2+} + 2e^- \longrightarrow Hg_2^{2+} \qquad E^\circ = +0.920 \text{ V}$$

$$Fe^{3+} + e^- \longrightarrow Fe^{2+} \qquad E^\circ = +0.771 \text{ V}$$

The only function of the inert electrode is to transport electrons to or from the ions in solution. The E° values refer to conditions such that the activities of the two ionic species are equal, which does not necessarily mean that the total concentrations of oxidized and reduced forms of the element are equal. In the presence of complex formers, especially, the tendency of the two oxidation states of the metal to form complexes may not be the same, so that an $E^{\circ\prime}$ based on total concentrations rather than activities of free ions can be either larger or smaller than the tabulated value of E°.

SIGN CONVENTIONS

We have chosen to write half-reactions as reductions, which gives E° values that are negative with respect to the SHE for those metals that are more powerful reducing agents than hydrogen, and positive values for those that are less powerful:

$$Cu^{2+} + 2e^- \longrightarrow Cu \qquad E^\circ = +0.337 \text{ V}$$

$$2H^+ + 2e^- \longrightarrow H_2 \qquad E^\circ = 0 \text{ V}$$

$$Zn^{2+} + 2e^- \longrightarrow Zn \qquad E^\circ = -0.763 \text{ V}$$

These values are consistent with experiment, for if a cell is constructed with electrodes of copper and zinc, each in contact with its own ions, the copper is the one that is observed to be positive, and the zinc negative. Only E° values written in this way should be called "standard electrode potentials." If we were to write a half-reaction as an oxidation, then the sign of the potential would have to be reversed. There are two conflicting conventions for determining the sign of the potential of an electrode. That followed here is in accord with the recommendations of the International Union of Pure and Applied Chemistry (IUPAC), meeting in Stockholm in July, 1953. A complete account of the several sign conventions and the IUPAC recommendations can be found in the literature.[4,5]

REVERSIBILITY

The terms *reversible* and *irreversible* are used with several different meanings, according to the context. In a purely chemical sense, a reaction is irreversible if its products either do not react with each other, or do so in such a way as to give products other than the original reactants. As an electrochemical example, consider a cell made up of zinc and silver/silver chloride electrodes in dilute hydrochloric acid. If this cell is short-circuited by an external connection, the half-reactions that occur are

$$Zn \longrightarrow Zn^{2+} + 2e^-$$

$$2AgCl_{(s)} + 2e^- \longrightarrow 2Ag + 2Cl^-$$

and the overall cell reaction is

$$Zn + 2AgCl_{(s)} \longrightarrow 2Ag + 2Cl^- + Zn^{2+}$$

However, if this cell is connected to a source of electricity at a high enough voltage to force current through it in the reverse direction, the reactions will be

$$2H^+ + 2e^- \longrightarrow H_2$$

$$2Ag + 2Cl^- \longrightarrow 2AgCl_{(s)} + 2e^-$$

and the complete reaction is

$$2Ag + 2H^+ + 2Cl^- \longrightarrow 2AgCl_{(s)} + H_2$$

Thus it is seen that the silver/silver chloride electrode is reversible, while the zinc/hydrochloric acid half-cell is not.

In a *thermodynamic* sense, a reaction is reversible only if an infinitesimal change in driving force will cause a change in direction, which is equivalent to saying that the system is in thermodynamic equilibrium. This implies that the reaction is fast enough to respond instantaneously to any small change in an independent variable. Thermodynamic reversibility is an ideal state that can only be approximated by real systems. If an electrochemical reaction is rapid enough that the departure from equilibrium is negligible, it can be considered reversible. A given reaction may be effectively reversible when observed by one technique (such as potential measurement with no current flowing) and yet deviate noticeably from reversibility when studied under slowly changing conditions, as in polarography, and become "totally" irreversible when subjected to rapid changes, as in certain fast-scan procedures.

POLARIZATION

An electrode (and hence a cell) is said to be *polarized* if its potential shows any departure from the value that would be predicted from the Nernst equation. This circumstance may occur, for example, when an arbitrary potential is impressed across a cell, or when a significant amount of current is drawn through it. Changes in potential due to actual changes in concentration of ions at the electrode surfaces are sometimes called *concentration polarization*. This expression is not recommended, however. The activities concerned should always be those of the ions actually present at the electrode surface.

OVERVOLTAGE

According to thermodynamic definitions, any half-cell is operating irreversibly if appreciable current is flowing. The actual potential of a half-cell under such conditions cannot be calculated, but it is always greater than the reversible potential computed from the Nernst equation (i.e., more negative for a cathode, more positive for an anode). The difference between the equilibrium potential and the actual potential is known as *overvoltage* or *overpotential*. Overvoltage[6] can be thought of as the extra driving force necessary to cause the reaction to take place at an appreciable rate. Its magnitude varies with current density (the current per unit area of the electrode), the temperature, and with the materials taking part in the reaction. Of particular importance is the overvoltage required to reduce H^+ ion (or water) to give hydrogen gas. This process, in the absence of overvoltage, would take place at 0 V (for the activity of H^+ ion equal to unity, the SHE). Figure 14-3 gives representative values of hydrogen overvoltage on a number of cathodes, all in 1 M hydrochloric acid solution.[7]

This overvoltage can be of real advantage in some circumstances. Cations of metals such as iron and zinc, for example, can be reduced to the free metals at a mercury cathode, even though their standard potentials are more negative than

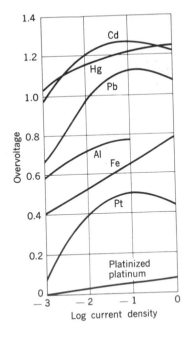

Figure 14-3 Hydrogen overvoltage on various metals as a function of current density (amperes per square centimeter). The electrolyte is 1 *M* HCl. (*John Wiley & Sons, Inc.*[6])

the SHE, because the high overvoltage of hydrogen on mercury prevents its liberation. At a platinum cathode these ions cannot be reduced from an aqueous solution, as the potential cannot exceed that required for hydrogen reduction.

ELECTROANALYTICAL METHODS

Listed here for reference are the principal analytical methods that depend on electrochemistry. Most of these are treated in detail in subsequent chapters.

1. *Potentiometry.* This is a direct analytical application of the Nernst equation through measurement of the potentials of nonpolarized electrodes with no current flowing.
2. *Chronopotentiometry.* According to this method, a known constant current is passed through the solution, and the potential appearing across the electrodes is observed as a function of time. The potential stays nearly constant for a period of time proportional to the concentration of the electroactive species. The related measurement of current following application of a constant potential is called *chronoamperometry.*
3. *Voltammetry* and *polarography.* These are methods of studying the composition of electrolytic solutions by plotting current-voltage curves. In the usual procedure, the voltage applied to a small polarizable electrode (relative to a

reference electrode) is increased negatively over a span of 1 or 2 V, and the resulting changes in current noted. *Voltammetry* is the general name for the method; the term *polarography* is usually restricted to applications of the dropping mercury electrode.

4. *Conductimetry.* In this analytical method, two identical inert electrodes are used, and the conductance (the reciprocal of resistance) between them is measured. Specific effects of the electrodes are eliminated as far as possible.

5. *Coulometry.* This is a method of analysis that involves the application of Faraday's laws of electrolysis, the equivalence between quantity of electricity and quantity of chemical change.

6. *Controlled-potential separations.* It is frequently possible to achieve quantitative separations by means of electrolytic oxidation or reduction at an electrode with carefully controlled potential. The quantity of separated substances can be measured either gravimetrically or coulometrically.

Interesting correlations of many of these electroanalytical methods have been presented in the literature.[8-10] These papers will be more readily appreciated *after* detailed study of the several methods individually. The concepts presented in this and the following four chapters are treated in much more detail in Ref. 11, to which the student is referred for further study.

PROBLEMS

14-1 Derive an expression for the half-cell potential for the class III electrode described above, in terms of the solubility products of Ag_2S and CdS.

14-2 The standard reduction potentials for $Cu^{2+} + 2e^- = Cu$ and for $Cu^+ + e^- = Cu$ are both listed in App. A. Calculate from them the standard reduction potential corresponding to the process $Cu^{2+} + e^- = Cu^+$.

REFERENCES

1. L. Meites, in *Handbook of Analytical Chemistry*, L. Meites (ed.), McGraw-Hill, New York, **1963**, table 5-1, p. 5-6.
2. N. H. Furman, in *Treatise on Analytical Chemistry*, I. M. Kolthoff and P. J. Elving (eds.), Wiley-Interscience, New York, **1963**; pt. I, vol. 4, p. 2294.
3. G. G. Rao and P. K. Rao, *Talanta*, **1963**, *10*, 1251; **1964**, *11*, 825.
4. M. L. McGlashen, *Pure Appl. Chem.*, **1973**, *21(1)*, 1.
5. T. S. Licht and A. J. deBéthune, *J. Chem. Educ.*, **1957**, *34*, 433.
6. J. O'M. Bockris, *J. Chem. Educ.*, **1971**, *48*, 352.
7. F. Daniels and R. A. Alberty, *Physical Chemistry*, (3d ed.), Wiley, New York, **1966**, p. 266.
8. I. M. Kolthoff, *Anal. Chem.*, **1954**, *26*, 1685.
9. C. N. Reilley, W. D. Cooke, and N. H. Furman, *Anal. Chem.*, **1951**, *23*, 1226.
10. W. H. Reinmuth, *Anal. Chem.*, **1960**, *32*, 1509.
11. B. H. Vassos and G. W. Ewing, *Electroanalytical Chemistry*, Wiley-Interscience, New York, **1983**.

CHAPTER

FIFTEEN

POTENTIOMETRY

As discussed in the previous chapter, the Nernst equation provides a simple relationship between the relative potential of an electrode and the concentration of a corresponding ionic species in solution. Thus measurement of the potential of a reversible electrode permits calculation of the activity or concentration of a component of the solution.

As an example, suppose we construct a cell with a silver electrode dipping into a solution of silver nitrate that is connected by a salt bridge to a saturated calomel reference electrode (SCE). The cell assembly is diagrammed in Fig. 15-1. The beaker on the left contains the solution of $AgNO_3$, and the side-tube on the right contains the SCE. The central beaker connects the KCl solution of the SCE with the salt bridge from the silver solution. The salt bridge is filled with an agar gel that contains ammonium nitrate to give electrolytic conduction. (This arrangement prevents contamination of the SCE by silver and of the silver nitrate by KCl; it also reduces the liquid-junction potential to negligible proportions.)

If an electronic voltmeter is connected to the two electrodes, the silver will be found to be positive, the SCE negative. Suppose the meter indicates a 0.450-V difference in potential between the electrodes. We can write

$$E_{Ag} = E_{Ag}^{\circ} + \frac{RT}{nF} \ln [Ag^+]$$

and

$$E_{SCE} = +0.246 \text{ V}$$

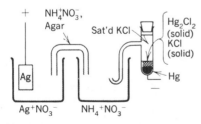

Figure 15-1 Cell assembly with silver and saturated calomel electrodes, schematic.

Subtraction then gives

$$E_{cell} = E_{Ag} - E_{SCE} = E°_{Ag} - E_{SCE} + \frac{RT}{nF} \ln [Ag^+]$$

Solving for log $[Ag^+]$† and noting that $n = 1$, we have (at 25°C)

$$\log [Ag^+] = \frac{E_{cell} - E°_{Ag} + E_{SCE}}{2.303(RT/nF)}$$

$$= \frac{0.450 - 0.799 + 0.246}{0.0591} = -1.74$$

$$[Ag^+] = \text{antilog} (-1.74) = 1.8 \times 10^{-2} \, M.$$

Notice that in combining two half-cells, as in the first step above (writing $E_{cell} = E_{Ag} - E_{SCE}$), the more negative is always subtracted from the more positive. This is the same convention mentioned previously as applied to the corresponding chemical equations, the oxidation half-reaction being subtracted from the reduction. This ensures a *positive* cell potential corresponding to a reaction written in the direction of spontaneous action.

Consider a cell consisting of a platinum electrode dipping into a solution nominally 0.1 M in iron(II) sulfate. The KCl salt bridge from an SCE is inserted directly into the same solution, since no harmful interaction can occur. A potential difference of 0.395 V is observed (at 25°C). The goal is to find the percentage of iron(II) that has been converted by air oxidation to iron(III). Starting with the expressions for the two half-cell potentials, the necessary calculations are as follows (note that $n = 1$):

$$E_{Pt} = E°_{Fe^{3+}/Fe^{2+}} + \frac{RT}{nF} \ln \frac{[Fe^{3+}]}{[Fe^{2+}]}$$

$$E_{SCE} = +0.246$$

$$E_{cell} = E_{Pt} - E_{SCE} = E°_{Fe^{3+}/Fe^{2+}} - E_{SCE} + 0.0591 \log \frac{[Fe^{3+}]}{[Fe^{2+}]}$$

$$\log \frac{[Fe^{3+}]}{[Fe^{2+}]} = \frac{E_{cell} - E°_{Fe^{3+}/Fe^{2+}} + E_{SCE}}{0.0591}$$

$$= \frac{0.395 - 0.771 + 0.246}{0.0591} = -2.20$$

$$\frac{[Fe^{3+}]}{[Fe^{2+}]} = \text{antilog} (-2.20) = 6.3 \times 10^{-3} = 0.63 \text{ percent}$$

which shows that 0.63 percent of the iron(II) had been oxidized.

† Remember that $\ln x = 2.303 \log x$. The quantity 2.303 (RT/F) occurs so frequently that it is worth while to memorize its value at 25°C, namely 0.0591. These factors are given more significant figures than may actually be warranted so that they can be immediately recognized, wherever they appear.

THE CONCENTRATION CELL

This designation is given to a highly symmetrical cell having two identical electrodes dipping into solutions that are the same in every respect except the concentration of the ion to which the electrodes are sensitive. The potential between the electrodes will then be related to the *ratio* of the two concentrations.

For example, in a chloride analysis, one silver/silver chloride electrode may dip into a solution of unknown chloride concentration $[Cl^-]_x$, while the other dips into a standard solution of which the concentration is $[Cl^-]_s = 0.1000\ M$. As shown in Eq. (14-17), the sign of the log term in the Nernst equation becomes negative; the constant terms, $E° + (RT/nF) \ln K_{sp}$ (equal to $+0.222$ V for the Ag/AgCl electrode at 25°C), are the same for both electrodes, hence drop out. Activity corrections can be neglected, even at relatively high concentrations, as their effect will be similar for the two solutions. The electrode potential for the standard is

$$E_s = +0.222 - 0.0591 \log 0.1000 = +0.281 \text{ V}$$

If the unknown solution is more concentrated, say $0.1500\ M$, then

$$E_x = +0.222 - 0.0591 \log 0.1500 = +0.271 \text{ V}$$

The potential of the cell is found, as usual, by subtracting the more negative from the more positive

$$E_{cell} = E_x - E_s = +0.010 \text{ V}$$

The measured potential (such as the $+0.010$ V above) may correspond to either of two unknown concentrations, so the concentration cell can give rise to ambiguous interpretation. This may be avoided by noting carefully the relative signs of standard and unknown.

The concentration cell provides a highly sensitive analytical tool[1] because in a method involving the comparison of two nearly identical solutions, most sources of error arising within the cell cancel out. This means that the overall precision of the method may very well be limited only by the measuring instrument. As in any potentiometric method, the sensitivity (at 25°C) is $0.0591/n$ volts for a tenfold change in concentrations. If the measurement were made relative to a universal reference electrode (i.e., *not* a concentration cell), a measuring instrument with a range of perhaps as much as 2 V would be needed, whereas with a concentration cell, a 20-mV instrument can serve. The latter permits 100 times the precision of the former.

ION-SELECTIVE MEMBRANE ELECTRODES

A whole class of very useful electrodes that show varying degrees of specificity and selectivity utilize a *membrane* to confine an inner reference solution and electrode, and at the same time make electrolytic contact with the outer (test) solution.[2] A few typical designs are shown in Fig. 15-2. The membrane in each of these electrodes acts by an ion-exchange mechanism.

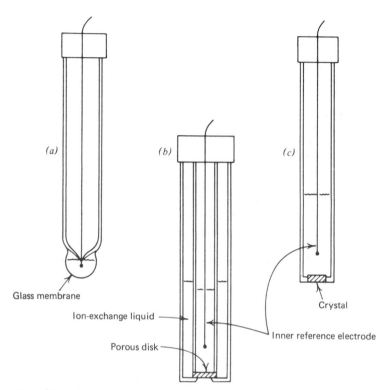

Figure 15-2 Ion-selective electrodes: (a) glass, (b) liquid ion exchange, (c) ionic crystal membrane.

The Glass Electrode

Electrode (a) in Fig. 15-2 is the familiar glass electrode used for pH measurements. It consists of a small bulb of pH-sensitive glass containing a chloride solution of known pH, and an internal reference electrode, usually silver/silver chloride or calomel. The glass is a partially hydrated aluminosilicate containing sodium or calcium ions and often small amounts of lanthanide ions. It is reactive to hydrogen ions in the sense that an ion can join an oxygen site on the lattice at the same time that another, on the opposite surface, leaves, thus maintaining electrical neutrality in the glass. An equilibrium is easily established with hydrogen ions in the inner and outer solutions, producing a potential

$$E = K + \frac{RT}{F} \ln \frac{(H^+)_{inner}}{(H^+)_{outer}} \tag{15-1}$$

K in this expression includes the difference between the characteristic potentials of inner and outer reference electrodes, the liquid-junction potential, and a small, unpredictable contribution known as the *asymmetry potential*, possibly due to physical strains in the glass.

By introducing the definition of pH,† Eq. (15-1) can be rewritten (at 25°C) as

$$E = K + 0.0591(\text{pH}_{\text{outer}} - \text{pH}_{\text{inner}}) \qquad (15\text{-}2)$$

In any given electrode the pH of the inner solution is constant, so we can combine it with K and drop subscripts, to give

$$E = K' + 0.0591 \text{ pH} \qquad (15\text{-}3)$$

In a practical pH meter, the constant K' is taken into account in the calibration procedure, whereby the electrode assembly is immersed in a standard buffer and the indicator arbitrarily made to show the correct value. The glass electrode is characterized by a "pH of zero potential," the point where the inner and outer solutions are at the same pH.

Combination probes containing both glass and reference electrodes are fabricated by many manufacturers. In most designs the reference electrode makes contact with a built-in salt bridge held in an annular space surrounding the glass electrode. The KCl solution serves as an electrostatic shield for the high-resistance glass electrode. The combination probe has become quite popular because of its convenience, though the cost is somewhat greater than for a pair of separate electrodes.

One shortcoming of the glass pH electrode is that an erroneously high reading is obtained in the presence of a large concentration of an alkali metal, the so-called *sodium error*. The previous equations are no longer adequate. The more complete relation, known as the Nernst–Eisenman equation, is

$$E = \text{constant} + \frac{RT}{F} \ln([\text{H}^+] + k_1[\text{Na}^+] + k_2[\text{K}^+] + \ldots) \qquad (15\text{-}4)$$

where the k's are *selectivity coefficients*. An acceptable pH electrode should have very small k values, 10^{-3} or less. These coefficients are not strictly constant, and cannot be used to calculate corrections for observed pH values. They are useful in determining the suitability of various electrodes for particular analytical situations.

Eisenman[4] and others have shown that the selectivity coefficients are related to exchange constants for an ion-exchange process taking place at the glass surface, and to the diffusion mobilities of the ions within the glass. For example, if consideration is limited to H^+ and Na^+ ions, the coefficient k_1 is given by

$$k_1 = \frac{(\text{H}^+)_{\text{sol}}(\text{Na}^+)_{\text{surf}} U_{\text{Na}^+}}{(\text{H}^+)_{\text{surf}}(\text{Na}^+)_{\text{sol}} U_{\text{H}^+}}$$

where the subscripts denote activities in solution and adsorbed on the glass surface; U_{Na^+} and U_{H^+} are the respective mobilities in the glass. Procedures are available for the precise determination of the effect of sodium ion on the potential of a glass electrode.[5]

Glass electrodes can be made with high sensitivity toward Na^+ and Ag^+ and only moderate pH response. This type of electrode can be used to measure either

---

† Although the pH scale is defined as the negative logarithm of the activity of hydrogen ions, it has been found expedient to set up a practical or working scale based on a series of buffer solutions prepared in a prescribed manner. A full discussion of both theoretical and practical aspects of the pH concept can be found in the monograph by Bates.[3]

Na^+ or Ag^+ ion if the other is absent or held constant, and if the solution is adequately buffered. A glass electrode sensitive to NH_4^+ ion is also available.

LIQUID-MEMBRANE ELECTRODES

Electrodes sensitive to a variety of cations or anions can be prepared with a membrane or barrier containing a liquid ion-exchange material.[4] This type of electrode is constructed as shown in Fig. 15-2b. A small disk of hydrophobic filter material forms the barrier between inner and outer electrolytes. The disk is in contact at its perimeter with an organic solvent, immiscible with water, held in the annular space. Dissolved in this solvent is a salt of the desired ion with a counterion of relatively high molecular weight and much greater solubility in the organic phase than in water. The solvent is pulled into the pores of the disk by capillarity, where it makes electrical contact with both aqueous solutions. Equilibrium is thus established between the common ion in the membrane and the solutions. The potential of the inner electrode follows a Nernst relation, just as does that of the glass electrode. Some examples of electrodes with liquid membranes are listed in Table 15-1.

Table 15-1 Representative ion-selective electrodes
(From Ref. 2 unless noted)

Liquid membranes		
Ion measured	Exchange site†	Principal selectivity constants
Ca^{2+}	$(RO)_2PO_2^-$	H^+ 10^7; Zn^{2+} 3.2; Fe^{2+} 0.80; Pb^{2+} 0.63; Cu^{2+} 0.27; Ni^{2+} 0.08; Sr^{2+} 0.02; Mg^{2+} 0.01; Ba^{2+} 0.01; Na^+ 0.0016
NO_3^-	NiL_3^{2+}	ClO_4^- 10^3; I^- 20; ClO_3^- 2; Br^- 0.9; S^{2-} 0.57; NO_2^- 0.06; Cl^- 0.006; SO_4^{2-} 0.0006
ClO_4^-	FeL_3^{2+}	OH^- 1.0; I^- 0.012; NO_3^- 0.0015; Cl^- 0.00022; SO_4^{2-} 0.00016
UO_2^{2+} [12]	a polyether‡	H^+ 0.016; Ag^+ 0.003; Pb^{2+} 0.0002; etc.

Solid-state membranes		
Ion measured	Membrane	Principal interferences
F^-	LaF_3	OH^-
Cl^-	$AgCl(Ag_2S)$	$Br^-, I^-, S^{2-}, NH_3, CN^-$
Br^-	$AgBr(Ag_2S)$	I^-, S^{2-}, NH_3, CN^-
I^-	$AgI(Ag_2S)$	S^{2-}, CN^-
SCN^-	$AgSCN(Ag_2S)$	$Br^-, I^-, S^{2-}, NH_3, CN^-$
S^{2-}, Ag^+	Ag_2S	Hg^{2+}
CN^-	$AgI(Ag_2S)$	I^-, S^{2-}
Cu^{2+}	$CuS(Ag_2S)$	Hg^{2+}, Ag^+
Pb^{2+}	$PbS(Ag_2S)$	Hg^{2+}, Ag^+, Cu^{2+}
Cd^{2+}	$CdS(Ag_2S)$	Hg^{2+}, Ag^+, Cu^{2+}

† The ligand L is a substituted 9,10-phenanthroline moiety.
‡ N,N′-diheptyl-N,N′,6,6-tetramethyl-4,8-dioxaundecanediamide.

It is also possible to construct an electrode of this general type without an internal reference solution. The ion-exchange material is incorporated into a polymer which is then coated directly onto a metal wire.[6,7] Although the theory of these electrodes is not entirely clear, they appear to be the electrical equivalents of the more elaborate versions.

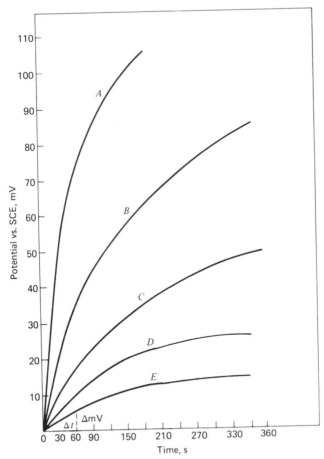

Figure 15-3 Response curves (potential against time) for the urease-catalyzed hydrolysis of urea. Urea concentration, 0.01 M; pH, 7.0; buffer, 0.1 M "tris." Units of urease are: A, 0.04; B, 0.016; C, 0.008; D, 0.004; E, 0.002. (*Analytical Chemistry.*[8])

DOUBLE-MEMBRANE ELECTRODES

The versatility of ion-selective membrane electrodes can sometimes be increased by the use of a second membrane. The partial pressure of CO_2 dissolved in blood plasma or other fluid is routinely measured with a glass electrode covered with a thin film of Teflon or other gas-permeable polymer. Trapped between the film and the glass is a layer of aqueous $NaHCO_3$ solution, about 0.01 M. In use, CO_2 diffuses through the plastic film, in an amount determined by its partial pressure in the sample. The resulting pH change in the bicarbonate solution is sensed by the glass electrode.

The inherent specificity of enzymes can sometimes be used to advantage in electrodes.[8] A second membrane consisting of a gel layer containing urease, for example, sensitizes an ammonium-ion glass electrode to urea. The enzyme-catalyzed hydrolysis of urea produces NH_4^+ ion at a *rate* proportional to the urea concentration.[9] The response is shown in Fig. 15-3. It will take several minutes for a steady potential to be reached, but a valid analysis can be obtained in less time by determining the initial slope. Other possible enzyme electrodes are reviewed in Refs. 10 and 11.

SOLID-STATE MEMBRANE ELECTRODES

Another important class of electrodes makes use of a wafer or pellet of crystalline material as the membrane. A prime example is the Orion† fluoride electrode, in which the membrane is a single crystal of lanthanum fluoride, LaF_3. Structurally this takes the form shown in Fig. 15-2c. The crystal lattice is such that fluoride ions can move about freely within an immobile framework of lanthanum ions. The response is completely specific to fluoride, as no other ions can penetrate into the crystal. The electrode shows true Nernstian response from approximately 10 to 10^{-6} M fluoride activity. It is limited in extremely dilute solutions by the finite solubility of the crystal. Equation (14-17) applies to this electrode, just as it does to the silver/silver chloride, so that the sign of the logarithmic term of the Nernst equation is negative

$$E = K - \frac{RT}{F} \ln (F^-) \qquad (15\text{-}5)$$

The fluoride electrode has become a particularly important analytical tool, because prior methods for the determination of this important ion involved time-consuming indirect methods of limited accuracy.

Comparable electrodes can be fabricated from a polycrystalline pressed pellet of silver sulfide, responsive to either Ag^+ or S^{2-} ions down to about 10^{-19} or 10^{-20} M.

Chloride, bromide, iodide, and thiocyanate electrodes can be made by pressing into a pellet a mixture of Ag_2S and the silver salt of the desired anion, AgX. As these salts are more soluble than is Ag_2S, the resulting equilibrium involves the

† Orion Research, Inc., Cambridge, Mass.

X^- anion and its counterpart in the test solutions. The Nernst equation takes the form

$$E = K - \frac{RT}{F} \ln (X^-) \qquad (15\text{-}6)$$

where K includes the log of the solubility product of AgX.

An analogous series of electrodes can be made by incorporating the sulfide of a second metal into the Ag_2S pellet. In the case of lead, for example (where $n = 2$), the applicable Nernst equation for this class III electrode is

$$E = K + \frac{RT}{2F} \ln (Pb^{2+}) \qquad (15\text{-}7)$$

Representative solid-state membrane electrodes are listed in Table 15-1.

The effects of extraneous ions on solid-state membrane electrodes contrast with such effects on liquid (and glass) ion-exchange types. In the case of liquid membranes, the effects are best described in terms of selectivity coefficients [Eq. (15-4)]. Interferences with solid-state electrodes, on the other hand, are primarily related to solubility products. For example,[6] an $AgBr(Ag_2S)$ electrode will cease responding to bromide ions and become effectively a thiocyanate electrode if the activity of SCN^- exceeds that of Br^- by the ratio of the K_{sp}'s, as then the AgBr on the surface of the electrode will convert to AgSCN. Lesser amounts of SCN^-, however, will have no deleterious effect.

These electrodes, based on solid-state membranes, are among the most convenient and useful detectors for cations and anions in solution that are available. It is to be expected that comparable electrodes will be developed for many other ions.[12]

Another type of selective electrode, invented by E. Pungor and manufactured in Hungary, consists of a silicone rubber membrane with an insoluble salt such as AgI imbedded in it like a "filler." The loaded membrane must be soaked for several hours before use, in a solution of the ion to which it is sensitized. These electrodes are not widely used in the United States.

REFERENCE ELECTRODES

The requirements for the reference electrode may be more severe with ion-selective electrodes than in pH measurements because of the greater accuracy often desired.[13] It is usually sufficient to measure pH to the nearest hundredth of a pH unit (± 0.6 mV), whereas measurements of ions other than H^+ may well need to be an order of magnitude better. Hence small variations in the reference electrode that would be negligible in pH measurements become important.

One of the most common reference electrode configurations for pH work utilizes a fiber of asbestos sealed through the glass at the site of the liquid junction.

The inner electrolyte (usually saturated KCl) is maintained at a slightly higher hydrostatic head than the test solution so that a slight outward flow of KCl will prevent contamination of the reference electrode. There is, however, some tendency for the fiber to become partially clogged with tiny crystals of KCl, preventing adequate flow and affecting the potential. It is desirable, when this may be a problem, to use an electrode with a sleeve-type liquid junction, providing greater flow.

POTENTIOMETRIC TITRATIONS

A great variety of titration reactions can be followed potentiometrically. The only requirement is that the reaction involves the addition or removal of some ion for which an electrode is available. The potential of the indicating electrode will change during the course of the titration, as dictated by the Nernst equation. The curves obtained when potential is plotted as a function of the amount of titrant added serve to identify the equivalence point or points as the points of steepest slope. As these curves are discussed in quantitative analysis texts, they will not be given detailed treatment here; Fig. 15-4 is a typical example.

The total change in voltage during a titration may well be only a small fraction of the mean potential difference between the two electrodes. If this is true, then the precision can be improved through the use of a concentration cell. The two compartments of the cell will contain identical electrodes, appropriate to the ion being titrated. In the reference side is placed a solution identical to that expected at the equivalence point. Then when the titration in the indicator vessel reaches equivalence, the potential difference will be zero. The increased precision results from the use of the measuring instrument in its most sensitive range.

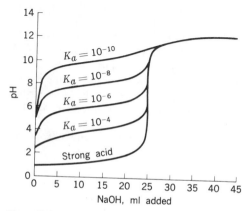

Figure 15-4 An example of potentiometric titration curves: Acids of various strengths titrated by NaOH. The acid dissociation constants are as marked.

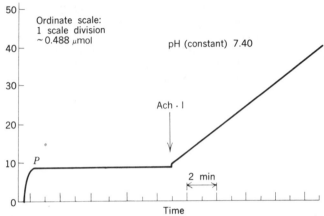

Figure 15-5 Titration of cholinesterase at constant pH. (*Acta Pharmacologica et Toxicologica.*[14])

Constant Potential Titrations

Another approach to potentiometric titration is to measure the amount of titrant needed to maintain the indicator electrode at a constant potential. The titration curve then becomes a plot of volume of standard solution added as a function of time. This procedure has been employed rather extensively in the field of enzymology.

For example, the enzyme cholinesterase acts to decompose acetylcholine, producing acetic acid in the process. The enzyme is highly sensitive to pH, and the medium must be held very close to pH 7.4 for the reaction to proceed optimally. This can be managed by the use of a pH meter connected to a servo system which controls a motor-driven syringe buret supplying NaOH solution as needed to maintain the pH constant. This equipment is known as a *pH-stat*. Figure 15-5 shows an example of a curve by which the cholinesterase activity of a sample of animal tissue was determined.[14] A 0.3-g portion of tissue was homogenized in physiological saline solution (0.9 percent NaCl). The pH was adjusted to 7.4 at point P, and held there for about 10 min to establish a base line showing that no acid was being liberated spontaneously. Then an excess of acetylcholine iodide (Ach.I) was added, whereupon the inflow of NaOH commenced. For this experiment the cholinesterase activity was determined from the slope to be 4.96×10^{-6} $mol \cdot g^{-1} \cdot min^{-1}$.

This general technique does not seem to have been applied extensively outside of biochemical work, but it is certainly of wide applicability.

INSTRUMENTATION

The Nernst equation is strictly valid only if no current passes through the cell. This imposes restrictions on the design of measuring instruments. There is no potential-measuring device that ensures truly zero current, but this condition can be approached closely enough for analytical purposes. The classical method is by the use of a precision potentiometer, an instrument in which the voltage of the cell is counterbalanced with an accurately measurable fraction of the voltage from a stable internal source. Potentiometers are seldom used in modern analytical laboratories.

The most prevalent instrument for measuring cell potentials is the *pH meter* (or *specific-ion meter*). This electronic voltmeter contains an amplifier that senses the signal voltage and produces a proportional meter deflection or numerical (digital) indication. The resistance of a glass electrode may be as high as $10^8 \ \Omega$, and if the error is to be held to 0.1 percent, the input resistance of the amplifier must not be less than $10^{11} \ \Omega$. This can easily be achieved with modern solid-state amplifiers.

There are many manufacturers of pH meters, each offering several models, some battery operated, some using the power lines. They fall roughly into three categories, with high, medium, and relatively low precision and accuracy (and price). The first group is primarily designed for research purposes, the second for general laboratory use, the third for field use where small size and rugged construction are more important than high precision.

A line-operated laboratory pH meter must have three controls on its panel, and may have a fourth. These are (1) a switch with "standby" and "operate" positions; (2) a calibration or standardization adjustment, which amounts to a zero offset with which to adjust the meter to read the correct value when the electrodes are immersed in a standard buffer; (3) a temperature compensator that permits alteration of the sensitivity to account for the temperature dependence of the Nernst potential. Some meters also have a scale selector that allows the instrument to cover the whole pH range (usually 0 to 14) or to fill the scale with a selected portion of that range, perhaps 2 or 3 pH units; this type is called an *expanded-scale pH meter*.

It is sometimes not realized that the temperature compensator acts to adjust the *slope* of the response curve, and therefore can be used to force the meter to give consistent readings for two standard buffers. Ideally, a pH meter set to 7 with a pH 7 buffer should read exactly 4 when tested with a buffer at pH 4, and similarly for pH 10. If it does not, a slight adjustment of the temperature knob will bring it to the correct reading. This should be followed by a repeat check at pH 7 and again at 4 or 10. This procedure inherently adjusts for the prevailing temperature.

Automatic Titrators

In industrial analytical laboratories and for some kinds of research problems, automatically operated potentiometric titrators are widely used. There are two classes of titrators, those in which a complete titration curve is plotted on chart paper, and those that act to close an electrically operated buret valve at the equivalence point. Those of the first type consist in essence of a pH meter connected to a strip-chart recorder. The titrant must be delivered at a constant rate. This is not possible from a conventional gravity-flow buret, so a constant-flow pump or motor-driven syringe must be used in its place.

The second type of titrator employs in its end-point detection system a special capacitive electronic circuit that will doubly differentiate the variations in potential that are fed into it from the electrodes. If the potential as a function of volume of reagent $E = f(V)$ is given by curve a of Fig. 15-6, then the derivative dE/dV is represented by curve b, and the second derivative d^2E/dV^2 by curve c. In the titrator, advantage is taken of the fact that the positive peak in curve c comes very slightly *before* the equivalence point. The first *decrease* in the second-derivative current triggers a relay that closes the buret stopcock. The mechanical inertia in the moving parts causes a delay that just offsets the advance warning given by the second-derivative curve, so that the flow of titrant is stopped at the right moment.

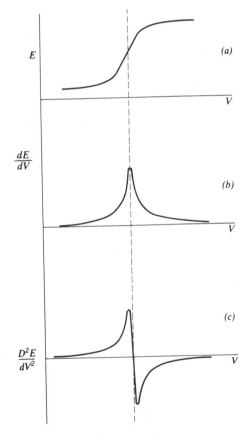

Figure 15-6 A potentiometric titration curve, shown as (a) the integral form, (b) the first derivative, and (c) the second derivative.

PROBLEMS

15-1 A cell is formed with a lead electrode in 0.015 M lead acetate and a cadmium electrode in 0.021 M cadmium sulfate. The two solutions are joined by a salt bridge containing ammonium nitrate. What is the potential of the cell at 25°C? (The activity coefficients in the two solutions can be considered equal.)

15-2 What is the pH of a solution at 25°C if a potential of 0.703 V is observed between a hydrogen electrode and an SHE placed therein?

15-3 A cell is set up as follows: silver electrode, unknown solution, salt bridge, saturated KCl solution, $Hg_2Cl_{2(s)}$, mercury electrode. (a) Which electrode is the reference and which the indicator? (b) What is the purpose of the salt bridge, and what electrolyte should it contain? (c) If the potential of the cell is found to be 0.300 V, with the silver electrode more positive than the mercury, what is the concentration of Ag^+ ion in the unknown?

15-4 A sample of lead was suspected of containing an impurity of silver. To analyze for this, a method using a concentration cell was selected. A 10.00-gram sample of the metal was dissolved in nitric acid and diluted to 100.0 ml. The cell was prepared by pipetting 25.00 ml of 0.1000 M silver nitrate into each of two beakers. Identical silver electrodes were inserted and the two solutions joined by an ammonium nitrate salt bridge. The potential difference between the electrodes was, as expected, zero. A 10.00-ml aliquot of the lead nitrate solution was added to one beaker and 10.00 ml of distilled water to the other, whereupon a potential of 0.070 mV appeared between the silver electrodes. Calculate the percentage of silver impurity in the lead. Estimate the precision of the analysis if the measuring instrument has a maximum uncertainty of ± 1 μV.

15-5 A cell is assembled with two platinum wires as electrodes dipping into separate beakers that are connected by a salt bridge, each beaker containing 25.00 ml of a mixture of Fe(II) and Fe(III) chlorides, each 1 M. Now 1.00 ml of a solution of tin(II) chloride is added to one side, causing a potential difference of 0.260 mV to appear between the electrodes. The reaction taking place is

$$SnCl_2 + 2FeCl_3 \longrightarrow 2FeCl_2 + SnCl_4$$

Compute the concentration of the $SnCl_2$ solution.

15-6 What is the maximum concentration of Cu^{2+} ion that can exist in solution in contact with metallic zinc?

15-7 Derive an equation for the potential of a CO_2 electrode as a function of the partial pressure of CO_2 in a sample.

15-8 The fluoride electrode can be used in class II to measure lanthanum ions, La^{3+}. Derive the relation between the potential and the La^{3+}-ion activity.

15-9 An aqueous solution (at pH 5.0) is to be examined for its free F^--ion concentration. A 100-ml portion of the solution, measured with a fluoride electrode, is found to give a reading of 120 mV against a suitable reference electrode. Exactly 1.00 ml of a 0.100 M solution of KF is added to the test solution with stirring, whereupon the potential changes to 108 mV. Calculate the F^--ion concentration in the sample. Assume 25°C.

15-10 A glass electrode gives the following potentials against a convenient reference electrode:

$[H^+]$	$[Na^+]$	E
10^{-10}	10^{-6}	-0.572
10^{-10}	10^{-7}	-0.588
10^{-12}	10^{-4}	-0.472

What is the value of k_1 in Eq. (15-4), if no other cations are present?

REFERENCES

1. N. H. Fµrman, in *Trace Analysis*, J. H. Yoe and H. J. Koch, Jr. (eds.), Wiley, New York, **1957**; chap. 9.
2. R. A. Durst (ed.), "Ion-Selective Electrodes," *Natl. Bur. Standards Spec. Publ.* 314, **1969**.
3. R. G. Bates, *Determination of pH: Theory and Practice*, (3d ed.), Wiley, New York, **1973**.
4. G. Eisenman, *Glass Electrodes for Hydrogen and Other Cations*, Dekker, New York, **1967**.
5. A. K. Covington and M. I. A. Ferra, *Anal. Chem.*, **1977**, *49*, 1363.
6. J. W. Ross, Jr., chap. 2 of Ref. 2.
7. C. R. Martin and H. Freiser, *J. Chem. Educ.*, **1980**, *57*, 512.
8. G. G. Guilbault, R. K. Smith, and J. G. Montalvo, Jr., *Anal. Chem.*, **1969**, *41*, 600.
9. A. Ansaldi and S. I. Epstein, *Anal. Chem.*, **1973**, *45*, 595.
10. H. H. Weetall, *Anal. Chem.*, **1974**, *46*, 602A.
11. L. D. Bowers and P. W. Carr. *Anal., Chem.*, **1976**, *48*, 544A.
12. J. Šenkyr, D. Ammann, P. C. Meier, W. E. Morf, E. Pretsch, and W. Simon, *Anal. Chem.*, **1979**, *51*, 786.
13. R. D. Caton, Jr., *J. Chem. Educ.*, **1973**, *50*, A571; **1974**, *51*, A7.
14. J. Jensen-Holm, H. H. Lausen, K. Milthers, and K. O. Møller, *Acta Pharmacol. Toxicol.*, **1959**, *15*, 384.

SIXTEEN

VOLTAMMETRY, POLAROGRAPHY, AND RELATED METHODS

The previous chapter dealt with potentials of electrodes in which no current was allowed to flow. We shall now investigate phenomena accompanied by the passage of appreciable current. In particular, we will be concerned with plotting curves showing the current as a function of the voltage on the electrode of interest (the *working electrode*). This general approach to the study of the composition of a solution is called *voltammetry*. The term *polarography* is limited to voltammetry at the dropping mercury electrode.

The passage of current necessitates a modification of the reference electrode, or better, the addition of a third electrode to the cell. The use of the same electrode as both reference and current carrier is undesirable in principle. To be used this way, an electrode must have low internal resistance in order not to introduce excessive error; a 10-mV error will result from only 10 μA flowing through 1000 Ω. In addition, the metal–solution interface in the reference electrode must have a much larger area than the working electrode so that the current density and hence any resulting polarization effects will be minimized. This can be satisfactory for currents less than about 10 μA if the working electrode is very small. The fiber-tip reference electrode intended for use with a pH meter has much too high a resistance for this application.

A three-electrode cell is greatly to be preferred in general voltammetry. The third (auxiliary) electrode carries the current, while the reference electrode only senses a potential but does not draw current. The auxiliary electrode can be simply a wire of platinum or silver, or it can be a mercury pool. The reference electrode, since it does not carry current, can be of any convenient physical form.

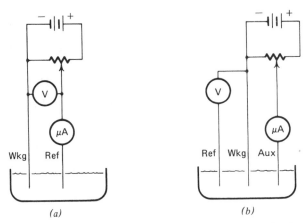

(a)   (b)

Figure 16-1 Two- and three-electrode cells for voltammetry and polarography. Wkg: working electrode; Ref: reference electrode; Aux: auxiliary electrode.

Another advantage to the three-electrode arrangement is that it can be used with high-resistance, nonaqueous or mixed solvent systems as well as with the more common low-resistance aqueous solutions. For this application, the tip of the reference electrode (or of a salt bridge leading to it) must be placed as close as possible to the working electrode, so as not to sense any significant portion of the voltage drop across the solution.

The two- and three-electrode cells are compared in Fig. 16-1. A variable voltage source and a microammeter are connected in series with the current-carrying electrodes. The actual potential at the working electrode relative to the reference electrode is measured by a suitable electronic voltmeter.

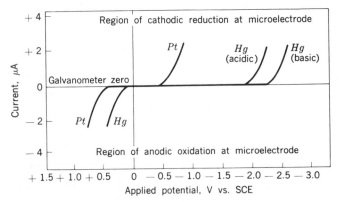

Figure 16-2 Conventions for plotting voltammograms. The curves labelled Pt or Hg indicate the approximate potential limits attainable at these electrodes.

The working electrode in voltammetry is inert, responding to whatever electroactive species may be present in solution. The choice of electrode depends largely on the range of potentials to be investigated. For potentials more positive than the SCE, the best choice is platinum. Mercury can be used at potentials more negative than about $+0.25$ V versus SCE. Platinum is limited in the positive direction by the oxidation of water $(2\,H_2O \rightarrow O_2 + 4\,H^+ + 4e^-)$, which occurs at about $+0.65$ V, depending on the pH. On the other hand, for negative potentials, platinum can only be used to about -0.45 V, at which point hydrogen is liberated $(2\,H^+ + 2e^- \rightarrow H_2$, or $2\,H_2O + 2e^- \rightarrow H_2 + 2\,OH^-)$, while mercury, due to its high overvoltage for hydrogen, can be utilized as far as -1.8 V in acid or -2.3 V in basic media. Figure 16-2 shows these limiting potentials graphically, and also indicates the conventions regarding the sign of the current and the method of plotting voltammetric curves.

DIFFUSION-LIMITED CURRENT

Consider an inert working microelectrode together with a silver wire as auxiliary electrode, and a saturated calomel reference in a deaerated, unstirred solution containing 0.1 M KCl and 10^{-3} M $PbCl_2$. Let us suppose that a switch is closed in the external circuit, suddenly applying -1.0 V to the working electrode relative to the SCE (Fig. 16-1b). This potential is great enough to reduce Pb^{2+} ion to the metal, but not to reduce water (at pH 7). K^+ ion would require a much higher potential, and there is nothing else that is reducible. At the auxiliary electrode (the anode) an amount of silver equivalent to the reduced lead is converted to AgCl, a process that has no effect on the working electrode.

Several things will happen: the electric field will cause both K^+ and Pb^{2+} ions to move toward the microelectrode and Cl^- ions to move in the opposite direction. The K^+ ions, not being reducible, will form a sheath (about one or two ions thick) around the electrode, and this will result in almost completely neutralizing the field, so far as the bulk of the solution is concerned. The Pb^{2+} ions will not contribute to this sheath, because they *are* reducible; every lead ion that approaches the electrode will immediately be discharged and deposited on the surface. But since the field has been neutralized by the K^+ ions, the only way the lead ions can reach the vicinity of the electrode is by *diffusion*. (Because of the requirement of overall electrical neutrality, the reverse movement of Cl^- ions will drop to the low level required to match the reduction of Pb^{2+} ions.)

The rate of movement of any species because of diffusion is proportional to the concentration gradient at any two points divided by the distance between them. In terms of the calculus

$$\frac{dN}{dt} = -D\frac{dC}{dx} \tag{16-1}$$

in which dN/dt is the number of moles passing a particular point in the solution per unit time, C refers to the concentration of the diffusing species, and D is a constant of proportionality called the *diffusion coefficient*. (The negative sign appears because the net diffusion is toward the *smaller* concentration.) This is *Fick's law.*[1]

Application of Fick's law to the electrolysis problem we are considering leads to the *Cottrell equation*

$$i = nFA\left(\frac{D}{\pi t}\right)^{1/2} C \tag{16-2}$$

where i is the electrolysis diffusion current (in μA) flowing at time t (s) from the start of the experiment, n is the number of electrons involved in the electrode reaction, F is the Faraday constant (96487 C per equivalent),† A is the area (cm^2) of the electrode, D is Fick's diffusion coefficient (cm$^2 \cdot$s^{-1}), and C is the bulk concentration of the electroactive species (mmol$\cdot$l^{-1}). The concentration is assumed to be zero at the electrode surface. The current i is taken as positive for cathodic reductions and negative for anodic oxidations. It is important to note the proportionality between the current and concentration; however, since the current falls off as the square root of time, rather than assuming a fixed value, this equation is not a convenient basis for analytical work.‡ A more practical relation will be derived in a later section.

THE DROPPING MERCURY ELECTRODE (DME)

The most widely used microelectrode is mercury in the form of a succession of tiny droplets emerging from a very fine bore glass capillary. This has several major advantages, in comparison to solid electrodes, to offset the inconvenience of handling mercury. One is the high hydrogen overvoltage of a mercury cathode; another is the fact that the electrode surface is continually being renewed, and hence cannot become fouled or poisoned. In addition, the increasing area of the DME during the lifetime of each drop more than offsets the decreasing current predicted by the Cottrell equation for an electrode of fixed area; this, as we shall see shortly, makes quantitative analysis much more practical.

The simplest cell for use in three-electrode polarography is merely a small beaker (100 or 150 ml) to contain the solution to be analyzed. Into this are dipped the tip of the DME capillary, a reference electrode, and a platinum wire as an auxiliary electrode (Fig. 16-3). The DME must be clamped firmly in a vertical position so that the mercury drops will be uniform. Also included should be a bubbling tube to admit inert gas for deoxygenation. Commercial cells usually have a plastic cover with holes to fit the several inserts. For the older, two-electrode instruments, the customary cell was in the shape of an H, with a low-resistance

---

† Note that C is the accepted symbol (abbreviation) for coulomb, whereas italic *C* is here defined as a concentration.

‡ Analysis by means of current-time curves at constant potential, which makes direct use of the Cottrell equation, is called *chronoamperometry*. It has some value in studies of the electron-transfer kinetics in irreversible systems.

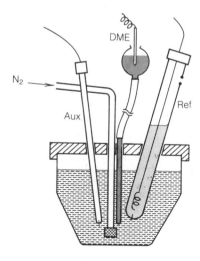

Figure 16-3 A three-electrode polarographic cell. The reference electrode can be of the type designed for pH meters.

SCE permanently installed in one side, the DME inserted in the other. The cross arm was filled with a plug of agar gel containing KCl, held in place with a glass frit.

The capillary for the dropping electrode is a section of glass tubing several centimeters long, with an internal diameter of 0.03 to 0.05 mm. It must be handled with care to prevent any aqueous solution from entering, since it is practically impossible to clean it out if it once becomes contaminated. After use, the capillary should be removed from the cell and rinsed with distilled water *while the mercury is still flowing*. It can then be clamped in air, protected from dust, and the mercury reservoir lowered to just stop the flow. It should *not* be left immersed in water.

To derive an equation for the DME corresponding to the Cottrell equation for stationary electrodes, we must make the assumptions that the rate of flow of mercury is constant and that the drop of mercury is spherical right up to the moment of separation. This leads to the *Ilkovič equation*

$$i_d = 708.2 \, nD^{1/2}m^{2/3}t^{1/6}C \tag{16-3}$$

where i_d is the *diffusion current* and m is the *rate* of flow of mercury (in $mg \cdot s^{-1}$). The numerical coefficient includes geometrical factors, the Faraday constant, and the density of mercury. If the current is plotted as a function of time, a fluctuating curve is obtained, as in Fig. 16-4, with a period of a few seconds. The drop time can be varied by changing the head of mercury or by dislodging the drops by tapping the capillary stem electromechanically at regular intervals. The natural drop time varies slightly with the applied potential, being greatest at about -0.5 V versus SCE.†

---

† This is the potential, known as the *electrocapillary maximum* (ECM), at which a mercury–water interface has a maximum interfacial tension. A mercury electrode when initially placed in water assumes the potential of the ECM.

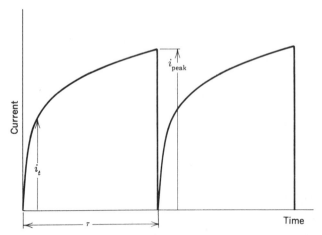

Figure 16-4 Current-time characteristic of the dropping mercury electrode, showing current increasing as the $\frac{1}{6}$-power of time.

Although the temperature does not enter explicitly into the Ilkovič equation, it is nevertheless important, as each factor in the equation (excepting n) is to some extent temperature-dependent. The chief effect is through the temperature coefficient of the diffusion constant D. The diffusion current increases by 1 or 2 percent per degree in the vicinity of room temperature. Hence the cell temperature should be controlled to within a few tenths of a degree for high-precision measurements. This is not needed for qualitative or semiquantitative work, however.

The diffusion current also varies from its normal value if the concentration of supporting electrolyte is less than 25 or 30 times that of the reducible substance. This is because, under these conditions, the reducible ions carry an appreciable fraction of the current. This *migration current* results from the electrostatic attraction or repulsion between the DME and the ions. Hence the observed current is increased slightly for the reduction of cations (coulombic attraction) and diminished (coulombic repulsion) for the reduction of anions, as a result of lowering the supporting electrolyte concentration, while it is unchanged for the reduction of nonionic species. This situation would invalidate the Ilkovič equation, since the transport of reducible substance to the electrode is no longer governed solely by diffusion.

VOLTAGE SCANNING POLAROGRAPHY

The previous section discussed current-time curves produced at constant potential. In practical polarography, however, more useful information can be obtained by sweeping the voltage applied to the DME, and recording the current. Curves of this type are produced by automatically recording *polarographs.*

In the simplest polarograph the potential applied to the cell is continuously increased, usually in the negative direction (i.e., the DME becoming more negative with respect to the SCE) and the current is recorded on a strip-chart recorder. As the potential changes linearly with time, and the recording paper moves at constant speed, the resulting curve (*polarogram*) can be interpreted as a true current-voltage plot.

Consider a cell such as that in Fig. 16-3, provided with DME, SCE, and platinum auxiliary electrodes, filled with an oxygen-free solution that is 0.1 M in KNO_3 and 0.001 M in Cd^{2+}. A polarogram obtained as outlined above will resemble that shown as curve a in Fig. 16-5. The most obvious feature of this curve is the series of deep serrations produced by successive drop-falls. These fluctuations complicate the interpretation of the current-voltage curves. They can be minimized by a number of instrumental techniques, one of which involves an electronic gating system such that the current is sampled only for a fraction of a second just

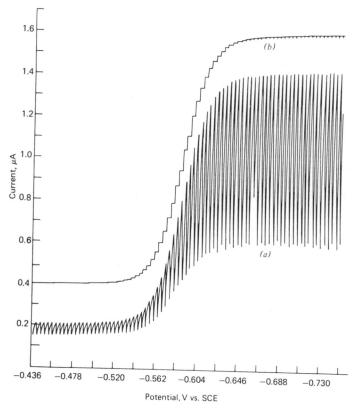

Figure 16-5 Comparison of polarograms (*a*) without and (*b*) with sampling circuitry. Curve (*b*) is displaced upward for clarity. The solution is 10^{-3} M Cd^{2+} in 1 M KNO_3. (*Courtesy of W. J. Mergens.*)

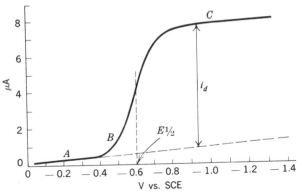

Figure 16-6 Idealized polarogram of 10^{-3} M Cd^{2+} in 0.1 M KCl. The solid line is the envelope of the actual polarogram.

before each drop-fall ("time-sampled" or "Tast" polarography). This presents the data in a more convenient form (curve b of Fig. 16-5).

To examine the phenomena taking place in the cell, it is convenient to use an idealized curve, such as Fig. 16-6. The rising portion of this curve is commonly known as a "polarographic wave." The curve divides itself into three regions. In region A the potential is too low to permit reduction of any of the substances known to be present. The small current that does flow is called the *residual current*; it can be explained as the sum total of currents due to the reduction of trace impurities (most commonly O_2), and a so-called *charging current* which results from the fact that the mercury–solution interface, with its sheath of unreducible ions, acts like a capacitor. As the voltage is increased during the scan, more and more charge is driven onto this capacitor, constituting a current. The residual current is small, and if care is taken to remove oxygen, it is reproducible and easily corrected for.

In the vicinity of B, the current starts to increase above the residual current level. This added current corresponds to the removal of Cd^{2+} ions from the solution at the surface of the electrode by reduction to Cd metal. The ions so removed are replaced by diffusion from the body of the solution.

At C the current shows a saturation effect caused by the total depletion of Cd^{2+} ions in the near vicinity of the DME. More Cd^{2+} ions continually reach the electrode by diffusion, so that a steady state equilibrium is established, with correspondingly constant current. The rate of diffusion is determined solely by the difference in concentration between the bulk solution and zero, the concentration at the electrode surface. The value of the limiting current at C, corrected for the residual current, is called the *diffusion current i_d*. It is directly dependent on the bulk concentration of the reducible species.

If the negative potential is increased beyond C, the current will rise slowly (parallel to the residual current curve) up to about $-2V$, where it again increases rapidly, corresponding to the reduction of some other component of the solution, possibly K^+ or H^+ ions.

THE SHAPE OF THE POLAROGRAPHIC WAVE

The equation for the current as a function of potential can be derived from the Nernst relation, provided that the reaction at the DME is reversible. This derivation will be illustrated here by the important special case of the reduction of a simple cation to a metal soluble in mercury. Since solutions studied polarographically are almost always very dilute, activity coefficients can be assumed to be unity. The same assumption applies to the activity coefficient of the metal dissolved in the amalgam.

The half-reaction can be written in the form

$$M^{n+} + ne^- \longrightarrow M_{Hg}$$

where M_{Hg} denotes the metal dissolved in mercury. The potential of the electrode is given by the Nernst equation as

$$E_{DME} = E^\circ - \frac{RT}{nF} \ln \left(\frac{[M]^s_{Hg}}{[M^{n+}]^s_{aq}} \right) \qquad (16\text{-}4)$$

where the superscript "s" signifies conditions at the mercury surface. Since the current i is limited by diffusion,† it follows that

$$i = k([M^{n+}]_{aq} - [M^{n+}]^s_{aq}) \qquad (16\text{-}5)$$

where $k = 708\, nD^{1/2}m^{2/3}t^{1/6}$. For the limiting current, i_d, $[M^{n+}]^s_{aq}$ becomes very small, and we can write

$$i_d = k[M^{n+}]_{aq} \qquad (16\text{-}6)$$

and thus

$$i = i_d - k[M^{n+}]^s_{aq} \qquad (16\text{-}7)$$

The concentration of M in the amalgam is proportional to the current, so that

$$i = k'[M]_{Hg} \qquad (16\text{-}8)$$

The constant k' differs from k only in that the diffusion coefficient D is replaced by D', a similar factor for M in the amalgam, so that

$$\frac{k}{k'} = \left(\frac{D}{D'} \right)^{1/2} \qquad (16\text{-}9)$$

The values of $[M]_{Hg}$ and $[M^{n+}]^s_{aq}$ from Eqs. (16-7) and (16-8) and the ratio of constants from Eq. (16-9) can be substituted into Eq. (16-4), to give

$$E_{DME} = E^\circ - \frac{RT}{2nF} \ln \left(\frac{D}{D'} \right) - \frac{RT}{nF} \ln \left(\frac{i}{i_d - i} \right) \qquad (16\text{-}10)$$

---

† Currents, in this discussion, are assumed to have been corrected for the residual current blank.

At the point where $i = i_d/2$, the last term drops out, and the potential is designated as the *half-wave potential*

$$E_{1/2} = E° - \frac{RT}{2nF} \ln \left(\frac{D}{D'} \right) \qquad (16\text{-}11)$$

From this we can write

$$E_{DME} = E_{1/2} - \frac{RT}{nF} \ln \left(\frac{i}{i_d - i} \right) \qquad (16\text{-}12)$$

The half-wave potential is an easily measured quantity, and as Eq. (16-11) shows, it is simply related to the standard potential $E°$. The diffusion coefficients D and D' are usually not greatly different in the absence of complexing agents, so that $E_{1/2}$ is normally not far from $E°$.

Equation (16-12) gives the form of the polarographic wave in terms of the parameters i_d and $E_{1/2}$, and provides a convenient method for establishing the value of n. The most direct measure of n is obtained by plotting values of $\log [i/(i_d - i)]$ against the potential E_{DME} (Fig. 16-7). The equation predicts a straight line with slope given by $2.303RT/nF$, or (at 25°C) $0.0591/n$. The point on this curve corresponding to $i = i_d/2$ will give a precise measure of $E_{1/2}$.

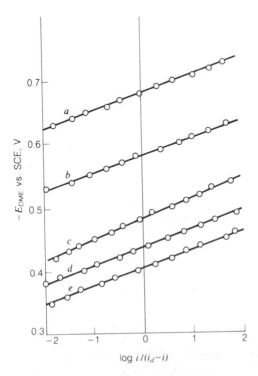

Figure 16-7 Plots of $-E_{DME}$ against log $[i/(i_d - i)]$ for the reduction of Pb^{2+} from the following media (*a*) 0.1 *M* NaOH, (*b*) 1 *M* $K_2C_2O_4$ (oxalate) at pH 9.0, (*c*) 0.5 *M* $Na_2C_4H_4O_6$ (tartrate) at pH 5.5, (*d*) 1 *M* KCl, (*e*) 1 *M* KNO_3. The mean slope is 29.8 ± 1.7 mV. The intersections of the vertical zero line with the experimental curves give the respective half-wave potentials. (*Wiley-Interscience.*[2])

The preceding derivation is concerned with the reduction of a simple hydrated ion. In the presence of a complex former, the half-wave potential is shifted to more negative values in accordance with the relation

$$E_{1/2} = E^\circ + \frac{RT}{nF} \ln K_c - \frac{pRT}{nF} \ln [X] \qquad (16\text{-}13)$$

where K_c is the instability constant of the complex, $[X]$ is the concentration of the complexing agent, and p is the number of moles of X that combines with one mole of the metal M. (This equation is based on the assumption that the diffusion coefficients involved are nearly equal.) Equation (16-12) is essentially unaltered by the presence of a complex, though the value of i_d for a given concentration may change slightly.

The discussion above was given in terms of cathodic reduction at the DME, as this is the most widely applicable condition. It is also valid, however, for anodic oxidations at the DME.

For the case of reduction to a metal that is insoluble in mercury (such as Fe or Cr) the equations would have to be modified, but this is of no great importance, since all known examples are irreversible so that the Nernst equation does not apply.

Another process that is important is the reduction (or oxidation) of one water-soluble species to another, for example, the reduction of Fe^{3+} to Fe^{2+} ions. If both forms of A in the general equation $A_{ox} + ne^- \rightleftharpoons A_{red}$ are present simultaneously in solution, the potential of the DME is given by

$$E_{DME} = E_{1/2} - \frac{RT}{nF} \ln \left(\frac{i - i_{d(a)}}{i_{d(c)} - i} \right) \qquad (16\text{-}14)$$

in which $i_{d(a)}$ represents an *anodic* diffusion current due to oxidation of A_{red}, and $i_{d(c)}$ is the *cathodic* diffusion current corresponding to the reduction of A_{ox}. The half-wave potential is

$$E_{1/2} = E^\circ - \frac{RT}{2nF} \ln \left(\frac{D_{ox}}{D_{red}} \right) \qquad (16\text{-}15)$$

Since the two diffusion coefficients are usually nearly equal, E°, the standard potential for the redox system, is very nearly equal to $E_{1/2}$. If either A_{ox} or A_{red} is absent from the solution, the corresponding i_d becomes zero, but the value of $E_{1/2}$ is unchanged. Figure 16-8 illustrates this for the case of Fe(III) and Fe(II)[2]. Curve (a) shows the reduction of Fe(III), curve (c) the oxidation of Fe(II), while (b) gives the curve for (almost) equal quantities of the two. The vertical lines indicate the half-wave potentials, which should be identical in this reversible system.

If two or more reducible species are present in the same solution, the polarogram will include waves for each, as shown in Fig. 16-9. The five cations in this figure have quite different properties: (1) Ag^+ is reduced so easily that its wave cannot be completely formed, though the diffusion plateau is well defined; (2) Tl^+ shows a reversible reduction with $n = 1$; (3) Cd^{2+} is also reversible, but the slope

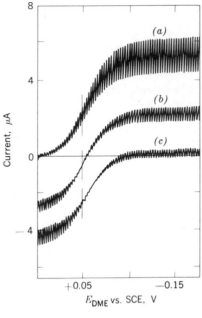

Figure 16-8 Polarograms of (a) 1.4 mM Fe(III), (b) 0.7 mM each of Fe(II) and Fe(III), and (c) 1.4 mM Fe(II). The supporting electrolyte in each case is saturated oxalic acid containing 0.0002 percent methyl red as a maximum suppressor. (*Wiley-Interscience*.[2])

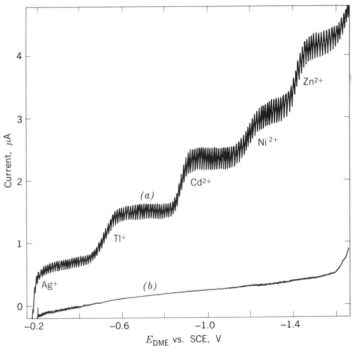

Figure 16-9 Polarograms of (a) a solution containing 0.1 M each of Ag^+, Tl^+, Cd^{2+}, Ni^{2+}, and Zn^{2+} in 1 M NH_3 and 1 M NH_4Cl, with 0.002 percent Triton X-100; (b) the supporting electrolyte alone. (*Wiley-Interscience*.[2])

shows that $n = 2$; (4) Ni^{2+} shows a more drawn-out curve, though $n = 2$, indicative of irreversibility; (5) Zn^{2+} resembles Cd^{2+} in showing a reversible wave with $n = 2$.

Maxima

Sometimes as the voltage is increased past the top of a polarographic wave, the current drops somewhat, instead of leveling off, creating a maximum in the curve. This may be only a slight hump, or it may be a sharp peak exceeding the true wave height by a factor of two or more. This phenomena is related to the tangential streaming motion of the solution past the surface of the expanding drop.

Maxima can usually be eliminated by the addition of an organic surfactant such as gelatin or certain dyes. The nonionic detergent Triton X-100† is particularly useful as a maximum suppressor. A 0.2 percent stock solution is convenient; 0.1 ml of this for each 10 ml of solution in the polarographic cell is usually satisfactory. Care must be taken not to use too much suppressor, as this may distort or even suppress the wave itself along with the maximum, and the half-wave potential may be shifted a few millivolts from its normal value.

Oxygen Interference

Dissolved oxygen is reducible at the DME in many media. An example of its effect on a polarogram is shown in Fig. 16-10, where two waves are seen. The first ($E_{1/2} = -0.05$ V vs. SCE) is caused by the reduction of oxygen from zero oxidation state to -1 (as in hydrogen peroxide); the second ($E_{1/2} = -0.9$ V) corresponds to the reduction from zero to -2 (as in water). The first of these two waves often shows a sharp maximum in the absence of a suppressor and in a dilute supporting electrolyte. This wave can be utilized in the analytical determination of dissolved oxygen, but more often it appears as an interferent of high nuisance value. Hence in most polarographic work provision must be made for the removal of oxygen. In alkaline solutions this can often be accomplished by adding a small amount of potassium sulfite which reduces the oxygen quantitatively. In any case the oxygen can be flushed out of the solution with an inert gas such as nitrogen, a process called *sparging*. Using a simple constricted glass tube this may take 20 to 30 min. The time can be cut to 2 or 3 min by substituting a fritted-glass gas disperser. The stream of gas must be discontinued while data are being taken, because of the undesirable stirring action. Mercury should be excluded from the solution until after the deaeration, since it may be oxidized by the dissolved oxygen. This means that the capillary should not be inserted into the cell prior to the removal of oxygen.

Instrumentation

A basic three-electrode polarograph can easily be assembled from standard electronic components, following the diagram of Fig. 16-11. This calls for three

† Rohm and Haas Company, Philadelphia.

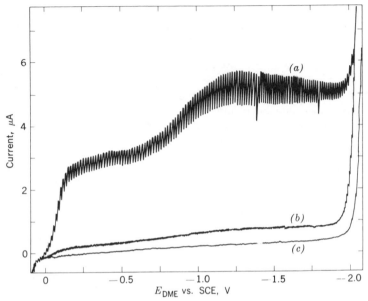

Figure 16-10 Polarograms of 0.1 *M* KCl: (*a*) saturated with air, showing the double wave of oxygen; (*b*) partially deaerated; (*c*) after complete deaeration. (*Wiley-Interscience.*[2])

operational amplifiers.† A linear ramp for scanning the voltage applied to the DME can be obtained from a single amplifier (no. 1 in the figure) with a capacitor connected from its output back to its input. If components E_1, R_1, and C_1 are constants, the output at E_2 will be given by

$$E_2 = -\frac{E_1}{R_1 C_1} \int_0^t dt = -\frac{E_1}{R_1 C_1} t \qquad (16\text{-}16)$$

† These amplifiers, described briefly in Chap. 3 in connection with photodetectors, are discussed more fully in Chap. 27.

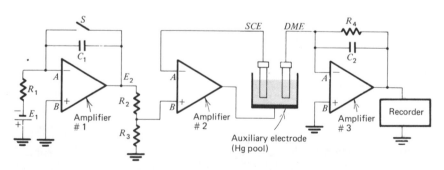

Figure 16-11 A three-electrode polarograph with operational amplifier circuitry.

This shows that the voltage at E_2 will increase linearly with time, its slope being determined by constants. Because of the negative sign, if E_1 is negative, then E_2 will be positive-going; this constitutes the *ramp* function.

An appropriate fraction of the ramp (determined by the magnitudes of R_2 and R_3) is applied to the B input of amplifier 2, which is thus kept at the ramp potential above ground. The only mode of response available to amplifier 2 is to emit current from its output to the auxiliary electrode. This current cannot go to the SCE, because the SCE connects only to the input of an amplifier and hence cannot carry current; therefore the current *must* flow through the DME and the resistor R_4. Amplifier 3 is forced to put out just enough current to equal that passing through the cell, in order to ensure the equality of potential at its two inputs. Because of this equality, the DME is essentially at ground potential at all times. The SCE, for a similar reason, is always at ramp potential above ground. The result is that amplifier 2 allows precisely the required amount of current to flow to maintain the SCE–DME potential difference at the desired linearly increasing voltage, with the DME negative-going. Hence the recorder will give the true polarogram. The function of capacitor C_2 is to reduce the amount of high-frequency electrical noise in the circuit. Resistor R_4 relates to the scale of the recorder. The switch S across the integrating capacitor is used to start the experiment; the moment of opening this switch corresponds to time zero. Range switching and zero offset are easily supplied, but are omitted from the figure for clarity.

Sampling Circuits

As mentioned earlier, one component of the residual current is due to the charging of the capacitance existing at the electrode–solution interface. As the DME is made more and more negative during the scan, increasing numbers of nonreducible cations are drawn into the cloud surrounding the electrode. The motion of these ions and of a like number of electrons within the metal constitute a transient current, often referred to as the *double-layer charging* (or *capacitive*) *current*. As with any capacitor, current can only flow if either the voltage is varying or the "plates" of the capacitor are changing in area or separation. In the case of the DME, the separation is the thickness of the double layer (the ions in the cloud and the electrons in the metal), which may be considered to be constant. The governing equation for the capacitive current is

$$I_c = K \frac{dA}{dt} + \frac{dE}{dt} \qquad (16\text{-}17)$$

where the constant K includes the dielectric constant and the separation, and where A is the area of the electrode surface. We can consider two cases: (1) the change of voltage dE/dt (the ramp) is slow enough to be negligible during the drop period, and (2) the measurement is made near the end of a drop life, where the rate of change of the area dA/dt is minimal.

It can be shown mathematically that, whereas the faradaic current increases as the one-sixth power of time, starting at zero with the birth of a new drop, the

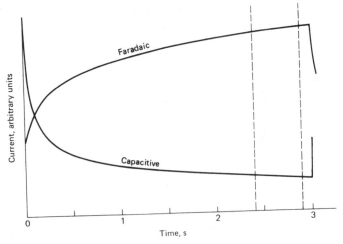

Figure 16-12 Growth of the faradaic current and simultaneous decrease of the capacitive (charging) current within the lifetime of a single mercury drop. The period between the vertical dashed lines is the optimum time for current measurements.

charging current is relatively large at the start and then decreases, following a minus one-third power curve. These relations (Fig. 16-12) show that the effect of the charging current will be least and that of the faradaic current greatest just before each drop of mercury falls. A very productive approach to increasing the signal-to-noise ratio lies in a gating or timing arrangement whereby current measurements are taken only during the last part of the growth of the drop.

The gating system can be synchronized with the DME either by detecting the drop fall with an electronic sensor or by dislodging the drop at a predetermined time. For example, in Fig. 16-12, a timing circuit can be designed to knock off the drop at 3-s intervals, and to permit the recorder to respond only between 2.4 and 2.9 s in the drop lifetime. During the 2.5 s when the current is *not* being sampled, the recorder will simply draw a horizontal straight-line segment. The result, as seen in curve *b* of Fig. 16-5, is much easier to measure quantitatively than is the unmodified polarogram.

Rapid-Scan Polarography

It is possible to sweep the applied voltage fast enough to obtain a complete polarogram within the last half-second of the drop life. The curve obtained by this method differs from a conventional polarogram, showing a peak of characteristic shape (Fig. 16-13). The reason for this shape is that the slow process of diffusion is unable to supply reducible material to the electrode fast enough to keep up with the rapidly increasing potential, so that a steady state is never attained. The

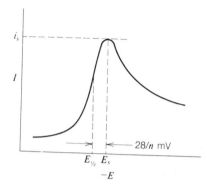

Figure 16-13 A typical rapid-scan polarogram, showing the relation between the summit and half-wave potentials.

summit potential E_s is given as a function of the half-wave potential by the relation

$$E_s = E_{1/2} - 1.1 \frac{RT}{nF} \tag{16-18}$$

which, at 25°C, becomes

$$E_s = E_{1/2} - \frac{0.028}{n} \quad \text{volts} \tag{16-19}$$

The value of current at the summit for a reversible system is given by the *Randles-Ševčik equation*, which is analogous to the Ilkovič equation, but includes the scan rate dE/dt

$$i_s = k n^{3/2} m^{2/3} t^{2/3} D^{1/2} \left(\frac{dE}{dt}\right)^{1/2} C \tag{16-20}$$

Figure 16-14 illustrates the curve obtained in a rapid-sweep experiment with two reducible species present. A quantitative analysis for the second species cannot

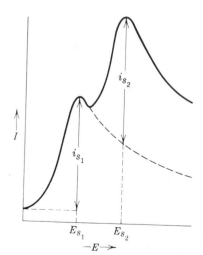

Figure 16-14 A rapid-scan polarogram of a mixture of two reducible species. The background current for the second peak must be extrapolated from the decay curve of the first peak.

be made with precision because of the necessity of extrapolating the first part of the curve to provide a background for the second.

CYCLIC VOLTAMMETRY

This is a modification of the rapid-scan technique wherein the direction of scanning is reversed following the reduction of interest. To accomplish this, a *triangular-wave* voltage is applied to the cell (Fig. 16-15a), rather than the simple ramp function. A typical curve obtained by this method is shown in part *b* of the figure.[3] The entire process takes place in a second or less, near the end of the life of a mercury drop. When the voltage is first applied, the current will start near the origin (*A*), and only residual current will flow until the potential is negative enough to effect the reduction of some species present, in this case zinc, whereupon a maximum appears, exactly analogous to that in Fig. 16-13. At point *D*, the direction of the scan is reversed, so that the voltage proceeds back toward zero at the same rate at which it had previously increased. The sudden drop (*D* to *E*) is caused by the reversal of the capacitive current. In the region *E* to *F*, the current, still cathodic, continues the process of depletion of zinc ions from the vicinity of the electrode that had been taking place in the *B*-to-*D* region. As the voltage reaches the point *F*, a diffusion-controlled steady state again comes into play, and the current drops to the *G-H* area, where it is essentially the residual capacitive current. In the *H-I-J* region, metallic zinc, the product of the prior reduction, is reoxidized, giving a diffusion-controlled anodic current. At *J*, the scan is again reversed. The current now shows an abrupt rise (*J* to *K*), essentially returning to the starting point.

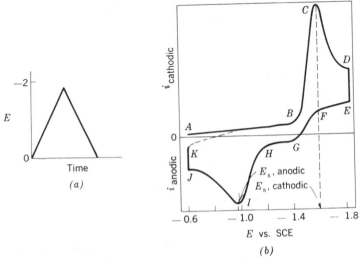

Figure 16-15 Cyclic voltammetry: (*a*) the triangular-wave excitation function; (*b*) a cyclic voltammogram obtained with 10^{-3} M Zn^{2+} in 2 M NH_3/NH_4Cl buffer. (*Academic Press*.[3])

The fact that the current at I is not equal in magnitude to that at C may be due partly to incomplete removal of zinc metal from the mercury drop, and partly to a difference between the diffusion coefficients for the aqueous species containing Zn(II), presumably $[Zn(NH_3)_4]^{2+}$ ion, on the one hand, and metallic zinc in the amalgam, on the other. The concentration gradient causing diffusion is clearly very unequal for the two species.

The electrode reaction used as an example here is rather irreversible, as shown by the large difference (about 0.6 V) between the cathodic and anodic summits. For a reversible process with $n = 2$, this difference (at 25°C) would be 0.028 V, as predicted by Eq. (16-19). This is another convenient way to determine the degree of reversibility.

Cyclic voltammetry is very useful in providing a convenient way of determining qualitatively how many reducible species are present, with an indication of their reversibility. It is useful in studies of electrode kinetics and species stability. It is not, however, often used for quantitative analysis per se.

DIFFERENTIAL PULSE POLAROGRAPHY (DPP)

In this modification of polarography, which has come to be even more widely used than the traditional (dc) form, a series of short electrical pulses are superimposed on the ramp, as shown in Fig. 16-16. The timing and magnitude of the pulses are variable, but reasonable values would call for 25-mV pulses lasting 50 ms, and repeated once for every drop of mercury, perhaps every 2 s. The current flowing through the cell is measured during, say, 15-ms "windows," just before the start and finish of each pulse, and the *difference* between them is displayed on the recorder. The effect of capacitance current is effectively cancelled out by this procedure, and the only quantity recorded reflects the increment of faradaic current corresponding to the difference in applied potential between points A and B in the figure, namely the pulse height, δE.

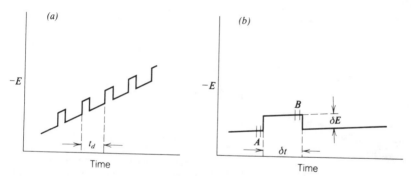

Figure 16-16 The excitation program in differential pulse polarography: (*a*) a train of pulses superimposed on a ramp voltage; (*b*) detail of a single pulse. The drop time is t_d, the pulse duration is δt.

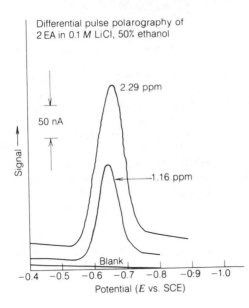

Figure 16-17 A differential pulse polarogram of 2-ethylanthraquinone (2EA). The peak height is closely proportional to concentration. (*E. G. & G. Princeton Applied Research Corporation.*)

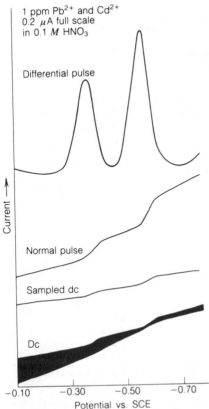

Figure 16-18 Polarogram of an equimolar mixture of Pb^{2+} and Cd^{2+} as determined by several techniques. The current sensitivity of the recorder is the same for all. (*E. G. & G. Princeton Applied Research Corporation.*)

The absence of charging current makes possible a considerable improvement in sensitivity. Concentrations of reducible species can be measured with adequate precision down to 10^{-8} M, in favorable cases, as compared to about 10^{-5} M for dc polarography. The DPP polarogram takes the shape of the derivative of the dc curve, as seen in Fig. 16-17.

Ac polarography is another modification, in which a small amplitude of alternating voltage is superimposed on the ramp, and the resulting ac current is measured. This suppresses the effect of charging current, and results in a polarogram resembling that of DPP (Fig. 16-17), with about the same sensitivity for reversible systems. Irreversible systems cannot be studied by this technique.

Figure 16-18 shows polarograms of lead and cadmium, both at 1 ppm, as determined by dc and pulse techniques. One of these is *normal pulse*, a method wherein the potential is returned to zero (vs. SCE) between pulses; it is useful if some component of the solution tends to "poison" the electrode by adsorption on the surface.

For further details of pulse and ac polarography, refer to Ref. 1.

QUALITATIVE ANALYSIS

Since the half-wave potential is characteristic of the species undergoing reduction or oxidation at the DME, this parameter can be used for its identification. The value of $E_{1/2}$ for a given substance depends on the nature of the supporting electrolyte, largely because of the differing tendency to form complex ions. A few representative values are listed in Table 16-1. The importance of wise selection of electrolyte can be seen by comparing the data for lead and cadmium. These cations have nearly identical half-wave potentials in NaOH, but are separated fairly well in KCl or H_3PO_4, and even further in KCN.

Many half-wave potential data are to be found in handbooks and monographs on polarography.[2,4] However, it is frequently expedient to plot polarograms of known substances for direct comparison with similar curves for unknowns. Published values lacking information as to the exact composition of the supporting electrolyte and the nature of the reference electrode are of little value for purposes of identification.

The half-wave potential can be determined graphically from a conventional polarogram, as shown in Fig. 16-19. Portions AB and DF of the curve are extended as shown, and a tangent is drawn to the curve at its inflection point C. The line GH is bisected, and a line JK is drawn parallel to AB and DF. The abscissa of the point of intersection of JK with the curve gives the value of $E_{1/2}$. This rather complicated procedure is necessary in the frequently encountered, nonideal case where DF is not as nearly parallel to AB as might be desired. According to the described procedure, slight errors of judgment in the location of the tangent line GH will have the least effect on the ultimate value of $E_{1/2}$. In evaluating $E_{1/2}$ from nonsampled polarograms, the upper envelope of the serrated curve should be used in the geometrical construction.

Table 16-1 Half-wave potentials of some common cations in various supporting electrolytes, V versus SCE†

		Supporting electrolyte			
Cation	KCl (0.1 M)	NH₃ (1 M) NH₄Cl (1 M)	NaOH (1 M)	H₃PO₄ (7.3 M)	KCN (1 M)
Cd²⁺	−0.60	−0.81	−0.78	−0.77	−1.18‡
Co²⁺	−1.20‡	−1.29‡	−1.46‡	−1.20‡	−1.13‡ [to Co(I)]
Cr³⁺	. . . . .§	−1.43‡ [to Cr(II)] −1.71‡ [to Cr(0)]	. . . . .	−1.02‡ [to Cr(II)]	−1.38 [to Cr(II)]
Cu²⁺	+0.04 [to Cu(I)] −0.22 [to Cu(0)]	−0.24 [to Cu(I)] −0.51 [to Cu(0)]	−0.41‡	−0.09	NR¶
Fe²⁺	−1.3‡	−1.49‡	. . . . .	. . . . .	. . . . .
Fe³⁺	. . . . .	. . . . .	−1.12†† [to Fe(II)] −1.74†† [to Fe(0)]	+0.06 [to Fe(II)]	. . . . .
Ni²⁺	−1.1‡	−1.10‡	. . . . .	−1.18	−1.36
Pb²⁺	−0.40	. . . . .	−0.76	−0.53	−0.72
Zn²⁺	−1.00	−1.35‡	−1.53	−1.13‡	NR

† From data published by Meites[2].
‡ Irreversible reduction.
§ . . . . . . indicates insufficient solubility or lacking information.
¶ NR indicates that the ion is not reducible in this medium.
†† 3 M KOH solution plus 3 percent mannitol.

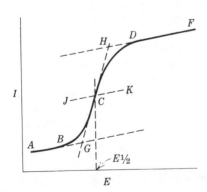

Figure 16-19 Graphical method of locating the half-wave potential in a polarogram.

QUANTITATIVE ANALYSIS

The magnitude of the diffusion current in dc polarography is related to the concentration of reducible species through the Ilković equation. Hence if the several factors of that equation are known or can be measured, the concentration can, in principle, be computed from the known current. This is usually impracticable, however, and a comparison method is preferable. The Ilković equation can be written in simplified form as

$$i_d = KC \qquad (16\text{-}21)$$

The proportionality constant can be evaluated by observations on known standard solutions.

For example, suppose cadmium is to be determined in a sample of zinc. A 0.1-g sample is dissolved in HCl, a few drops of Triton X-100 added, and the solution diluted to a known volume with 1.0 M KCl. A portion is placed in the polarographic cell and sparged with nitrogen. A preliminary polarogram is recorded, using either dc or DPP. The potential range from about -0.4 to -0.8 V versus SCE is adequate for this analysis. A wave at about -0.64 V in this trial polarogram will show qualitatively whether or not cadmium is present. The reduction potential of zinc is so far negative that it will not interfere with the cadmium wave. If cadmium proves to be present, the preliminary curve will give an idea of the relative dilution needed to give the best analysis. If the solution is already too dilute, the sensitivity can be increased; if it is too concentrated, further dilution with KCl solution is called for. Another polarogram is now recorded for the final analysis. A standard solution of $CdCl_2$ in 1.0 M KCl must also be prepared at about the same final dilution, and a polarogram recorded for it. The resulting curves will resemble Fig. 16-20. The values of i_d for both standard and unknown are measured from the graph, and the concentration in the unknown determined by a simple proportion. Alternatively a calibration curve can be prepared from a series of known concentrations.

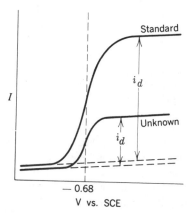

Figure 16-20 Dc polarograms of a standard and an unknown, slightly offset vertically for clarity.

The method of *standard addition* can be used to advantage in polarography. In this technique a known amount of a standard solution is added to the sample under test; comparison of polarograms taken before and after the addition contain all the information needed to complete the analysis. The advantage is that the two polarograms to be compared will have been determined under identical conditions. Details of the method are presented in Chap. 26.

All quantitative polarographic measurements must take into account the residual current. If a considerable voltage range is scanned before the start of a wave, the residual current can be approximated by extrapolation, as in Fig. 16-20. Otherwise, it may be necessary to run a blank. This would be the only way, for instance, to measure the height of the first oxygen wave in Fig. 16-10. For small concentrations, where the effect is greatest, some automatic method of compensation is called for. This can sometimes be provided by a device that feeds an extra small component of current in opposition to the cell current. This added current, which is proportional to the scanning voltage, must be carefully selected to compensate for the resistive losses in the solution. This cannot give complete compensation, because the residual current is not strictly linear, but it can often extend the useful range of polarography by a factor of ten or so.

Another limitation to quantitative precision in polarography appears when the waves corresponding to two reducible species are relatively close together. If they are so close that no horizontal segment is discernible between them, the individual diffusion currents cannot be measured directly. It may be possible to resolve the difficulty by changing to a different supporting electrolyte or adding a complex forming reagent. This effect is less likely to be troublesome with DPP than with dc polarography because of the derivative shape of the curves.

ORGANIC POLAROGRAPHY

Polarography presents an important tool for analysis and structure determination in organic chemistry. The principles are no different from those previously discussed. The product of electrochemical action is never soluble in mercury, but is almost always soluble in the same solvent as the original sample. Any solvent that will dissolve an electrolyte is potentially useful for polarography. Various alcohols or ketones, pure or mixed with water, have been used, as have dimethylformamide, acetonitrile, ethylenediamine, and others. Various quaternary ammonium salts, such as tetrabutylammonium iodide, are readily soluble in organic solvents and will serve as supporting electrolytes. As an example, see Fig. 16-17, a DPP polarogram of 2-ethylanthraquinone in 50 percent aqueous ethanol, with LiCl as supporting electrolyte.

Many classes of organic compounds can be reduced at the DME. Among them can be mentioned compounds with conjugated unsaturation; many carbonyl compounds; halogen compounds; quinones; hydroxylamines; nitro-, nitroso-, azo-, and azoxy- compounds; amine oxides; diazonium salts; many sulfur-containing and hetrocyclic compounds; peroxides; and reducing sugars. For details, the literature should be consulted.[5] The pH and ionic strength of solutions tend to be more important in organic than in inorganic applications, because H^+ ion is almost always involved in organic reductions.

A typical example of an organic application is the analysis of aromatic carbonyl compounds.[5] The following half-wave potentials (vs. SCE) were observed in a supporting electrolyte of LiOH in aqueous ethanol: benzaldehyde, -1.51 V; n-propyl phenyl ketone, -1.75; isopropyl phenyl ketone, -1.82; $tert$-butyl phenyl ketone, -1.92. The waves were clearly defined, and the diffusion currents were linear with concentration over the range 0.2 to 2.5 mM.

OTHER AMPEROMETRIC METHODS

A number of analytical techniques that involve measurement of currents at prescribed potentials can conveniently be treated here. Some of these are occasionally referred to as "polarographic," even though the DME is not used.

The Oxygen Electrode

Molecular oxygen in solution can be measured with a membrane electrode operated amperometrically, the so-called *Clark oxygen sensor*. The cell consists of an inert metallic cathode covered by a gas-permeable membrane of Teflon or a silicone, and an anode of silver, with a 1.5-V battery in series (Fig. 16-21). Current can only flow as the result of oxygen diffusing from the sample through the membrane to the cathode where it is reduced to water. The necessary hydrogen ion is supplied by the internal buffer. The minute current that flows converts the equivalent amount of silver to AgCl at the anode. The current is proportional to the dissolved oxygen concentration over the range of 1 to 10 mg/l.

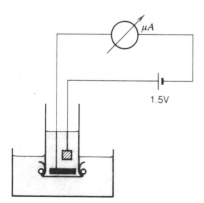

Figure 16-21 The Clark oxygen sensing electrode assembly. The microammeter can be replaced with operational amplifier circuitry.

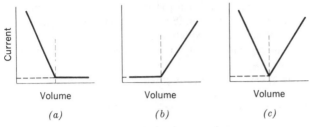

Figure 16-22 Typical amperometric titration curves.

Amperometric Titration

It is possible to carry out a titration in a voltammetric electrolysis cell and to follow its progress by observing the diffusion current after successive additions of reagent. Since the diffusion current is generally proportional to concentration, the titration curve consists of two straight-line segments intersecting at the equivalence point. Three types of curves can be distinguished (Fig. 16-22). Curve (a) results from the titration of a reducible species by a nonreducible reagent. An example is the titration of lead ion in KNO_3 by oxalate, with the DME cathode at -1.0 V (vs. SCE). The initial diffusion current is relatively high, then decreases regularly as the Pb^{2+} ion is removed by precipitation with oxalate. After the equivalence point is reached, further increments of oxalate have no effect on the current.

The reverse titration, oxalate by lead ion, under similar conditions, will give a curve such as (b) in the figure. The Pb^{2+} ion cannot accumulate in solution and gives a diffusion current until all the oxalate is precipitated.

Curve (c) results from the titration of lead by dichromate at -1.0 V, where both Pb^{2+} and $Cr_2O_7^{2-}$ ions are reducible at the DME.

Amperometric titration is applicable to many redox and complexation reactions, as well as to precipitations. It is inherently capable of greater accuracy than the corresponding nontitrative polarographic methods, since each analysis involves a number of separate determinations for which random errors tend to cancel.

The Rotating Platinum Electrode

The use of a rotating platinum electrode in place of the DME in titrimetry increases sensitivity because of the disruption of the diffusion layer by the stirring action of the electrode. The electrode is usually fabricated with a 2- or 3-mm length of platinum wire extending horizontally from its vertical glass supporting tube. The tube is rotated at a few hundred revolutions per minute, and this rate must be held quite constant to obtain consistent results.

An excellent example of the use of the rotating platinum electrode is the titration of arsenic(III) by BrO_3^- in the presence of Br^- ion.[6] The As(III) solution

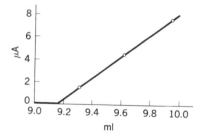

Figure 16-23 Amperometric titration of As(III) by BrO_3^- ion. (*Journal of Physical Chemistry.*[6])

is made $1\,M$ in HCl and $0.05\,M$ in KBr. The applied potential is $+0.2$ to $0.3\,V$ (vs. SCE). The reaction is

$$3\,AsO_2^- + BrO_3^- \longrightarrow 3\,AsO_3^- + Br^-$$

The bromide serves as an indicator, since only after the As(III) is completely reacted can the bromide be oxidized

$$BrO_3^- + 5\,Br^- + 6\,H^+ \longrightarrow 3\,Br_2 + 3\,H_2O$$

Of all the substances present, free bromine is the only one that is reducible at the specified potential. Figure 16-23 shows the curve resulting from the titration of 100 ml of a $9.18 \times 10^{-4}\,M$ solution of arsenious acid by $0.0100\,M\,KBrO_3$. At this applied potential oxygen is not reduced, hence it is not necessary to sparge the solution prior to analysis.

The number of titrations to which the amperometric method can be applied is much greater than that for potentiometric titration, because the electrodes are nonspecific. There are so many ions and molecules that yield voltammetric waves at either mercury or platinum electrodes that there is a good possibility of finding a suitable reagent for the direct or indirect titration of nearly any substance. The method is well suited to the precise determination of low concentrations.

Biamperometric Titrations

A simplified procedure is made possible by impressing a small potential across two identical inert electrodes. The equipment required consists merely of a source of about 50 to $100\,mV$ and a galvanometer. No current can flow between the electrodes unless both members of a reversible redox pair are present in solution. For example, if both Fe^{2+} and Fe^{3+} are present, current will be able to pass because the Fe^{2+} can be oxidized at one electrode while Fe^{3+} is being reduced at the other. The potentials required for these two processes are essentially equal, so even a few millivolts will be sufficient to produce a current.

Some systems that are not reversible will also permit current to flow. H_2O_2, for example, is oxidized at the anode to give oxygen and simultaneously reduced at the cathode to give OH^- ions. The Mn(VII)/Mn(II) couple is not reversible, but nevertheless permits electrolysis, as Mn^{2+} is oxidized anodically to MnO_2, and MnO_4^- undergoes cathodic reduction, also leading to MnO_2. Some other

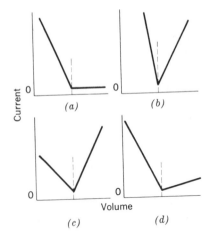

Figure 16-24 Selected biamperometric titration curves: (a) I_2 by $Na_2S_2O_3$; (b) Fe(II) by Ce(IV); (c) V(V) by Fe(II); (d) Fe(CN)$_6^{4-}$ by Ce(IV). (*Analytical Chemistry.*[7])

electrolyzable systems are: I_2/I^-, Br_2/Br^-, Ce^{4+}/Ce^{3+}, $Fe(CN)_6^{3-}/Fe(CN)_6^{4-}$, Ti^{4+}/Ti^{3+}, VO_3^-/VO^{2+}.

Curves for a few titrations performed in this manner are shown in Fig. 16-24.[7] The titration of iodine by thiosulfate (curve a) is one of the earliest reactions to be followed by this technique; it is widely used in the Karl Fischer determination of water. The shape of the curve can be explained as follows: Prior to the equivalence point, both free iodine and iodide ions are present in the solution, and so current can flow. As the titration proceeds, iodine is reduced to iodide; at the equivalence point no free iodine remains, and no current can flow. Beyond the equivalence point, as more thiosulfate is added, no current can flow, as the thiosulfate/tetrathionate pair does not constitute a reversible system.

In the titration of Fe(II) by Ce(IV) (curve b), on the other hand, current can flow on both sides of equivalence, as both the iron and cerium pairs form reversible couples. There is a point of (nearly) zero current corresponding to the complete removal of Fe^{2+} ions before excess Ce^{4+} ions have been added.

The other curves can be interpreted along similar lines. The end points in all these titrations are sharply defined, as the current drops essentially to zero.

PROBLEMS

16-1 A 1.000-g sample of zinc metal is dissolved in 50 ml of HCl and diluted to 250 ml. A 25.00-ml aliquot is transferred to a polarographic cell, a few drops of maximum suppressor added, and oxygen is flushed out. A polarogram is recorded in the range of 0 to -1 V against a mercury pool electrode. A wave appears with $E_{1/2} = -0.65$ V, with $i_d = 7.6$ cm (recorder deflection). A 5.00-ml portion of 5×10^{-4} M CdCl$_2$ is added directly to the polarograph cell that already contains the zinc solution, oxygen is again flushed out, and a second polarogram recorded. The wave shows the same $E_{1/2}$, but the i_d is increased to 18.5 cm. Calculate the percent by weight of cadmium impurity in the zinc metal. Do not overlook the dilution effect. (Note that the supporting electrolyte is HCl + ZnCl$_2$.)

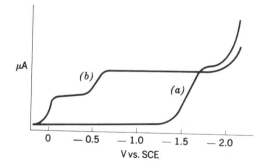

μA

(b)

(a)

0   — 0.5   — 1.0   — 1.5   — 2.0

V vs. SCE

Figure 16-25 Polarograms of (a) cupron, and (b) Cu(II) in NH_3/NH_4Cl buffer. (*Industrial and Engineering Chemistry, Analytical Edition.*[8])

16-2 A 5×10^{-3} M solution of $CdCl_2$ in 0.1 M KCl shows a diffusion current at -0.8 V (vs. SCE) of 50.0 μA. The mercury is dropping at a rate of 18.0 drops per min. Ten drops are collected and found to weigh 3.82×10^{-2} g. (a) Calculate the diffusion coefficient D. (b) If the capillary is replaced by another, for which the drop time is 3.0 s, and ten drops weigh 4.20×10^{-2} g, what will be the new value of the diffusion current?

16-3 Cupron (α-benzoinoxime) is a precipitating agent for Cu(II).[8] In a medium consisting of 0.1 M NH_4Cl and 0.05 M NH_3 (pH = 9), cupron is reduced at the DME, giving a wave with $E_{1/2} = -1.63$ V (vs. SCE), (curve a, Fig. 16-25). The double wave of copper in the same medium is shown at b. Sketch the curves that would be found in the amperometric titration of Cu(II) by cupron at applied potentials of -1.0 V and -1.8 V. Which potential would be preferred for the titration of copper in the absence of interfering substances? Which would be more liable to interference by reducible impurities?

16-4 Small concentrations (0.1 to 10 ppm) of nitrate ion can be determined polarographically in 0.1 M zirconyl chloride ($ZrOCl_2$) as supporting electrolyte.[9] The difference in diffusion currents before and after reduction of nitrate by ferrous ammonium sulfate is measured with the DME at -1.2 V vs. SCE. The following data are recorded for two standards and an unknown:

Solution	Diffusion current (μA)	
	Before reduction	After reduction
10.0 ppm	87.0	22.0
5.0 ppm	48.5	15.2
Unknown	59.0	17.0

Calculate the concentration of nitrate in the unknown.

16-5 Calculate the values of E_{DME} corresponding to currents of 1, 2, 3 μA, etc., up to 9 μA, for three hypothetical reductions in each of which $E_{1/2} = -1.000$ V (vs. SCE), and $i_d = 10$ μA, but for which $n = 1, 2,$ and 3, respectively, at 25°C. Plot these data on a single graph so that the three curves intersect at the half-wave point. For the same data, plot on another sheet the quantity log $[i/(i_d - i)]$ as abscissas against E_{DME} as ordinates. Comment on the closeness of agreement between your curves and the appropriate equations in the text.

16-6 Ag^+ ion in $NaClO_4$ as supporting electrolyte is reducible with the DME at the same potential as the SCE. Cl^- in the same medium gives an anodic wave with $E_{1/2} = +0.25$ V versus SCE. It is possible to determine whether the complex $AgCl_2^-$ is reducible under these conditions by titrating Ag^+ by Cl^-, amperometrically, at the DME. Sketch and explain the titration curves that might result.

16-7 The polarograms shown in Fig. 16-5 were taken with a three-electrode cell assembly. Suppose the same solution was run in a two-electrode cell, in which the resistance of the reference electrode was 10 kΩ. What errors (if any) would be caused in (a) the half-wave potential, and (b) the diffusion current?

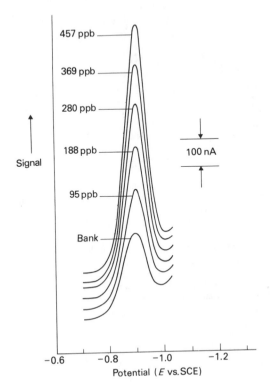

Figure 16-26 Differential pulse polarography of ammonia in 0.4 M acetate buffer at pH 4, and 37% formaldehyde. (*E. G. & G. Princeton Applied Research Corporation.*)

16-8 The Cottrell equation, Eq. (16-2), can be used to estimate the value of the diffusion coefficient. Suppose the following parameters are imposed: $n = 2$; volume of Hg drop = 0.5 mm³; drop time = 2 s; concentration = 2×10^{-4} M; i_d (measured) = 0.520 μA. Calculate D.

Useful formulas: The surface area of a sphere is $A = 4\pi r^2$, and the volume is $(4/3)\pi r^3$, where r is the radius.

16-9 The effective capacitance of the double layer surrounding a mercury drop at the DME can amount to several microfarads. Suppose that in a particular case it is 5.0 μF at an applied voltage of -1.0 V with respect to the electrocapillary maximum. (*a*) How many electrons are stored on the drop? (*b*) If the drops fall at the rate of 1 every 5 s, what is the equivalent current caused by transporting these electrons to ground?

16-10 Ammonia reacts with formaldehyde in an acetate buffer to give hexamethylenetetramine, according to the reaction: $4NH_3 + 6CH_2O \rightarrow C_6H_{12}N_4 + 6H_2O$. The product is reducible at the DME. Figure 16-26 shows a series of DPP peaks prepared under the following conditions: Supporting electrolyte, equal parts of 0.4 M acetate buffer (pH 4) and 37 percent formaldehyde; stock solution, 30.2 mg NH₄Cl in 1 liter deionized water (i.e., 9.6 ppm NH₃); increments, 100 μl aliquots added to 10.0 ml deoxygenated electrolyte; drop time, 1 s.

(*a*) Prepare a calibration curve of peak current (corrected for the blank) against the concentration of added NH₃ (calculated as ppb that would be in the solution if the formaldehyde were not present).

(*b*) A 10.0-l volume of tank nitrogen (at standard temperature and pressure) was bubbled through a portion of supporting electrolyte, which was then analyzed by DPP. A corrected peak current of 0.432 μA was recorded. Calculate the ammonia content of the nitrogen, in parts per million.

16-11 Suppose that the solution surrounding a Clark oxygen sensor contains 5 mg of O_2 per liter, and that this results in a current of 10 μA. Calculate the number of moles of O_2 that actually diffuse through the membrane and are reduced per minute. How does this relate to the 5 mg of O_2 per liter?

REFERENCES

1. B. H. Vassos and G. W. Ewing, *Electroanalytical Chemistry*, Wiley-Interscience, New York, **1983**, p. 218.
2. L. Meites, *Polarographic Techniques*, (2d ed.), Wiley-Interscience, New York, **1965**.
3. H. Schmidt and M. von Stackelberg, *Modern Polarographic Methods*, Academic Press, New York, **1963**.
4. L. Meites, in *Handbook of Analytical Chemistry*, L. Meites (ed.), McGraw-Hill, New York, **1963**, p. 5-38.
5. P. Zuman, *Organic Polarographic Analysis*, Macmillan, New York, **1964**.
6. H. A. Laitinen and I. M. Kolthoff, *J. Phys. Chem.*, **1941**, *45*, 1079.
7. K. G. Stone and H. G. Scholten, *Anal. Chem.*, **1952**, *24*, 671.
8. A. Langer, *Ind. Eng. Chem., Anal. Ed.*, **1942**, *14*, 283.
9. M. C. Rand and H. Heukelekian, *Anal. Chem.*, **1953**, *25*, 878.

SEVENTEEN

ELECTRODEPOSITION AND COULOMETRY

The cathodic deposition of transition metals for analytical purposes is undoubtedly the oldest of electroanalytical techniques. Since the mid-nineteenth century, the coinage metals have been determined as major constituents of alloys and ores by electrodeposition onto a preweighed cathode. Conventionally this has been carried out with current densities as high as a few tenths A/cm^2, which is much too large to approximate thermodynamic equilibrium. Selective deposition of metals could be achieved in some cases by the addition of complexing agents. In other cases, the use of mercury as cathode material allowed separations based on the high overvoltage required for the reduction of hydrogen ions.[1]

The technique can be improved by the use of a *potentiostat*. This instrument can control the potential of the cathode of the electrolysis cell relative to a reference electrode. Figure 17-1 shows the design of a potentiostat using operational amplifiers. Comparison with Fig. 16-11 will reveal that this potentiostat has much in common with a polarograph. For the present purpose, a constant potential is desired, so the ramp generator is replaced with an adjustable voltage source. If more current is needed than the usual operational amplifier can handle, a *booster* amplifier is added within the feedback loop of amplifier 1, the control amplifier. The current-to-voltage converter (amplifier 2) must be able to produce the same current, so it also must have a booster. (These boosters can be thought of as power output stages added to their respective operational amplifiers.) If the instrument is to be used with gravimetric determination of the deposited metal, the working electrode can be grounded directly, and amplifier 2 and the recorder omitted.

In controlled-cathode electrolysis, at a potential where only a single species is reducible, the *current* is limited by diffusion (even in the presence of stirring), and

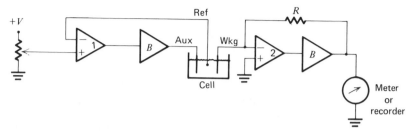

Figure 17-1 A potentiostat using operational amplifier circuitry. The amplifiers marked B are boosters which permit operation with greater currents than the operational amplifiers alone can handle.

hence is proportional to the concentration of the reducible species. Therefore both current and concentration will fall off exponentially with time, and we can write

$$\frac{C_t}{C_0} = \frac{i_t}{i_0} = 10^{-kt} \qquad (17\text{-}1)$$

where C_t represents the concentration at time t, C_0 that at time $t = 0$, i_t and i_0 are the corresponding currents. The constant k is given by DAS/V, where D is the diffusion coefficient, A is the area of the cathode, V is the volume of the solution, and S is a quantity proportional to the rate of stirring. A plot of log i against t will give a straight line with a negative slope equal to k. From this plot one can determine the time required to deposit any given fraction of the desired species. For instance, in an example quoted by Lingane[2] for the deposition of copper, k was found to be 0.15 min^{-1}, from which it follows arithmetically that deposition was 99 percent complete in 13 min and 99.9 percent in 20 min.

Controlled potential electrolysis is useful in some fields of chemistry other than analytical. In synthesis involving electrolytic oxidation or reduction, improved operation results from potential control. Se(II) and Te(II) have been prepared in this way, as has tungsten in both (III) and (V) oxidation states. Various pinacols, hydroxylamines, and others, have been reported in near 100 percent yields. Electrodeposition provides a valuable method of separation of radioactive nuclides in submicrogram amounts.

COULOMETRY

An even more powerful method of electrical measurement requires integration. According to Faraday's law of electrochemical equivalence, the amount of chemical reaction produced by electrolysis is proportional to the quantity of electricity passed. This quantity, expressed in coulombs, is measured by the time integral of the current

$$Q = \int i \, dt \qquad (17\text{-}2)$$

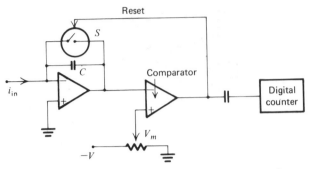

Figure 17-2 An integrator with digital readout, to be used as a coulometer.

Application of this relation, known as *coulometric analysis*, permits the quantitative determination of any substance that can be made to undergo an electrochemical reaction with 100 percent current efficiency (i.e., no side reactions).

Two procedures are possible: operation at constant current, so that the amount of material reacted is proportional to the elapsed time, and operation at constant potential, in which case the current decreases exponentially to practically zero. Both procedures have important areas of application.

The quantity Q can be measured directly by any of a number of kinds of integrators,[3] including chemical, electromechanical, or electronic types. One of these that is easily assembled in the laboratory uses operational amplifiers, as in Fig. 17-2. The current i_{in} flows to the input of the amplifier, but since it cannot enter the amplifier itself, it must go to charging the capacitor C, just as in the ramp generator for polarography. If Q were limited to about 1 mC,† then a single integrating amplifier would suffice, but in most applications many times this amount must be measured. One way this can be done is by means of the additional components shown in the figure. When the voltage across the capacitor builds up to a predetermined value, equal to V_m, the second amplifier, which has no feedback (a *comparator*, see Chap. 27), suddenly changes its output from -10 to $+10$ V. This discharges the capacitor by activating a voltage-controlled gate (i.e., switch S, which may be a relay or an appropriate semiconductor device). The comparator then returns to its previous state, leaving the capacitor free to charge up again. Each time the comparator goes positive, a count registers on the digital counter, thus giving a quantitative measure of Q.[3,4]

Constant Potential Coulometry

In this analytical technique metals can be separated according to their formal reduction potentials, as discussed in Chap. 14 (see Figs. 14-1 and 14-2). The current drawn by the electrolysis cell at constant potential is dependent on the concentra-

† Millicoulomb.

tion of the species being reduced, and hence decreases as the reaction proceeds, in accordance with Eq. (17-1). In principle, this is no different from classical electrodeposition, except in the method of reading the results: the final measurement is electrical rather than gravimetric.

The controlled potential technique is widely applicable to the determination of small concentrations of electroactive species. An excellent example[5] is the determination of plutonium (6- to 12-mg portions) to a relative standard deviation of 0.06 percent. An ion-exchange procedure was necessary to remove interferences. The reference gives details of a highly precise method of treating the data.

Constant Current Coulometry

An indirect coulometric analysis normally consists of the electrolytic generation of a soluble species that will react quantitatively with the substance to be determined. This falls within the broad definition of titration, the reagent being generated in situ rather than delivered from a buret. Hence the method is known as *coulometric titration*. As in any titration, an independent property of the chemical system must be monitored to establish the equivalence point in the reaction.

The principle of coulometric titration is best introduced through an example. Let us consider the determination of Fe(III) in a solution containing HBr, by cathodic reduction to Fe(II). This is accomplished with the aid of a platinum cathode and silver anode. Suppose that we first attempt a *direct* reduction. Curve 1 of Fig. 17-3 depicts the pertinent voltammogram, showing two waves, one corresponding to the reduction of the $FeBr_2^-$ ion, the other to that of H^+. If we force a constant current of magnitude a to pass through this cell, the cathode potential will initially assume the value $+0.40$ V (approximately) versus the SCE, where curves 1 and a intersect. As the electrolysis proceeds and iron is reduced, the plateau corresponding to the diffusion current of $FeBr_2^-$ is progressively lowered until the cathode potential suddenly jumps to about -0.3 V (curve 2), corresponding to the reduction of H^+ ions. From this point on, Fe(III) is reduced

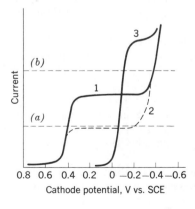

Figure 17-3 Current-voltage curves of Fe(III) (curve 1), and Ti(V) (curve 3), in HBr, as observed with a platinum cathode and SCE. Curve 2 is the same as 1, but for a smaller concentration of Fe(III).

and H_2 is liberated simultaneously, so that the current efficiency with regard to the reduction of iron falls below 100 percent, invalidating the analysis.

Let us now repeat the experiment after adding a considerable excess of titanium(IV). This is reducible to Ti(III) in the presence of acid, at a potential slightly more negative than that of the SCE (curve 3). If again the current is established at level a, the iron will be reduced as before until its diffusion current is lowered to a, but at that point the potential will jump only to -0.05 rather than -0.3 V. From there on both Fe and Ti will be reduced, but this does not result in any loss, since Ti(III) reacts quantitatively with Fe(III), so that the net result is the reduction of one iron atom per electron, no matter whether directly or indirectly, maintaining the current efficiency at 100 percent as required. (If the current had been set at level b rather than a, then the two metals would have been reduced simultaneously from the very beginning, but the result would have been the same.)

The end point in this reaction is the point in time when the quantity of electricity passed is just equivalent to the total amount of Fe(III) originally present in the sample. There are many ways in which this point can be identified. Among them are: potentiometry with platinum and SCE electrodes; amperometry at about $+0.25$ V; a biamperometric observation; a photometric method involving the addition of KSCN or other chromogenic reagent for Fe(III). Of these, the biamperometric technique is likely to be the simplest to implement.

In the experiment just outlined, the anodic reaction was $Ag + Br^- \rightarrow AgBr + e^-$. This produced no interference, because of the insolubility of the product. In many titrations, however, a soluble product will be formed at the counterelectrode, and if no precaution is taken, it will react at the generator electrode, diminishing the current efficiency. If, in the example above, a platinum anode had been selected rather than silver, the anodic reaction would have been $2Br^- \rightarrow Br_2 + 2e^-$; the bromine produced would have circulated throughout the solution and would have been reduced at the cathode, or have reacted with Fe(II). To avoid this kind of difficulty, the counterelectrode (i.e., the anode, for a reduction) can be shielded with a glass tube with a fritted tip to discourage convection. Often this is adequate, but in other cases it falls short of eliminating the source of error, and it may be necessary to resort to an agar-gel salt bridge or other device.

A small bed of an ion-exchange resin within the fritted glass shield will sometimes serve to prevent such interferences.[6] Suppose, for example, that we wish to titrate a base by coulometric generation of H^+ ions. The generator electrode will be the anode, and its half-reaction the familiar $H_2O \rightarrow \frac{1}{2}O_2 + 2H^+ + 2e^-$. At the cathode the complementary reaction, $2e^- + 2H_2O \rightarrow H_2 + 2OH^-$, will take place. Obviously the OH^- ion produced at the cathode must not be allowed to mix with the solution being titrated. An ion-exchange resin charged with chloride will replace the OH^- ions with Cl^-, removing the difficulty. This principle appears not to have received the study it deserves.

In Fig. 17-4 is shown schematically an apparatus suitable for the titration of acid. The generator and counter-electrodes are connected to a constant-current

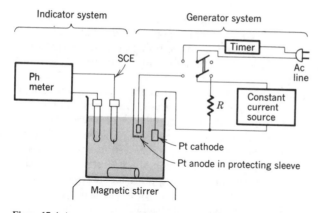

Figure 17-4 Apparatus for coulometric titration at constant current with potentiometric end-point detection. Resistor R serves as a load for the current source when in the standby mode.

source with an associated timer, while the indicator pair are the conventional glass and reference system of a pH meter. (Constant-current sources are easily constructed from standard electronic components—see Chap. 27.)

A large number of reagents can be generated electrolytically, including H^+, OH^-, Ag^+, and other metal cations, oxidants such as Ce(IV), Mn(III), Ag(II), Cl_2, Br_2, I_2, and $Fe(CN)_6^{3-}$, reductants including Fe(II), $Fe(CN)_6^{4-}$, Ti(III), $CuBr_2^-$, and Sn(II), and complexogens such as EDTA and CN^-. By one or another of these reagents it is possible to substitute coulometric counterparts for practically all the procedures of classical volumetric titrimetry. This presents the great practical advantage that it is not necessary to prepare and store standardized solutions.[7] The primary standard for coulometric titration is the combination of a constant-current source and an electronic timer, which are applied to *all* titrations, no matter what their chemical nature. Coulometric titration also has the advantage that it is applicable to samples one or two orders of magnitude smaller than conventional procedures (samples of 0.1 down to 0.001 milliequivalents are usual, compared with 1 to 10 meq for volumetric titrations). Furthermore, some reagents, such as Mn(III), Ag(II), $CuBr_2^-$, and Cl_2, can be employed even though they are unstable or otherwise not suited for volumetric use.

The precision possible in coulometric titration can easily equal or exceed that attainable by volumetric procedures. Eckfeld and Shaffer[8] have reported a careful study of precision in coulometric neutralization. They could measure the quantity of charge to about ± 0.004 percent. One simple but effective precaution was to provide a slow flow of indifferent electrolyte in a salt bridge, thus eliminating all possibility of contamination or loss of sample through the fritted glass. This paper should be studied by anyone attempting precise work in coulometric titrimetry.

The coulometric method is less suitable for larger concentrations, and this is its chief limitation. The reason is that for large samples, it would be necessary to operate with much larger currents or longer times. Either of these alternatives is likely to reduce the current efficiency by providing more opportunity for side reactions to occur.

Coulometric *pretitration* is often advisable. After the titration apparatus is assembled, a small portion of the material to be titrated is inserted and the electrolysis allowed to proceed until the desired endpoint is observed. Then the measured sample is added and titrated to a second endpoint. This ensures that any impurity that can react with the generated titrant is removed in advance. It also obviates any uncertainty about the surface condition of the electrodes (an oxide film, for example). The titration curve will have the appearance shown in Fig. 17-5. The material pretitrated reacts with generated reagent from time t_0 to t_1, following which reagent accumulates (at A). The sample is then added; it reacts immediately with the portion of reagent that has just been generated, returning the curve to zero (at B), and then continues to react with generated titrant until the curve rises again at C. The two sloping portions of the curve are extrapolated back to the zero level at D and E, and the time between these two points, $t_2 - t_1$, is taken as the electrolysis time. The slopes at A and C will differ if appreciable dilution has occurred with the addition of the sample.

Coulometric titration is more easily automated than other forms of titration, in that no mechanical components such as pumps or burets are involved. Passage of a constant current provides a linear time base for the titration. Coulometric generation can readily be adapted to an all-electronic version of the pH-stat discussed in Chap. 15.

Several automatic or semiautomatic coulometric titrators are available commercially. There are also a number of continuous analyzers for flow-stream monitoring, in which a recorder indicates the magnitude of current needed to maintain constant the concentration of some component by causing it to react with an electrogenerated reagent. These are often called "coulometric," though "amperometric" might be a more appropriate term.

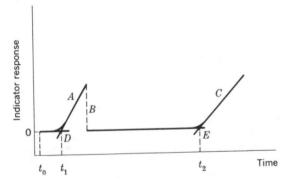

Figure 17-5 Coulometric titration curve illustrating pretitration. The vertical axis refers to the output of any detector (photometric, amperometric, etc.) that shows a linear response with concentration.

ELECTROLYTIC PRECONCENTRATION

In the analysis of solutions containing trace amounts of transition metals, some method of increasing the concentration prior to analysis is often essential. Of the several possible techniques for doing this, one of the best is cathodic electro-deposition. Electrolysis can be continued as long as necessary to accumulate sufficient metal for subsequent analysis. If the cathode is made sufficiently negative, all reducible metals present will be deposited together, but some degree of selective deposition can be effected by potentiostatic control. Electrolysis can sometimes be carried to exhaustion, but this may be impossible or require inordinately long times, so more commonly deposition is continued for a specific period only.

The choice of electrode on which deposition is to take place will depend on the method selected for final determination. Analysis by electrochemical means is the most widely used, and for this a mercury electrode is usually to be preferred (see the next section). For photometric analysis, the metals must be stripped off the cathode, either electrolytically or by acid attack, and a platinum electrode is satisfactory. Deposition on pyrolytic graphite for subsequent analysis by x-ray fluorescence was mentioned in Chap. 11.[9]

STRIPPING ANALYSIS[10–12]

This term refers to the analysis of a mixed deposit of metals by anodic voltam-metry. In a typical procedure, a portion of solution is electrolyzed for perhaps 20 or 30 min with a small mercury cathode, at a suitable potential to reduce all metals up to the limit imposed by the hydrogen overvoltage. The mercury electrode is then made the anode and the voltage is swept in the positive-going direction, stripping off the metals deposited during the previous step. The stripping process is carried out under voltammetric conditions in a time of 2 or 3 min.

A widely used electrode for stripping analysis is a *hanging mercury drop electrode* (HMDE). Such a drop can be formed at the tip of a mercury-filled capil-lary attached to a micrometer plunger assembly, so that a turn of the micrometer through a measured angle will extrude an exactly reproducible quantity of mercury. A less expensive device for forming a mercury drop, and one that can be homebuilt, is illustrated in Fig. 17-6. A small plastic spoon or scoop (S) is held beneath a standard polarographic capillary (C) until it has collected one or more drops of mercury; the scoop is then rotated and raised so that the mercury will make contact with the tip of a platinum wire sealed into a glass tube (E), where it will adhere.

A solid electrode cannot be used satisfactorily with voltammetric stripping, because atoms of a minor constituent of the plated mixture may be covered or trapped by a major constituent, and hence will not be completely reoxidized. This difficulty does not arise with metals dissolved in mercury. Sometimes carbon electrodes, preplated with a little mercury, can be used in place of the HMDE.

In analytical stripping as carried out by anodic voltammetry, a series of peaks appear on the current-voltage curve corresponding to successively oxidized

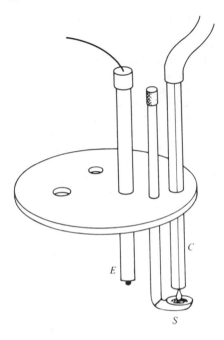

Figure 17-6 Hanging mercury-drop electrode assembly held in a plastic beaker cover. Mercury drops can be transferred by scoop S from capillary C to the platinum-tipped electrode E.

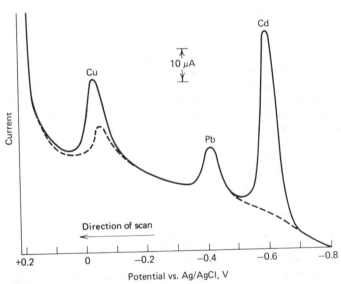

Figure 17-7 Anodic stripping voltammogram. The dashed line represents a blank. For details, see text. (*Journal of Chemical Education.*[10])

metals. The quantity of each can be determined from the height of the peak, measured from a baseline established in a blank run. Figure 17-7 shows the result of an experiment reported by Ellis.[10] The solution contained equal quantities (2×10^{-7} M) of Cu^{2+} and Cd^{2+}. Deposition was for 5 min at -1.0 V (vs. Ag/AgCl). Note that the reagent blank (dashed line) showed appreciable amounts of both Cu^{2+} and Pb^{2+}, even though the sample was thought to be free of lead. This is not uncommon in stripping analysis; the method is so extremely sensitive that supposedly pure solvents and reagents are often found to contain unsuspected trace metals.

PROBLEMS

17-1 A constant current of 15.0 mA is allowed to flow for exactly 10 min through a number of electrolytic cells connected in series. All electrodes are platinum. The cells contain an excess of the electrolytes listed. For each, determine what substance will be formed at each electrode, and calculate the quantities of each, in milligrams if solid or liquid, in milliliters (at standard temperature and pressure) if gaseous:

(a) $Cu(NO_3)_2$ (c) $K_4Fe(CN)_6$ (e) $Pb(ClO_4)_2$
(b) NaOH   (d) HgI_2 (f) $Ag(NH_3)_2Cl$

17-2 A cadmium amalgam containing 12 percent cadmium by weight is to be prepared for use in a Weston standard cell. Starting with 20 g of mercury, how long should electrolysis of $CdCl_2$ solution continue (at 200 mA) in order to produce the requisite amount of cadmium?

17-3 Cerium(IV) is to be determined by coulometric titration with electrogenerated Fe^{2+} ion. The end point is observed potentiometrically with platinum and SCE electrodes connected to a pH meter operating in the millivolt mode. Preliminary studies show that the potential of the platinum wire indicator electrode should be $+0.800$ V vs. SCE. The acidified solution contained 0.0005 mol of Fe^{3+} in a volume of 250 ml. Interfering substances were removed by a preliminary titration of the same type. For this purpose about 0.2 μmol of Ce(IV) was added, and current passed through until the indicator showed $+0.800$ V. Then a 1.00-ml portion of the unknown solution was added, and generation was continued until the end point was reached again. The data shown in the accompanying table were taken. The coulometer readings are in arbitrary units, such that a change of 1 unit corresponds to 4.79×10^{-4} μequivalent. Calculate the concentration of the unknown in micrograms of cerium per milliliter.

Time, s	Coulometer reading	Potential, Pt/SCE
Preliminary titration		
. . . .	20	$+0.830$
436.0	120	0.801
472.8	170	0.790
Analysis titration		
472.8	170	0.893
. . . .	470	0.861
. . . .	720	0.820
. . . .	750	0.814
. . . .	770	0.810
925.0	790	0.803
939.5	810	0.794

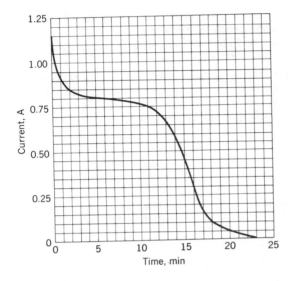

Figure 17-8 Current-time curve for the deposition of copper from a sample.

17-4 The copper from a 0.400-g sample of brass was deposited electrolytically with a suitably controlled cathode potential. The cell was connected in series with a recording ammeter. The record obtained is reproduced in Fig. 17-8. The current-time integral can be approximated by counting the squares beneath the curve or by the method of trapezoids. Perform this integration and compute the percentage of copper in the alloy. Why does this curve not follow the exponential law?

17-5 What current (in milliamperes) would be required for constant-current coulometry, so that a seconds timer would read directly in microequivalents of electrode reaction?

17-6 Anthranilic acid (o-aminobenzoic acid) can be brominated by electrolytically generated bromine at pH 4, to produce tribromoaniline. It has been shown[13] that small amounts of copper can be determined by precipitating Cu(II) anthranilate, $Cu(C_6H_4NH_2CO_2)_2$, dissolving the precipitate, and titrating the liberated anthranilic acid coulometrically.

The copper in a 1.000-g sample of a biological material is converted to ionic form, and precipitated with excess anthranilic acid. The precipitate is filtered, washed, and redissolved. The acid is then brominated with a constant current of 6.43 mA. The time required is 22.40 min. Calculate the amount of copper in the original sample, in parts per million.

17-7 A sample of lake water was to be analyzed for Cu, Pb, and Cd by stripping analysis. The electrode consisted of a film of mercury held on a carbon support. In one experiment the potential of the electrode was held at -1.0 V (vs. SCE) for 90 min in a 200-ml sample, by which time the current had dropped to a negligible value. The electrode was then scanned anodically. Integration of the three resulting peaks indicated 12.5 μC at the potential relating to Cd, 41.0 μC for Pb, and 38.2 μC for Cu. Calculate the concentration of each metal in the original sample, in terms of parts per billion (parts per 10^9).

17-8 A solution 10^{-8} M in Cu^{2+} is to be deposited into a mercury drop electrode prior to anodic stripping analysis. If the volume of the drop is 0.0010 cm^3, and the electrolysis current is 0.500 μA, how long must the plating process be continued to make the concentration in the amalgam 10^{-3} M?

17-9 Silver, as a major component of an alloy, can be determined quantitatively by controlled potential coulometry. The supporting electrolyte is 0.1 M H_2SO_4, to which sulfamic acid should be added if any nitric acid is present. In order to avoid chloride contamination, the reference electrode selected is Hg/Hg_2SO_4 (sat K_2SO_4), the potential of which is -0.579 V (vs. SHE, at 25°C). The cell potential for the deposition of silver is set at -0.25 V. In a particular analysis, a 1.000-g sample of a brazing alloy was dissolved in mixed nitric and sulfuric acids, excess HNO_3 and oxides of nitrogen were boiled off, the solution was transferred to a 250-ml volumetric flask and diluted to the mark with deionized water. An aliquot of 0.500 ml was added to a portion of the supporting electrolyte and electrolyzed, requiring 1.198 coulombs.

(a) Reconcile the selected electrolysis potential with Fig. 14-1.

(b) Calculate the percent silver in the alloy.

REFERENCES

1. J. A. Maxwell and R. P. Graham, *Chem. Rev.*, **1950**, *46*, 471.
2. J. J. Lingane, *Electroanalytical Chemistry*, 2d ed., Wiley-Interscience, New York, **1958**.
3. G. W. Ewing, *J. Chem. Educ.*, **1972**, *49*, A333.
4. S. R. Pareles, *Anal. Chem.*, **1973**, *45*, 998.
5. M. K. Holland, J. R. Weiss, and C. E. Pietri, *Anal. Chem.*, **1978**, *50*, 236.
6. U. Eisner, J. M. Rottschafer, F. J. Berlandi, and H. B. Mark, Jr., *Anal. Chem.*, **1967**, *39*, 1466.
7. G. W. Ewing, *Am. Lab.*, **1981**, *13(6)*, 16.
8. E. L. Eckfeldt and E. W. Shaffer, Jr., *Anal. Chem.*, **1965**, *37*, 1534.
9. B. H. Vassos, R. F. Hirsch, and H. Letterman, *Anal. Chem.*, **1973**, *45*, 792.
10. W. D. Ellis, *J. Chem. Educ.*, **1973**, *50*, A131.
11. B. H. Vassos and G. W. Ewing, *Electroanalytical Chemistry*, Wiley, New York, **1983**, chap. 10.
12. I. Shain, in *Treatise on Analytical Chemistry*, I. M. Kolthoff and P. J. Elving (eds.), Wiley-Interscience, New York, **1963**, pt. I, vol. 4, chap. 50.
13. L. G. Hargis and D. F. Boltz, *Talanta*, **1964**, *11*, 57.

EIGHTEEN

CONDUCTIMETRY

The preceding chapters have dealt with specific electrochemical reactions at electrode surfaces. Nonfaradaic currents (those not accompanied by chemical effects) have been treated as *noise*, undesirable phenomena tending to obscure the desired information. Now we will consider one nonfaradaic quantity that can carry useful information: electrolytic conductance.

A cell consisting of two platinum electrodes in an ionic solution can be represented by an equivalent electrical circuit made up of resistances and capacitances, as in Fig. 18-1. In this diagram, R_{L1} and R_{L2} represent the resistances of the connecting wires (usually negligible), C_{DL1} and C_{DL2} are the double-layer capacitances at the two electrodes, C_P is the interelectrode capacitance (in parallel with the cell), and R_{sol} is the resistance of the solution between the electrodes. The components marked R_{F1} and R_{F2} represent the *faradaic resistances* at the two electrodes, i.e., the electrical equivalent of any possible electrode reactions. If a constant (dc) potential is impressed on this network, nothing will happen except for a brief transient, provided the voltage is small enough that no electrochemical process can occur. If the voltage is higher, then current will flow through the R_F components and R_{sol}.

On the other hand, if an ac potential is applied, alternating current will flow through the C_{DL}'s and R_{sol}, and at the same time through C_P. Each C_{DL} provides such an easy path for alternating current that voltage cannot build up across the corresponding R_F to the point where faradaic current can flow. Hence if C_P can be kept negligibly small and the C_{DL}'s large, the effect of R_{sol} can be studied by itself. In practice the double-layer capacitance can be increased many times by coating the platinum electrodes with spongy platinum black (*platinizing*) which greatly

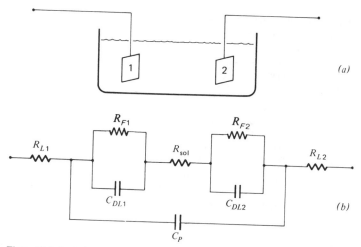

Figure 18-1 A conductance cell (a) and its equivalent circuit (b).

increases the effective surface area. C_P becomes significant only with high-resistance solutions, when large electrodes close together must be selected in order to keep resistance measurements within the range of the measuring instrument.

THEORY

The *conductance* L of a solution, expressed in siemens,† is defined as the reciprocal of the resistance. It is related to the ratio of the area a of the electrodes and to the distance d between them, and to the total ionic concentration by the expression

$$L = 10^{-3}(a/d)\sum_i z_i C_i \lambda_i \tag{18-1}$$

The ratio a/d is a geometric property of the cell, and its reciprocal is defined as the *cell constant*, designated by θ, with the units of cm^{-1}. C_i in Eq. (18-1) is the molar concentration of the ith ion with charge z_i, and λ_i is the corresponding equivalent ionic conductivity. The summation covers all ions of both signs.

The quantity λ is a property of ions that gives quantitative information about their relative contributions to the conductance of a solution. Its value is to some extent dependent on the total ionic concentration of the solution, increasing with increasing dilution. It is convenient to tabulate numerical values of λ_0, the limiting value of λ, as the concentration approaches zero (infinite dilution). This differs from the *ionic mobility* by the factor F (the Faraday constant). Representative values are given in Table 18-1.

---

† The siemens is the SI unit of conductance. It is equivalent to the formerly used unit "mho." The general symbol for conductance is G, but for electrolytic conductance, L is usually used instead.

Table 18-1 Equivalent ionic conductivity at infinite dilution (in units of $S \cdot cm^2 \cdot mol^{-1}$, at 25°C)†

Cations	λ_0	Anions	λ_0
H^+	349.8	OH^-	198.6
$\frac{1}{3}Co(NH_3)_6^{3+}$	102.3	$\frac{1}{4}Fe(CN)_6^{4-}$	110.5
K^+	73.5	$\frac{1}{3}Fe(CN)_6^{3-}$	101.0
NH_4^+	73.5	$\frac{1}{3}Co(CN)_6^{3-}$	98.9
$\frac{1}{2}Pb^{2+}$	69.5	$\frac{1}{2}SO_4^{2-}$	80.0
$\frac{1}{3}La^{3+}$	69.5	Br^-	78.1
$\frac{1}{3}Fe^{3+}$	68.0	I^-	76.8
$\frac{1}{2}Ba^{2+}$	63.6	Cl^-	76.4
Ag^+	61.9	NO_3^-	71.4
$\frac{1}{2}Ca^{2+}$	59.5	$\frac{1}{2}CO_3^{2-}$	69.3
$\frac{1}{2}Cu^{2+}$	53.6	$\frac{1}{2}C_2O_4^{2-}$	74.2
$\frac{1}{2}Fe^{2+}$	54.0	ClO_4^-	67.3
$\frac{1}{2}Mg^{2+}$	53.1	HCO_3^-	44.5
$\frac{1}{2}Zn^{2+}$	52.8	$CH_3CO_2^-$	40.9
Na^+	50.1	$HC_2O_4^-$	40.2
Li^+	38.7	$C_6H_5CO_2^-$	32.4
$(n\text{-Bu})_4N^+$	19.5		

† Data mainly from Frankenthal.[1]

For some applications, it is necessary to know the cell constant θ. Direct geometrical measurement is impracticable except in cells specifically designed for the purpose, so it is generally determined from measurements on solutions of known *specific conductance* ($\kappa = L\theta$). Some values useful for calibration purposes are listed in Table 18-2.

Table 18-2 Specific conductances of KCl solutions at 25°C[2]

Concentration, $g \cdot kg^{-1}$ of solution	κ, $S \cdot cm^{-1}$
71.1352	0.11134
7.41913	0.012856
0.74526	0.0014088

INSTRUMENTATION

The traditional instrument for measuring electrolytic conductance is the Wheatstone bridge, modified for ac operation (Fig. 18-2). The bridge is energized from the source E, either at 1 kHz or at the power line frequency. The arms R_1 and R_2 can be selected by the switch to give precise ratios of 0.1, 1, or 10. R_x represents

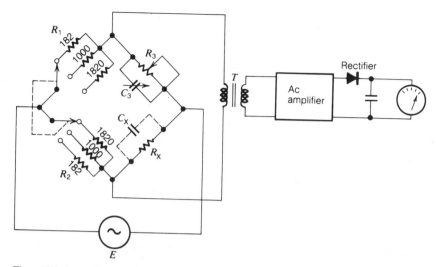

Figure 18-2 An ac Wheatstone bridge for conductance measurements. The 2-pole, 3-throw switch permits choice of 0.1, 1, or 10 as ratios.

the resistance of the conductance cell, shunted by the capacitance C_x. (C_x is actually the effective combination of the several capacitances shown in Fig. 18-1.) R_3 is a precision variable resistor with a calibrated dial, shunted by a small variable capacitor C_3 with which to balance out the cell capacitance C_x.

The alternating potential appearing across the diagonal of the bridge is amplified, rectified, and metered. In use the selector switch and the dial of R_3 are adjusted until the meter shows zero deflection, at which point the resistance of the cell is given by

$$R_x = \frac{R_1}{R_2} R_3 \qquad (18\text{-}2)$$

and its conductance by

$$L_x = \frac{R_2}{R_1 R_3} \qquad (18\text{-}3)$$

Another approach to the measurement of conductance is based on an operational amplifier control circuit, Fig. 18-3. Because of the ability of the amplifier to maintain equality of the potentials of its two inputs, the ac voltage E_{in} appears directly across the cell, but the current that this produces through the cell is balanced by an equal current from the amplifier's output through a selected feedback resistor R_f. The output voltage E_0 is given by

$$E_0 = E_{in}\left(\frac{R_f}{R_x} + 1\right) = E_{in}(R_f L_x + 1) \qquad (18\text{-}4)$$

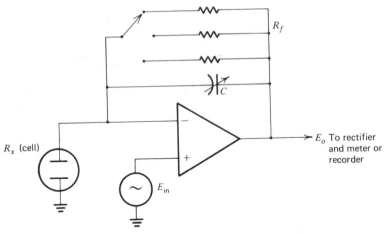

Figure 18-3 An operational amplifier circuit for conductance measurements.

If R_f is large enough, the 1 can be neglected and the output ac voltage will be proportional to the solution conductance. A more elaborate version is described by Mueller et al.[3] Note that this apparatus does not require balancing like a bridge, but gives a continuous reading.

APPLICATIONS

Most applications of conductance measurements are concerned with aqueous solutions. Figure 18-4 shows specific conductances and resistances for a number of materials. Water itself is a very poor conductor. Its specific conductance, due to dissociation into H_3O^+ and OH^- ions, is approximately 5×10^{-8} S·cm^{-1} at 25°C, but ordinary distilled or deionized water falls far short of this. Water stills and demineralizers are often provided with conductance monitors.

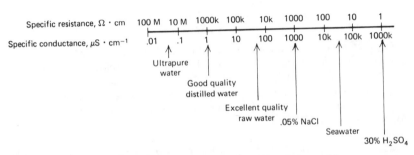

Figure 18-4 Specific resistance and conductance ranges for some typical materials.

Solutions of strong electrolytes show a nearly linear increase in conductance with concentration up to about 10 to 20 percent by weight. At higher concentrations, the conductance decreases again, as interionic attraction hinders free movement of ions through the solution. Many special-purpose conductance meters are available, calibrated for particular solutes, bearing scales such as "0 to 30 ppm NaCl," or "2 to 25 percent H_2SO_4."

CONDUCTOMETRIC TITRATIONS

The conductance method can be used to follow the course of a titration, provided that there is a significant difference in conductance between the original solution and the reagent or the products of reaction. It is not necessary to know the cell constant, since relative values are sufficient to permit locating the equivalence point. It is essential, however, that the spacing of the electrodes does not change during the titration.

The contribution of any ion to the conductance of a solution is proportional to its concentration, but in a titration, as reagent is added, so also is more water, and the change in conductance must be corrected for the effect of dilution. Hydrolysis of reactants or products, or partial solubility of a precipitate, may also cause departures from linearity.

The shape of a titration curve can be predicted easily. The concentration of each ion at successive points in the titration is calculated by the usual methods based on stoichiometry, equilibria, and dilution. The concentrations, multiplied by the λ_0 value from Table 18-1, give the relative contributions of the ion, and summation of all ions present yields the titration curve. For an example, the titration of HCl by NaOH, see Fig. 18-5. The signal, proportional to the conductance, is shown at (a); it can be resolved into the contributions of the various ions as in (b).

Conductometric titrations are not used as much as formerly, at least in part because of the lack of specificity of the method.

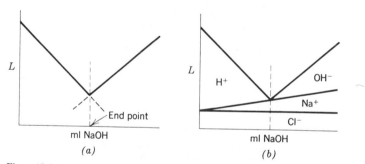

Figure 18-5 Conductometric titration curve for the titration of HCl by NaOH: (a) instrument response; (b) same, showing the contributions of specific ions. The dilution effect is assumed to be negligible.

Radiofrequency Conductimetry (Oscillometry)

If the frequency of the oscillator powering the conductance meter is raised from the usual 1 kHz into the megahertz region, the necessary instrumentation changes considerably, as does the mathematical theory, but the resulting information is not greatly different. For further details the reader is referred to the literature.[4-6]

PROBLEMS

18-1 It has been established[7] that the specific conductance of seawater at 25°C depends on the salinity S according to the relation

$$\kappa = 1.82 \times 10^{-3} S - 1.28 \times 10^{-5} S^2 + 1.18 \times 10^{-7} S^3$$

where S is expressed in grams of salts per kilogram of water. The average value of S for undiluted seawater is 35.0.

A sample of water taken near the mouth of a river showed a specific conductance of $1.47 \times 10^{-2} S \cdot cm^{-1}$. What is its salinity? How much fresh water has been mixed with each kilogram of seawater at this location? (Assume that the conductance of the river water is negligible, and that differences in density have no effect.)

18-2 Sketch on one graph the curves you would predict for the conductometric titration of $0.001\ M$ $AgNO_3$ by $0.010\ M$ solutions of each of the following: HCl, KCl, NH_4Cl, $CaCl_2$, NaCl, and LiCl. Which would result in the greatest precision? Explain.

18-3 The conductometric titration of organic bases by BBr_3, and vice versa, has been reported.[8] Various aprotic solvents were usable. For example, an inverted V-shaped conductance curve was obtained when BBr_3 in nitrobenzene was titrated with quinoline. Outline the reactions involved, and sketch a titration curve showing graphically the contributions of the various species to the total conductance. (It will be necessary to refer to the original paper for details.)

18-4 A reference solution was made up containing 3.7096 g of KCl in enough water to make up 500.0 g of solution (cf. Table 18-2). The conductance of a certain cell filled with this solution was found to be $L = 0.05327$ S. What was the cell constant?

18-5 Whereas both Ag_2SO_4 and $BaCl_2$ are freely soluble, AgCl and $BaSO_4$ both have solubility products about 10^{-10}, and so a titration of Ag_2SO_4 by $BaCl_2$ is easily followed conductometrically. By application of Eq. (18-1) and the data given in Table 18-1, calculate the conductance in a titration vessel (with $\theta = 0.452\ cm^{-1}$) corresponding to the points listed below, in the titration of $0.1\ M$ Ag_2SO_4 by $1.0\ M$ $BaCl_2$ (the dilution effect can be neglected):

(a) the initial solution (Ag_2SO_4 only)
(b) after addition of one-half of the equivalent amount of $BaCl_2$
(c) at the equivalence point
(d) after the addition of 1 equivalent beyond the equivalence point

Sketch the resulting titration curve.

REFERENCES

1. R. P. Frankenthal, in *Handbook of Analytical Chemistry*, L. Meites (ed.), McGraw-Hill, New York, **1963**, p. 5-29 ff.
2. G. Jones and B. C. Bradshaw, *J. Am. Chem. Soc.*, **1933**, 55, 1780.
3. T. R. Mueller, R. W. Stelzner, D. J. Fisher, and H. C. Jones, *Anal. Chem.*, **1965**, 37, 13.

4. C. N. Reilley, in *New Instrumental Methods in Electrochemistry*, P. Delahay (ed.), Wiley-Interscience, New York, **1954**, chap. 15.
5. E. Pungor, *Oscillometry and Conductometry*, Pergamon, New York, **1965**.
6. G. Svehla, in *Essays on Analytical Chemistry*, E. Wänninen (ed.), Pergamon, Oxford, **1977**, p. 233.
7. E. Ruppin, *Z. anorg. Chem.*, **1908**, *49*, 190.
8. M. C. Henry, J. F. Hazel, and W. M. McNabb, *Anal. Chim. Acta*, **1956**, *15*, 187.

NINETEEN

INTRODUCTION TO CHROMATOGRAPHY

In the analysis of a great many chemical systems, the first step must be separation of the components of a mixture. Of the many methods of separation, one of the most common and most versatile is chromatography. This is a dynamic process involving two immiscible phases, one mobile, the other stationary. The mobile phase can be either a gas or a liquid, while the stationary phase can be porous or granular solid, or a thin liquid film adsorbed on a solid.

The field is usually divided for convenience into the area of *gas chromatography* (GC) and *liquid chromatography* (LC). Also useful are *paper chromatography* (PC) and *thin-layer chromatography* (TLC), but these, not being primarily instrumental, are not treated in this book. In this chapter we will examine those theoretical aspects that are common to both GC and LC, and in subsequent chapters take up the instrumental and practical features of each.

The chromatographic process is easily visualized on a qualitative basis. Consider a column packed with a granular solid (Fig. 19-1), with a fluid flowing through it. A species X, dissolved in the fluid, is carried along with it, but also tends to be held on the surface of the solid by adsorption or other mechanism. Any given molecule of X spends part of its time in the mobile phase and moves forward with it, and part of its time held immobile on the solid surface. Separation of two such solutes, X and Y, depends on the difference of their relative affinities for the two phases, so that one spends more time than the other in the mobile phase, and hence arrives sooner at the far end of the column.

It is convenient to introduce a parameter called the *partition ratio*, conventionally designated by k'. This is defined as

$$k' = \frac{n_s}{n_m} \tag{19-1}$$

Figure 19-1 A section of a packed chromatographic column.

where n_s and n_m are the number of moles of solute X present in the stationary and mobile phases, respectively. This is a measure of the retention of compound X, and is a property of a particular combination of fixed and mobile phases for a given solute. The extent to which two substances can be separated is expressed by a *relative retention*, denoted by α:

$$\alpha = \frac{k_2'}{k_1'} \tag{19-2}$$

The larger the value of n_s, the number of moles of solute in the stationary phase, the longer will be the time required for its elution, and since the subscripts on the k's in Eq. (19-2) are assigned in the order of elution, it follows that α will always be greater than unity.

In order to achieve a good separation, the sample must be injected onto the column in one small, compact dose, so that all components start their trip through the column at the same instant. A suitable detector at the output will generate peaks corresponding to the emergence of the various components, resulting in a recorder trace such as that in Fig. 19-2. Peaks are shown for four substances present in the sample, of which t_1 is the least, and t_4 the most tightly held by the stationary phase.

Components are separated more and more completely as they move through the column. Thus a long column tends to enhance peak resolution. However, diffusion, both upstream and downstream, tends to broaden the moving zone occupied by each component. Broadening due to this cause is proportional to the

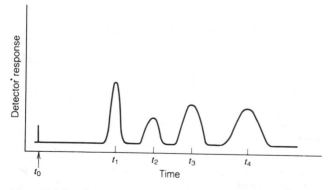

Figure 19-2 A well-resolved chromatogram of a four-component mixture.

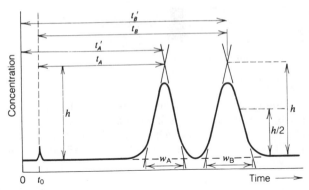

Figure 19-3 A two-component chromatogram, showing the definitions of various parameters. The peak at t_0 corresponds to an unretained component.

square root of the time spent in the column. The broader the peaks, the less precisely can their positions be determined, and this puts a practical limit on the length of columns.

The parameters needed for the description of chromatographic peaks are indicated in Fig. 19-3. The level marked $h/2$ is located at half the height of a triangle formed by drawing tangents to the curve at the points of inflection.† The width of each peak (w) is a measure of the statistical distribution of the retention time of individual molecules. The *standard deviation* from the mean, denoted by σ, is equal to one-half the width at the half-height level (the HWHM),‡ and hence, by geometry, it is also equal to $w/4$. The relation between width and retention time is given by

$$\frac{w_A}{w_B} = \left(\frac{t_A}{t_B}\right)^{1/2} \tag{19-3}$$

THEORY OF CHROMATOGRAPHIC MIGRATION

The theory of migration is based on the repeated transfer of solute molecules back and forth between phases as the solute is being swept down the column. Any one molecule (on the average) will spend time t_s in the stationary phase and time t_m in the mobile phase, as it passes through the column. During the time t_m, it moves forward with the velocity of the carrier, v; during time t_s it does not move forward at all. Its motion, then, is stepwise, as it transfers into and out of the

---

† It can be shown mathematically that this is $1/\sqrt{e}$ times the actual peak height. This factor (0.607) is derived from the equation for a gaussian distribution curve, hence is only approximate for real peaks.
‡ HWHM = half width at half maximum.

mobile phase. The relative magnitudes of t_s and t_m determine how quickly the solute moves down the column.

The various factors contributing to the efficiency of separation may be described by the concept of the height equivalent to a theoretical plate (HETP). A *theoretical plate* is a fictitious concept that does not correspond to any actual entity in the column. For evaluation purposes it is a very convenient parameter, which is its only raison d'être. It is defined as the ratio of the standard deviation squared (the *variance*) to the length of the column, $H = \sigma^2/L$. This is the length within the column that is able to achieve equilibrium between phases under a particular set of conditions (flow rate, temperature, etc.). For high efficiency, a large number N of theoretical plates is desirable, and to avoid very long columns, the HETP must be as short as possible. The lower the HETP, the more efficient the column.

The number of theoretical plates in the column is given by $16(x/w)^2$, where x and w are defined as shown in Fig. 19-2. The quantities x and w must be in the same units, and are conveniently measured on a chromatogram, usually in centimeters. The relation is:

$$N = \frac{L}{H} = 16\left(\frac{x}{w}\right)^2 \quad \text{or} \quad N_{\text{eff}} = \frac{L}{H_{\text{eff}}} = 16\left(\frac{x'}{w}\right)^2 \tag{19-4}$$

where N_{eff} and H_{eff} are effective parameters, which gives

$$H = \frac{L}{N} = \frac{L}{16}\left(\frac{w}{x}\right)^2 \quad \text{or} \quad H_{\text{eff}} = \frac{L}{N_{\text{eff}}} = \frac{L}{16}\left(\frac{w}{x'}\right)^2 \tag{19-5}$$

Since H is a constant for a given system, this relation shows that x and w must vary together, so that for several peaks in the same chromatogram, the longer the retention time (i.e., the longer is x), so also will w be larger, and the peaks broader. It is clearly desirable for w, and hence for H, to be as small as possible for best resolution.

It has been shown by many workers that the HETP can be expressed by a relation, known as the *van Deemter equation*, of the form

$$H = A + \frac{B}{v} + Cv \tag{19-6}$$

where A, B, and C are approximately constant for a given system, and v is the velocity of the carrier fluid in centimeters per second.

The A term arises from the fact that not all solute molecules in the mobile phase travel exactly the same distance in passing through the column, an effect that is increased by nonuniformity of particle size. It is given by the relation

$$A = Kv(D_m + Pd_p v) \tag{19-7}$$

where D_m designates the diffusion coefficient of the solute in the mobile phase, d_p is the average diameter of the solid particles, and both K and P are constants depending on the irregularity of the packing material.

The B term, which becomes less important as v increases, is given by

$$B = 2\gamma(D_m + k'D_s) \tag{19-8}$$

in which D_s is the diffusion coefficient of the solute within the stationary phase, γ is the ratio of the effective forward velocity of the solute molecules to the velocity of the carrier, and k' is the partition ratio. B is concerned with the longitudinal diffusion of the solute. The B/v term can be lowered either by decreasing the temperature or increasing the flow rate.

The term in Cv, which predominates at higher flow rates, is contributed by transverse diffusion in the mobile phase, caused by different channels among the solid particles, and by the kinetic lag in attaining equilibrium between phases. The pertinent relation is

$$C = q\left(\frac{k'}{(1 + k')^2}\right)\left(\frac{d_s^2}{D_s}\right) + \frac{wd_p^2}{D_m} \tag{19-9}$$

where q is a geometrical factor depending on particle size and uniformity, d is the thickness of the liquid layer (if the particles are coated with liquid) or the diameter of the uncoated particles, and w is another parameter depending on the packing.

The van Deemter equation is plotted in Fig. 19-4 to show the qualitative relations among the three terms. There is an optimum flow rate v_{opt} for the system, at which H is a minimum. The optimum velocity will not be the same for the different components of a mixture, and should be selected for the components most difficult to separate. Chromatographers often choose to use a velocity greater than theoretical optimum in order to cut the time of analysis, even though this lessens the resolution somewhat. As the slopes of the left and right segments of the curve suggest, it is very harmful to be on the low-flow side of the optimum.

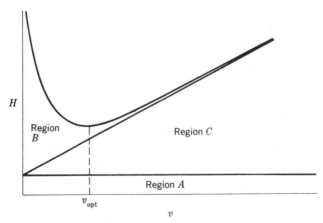

Figure 19-4 A plot of the van Deemter equation for a gas chromatogram. In a similar plot for LC the minimum (v_{opt}) would be so far to the left as to be nearly indistinguishable from the vertical axis.

The van Deemter equation was originally derived for gas chromatography. In liquid chromatography the relation is more complicated than Eq. (19-6), in that the quantity C includes several additional terms. The minimum in the curve gives a value of v_{opt} that is some 10^4 times smaller than in GC, and thus is much too low for convenient use.

Retention Time and Volume

The time elapsed between the injection of a sample onto the column and the elution of a component (measured at its peak) is defined as the *retention time* t_R. It is often more convenient to use an adjusted retention time t'_R, corrected for the time of passage of an unretained component through the column. In GC, air is often satisfactory as such an unretained component: $t'_R = t_R - t_{air}$. In LC, no substance is widely useful for this purpose, and one can only be selected as useful within a given system.

Measurements can also be expressed in terms of the *transition volume* V_R, related to the retention time through the flow rate F†

$$V_R = t_R F \qquad (19\text{-}10)$$

The retention volume can be corrected to allow measurements from an unretained peak

$$V'_R = t_R F - t_{air} F = t'_R F \qquad (19\text{-}11)$$

In GC, correction must be made for the difference in pressure at the two ends of the column. A temperature correction is also required. These factors can be combined to give

$$V_g = t'_R F j \frac{273}{T_c} \frac{1}{W_s} \qquad (19\text{-}12)$$

where j is the pressure correction,‡ T_c is the temperature of the column in kelvins, and W_s is the weight of stationary phase in the column. V_g represents the volume of carrier fluid required to move one-half of the solute through a hypothetical column containing 1 g of stationary phase at 0°C, and causing no pressure drop. V_g provides a convenient way in which to report retention data.

---

† F has units of $cm^3 \cdot s^{-1}$, contrasted with the linear velocity v in $cm \cdot s^{-1}$, as used in the van Deemter equation.

‡ The factor j for GC is given by

$$j = \frac{3[(P_i/P_o)^2 - 1]}{2[(P_i/P_o)^3 - 1]}$$

where P_i and P_o are the inlet and outlet pressures. The factor can be as low as 0.5, corresponding to $P_i/P_o = 2.75$. The correction is not needed in LC, since liquids are not compressible.

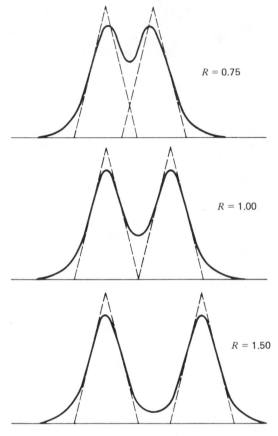

Figure 19-5 Two peaks of equal height, for which the resolution R has various values, as marked. The dashed lines are the triangular approximations to the peaks.

Resolution

The resolution is a measure of the degree of separation of adjacent peaks. It is defined as

$$R = \frac{t_{R(A)} - t_{R(B)}}{4\sigma} = \frac{t_{R(A)} - t_{R(B)}}{0.5(w_{(A)} + w_{(B)})} \qquad (19\text{-}13)$$

Figure 19-5 shows a pair of equal peaks for several values of R. Resolution is generally considered to be complete for $R = 1.5$.

PROBLEMS

19-1 (a) Starting with Eq. (19-5), derive an expression for the ratio H_{eff}/H as a function of k'.
  (b) Under what conditions are H_{eff} and H essentially equal?

19-2 Determine the dimensions (units) for all quantities in Eqs. (19-6) through (19-9).

19-3 By differentiation of Eq. (19-6), derive an expression for the minimum flow rate in terms of the parameters A, B, and C.

19-4 Assuming that the chromatogram of Fig. 19-3 was obtained with a column of length 0.5 m, estimate the effective number of theoretical plates and the corresponding plate height, as determined for each peak. How closely is Eq. (19-3) obeyed? Take the measurements needed directly from the figure, in millimeters.

19-5 By combining Eqs. (19-4) and (19-13), show that the resolution can be expressed by

$$R = \frac{t'_A - t'_B}{t'} \cdot \frac{\sqrt{N}}{4}$$

where $t' = 0.5(t'_A + t'_B)$, and $N = 0.5(N_A + N_B)$.

GENERAL REFERENCES

1. S. Dal Nogare and R. S. Juvet, Jr., *Gas-Liquid Chromatography: Theory and Practice*, Wiley-Interscience, New York, 1962.
2. J. C. Giddings, *Dynamics of Chromatography*, pt. I, vol. I, Dekker, New York, 1965.
3. E. Heftmann (ed.), *Chromatography, a Laboratory Handbook of Chromatographic and Electrophoretic Methods*, Van Nostrand Reinhold, New York, 1975.
4. L. R. Snyder and J. J. Kirkland, *Introduction to Modern Liquid Chromatography*, (2d ed.), Wiley-Interscience, New York, 1979.

TWENTY

GAS CHROMATOGRAPHY

Of all the separation methods, this technique is one of the most extensively used for analytical purposes. It provides a quick and easy way of determining the number of components in a mixture, including the presence of impurities, and in many cases, prima facie evidence of the identity of a compound. The chief requirement is some degree of stability at the temperature necessary to maintain the substance in the gas state. Thus a gas chromatograph (GC) is an essential tool for the chemist concerned with the synthesis or characterization of compounds of moderate molecular weight.

Figure 20-1 shows schematically the essential parts of a GC. There is much latitude between a basic unit that will serve for many identifications, and a highly sophisticated instrument suitable for the varied and stringent requirements of

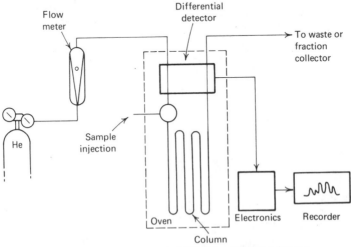

Figure 20-1 Schematic diagram of a typical GC with a differential detector.

research. We will consider first the physicochemical systems—the choice of materials for the fixed and mobile phases—and then the detailed instrumental features.

THE STATIONARY PHASE

GC is divided into two subclasses, according to the nature of the stationary phase. In one [called *gas-solid chromatography* (GSC)], the fixed phase consists of a solid material such as granular silica, alumina, or carbon. The separation process involves adsorption on the solid surface. GSC is quite limited in applicability, largely because of the tailing caused by nonlinear adsorption isotherms, partly because of excessive retention of reactive gases, which reduces the available area. Surface catalysis may also play a restricting role. GSC is of chief value in the separation of permanent gases and low-boiling hydrocarbons.

By far the more important class is *gas-liquid chromatography* (GLC),[1] in which the fixed phase is a nonvolatile liquid held as a thin layer on a solid substrate. The solid support ideally should have no effect on the chromatographic process, but only serve as a mechanical matrix for the liquid phase. The most common support is *diatomaceous earth*, also known as *kieselguhr*, which is available in many forms. This highly porous siliceous material is prepared in either of two general ways. It may be treated with alkali and calcined, giving a white product with some residual alkalinity, or it may be calcined with a binder but without the alkaline flux. In the latter case, the product is red or pink, is somewhat acid, and is known as crushed *firebrick*. The particle size should be fairly uniform and not too fine. Typical diameter ranges are 60 to 80 mesh (about 0.25 to 0.18 mm), 80 to 100 mesh (0.18 to 0.15 mm), and 100 to 120 mesh (0.15 to 0.13 mm). The smaller the grains, the more pressure is required to force gas through the columns.

Diatomaceous earth, being a form of hydrated silica, contains many free —OH groups on its surface. These can serve as sites at which solute molecules can be adsorbed. This is undesirable in GLC, because it results in a sluggish release of solute from the liquid film to the carrier gas, as evidenced by *tailing* of the peaks. This effect can be reduced by the use of a polar liquid phase that is itself adsorbed strongly onto the solid. Sometimes more effective is treatment of the solid with a *silanizing agent* such as hexamethyldisilazane (HMDS), which converts the $Si—O—H$ groups to the innocuous $Si—O—Si(CH_3)_3$:

$$-\overset{|}{\underset{|}{Si}}-O-\overset{|}{\underset{|}{Si}}- \ + \ [(CH_3)_3Si]_2NH$$

OH   OH   (HMDS)

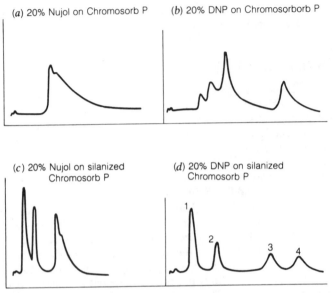

(a) 20% Nujol on Chromosorb P   (b) 20% DNP on Chromosorborb P

(c) 20% Nujol on silanized Chromosorb P   (d) 20% DNP on silanized Chromosorb P

Figure 20-2 Tailing due to adsorption on Chromosorb P, and its reduction following silanization. The solutes are: (1) ethanol, (2) methyl ethyl ketone, (3) methyl propyl ketone, (4) *n*-butanol. (*Wiley-Interscience.*[2])

Figure 20-2 illustrates these points with chromatograms of mixed polar solvents under several conditions.[2] In (a) is shown the result of using the non-polar liquid Nujol coated on a firebrick support (Chromosorb P); the asymmetry (tailing) is so marked as to make the chromatogram worthless. Changing to the more polar solvent dinonyl phthalate (DNP) at (b) is an improvement, as is treatment with a silanizing agent (c). Only when both of these improvements are introduced (d) is an acceptable recording produced.

Capillary Columns

The granular packing material can be eliminated by the use of a long capillary of glass or fused silica, in which the walls serve as support for the stationary liquid phase. Typical dimensions are 0.2 mm inside diameter and 50 to 100 m in length. Such columns can be extremely efficient, with HETP of the order of 1 mm, so that the column may contain as many as 500,000 theoretical plates, compared to standard packed columns for which 5000 plates is typical.

Capillary columns are especially useful for separating the components of complex mixtures (see, for example, Fig. 20-3). They require special precautions and techniques with respect to sample handling and coupling to detectors, as will be described later.

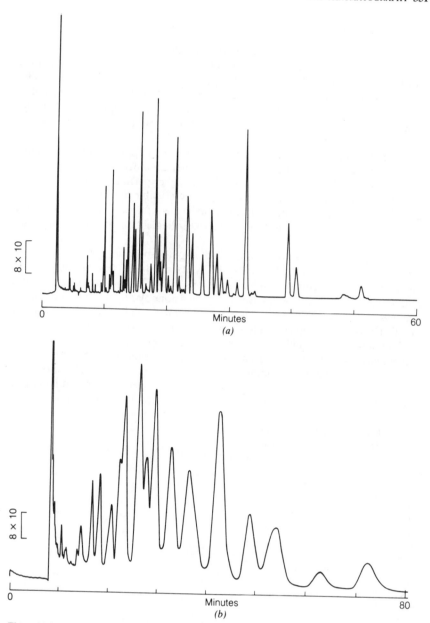

Figure 20-3 Comparison of gas chromatograms taken on: (a) a glass capillary column, and (b) a packed column. Both use the same stationary liquid and same temperature. The sample size was 30 times larger in (b) than in (a), and the flow rate much greater (*Journal of High Resolution Chromatography & Chromatographic Communications.*[3])

THE STATIONARY LIQUID PHASE

Hundreds of materials have been reported as suitable liquid phases for specific separations. Many of these are waxes, rubbers, or glasses at room temperature, but become liquids at the operating temperature of the GC column. They differ for the most part with respect to their degree of polarity and the temperature range over which they can be used. For the majority of applications a limited number of liquids will suffice. Table 20-1 lists a few representative liquids that will provide a versatile selection.

The temperatures quoted in the table represent an approximate useful range, but since they also depend on other factors, they are not to be considered hard restrictions. Thus some detectors will tolerate higher partial pressures of volatile stationary liquid than others. Also, it may be permissible to heat a column to the upper limit cited or even beyond, if it is held there for only a very short time. The lower limit depends on such factors as solidification or greatly increased viscosity.

The *polarity* of the liquid phase is not usually specified in terms of the dielectric constant, but rather empirically by its ability to separate appropriate compounds under chromatographic conditions. Nonpolar solutes such as pentane, butane, and propane, can be resolved easily on a nonpolar liquid such as squalane, whereas their peaks fall much closer together on a column containing a polar liquid. The converse applies to the separation of polar solutes such as alcohols.

The amount of liquid carried by the solid support is specified in terms of percent *loading* by weight. The usual coating procedure for standard columns calls for dissolving the required amount of liquid in a volatile solvent. The dried solid support is thoroughly mixed with the solution in an open container, followed by removal of the solvent by evaporation. The solid with its liquid coating has the

Table 20-1 Some stationary phase liquids

Material	Temperature range, °C
Nonpolar liquids	
Apiezon L	50–300
Silicone DC-200	50–350
Silicone SE-30	50–350
Squalane	20–150
Intermediate liquids	
Silicone DC-QF-1	0–275
Silicone OV-17	0–280
Polar liquids	
Carbowax 20M	60–225
Diethylene glycol succinate	20–200
Ethylene glycol adipate	20–190

appearance of a free-flowing sand, which can be poured into a long straight metal tube, with tapping or vibration to promote even packing. The tube, fitted with gas-tight connectors, may be coiled loosely after packing.

Coating a liquid phase onto the walls of a capillary column is a more difficult procedure. Many liquids tend to form droplets rather than a continuous film. This tendency can be minimized by roughening the surface with dry HCl or other reagent. The pretreated capillary is then filled with a solution of the desired liquid in a volatile solvent, and the solvent evaporated at reduced pressure and elevated temperature.

Capillary columns have such high efficiency that satisfactory separations can often be achieved even if the stationary phase is not ideal with respect to polarity. Hence it may be sufficient to keep on hand only two columns, one polar, the other nonpolar, to meet the needs of the majority of applications.[4]

There is another type of column packing that can be considered intermediate between the bare solids of GSC and the coated supports of GLC. This packing consists of porous beads of a cross-linked organic polymer such as copolymerized styrene and divinylbenzene. The maximum temperature is about 250°C. It appears that the components of the sample distribute themselves between the gas phase and the amorphous beads, the latter acting more like a solvent than an adsorbent. These materials give remarkably clean separations. They are available under various trade names, including Porapak (Waters), Chemipak (Gasukuro Kogyo), and the Chromosorb-100 series (Johns Manville).

Most packed or coated columns require further conditioning before use. This operation involves flushing with dry carrier gas for a few hours at the highest permissible temperature, to flush out any volatiles that might cause interference.

Bonded Phases

Many conventional liquid phases suffer from volatility, especially at high temperatures. Even a small amount of volatilization will distort the background in a chromatogram, and thus interfere with observation and measurement of trace components of a sample. This difficulty can be nearly eliminated by the use of organic compounds that are covalently bonded to the support.[5] For example, a diatomaceous earth material can be treated with a chlorosilane that has long-chain aliphatic, aromatic, or glycolic substituents. The flowing gas only encounters the organic moieties, which act like solvents, while the molecules are firmly anchored and cannot volatilize. Bonded stationary phases are quite popular in spite of their greater cost.

CARRIER GAS

By far the most common carrier gas is helium. A principal reason for this choice is that one of the most useful detectors depends on the thermal conductivity of the gas, a property that is much greater for hydrogen and helium than for any other gases. However, because of their low density, greater flow rates are required for either of these than for heavier gases, in order to reduce diffusion effects that would cause peak broadening. Hydrogen has two drawbacks that militate against its use: one is its fire- and explosion-hazard, the other is its chemical reactivity toward reducible or unsaturated samples.† Other gases, such as argon or nitrogen, are required for certain detectors, as will be detailed later.

SAMPLE INJECTION

An outstanding feature of GC is its ability to utilize small samples—from 0.01 to 50 μl of a liquid. There are two common methods of introducing the sample: by valve and by syringe. The syringe technique is the most widely used. The device employed is essentially the same as the medical hypodermic syringe, and is available in many calibrated sizes to deliver from 0.01 μl up. The chromatograph is provided with an inlet port sealed with a replaceable rubber septum through which the needle can be inserted. Syringes can be used with gases or low-viscosity liquid samples. The region into which the needle projects must be heated in order to vaporize the sample instantly, but overheating of the rubber septum must be avoided, as it can evolve a surprising amount of gas to contaminate the sample.

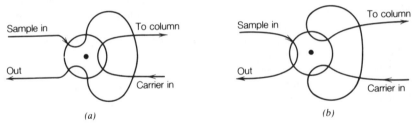

(a)   *(b)*

Figure 20-4 A six-port sampling valve.

The valve method is convenient for sampling gas streams. Figure 20-4 shows how a six-port valve can be used to measure out and introduce a gaseous sample. In position (*a*) the stream to be sampled flows through a loop of calibrated volume, while the carrier gas alone passes through the column. Upon turning the valve through 60° to position (*b*), the loop is placed in the carrier gas stream and the entrapped sample is swept along to the column.

The insertion of liquid samples onto a capillary column requires special precautions to avoid overloading. The volume delivered to the column cannot exceed about 0.2 μl, and less (ca. 0.01 μl) is preferable. A precision syringe capable of measuring such a small amount accurately is both expensive and fragile. Alternatively a flow-splitter may be used. In this device the stream of gas is divided following sample injection, so that a large fraction (30 to 90 percent) is vented while the remainder goes to the column. For an interesting account of the problems involved, and how one manufacturer has solved them, see Ref. 7. Continued interest in this field has resulted in two new devices described in the same issue of *Analytical Chemistry*.[8,9]

---

† Hydrogen has a specific advantage, however, in that it can be generated electrolytically. An ingenious application to a self-contained GC for use in space vehicles is described in Ref. 6.

SOLID SAMPLES†

Solids can only be analyzed directly by GC if they have high enough vapor pressure to ensure immediate volatilization in the heated inlet space. They can often be injected as solutions in a suitable volatile solvent. Many nonvolatile solids can be decomposed thermally to produce characteristic gaseous products that can be chromatographed. This procedure is known as *pyrolysis GC* or *PGC*.[10] The sample is placed directly into a small coil of platinum wire where it can be heated to several hundred degrees Celsius in a few milliseconds while the carrier gas is flowing over it. The pyrolysis products are passed directly onto the column.

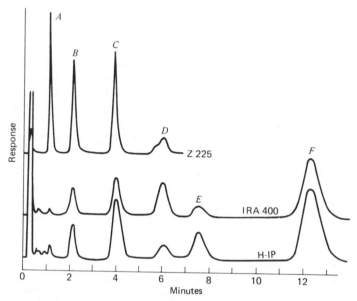

Figure 20-5 Pyrolysis gas chromatograms of three ion-exchange resins at 100°C. The column was a polyphenyl ether supported on Celite. The fragments are: *A*, benzene; *B*, toluene; *C*, xylene and ethylbenzene (unresolved); *D*, styrene; *E*, ethyltoluene; and *F*, vinyltoluene. (*Analytical Chemistry*.[11])

Better control of the final temperature can be achieved by high-frequency induction heating. The sample is held on a wire or strip made of a ferromagnetic alloy of nickel and iron or cobalt. Each such alloy is characterized by a temperature, called the Curie point, where it loses its ferromagnetic quality, becoming paramagnetic, which means that it can no longer absorb RF energy. Often, though, the rate of heating is more important than the final temperature.[10]

Pyrolysis GC is a particularly good method of studying polymeric materials. An example is shown in Fig. 20-5.[11]

† The present trend is to displace GC in favor of LC for analysis of those solid samples that are soluble in suitable solvents; see Chap. 21.

Another path by which nonvolatile solids can be studied by GC involves the formation of volatile chemical derivatives. An example of this method is the separation of amino acids as the *N*-acetyl or *n*-amyl esters on a Carbowax column.[12] Another useful series of derivatives can be prepared by silanization, the insertion of di- or tri-methylsilyl groups in place of labile hydrogen, as in —OH, —COOH, —SH, and —NH$_2$ groups.[13] This was originally reported for the chromatography of sugars, but is applicable to many other classes of compounds. An interesting example of derivatization is the separation of beryllium from other trace metallic elements in lunar and meteoritic rocks, via the chelate with trifluoroacetylacetone.[14]

DETECTORS

In principle, the measurement of any property that has different values for different gases can be incorporated into a GC detector, and several dozen have been described. Detectors can be grouped into two major families. In the first family are those that give a response proportional to the *concentration* of sample (expressed in mole fraction), but are independent of the rate of flow of the gas. The response of second family detectors depends upon the *rate* at which the sample is delivered to the sensing element, but the extent of dilution by carrier gas is irrelevant.

First Family Detectors

This group includes devices that sense passively some physical property of the gas without reacting with it chemically. By far the most important in this class are the thermal-conductivity (TC) and electron-capture (EC) detectors. Also included are little-used detectors based on the absorption of UV or IR radiation.

The thermal-conductivity detector†[15] This device consists of a block of metal with two (or four) cylindrical cavities machined into it. Each cavity is provided with a centrally positioned thin-wire filament (Fig. 20-6). These resistive elements form the arms of a Wheatstone bridge, with the gas flowing around them as indicated in Fig. 20-7. Sufficient current is passed through the bridge to maintain the filaments a few degrees warmer than the metal block. The bridge is balanced initially (by adjustment of R_5) with pure helium flowing around all filaments. When a slug of sample component comes along, the temperature of the filament R_2 (in a), or R_2 and R_3 (in b), will increase because the sample gases (see Table 20-2) will always be much poorer conductors of heat than helium (hydrogen is the only exception). The temperature coefficient of resistance of the filament wires produces an electrical unbalance condition in the bridge that is amplified and displayed by the recorder.

In some models the filaments are replaced with *thermistors*, which are semiconductor devices with large negative temperature coefficients. These are more

† Sometimes called a *katharometer*.

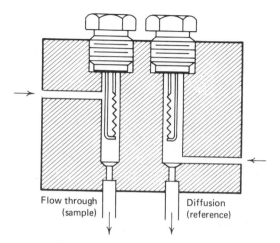

Flow through
(sample)

Diffusion
(reference)

Figure 20-6 One form of a TC detector. The gas on the reference side is allowed to enter the chamber only by diffusion, giving greater stability, whereas on the sample side the gas flows directly through, giving greater speed of response. (*Gow-Mac Instrument Company.*)

sensitive than metal filaments, at room temperature, but somewhat less so at elevated temperatures.

The electron-capture detector For many years GC made use of TC detectors almost exclusively, but with the advent of capillary columns, which are limited to smaller samples, greater sensitivity was required.

One method of detection that can give greater sensitivity is a modification of the ionization chamber long used for radiation detection.[16] The effluent from the chromatographic column is allowed to flow through such a chamber, where it is subjected to a constant flux of beta-ray electrons from a permanently installed radioisotope (Fig. 20-8). A titanium foil containing adsorbed tritium makes the most satisfactory source, though ^{63}Ni can be used. Both are pure beta sources, which makes for easy shielding against radiation hazard.

A small current (nanoamperes) normally flows through the chamber, carried by the gaseous ions. Organic compounds eluted from the column interfere with

Table 20-2 Thermal conductivities of a few gases $(cal \cdot s^{-1} \cdot cm^{-1} \cdot K^{-1})$

Gas	Thermal conductivity
H_2	44.5
He	36.0
Ne	11.6
CH_4	8.18
O_2	6.35
N_2	6.24
CO_2	3.96
CH_3OH	3.68
Organic gases	1–4

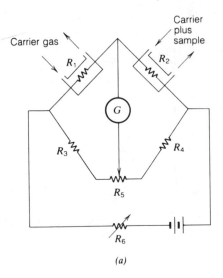

(a)

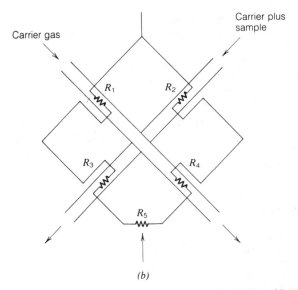

(b)

Figure 20-7 Electrical circuit for a TC detector. (a) A bridge with two active arms, and (b) one with all four arms active. Resistor R_5 provides an initial balance adjustment. In practice, the galvanometer G is replaced by an electronic amplifier and recorder. The circuitry external to the actual bridge can be identical in (a) and (b).

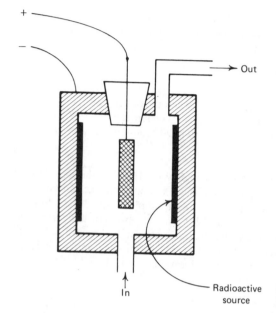

→ Out

↑ In

Radioactive source

Figure 20-8 An electron-capture detector, schematic.

this current by electron transfer, becoming themselves ionized in the process. The organic ions, however, are less mobile than ions of the carrier gas, usually nitrogen, and so the current is diminished. Argon can be used as carrier, but it tends to be excited to a metastable state by the beta radiation, and a quenching gas, such as methane, must be added.

The electron-capture detector is particularly sensitive to halogenated compounds. It was largely due to this detector that the ubiquitous distribution of pesticides in the world environment became evident.

In these first-family detectors, the signal response is proportional to x_s, the mole fraction of solute, which is a dimensionless quantity, and the area beneath a peak on the chromatogram is given by $x_s \, dt$. But $x_s = v_s/(v_s + v_c)$, in which the denominator is v, the sum of the flow rates of carrier and sample. So we can write

$$A = \int x_s \, dt = \int \frac{v_s}{v_s + v_c} \, dt \qquad (20\text{-}1)$$

This area is proportional to m, the mass of substance giving rise to the peak, only if v is held constant, which is not a simple matter experimentally (flow regulators exert control over v_c only). Since very small samples will have negligible effect on v, it follows that

$$A = \frac{1}{v} \int v_s \, dt = \frac{1}{v} \int \frac{dm}{dt} \, dt = \frac{m}{v} \qquad (20\text{-}2)$$

Hence, if the measurement is to be absolute, the measured area must be multiplied by the flow rate. For determinations relative to a standard, this factor can be included in the overall calibration.

Second Family Detectors

Most organic compounds are readily burned when introduced into a hydrogen–oxygen flame, producing ions and, in some cases, characteristic UV or visible radiation. Remarkably sensitive GC detectors have been devised that are based on flame measurements.

The flame-ionization detector (FID) In this widely used device, the ions formed during the combustion of the sample are collected at a charged electrode, and the resulting current measured with an electrometer amplifier (p. 214 of Ref. 1). Figure 20-9 is a diagrammatic sketch of an FID. The carrier gas (usually nitrogen) emerging from the column is mixed with an equal volume of hydrogen and burned at a metallic jet in an atmosphere of air. The jet (or a surrounding ring) is made the negative electrode, and a loop or cylinder of inert metal surrounding the flame is

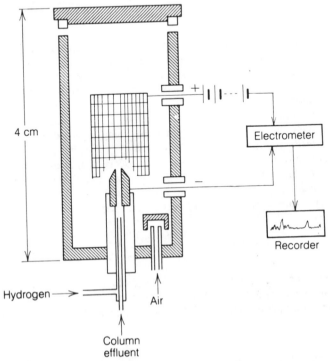

Figure 20-9 A hydrogen-flame ionization detector (FID). (*Barber-Colman Company.*)

made positive. The sensitivity to organic solutes varies roughly in proportion to the number of carbon atoms; it is perhaps a thousandfold more sensitive than the TC detector. The FID is an excellent general-purpose detector, particularly with capillary columns, because of its great sensitivity. Its lack of dependence on flow rate makes it convenient for quantitative analytical measurements.

The FID can be made almost solely responsive to organophosphorus compounds, even in submicrogram amounts, by the incorporation of a block of CsBr or Rb_2SO_4 as part of the structure immediately surrounding the flame.[17] The flame is operated in a hydrogen-rich mode, rather than oxygen-rich, as in the unmodified detector. The physical basis on which this detector works has not been entirely elucidated. It is the detector of choice for measuring trace levels of phosphate pesticides.

It is also possible to optimize the FID for the determination of organosilicon compounds.[18] This permits observation of silanized alcohols, amines, and others in the presence of such compounds as hydrocarbons that do not react with the silanizing reagent.

The flame-photometric detector This detector is based on measurement of the luminous emission from a hydrogen-rich flame in the presence of compounds containing either sulfur or phosphorus. These elements produce emissions at 394 and 526 nm, respectively.[19] The detector (Fig. 20-10) consists of a hydrogen–air burner with a photomultiplier detector optically coupled to it. The optical path is located so that only the upper part of the flame is observed, as this portion does not emit appreciably in the absence of S or P. Interchangeable optical filters permit selection of one or the other of the two elements.

Due to the fact that the entire sample component is consumed in any flame detector, the integrated area beneath the signal-time (or signal-volume) curve must correspond exactly to the mass m of substance detected. The height of the

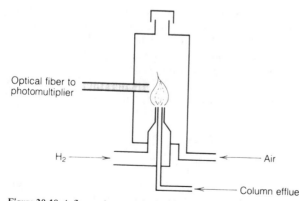

Figure 20-10 A flame-photometric detector. Light from the flame is conducted by a fiber-optic link to a photomultiplier, which may be at some distance.

Table 20-3 GC detectors, comparative data[17]

Detector†	D‡	Linear range
TC	10^{-12} g·ml^{-1}	10^5
FID	10^{-12} g·s^{-1}	10^7
ECD(T)	10^{-14} g·ml^{-1}	10^4
FID(P)	10^{-15} g·s^{-1}	10^3
FPD(P)	10^{-12} g·s^{-1}	None
IR	"High μg"	None
MS	"High μg"	10^6

† TC, thermal conductivity; FID, flame ionization; ECD(T), electron capture (tritium); FID(P), flame ionization, for phosphorus; FPD(P), flame photometric, for phosphorus; IR, infrared detector; MS, mass spectral detector.

‡ Detectivity, $D = N/S$, where N is an equivalent noise voltage and S is a sensitivity parameter.

curve at any point is proportional to the mass flow rate of the sample, $v_s = dm/dt$; hence the area beneath the recorded curve is given by

$$A = \int v_s \, dt = \int \frac{dm}{dt} \, dt = m \qquad (20\text{-}3)$$

and thus m is obtained directly.

Detector Scavenging

An important feature of all analytical chromatography is the dead volume of the system, including especially the detector. With a standard packed GC column, the rate of flow of gas is adequate to keep the detector flushed out. But with a capillary column, the rate may be too slow, so that the contents of the detector tend to become stagnant, thus broadening the peaks that the column has just cleanly separated. It is essential that the detector have as little hold-up volume as possible, but there are practical limits to this approach. The problem can usually be eliminated by providing an extra supply of pure carrier gas directly into the detector, to keep it flushed out. This is called *scavenging.*

Sensitivities of various detectors are listed in Table 20-3.[17] These data are to be taken as representative only, since the limits may vary with slight changes in chromatographic conditions.

DUAL DETECTION

Since different detectors have different sensitivities for various classes of compounds, additional information about samples can often be obtained by the use of two detectors simultaneously at the output of the same column. The two

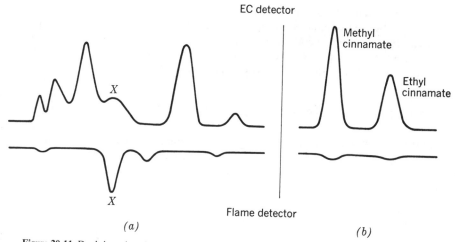

Figure 20-11 Dual detection GC of the high-boiling constituents of peppermint oil. In (a), the peak marked X was initially thought to be due to methyl cinnamate, which has nearly the same retention time. The results in (b) on authentic methyl cinnamate show much greater response for the ECD than the FID, whereas X was seen more easily by the FID, ruling out methyl cinnamate as the identity of X. (*Varian Aerograph.*)

detectors can be placed in series, so that the column effluent passes first through one then the other, provided that the first is nondestructive. Alternatively the two detectors can be connected in parallel with a flow-splitting device to direct part of the gas to each detector.

Figure 20-11 shows an example,[20] in which dual traces were taken from EC and FID detectors. Several peaks can be seen in each trace that are absent or much less pronounced in the other. The relative responses of a number of compounds to these two detectors are given in Table 20-4. It is evident that a dual record like this can be of great help in identifications. The occurrence of a peak in one trace and not in the other can rule some compounds out of consideration, although it can never alone prove an identity.

Table 20-4 Approximate ratio of sensitivities, electron capture to flame ionization[20]

Hexane	10^{-6}	Methyl salicylate	1.2
Carvone	0.01	Diethyl maleate	53
Pulegone	0.01	Diacetyl	53
Menthol	0.1	Ethyl cinnamate	65
Ethyl crotonate	0.9	Benzylideneacetone	65
Benzaldehyde	1.0	Cinnamaldehyde	200
Anisdaldehyde	1.0	Carbon tetrachloride	10^6

Aue and Hill[21] have adapted a flame detector so that ions and photons can both be observed simultaneously. They found this arrangement to be particularly successful with organometallic compounds, where the spectroscopic detector could be set at the appropriate wavelength to observe the atomic emission from the metal. The organic portions were detected by the FID.

TEMPERATURE PROGRAMMING[22]

In the separation of a number of compounds of similar type but widely varying in volatility, a difficulty arises if the experiment is carried out at constant temperature.

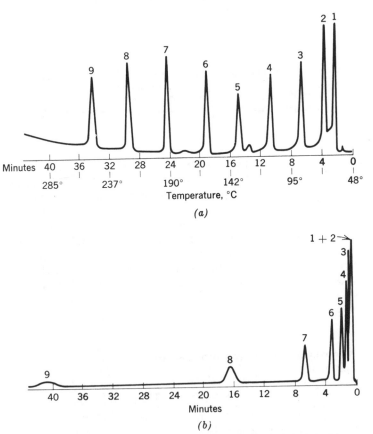

Figure 20-12 The effect of temperature programming on the GC of alcohols: (*a*) programmed temperature chromatogram, (*b*) isothermal chromatogram. Note that time runs to the left in this recording. The components are: (1) methanol, (2) ethanol, (3) 1-propanol, (4) 1-butanol, (5) 1-pentanol, (6) cyclohexanol, (7) 1-octanol, (8) 1-decanol, and (9) 1-dodecanol. (*Analytical Chemistry.*[23])

The low-boiling components are eluted quickly, and bunch together on the chromatogram, while the less volatile species take much longer to emerge, and their peaks are accordingly broader and shallower. This can be overcome by raising the temperature of the entire column at a uniform rate. When this is done, the partition coefficients of the compounds, which are temperature-dependent, are altered, and the result is that the peaks are much more evenly distributed along the chromatogram, and more equal in width. Figure 20-12, taken from the original paper on the subject, illustrates this concept.[23]

This figure shows an increasing baseline on going to higher temperatures (to the left in the figure), that is characteristic of programmed-temperature GC. It is due to increased *bleeding* or volatilization of the stationary phase, which would not be evident if the column were held at constant temperature. In Fig. 20-12, the effect is not very pronounced, but sometimes it can be so severe as to vitiate the analysis. This can be minimized or even eliminated by the use of two parallel columns with identical packing, placed in the same oven. The two columns should have identical detectors, or the effluents from the two columns should pass through opposite sides of the same TC bridge. The carrier gas is split into two streams *before* entering the columns, and the sample is inserted into one side only. The detectors are connected electrically so as to balance out the effect of the bleeding liquid phase, which is the same in the two columns. Note the similarity in this principle to the use of double-beam optics in spectrophotometry.

COMMERCIAL GAS CHROMATOGRAPHS

Flexible GC instruments suitable for exacting research are mostly modular in construction. The user can maintain a large inventory of interchangeable columns, and quickly install any selected one (or pair) as appropriate for a particular application. Likewise, any of several detectors can be selected. Temperature-programming controls are built in. The recorder is often a separate unit, rather than being incorporated into the main instrument chassis, as is customary with spectrophotometers.

If the chromatograph is intended for a single purpose, as it might well be in a quality-control laboratory, only a single detector and column type need be purchased. There are also several stripped-down chromatographs, usually equipped only with a TC detector and manual temperature control, that are fully adequate for many routine analyses.

All but the low-budget models are now equipped with built-in microcomputer controls, accessible from a keyboard. This is of great assistance in setting up the conditions for a particular analysis. In some instruments the computer also controls the plotter and can print elution times and peak areas for each maximum on the chromatogram. Figure 20-13 shows the type of printout that can be obtained from one commercial model.[24]

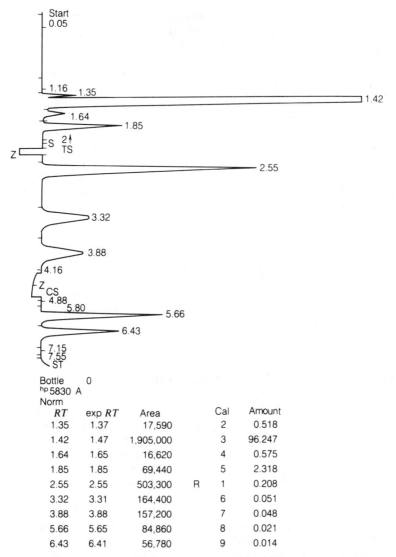

RT	exp *RT*	Area	Cal	Amount
1.35	1.37	17,590	2	0.518
1.42	1.47	1,905,000	3	96.247
1.64	1.65	16,620	4	0.575
1.85	1.85	69,440	5	2.318
2.55	2.55	503,300 R	1	0.208
3.32	3.31	164,400	6	0.051
3.88	3.88	157,200	7	0.048
5.66	5.65	84,860	8	0.021
6.43	6.41	56,780	9	0.014

Figure 20-13 Printout of a computer-controlled GC. The numbers against individual peaks are retention times. Note the large dynamic range, as both minor and major components are measured, as seen in the "Area" column. The sample was a natural gas. (*American Laboratory*.[24])

QUALITATIVE ANALYSIS

A certain amount of qualitative information can be obtained from the selectivity of various column liquids and detectors, but this approach will seldom go farther than to identify the class to which a compound belongs. For further information, one must turn to observation of *retention times*, the elapsed time between the injection of the sample and its appearance at the detector. For a given column, flow rate, and temperature, the retention time of a particular compound will be a constant, but it is not practicable to convert such data from one set of conditions to another except by some application of the internal standard principle. Various suggestions have been made as to the best way of doing this.

Relative retention times are often specified. In the determination of these values, a standard substance is added to the mixture prior to running through the column, and retention times are taken relative to this internal standard. *n*-Pentane is widely used for this purpose, but for work on a polar column at an elevated temperature, some other substance, such as methyl palmitate, may be more appropriate.

There are a number of semiempirical relations between relative retention data and other parameters. A plot of the logarithm of retention times against the number of carbon atoms in a homologous series of compounds in a nonpolar liquid phase gives a family of parallel lines, as shown in Fig. 20-14. The slope indicates that the retention time approximately doubles for the addition of one

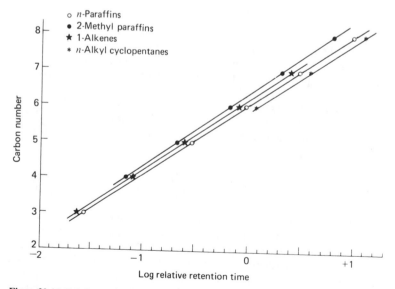

Figure 20-14 Relative retention times as a function of carbon number for several series of hydrocarbons. Plotted from data of Ladon and Sandler.[25]

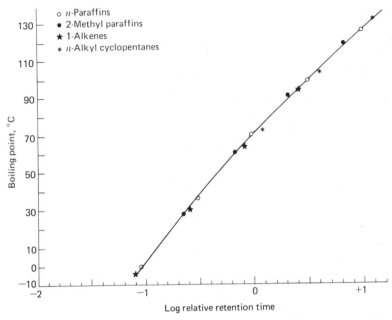

Figure 20-15 Relative retention times as a function of boiling points. Plotted from data of Ladon and Sandler.[25]

CH_2 group to an aliphatic chain. Since boiling points also relate to chain length, it is to be expected that they will likewise give linear plots against the log of retention time. Figure 20-15 shows a boiling-point plot for the same data as in Fig. 20-14. Note that the several parallel lines of Fig. 20-14 have now merged into a single, nearly straight line.

A decided improvement is offered by the *Kováts retention index* system, which presents a uniform scale rather than a single fixed point for comparison.[26] The retention index I was originally defined in terms of volumes, but we will use the equivalent time expression

$$I = 100 \left[\frac{\log t'_x - \log t'_z}{\log t'_{z+1} - \log t'_z} + z \right] \qquad (20\text{-}4)$$

where t'_x is the adjusted retention time for substance x, t'_z and t'_{z+1} are the corresponding times for normal hydrocarbons with z and $z + 1$ carbon atoms, respectively. The logs are used because, as we have seen, this function produces a linear scale for successive hydrocarbons. This definition of I requires that t'_x lies between t'_z and t'_{z+1}. The index is nearly linear with temperature, at least over short ranges.

Even more information can be obtained by comparing the Kováts indices for the same series of compounds as separated on polar and nonpolar stationary phases. Index differences (ΔI) between columns can yield supporting data related to molecular structure. The details of the method can be found in a report by Schomburg,[27] who has applied it to a series of 156 hydrocarbons containing the cyclopropane ring.

Simulated Distillation

GC has found a valuable area of application as a replacement for analytical distillation, particularly in the petroleum field. A high-precision fractional distillation takes something like 100 h for completion, hence is useless for refinery control purposes. Equally good or even better results can be obtained by dual-column, temperature-programmed GC in only 1 h.[28] A computer continuously integrates the detector signal and prints the accumulated total at intervals of a few seconds. These data, plotted against column temperature, give a curve identical in shape to that produced by the 100-h distillation. A correction must be made to the temperature scale if true boiling points are needed, because the partial pressure of a component in the carrier gas is not 1 atm, as required by the definition of the boiling point.

QUANTITATIVE ANALYSIS

For known substances, quantitative determinations are generally performed on the recorded chromatogram. If the peaks are sharp and narrow, little error results from simple height measurement. For broader peaks the included area must be determined. Many GCs have built-in integrators, but lacking this facility, the simplest way is to make use of the triangular approximation of the gaussian curve, mentioned in the preceding chapter, whereby the area is equated to the height multiplied by half the base width (Fig. 19-3).

One procedure for quantitative analysis involves the collection of sample components as they are eluted from the column or after passing through any non-destructive detector. Each sample can then be analyzed in any appropriate manner. The apparatus can take many forms, from a test tube standing in a paper cup full of ice, to elaborate automated and refrigerated sample collectors. This is not usually done simply for quantitation, but for further study and identification.

GC AS A MEMBER OF A TEAM

GC can play a valuable role in combination with any other instrumental technique that can accept gaseous or volatile liquid samples. The most significant of these are mass spectrometry (GC/MS) and infrared spectrophotometry (GC/IR). It is even possible to use both at the same time.[29]

The combination of GC with mass spectroscopic techniques is especially fruitful. The mass spectrometer is at its best when presented with a small gas-phase

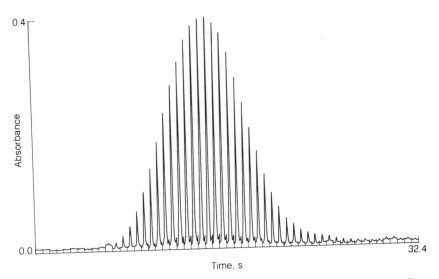

Figure 20-16 IR detection of dimethyl fumarate. The sample contained 2 μg; the flow was split so that half went to a FID, the other half to a Fourier-transform IR spectrophotometer. (*Applied Spectroscopy.*[33])

sample consisting of a single substance, a condition easily met by the effluent corresponding to a particular GC peak. The major problem in interfacing the two is the need for removal of the carrier gas, which would swamp the pumping system in conventional mass spectrometers. Further discussion will be found in Chap. 22.

In the case of GC/IR, two options are available. The greatest sensitivity can be obtained, at the expense of speed, by trapping successive sample components as they emerge from the GC, then recording their spectra with a conventional IR spectrophotometer. Transfer lines can be arranged to permit the gas to flow directly into a special absorption cell where it can be isolated by a valve while a spectrum is being recorded.[30]

The other possibility is to design an IR spectrophotometer that can operate fast enough to collect a spectrum "on the fly." With older IR detectors this could not be done, but the introduction of pyroelectric detectors has made it feasible.[31,32] Fourier-transform IR, with its inherently high speed, is better yet.

Figure 20-16 shows a GC/FTIR application in which the chromatographic peak for dimethyl fumarate was tested for identity and homogeneity.[33] The IR carbonyl band (1650 to 1850 cm^{-1}) was scanned repeatedly, at 0.6 s per scan, showing a single strong absorption each time. Another application is seen in Fig. 20-17.[34] The spectrophotometer is programmed to monitor several regions, averaging the response over the designated wave-number range, and to plot the result against elution time. From the graph so produced, one can deduce the class of compound represented by each chromatographic peak.

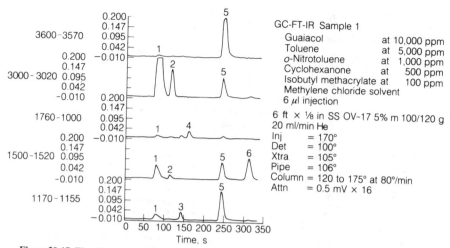

Figure 20-17 Five IR channels of GC effluents. (*Nicolet Instrument Corporation.*)

PROBLEMS

20-1 It is sometimes advantageous to analyze a hydrocarbon mixture quantitatively by oxidizing the column effluent prior to detection. The water vapor formed can be removed by a trap, and the CO_2 admitted to the TC detector. In a particular experiment, seven components gave peaks with integrated areas as follows:

Peak	Compound	Relative area
1	*n*-Pentane	2.00
2	*n*-Hexane	5.72
3	3-Methylhexane	2.21
4	*n*-Heptane	8.15
5	2,2,4-Trimethylpentane	1.92
6	Toluene	3.16
7	*n*-Octane	5.05

(*a*) Point out some advantages and disadvantages of this preoxidation procedure.
(*b*) Should the oxidation step precede or follow passage through the column, and why?
(*c*) Compute the composition of the sample giving rise to the data cited, in terms of mole percent of total hydrocarbons.

20-2 A chromatogram shows peaks as follows, in terms of distance from the injection point as measured on the recording paper:

Compound	Distance, cm
Air	2.2
n-Hexane	8.5
Cyclohexane	14.6
n-Heptane	15.9
Toluene	18.7
n-Octane	31.5

Calculate the Kováts indices for toluene and cyclohexane.

20-3 Two components, A and B, were found, in a particular GLC chromatogram, to give peaks at 5.0 and 7.0 cm on the chart paper, measured from the point of injection. An air peak appeared at 1.0 cm. Other pertinent data were:

Chart speed	$6 \text{ cm} \cdot \text{min}^{-1}$
Flow rate, F	$10 \text{ cm}^3 \cdot \text{s}^{-1}$
Pressure at top of column, P_i	2 atm
Pressure at bottom, P_o	1 atm
Column temperature, T_c	100°C
Weight of stationary phase, W_s	60 g
Density of stationary phase, ρ_s	$2 \text{ g} \cdot \text{cm}^{-3}$

For each component, calculate V_g. (See Chap. 19.)

20-4 Submicrogram quantities of cyanide can be determined by GC following conversion to cyanogen chloride, CNCl.[34] The reagent is aqueous chloramine-T (sodium p-toluenesulfonchloramide). The product CNCl is extracted with a specified quantity of hexane and injected onto a GC column. The carrier gas is argon with 5 percent methane. The EC detector gives a retention time of 2.4 min for CNCl and 4.8 min for hexane under the experimental conditions reported. The hexane peak serves as an internal standard. Calibration showed an average slope of $2.53 \text{ ml} \cdot \mu\text{g}^{-1}$ for a plot of the ratio of peak areas (CHCl/hexane) against concentration of CN^{-1} ion. A 1-ml sample of blood (from the coroner's office) was processed as described; a CNCl peak with an area of 31.61 units was recorded, along with a hexane peak of 0.2333 unit. What was the cyanide content of the blood, in $g \cdot ml^{-1}$?

20-5 The relative separating ability of a packed (p) and a capillary (c) column can be defined as

$$F = \frac{M_{\max(c)}}{M_{\max(p)}} \tag{20-5}$$

where $M_{\max}$ is the maximum flow rate. The relation of $M_{\max}$ to m, the total mass injected (the same for both columns), is given for a second-family detector by

$$m = 2 \int_0^\infty M \, dz \tag{20-6}$$

where z is the time coordinate taken relative to the peak maximum, combined with the equation for a gaussian curve

$$M = M_{\max} \exp\left(-\frac{1}{2\sigma^2} z^2\right) \tag{20-7}$$

The final expression is

$$F = \frac{\sigma_p}{\sigma_c} \tag{20-8}$$

which is equivalent to

$$F = \frac{t_{R,p}}{t_{R,c}} \left(\frac{N_c}{N_p}\right)^{1/2} \tag{20-9}$$

where t_R is the retention time and N is the number of theoretical plates.[3]

(a) Derive Eq. (20-8) and justify its equivalence to Eq. (20-9).
(b) Derive a comparable equation for first-family detectors.

20-6 A refinery product is to be analyzed by GC for its content of methylethylketone (MEK) and toluene. It was decided to use t-butylbenzene (tBB) as an internal standard. The following results were obtained with a column coated with 1,2,3-tris(2-cyanoxy)propane:

	Standard		Unknown	
	wt %	pk hts	wt %	pk hts
MEK	0.050	3.20	. . . .	3.20
Toluene	0.050	4.70	. . . .	5.21
*t*BB	0.050	4.20	0.045	4.11

What were the weight-percentages of MEK and toluene in the sample?

20-7 Two solutes are reported as having specific retention volumes [V_g, Eq. (19-12)] of 24.0 and 20,0 ml per gram of stationary phase. Calculate the expected elution times for a column with the same stationary phase, given the following data:

Column temperature	27°C
Gas pressure at injection port	2.20 atm
Gas pressure at end of column	1.00 atm
Weight of stationary phase	3.50 g
Flow rate	3.20 ml/s

REFERENCES

1. H. M. McNair, in *Chromatography, a Handbook of Chromatographic and Electrophoretic Methods*, (3d ed.), E. Heftmann (ed.), Van Nostrand Reinhold, New York, **1975**, chap. 9.
2. S. Dal Nogare and R. S. Juvet, Jr., *Gas-Liquid Chromatography*, Wiley-Interscience, New York, **1962**.
3. F. J. Yang and S. P. Cram, *J. High Res. Chromatogr. Chromatogr. Commun.*, **1979**, *2*, 487.
4. M. Novotny, *Anal. Chem.*, **1978**, *50*, 17A.
5. E. Grushka and E. J. Kikta, Jr., *Anal. Chem.*, **1977**, *49*, 1004A.
6. M. R. Stevens, C. E. Giffin, G. R. Shoemake, and P. G. Simmonds, *Rev. Sci. Instrum.*, **1972**, *43*, 1530.
7. L. S. Ettre and J. E. Purcell, in *Progress in Analytical Chemistry*, vol. 8, I. L. Simmons and G. W. Ewing (eds.), Plenum Press, New York, **1975**, p. 119.
8. F.-S. Wang, H. Shanfield, and A. Zlatkis, *Anal. Chem.*, **1982**, *54*, 1886.
9. T. L. Peters, T. J. Nestrick, and L. L. Lamparski, *Anal. Chem.*, **1982**, *54*, 1893.
10. C. J. Wolf, M. A. Grayson, and D. L. Fanter, *Anal. Chem.*, **1980**, *52*, 348A.
11. J. R. Parrish, *Anal. Chem.*, **1973**, *45*, 1659.
12. D. E. Johnson, S. J. Scott, and A. Meister, *Anal. Chem.*, **1961**, *33*, 669.
13. C. C. Sweeley, R. Bentley, M. Makita, and W. W. Wells, *J. Am. Chem. Soc.*, **1963**, *85*, 2497.
14. K. J. Eisentraut, D. J. Griest, and R. E. Sievers, *Anal. Chem.*, **1971**, *43*, 2003.
15. T. Johns and A. C. Stapp, *J. Chromatogr.*, **1973**, *11*, 234.
16. C. A. Burgett, *Res./Dev.*, **1974**, *25(11)*, 28.
17. C. H. Hartmann, *Anal. Chem.*, **1971**, *43(2)*, 113A.
18. M. A. Osman, H. H. Hill, Jr., M. W. Holdren, and H. H. Westberg, *Anal. Chem.*, **1979**, *51*, 1286.
19. S. S. Brody and J. E. Chaney, *J. Gas Chromatogr.*, **1966**, *4*, 42.
20. C. H. Hartmann, et al., *Aerograph Res. Notes* (Varian Aerograph, Walnut Creek, CA), **1963** (fall), **1966** (spring).
21. W. A. Aue and H. H. Hill, Jr., *Anal. Chem.*, **1973**, *45*, 729.
22. W. E. Harris and H. Habgood, *Programmed Temperature Gas Chromatography*, Wiley, New York, **1966**.
23. S. Dal Nogare and C. E. Bennett, *Anal. Chem.*, **1958**, *30*, 1157.
24. G. V. Peterson and J. S. Poole, *Am. Lab.*, **1974**, *6(5)*, 70.
25. A. W. Ladon and S. Sandler, *Anal. Chem.*, **1973**, *45*, 921.

26. L. S. Ettre, *Anal. Chem.* **1964**, *36(8)*, 31A.
27. G. Schomburg and G. Dielmann, *Anal. Chem.*, **1973**, *45*, 1647.
28. L. E. Green, L. J. Schmauch, and J. C. Worman, *Anal. Chem.*, **1964**, *36*, 1512.
29. C. L. Wilkins, G. N. Giss, G. M. Brissey, and S. Steiner, *Anal. Chem.*, **1981**, *53*, 113.
30. R. F. Brady, Jr., *Anal. Chem.*, **1975**, *47*, 1425.
31. G. J. Penzias, *Anal. Chem.*, **1973**, *45*, 890.
32. J. O. Lephardt and B. J. Bulkin, *Anal. Chem.*, **1973**, *45*, 706.
33. D. L. Wall and A. W. Mantz, *Appl. Spectrosc.*, **1977**, *31*, 552.
34. J. C. Valentour, V. Aggarwal, and I. Sunshine, *Anal. Chem.*, **1974**, *46*, 924.

General reference (added in proof)

H. M. McNair and E. J. Bonelli, *Basic Gas Chromatography* (5th ed.), Varian Instrument Division, Palo Alto, CA., **1969**.

TWENTY-ONE

LIQUID CHROMATOGRAPHY

The earliest form of chromatography to be seriously studied as an analytical tool was the separation of natural materials, such as plant pigments, from solution. Liquid chromatography was eclipsed for many years because of the tremendous success of its gas analog. Recently, however, it has met with renewed interest as a result of the application of modern design principles.[1-3]

In the older technique a glass column, perhaps 1 by 30 cm, was filled with a granular solid, and the carrier liquid containing the sample was poured through. The chief difficulty was slow speed. If the granules were small enough to give good separation, then the delivery under gravity alone might decrease to a few drops per minute. The obvious way to increase the throughput is to exert a force on the liquid by a positive-displacement pump or by gas pressure. Older apparatus could not survive the necessary high pressure, so major developments had to await a complete redesign of the system.

Liquid chromatography has the major advantage over GC of operating at a lower temperature, the range being limited only by the freezing and boiling points of the solvent. This means that LC is a viable technique for the separation of thermally unstable molecules such as proteins that cannot be volatilized without decomposition.

As an example of the kind of progress that has been made in LC, consider the separation of nucleosides.[1] Uridine, guanosine, adenosine, and cytidine could be cleanly separated in 1967 in one hour, using a 6-mm diameter column at a pressure of 10 to 20 psig.† Two years later the same separation took 24 min in a

† psig = pounds per square inch, gauge, i.e., above atmospheric pressure. 1 psig = (51.7 + 760.0) torr = 812 torr = 108 kPa (kilopascals).

375

1-mm column at 400 psig, and in 1970, in the same column, only 1.25 min was required at 5000 psig. Clearly, apparatus to operate at such high pressures must involve highly specialized design features. In the present treatment, we will be concerned only with modern high-pressure systems, often designated as HPLC, for high-performance liquid chromatography. An excellent brief description of the state of LC in 1982 can be found in a review paper by Freeman.[4]

The flow diagram of a versatile liquid chromatograph is shown in Fig. 21-1. Two solvent reservoirs, A and B, are provided to facilitate using mixed solvents for the liquid phase. Associated with each reservoir is a heated degassing chamber to remove dissolved air that might otherwise cause bubbles in the column. A special valve permits the use of either solvent alone or a mixture of the two in any proportion. The valve can be driven, if desired, by a geared-down motor, so that the proportions of the two solvents can be changed gradually during the course of a chromatographic separation, a procedure known as *gradient elution*.

From the mixing valve, the liquid is pumped at high pressure into the chromatograph, which is enclosed within a controlled-temperature chamber. The liquid first passes through a coil of tubing to bring it to the working temperature, and then through a *precolumn* loaded with the same packing material as the main column. The precolumn ensures that the mobile liquid is equilibrated with the material of the analytical column. It also acts as a filter to remove any residual suspended matter.

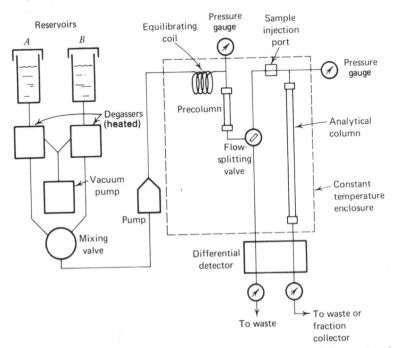

Figure 21-1 Flow diagram for a typical liquid chromatograph, with provision for gradient elution.

The sample is introduced between the pre- and main columns, either by syringe or valve, as in GC. The column effluent passes through one side of a differential detector to a fraction collector or to waste. The reference stream for the detector is split off from the main stream just prior to the sample injection point.

In simpler, less expensive units, temperature control is often omitted, which obviates the need for the temperature equilibrating coil of Fig. 21-1. The precolumn, also, is sometimes omitted, and as we will see, not all detectors are differential in nature.

Pumps

The high pressure that must be applied to the mobile liquid to force it through the column at a satisfactory rate can be obtained either by a motor-driven pump or by pressure transfer from a cylinder of compressed air or nitrogen. The latter method requires a diaphragm or piston to keep the gas from direct contact with the liquid, as otherwise considerable amounts would dissolve, to reappear as bubbles in the column and detector.

The pump is more widely used. It can be either a reciprocating pump, or a single-stroke type, essentially a large capacity motor-driven syringe. Most LC detectors are flow-sensitive, so the pump must be able to deliver liquid at a constant rate without pulsations. Manufacturers use various ingenious methods to achieve this condition (p. 159 of Ref. 2). One way is to provide two cylinders and pistons, so timed that one fills quickly while the other delivers slowly, and then takes over the delivery function as its mate becomes empty, after which the cycle repeats.

Columns

Columns for LC are usually made of stainless steel tubing, some 2 to 5 mm inside diameter, and 10 to 30 cm in length. They can be purchased ready packed, or can be packed by the user.† Column connections are made with flexible stainless steel tubing, usually about 1.5 mm outside diameter. It is imperative that dead volume in all the fittings be kept to the absolute minimum to avoid loss of resolution.

The nature of the packing material depends on the type of separation desired, and will be described in subsequent paragraphs.

CLASSES OF LIQUID CHROMATOGRAPHY

In the treatment of GC, we noted two distinct mechanisms by which the sample constituents can be retarded: by interaction with a solid (GSC), or with an immobilized liquid (GLC). There was also an intermediate class, where the active, liquid-like, material is bonded onto the solid support. These mechanisms are still operative in LC, but others must also be recognized, resulting from interaction between solvent and solutes.

---

† Special precautions must be taken in packing LC columns (see pp. 206 ff. of Ref. 3).

LIQUID-SOLID CHROMATOGRAPHY (LSC)

This is the case in which the retarding force involves the adsorption of solute molecules at hydroxyl-group sites on silica or alumina substrates. Polar molecules are held more strongly than nonpolar, and the usual order of elution is (p. 361 of Ref. 3):

saturated hydrocarbons (small k') < olefins < aromatic hydrocarbons

$\cong$ organic halides < sulfides < ethers < nitro-compounds

< esters $\cong$ aldehydes $\cong$ ketones < alcohols $\cong$ amines < sulfones

< sulfoxides < amides < carboxylic acids (large k')

(The symbol k' is the partition ratio introduced in Chap. 19.) The strength of adsorption is generally characteristic of functional groups in organic compounds, hence this method is particularly useful in separating classes of compounds. There may also be steric effects, so that positional isomers, such as cis-trans pairs, can sometimes be resolved.

A major difficulty in quantitative separations by LSC is caused by the non-linear adsorption isotherms encountered as the concentration of solute is raised. It is desirable to have the linear region (i.e., where the amount adsorbed is proportional to the concentration) extend as far as possible. In practice it is found that this linear region is longer for weakly adsorbed species than for those that are strongly adsorbed. This is interpreted as indicating discrete adsorption sites active with respect to dipole and hydrogen-bond interactions, whereas the weaker van der Waals forces can be effective over a larger area.

The reactivity of an adsorbent can be reduced by adding a small amount of water along with the mobile solvent. The water molecules become selectively adsorbed on the most active sites, leaving available the somewhat less active ones. This has the effect of increasing markedly the linear region for organic solutes. The adsorption of water is reversible, so the activity of the solid can be altered by changing the water content of the solvent.

LIQUID-LIQUID CHROMATOGRAPHY (LLC)

In this category, also known as *partition chromatography*, we consider systems in which the granular solid serves only as a mechanical support for a stationary phase, just as in GLC, while a second liquid forms the mobile phase. Because of the requirement that the two liquids be immiscible, it follows that they will differ markedly in degree of polarity. Either the more polar or the less polar liquid may be immobilized. Most commonly a polar solvent, such as alcohol or water, is adsorbed on a porous support of silica, alumina, or magnesium silicate. A non-polar solvent can be held on the same substrates following silanization, which renders them hydrophobic; this is sometimes called *reverse-phase* partition chromatography. Figure 21-2 shows a pair of chromatograms obtained in the

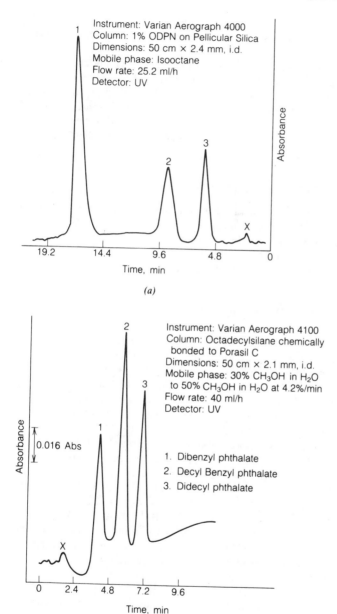

Figure 21-2 LLC chromatograms of phthalate ester plasticizers: (*a*) normal phase, (*b*) reverse phase. Note that the time scales are reversed. (*Varian Aerograph.*[1])

analysis of a mixture of phthalate esters by normal and reverse-phase LLC.[1] Note that time is plotted in opposite directions to emphasize the reversed sequence of elution.

LLC is more effective than LSC in separating similar compounds, such as members of a homologous series. A practical advantage of LLC as contrasted with LSC is the ease with which the immobilized film can be washed off and replaced without the need of repacking the column. On the other hand, this ease of removal leads to bleeding of the coating liquid. In LSC, the active sites can become poisoned by the irreversible adsorption of highly active compounds, and there is usually no way to rejuvenate the column.

Bonded Phase Liquid Chromatography (BPC)

This class uses the same types of packings as in the corresponding GC technique. It is comparable to LLC in its separating ability, and has largely replaced it, even though more expensive. The principal advantage is the permanence of the stationary phase, which practically eliminates bleeding. The chromatogram shown in Fig. 21-2b was prepared with a BPC column.

ION-EXCHANGE CHROMATOGRAPHY

Ion-exchange resins consist of highly polymerized, cross-linked, organic materials containing a large number of acidic or basic groups. Although the resins are insoluble in water, the active groups are hydrophilic and have varying degrees of affinity for ionic solutes. There are four types of resins, which are listed with some illustrative examples in Table 21-1. The useful pH ranges are significant. Below pH 5 the weak acid resins are so slightly dissociated that cation exchange is negligible; the converse is true for weakly basic types above pH 9.

Three examples will be described to show the versatility of ion-exchange chromatography. The first is the separation of simple cations on a strongly acid exchanger. For monovalent ions, the relative affinities are: $Li^+ < H^+ < Na^+ < NH_4^+ < K^+ < Rb^+ < Cs^+ < Ag^+ < Tl^+$ (that is, Li^+ is held least strongly on the resin). A similar scale for divalent ions is $UO_2^{2+} < Mg^{2+} < Zn^{2+} < Co^{2+} < Cu^{2+} < Cd^{2+} < Ni^{2+} < Ca^{2+} < Sr^{2+} < Pb^{2+} < Ba^{2+}$. Figure 21-3 shows the complete separation of Na^+ and K^+ ions.[5] The mixed sample was placed on the top of a column and eluted with 0.7 M HCl. The dashed curve represents theoretical predictions based on gaussian distributions. The average HETP was 0.5 mm.

The next example (Fig. 21-4) is the separation of a number of transition metal ions on a strongly basic anion-exchange resin.[6] The resin was first converted to the chloride form by treatment with 12 M HCl. After insertion of the sample, elution was carried out with successively more dilute HCl. The Ni(II) was not retained at all, even in concentrated HCl. Dilution to 6 M HCl caused the elution of Mn(II); Co(II) came out at 4 M, Cu(II) at 2.5 M, Fe(III) at 0.5 M, and Zn(II) only at 0.005 M. This sequence reflects the relative stabilities of the complex

Table 21-1 Ion-exchange resins for chromatography†

Resin class	Nature of resin	Effective pH range	Chromatographic applications
1. Strongly acidic cation exchange	Sulfonated polystyrene	1–14	Fractionation of cations; inorganic separations; lanthanides; B vitamins; peptides; amino acids
2. Weakly acidic cation exchange	Carboxylic polymethacrylate	5–14	Fractionation of cations; biochemical separations; transition elements; amino acids; organic bases; antibiotics
3. Strongly basic anion exchange	Quaternary ammonium polystyrene	0–12	Fractionation of anions; halogens; alkaloids; vitamin B complexes; fatty acids
4. Weakly basic anion exchange	Polyamine polystyrene or phenolformaldehyde	0–9	Fractionation of anionic complexes of metals; anions of differing valence; amino acids; vitamins

† From data on Amberlite resins, Rohm & Haas Company, Philadelphia, Pa., via Malinckrodt Chemical Works, St. Louis, Mo.

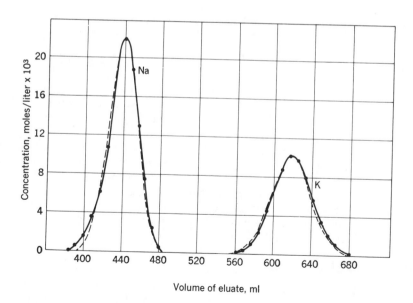

Figure 21-3 Ion-exchange separation of sodium and potassium ions on a cation-exchange resin, Dowex-50, eluted with 0.7 M HCl. (*Analytical Chemistry.*[5])

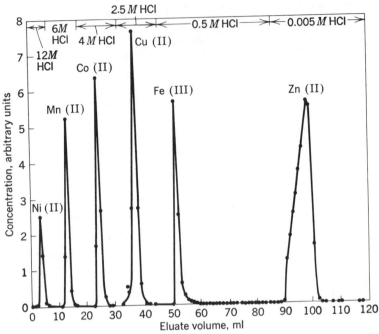

Figure 21-4 Ion-exchange separation of several transition metals on an anion-exchange resin, Dowex-1, eluted with successively more dilute HCl. (*Journal of the American Chemical Society.*[6])

chloride anions in reactions such as $CoCl_4^{2-} \rightleftharpoons Co^{2+} + 4Cl^-$, as well as the varying affinity of the resin for these ions and for the chloride ion.

Ion-exchange chromatography is a very valuable tool in the separation of complex mixtures of compounds of biochemical interest. Scott and coworkers[7] have resolved peaks corresponding to over 100 constituents of urine, using parallel columns of anion and cation exchangers.

Figure 21-5 shows 46 identified peaks in an ion-exchange chromatogram of mixed amino acids, observed with a photometric detector. Several manufacturers offer special-purpose chromatographs for the analysis of amino-acid mixtures.

It should be mentioned that ion exchange has important analytical applications other than chromatographic. These include removal of ionic interferences, and preconcentration of trace ionic materials. The reader is referred to the literature for further discussion (Ref. 8 and references included therein).

Ion-Pair Chromatography (IPC)

This is a special case of LLC or BPC, that is applicable to ionizable solutes consisting of a cation C^+ and anion A^- that are individually soluble in water, but for which the ion pair C^+A^- is soluble only in a nonaqueous solvent. Columns for IPC can be packed with a liquid-coated solid or with a chemically bonded material. They can operate in either the normal or the reverse-phase mode.

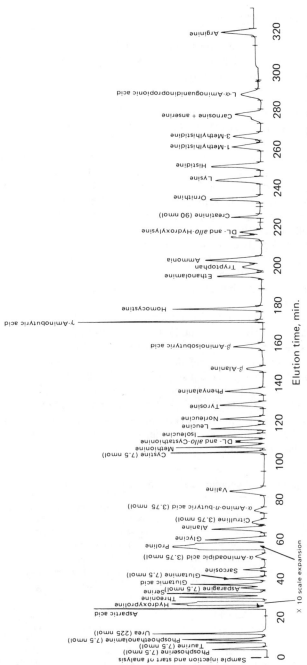

Figure 21-5 Ion-exchange separation of amino acids from a calibration mixture. Detection was via the ninhydrin reaction, with photometric measurements at 590 nm. The vertical scale is in absorbance units. (*Durram Instrument Corporation.*)

IPC is very effective in separating carboxylic and sulfonic acids using a tetraalkylammonium counter-ion, or amines with perchlorate as counter-ion. For more details, see pp. 453 ff. of Ref. 3.

MOLECULAR SIEVES AND SIZE-EXCLUSION CHROMATOGRAPHY (SEC)[9]

The term *molecular sieve* refers to a class of highly porous natural and synthetic crystalline materials, including *zeolites*, in which all the pores are of the same size.[10] The synthetic varieties are available in granular form with pore diameters from about 0.4 to 1.5 nm, the same order of magnitude as the dimensions of low molecular weight organic molecules. Molecules appreciably smaller than the pore size readily diffuse into the interior of the grains and are strongly adsorbed there, while molecules larger than the pores obviously cannot enter at all.

Sieve materials used in columns provide efficient removal of small molecules from a flowing stream, allowing larger ones to pass through unhindered. Table 21-2 lists some materials that are adsorbed by the several sieve types from one manufacturer. This kind of separation can clearly be of great value. Since this separation is not based on any distribution ratio, the mathematical relationships of Chap. 19 do not apply, and the method is not strictly chromatographic.

An extension of the molecular sieve concept that does obey the laws of chromatography is known as *gel permeation* or *gel filtration* chromatography (GPC or GFC). The stationary phase consists of beads of porous polymeric material. Among the most widely used are the previously mentioned copolymer of styrene and divinylbenzene (PS-DVB), and a variety of polyacrylamide gels. These materials have much larger pores than zeolites, and must be saturated with solvent prior to use. The solvent causes the particles to swell considerably, one of the attributes of a gel. The sieving effect is of such a magnitude that it is convenient

Table 21-2 Separation of components on Linde molecular sieves†

Adsorbed on both 4A and 5A	Adsorbed on 5A but not on 4A	Adsorbed on 13X but not on 4A or 5A
Ethane, propane	Propane and higher *n*-paraffins	Branched paraffins
Ethylene, acetylene	Butene and higher *n*-olefins	Benzene and other aromatics
Methanol, ethanol, *n*-propanol	*n*-Butanol and higher *n*-alcohols	Branched, secondary, and tertiary alcohols
	Cyclopropane	Cyclohexane
Water, ammonia, carbon dioxide, hydrogen sulfide	Freon-12	Carbon tetrachloride, sulfur hexafluoride, boron trifluoride

† From publications of the Linde Division of Union Carbide Corporation, via H. C. Mattraw and F. D. Leipziger, in *Treatise on Analytical Chemistry*, I. M. Kolthoff and P. J. Elving (eds.), pt. I, vol. 2, p. 1102, Wiley-Interscience, New York, **1961**. The pore sizes of the sieves are as follows: 4A, 0.4 nm (4 Å); 5A, 0.5 nm; 13X, 1.0 nm. At temperatures below about $-30°C$, appreciable quantities of carbon monoxide, nitrogen, oxygen, and methane are adsorbed on both 4A and 5A.

Table 21-3 Limiting molecular weights retained by μStyragel beads†

Pore size, nm	M.W. limit
10	700
50	$(0.05 \text{ to } 1) \times 10^4$
100	$(0.1 \text{ to } 20) \times 10^4$
10^3	$(1 \text{ to } 20) \times 10^4$
10^4	$(1 \text{ to } 20) \times 10^5$
10^5	$(5 \text{ to } > 10) \times 10^6$

† Courtesy of Waters Associates.

to specify it in terms of the molecular weight of a solute that is just excluded. Table 21-3 gives such data for several grades of μStyragel, a PS-DVB product of Waters Associates. The exclusion limits are rather wide, because the shape of the molecules (globular, linear, folded, etc.) will have considerable effect.

Figure 21-6 is a typical SEC chromatogram. Notice that the first peak to be eluted corresponds to the largest molecular-weight species in the sample, since this is not retained by the gel.

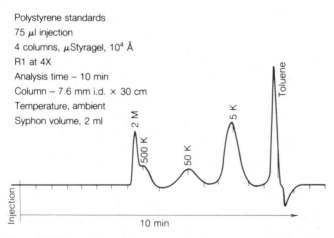

Polystyrene standards
75 μl injection
4 columns, μStyragel, 10^4 Å
R1 at 4X
Analysis time – 10 min
Column – 7.6 mm i.d. × 30 cm
Temperature, ambient
Syphon volume, 2 ml

10 min

Figure 21-6 Size-exclusion chromatogram of polystyrene standards in toluene. Noted on the curve are the molecular weights corresponding to the several peaks. (*Waters Associates.*)

GRADIENT ELUTION

The LC methods described so far are *isocratic*, that is, a single mobile liquid phase is used throughout an experiment. Such methods are readily applicable to the

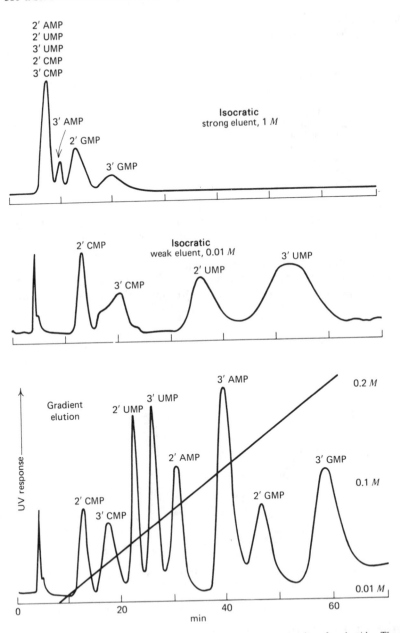

Figure 21-7 Comparison of gradient and isocratic elution in the separation of nucleotides. The sloping line in the lower chart represents the concentration of the eluting liquid, against the molarity scale at the right. The abbreviations are standard designations of various nucleotides. (*Varian Aerograph.*[1])

separation of materials of similar type, where column and solvent can be selected for optimum results. For complex mixtures, however, where components to be separated include a wide range of polarities, isocratic procedures are not adequate. The retention times (or k' values) are too dissimilar, and the peaks tend to crowd together near the start, while later peaks are broadened too greatly to be measured with accuracy.

This problem can be greatly reduced by means of *gradient elution*, using the mixing apparatus shown in Fig. 21-1. The composition of the solvent is changed gradually as the chromatogram is developed, starting with a "weak" solvent (i.e., one that gives large k' values) and proceding to a "stronger" solvent (smaller k'). The result is a dramatic improvement in the chromatograms, with peaks well resolved. Figure 21-7 shows chromatograms of the same mixture with and without gradient elution.[1] Figure 21-4 is an example of stepwise gradient elution in ion-exchange chromatography.

It may be noted that gradient elution plays a role in LC comparable to that of temperature programming in GC.

DETECTORS

Photometric Detectors

One of the more popular LC detectors depends on the measurement of UV (or visible) absorption. The optical system for such a detector must be carefully designed so that enough radiant energy can be made to pass through the narrow absorption cells, which are limited to about 1-mm diameter to avoid dead space. A typical photometer is diagrammed in Fig. 21-8. The sample and reference cells consist of cylindrical channels drilled in a block of stainless steel or Teflon and closed by silica windows. UV radiation from the lamp, collimated by a lens,

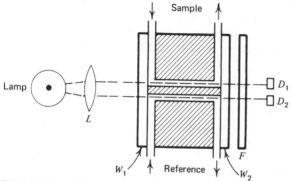

Figure 21-8 A typical photometric LC detector. L: collimating lens; W_1 and W_2: UV-transmitting windows; F, filter; D_1 and D_2: photocells.

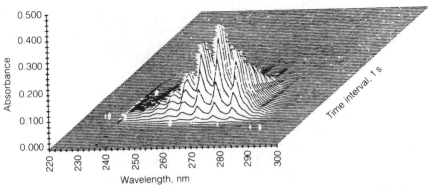

Figure 21-9 Multiwavelength monitoring of benzene in acetonitrile, as it elutes from an LC column. The detector is an array of photodiodes. (*Science.*[11])

passes through the two channels to dual photocells. The source is commonly a low-pressure mercury arc, which gives most of its output at 254 nm. Some models are provided with a fluorescent converter to provide an alternative wavelength band centered at 280 nm. This is a small silica plate coated with a suitable phosphor, which absorbs at 254 and emits at 280 nm. One or both of these wavelengths are absorbed by many important classes of compounds.

To be more generally useful in terms of selectivity, a spectrophotometer, with its continuously variable wavelength, is desirable, even though there will be some loss of sensitivity. A number of spectrophotometers are available with the necessary condensing optics to give a narrow intense beam of radiation. They provide an additional degree of selectivity not possessed by other LC detectors, in being able to discriminate between various components of the column effluent.

Hewlett-Packard has designed a spectrophotometric detector that uses an array of 211 photodiodes fabricated on a single silicon substrate.[11] This permits simultaneous measurement of a large number of narrow wavelength bands. The information from the array is processed by a computer at a rate of 22,500 data points per second, and stored in memory for subsequent plotting. Figure 21-9 illustrates the kind of three-dimensional spectrochromatogram that can be obtained.

Refractometric Detectors

Another important detector for LC is the *differential refractometer*. Differences in the index of refraction can be measured to about 1 part in 10^7, which corresponds to a few parts per million of an organic solute in water (this estimate is based on handbook values for maltose at 25°C). This provides a method of detection that is nonspecific, and depends for its sensitivity solely on the considerable difference in the index between solvent and solutes. The advantage of refractive index detection is that it can be employed with solvents whose physical properties (such as UV absorption) might interfere with other modes of detection. The disadvantage is that it cannot be used with gradient elution, because the change in index due to solvent programming completely overwhelms any signals produced by the eluted components.

Figure 21-10 shows the principles of operation of two refractometric detectors. The form in (*a*) is based on the angular displacement of a light beam on passing through two liquid-filled prisms. If the two liquids are identical, the displacement will be nil, but even a change of a few parts per million in the refractive index will make a detectable difference in the angle of the beam. The photodetector is sensitive

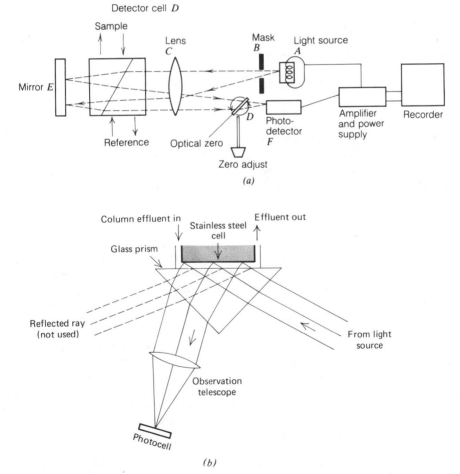

Figure 21-10 Refractometric LC detectors. (*a*) Waters Associates; (*b*) Laboratory Data Control.

to the location of the light beam rather than to its intensity, so that its output changes as the beam moves across it. The zero-adjusting device is merely a glass plate that can be turned so as to displace the light beam slightly.

The detection system in (b) depends on the relative intensity of light reflected from and transmitted through an interface between two transparent media. The effluent stream is led through a narrow passage between one face of a 45° glass prism and a steel plate. A collimated beam of light enters the prism as shown; it is partly reflected at the interface with the liquid, and partly transmitted to produce a lighted spot on the steel backplate. The steel plate is observed through a telescope fitted with a photocell. It can be shown mathematically that, provided the angle of incidence is chosen correctly (a little less than the critical angle of total reflection), then the power of the observed radiation will depend linearly on the index of refraction of the liquid. The light source and focusing optics must be mounted on an arm that can be rotated through a small angle around the prism to make the initial adjustment.

These two refractometric detectors are about equal in sensitivity, being able to detect a change in index of 1 part in 10^7. The deflection type (Fig. 21-10a) is more convenient to operate, but has a smaller linear range than that of b.

Other Detectors

A detector related to UV absorption is based on *fluorescence* measurements, following excitation with the 254-nm line of the mercury arc.[12] This highly selective and sensitive detector is especially important in biochemical applications. Users must always be alert to the possibility of quenching by other solution components or by dissolved oxygen.

Yet another technique for identifying and measuring column eluates is by a *reaction detector*. The liquid stream from the column is mixed continuously with a substance that will react with the expected species to form an absorbing or fluorescing product. The combined flow is then passed through an appropriate optical detector. An application of this principle uses the reagent fluorescamine (Fluoram) in the determination of proteins and amino acids.[13] This polycyclic aromatic compound reacts with primary amines to give products that fluoresce strongly at 475 nm upon excitation at 390 nm.

The *dielectric constant detector*[14] utilizes a narrow space between two metal electrodes as a capacitor. The column effluent, passing through this channel, causes a variation in the capacitance according to its dielectric constant, ϵ. LC solvents vary greatly in their ϵ-values, from about 2 for symmetrical molecules such as benzene and cyclohexane to greater than 180 for such a highly polar compound as methylformamide. Deviations seen by the detector can give either positive or negative peaks, according to whether the solute component has an ϵ greater or less than that of the solvent. This provides a detector of wide utility, somewhat more sensitive than that based on the refractive index.

Electrochemical detection, either amperometric or coulometric, is a useful adjunct to LC. It is applicable to reverse-phase chromatography wherein the components of the sample are electroactive.[15] In its simplest form an inert working electrode is maintained by a potentiostat at a point on the diffusion-limited plateau of a desired component, and the current is recorded as a function of time while the elution proceeds. For easily reduced (or oxidized) species, this works well, but if a considerable voltage has to be supplied, the method loses both sensitivity and selectivity.

In a modification of this method, two working electrodes are connected to separate potentiostats. The electrodes can be arranged in any of several geometries to achieve different objectives,[16] but the most useful arrangement is sequential.[17,18] The effluent from the LC column passes the first electrode, where an electrochemical reaction takes place, giving products which are detected at the second electrode. This combination gives greatly improved selectivity and sensitivity over that of a single stage. Figure 21-11 shows the kind of results that can be obtained.[16] In each of the three dual chromatograms, the upper curve (w_1) is the same, corresponding to anodic current at the first (upstream) electrode, which was held at $+1.10$ V (vs. Ag/AgCl). In part (A), the second electrode was set at $+0.95$ V; the peaks here are smaller because of partial depletion at the first electrode. In (B), the second electrode was held at $+0.35$ V, at which potential

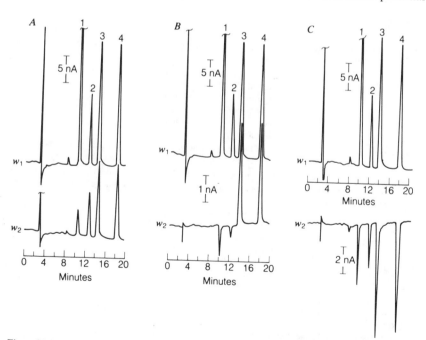

Figure 21-11 Dual-electrode chromatograms for mixtures of four phenolic acids: (1) 4-hydroxybenzoic acid, (2) vanillic acid, (3) caffeic acid, (4) 4-methylcatechol. Electrodes: glassy carbon vs. Ag/AgCl. Anodic current plotted upward, cathodic downward; for potentials, see text. The peak at about 3 min is due to a nonretained component of the solution. (*Analytical Chemistry*.[15])

compounds 1 and 2 that were oxidized at the prior electrode are re-reduced. In (C), the second electrode is at 0.0 V, and all four compounds are re-reduced.

An *ionic conductance detector* is often used in ion-exchange chromatography. A major difficulty is associated with the conductance of the carrier liquid, which necessarily contains relatively high concentrations of electrolytes. Small and co-workers[19] have described a procedure, subsequently known as *ion chromatography*, that can alleviate this difficulty. They inserted a second column, following the conventional ion-exchange column in which the ions are separated. The function of the added column is to remove the supporting electrolyte without affecting the ions of interest. For example, they show an excellent resolution of the alkali metal ions eluted with 0.01 M HCl. The HCl was neutralized in the secondary column by an anion-exchange resin in the OH^- form:

$$HCl + resin.OH^- \longrightarrow resin.Cl^- + H_2O$$

The replacement of HCl by H_2O leaves the conductance detector free to respond to the alkali cations. The authors show analogous methods of detecting anions and amines.

PROBLEMS

21-1 In a separation of nucleosides on an LC column using a UV detector, peaks appeared that were identified as follows:

Air	4.0 min
Uridine	30 min
Inosine	43 min
Guanosine	57 min
Adenosine	71 min
Cytidine	96 min

On another column of different dimensions, but packed with the same stationary phase, the air peak came at 5.0 min, and uridine at 53 min. Another component was eluted at 100 min. Identify it.

21-2 A mixture of normal paraffins in tetrahydrofuran (THF) was chromatographed by an SEC procedure on 10-nm μStyragel. The response of the refractive index (RI) and dielectric constant (DC) detectors were as follows:[13]

Compound	RI	DC	Retention time
C_6H_{14}	45	44	11.8 min
$C_{10}H_{22}$	1	50	10.5 min
$C_{14}H_{30}$	−29	52	9.4 min

(a) Did these compounds elute in the expected sequence? Explain.

(b) In what sequence would they have eluted in normal-phase LLC, in reverse-phase LLC, and in LSC?

(c) Account for the fact that $C_{14}H_{30}$ gave a negative reading with the RI detector but positive with the DC.

21-3 Devise, in principle, a detector in which amino acids will react, as they are eluted, with a ninhydrin solution to give the colored products identified in Fig. 21-5, without loss of resolution. Speculate on the possibility of reacting the mixed amino acids with the ninhydrin prior to separation on the column.

The reaction scheme is

Ninhydrin

(Blue)

21-4 A solid sample consists of the nitrates of sodium and potassium. A 5.00-g portion was dissolved in enough deionized water to make 1.00 liter. Of this, 50.0 ml was passed through a Dowex-50 ion-exchange column in the H^+ form. The acid released was eluted with water. When the elution was complete, as shown by an electrolytic conductance monitor, the eluted acid was titrated with 0.1032 M NaOH, requiring 27.90 ml to reach a methyl orange end point. What was the percentage composition of the sample?

REFERENCES

1. E. J. Johnson and R. Stevenson, *Basic Liquid Chromatography*, Varian Associates, Palo Alto, **1978**.
2. H. Veening, in *Topics in Chemical Instrumentation*, G. W. Ewing (ed.), vol. 2, American Chemical Society, Washington, **1977**, p. 148.
3. L. R. Snyder and J. J. Kirkland, *Introduction to Modern Liquid Chromatography* (2d ed.), Wiley-Interscience, New York, **1979**.
4. D. H. Freeman, *Science*, **1982**, *218*, 235.
5. J. Beukenkamp and W. Rieman, III, *Anal. Chem.*, **1950**, *22*, 582.
6. K. A. Kraus and G. E. Moore, *J. Am. Chem. Soc.*, **1953**, 75, 1460.
7. C. D. Scott, D. C. Chilcote, and N. E. Lee, *Anal. Chem.*, **1972**, 44, 85.
8. I. M. Kolthoff, E. B. Sandell, E. J. Meehan, and S. Bruckenstein, *Quantitative Chemical Analysis* (4th ed.). Macmillan. New York. **1969**, p. 291.

9. W. W. Yau, J. J. Kirkland, and D. D. Bly, *Modern Size-Exclusion Liquid Chromatography*, Wiley, New York, 1979.

10. W. M. Meier and J. B. Uytterhoeven (eds.), *Molecular Sieves*, Advances in Chemistry No. 121, American Chemical Society, Washington, 1973.

11. J. C. Miller, S. A. George, and B. G. Willis, *Science*, 1982, *218*, 241.

12. J. W. Lyons and L. R. Faulkner, *Anal. Chem.*, 1982, *54*, 1960.

13. S. Udenfriend, S. Stein, P. Böhlen, W. Dairman, W. Leimgruber, and M. Weigele, *Science*, 1972, *178*, 871.

14. L. V. Benningfield, Jr., and R. A. Mowery, Jr., *J. Chromatogr. Sci.*, 1981, *19*, 115.

15. P. T. Kissinger, *Anal. Chem.*, 1977, *49*, 447A.

16. D. A. Roston and P. T. Kissinger, *Anal. Chem.*, 1982, *54*, 429.

17. R. W. Andrews, C. Schubert, J. Morrison, E. W. Zink, and W. R. Matson, *Am. Lab.*, 1982, *14(10)*, 140.

18. W. A. MacCrehan and R. A. Durst, *Anal. Chem.*, 1981, *53*, 1700.

19. H. Small, T. S. Stevens, and W. C. Bauman, *Anal. Chem.*, 1975, *47*, 1801.

MASS SPECTROMETRY

The mass spectrometer is an instrument that will sort out charged gas molecules (ions) according to their masses. It has no real connection with optical spectroscopy, but the names *mass spectrometer* and *mass spectrograph* were chosen by analogy, because the early instruments produced a photographic record resembling an optical line spectrum.

INSTRUMENTATION

There are several distinct types of mass spectrometers, but all must possess components to perform the following functions (Fig. 22-1): (1) ionization of the sample, (2) acceleration of the ions by an electric field, (3) dispersion of the ions according to their mass-to-charge ratio, and (4) detection of the ions to produce a corresponding electrical signal. These functions will be described in the paragraphs that follow.

Since the mass spectrometer depends on a stream of gaseous ions following well-defined trajectories through combinations of electric and magnetic fields, it is essential that all parts from ion source to detector be evacuated. The pressure must generally be no greater than about 10^{-3} Pa (about 10^{-5} torr). This requires efficient and continuous pumping, for which either ion pumps or oil-diffusion pumps trapped with liquid nitrogen are most commonly used. An accurate and sensitive pressure gauge is essential. A typical vacuum system is shown in Fig. 22-2.

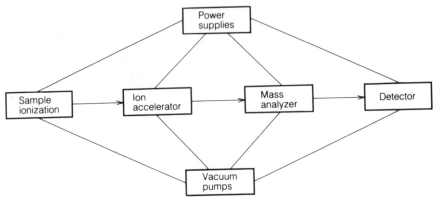

Figure 22-1 Block diagram of a typical mass spectrometer.

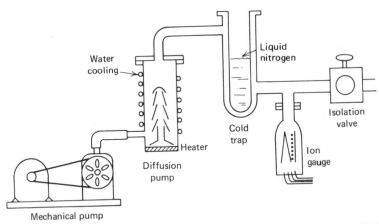

Figure 22-2 Typical vacuum system for a mass spectrometer. The ion gauge is a common device for measuring a vacuum.

ION SOURCES

Up until the early 1970s, mass spectra could only be obtained for gases or materials with sufficient vapor pressure to be converted to gases at the reduced pressure of the mass spectrometer. Since then techniques for producing gaseous ions from solids and high-boiling liquids have been introduced.

Once the sample has been converted to a low-pressure gas, ions can be formed by bombardment with a stream of electrons from a hot filament, a process known as *electron-impact* (EI) *ionization*. Ions can also be formed by a secondary process originating in an ion-molecule reaction in the gas phase. This is called *chemical*

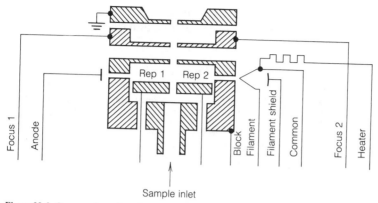

Figure 22-3 Cross section of an electron impact ion source. The filament and anode define the electron beam. The ions are formed in the space just above the repellers (marked " Rep "). A positive charge on the repellers, together with a negative potential on the focus electrodes, cause positive ions to be accelerated upward in the diagram.

ionization (CI). Other mechanisms for providing the energy for ion formation in gases have been developed, but are of less general applicability.

Gaseous ions can be obtained from solid samples by variations of a procedure known as *desorption* (though this term is not always descriptive of the process taking place).[1] Energy is delivered to the surface of the sample by a beam of ions or of neutral atoms. The impact causes a miniature explosion in which a small fraction of the surface molecules are ejected and at the same time ionized. Desorption can also be produced by means of a laser beam or by application of an electrostatic field.

Electron Impact Ionization (EI)

Figure 22-3 shows the basic structure of a typical EI source unit. The sample is introduced as a gas at low pressure into a cavity in a metal block, where it is exposed to a beam of electrons. An accelerating potential of 70 V is applied between a heated tungsten or rhenium filament and an electron trap. This potential gives the electrons sufficient energy to ionize nearly any interatomic bonds.

. Positive ions† are extracted from the cavity where they were formed, by an electrostatic field applied between a positive repeller electrode and a negative accelerator. They pass through a narrow orifice or slit and several focusing electrodes into the mass analyzer.

For proper subsequent focusing, the ions emerging from the source should be as nearly uniform in kinetic energy as possible. During acceleration they acquire

---

† Bombardment of molecules by energetic electrons usually produces more positive ions than negative, and so the majority of mass spectral applications involve positive ions only. If negative ions are to be studied, the sign of the ion-accelerating potential must be reversed.

energy $E = zV$, where z represents the charge on the ion, and V is the applied potential. The kinetic energy of the ions as they pass through the slit is given by

$$E_{kin} = zV + E_0 = \tfrac{1}{2}mv^2 \tag{22-1}$$

where m is the mass of the ion, v is its velocity, and E_0 is the kinetic energy that the ion may have been given as a result of the ionizing impact prior to acceleration. The energy of the emerging ions will always have a finite spread because of variations in E_0 and because of the fact that ions are formed at different distances from the slit. Careful design of the source structure can minimize this spread so that it can usually be neglected for low-resolution spectrometers.

Rearrangement of Eq. (22-1) with omission of E_0 gives

$$v = \sqrt{\frac{2V}{m/z}} \tag{22-2}$$

which shows that the ions move with velocities related to their mass-to-charge ratio, m/z, usually called the *mass number*,† sometimes specified in terms of "atomic mass units" (amu).

There are a number of methods for introducing samples into the ionization source, the choice depending on physical properties such as melting point or vapor pressure. Many spectrometers will accept samples introduced in more than one way. If the sample is a gas or a volatile liquid, it is best handled by allowing it to expand into a previously evacuated glass or metal container which communicates with the source via a tiny orifice called a *pinhole* or *molecular leak* (Fig. 22-4).

The molecular leak may consist of one or more needle holes in a thin gold membrane. The holes must be small compared to the mean free path of the gas molecules; a diameter of 0.01 mm is about right. This ensures conformity to Graham's law of effusion: Gases will pass through an orifice at a rate inversely proportional to the square roots of their molecular weights. The molecules that escape ionization follow this same law in diffusing out of the ion source, so the relative partial pressures of different gases will be the same within the source as they were in the external reservoir, an essential condition for quantitative analysis. The expansion flask will contain enough sample to run many duplicate spectra.

Organic solids that cannot be handled as vapors can be introduced into the source by means of a *probe*, typically a stainless steel rod 6 mm in diameter and 25 cm long, bearing a tiny cup at its tip to hold the sample. The probe is inserted through a vacuum lock (Fig. 22-4), and heated electrically. A milligram or less of sample is sufficient to give a satisfactory spectrum, but the sample does not last very long before being pumped down to nothing.

Electron impact is a rather harsh method of producing ions which tends to break the target molecules into a large number of fragments. It can be useful as a fingerprinting technique, and can give much information about the relative strengths of different atomic bonds, but it can also be confusing, particularly with

† The mass number is very commonly designated by m/e rather than m/z, where e is expressed in units of electronic charge, and thus is numerically equal to z.

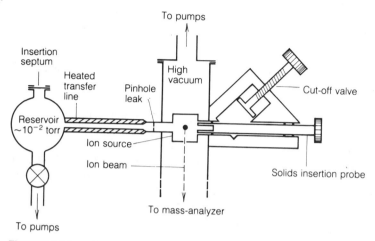

Figure 22-4 Schematic portrayal of a versatile system for introducing samples in a mass spectrometer. Gases or volatile liquids are injected by syringe or by valve to the large reservoir at the left, from which they enter the ion source through a pinhole leak. Solids are inserted by means of the probe entering from the right. The diagonal valve isolates the vacuum system from the outside atmosphere while the probe is being inserted or withdrawn.

multicomponent samples. The interpretation of fragmentation patterns will be described briefly in a later paragraph.

Chemical Ionization (CI)

In this technique,[2] the sample is diluted with a large excess (perhaps $10^4:1$) of a "reagent" gas before being subjected to the electron beam. The probability of a primary ionizing collision between an electron and a molecule of the sample is now negligibly small, so that primary ions are formed almost entirely from the reagent molecules. The gases commonly used as reagents are low molecular weight compounds such as CH_4, $i\text{-}C_4H_{10}$, NH_3, and the inert gases He and Ar.

Secondary ions are formed either by transfer of a hydrogen atom or of an electron. With methane, for example, reactions such as the following occur:

$$CH_4 + e^- \longrightarrow CH_4^+ + 2e^-$$

$$CH_4 + e^- \longrightarrow CH_3^+ + H + 2e^-$$

$$CH_4^+ + CH_4 \longrightarrow CH_5^+ + CH_3$$

$$CH_3^+ + CH_4 \longrightarrow C_2H_5^+ + H_2$$

$$R\text{-}CH_3 + CH_5^+ \longrightarrow R\text{-}CH_4^+ + CH_4$$

In the last step, $R\text{-}CH_3$ represents a sample molecule. The product ion $R\text{-}CH_4^+$, can be symbolized as $(M + H)^+$, where M represents the original molecule.

Studies have shown that the species CH_5^+ and $C_2H_5^+$ together make up nearly 90 percent of the ions present in this system.

The mass spectra from CI sources are markedly different from EI spectra, and produce a different kind of information about ionization processes. The CI spectra are much simpler, with fewer peaks, hence are often easier to interpret. Figure 22-5 shows the mass spectra of a compound as produced by the two types of sources.

The physical structure of the source chamber for CI, as well as the accompanying vacuum system, must be specially designed to permit maintaining a pressure ratio perhaps as great at 10^5 on the two sides of the slit.

As an interesting application of an unusual reagent gas, consider the study of alcohols in the presence of an excess of nitric oxide.[3] The ions resulting from the

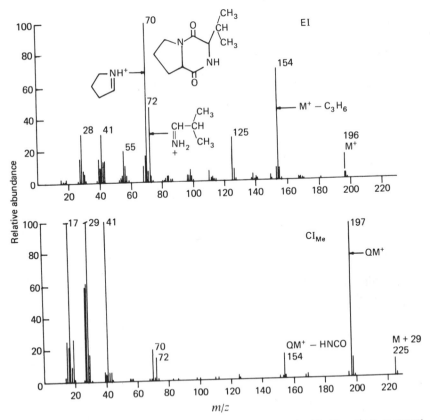

Figure 22-5 Mass spectra of diketopiperazine by EI ionization and by CI with methane as reagent. Note the great sensitivity of the $(M + H)^+$ peak, designated "QM^+" for "quasi-molecular" ion. The peak at 225 represents the addition of $C_2H_5^+$, and serves to verify that the molecular ion must be 196. This is an example of a computer-reconstructed spectrum. (*Finnigan Corporation.*)

different classes of alcohols are as follows:

Ion	Alcohols		
	Primary	Secondary	Tertiary
$(M - 1)^+$	×	×	
$(M - 2 + NO)^+$	×	×	
$(M - 3)^+$	×		
$(M - OH)^+$		×	×
$(M + NO)^+$	×		

By observation of these ions, both the class of an alcohol and its molecular weight can be determined.

Secondary Ion Mass Spectrometry (SIMS)[4]

In SIMS, a solid sample is subjected to a beam of ions from an auxiliary source similar to that shown in Fig. 12-20. The most often used ions are Ar^+ and O_2^+. If the sample is nonconducting, precautions must be taken against the buildup of a positive electrostatic charge on the surface that would interfere with proper focusing. This can be controlled by flooding the sample with low-energy electrons from an electron gun. A finely powdered sample mounted on a conducting substrate may dissipate the charge adequately.[5] Organic samples are generally coated, by adsorption or otherwise, on a substrate of a metal such as silver.

The formation of ions, which may be of either sign, can follow several mechanisms:[4] (1) a molecule, M, can attach itself by a process called *cationization* to a charged atom of the substrate metal Ag^+, to give an organometallic species $(M + Ag)^+$; (2) the molecule of M can ionize by a process of electron transfer to give radical ions, $M \cdot^+$ or $M \cdot^-$; (3) ions originating from organic salts can be ejected from the sample by direct transfer of momentum from the primary ions. Figure 22-6 includes examples of ion patterns formed by each of these mechanisms. The various lighter ions arise from unimolecular reactions in the gas phase.

An interesting development is the direct examination of paper chromatograms by SIMS, as demonstrated by Day et al.[4]

Fast Atom Bombardment (FAB)

This technique differs from SIMS only in that the bombarding beam consists of neutral atoms rather than ions. The atom gun is essentially the same as that for an ion beam, but its geometry is such that ions have a chance to react with neutrals or with secondary electrons in such a way as to lose their charge while retaining their momentum. Possible processes are:

$$\underset{\rightarrow}{A}^+ + A \longrightarrow \underset{\rightarrow}{A} + A^+$$

and

$$\underset{\rightarrow}{A}^+ + e^- \longrightarrow \underset{\rightarrow}{A}$$

(a)

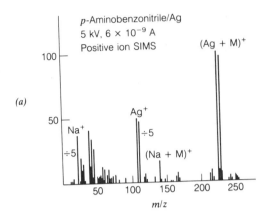

(b)

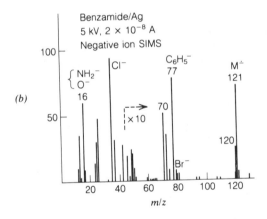

(c)

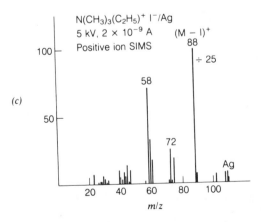

Figure 22-6 SIMS spectra illustrating three different ionization processes: (a) attachment of a silver cation to the molecule; (b) electron attachment giving a negative ion-radical; (c) loss of a counterion (iodide), leaving the quaternary ammonium ion to be recorded. The notation "/Ag" in the legend means that the organic substance was deposited on a silver substrate for insertion into the spectrometer. The presence of Na^+ in (a) and of Cl^- in (b) are due to an impurity of NaCl. (*Analytical Chemistry.*[4])

where the arrows indicate forward momentum. The atomic beam, as it leaves the gun, also contains ions, which must be removed by an electrostatic deflector.[6,7] Argon atoms form an acceptable beam, but the more expensive xenon gives greater sensitivity.[8]

The effect of the fast atoms on the target molecules is not greatly different from that seen with ions in SIMS. The principal advantage of FAB is its compatibility with magnetic sector spectrometers, which would defocus an incoming beam of ions.[1,8]

FAB has been found to be very useful for the study of complex biological or pharmaceutical molecules. Such organic compounds may be dissolved in a drop of glycerol held on a stainless steel probe. The glycerol has a low enough vapor pressure that only traces of its presence can be discerned in the mass spectrum.[8] The use of a solvent has the advantage that the supply of sample molecules on the surface is continually renewed by diffusion.[7]

MASS ANALYZERS

There are several possible ways in which ions can be separated by mass number. Only the most widely used methods will be discussed here.

Passage of charged particles through a magnetic field results in a circular trajectory of radius given by

$$r = \frac{mv}{zB} \qquad (22\text{-}3)$$

where v is the accelerating voltage and B is the magnetic field strength. It can easily be shown geometrically that a homogeneous beam of ions diverging from a slit can be brought to a focus by a magnetic field in the shape of a sector† (Fig. 22-7). This is the basis of the *magnetic sector* mass spectrometer. As seen in Eq. (22-1), the ions emerging from the source have (nearly) uniform kinetic energy. In order to come to a sharp focus, Eq. (22-3) shows that they must also have equal momentum (mv). The radius of the trajectory is obtained from a combination of these two equations

$$r = \frac{1}{B} \sqrt{2V \frac{m}{z}} \qquad (22\text{-}4)$$

This equation demonstrates that every species of ion, characterized by a particular value of m/z, will follow its own curve for a given magnetic field strength. The spectrometer is provided with an exit slit, as shown in Fig. 22-7a, that will isolate those ions for which the path has just the right radius of curvature. According to Eq. (22-4), for the selected ions, the m/z ratio equals $k(B^2/V)$, where k is a constant of the apparatus. Hence a range of masses can be scanned by varying either B or V, keeping the other constant.

† The geometric construction requires that the two slits and the apex of the sector be colinear, as shown in the figure. Sectors of 60, 90, and 180° are used in commercial instruments.

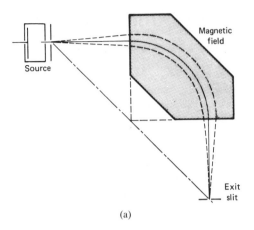

(a)

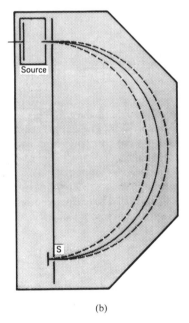

(b)

Figure 22-7 Magnetic sector spectrometers: (a) 90°; (b) 180 . The source in each is similar to that of Fig. 22-3.

The resolution of the sector mass analyzer is limited because of the spread of kinetic energies, and also because the boundaries of the magnetic field cannot be sharply defined. It can be improved by correcting either of these features. The magnetic boundary effect can be eliminated through the use of a "sector" of 180°, with both source and detector immersed in the magnetic field (Fig. 22-7b). This design, however, is rather awkward to use because of the need to locate the source and collector in the confined space between the magnetic pole pieces.

DOUBLE-FOCUS INSTRUMENTS

The beam of ions can be rendered isoenergetic by means of an electrostatic sector (Fig. 22-8). The beam assumes a circular path in passing through the annular space between two concentric cylindrical electrodes. The radius r and the applied field E determine the energy of the particles that can pass, according to the relation

$$\frac{1}{2}mv^2 = \frac{zEr}{2} \qquad (22-5)$$

This can be rearranged to give

$$\frac{m}{z} = \frac{Er}{v^2} \qquad (22-6)$$

which shows that the mass number of ions passing through the sector can be controlled by means of the applied potential. This electric sector, sometimes called an *energy filter*, can be used in conjunction with a magnetic sector to form a *double-focus* mass spectrometer, i.e., one that focuses the ions both in energy and in mass.

There are two double-focus designs in common use. One of these, the Nier–Johnson (Fig. 22-9), uses 90° sectors with an intermediate slit. The other, using

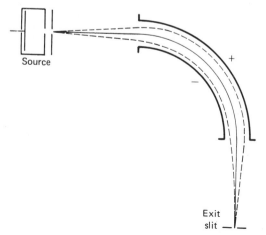

Source

+

−

Exit
slit

Figure 22-8 A cylindrical electrostatic sector energy filter.

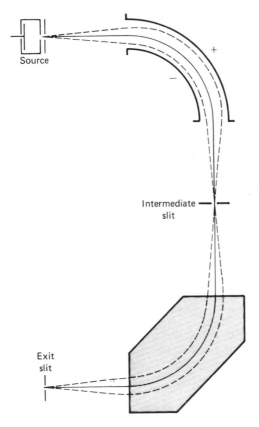

Source

Intermediate slit

Exit slit

Figure 22-9 A Nier–Johnson double-focus mass analyzer.

Mattauch–Herzog geometry (Fig. 22-10), uses an electric sector with an angle of 31.83°. At this angle, the effect of the sector is to collimate the ion beam, analogous to forming an optical virtual image at infinity. This means that all ions enter the magnetic field at normal incidence, thereby minimizing the edge effect. The magnetic sector has an angle of 135°, which brings each ionic species to a focus at the far boundary of the field. An important feature of this design is that all masses are focused simultaneously along a plane surface, the focal plane, which makes possible direct photographic recording. This is not true of any other common design of mass spectrometer.

Resolution

The term *resolution* is unfortunately not always used in the same sense. According to the most widely used definition, the resolution is the ratio $M/\Delta M$, where ΔM is the difference in mass numbers that will give a valley of 10 percent above the

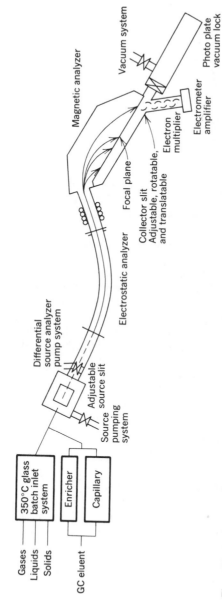

Figure 22-10 Schematic diagram of a double-focus mass spectrometer according to the Mattauch–Herzog design.

Gases
Liquids
Solids

350°C glass batch inlet system

GC eluent

Enricher

Capillary

Source pumping system

Adjustable source slit

Differential source analyzer pump system

Electrostatic analyzer

Magnetic analyzer

Vacuum system

Focal plane

Collector slit
Adjustable, rotatable, and translatable

Electron multiplier

Electrometer amplifier

Photo plate vacuum lock

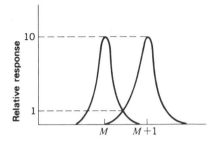

Figure 22-11 Illustrating the definition of resolution as used in mass spectrometry.

base line between peaks of mass numbers M and $M + \Delta M$, for two peaks of equal height (Fig. 22-11). Resolution is usually considered to be satisfactory if ΔM is less than 1. In many types of spectrometer, the resolution becomes progressively poorer as one goes to larger masses. The highest mass number that will just resolve two equal peaks, the *unit resolution*, serves as a figure of merit. If this criterion is met for masses up to 600 and 601, for example, the spectrometer is said to have unit resolution of 600.

The unit resolution of a magnetic sector spectrometer may go as high as about 5000, whereas that of a double-focus design may reach 50,000 or even higher. This cannot be taken to imply that an instrument of the latter type is able to observe mass numbers as high as 50,000, but that it is possible to distinguish species in which the difference in mass is correspondingly less than one mass unit.

A double-focus spectrometer can easily resolve peaks due to ions with the same nominal molecular weight but different elemental composition. Examples are: N_2 (28.0061), CO (27.9949), and C_2H_4 (28.0313), or a series such as $C_5H_4N_4O$ (136.0385), $C_6H_6N_3O$ (136.0511), $C_7H_8N_2O$ (136.0637), $C_8H_{10}NO$ (136.0762), and $C_9H_{12}O$ (136.0889). The establishment of empirical formulas from high-resolution mass spectral data is not a trivial task, but one that can be handled by a suitable computer algorithm.[9]

QUADRUPOLE MASS ANALYZERS

The quadrupole mass analyzer (also known as a *quadrupole mass filter*) is a device with which ions can be separated according to their m/z ratios without the need for a heavy magnet. It consists of four metal rods, precisely straight and parallel, so positioned that the ion beam shoots down the center of the array (Fig. 22-12). A circular orifice rather than a slit is used as the inlet port. Diagonally opposite rods are connected together electrically, and the two pairs connected to opposite poles of a dc source and also to an RF oscillator.

Neither the dc nor the ac field has any effect on the forward motion of the ions, but lateral motion will be produced by these interacting fields. This can be analyzed[11] in terms of the coordinate system shown in Fig. 22-13. If the rods were

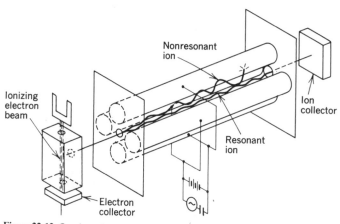

Figure 22-12 Quadrupole mass spectrometer. Scanning may be accomplished by varying the dc and RF voltages while keeping their ratio constant. (*Research and Development*.[10])

of symmetric hyperbolic cross section, then the potential ϕ at any point (x, y) would be given as a function of time t by the equation

$$\phi = (V_{dc} + V_{RF} \cos \omega t)\left[\frac{x^2 - y^2}{r^2}\right] \tag{22-7}$$

where V_{dc} is the applied direct potential, V_{RF} is the amplitude of the ac voltage of frequency ω rad·s^{-1}, and r the radial dimension defined in Fig. 22-13. This relation is very nearly correct even when the hyperbolic rods are replaced by less expensive cylindrical ones.

The force acting laterally on an ion of unit charge z is obtained by differentiating with respect to x and y

$$F_x = -z\frac{\partial\phi}{\partial x} = -z\frac{(V_{dc} + V_{RF} \cos \omega t)x}{r^2}$$

$$F_y = -z\frac{\partial\phi}{\partial y} = -z\frac{(V_{dc} + V_{RF} \cos \omega t)y}{r^2} \tag{22-8}$$

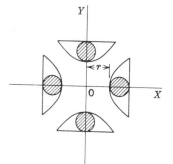

Figure 22-13 Geometry of the rod assembly in a quadrupole array. The ions move along the Z axis, perpendicular to the plane of the paper.

Then, since acceleration can be equated to the ratio of force to mass, we can write as the equations of motion for an ion of mass m and charge z

$$\frac{d^2x}{dt^2} + \frac{2}{r^2(m/z)}(V_{dc} + V_{RF}\cos \omega t)x = 0$$

$$\frac{d^2y}{dt^2} + \frac{2}{r^2(m/z)}(V_{dc} + V_{RF}\cos \omega t)y = 0$$

(22-9)

These equations indicate that the motions of the ions will have a periodic component of frequency ω, but will also be dependent on the m/z ratio. A further mathematical treatment will show that for $V_{dc}/V_{RF} < 0.168$, there is only a narrow range of frequencies for which the ionic trajectories are stable (i.e., not divergent) with respect to both the x and y coordinates. Outside this range, the ions will collide with one or the other set of rods. Maximum resolution is obtained with the V_{dc}/V_{RF} ratio approaching as closely as possible the limiting value 0.168. If the ratio is allowed to become larger than this, no frequency exists for which a stable trajectory can be found, no matter what the m/z value may be. Mass selection can be achieved by varying simultaneously the dc and RF voltages, while keeping the frequency constant. Commercial quadrupole spectrometers have mass number ranges as high as 1500.

TIME OF FLIGHT MASS ANALYZERS

The instruments so far described produce a steady beam of ions for any given setting of the controls. It is possible, however, to apply the accelerating potential intermittently, to give a beam that is segmented or pulsed. This permits sorting the ions by their velocities, which is tantamount to mass sorting. The *time-of-flight* (TOF) mass spectrometer operates on this principle (Fig. 22-14).[12,13] An

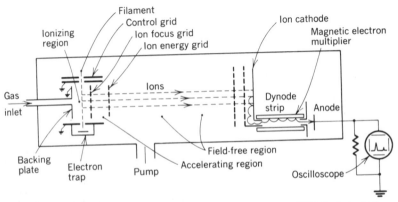

Figure 22-14 Schematic diagram of a time-of-flight mass spectrometer. (*CVC Products, Inc.*)

electron beam ionizes the sample, using either EI or CI techniques. An accelerating potential of the order of 2000 V is applied to a grid, in the form of a voltage pulse lasting 1 μs or less, and repeated some 20,000 times per second. This positive pulse accelerates the ions into a long field-free drift tube, through which the ions move at their own velocities. Since all ions receive the same energy, the velocity each acquires is proportional to its $(z/m)^{1/2}$ [cf. Eq. (22-2)]. The ions, after traversing the field-free region, impinge on a detector. The time of transit is given by

$$t_t = \frac{L}{\sqrt{2V}} \sqrt{\frac{m}{z}} \qquad (22\text{-}10)$$

where L is the length of the drift tube and V is the accelerating voltage. (Note that e, the coulombic charge on the electron, must be used here rather than z, if calculations are to be made.) Computation based on $L = 1$ m, $V = 2$ kV, $m = 1.67 \times 10^{-27}$ kg, and $e = 1.60 \times 10^{-19}$ C, gives 1.58 μs transit time for a proton. Transit times for a few ions are:

H^+	1.58 μs
N_2^+	8.37 μs
O_2^+	8.94 μs
Xe^+	18.17 μs

The detector shown in Fig. 22-14 is a specially designed electron multiplier with the rapid response needed to avoid overlap of successive pulses. It consists of a pair of glass plates coated with a high-resistance metallic film. An electric gradient is impressed along the length of the plates, crossed by the field from a series of small permanent magnets. The ions impinge on one of these plates, as shown, and the emitted secondary electrons follow circular arcs to a location farther down the plate, where the process is repeated. Eventually the amplified stream of electrons strikes an anode connected to the readout device. The oscilloscope can be replaced by an electronic gating system that sends successive pulses to a high-speed recorder.[13]

TOF spectrometers can observe mass numbers up to about 1500 with unit resolution of 500 to 600.

FOURIER TRANSFORM MASS SPECTROMETRY (FTMS)

In previous chapters we have seen the great impact of Fourier-transform techniques on IR and NMR spectroscopies. In the last few years, a comparable development has arisen in mass spectroscopy, that, in the opinion of some experts, may well point to the future of MS.[14]

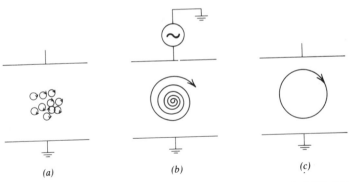

Figure 22-15 Ionic orbits in a magnetic field. In each case the magnetic field is perpendicular to the plane of the paper: (a) many ions in small orbits in random phase relations with respect to each other; (b) under RF excitation, all ions revolve in phase in expanding orbits; (c) same, after removal of the excitation.

FTMS is based on an older technique known as *ion-cyclotron resonance* (ICR); see, for example, Ref. 15. This was never a very successful method except for kinetic studies of gas-phase ion–molecule reactions. The acceptable mass range was limited to about 280 with unit resolution at 200. With the advent of FT methods, as we shall see, the mass range can be extended to well above 1000, with resolution at least as good as with double-focus sector spectrometers.

The heart of an ICR spectrometer (with or without the FT feature) is a rectangular compartment, a few centimeters on a side, within which sample molecules are ionized in the presence of a constant magnetic field. The ions as they are formed will be in random motion, and being in a magnetic field, they will be constrained to follow circular trajectories at a frequency called the *cyclotron frequency*

$$\omega_C = \frac{Be}{m/z} \tag{22-11}$$

where B is the magnetic field strength and e is the electronic charge (Fig. 22-15a). To give sufficient time for the separation of ions they must be retained for some time (several tenths of a second) within the field. This is accomplished by trapping them in a potential well formed by placing a positive potential (~ 1.0 V) on the sideplates and a negative potential (~ -0.5 V) on the upper and lower plates and the two end plates (Fig. 22-16).

Mass discrimination is made possible by the application of a variable RF field at frequency ω_1 across the top and bottom plates. If the frequency is adjusted to resonate with the cyclotron frequency ($\omega_1 = \omega_C$), the ions will absorb energy, thus increasing their velocity and the radius of their trajectory (Fig. 22-15b). All ions of the given m/z ratio will circulate in phase with the RF excitation. If ions of many different masses are present, only those in resonance will respond.

There are basically two approaches to detection of the resonance condition. In the older ICR spectrometers the RF excitation was supplied by a special circuit called a marginal oscillator, such that the energy withdrawn by the ionic resonance could be measured accurately. This only works above about 75 kHz, which limits the mass number attainable. The improved method requires scanning the entire frequency range of interest (~ 20 kHz to 1 MHz, if $B = 1.2$ T) in about 1 ms. This causes *all* ions within the applicable mass range to circulate in phase, a condition that persists after the excitation is removed (Fig. 22-15c). These circulating ions induce an image current in the upper and lower plates, and this can be sensed by an electronic amplifier. The signal so obtained is a composite of signals from all ions, and hence contains all the information about the sample that can be produced by this kind of mass spectrometer. Conversion to a conventional mass spectral display requires Fourier transformation.

Figure 22-17 shows a typical example of the composite signal and its transform.[16,17] The ability of FTMS to distinguish between ions of the same nominal molecular weight is demonstrated by Fig. 22-18; in this it is easily the equal of high-resolution, double-focus, sector spectrometers.

FTMS shows the equivalent of the Fellgett advantage mentioned in connection with FTIR, namely that all ions present are observed simultaneously rather than sequentially.[18] The Jacquinot advantage also applies, since there are no slits to restrict the effective sample size.

Chemical ionization takes rather a different aspect with FTMS. Since the primary ions can be held (trapped) in the active field area for some time (up to many seconds), the probability of a reactive collision occurring is quite large, even at low pressure. Even without an added reagent, ions of the sample can react with other fragments or with neutral molecules of the sample itself, a phenomenon known as *self-CI*. Reference 19 gives a full discussion of FTMS-CI.

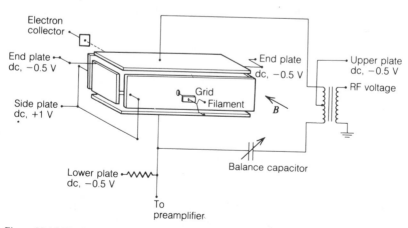

Figure 22-16 The heart of a Fourier-transform, ion-cyclotron resonance mass spectrometer. The volume occupied is about 10 cm³. (*Analytical Chemistry.*[14])

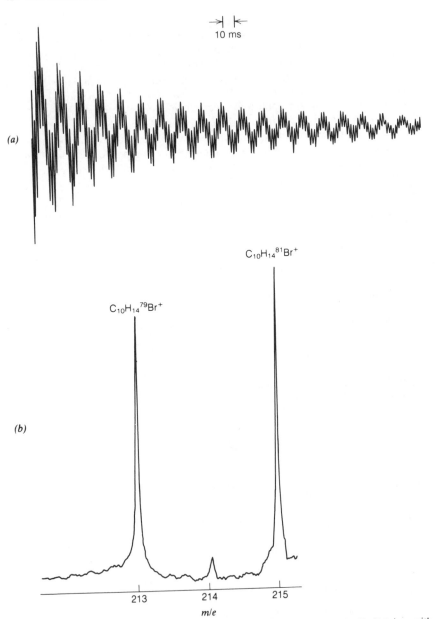

Figure 22-17 Partial mass spectrogram of dibromoadamantane, showing the $C_{10}H_{14}Br^-$ ions with both the 79 and 81 isotopes of bromine at mass numbers 213 and 215: (a) the time domain ICR interferogram; (b) the spectrum obtained by Fourier transformation of the signal in (a). (*Journal of Chemical Physics*.[16])

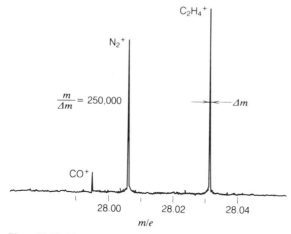

Figure 22-18 High-resolution FTMS spectrum of a ternary mixture of N_2, C_2H_4, and CO, in the vicinity of mass number 28. The resolution, $m/\Delta m$, was 250,000. (*Plenum Press.*[17])

MS DETECTORS

Ion detectors are of three types: a simple collector known as a Faraday cup, an electron multiplier, and a photographic plate.

The *Faraday cup* is the least elaborate, and also the least sensitive, of these detectors. It is used in many spectrometers where extreme sensitivity is not needed, because of its convenience and low cost. It consists of an insulated conductor directly connected to an electrometer amplifier. Its cup shape lessens the likelihood of escape of secondary electrons liberated by ion impact.

The *electron multiplier* is operationally the same as the photomultiplier, either conventional or channel type, with the primary cathode optimized for the detection of ions rather than photons. Being immersed in the spectrometer vacuum, it does not need the glass envelope of the usual photomultiplier. The sensitivity is perhaps 1000 times greater than that of the Faraday cup.

Photographic detection is only usable with Mattauch–Herzog instruments. Because the photoplate integrates the ion signal over a period of time, it is capable of greater sensitivity than any other detector. It can also make more effective use of the high-resolution capability of the double-focus spectrometer. The plates are processed by the usual photographic techniques and read with the aid of a densitometer.

Data Recording

The peaks appearing in a mass spectrum are often extremely sharp and numerous. Analog recording requires an unusually fast-responding recorder of the type known as *oscillographic*, in which a light beam is reflected by a low-inertia galvanometer

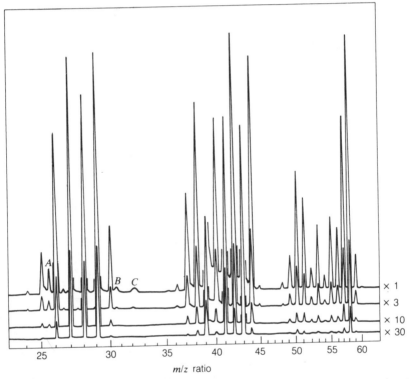

Figure 22-19 The mass spectrum of *n*-butane (molecular weight 58) as recorded on a magnetic sector mass spectrometer. Simultaneous tracings by galvanometers of different sensitivities provide a dynamic range of about 30,000. The maximum marked *A* is due to a doubly-charged ion; those at *B* and *C* to metastable ions. (*E. I. Du Pont de Nemours & Co.*)

onto a moving strip of photosensitive paper. One type includes several channels of graded sensitivity, so that several traces are made at the same time (Fig. 22-19). The sensitivity relations between the traces are known accurately, and the peak height can be measured on the trace that gives the largest deflection within the limits of the paper. Further sophistication in data handling depends on the presence of a computer, which can present the spectral results in any desired format.

FRAGMENTATION PATTERNS

The series of ionic fragments observed for a given compound can be considerably different for different modes of operation. Consider first the sequence of events taking place within an electron-impact ion source, as the electron energy is in-

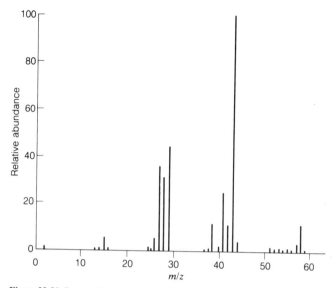

Figure 22-20 Bar-graph representation of the mass spectrum of *n*-butane.

creased through its useful range. Let us assume that an organic compound with several carbon atoms is present in the gas phase. The first ionization potential of such a compound is between 8 and 12 eV.† At lower potentials no positive ions will be formed. The first ion to appear will result from the removal of one electron from the molecule, hence it is called the *molecular ion* or *parent ion*. As the potential is increased, other bonds in the molecule will be broken, each characterized by an *appearance potential*, at which it first becomes evident. Hence mass spectrometry can provide information about ionization potentials and relative bond strengths.

The majority of EI or CI mass spectra are recorded with a 70-V electron beam, energetic enough to break any bonds likely to be present. Each compound yields a characteristic series of fragments, called its *fragmentation pattern* or *cracking pattern*. Such patterns are commonly presented as a bar graph, as shown in Fig. 22-20, which is the equivalent of Fig. 22-19, the mass spectrum of *n*-butane. Note that the molecular ion ($m/z = 58$) gives a relatively small peak, while the peak at 43 is the most intense. (The largest peak in a spectrum is called the *base peak*; it often is not the molecular peak.) This indicates that a fragment of mass number 43 is more resistant to further cleavage than was the parent molecule itself. In this case it must have been formed by the loss of a fragment of mass $58 - 43 = 15$, clearly a methyl group, so the base peak is due to the $C_3H_7^+$ ion. The small peak at $59 (= M + 1)$ is due to the presence of ^{13}C and ^2H in their natural abundances,

---

† The ionization potential of a compound or element is the energy in electronvolts necessary to remove the least strongly held electron to an infinite distance. In EI, this may be taken as the accelerating potential in the electron beam.

and is an example of an *isotope satellite* peak. An occasional small peak at a half-integral mass number, such as that at 25.5 in Fig. 22-19, is due to a doubly charged ion (mass 51); the large peak at 29 may include both $C_4H_{10}^{2+}$ and $C_2H_5^+$ ions.

It has already been pointed out that the spectra resulting from CI procedures are usually much simpler than EI, showing the molecular ion as a strong peak.

Mass spectra, even with only moderate resolution, can provide a wealth of information related to the composition and structure of a sample. In addition to the molecular weight, important fragments can often be identified, including such groups as phenyl (mass 77) or benzyl (91). A series of peaks such as 15, 29, 43, 57, 71, 85, etc., separated by units of 14 (CH_2), suggest a long aliphatic chain. Primary alcohols and amines are often identified by the presence of the $-CH_2OH$ peak at 31 or the $-CH_2NH_2$ peak at 30 amu. A unique application involves isotopes. ^{35}Cl and ^{37}Cl, and fragments containing them, are often identified from their characteristic two peaks with intensity ratios of approximately 3:1, separated by two amu. Similarly, ^{79}Br and ^{81}Br are also separated by 2 amu, but have almost identical intensities. Thus the presence of certain elements is often readily apparent from fragmentation patterns. The detailed procedure for deriving elemental composition and molecular structure are much too detailed to include here. There are many books devoted to this subject.[11,20]

Metastable Ions

Some of the ions that are produced in the ion source are inherently unstable, but nevertheless have finite lifetimes. These *metastable ions* are likely to decompose during their passage through the spectrometer. The new fragments formed when such an ion breaks down must include at least one ion of the same charge, that will be propagated through the mass analyzer. This will result in a rather broad maximum in the spectrum, since ions formed in different locations will not be focused together. In Fig. 22-19, two small rounded bumps are visible (marked *B* and *C*) that are due to metastables. The most sensitive trace in the same figure (labeled " × 1") shows a broad rise in background level from about 39 to 44 on the mass number scale, presumably due to metastables. (Compare this to the even background in the 49 to 59 region.) Observations of metastable ions can be of considerable use in studies of organic mechanisms.[21]

Negative Ions

In the discussion of mass spectrometry so far, scant attention has been paid to the possibility of utilizing ions with a negative charge. Positive ions predominate in EI ionization of gases, at least in part because of their greater stability. A negative ion can lose its extra electron more easily than a positive ion can lose an excess proton or gain another electron.

Most mass spectrometers can be used for negative ion analysis as well as positive, by reversing all potentials and the directions of all magnetic fields. In some this requires only throwing a switch, but in others some rewiring will be needed.

In CI, particularly, the observation of negative ions can be quite fruitful.[22] The spectra are simpler and can be remarkably selective. For example, sub-picogram amounts of chlorinated hydrocarbons, such as the insecticide DDT, can be measured, with 90 percent isobutane plus 10 percent methylene chloride as reagent, whereas an ester, methyl stearate, gives no observable ions.[22] In another report, the determination of mercaptans was carried out using cyclohexane as combined solvent and reagent, with an apparent limit of about 10 ppm.[23]

QUALITATIVE ANALYSIS

The identification of unknown materials by MS requires definite assignment of mass numbers to peaks on a chart. Mass spectrometers that are equipped with computers can identify the peaks as they are formed, and mark the record accordingly. Without this feature, mass assignments can be difficult, becoming less certain as the mass increases. For a magnetic deflection instrument in which the magnetic field B is scanned at a constant rate, Eq. (22-4) tells us that the mass-number scale is linear, so that in principle two mass identifications will calibrate the entire spectrum. However, it is often necessary or desirable to scan the field exponentially, or to scan by varying the accelerating potential. In such cases, a nonlinear m/z scale results, and calibration with known compounds must be used. At the lower end of the scale, peaks due to the components of air (Fig. 22-21) will identify mass positions. For a convenient spot check, mercury vapor can be used, giving a characteristic isotopic pattern at mass numbers 198 to 204. For a more inclusive calibration, *perfluorokerosene* (PFK) is often suitable. McLafferty[20]

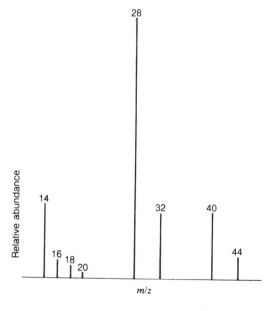

Figure 22-21 The mass spectrum of air.

has given a "partial" list of 73 fragment peaks from this mixture of fluorocarbons. Peaks appear at 69 (CF_3^+), 93 ($C_3F_3^+$), 105 ($C_4F_3^+$), 131 ($C_3F_5^+$), and homologous peaks greater than these by increments of 50 (CF_2). PFK can be run immediately preceding or following an unknown, with no change in controls between, or it can be mixed with the unknown. The latter method, used primarily with high-dispersion instruments, is possible because the mass of fluorine-containing compounds are different from others, and hence do not exactly overlap. Once the m/z values have been assigned to various peaks, the corresponding fragment species, and subsequently the parent molecule, can be identified.[20]

QUANTITATIVE ANALYSIS

The fragmentation patterns of the components of a mixture are additive; hence mixtures can be analyzed if spectra for the several components, run under the same conditions, are at hand. The calculation involves a set of n simultaneous equations in n unknowns for a mixture of n components, an easy task for a small computer. With components present to more than about 10 mole percent, precision and accuracy may be within ± 0.5 mole percent (at 90 percent confidence level). Mixtures of this order are better handled with a GC input, discussed in the next section.

The mass spectrometer can be used in tracer studies, utilizing compounds enriched with stable isotopes that are in low natural abundance, such as ^2H, ^{13}C, ^{33}S, and ^{40}K, among many others. Some isotopes should be avoided because of potential interference; thus ^{58}Fe would be a poor choice for an iron tracer, as it is indistinguishable from ^{58}Ni, except at highest resolution. The technique of *isotope dilution* is often used in tracer studies; it is described in detail in Chap. 24, as it is used more widely with radioactive isotopes.

GC/MS AND LC/MS

As mentioned in Chap. 20, the combination of gas chromatography with mass spectrometry can be particularly fruitful. The symbiotic relationship of these two methods makes an interesting study in the development of analytical instrumentation, as the first of a growing class of "hyphenated" techniques.

There has been an unwarranted tendency to think of one member of this partnership as virtually an appendage of the other. Either the mass spectrometer is an elaborate GC detector, or the GC is a superior sample-handling system for the mass spectrometer. Neither of these concepts does justice to the combined instrument, which is much more than merely the sum of its parts. The MS is not very well adapted to the analysis of mixtures of similar substances, because of the multiplicity of fragment ions. On the other hand, a GC has no inherent ability to identify the components of a mixture. The combined instrument, however, is unexcelled in analyzing complex samples, as long as they have sufficient vapor pressure and thermal stability. The GC detector provides a quantitative measure of each component, while the MS establishes its identity.

There are two major factors that must be considered in designing a satisfactory GC/MS instrument. First is the carrier gas, which cannot be tolerated by the vacuum of the MS, and second is the required compatibility of the two parts with respect to speed. Let us examine these two features in some detail.

The pressure of the gas stream exiting from a GC is essentially atmospheric, whereas that admitted to the ionizing source of the MS cannot be greater than about 10^{-3} Pa for EI or 10 Pa for CI (1 atm is approximately 10^5 Pa). The amount of a sample constituent, however, is generally only a very small fraction of the eluent from the GC. Thus a reduction of pressure will not provide a detectable amount of sample, and it is necessary to separate the carrier gas from the sample. This can be accomplished by means of a separator based on physical properties of the gases. One such separator is that designed by Biemann and his collaborators,[24] and shown in Fig. 22-22. The gas mixture, in which the carrier must be either H_2 or He, is passed through a porous tube surrounded by a jacket connected to a vacuum pump. The low molecular weight carrier gas easily diffuses through the porous walls and is pumped away, while the heavier sample molecules, with their greater momentum, continue on to the mass spectrometer. This and several other separators are described in Ref. 25.

In principle, nearly any mass spectrometer can be used in conjunction with GC, but a number of parameters may limit the choice. It may not be possible to scan the magnetic field of a sector spectrometer fast enough to record an entire fragmentation spectrum during the elution of a single chromatographic peak, although the electric accelerating potential may well be capable of more rapid scanning. Quadrupole spectrometers have the required speed, but their resolution is less than might be desired. Fourier-transform ICR spectrometers are ideal for this service.[26]

GC/MS can be operated in either of two modes: In one mode, the MS unit is preset to a particular mass number corresponding to a unique ion from the substance sought; this will identify the chromatographic peak that contains this substance. Quadrupole or FTMS spectrometers can be programmed to monitor

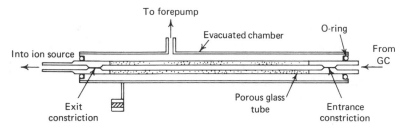

Figure 22-22 An enrichment system linking a mass spectrometer and a gas chromatograph. (*Analytical Chemistry.*[24])

several specific mass numbers sequentially on a time scale much faster than that of the GC, hence permitting the identification of several substances simultaneously.

In the other mode, a complete mass spectrum can be recorded for each component eluted from the GC. This will clearly require high-speed MS scanning with the observed spectra being placed in computer memory for subsequent reduction. Both of these procedures are illustrated in a study of trace organic compounds found in the fly ash from a municipal incinerator.[27] Some 99 distinct compounds were observed; all but 15 of these were positively identified, and of those 15, all but one were unambiguously assigned to particular structural classes.

Many mass spectrometers are equipped with an auxiliary electrode, usually just outside the ionization source, that intercepts a small fraction of the ions before they are separated in the mass analyzer. This was originally intended as an aid in the adjustment of the ion source, but it is very useful in connection with a GC, as its current can be recorded to constitute a nonselective GC detector.

LC/MS is more difficult to instrument than is GC/MS. Several techniques have been suggested for doing this,[28] but only two of these are important enough to warrant description here.

The first method involves removing the solvent by evaporation, before introduction into the mass spectrometer. This can be done by using a moving band of stainless steel or an inert plastic to transport the sample from one point to another (Fig. 22-23). The effluent from the LC is split (at 1 in the figure), and a selected fraction (up to about 1 ml/min) is deposited on the band 2. An infrared heater 3 evaporates the solvent. The band passes through two successive chambers 4 where the solvent vapors are pumped off. In region 5 the band is heated to desorb the molecules of solute where they will diffuse into the ionizing chamber of the mass spectrometer. The heater at 6 removes any residual material, so that the band will be ready for reuse. The power to drive the band is delivered by the two rollers at 7. This system is very effective with nonpolar liquids. With polar solvents, a higher evaporation temperature and lighter loading of the band are needed to give satisfactory results.

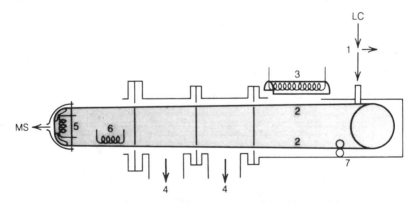

Figure 22-23 Schematic diagram (side view) of a moving-band GC interface. (*Finnigan Corporation.*)

The second method for interfacing LC with MS is by the direct injection of effluent, including sample components together with solvent, into the mass spectrometer. The liquid is passed through a capillary to a pinhole orifice in the wall of the ionization chamber. At this point the solvent plays the role of CI reagent in producing ions from the solutes. Such solvents as water, methanol, or acetonitrile are appropriate.

TANDEM MASS SPECTROMETRY (MS/MS)

The function of the chromatograph in the preceding paragraphs is to separate the constituents of a mixture so that one species at a time is presented to the mass analyzer. In a somewhat analogous manner, one mass analyzer can be used to select an ion of a specified mass number to be sent on to a second analyzer for identification.

For example, suppose a mixture of similar organic compounds is ionized by a CI process so that the molecular ions predominate. A conventional mass spectrometer will show a series of maxima, one for each compound, but generally will not give sufficient information for the identification of the individual components. In a tandem spectrometer, the parameters can be adjusted so that ions of one mass number only are allowed to pass through the slit separating the first and second analyzers. These ions are then subjected to further ionization by collision with molecules of an added gas such as helium, to give characteristic fragments that are then dispersed by the second analyzer.

As another example, consider the identification of isomers, all of which have the same molecular ion, as in Fig. 22-24.[29] The three compounds all have a molecular weight of 182, and all give a parent ion $(M - H)^-$ at 181. The secondary fragmentation patterns are easily distinguished for identification.

In another mode of operation, the primary analyzer can be scanned while holding the secondary at the mass number corresponding to an ion with diagnostic importance. Figure 22-25 shows such a case, arising in determining the constituents of nutmeg.[29]

Instrumentation for MS/MS

Much of the earlier work was performed with a modified double-focus spectrometer of the Nier–Johnson type, in which the geometry was reversed so that the ions passed through the magnetic sector before the electric sector. When a primary ion of mass m_1 is fragmented to give a daughter ion of mass m_2, the kinetic energy of the latter is directly related to the ratio m_2/m_1, and hence an energy analyzer (the electric sector) can become a valid mass analyzer. This is subject to considerable spread, however, because of variations in translational energy of the ions. Superior results can be obtained by using two intact Nier–Johnson spectrometers,[30] but this is too expensive for wide usage.

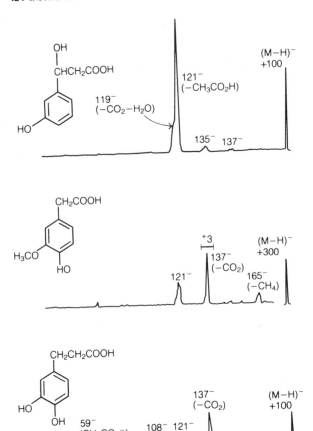

Figure 22-24 Negative daughter ions generated from carboxylate ions, as observed in MS/MS with a magnetic deflection instrument. The three acids can be identified through these spectra. (*Chemical and Engineering News.*[29])

More reasonable in cost, and nearly as good in performance, is a tandem spectrometer using quadrupole elements.[31] This is shown in Fig. 22-26. The instrument actually consists of three quadrupole segments, of which no. 2 is operated with RF only (no dc) applied to the rods. In this mode, the quadrupole cannot provide mass discrimination, but it does bring all ions to a common focus at the exit port. This segment serves as the collision chamber where secondary ionization takes place.

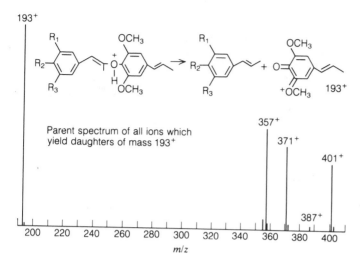

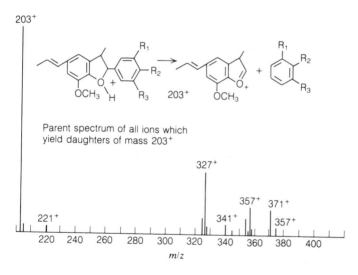

Figure 22-25 Parent ion spectra of nutmeg constituents. The two scans are molecular-weight profiles of all compounds that produce daughter ions of mass numbers 193 and 203 by reactions such as those shown. The data are from a quadrupole mass spectrometer. (*Chemical and Engineering News.*[29])

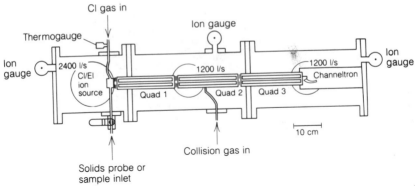

Figure 22-26 Diagram of a triple-quadrupole mass spectrometer. The large circles in the rear wall are connections to the vacuum pumps. (*Analytical Chemistry.*[31])

PROBLEMS

22-1 An ion of mass $m = 100$ amu and charge $z = 1$, is accelerated with a potential of $V = 1$ kV. Calculate its velocity in meters per second.

22-2 The ion of Prob. 22-1 encounters a magnetic field, the geometry of which requires a trajectory with radius $r_1 = 10$ cm for the ions to reach the exit slit. What must be the field strength in teslas?

22-3 The ion of Probs. 22-1 and 22-2 now enters an electrostatic sector with radius $r_2 = 12$ cm. What should be the potential E in kilovolts to enable the ion to pass to the detector?

22-4 A time-of-flight mass spectrometer has a drift tube 85.0 cm long. If the accelerating potential is 2.00 kV, calculate the difference in arrival times of ions with mass numbers 300 and 301.

22-5 Account for each of the major ions in the mass spectra of Figs. 22-19 and 22-21.

22-6 An organic compound is analyzed for its N content by isotope dilution.[32] A measured amount of the compound containing ^{15}N in place of ^{14}N is added. After conversion of all the nitrogen to N_2, a mass spectrometer shows the following peak heights:

m/e	28	29	30
Height	978.5	360.6	52.5

Calculate the percent of the nitrogen which is ^{15}N.

22-7 An isotope dilution method for the determination of C in submilligram quantities with ^{13}C tracer has been reported by Boos et al.[33] The sample is mixed with a portion of succinic acid, $C_4H_6O_4$, which contains about 30 atom percent ^{13}C. The mixture is oxidized to CO_2 and H_2O, and the resulting CO_2 examined in a mass spectrometer. The ratio of mass 45 to 44 (corrected for the natural isotopic composition of O) is taken as the $^{13}C/^{12}C$ ratio, designated r. In natural C, the abundance of ^{13}C is 1.11 percent and ^{12}C 98.9 percent, which must be taken into account. The equations are as follows:

$$^{13}C_S = W_T\left(\frac{4}{119.3}\right)\left(\frac{r_T}{r_T + 1}\right) + W_S\left(\frac{X_C}{12.01}\right)(0.0111)$$

$$^{12}C_S = W_T\left(\frac{4}{119.3}\right)\left(\frac{1}{r_T + 1}\right) + W_S\left(\frac{X_C}{12.01}\right)(0.989)$$

$$r_S = \frac{^{13}C_S}{^{12}C_S}$$

where $^{12}C_S$ and $^{13}C_S$ represent the numbers of milligram atoms of the respective isotopes present in the mixed sample, r_S is the observed ratio, W_T and W_S are the weights in milligrams of tracer and sample, r_T is the ratio for pure tracer compound oxidized in the same manner, and X_C is the quantity sought, the weight fraction of C in the unknown.

(a) Explain the above equations, and from them derive an expression for X_C in terms of W_S, W_T, and r_S.

(b) In a particular analysis, 0.156 mg of sample and 0.181 mg of tracer were taken. The ratio r_S was found to be 0.206. The tracer contained 31.41 percent of its carbon as ^{13}C. Calculate the percent C in the sample.

22-8 The mass spectrum of a sample of an alcohol was run using NO as CI reagent. The following results were obtained:

m/z	Relative peak height
17	low
20	medium
31	low
120	low
134	medium
136	high
155	medium
157	medium

What conclusions can you draw about the sample?

22-9 Ramseyer and Morrison[34] have published a comprehensive treatment of the analysis of organic materials for trace metals, using SIMS. One of the samples they analyzed was the NBS Standard Reference Material called "Orchard Leaves," which is certified to contain, among other elements, $(2.09 + 0.030\%)$ ppm of calcium and $(1.47 \pm 0.03\%)$ ppm of potassium. The authors, through careful measurements with the SIMS apparatus, developed a table of relative sensitivity factors (RSF), defined as

$$RSF_{x,k} = \frac{(i_x/C_x f_x)}{(i_K/C_K f_K)}$$

where i is the secondary ion intensity (in counts per second), C is the concentration, and f is the isotopic abundance. Subscripts x and K refer to the element to be determined and to potassium, selected as a reference element. Suppose a particular sample, with a matrix comparable to that of orchard leaves, gives intensities:

$$i_{Ca} = 7.2 \times 10^4 \text{ cps for } ^{40}Ca$$

$$i_K = 1.3 \times 10^5 \text{ cps for } ^{39}K$$

What is the concentration of calcium? (The isotopic abundance of ^{39}K is 93.1%, and of ^{40}Ca is 96.9%.)

22-10 The molecular weight of benzophenone and azobenzene are, respectively, 182.2214 and 182.2244.

(a) Would it be possible to distinguish between these two compounds, each in a pure state, with a mass spectrometer with unit resolution of 1000?

(b) Could mixtures of the two be analyzed?

REFERENCES

1. K. L. Busch and R. G. Cooks, *Science*, **1982**, *218*, 247.
2. B. Munson, *Anal. Chem.*, **1977**, *49*, 772A.
3. D. F. Hunt, T. M. Harvey, W. C. Brumley, J. F. Ryan, III, and J. W. Russell, *Anal. Chem.*, **1982**, *54*, 492.

4. R. J. Day, S. E. Unger, and R. G. Cooks, *Anal. Chem.*, **1980**, *52*, 557A.

5. W. H. Christie, R. E. Eby, R. J. Warmack, and L. Landau, *Anal. Chem.*, **1981**, *53*, 13.

6. K. L. Rinehart, Jr., *Science*, **1982**, *218*, 254.

7. M. Barber, R. S. Bordoli, G. J. Elliott, R. D. Sedgwick, and A. N. Tyler, *Anal. Chem.*, **1982**, *54*, 645A.

8. S. A. Martin, C. E. Costello, and K. Biemann, *Anal. Chem.*, **1982**, *54*, 2362.

9. R. G. Dromey and G. T. Foyster, *Anal. Chem.*, **1980**, *52*, 394.

10. D. Lichtman, *Res. Dev.*, **1964**, *15(2)*, 52.

11. J. B. Farmer, in *Mass Spectrometry*, C. A. McDowell (ed.), McGraw-Hill, New York, **1963**, chap. 2.

12. W. C. Wiley, *Science*, **1956**, *124*, 817.

13. W. McFadden, *Techniques of Combined Gas Chromatography/Mass Spectroscopy*, Wiley, New York, **1973**, pp. 46 ff.

14. R. L. Hunter and R. T. McIver, Jr., *Anal. Chem.*, **1979**, *51*, 699.

15. J. D. Baldeschweiler and S. S. Woodgate, *Acc. Chem. Res.*, **1971**, *4*, 114.

16. M. B. Comisarow and A. G. Marshall, *J. Chem. Phys.*, **1975**, *62*, 293.

17. M. B. Comisarow, in *Transform Techniques in Chemistry*, P. R. Griffiths (ed.), Plenum Press, New York, **1978**, chap. 10.

18. A. G. Marshall, *Anal. Chem.*, **1979**, *51*, 1710.

19. S. Ghaderi, P. S. Kulkarni, E. B. Ledford, Jr., C. L. Wilkens, and M. L. Gross, *Anal. Chem.*, **1981**, *53*, 428.

20. F. W. McLafferty, *Interpretation of Mass Spectra* (3d ed.), University Science Books, Mill Valley, CA, **1980**.

21. K. R. Jennings, in *Mass Spectrometry: Techniques and Applications*, G. W. A. Milne (ed.), Wiley-Interscience, New York, **1971**, pp. 419 ff.

22. R. C. Daugherty, *Anal. Chem.*, **1981**, *53*, 625A.

23. H. Knof, R. Large, and G. Albers, *Anal. Chem.*, **1976**, *48*, 2120.

24. J. T. Watson and K. Biemann, *Anal. Chem.*, **1965**, *37*, 844.

25. R. Ryhage and S. Wikström, in *Mass Spectrometry: Techniques and Applications*, G. W. A. Milne (ed.), Wiley-Interscience, New York, **1971**, pp. 91 ff.

26. C. L. Wilkins, G. N. Giss, R. L. White, G. M. Brissey, and E. C. Onyiriuka, *Anal. Chem.*, **1982**, *54*, 2260.

27. G. A. Eiceman, R. E. Clement, and F. W. Karasek, *Anal. Chem.*, **1979**, *51*, 2343.

28. P. J. Arpino and G. Guiochon, *Anal. Chem.*, **1979**, *51*, 682A.

29. R. G. Cooks and G. L. Glish, *Chem. Eng. News*, **1981**, *59(48)*, 40.

30. F. W. McLafferty, P. J. Todd, D. C. McGilvery, and M. A. Baldwin, *J. Am. Chem. Soc.*, **1980**, *102*, 3360.

31. R. A. Yost and C. G. Enke, *Anal. Chem.*, **1979**, *51*, 1251A.

32. A. V. Grosse, S. G. Hindin, and A. D. Kirshenbaum, *Anal. Chem.*, **1949**, *21*, 386.

33. R. N. Boos, S. L. Jones, and N. R. Trenner, *Anal. Chem.*, **1956**, *28*, 390.

34. G. O. Ramseyer and G. H. Morrison, *Anal. Chem.*, **1983**, *55*, 1963.

TWENTY-THREE

THERMOMETRIC METHODS

Many of the analytical methods discussed in previous chapters have significant temperature coefficients, but the analyst's interest in them is generally directed only toward the optimization of working parameters. This chapter will be concerned with a number of techniques in which some property of the system is measured as a function of temperature, or where measurement of the heat evolved or absorbed by a reaction provides analytical information. These methods are listed for reference in Table 23-1. Other comparable procedures, less used, are not included. (For further details, see Refs. 1 and 2.)

Table 23-1 Thermoanalytical methods

Designation	Property measured	Apparatus
Thermogravimetry (TGA)	Change in weight	Thermobalance
Derivative thermogravimetry (DTG)	Rate of weight change	Thermobalance
Differential thermal analysis (DTA)	Heat evolved or absorbed	Differential thermometer
Scanning calorimetry (DSC)	Heat evolved or absorbed	Differential calorimeter
Thermometric titration	Change of temperature	Adiabatic calorimeter
Direct injection enthalpimetry	Heat evolved or absorbed	Adiabatic calorimeter

THERMOGRAVIMETRIC ANALYSIS (TGA)

This is a technique whereby the weight of a sample can be followed over a period of time while its temperature is being raised linearly. Several examples of thermograms obtained by this procedure are shown in Fig. 23-1.[3] Curve 1 shows the

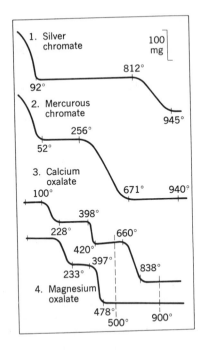

Figure 23-1 Examples of thermogravimetric analysis. (*American Elsevier.*[(3)])

weight of a precipitate of silver chromate, collected in a filtering crucible. The initial drop in weight represents the loss of excess wash water. Just above 92°C the weight becomes constant and remains so to about 812°C. From there to 945°C oxygen is expelled. A careful analysis of the loss in weight shows that the decomposition must proceed according to the reaction $Ag_2CrO_4 \rightarrow O_2 + Ag + AgCrO_2$. The residue is thus a mixture of silver and silver chromite. It follows that the silver chromate precipitate, to be used in a gravimetric chromium analysis, may be dried anywhere in the plateau region between about 100 and 800°C, showing that the convenient temperature of 110°C is satisfactory. (Laboratory directions in older textbooks specified exactly 135°C.)

Curve 2 of Fig. 23-1 shows a heating curve for mercury(I) chromate. This compound is stable between about 52 and 256°C and then decomposes according to the reaction $Hg_2CrO_4 \rightarrow Hg_2O + CrO_3$. The Hg_2O is lost by sublimation, and the CrO_3 remains at constant weight above 671°C. Because of the high atomic weight of mercury, the precipitate of Hg_2CrO_4 provides a favorable gravimetric factor for the determination of chromium. Again, drying at 110°C is acceptable.

Much of the reported work in thermogravimetry has been directed in this way toward establishing optimum temperature ranges for drying or igniting precipitates for conventional gravimetric analysis. The technique, however, has a much wider potential than this. Consider, for example, curves 3 and 4 of Fig. 23-1. A significant difference is observed between the oxalates of calcium and magnesium, which permits their simultaneous determination. Calcium oxalate decomposes in two steps: $CaC_2O_4 \rightarrow CaCO_3 + CO$, followed by $CaCO_3 \rightarrow CaO + CO_2$. Magnesium oxalate, however, does not pass through the carbonate stage: $MgC_2O_4 \rightarrow MgO + CO + CO_2$. The ranges of stability are:

$CaC_2O_4 \cdot H_2O$	$<100°C$		
CaC_2O_4	228–398	MgC_2O_4	233–397°C
$CaCO_3$	420–660		
CaO	>840	MgO	>480

Thus at 500°C, calcium carbonate and magnesium oxide are stable, while at 900°C both metals exist as the simple oxides. Comparison of the weights at these two temperatures will permit calculation of the amounts of both elements in the original sample.

The limiting temperatures of the various segments in thermograms, such as those of Fig. 23-1, cannot be considered exactly reproducible. The thermogravimetric method is dynamic, and the system is never at equilibrium. Hence the temperatures of distinctive features on the curve will depend to some extent on such factors as the rate of heating and the sample size.

Thermobalances

Recording analytical balances with provision for controlled heating of the sample are called *thermobalances*. Most modern examples are electronically self-balancing, single-pan balances. The oven or furnace for sample heating is often installed beneath the balance, so that the sample pan can be suspended directly from the balance beam. This requires stringent precautions against air convection from the hot furnace interfering with the operation of the balance. The electronic recording mechanism either plots a graph of weight against time or, with an XY-recorder, directly against temperature. If plotted against time, it is advisable to display the temperature simultaneously with a second pen; examples of temperature programming can be seen in curves 1 and 2 of Fig. 23-4.

Derivative Thermogravimetric Analysis (DTG)

It is often advantageous to be able to compare a thermogram with its first derivative, as in Fig. 23-2.[3] The plateau in the thermogram at 700°C is clear enough, but the shoulder at about 870°C can be pinpointed much more exactly with the aid of the derivative curve.

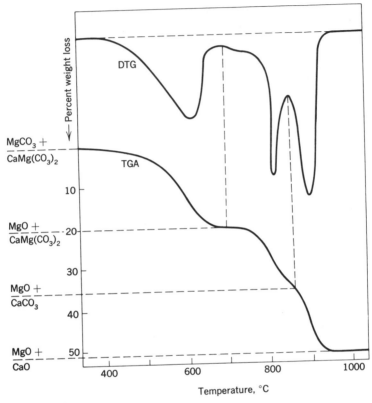

Figure 23-2 The relation between a TGA curve and its derivative (DTG), for the pyrolysis of mixed calcium and magnesium carbonates. (*Hungarian Scientific Instruments.*[4])

DIFFERENTIAL THERMAL ANALYSIS (DTA)

This is a technique by which phase transitions or chemical reactions can be followed through observation of heat absorbed or liberated. It is especially suited to studies of structural changes within a solid at elevated temperatures, where few other methods are available.

The temperature difference between a sample and an inert reference material is monitored while both are subjected to a linearly increasing environmental temperature. Figure 23-3 illustrates the principle. Two small crucibles, placed in suitably shaped cavities in a metal block, contain sample (S) and reference (R). The two junctions of a thermocouple are inserted into the crucibles so as to give directly the temperature difference between them. A separate thermocouple is placed in cavity B to measure the temperature of the block. The whole assembly is then heated under the control of a linear programmer. The reference material must be selected on the basis of thermal stability, showing no phase changes or decomposition within the range of temperatures to be covered. Alumina (Al_2O_3) is often used for this purpose.

With constant heating, any transition or thermally induced reaction in the sample will be recorded as a peak or dip in an otherwise straight line. An endothermic process will cause the thermocouple junction in the sample to lag behind the junction in the reference material, and hence develop a voltage, whereas an exothermic event will produce a voltage of opposite sign. It is customary to plot exotherms upward and endotherms downward.

Clearly, if the temperature of the block were to be held at any constant level, both sample and reference would soon attain an equilibrium and no voltage would be observed. Hence it is evident that this is a dynamic rather than a static process. It is essential that the rate of heating of the block be constant and accurately reproducible from one experiment to another if results are to be comparable.

The usual mode of operation is to supply heat to the samples, and therefore endothermic events are more likely to occur than exothermic. When an exotherm does occur, it is often caused by a secondary process. As an example, consider the curves of Fig. 23-4.[5] Curve 1 is essentially the same as curve 3 of Fig. 23-1; the slight differences result from differing instrumental conditions. Curve 2 represents the same type of experiment, but with the sample in an atmosphere of CO_2 rather than air; as would be expected, no difference is evident until the decomposition temperature of $CaCO_3$ is reached, which now requires a higher temperature.

Curve 3 is a differential thermogram (DTA curve), also showing the decomposition of CaC_2O_4 in an atmosphere of CO_2. It is seen that the three points of weight loss correspond to three endothermic processes, as it requires energy to break the bonds in the successive elimination of H_2O, CO, and CO_2. By contrast, the second peak in curve 4, where the atmosphere is air, is sharply exothermic, caused by the combustion of CO in air at the temperature of the furnace.

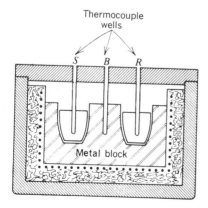

Figure 23-3 Illustrating, in principle, the construction of a DTA apparatus. The row of dots surrounding the metal block represent the electrical heater.

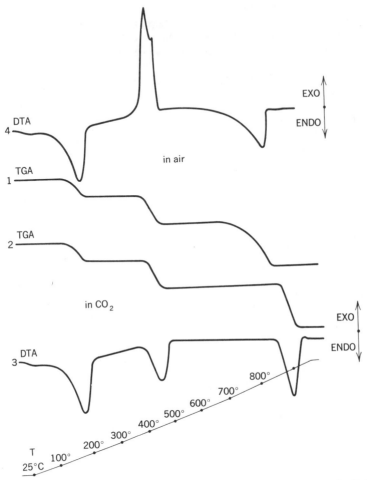

Figure 23-4 Simultaneous DTA-TGA diagram of the decomposition of $CaC_2O_4 \cdot H_2O$ in air and in CO_2. (*Plenum Press.*[5])

There is some similarity between a differential thermogram (DTA curve) and a derivative DTG curve, but the information contained in the two is different. The DTG curve can only demonstrate alterations in weight, whereas DTA reveals energy changes, regardless of change or constancy of weight. Figure 23-5 shows an interesting case, in which a pronounced endotherm in DTA (at 950°C) does not show up at all in either TGA or DTG; this is evidence of a crystalline transition from rhombic to hexagonal modifications of $SrCO_3$, which of course does not involve any change in weight.

DTA Apparatus

Figure 23-6 shows schematically the essential parts of a DTA apparatus, including provision for bathing the samples with a controlled atmosphere; the gas can be made to flow *through* the bed of particulate sample, thereby flushing away any gaseous products of decomposition. In this apparatus, as well as in some models of thermobalance, a gas chromatograph connected so as to monitor evolved gases, can be helpful in gathering information about a system.

Scanning Calorimetric DTA

Conventional DTA can give good qualitative data about temperatures and signs of transitions, but it is difficult to obtain quantitative information about the sample or the heat of transition. This difficulty arises from the importance of frequently unknown factors, such as the specific heats and thermal conductivities of the sample both before and after the transition. The rate of heating, placement of thermocouples, and other instrumental parameters will also affect the areas beneath endotherms or exotherms.

Quantitative results can be obtained by converting the sample compartment of a DTA apparatus into a differential calorimeter.[6] Typical is an instrument called a *differential scanning calorimeter* (DSC), in which the calorimeter is of the isothermal type.[7] Each sample holder (unknown and reference) is provided with

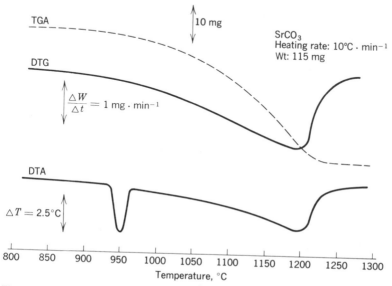

Figure 23-5 The decomposition of $SrCO_3$ in air, showing the rhombic-hexagonal crystalline transition, visible in DTA but not in DTG. (*Mettler Instrument Corporation.*)

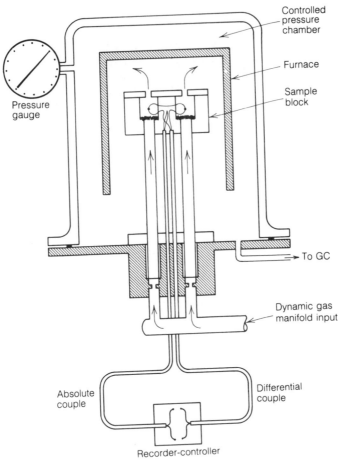

Figure 23-6 Schematic diagram of one type of DTA apparatus. (*Columbia Scientific Industries.*)

its own resistive heater. When the differential thermocouple starts to register a voltage, an automatic control loop sends just enough power into whichever of the samples is the cooler, to counteract the trend and keep the two temperatures within a very small fraction of a degree of equality. A second electronic control loop forces the temperature of the reference (hence effectively of both) to increase linearly with time. The recorder traces out the amount of electric power that had to be delivered to one or the other of the two samples to maintain isothermal conditions. The resulting thermogram resembles conventional DTA, but the area beneath a peak is an *exact* measure of the energy supplied to the unknown to compensate for an endothermic event, or to the reference material to equal the energy emitted in the unknown when an exothermic event takes place. Differences in thermal conductivity, heat capacity, etc., are now irrelevant. Several firms have comparable instruments, differing in the details of operation.

Figure 23-7 compares the DTA and DSC curves for $CuSO_4 \cdot 5H_2O$. In the DTA plot, the temperature ramp is perturbed somewhat by the thermal events occurring in the sample, whereas no such effect is possible in DSC, and the peaks are more regular in shape.

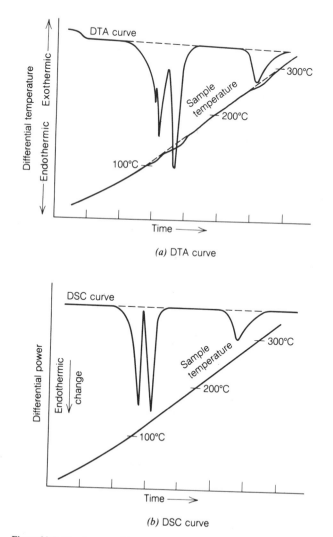

(a) DTA curve

(b) DSC curve

Figure 23-7 The decomposition of $CuSO_4 \cdot 5H_2O$: (a) DTA curve, and (b) the comparable curve from DSC. The three endotherms correspond to the loss of two, two, and one molecules of H_2O, respectively.

A scanning calorimeter provides a convenient means for the precise determination of impurity limits in highly purified organic compounds, through observation of the melting point depression.[8, 9] Experimental and calculational details are given in the references. The standard deviation of the results is reported to be ± 4 percent of the impurity measured.

THERMOMETRIC TITRIMETRY[10]

Since practically all chemical reactions are accompanied by a heat effect, the course of a reaction can be followed by observing the heat liberated or absorbed. Such a measurement can be made by titration in a small adiabatic calorimeter. A suitable calorimeter can easily be assembled from a pair of small Dewar flasks or insulated beakers. The temperature change can be read with a thermocouple or a thermistor thermometer. Thermometric titration can readily be automated, and several companies make equipment for the purpose. In most models titrant is added at a constant rate by a syringe pump or its equivalent, and the difference in temperature between the contents of the analytical and reference containers is plotted on a strip-chart recorder.

A large variety of titration reactions have been followed with success. These include neutralizations of both strong and weak acids and bases, precipitations, redox reactions, and complex formations. Any solvent can be used; besides water, work has been reported in acetic acid, carbon tetrachloride, benzene, nitrobenzene, and the fused eutectic of lithium and potassium nitrates. Reported precision is usually better than ± 1 percent standard deviation, sometimes much better.

It is essential that the two reacting solutions do not differ appreciably with respect to extraneous materials that would contribute noticeable heat effects, either by reaction with each other or with the solvent (heat of dilution). For example, in the titration of Fe(II) with $K_2Cr_2O_7$, both sample and titrant must have the same concentration of sulfuric acid. There is much merit in a system with two identical pumps adding equal amounts of reagent to the two calorimetric vessels. This eliminates the effects of the heat of dilution and any other sources of common-mode interference.[11]

As pointed out by Jordan,[10] thermometric titrimetry is the only common method of titration not based solely on considerations of the change in free energy ΔG, hence on the equilibrium constant of the reaction. The quantity measured is ΔH, not ΔG, in the familiar thermodynamic relation $\Delta H = \Delta G + T \Delta S$. Hence thermometric titrations may give useful results even if ΔG is zero or positive. A few examples will indicate the value of this approach.

Boric acid is an extremely weak acid, with a first ionization constant $K_1 = 5.8 \times 10^{-10}$ at 25°C. A straightforward thermodynamic calculation gives, for the reaction with OH^- ion,

$$H_3BO_3 + OH^- \rightleftharpoons H_2BO_3^- + H_2O \qquad (23\text{-}1)$$

a $\Delta G°$ value of -6.5 kcal/mol, corresponding to a neutralization constant $K_n = K_1/K_w = 5.8 \times 10^4$. This may be compared to the neutralization of a strong acid for which $K_n = 10^{14}$ and $\Delta G° = -19.2$ kcal/mol. Because of the small value of $\Delta G°$ for reaction (23-1), boric acid cannot be titrated successfully by any method that depends on the pH (such as potentiometric or photometric techniques), since the hydrogen–ion activity is determined by the equilibrium constant.

However, it so happens that the entropy term $T \Delta S°$ is -3.7 kcal/mol for boric acid, compared to $+5.7$ for HCl. These terms combine to give enthalpies of neutralization of -10.2 kcal/mol for boric acid and -13.5 for HCl, from which it is evident that they can be titrated thermometrically with equal ease. This is illustrated in Fig. 23-8.[12]

Another interesting case is the titration of calcium and magnesium with EDTA. The stability constants of the chelates differ by less than two orders of magnitude, and titrations based on an indicator cannot resolve them. However, the entropy change of the reaction of Mg^{2+} with EDTA is twice that for the Ca^{2+} reaction. This not only gives a distinct difference in ΔH values, but it actually changes the sign: $\Delta H°$ is $+5.5$ kcal/mol for the magnesium reaction and -5.7 for calcium. A titration curve for a mixture of the two is shown in Fig. 23-9.[10]

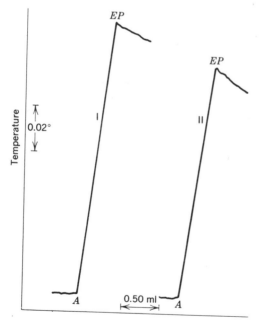

Figure 23-8 Typical thermometric titration curves, in 0.01 M aqueous solutions: (I) HCl, and (II) H₃BO₃, titrated by NaOH. The titrations start at A and reach endpoints at EP. (*Record of Chemical Progress.*[8])

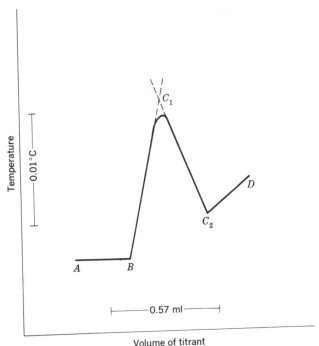

Figure 23-9 Thermometric titration of a mixture of 0.25 mmol each of Ca^{2+} and Mg^{2+} ions with EDTA. The titration was started at B, and showed a calcium endpoint extrapolated to C_1 and a magnesium endpoint at C_2. The C_2 to D region represents addition of excess reagent. (*Wiley-Interscience.*[11])

ENTHALPIMETRY

This is a method, related to thermometric titrimetry, that can provide not only stoichiometric information, but also ΔH, the molar enthalpy change. This procedure, called *direct injection enthalpimetry* (DIE),[11, 13] involves the insertion, all at once, of a measured, excess portion of a reagent solution into a sample contained in a small adiabatic calorimeter.

Figure 23-10 presents a generalized curve that might be obtained from a DIE experiment. Segment AB is a preliminary trace on the recorder, to establish a base line. The reagent is injected at point B. In the vicinity of C, the trace often shows curvature rather than a sharp break, and this can be related to the equilibrium constant (hence to $\Delta G°$) for the reaction. From C to D, the curve commonly rises as shown, corresponding to the heat of dilution of the reagent; it may, however, slope downward, indicating that the dilution is endothermic (which is unusual) or that the reagent is cooler than the contents of the titration vessel. The temperature change that can rightly be ascribed to the reaction is ΔT, from B to the

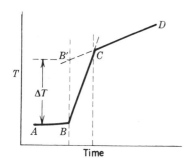

Figure 23-10 Idealized enthalpometric curve. The sample was injected at time *B*.

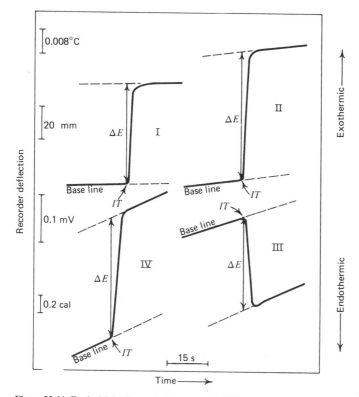

Figure 23-11 Typical injection enthalpograms: (I) HCl treated with excess NaOH; (II) H_3BO_3 with excess NaOH; (III) Mg^{2+} with excess EDTA; (IV) Pb^{2+} with excess EDTA. Sample quantities were of the order of 0.1 mmol in 25 ml. At time *IT*, 0.300 ml of 1 *M* reagent was injected. ΔE is the extrapolated imbalance potential of the thermistor bridge. (*Analytical Chemistry*.[14])

extrapolated intersection of CD with the zero time ordinate. ΔT is proportional to the total amount of heat liberated, $Q = -N \Delta H$, where N is the number of moles reacting, and ΔH is the heat absorbed per mole. The proportionality constant k is the heat capacity of the vessel and its contents, in kilocalories per kelvin, so that

$$T = \frac{Q}{k} = -\frac{N \Delta H}{k} \qquad (23\text{-}2)$$

The numerical value of k can be determined by a simple calibration step, for example, by a known amount of electrical heating. Then N can be determined if $\Delta H°$ is known, or vice versa, if we make the assumption that ΔH and $\Delta H°$ do not differ materially.

Figure 23-11 shows a few examples of injection enthalpograms.[14] This technique can be of very general applicability and high sensitivity. Three nanomoles of nitrite has been reported determined by DIE, with a precision of ± 5 percent, through the reaction with sulfamic acid.[15]

PROBLEMS

23-1 Figure 23-12*a* shows the TGA curves for the anhydrous salts AgNO$_3$ (550 mg), and Cu(NO$_3$)$_2$ (285 mg). Figure 23-12*b* is a TGA curve taken on a binary mixture of these two salts.

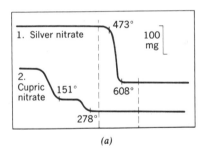

(a)

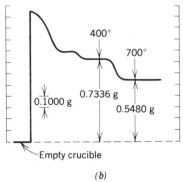

(b)

Figure 23-12 TGA curves for silver and copper nitrates and their mixtures. The samples were dried in air to drive off excess moisture before heating: (*a*) standard curves; (*b*) a mixture. (*Standard curves from American Elsevier.*[3])

(*a*) From rough measurements on the curves of the pure compounds, determine what species are stable at 400 and at 700°C.

(*b*) What was the composition of the mixture?

23-2 "Microcosmic salt," $Na(NH_4)HPO_4 \cdot 4H_2O$, upon heating, first liberates four molecules of H_2O, then another H_2O and a molecule of NH_3, to end up as stable $NaPO_3$. Sketch the curves you might expect to get from a study of this compound (*a*) with a thermobalance, and (*b*) by DTA.

23-3 What is the end product of the pyrolysis of $SrCO_3$, as shown by Fig. 23-5?

23-4 The relation between the mole fraction x_s of solute and the melting point depression ΔT is given in physical chemistry texts as

$$\Delta T = - \frac{RT_0^2}{\Delta H_f} \cdot x_s$$

where ΔH_f is the heat of fusion in $cal \cdot mol^{-1}$, T_0 is the melting point of the solvent in kelvins, and R is the gas constant ($1.987 \; cal \cdot K^{-1} \cdot mol^{-1}$). A DSC curve[8] for 2.285 mg of a "pure" compound A (molecular weight = 263.12) gave a peak with measured area of 3302 planimeter units (1 unit corresponded to 0.0199 mcal), at $T_0 = 308.9$ K. Determine ΔH_f (in $cal \cdot mol^{-1}$), and from it the mole percent (100 × mole fraction) of impurity in A. The observed ΔT was 0.112 K.

23-5 Small amounts of barium are to be determined by DIE, in which the samples are injected into excess HSO_4^- in 0.1 M HCl. The literature states that for the reaction $HSO_4^- + Ba^{2+} \rightarrow BaSO_4(s) + H^+$, $\Delta H° = -11.1 \; kcal \cdot mol^{-1}$. (The heat capacity of the dilute solutions used can be assumed to be the same as for water, $1 \; cal \cdot g^{-1} \cdot K^{-1}$, and the density to be $1 \; g \cdot ml^{-1}$.) In a particular experiment, 2.00 ml of sample was injected into 18.00 ml of reagent, resulting in a temperature rise of $\Delta T = 0.278$ K. What was the $[Ba^{2+}]$ concentration in the sample?

REFERENCES

1. T. Daniels, *Thermal Analysis*, Wiley, New York, **1973**.
2. W. W. Wendlandt and P. K. Gallagher, in *Thermal Characterization of Polymeric Materials*, E. A. Turi (ed.), Academic Press, New York, **1981**.
3. C. Duval, *Inorganic Thermogravimetric Analysis*, (2d ed.), American Elsevier, New York, **1963**.
4. F. Paulik, J. Paulik, and L. Erdey, *Hung. Sci. Instrum.*, **1964**, *1*, 3.
5. H. P. Vaughn and W. G. Wiedemann, in *Vacuum Microbalance Techniques*, P. M. Waters (ed.), Plenum Press, New York, **1965**.
6. Pages 86 and 122 of Ref. 1.
7. E. S. Watson, M. J. O'Neill, J. Justin, and N. Brenner, *Anal. Chem.*, **1964**, *36*, 1233.
8. C. Plato and A. R. Glasgow, Jr., *Anal. Chem.*, **1969**, *41*, 330.
9. C. Plato, *Anal. Chem.*, **1972**, *44*, 1531.
10. J. Jordan, in *Treatise on Analytical Chemistry*, I. M. Kolthoff and P. J. Elving (eds.), Wiley-Interscience, New York, **1968**, pt. I, vol. 8, chap. 91.
11. B. H. Vassos and R. A. Rodriguez, *Anal. Chem.*, **1981**, *53*, 135.
12. J. Jordan, *Rec. Chem. Progr.*, **1958**, *19*, 193.
13. G. A. Vaughn, *Thermodynamic and Enthalpometric Titrimetry*, Van Nostrand-Reinhold, London, **1973**.
14. J. C. Wasilewski, P. T.-S. Pei, and J. Jordan, *Anal. Chem.*, **1964**, *36*, 2131.
15. L. D. Hansen, B. E. Richter, and D. J. Eatough, *Anal. Chem.*, **1977**, *49*, 1779.

TWENTY-FOUR

NUCLEAR METHODS

Those properties of atomic nuclei that are of analytical significance include nuclear masses and spins, both considered in previous chapters. Also important is the ability of some nuclei to undergo specific reactions. Such reactions include spontaneous radioactive decay accompanied by the release of particulate and electromagnetic radiation, on the one hand, and on the other, addition reactions in which the nucleus combines with a neutron or other particle. A related topic is Mössbauer spectroscopy, based on resonance absorption of gamma photons by certain nuclei.

RADIOACTIVITY

Although it may be assumed that the reader has a knowledge of the rudiments of radioactive phenomena, it will be appropriate to summarize those principles for future reference.

Nearly all known elements exist in several isotopic forms. Many of these do not occur in nature, but can be formed artificially by various procedures, starting with suitable isotopes of the same or other elements. The nuclei of most artificially prepared isotopes, and of many naturally occurring ones, are unstable in that they tend to disintegrate spontaneously with the ejection of particles or photons. The other product of the disintegration is a residual nucleus slightly lighter in mass than

444

before. Several different types of particles are ejected by radioactive substances. Those of importance for our purposes (see Table 24-1) are the electron, the positron (positive electron), the alpha particle, and the neutron. The emission of these particles is frequently, but not always, accompanied by the radiation of energy as gamma rays. Another mode of radioactive decay is the spontaneous capture by the nucleus of an electron from the K level. This process, known as *electron capture*, or *K-capture*, gives rise to the emission of the K x-rays characteristic of the element.

Table 24-1 Particles produced in radioactive decay

Particle	Symbol	Mass†	Charge‡	Penetrating power	Ionizing power
Electron	β^-	5.439×10^{-4}	-1	Medium	Medium
Positron	β^+	5.439×10^{-4}	$+1$	Medium	Medium
Alpha particle	α	3.9948	$+2$	Low	High
Neutron	n	1.0000	0	Very high	Nil
Photon (gamma ray)	γ	0	0	Very high	Very low

† Relative to the neutron.
‡ In units of 1.60240×10^{-19} C.

The particles and radiations from different nuclei vary widely in their energy content and in the rate at which they are produced. Both of these properties are characteristic of the particular isotope that is disintegrating, and can be used in its identification.

The frequency of occurrence of atomic disintegrations is related to a property of each isotope called its *half-life*. This is the time required for half of any sample to disintegrate. The half-life varies among the known active materials from millionths of a second to millions of years. The half-lives at either extreme cannot be measured directly, but can be inferred from other evidence. Isotopes of very short life are not useful for analytical purposes, simply because they disappear too quickly. On the other hand, isotopes of very long lifetimes are difficult to apply because their disintegrations are too infrequent. Isotopes useful for analytical applications are those with half-lives roughly between a few hours and a few thousand years. If experiments can be carried out quickly in the same laboratory where the radio-active material is prepared, then the lower limit can be reduced to 10 min or so. The length of any experiment generally should not exceed about 10 times the half-life of the isotope employed.

A number of radioisotopes that have been found useful in analytical applications are given in Table 24-2. Radioisotopes may be used as sources of radiations, or as tracers to follow some reaction or process and assist in determining its extent. Before turning to these applications, we shall discuss the methods of detection and measurement.

Table 24-2 Radioisotopes used in analysis†

Isotope	Type of decay‡	Half-life	Energy of radiation, MeV	
			Particles	Gamma transitions
^{3}H	β^-	12.26 years	0.0186	None
^{14}C	β^-	5720 years	0.155	None
^{22}Na	β^+ (90%) EC (10%)	2.58 years	0.545	1.27
^{32}P	β^-	14.3 days	1.71	None
^{35}S	β^-	87 days	0.167	None
^{36}Cl	β^-	3.0×10^5 years	0.714	None
^{40}K	β^- (89%) EC (11%)	1.27×10^9 years	1.32	1.46
^{42}K	β^-	12.36 hours	3.55 (75%) 1.98 (25%)	1.52 (25%)
^{45}Ca	β^-	165 days	0.255	0.32
^{51}Cr	EC	27.8 days	. . . .	0.32 (8%)
^{55}Fe	EC	2.60 years	. . . .	None
^{59}Fe	β^-	45 days	0.460 (50%) 0.27 (50%)	1.29, 1.10
^{57}Co	EC	270 days	. . . .	0.122, 0.0144, 0.136
^{60}Co	β^-	5.26 years	0.32	1.333, 1.173
^{65}Zn	EC (97.5%) β^+ (2.5%)	245 days	0.33	1.11
^{85}Kr	β^-	10.6 years	0.67	(γ)
^{90}Sr	β^-	29 years	0.54	None
^{90}Y	β^-	64 hours	2.27	(γ)
^{95}Zr	β^-	65 days	0.36, 0.40	0.72, 0.76
^{95}Nb	β^-	35.1 days	0.16	0.77
^{110}Ag	β^-	253 days	0.085 (58%)	0.44, 2.46
^{119m}Sn	IT	250 days	. . . .	0.065, 0.024
^{131}I	β^-	8.06 days	0.60 (87.2%) (others)	0.364 (80.9%) (others)
^{137}Cs	β^-	30 years	0.51 (92%) 1.17 (8%)	0.662 (from ^{137m}Ba daughter)
^{133}Ba	EC	7.2 years	. . . .	0.360, 0.292, 0.081, 0.070
^{140}La	β^-	40.2 hours	1.34 (70%) (others)	0.49, 0.82, 1.60 (others)
^{147}Pm	β^-	2.65 years	0.225	(γ)
^{170}Tm	β^-	127 days	0.97 (76%) 0.88 (24%)	0.084
^{203}Hg	β^-	47 days	0.21	0.28
^{198}Au	β^-	2.70 days	0.96 (others)	0.412 (others)
^{204}Tl	β^- (98%) EC (2%)	3.80 years	0.76	None
^{210}Pb	β^-	22 years	0.015, 0.061	0.046

† Data selected from extensive tabulation by Friedlander, Kennedy, Macias, and Miller.[1]

‡ EC = electron capture; IT = internal transition.

DETECTORS OF RADIATIONS

The detectors described in Chap. 11 for use with x-rays are also applicable in the detection of radioactivity. Gamma rays are, of course, physically indistinguishable from x-rays. Particulate radiations (except for neutrons) have less penetrating power, hence will suffer loss of energy in passing through the walls or surface layers of some types of detectors, even though once in the sensitive region, they may be easily detectable.

   Photographic detection is used primarily for mapping the distribution of radio-active materials on a solid surface, a process known as *autoradiography* or *radio-autography*.

Scintillation Counters[3]

When a ray or particle strikes a suitable fluorescent material, a tiny flash of visible light is emitted. Counting such *scintillations* therefore provides a measure of the number of incident particles or photons. The circuitry used for this purpose is similar to that described in Chap. 3 for photon counting in the UV.

   Scintillators can be either solid or liquid. The most-used solid is thallium-activated sodium iodide. It can be shaped as in Fig. 24-1, to accept samples inserted in a cylindrical well thus providing a high efficiency for collection of radiations. A pair of scintillators can be arranged to enclose a relatively small sample as in a sandwich, so that essentially all the emitted radiation is caught by the detector. This is referred to as 4π geometry. Good optical contact between the scintillator and photomultiplier is essential, and the surrounding walls should be highly reflective to minimize loss of light. The whole assembly must be shielded with lead or other high-density material, to reduce background interference.

   For quantitative measurements of isotopes that emit low-energy beta particles, such as ^{14}C, ^{35}S, and especially ^3H (tritium), it is preferable to use a *liquid scintillator* in which the active compound can be dissolved. This ensures maximum efficiency

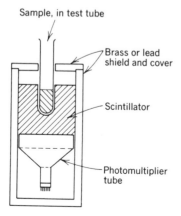

Sample, in test tube

Brass or lead
shield and cover

Scintillator

Photomultiplier
tube

Figure 24-1 A well scintillation counter. schematic.

in the production of scintillations from betas. A number of organic compounds will act as scintillators when dissolved in suitable solvents. These include anthracene, 1,4-diphenylbenzene, 2,5-diphenyloxazole (PPO), α-naphthylphenyloxazole (NPO), and phenylbiphenyloxadiazole (PBD). Of these, PPO is the most effective, but its emitted radiation is in the UV, and readily absorbed by many solvents. It is customary to mix with PPO a secondary scintillator that will translate (through a fluorescence mechanism) the UV scintillations into the visible region. The most common secondary scintillator is 1,4-bis-2-(5-phenyloxazolyl)-benzene (POPOP) or its dimethyl derivative (dimethyl-POPOP). A recommended solution contains 5 g/l PPO and 0.3 g/l dimethyl-POPOP in toluene.

When working with such low-level activity, special precautions must be taken to distinguish pulses produced by scintillations from spurious pulses arising in the photomultiplier, caused either by stray or cosmic radiation, or by shot-effect noise. This can be accomplished by using two identical photomultipliers looking at the same scintillator and connected in a *coincidence circuit* (Fig. 24-2). This consists of an electronic unit called an AND-gate, that will transmit a signal to the counting equipment only when it receives *simultaneous* pulses from the two photomultipliers. The shot noise, being random, will occasionally produce simultaneous signals and, if necessary, this source of undesired counts can be reduced still further by a triple coincidence circuit with three photomultipliers. The noise originating in the photomultipliers can be decreased also by refrigeration, which reduces the thermal motion of electrons.

Scintillation counting is inherently proportional, in that the energy in each flash of light is determined by the energy of the particle or photon that originated it. The proportionality can be maintained through the detector and amplifier to the ultimate record.

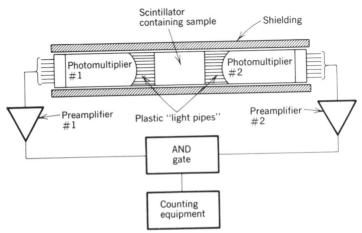

Figure 24-2 Liquid scintillation counting assembly with provision for coincidence counting. The sample, photomultipliers, and preamplifiers can be refrigerated to reduce electrical noise.

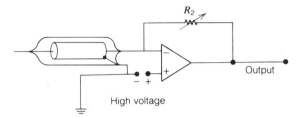

Figure 24-3 Operational amplifier circuit for a gas ionization counter.

Gas Ionization Detectors

Nuclear radiations, other than neutrons, produce some degree of ionization in many materials (see Table 24-1). Measurement of this ionization in gases or in semiconductors provides a very general method of detecting nuclear decay.

Let us consider the phenomena that take place in a gas-filled vessel as the potential is gradually increased across a pair of electrodes. One electrode is a grounded metallic cylinder, perhaps 1 cm in diameter and 5 cm in length, with a wire passing along the axis of the cylinder as the second electrode (Fig. 24-3). The central wire is connected to the inverting input of an operational amplifier,† the noninverting input of which is given a variable positive potential. Since an operational amplifier acts by forcing its two inputs to assume the same potential, this connection places the dc voltage from the power supply directly across the electrodes of the detector. The current that will flow must pass through the feedback resistor R. A corresponding voltage will appear at the output that can be amplified if necessary and displayed on a recorder.

Now suppose that the gas in the detector is subjected to a small source of beta particles at a rate of about 1000 per second. At a very low potential, near the origin in Fig. 24-4, the ions will recombine with each other as fast as they are formed, but as the voltage is increased through the region marked A, more and more ions will reach the electrodes, giving rise to measurable current. In the B region, the field is strong enough to collect essentially *all* ions. This produces a plateau of about 100 V in the curve, since an increase in voltage within this range will not result in any more ions being collected. A detector operating in this region is known as an *ionization chamber*. The current is proportional to the number of ions formed and to their energy content, but is so small (nanoamperes) that the external electronics must have very high gain to give a useful output. If the amplifier has a fast response time, individual pulses may be seen, corresponding to successive beta particles, but it is difficult to provide a small enough time constant together with the necessary high gain, so that ionization chambers are usually operated in the current mode.

If the voltage is raised into region C, the ions are accelerated by the field until they acquire sufficient energy to cause further ionization by collision, giving an

---

† This amplifier must be specially designed to withstand the high voltages involved.

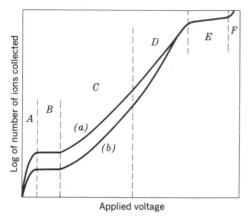

Figure 24-4 Number of ions collected, as a function of the applied voltage in a gas ionization counter. Curve (*a*), alpha particles; (*b*) beta particles. Note that the voltage axis is not drawn to scale; a counter optimized for one region may not operate satisfactorily in other regions. (*Van Nostrand.*[2])

internal gain of perhaps a thousandfold. This means that the pulses arising from individual beta particles become larger, but still retain their proportionality to the energy of the original betas. A device operating in this mode is called a *gas proportional counter*. Close regulation of the potential (which is usually 1000 to 2000 V) is essential, since the operating point (Fig. 24-4) is not on a plateau.

Increasing the voltage into region *D* produces greatly increased secondary ionization, and the pulse size can no longer be assumed to be proportional to the energy content of the original ionizing particle. At *E* a region is reached where, over a band of 100 or 200 V, all pulses have nearly equal magnitude, regardless of the energy of the ionizing particle. This is the *Geiger counter* region, which is excellent for counting particles where energy information is not required. The pulses are so large that little if any amplification is needed, which simplifies the design of portable survey meters. Even though pulse-height discrimination is not possible, it is easy to distinguish between beta and gamma radiation by inserting an aluminum shield, as this will exclude betas without affecting gamma rays.

If the voltage is raised further yet, into region *F*, the tube breaks into a self-sustaining glow discharge.

The operating regions for Geiger and proportional counters must be determined by plotting the counting rate, in counts per minute, for a fixed source of radiation, as the voltage is raised. Precautions must be taken to prevent the positive ions, which are accelerated toward the outer (negative) electrode, from causing secondary electron emission. Such electrons would be accelerated toward the central wire, and would produce secondary ionization of the gas that might initiate a continuing glow discharge. This can be avoided by adding to the fill gas a few percent of an organic vapor (methane or a volatile alcohol) or a halogen. The positive ions transfer their excess energy to the additive rather than to the electrode.

A modification of the proportional counter that is particularly convenient for weakly penetrating radiations is the *windowless flow counter*, in which the gas (e.g., argon–10 percent methane) is allowed to flow slowly through the detector. This

Figure 24-5 Typical sample and detector assembly for planchet counting, surrounded by heavy metal shielding. The overall height is about 40 cm, and the weight 90 kg. (*Radiation Counter Laboratories, Inc.*)

obviates the slow deterioration of the organic additive, and also permits the sample to be placed directly inside the counter itself.

Figure 24-5 shows the type of enclosure that is often used with an end-window counter tube. The sample is mounted on a stainless steel or aluminum disk or shallow cup called a *planchet*, and placed on a movable shelf beneath the counter. The distance from the counter to the sample can be adjusted to accommodate samples of varying strength. Aluminum absorbers can be inserted easily if required.

Semiconductor Detectors

Excellent proportional detectors can be constructed of silicon or germanium.[4] There are two techniques by which crystals of these elements are prepared for use as detectors. In both, the objective is to have a sensitive volume within which absorbed radiation will displace electrons from their normal locations, producing electron-hole pairs.

In one technique, a *pn* junction† is established just beneath the crystal surface. Both upper and lower surfaces are made conducting by deposition of a thin metallic film. The resulting diode is connected electrically with a reverse bias, so that electrons are pulled away from the junction on the *n* side while positive holes are pulled away on the *p* side. This procedure causes the formation of a *depletion region*, the thickness of which can be varied from 0 up to about 1 mm by control of the applied voltage.

† See Chap. 27 for a discussion of semiconductor properties and devices.

According to the second technique, ions of lithium are diffused or *drifted* into the crystals under the influence of an electric field; the lithium has the effect of "cleaning up" or compensating the natural charge carriers, so that when a field is applied across the treated crystal the effective depletion layer will be much deeper, perhaps as thick as 1 cm. Lithium-drifted germanium detectors must be kept at liquid-nitrogen temperature (77 K), whether in use or not, because the lithium ions are sufficiently mobile at room temperature to destroy the geometry of the depletion layer.

The thin depletion layers of the less expensive surface-junction detectors are sufficient for the detection of alpha and beta particles, that cannot penetrate deeply, but the thicker depletion region of a lithium-drifted detector, together with the larger absorption coefficient of germanium as compared to silicon, makes the lithium-drifted germanium detector by far the best for gamma-ray spectroscopy.

These detectors are used in a manner quite analogous to gas proportional detectors. The pairs of electrons and holes produced in the depletion region by absorbed radiation are accelerated toward the respective electrodes, forming a current proportional to the energy of the ionizing particle or photon. A sensitive, noise-free, electrometer amplifier is required, since the currents are only a few microamperes.

BACKGROUND

Radiation is always present in the environment, so that any detector of radio-activity will show a finite response even in the absence of a sample. This radiation is due in part to the natural radioactivity of the surroundings, and in part to cosmic rays. By shielding the counter with 5 to 10 cm of lead, it can be reduced markedly, to perhaps 15 to 20 counts per minute. A much higher background count, or a sudden increase, may indicate accidental contamination of the immediate surroundings with radioactive matter, or it may indicate incipient failure of the counter itself. All measurements of activities must be corrected for background count before any quantitative use or interpretation can be undertaken.

ELECTRONIC SCALERS

To make quantitative measurements of radioactive isotopes, a facility must be provided for counting the pulses coming from the detector. A decimal scaling circuit is commonly used for this purpose. This is an electronic device that will transmit to its output only every *tenth* pulse that is presented to its input. These units can be operated in cascade as needed to express the data with sufficient precision. They are directly connected to a digital numerical readout. Scalers are usually provided with a timing circuit so that the count can be continued for a predetermined period of time. Alternatively, the time required to reach a pre-determined count can be measured.

Radioactive decay is statistical in nature, that is, the exact number of atoms that will disintegrate and eject particles in any particular second is governed by the laws of probability. Observed counts are significant only when a large enough number of them have been accumulated to permit a valid statistical analysis. This aspect of the subject is essential to its intelligent application.[5, 6] Only a brief summary of those features of importance to analytical uses is given here.

The most convenient criterion of the validity of a series of measurements is the *standard deviation*, σ. For radioactivity measurements in which the half-life of the decaying isotope is long compared to the duration of the experiment, the standard deviation is given by the square root of n, the total number of counts. Hence the results of an experiment can be expressed as $n \pm \sqrt{n}$. This shows the advantage of determining the time for a predetermined count, namely, that it results in uniform precision.

The background count is also statistical in nature. If σ_s, σ_b, and σ_t represent the standard deviations of the sample, background, and total counts, respectively, then it follows that

$$\sigma_s = (\sigma_t^2 + \sigma_b^2)^{1/2} \tag{24-1}$$

There are two ways of handling this: the background can be counted long enough that $\sigma_b \ll \sigma_t$, and hence can be neglected. Alternatively, the ratio of counting times t_t for the sample (which includes background) and t_b for the background alone, that will give the best precision in the least time can be estimated from the relation

$$\frac{t_t}{t_b} = \left(\frac{R_t}{R_b}\right)^{1/2} \tag{24-2}$$

where the R's refer to the respective count rates, which need only be known roughly from a preliminary measurement.

As an example, suppose a preliminary experiment shows the approximate activities for sample and background to be $R_t = 1000$ cpm (counts per minute) and $R_b = 40$ cpm. The time ratio should be $t_t/t_b = (1000/40)^{1/2} = 5$. If a precision of 1 percent standard deviation is desired, the total count must be 10,000 counts (because $\sqrt{10,000} = 100$, which is 1 percent of the count), so this means that the counting must be continued for 10 min. Hence the background count should be taken for one-fifth of 10 min, or 2 min. The total count for the sample will be, let us say, 10,025 counts, which gives

$$R_t = \frac{10,025 \pm \sqrt{10,025}}{10} = 1002.5 \pm 10.01 \text{ cpm}$$

Similarly, the background count might be 81, giving

$$R_b = \frac{81 \pm \sqrt{81}}{2} = 40.5 \pm 4.5 \text{ cpm}$$

Hence, [using Eq. (24-1)], the corrected rate for the sample alone is

$$R_s = (1002.5 - 40.5) \pm [(10.01)^2 + (4.5)^2]^{1/2}$$
$$= 962 \pm 11 \text{ cpm}$$

Another potential source of error is due to the occurrence of *coincidences*, here defined as two pulses coming so close together that the counter cannot recover from one pulse quickly enough to respond to the next. The recovery time τ varies considerably from one type of detector to another. The governing relation is

$$R' = R + R^2\tau \tag{24-3}$$

where R is the observed count rate and R' is the true or corrected rate.

It should be realized that in many detector configurations, only a fraction of the radiation from a sample can enter the counter. With a single, end-window counter, the geometric efficiency is always well below 50 percent. Such a low efficiency is often tolerated because the layout of equipment is simpler than required for 4π geometry. It is always important to maintain constant geometry for determinations that are to be compared with one another. This is facilitated with apparatus like that of Fig. 24-5. Precautions must be taken against the effects of partial absorption of radiations by such materials as solvent or filter paper.

Pulse Height Analysis

Ionizing particles and photons from different radioisotopes vary widely in their energy content, as shown in Table 24-2. Individual active species can often be identified by observation of these energy values. One method is by the use of

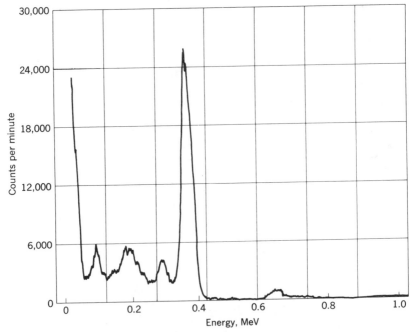

Figure 24-6 Gamma radiation spectrum of ^{131}I. (*Nuclear-Chicago Corporation.*)

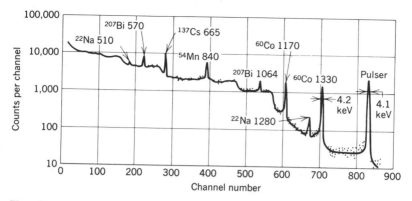

Figure 24-7 A spectrum of gamma radiation recorded with a lithium-drifted detector and multichannel analyzer. The figures are energies in kiloelectronvolts. The "pulser" peak results from a local oscillator, and gives an internal standard for dead-time corrections. (*Isotopes, Inc.*)

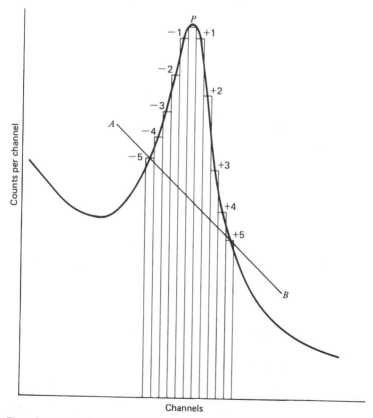

Figure 24-8 A peak for a single species from a gamma spectrum, showing the Covell method of quantitative evaluation.

standard absorbers, known thicknesses of aluminum for less energetic particles, or lead for gamma rays, placed between the sample and detector. The *half-thickness*, i.e., the thickness of metal that will cut the activity to half its value, can be translated into its energy equivalent by a calibration curve.

A more elegant method is by a pulse-height analysis made with any type of proportional counter.[6] The instrument to do this is the *multichannel analyzer* described in Chap. 11. Figure 24-6 shows the spectrum of radiations from ^{131}I, and Fig. 24-7 a similar spectrum of a mixture of gamma-emitters, both obtained with multichannel analyzers.

For quantitative results, the area beneath each peak must be measured accurately, a procedure often complicated by the lack of a well-defined base line. Covell has shown,[8] on a firm statistical basis, that a valid measure of the area can be obtained by a procedure illustrated in Fig. 24-8, where each vertical segment represents one channel of the analyzer. The line AB is drawn to intersect the curve an equal number of channels below and above the peak (at channels $P - 5$ and $P + 5$ in the figure). The area enclosed between the curve and this line, measured with a planimeter, is proportional to the intensity of the corresponding radiation.

NEUTRON COUNTING

Since neutrons are not charged, they do not produce ionization in a gas by any direct process. They can, however, be detected in a counter filled with gaseous BF_3, because neutrons react very readily with the ^{10}B nucleus to produce ^7Li and alpha particles, the $^{10}B(n, \alpha)^7Li$ reaction.† The resultant alpha particles trigger the counter in the usual way. Neutrons can also be detected with a scintillation counter into which a boron compound has been incorporated.

Low-energy neutrons can be diffracted in a crystal spectrometer, very much as can x-rays, since their deBroglie wavelength ($\lambda = h/mv$) is in the x-ray region. Another method involves selection according to velocities, whereby the neutrons pass through a measured course in a time-of-flight tube, resulting in a spectrum. The details of these instruments are described elsewhere.[9]

The selective absorption of neutrons of varying energy content is an extremely powerful analytical tool, but unfortunately for general application, it requires such a strong flux of neutrons that only a large nuclear reactor can supply it. A less powerful source can be applied to the absorptiometric determination of a few elements that have isotopes with unusually high absorptive power (*cross section*), particularly B, Cd, Li, Hg, Ir, In, Au, Ag, and several lanthanides.

Analytical Applications of Radioactive Sources

The absorption of alpha and beta particles is potentially useful for analytical purposes. Because of their low penetrating power, alpha rays are best suited for

---

† According to this notation, the first symbol within the parentheses designates the particle that reacts with the nucleus written to its left, generating the second particle in the parentheses and the residual nucleus written to the right.

the analysis of gases. A process has been described[10] in which an alpha source (^{210}Po in an aged preparation of "radium-D," ^{210}Pb) was placed inside an ionization chamber that also served as the sample container. Under conditions of constant pressure and potential, the current through the chamber is a function only of gas composition. In favorable cases, binary gas mixtures can be analyzed with a precision of ± 0.2 to 0.3 mole percent, by reference to a calibration curve prepared from measurements on known mixtures. This method has been used commercially in the detection of such toxic gases as $Ni(CO)_4$ and $Pb(C_2H_5)_4$ in air, in the parts-per-billion range.† The absorption of beta particles has also been applied to analysis, primarily of liquids. The absorption of betas by chemical species is almost entirely due to electron–electron interactions. Elementary considerations show that hydrogen has a greater number of electrons per unit weight than any other element, by at least a factor of 2. This renders the method particularly sensitive to the presence of hydrogen. This has been made the basis of an instrument for determining the H/C ratio in petroleum products.[11,12]

The use of gamma sources in place of conventional x-ray tubes has been discussed in Chap. 11. The application of tritium and other beta emitters in electron-capture GC detectors has been described in Chap. 20.

RADIOACTIVE TRACERS

The ease with which the presence of active isotopes can be detected and the precision with which they can be measured, even in very small quantities, leads to a variety of versatile analytical procedures. The most general techniques are activation analysis and isotope dilution.

ACTIVATION ANALYSIS

A great many elements become radioactive when bombarded with particles such as neutrons, protons, deuterons, and alpha particles. Neutron activation is the most widely used, and so will be examined most extensively.

Consider the exposure of various samples to neutrons of "thermal" velocities, i.e., with kinetic energy less than about 0.2 eV. The target nucleus typically captures a neutron to give a new nucleus with mass greater by 1 unit, but with the same positive charge. This is, of course, an isotope of the original species. The new nucleus is in many cases unstable and spontaneously decomposes by emitting a particle or gamma photon (or both); in other words, it is radioactive. The active isotopes formed in this way from the various elements vary widely in half-life, and in many instances can be identified by this property together with other pertinent information such as the gamma-ray energy spectrum.

Neutron activation can be used for analysis by subjecting a sample to neutron bombardment in a nuclear reactor. Radioactivity will be induced in each of the

---

† Mine Safety Appliances Co., Pittsburgh.

elements present that are capable of being so activated. The induced radioactivity in the sample can then be plotted against time, to give a *decay curve*. This curve is generally complex, being the summation of the activities of all the active species present. The individual species can be identified with the help of a computer, by a process of deconvolution. The half-life of the longest-lived component can be determined from the later portions of the curve, after more transient substances have virtually vanished. The activity due to this isotope can then be subtracted ("stripped away") from the readings for shorter times. Then the next longest-lived can similarly be identified and stripped away, then the next, and so on.

For example, the analysis of an aluminum alloy was described in one of the earliest reports of this method.[13]† A small sample of the metal (about 25 mg) was placed in a nuclear reactor for 5 min. The subsequent activity was followed with a standard counting apparatus for about 60 h (Fig. 24-9). Natural aluminum has only a single isotope, ^{27}Al. Capture of a neutron creates ^{28}Al, which decays by β-emission to give ^{28}Si, a stable species. Since the sample was primarily aluminum, the radiation due to ^{28}Al was very strong, but since its half-life is only 2.3 min, a half-hour wait allowed most of it to disappear.

It is seen from the figure that the activity (on a logarithmic scale) is a linear function of time after about 40 h. This straight-line portion, extrapolated backward, gives the activity at any time due to an isotope with a half-life of about 15 h, as determined from this graph. This is identified from a table of isotopes to be ^{24}Na, with a known half-life of 15.0 h. The plot also shows a linear region extending from 1 to about 18 h, which must be due to an isotope of half-life close to 2.5 h, determined to be ^{56}Mn (2.58 h).

Rather than plotting the complete decay curve, the desired results can be obtained by recording gamma-ray spectra at selected times following irradiation. A recent report from the U.S. Environmental Protection Agency[14] describes the simultaneous determination of 26 elements in urban air, as collected on fiberglass filters. Each sample was irradiated for 4 h, then, after a cooling-off period of 10 days, counted with a lithium-drifted germanium detector and a 2048-channel pulse-height analyzer. Figure 24-10 shows a typical plot of data as processed by a computer.

The sensitivity of analyses by means of neutron activation depends on the neutron flux, on the ability of the element sought to capture neutrons (the *neutron-capture cross section*), and on the half-life of the induced activity. The governing relation[4] is:

$$A = N\sigma\phi\left[1 - \exp\left(-\frac{0.693t}{T_{1/2}}\right)\right] \tag{24-4}$$

where A is the induced activity at the end of the irradiation (cps), N is the number of atoms of the isotope present in the sample, σ is the neutron-capture cross section (cm^2), ϕ is the flux (neutrons·cm^{-2}·s^{-1}), t is the time of irradiation, and $T_{1/2}$ is the

† The experiment described was performed without the benefit of a computer.

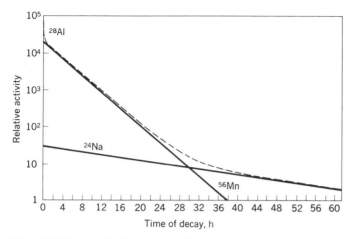

Figure 24-9 The analysis of an aluminum alloy by neutron activation. (*Analytical Chemistry*.[13])

half-life of the product. ($T_{1/2}$ and t must be in the same units.) Quantitative analyses are rarely based on calculations from this equation (although this was done in Ref. 13), as sufficiently reliable data are seldom available. As a further complication, ϕ may not be homogeneous and may vary with time. For practical purposes, standard samples are irradiated simultaneously with unknowns, and the analysis carried out by simple comparison.

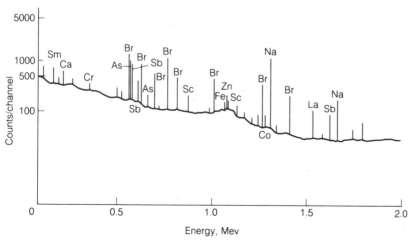

Figure 24-10 The gamma spectrum of atmospheric particulates from an urban atmosphere, following neutron activation. (*Analytical Chemistry*.[14])

If a large nuclear reactor is available for irradiation, in favorable cases as little as 10^{-10} g of an element can be detected. For less powerful neutron sources, the method is limited to those elements that have particularly favorable nuclear properties. For example, a neutron source consisting of 25 mg of Ra mixed with 250 mg of Be produces neutrons by the ^{9}Be$(\alpha, n)^{12}$C reaction with a flux of about 100 neutrons·cm^{-2}·s^{-1}. This can be used to activate only Rh, Ag, In, Ir, and Dy, but can offer a convenient and accurate method for these elements. A source composed of ^{124}Sb and Be, with a flux of 10^3 to 10^4 will activate about 19 elements. A nuclear reactor may have a flux as great as 10^{14}, and will activate nearly all the elements heavier than oxygen, but with greatly differing sensitivities. For some elements (In, Re, Ir, Sm, Eu, Dy, Ho, Lu, V, As, Sb) activation analysis appears to be capable of greater sensitivity than strictly chemical methods, whereas for others (Fe, Ca, Pb, Bi, Zn, Cd, Na, K) activation is no better than, or distinctly inferior to, chemical procedures.[15]

Activation by Species Other than Neutrons

Activation can also be produced by bombardment with charged particles, including protons ^{1}H$^+$, deuterons ^{2}H$^+$, tritons ^{3}H$^+$, and helium nuclei ^{3}He^{2+} and ^{4}He^{2+}.[16] The required energies in the tens of megaelectronvolts can be obtained from linear accelerators, Van de Graaff generators, or cyclotrons. The nuclear reactions that occur follow the same general principle as with neutrons: the projectile particle is captured by the target nucleus to give a product larger in both mass and charge. The new nucleus is likely to be unstable, and to disintegrate with the ejection of measurable particles or photons or both. The method can be very sensitive, particularly for the light elements (B, C, N, O) for which the detection limits are less than 1 part in 10^9. For further details, consult Refs. 16–18.

Activation by electromagnetic radiation is also possible. Gamma rays from ^{124}Sb have been used to activate ^{9}Be, and those from ^{24}Na for the measurement of deuterium in water.[19] These sources produce the most energetic gammas of any isotopes with a long enough lifetime to be practical, and ^{9}Be and ^{2}H are the only nuclei that can be activated by them, respectively. For wider applicability, bremsstrahlung radiation produced by the absorption of high-energy electrons in a high atomic weight target must be used. For some elements (F, Fe, Pb) the sensitivity is better than with neutron activation. In other cases, matrix interferences are eliminated, making the method attractive.

ISOTOPE DILUTION

This technique is applicable where a compound can be isolated in a pure state but with only a poor yield. A known quantity of the same substance containing an active isotope is added to the unknown and thoroughly mixed with it. A portion of the pure substance (radioactive and inert forms combined) is then isolated from the mixture and its activity determined. A simple calculation then gives the amount of the substance in the original sample.

Consider a solution that contains W grams of a compound to be determined. To the solution is added a portion of the same compound that is *tagged* with a radioactive atom; the added portion weighs w grams and has an activity of A cpm and a specific activity $S_0 = A/w$. After mixing, g grams of the compound is isolated in a pure state and found to have an activity of B cpm and specific activity $S = B/g$. The total amount of activity (assuming the loss by decay to be negligible) must be the same after mixing as before, or

$$wS_0 = (W + w)S \qquad (24\text{-}5)$$

from which it follows that

$$W = g \frac{A}{B} - w \qquad (24\text{-}6)$$

If the added material is highly active, then the amount added, w, can be very small relative to W, and Eq. (24-6) reduces to

$$W = g \frac{A}{B} \qquad (24\text{-}7)$$

Suppose the amount of glycine in a mixture of amino acids is desired. Glycine can be isolated chemically, but only with a low yield, which makes isotope dilution an appropriate technique. We start by obtaining a sample of glycine that contains an atom of ^{14}C in perhaps one in every million of its molecules. This preparation is determined to have a specific activity, corrected for background, of 25,000 cpm per gram. A 0.500-g portion of this active material is mixed with the unknown. From the mix a 0.200-g sample of pure glycine is recovered, and found to have a specific activity of 1250 counts per 10 min. The background is 100 counts per 5 min. The data can be summarized as follows:

$$w = 0.500 \text{ g}$$
$$S_0 = 25,000 \text{ cpm per gram}$$
$$A = wS_0 = 12,500 \text{ cpm}$$
$$g = 0.200 \text{ g}$$
$$B = (1250/10) - (100/5) = 105 \text{ cpm}$$

from which

$$W = g \frac{A}{B} - w = 0.200 \frac{12,500}{105} - 0.500$$

$$= 23.2 \text{ g}$$

which is the required weight of glycine in the sample. If w had been neglected, the resulting error would have been about 2 percent, whereas the counting error is about 3.5 percent.

A further illustration is provided by published work[20] on the electrogravi-metric determination of Co in steel. The reason for using isotope dilution was that Co, deposited anodically as Co_2O_3, is apt to form a poorly adherent layer. This precludes a conventional gravimetric determination, but loss of some particles is not objectionable in isotope dilution. A standard curve was prepared by adding equal aliquots of ^{60}Co to samples containing various known amounts of Co, then electrolyzing in a standardized manner. The unknown was fortified by an aliquot of ^{60}Co immediately upon dissolution of the steel sample. Cobalt was then deposited, the deposit weighed and its activity measured, and the amount in the original sample determined by reference to the calibration curve. Standard deviations varied from 0.005 to 0.025 percent.

The use of a standard curve in this way tends to eliminate some sources of error, in much the same way that a blank determination does in many analyses. However, in some applications, the answer is best obtained directly from the equations given above.

MÖSSBAUER SPECTROSCOPY[1,21,22]

This term designates a study of the resonance fluorescence of gamma radiation. It is comparable to resonance fluorescence in optical regions, but involves *intra-nuclear* rather than atomic energy levels. An important characteristic of this radiation, under optimum conditions of measurement, is the extreme sharpness of the lines. The resonance gamma ray of ^{67}Zn, for example, has a width at half-height of only 4.8×10^{-11} eV, about 2 parts in 10^{15} of the photon energy which is approximately 93 keV. This may be compared with the Zn K x-ray, which has a half-height width of 4.7×10^{-8} eV for a photon of 8.6 keV, or about 2 parts in 10^{11}, about 10,000 times broader than the gamma radiation.

The most extensively studied element is iron, because the nuclear energy levels of the ^{57}Fe isotope are most easily accessible. This species has a metastable level 14.4 keV above the stable ground state, and the transition between these levels produces gammas that are readily absorbed by ground-state ^{57}Fe nuclei. To obtain atoms of ^{57}Fe with excited nuclei, one starts with ^{57}Co, which has a 267-day half-life, decaying by electron-capture to produce the desired $^{57}Fe*$.† The latter immediately emits its excess energy as a 14.4 keV gamma photon. This photon can be absorbed by a ground-state ^{57}Fe nucleus, with which it resonates. The sequence of events can be depicted as

$$^{56}Fe \xrightarrow[(a)]{(d,n)} {}^{57}Co \xrightarrow[(b)]{EC267d} {}^{57}Fe* \xrightarrow[(c)]{-\gamma} {}^{57}Fe$$

† The asterisk here signifies an energetically excited nucleus.

The corresponding nuclei in the sample absorb the photon as follows:

$$^{57}Fe \xrightarrow[(d)]{+\gamma} {}^{57}Fe*$$

Process (a), the capture of a deuteron and concomitant loss of a neutron, takes place in a cyclotron during the preparation of the ^{57}Co precursor. The ^{57}Co is allowed to diffuse into the surface layers of a metal foil that is subsequently used as the "source" in the Mössbauer apparatus. The half-life of $^{57}Fe*$ with respect to the emission of the photon (c) is so much shorter than 267 days (b) that effectively one gamma is produced every time a ^{57}Co nucleus disintegrates. The absorber (the sample) can be ordinary iron in any chemical form, as the natural abundance of ^{57}Fe is adequate (about 2.2 percent) to give useful sensitivity.

Since the frequency bands are so narrow, extremely slight changes in the energy states of the absorbing nuclei can shift the frequency at which absorption can occur by more than the line width of the primary radiation, so that no absorption can take place. The effect of the state of chemical combination on the nuclear levels can be of just this order of magnitude. Such a *chemical shift* can be observed and measured by imposing a translational motion on either the emitter or absorber, in such a way that the resulting Doppler shift will exactly compensate for the chemical shift. The required motion turns out to be of the order of a few mm · s^{-1}, hence is easily realizable in practice.

Figure 24-11a shows the block diagram of a typical Mössbauer apparatus. In principle, either source or absorber can be made movable, but as the absorbing sample must often be refrigerated to reduce lattice vibrations, it is more convenient to move the source. A motor designed to produce reciprocating linear motion is driven by a signal generator programmed to give constant *acceleration*, first in one direction then the other (Fig. 24-11b). With this type of motion, a whole range of *velocities* is covered in each cycle; the *displacement* follows a parabolic curve.

The signal from the detector is fed through a single-channel analyzer, to restrict the response to a single resonant gamma ray. From there it passes to a multichannel analyzer synchronized with the signal generator. This assigns each channel to a specific narrow increment of velocities, so the built-in oscilloscope displays the response as a function of source velocity.

Figure 24-12 shows a representative Mössbauer spectrum, taken on several samples of lunar rocks.[23] Comparison with known materials served to identify two iron minerals. Mössbauer spectra can give information about valence states and crystal structures of any compounds or alloys containing the elements to which it is sensitive. It is restricted, however, to a few elements. By far the greatest amount of work has been done with ^{57}Fe, ^{61}Ni, and ^{119}Sn. There are about 30 elements in which the effect has been observed, and some 20 more in which it is to be expected. Many of these elements owe their response only to low-percentage isotopes, or for other reasons are not easily worked with. The importance of Fe, Ni, and Sn chemistries is great enough to ensure this technique a place among instrumental methods.

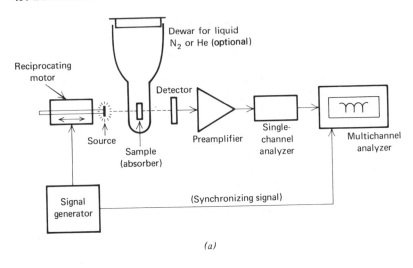

(a)

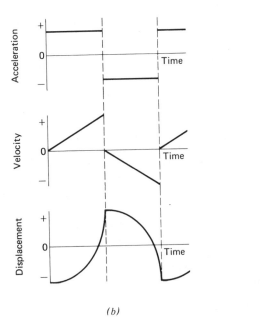

(b)

Figure 24-11 A Mössbauer spectrometer: (*a*). block diagram; (*b*). the corresponding time sequence.

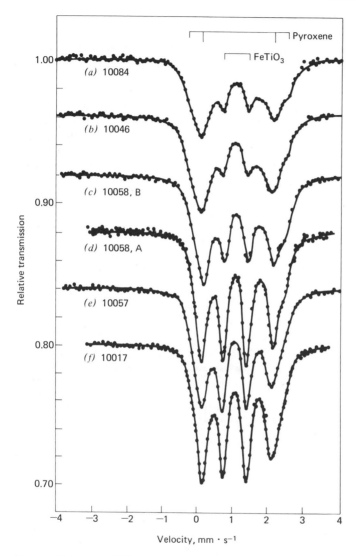

Figure 24-12 A series of Mössbauer spectra of six samples of lunar rocks and dust, showing varying proportions of $FeTiO_3$ and pyroxene, an iron-bearing silicate mineral. The numbers identify particular lunar samples. (*American Laboratory.*[23])

SAFETY PRECAUTIONS

The small amounts of radioactive materials needed for tracer experiments do not generally present radiation hazards that are difficult to guard against. Alpha- or beta-labeled isotopes are safe if kept in ordinary glass or metal containers, but when out of those containers, they should be handled with tongs and the operator should wear rubber or plastic gloves. Gamma emitters may require more extensive shielding, perhaps a few centimeters of lead, depending on the photon energy of the specific isotope. Pipetting by mouth, not advisable under any conditions, is NEVER to be sanctioned with radioactive solutions.

A survey meter should always be available so· that cleanup of accidental spillage can be checked. Often the hazard to the experimenter is less than the chance of contaminating the laboratory so that the background count is increased unduly. Most active tracer materials are as safe to use in the laboratory as such more familiar materials as silver nitrate. Safety precautions are no more exacting, merely of a different type.

Active materials in larger than trace quantities do, of course, require more elaborate safety measures, descriptions of which are readily available elsewhere.[1]

It should be noted that the possession and use of radioisotopes in the United States may require licensing by the Nuclear Regulatory Commission.

PROBLEMS

24-1 The term "coincidence" designates something to be desired in connection with scintillations, and something to be avoided when discussing statistics. Explain this seeming paradox.

24-2 A particular ionization chamber filled with air at normal pressure presents a path length of 8 cm to the beta particles from a moderately energetic source with 1000 disintegrations per minute. The geometrical efficiency is 50 percent. It has been established that beta rays produce an average of 10 ion pairs per millimeter of path in air. Calculate the magnitude of the current produced. (The electronic charge is 1.6×10^{-19} C.)

24-3 A method for the simultaneous determination of U and Th in minerals[23] requires (1) measurement of combined U and Th by radioactivity, and (2) determination of the Th/U ratio by x-ray emission spectroscopy. The combined radioactivity is expressed as percent equivalent uranium, namely, that amount of U in pitchblende necessary to give an equal activity. The Th/U ratio is taken as the ratio of peak heights for the x-ray lines: Th $L\alpha$ and U $L\alpha$. The U and Th contents are given by the relation $x + 0.2xy$ = percent equivalent U, where x is the weight percent of U and y is the Th/U weight ratio. For a particular counting apparatus, 1 percent equivalent U corresponds to 2100 cpm above background. A 1.000-g sample of a monazite sand, when prepared and counted according to the standard procedure, gave 2780 cpm (corrected for background). X-ray examination gave peak heights of 72.3 scale divisions for Th $L\alpha$ and 1.58 divisions for U $L\alpha$. Compute the U and Th contents of the sample in terms of weight percent.

24-4 A mixture is to be assayed for its penicillin content by isotope dilution. A 10.00-mg portion of radioactive penicillin with an activity of 4500 cpm per milligram is added to the given specimen. From the mixture it is possible to isolate only 0.35 mg of pure crystalline penicillin. Its activity is determined to be 390 cpm per milligram. (Background corrections have been applied.) What was the penicillin content of the sample, in grams?

24-5 According to the *reverse isotope dilution* method, a weight w of inactive compound is added to a preparation containing an unknown amount W of an active form of the same compound, which has a specific activity of S_0. A sample is then isolated in pure form, weighed, and counted. Show mathematically that Eq. (24-6) applies in this case.

24-6 A method has been described[25] for the determination of the oxidation products of propane by inverse isotope dilution. The sample to be oxidized was enriched in propane tagged with ^{14}C. Among the products was found a considerable quantity of active 2-propanol. To the mixed products was added a measured amount of inactive 2-propanol, and a portion isolated by conventional methods. The following data were obtained. (The symbol μCi stands for *microcurie*, an alternative unit for activity.)

Quantity of active propane	10 mmol
Specific activity of sample	72.8 μCi·mmol^{-1}
Inactive propanol added	16 mmol
Specific activity of propanol	5.8 μCi·mmol^{-1}

Compute the percent of propane converted to 2-propanol.

24-7 In a study of the solubilities of slightly soluble salts, the concentrations of oxalate solutions in the parts-per-million range are to be determined by precipitation of $^{45}CaC_2O_4$. Calculate the oxalate concentration (in parts per million) in a sample from the following data: A standard solution is prepared that is 0.680 M in $CaCl_2$ with a ^{45}Ca activity of 20,000 cpm per ml (corrected). To a 100-ml sample of trace oxalate solution is added 5.00 ml of the standard solution. No precipitate is visible beyond a slight turbidity. A few drops of $FeCl_3$ is added, and the solution made alkaline with ammonia to precipitate $Fe(OH)_3$. The precipitate is collected on a small filter paper with suction, washed once, dried, and counted. The counting apparatus is known from prior experiments to have a 30.0 percent efficiency. The time required for a preset count of 6000 is 18.60 min. The background is 150 counts per 5 min. (The efficiency correction is not to be applied to the standard.)

24-8 The beta radiation from an active source is to be measured with a Geiger counter. The maximum uncertainty permitted is ± 1 percent. Counts recorded at the ends of successive 5-min periods for sample and background are as follows:

Time, min	0	5	10	15	20	25	30
Background, cpm	0	127	249	377	502	672	793
Sample, cpm	0	2155	4297	6451	8602	10,749	12,907

(a) What is the minimum time over which the count must be taken to give the required precision?
(b) How long would the background have to be counted?
(c) What is the actual corrected count in counts per minute, with precision limits?

24-9 A neutron activation procedure is desired for the determination of trace levels of silver and zinc in alloys. Handbook tables give the following data (Cd, In, Cu, and Au are included as likely to be present in the same samples):

Reaction	Natural abundance, %	Product Half-life	Product activity
$^{64}Zn(n,\gamma)^{65}Zn$	48.9	244 d	EC
$^{66}Zn(n,\gamma)^{67}Zn$	27.8	Stable	
$^{67}Zn(n,\gamma)^{68}Zn$	4.1	Stable	
†$^{68}Zn(n,\gamma)^{69}Zn$	18.6	58 m	β
†$^{68}Zn(n,\gamma)^{69m}Zn$	18.6	13.9 h	β
$^{70}Zn(n,\gamma)^{71}Zn$	0.62	2.4 m	β
$^{107}Ag(n,\gamma)^{108}Ag$	51.8	2.42 m	EC, β
†$^{109}Ag(n,\gamma)^{110}Ag$	48.2	24.4 s	β
†$^{109}Ag(n,\gamma)^{110m}Ag$	48.2	253 d	β
$^{110}Cd(n,p)^{110m}Ag$	12.4	253 d	β
$^{114}Cd(n,\alpha)^{115}Cd$	28.9	53.5 h	β
$^{113}In(n,\gamma)^{110m}Ag$	4.28	253 d	β
$^{115}In(n,\gamma)^{116}In$	95.7	14 s	β
$^{197}Au(n,\gamma)^{198}Au$	100.0	2.69 d	β
$^{63}Cu(n,\gamma)^{64}Cu$	69.1	12.9 h	EC, β
$^{65}Cu(n,\gamma)^{66}Cu$	30.9	5.10 m	β

† ^{68}Zn goes 99% to ^{69}Zn and 1% to the metastable ^{69m}Zn.
^{109}Ag goes 96% to ^{110}Ag and 4% to ^{110m}Ag.

Following neutron irradiation, the sample should be placed in an automatic counting apparatus that will record the total activity at, say, 2-hour intervals for a period of 30 days. At the end of this waiting period, the sample is dissolved, and inactive silver and zinc perchlorates added as carriers. The solution is then electrolyzed at an appropriate potential to separate silver from zinc, and the activities of the two portions are determined.

(a) Which isotopes are actually utilized for the Ag and Zn determinations?

(b) Note that both ^{110}Cd and ^{113}In can be activated by neutrons to give ^{110m}Ag, thus becoming potential sources of error. The ^{110}Cd can be corrected for by observing the decay of ^{115}Cd. Explain how this would be done. How might the ^{113}In interference be eliminated?

(c) Explain what is meant by the symbol "m" in ^{110m}Ag and ^{69m}Zn.

(d) Would you expect any interference from Cu and gold due to (n, p) or (n, α) processes? Why?

(e) Both ^{66}Zn and ^{67}Zn can capture neutrons, yet they do not produce radiations. Explain this.

REFERENCES

1. G. Friedlander, J. W. Kennedy, E. S. Macias, and J. M. Miller, *Nuclear and Radiochemistry*, (3d ed.), Wiley-Interscience, New York, **1981**.
2. R. L. Hahn, in *Guide to Activation Analysis*, W. S. Lyon, Jr. (ed.), Van Nostrand, Princeton, **1964**, p. 63.
3. D. L. Horrocks, *Applications of Liquid Scintillation Counting*, Academic Press, New York, **1974**.
4. P. J. Ouseph, *Introduction to Nuclear Radiation Detectors*, Plenum Press, New York, **1975**.
5. Chap. 9 of Ref 1.
6. Chap. 18 of Ref. 3.
7. W. A. Ross, "Multichannel Analyzers," in *Instrumentation in Applied Nuclear Chemistry*, J. Krugers (ed.), Plenum Press, New York, **1973**.
8. D. F. Covell, *Anal. Chem.*, **1959**, *31*, 1785.
9. G. W. Leddicote, "Neutron Absorption and Scattering Techniques of Analysis," in *Treatise on Analytical Chemistry*, I. M. Kolthoff, P. J. Elving, and E. B. Sandell (eds.), pt. I, vol. 6, chap. 69, Wiley-Interscience, New York, **1965**.
10. P. F. Deisler, Jr., K. W. McHenry, Jr., and R. H. Wilhelm, *Anal. Chem.*, **1955**, 27, 1366.
11. R. B. Jacobs, L. G. Lewis, and F. J. Piehl, *Anal. Chem.*, **1956**, *28*, 324.
12. V. N. Smith and J. W. Otvos, *Anal. Chem.*, **1954**, *26*, 359.
13. G. E. Boyd, *Anal. Chem.*, **1949**, *21*, 335.
14. J. P. F. Lambert and F. W. Wilshire, *Anal. Chem.*, **1979**, *51*, 1346.
15. V. P. Guinn, in *Techniques of Chemistry, Vol. I, Physical Methods of Chemistry*, A. Weissberger and B. W. Rossiter (eds.), pt. III-D, chap. 7, Wiley-Interscience, New York, **1972**.
16. E. A. Schweikert, *Anal. Chem.*, **1980**, *52*, 827A.
17. C. S. Sastri, H. Petri, and G. Erdtmann, *Anal. Chem.*, **1977**, *49*, 1510.
18. R. B. Boulton and G. T. Ewan, *Anal. Chem.*, **1977**, *49*, 1297.
19. G. J. Lutz, *Anal. Chem.*, **1971**, *43*, 93.
20. D. Salyer and T. R. Sweet, *Anal. Chem.*, **1956**, *28*, 61; **1957**, *29*, 2.
21. R. H. Herber and Y. Hazony, in *Techniques of Chemistry, Vol. I, Physical Methods of Chemistry*, A. Weissberger and B. W. Rossiter (eds.), pt. III-D, chap. 4, Wiley-Interscience, New York, **1972**.
22. J. G. Stevens and G. K. Shemoy, *Mössbauer Spectroscopy and its Chemical Applications*, Advances in Chemistry Series, no. 194, American Chemical Society, Washington, **1981**.
23. A. H. Muir, Jr., R. M. Housley, R. W. Grant, M. Abdel-Gawad, and M. Blander, *Am. Lab.*, **1970**, *2(11)*, 8.
24. W. J. Campbell and H. F. Carl, *Anal. Chem.*, **1955**, *27*, 1884.
25. W. H. Clingman, Jr., and H. H. Hammen, *Anal. Chem.*, **1960**, *32*, 323.

TWENTY-FIVE
AUTOMATIC ANALYZERS

AUTOMATION VERSUS MECHANIZATION

Many of the instruments described in previous chapters in this book are highly mechanized, meaning that built-in electrical and mechanical devices relieve the operator of explicit care of many details. Such mechanization permits much more effective utilization of the analytical capabilities of the instrument than could be attained by purely manual operation. This is especially true where the method involves scanning one variable while continuously measuring another.

As an example, consider the infrared spectrophotometer. Even if the electro-mechanical aids usually taken for granted were omitted and all work done manually, equally valid spectra could be obtained. An experienced operator would need at least 5 or 10 min to set the prism or grating to the desired wavelength, adjust the slit width, measure the transmittance of both sample and blank, and record the data in a notebook. This would have to be repeated many hundreds of times to cover the 2 to 20 μm range. The data would have to be calculated point by point, and then plotted on graph paper. It might take a week to complete a single high-resolution spectrum. Clearly the mechanization of such an instrument permits not only great savings of time, but also greater freedom from error caused by fatigue.

Of course an automatic recording spectrophotometer will have its own potential sources of error. Imperfections and malfunction of mechanical parts can produce both systematic and random errors that may be difficult to track down and eliminate. But instrumental errors of this sort can generally be reduced by careful design and skillful construction, and the residual inaccuracies further diminished by overall calibration procedures. It is essential that calibration should be repeated routinely at frequent intervals to ensure the integrity of the system. Any changes in the instrument brought about by mechanical wear of moving parts and slow drift of the characteristics of electronic parts will be compensated to a considerable extent by this procedure.

The term *automation*, on the other hand, is usually taken to mean more than mere automatic operation of an instrument. It refers to a *system*, often consisting of one major instrument, such as a spectrophotometer, together with various other components to enable it to examine numerous samples in close succession and record the results. This type of automatic analysis is valuable whenever a large number of similar determinations must be carried out on a routine basis. Much impetus in this direction has stemmed from the needs of clinical laboratories, but automated instruments are also extensively used in quality control laboratories in chemical, pharmaceutical, metallurgical, and other industries.

In principle, a machine can be designed to duplicate any procedures that a human operator might carry out. Mechanical operations, such as dissolving, pipetting, and diluting, can be performed by a machine with better efficiency than by a human.[1,2] That this is also true of those crucial steps involving decision-making is not so obvious. An experienced chemist or technician, by observing the progress of a reaction, can determine when it has reached completion, and decide accordingly what the next step should be. A machine can be programmed to do this too, by making quantitative measurements followed by logical decisions based on those measurements. The machine has the advantage over the human that the correctness of its judgment will not falter because of fatigue and tedium.

The machine, however, does not excel at recognizing unusual occurrences that do not follow the expected patterns. A successful automatic analyzer must be able to recognize these unusual responses, at least to the extent that it will call the operator's attention to anything out of the ordinary.

Another requirement of an automatic analysis system is that of bookkeeping. There must be no discrepancy between the sequence of samples fed into the analyzer and the sequence of answers coming out. This may be difficult in multistep analyses, where a number of samples are in progress simultaneously.

Most automated analytical systems are built around one major instrumental approach. Sample handling, reagent addition, and other features are available if required, often supplied as discrete modules. In most cases the chemistry of specific analytical procedures is adapted from standard nonautomated methods. Minor changes are often made for reasons of convenience, so that all procedures to be used on a given instrument will fit into the same format in such features as time and temperature required for color development.

Automatic analyzers fall into two general classes: continuous-flow systems, and batch oriented types. Both have specific advantages and areas of usefulness. In the remainder of this chapter, a few representative examples of automated instruments of both kinds will be examined. The emphasis will be on the chemical and mechanical features, rather than on the perquisite electronics. The latter, particulary control by microprocessors, will be postponed to later chapters.

CONTINUOUS-FLOW SYSTEMS

Imagine a stream of color-forming reagent solution passing through a length of plastic tubing to a filter photometer equipped with a flow-through cuvet. Suppose now that a small portion of a sample solution is injected by a hypodermic syringe into the reagent some distance upstream from the photometer, as in Fig. 25-1. A colored slug or zone of sample will be formed, and will travel along the tube to the photometer. The detector will show a response as the colored material passes through the cuvet, and the integrated signal will relate directly to the amount of sample.

For such a system to give satisfactory results, several criteria must be met. The extent of the reaction must be exactly reproducible, and the integrity of samples must be maintained. One way of ensuring that these requirements are met is to segment the flowing stream by a series of air bubbles.[3,4] The action of the bubbles is to create turbulence in each segment of solution so that mixing is complete within that small volume. They also assist in cleaning the tube between samples. An inconvenience caused by the presence of the air bubbles is the need of a special "debubbler" to remove them prior to entrance into the detector.

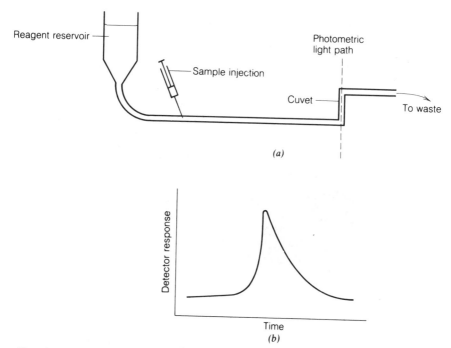

Figure 25-1 Illustrating the principle of continuous-flow analysis: (*a*) schematic of a typical apparatus; (*b*) detector response.

Another approach is to use a narrow-bore tube (~ 0.5 mm) without air segmentation. Under these conditions the flow is laminar. The mixing of sample and reagent is reproducible, though less than complete, being principally the result of diffusion.[5,6] This method, known as *flow-injection analysis* (FIA), is of more recent development than the air-segmented, and appears to be preferable in terms of increased speed of operation and reduced expense, though it appears to be less easily adapted to multistep analytical procedures. The two methods are capable of similar precision (within 1 or 2 percent). Both can be applied to a wide variety of analyses, using photometric and electrochemical detection techniques.

A typical example of flow analysis is the determination of calcium in blood serum by the air-segmented method. Figure 25-2 shows the pertinent apparatus, as supplied by one manufacturer, and Fig. 25-3 the schematic diagram. In the latter figure, the nine numbered horizontal lines at the right represent utilized channels in the standard 14-channel peristaltic pump; the related decimal fraction is the inside diameter (in inches) of the correct plastic tubing. In operation, dilute HCl is pumped through channel 4 and mixed with air (channel 2) at a T-connection. The flow rates are such that the acid stream is segmented by air bubbles spaced at about 1-cm intervals. The sample (serum or plasma) is pumped through channel 6 to join with the HCl stream. The next step is dialysis; the acidified sample is passed through a long spiral passage provided with a cellophane septum. In an identical passage on the other side of the septum flows a similarly segmented stream of HCl from pump channels 8 and 10. Ionic components of the sample (including Ca^{2+} and Mg^{2+}) diffuse into the second stream, while protein and other large organic molecules cannot pass the barrier and are pumped to waste.

Figure 25-2 General view of a continuous-flow analyzer: the Technicon AutoAnalyzer. From right to left, the modules are: sample turntable, peristaltic pump (with plastic cover), thermostated bath containing mixing coils, photometric analyzer beneath the strip-chart recorder, and computer controls. (*Technicon Instruments Corporation.*)

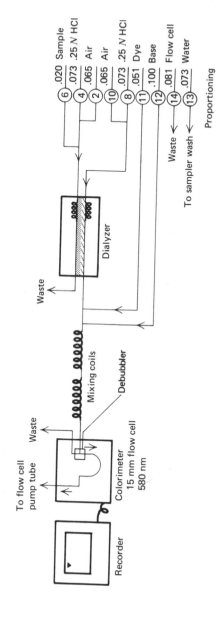

Figure 25-3 Technicon AutoAnalyzer flow sheet for calcium determination. (*Technicon Instruments Corporation.*)

473

At this point a reagent solution containing the dye cresolphthalein and 8-quinolinol (to suppress Mg^{2+} interference) is added, followed immediately by a 0.5 M solution of diethylamine. Sample and reagent are mixed thoroughly by passage through a mixing coil, and then flow into the photometer. Here the air bubbles are removed from the liquid stream, which then passes through the cuvet and pump channel 14 to waste. Channel 13 pumps water to rinse the sampling device. The entire procedure is capable of as many as 60 determinations per hour. Each sample is preceded by a wash cycle to remove traces of any former sample. Standard solutions are interspersed at intervals for calibration. The results are plotted on a strip-chart recorder.

BATCH PROCESSES

Mettler Instrument Corporation

Mettler has designed an automated analytical system based on titration. Any type of reaction capable of giving a potentiometric end point with ion-selective, pH, or redox electrodes can be implemented. Motor-driven syringe burets of several different capacities are easily interchanged. The controls are flexible, so that the titration can be stopped at the end point or a continuing curve can be recorded well past the end point. Alternatively, data can be displayed or printed out in either analog or digital form, or fed directly to a computer.

In a fully extended system, samples are weighed (on an electronic balance) directly into a series of up to 44 beakers. These are transported sequentially by a pneumatic drive to the titration head, where each is titrated. The results are calculated automatically and printed out on paper tape.

American Monitor Corporation

The "Programmachem" automates photometric analyses (primarily clinical) within the wavelength range 325 to 800 nm, with a grating spectrophotometer. As many as 89 samples can be loaded into the instrument at one time, and analyzed at the rate of 350 per hour. As each liquid sample is rotated in turn to the operating position, a probe dips into it and withdraws an accurately measured aliquot which it then transfers to a reaction tube. Here it is diluted, and reagent added to develop a color. Absorbance measurement at a preselected wavelength completes the analysis. The results are computed internally and printed out on a paper strip.

Reagent solutions for as many as 25 different tests are stored in the Programmachem cabinet, and selected according to instructions punched into a program card. In common with most automatic analyzers, this one is intended for applications in which a large number of similar determinations are required, but where it may be desirable to change over quickly to a different analysis. The operator can run a series of blood glucose determinations, for example, and then change to cholesterol merely by inserting the proper program card and initiating a purge cycle to rid the system of the previous reagents.

E. I. Du Pont de Nemours & Company

The Du Pont Automatic Clinical Analyzer (ACA) follows a unique plan. A set of reagents for a single determination are premeasured by the manufacturer and encapsulated in a special plastic kit or pack, which also serves as the reaction chamber and cuvet for the ultimate photometric determination. Packs for certain tests contain individual disposable chromatographic columns to isolate specific constituents or molecular-weight fractions.

A separate pack is used for each test performed on each sample. Each pack carries both the printed name of the test (for the benefit of the operator) and a binary code to instruct the analyzer. The instrument is programmed by insertion of the appropriate pack or packs behind each sample container in an input tray. The analyzer automatically injects a portion of the sample into each pack in succession, mixes the reagents, waits a preset length of time, forms a precise optical cell within the transparent pack walls, and measures the reaction product photometrically. These operations are precisely controlled and monitored by a built-in computer which also calculates the concentrations and prints out a report sheet for each sample. This report contains all the test results on that sample, together with the patient identification.

Figure 25-4 shows one of the analysis packs. As many as seven reagents are located in inner sealed pouches, to be broken open at the appropriate points in the cycle. After automatic injection of the sample followed by diluent, the pack is clipped to a moving chain to be transported from station to station through the apparatus shown in Fig. 25-5. After being heated to 37°C, the pack is pressed

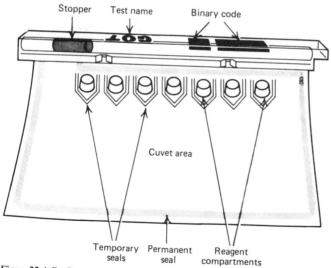

Figure 25-4 Du Pont ACA plastic analytical pack, showing seven reagent pouches. The digital code can be read by the instrument to identify the test to be performed. The sample is inserted through a tube from the left, shown closed with a stopper. (*E. I. Du Pont de Nemours & Co.*)

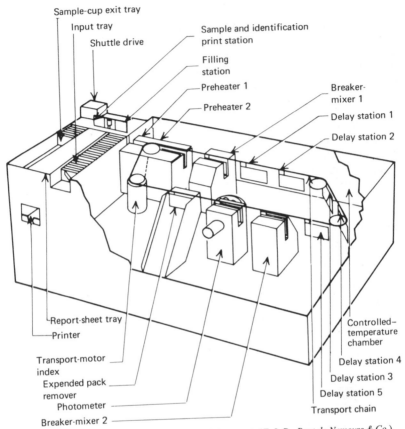

Figure 25-5 Cutaway plan of the Du Pont ACA instrument. (*E. I. Du Pont de Nemours & Co.*)

between jaws to break the first four of the seven reagent pouches, mixing their contents with the sample. The pack then passes through five delay stations to give adequate time (about 3 min) for full color development to occur, before the release of the remaining three reagents. The pack next moves to the photometer station where it is pressed between silica plates to form a cuvet exactly 1 cm thick. The photometer uses interference filters to isolate wavelength bands within the range of 340 to 600 nm. The expended pack is automatically discarded.

GeMSAEC Centrifugal Analyzer†

The analytical system designated by this acronym is built around a specially designed centrifuge.[7] All necessary dilutions and additions of reagents, as well

---

† The acronym stands for the original sponsors, the Institute of General Medical Sciences and the U.S. Atomic Energy Commission; the work was carried out at the Oak Ridge National Laboratory.

as spectrophotometric measurements, are carried out while the centrifuge is in motion. Figure 25-6[8,9] shows (a) a reagent and sample preloaded into cavities in a plastic rotor. Part (b) depicts the result of spinning the rotor; centrifugal force mixes the liquids and transfers them to a third cavity. In (c) the mixed solution is transferred further to a position where a light beam can pass vertically through the solution. In another form of rotor, a reagent can be added equally to all stations while the centrifuge is rotating.

The photomultiplier detector sees a continuing series of pulses, each corresponding to one sample space in the rotor, separated by dark intervals. Standards and blanks are included in each loaded rotor of 17 or more positions. A computer corrects for dark current, calculates concentrations, and averages the results over many rotations of the centrifuge.

The GeMSAEC equipment is now available commercially, and is finding many applications.

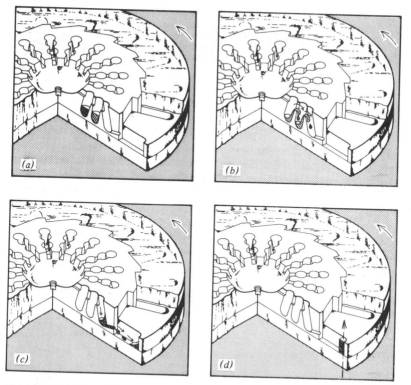

Figure 25-6 Principle of operation of the GeMSAEC centrifugal analyzer. (a) Reagent and sample loaded in place; (b) the same, in process of transfer; (c) the same, being further transferred into position for optical observation, shown in (d). The vertical dashed line in (d) shows the path of the light beam for photometric measurement. (*Analytical Chemistry.*[8])

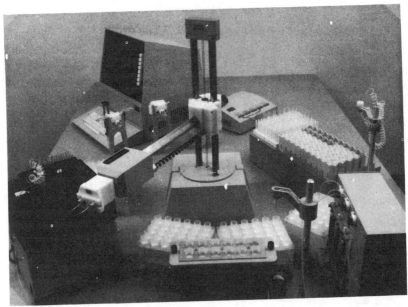

Figure 25-7 A laboratory robot: a computer-controlled arm and hand for manipulating samples. (*Zymark Corporation.*)

Zymark Corporation

This company is devoted to the improvement of laboratory procedures through *robotics*, the use of mechanical devices under computer control, to manipulate samples. An example is the "robot" shown in Fig. 25-7. This consists of a "hand" held by an "arm," that can be made to move vertically, radially, and circularly. The "fingers" can, for example, pick up a sample tube from a rack, hold it under a pipet tip (front, left) for the addition of reagent, shake it, place it in a photometer (front, right), then place it in another rack for discard. It can do all this without making mistakes or getting tired. The information from the photometer, together with sample identification codes, is entered into computer memory for future printing out.

This represents a new kind of technology that will undoubtedly become more prevalent in the future.

REFERENCES

1. D. A. Burns, *Anal. Chem.*, **1981**, *53*, 1403A.
2. G. D. Owens and R. J. Eckstein, *Anal. Chem.*, **1982**, 54, 2347.
3. L. T. Skeggs, *Anal. Chem.*, **1966**, *38*(6), 31A; see also literature of Technicon Instruments Corporation.

4. J. Salpeter and F. LaPerch, *Am. Lab.*, **1981**, *13(9)*, 78.
5. D. Betteridge, *Anal. Chem.*, **1978**, *50*, 832A.
6. J. Ruzicka and E. H. Hansen, *Flow Injection Analysis*, Wiley-Interscience, New York, **1981**.
7. N. G. Anderson, *Science*, **1969**, *166*, 317.
8. C. D. Scott and C. A. Burtis, *Anal. Chem.*, **1973**, *45*, 327A.
9. T. O. Tiffany, C. A. Burtis, J. C. Mailen, and L. H. Thacker, *Anal. Chem.*, **1973**, *45*, 1716.

TWENTY-SIX

GENERAL CONSIDERATIONS IN ANALYSIS

We have now completed a survey of some of the most useful analytical methods available to the chemist. We must now give some consideration to the problem of choosing the most appropriate method for any analytical problem that may arise.

Suppose that you, as an analytical chemist, are asked to devise a procedure for the quantitative determination of substance X. Here is a checklist of some of the questions you might ask before undertaking the task:

1. Why is the analysis desired? Is the sample a representative one? If not, it may make no sense to analyze it.
2. What is the matrix or host material in which the desired substance is found?
3. What impurities are likely to be present, and in approximately what concentrations?
4. What range of quantities can be expected for X?
5. What degree of precision and accuracy is required?
6. What reference standards are available?
7. Is the analysis to be performed in the laboratory, in a plant location, or in the field?
8. How many samples are expected per day?
9. Is it essential that the answers be obtained quickly, and if so, how quickly?
10. Is long-term reliability required, as for continuous unattended operation, and to what extent can it be traded off to lower the cost of equipment?
11. In what physical form is the answer desired (written report, analog recording, etc.)?
12. What special or unusual facilities are available that might affect the selection of a method (e.g., an atomic reactor)?

It may happen that some compromise is necessary. High precision may not be compatible with speed, for instance. Ultimately, personal preference may well be the deciding factor, if other considerations are about equal. Thus photometric and polarographic methods may give about the same accuracy with similarly dilute solutions (although they may differ in selectivity), and the time consumed and cost of apparatus are similar. The analyst is then free to choose the method with which he or she is more familiar.

SENSITIVITY AND DETECTION LIMITS

The sensitivity S of an analytical method or instrument may be defined as the ratio of the change in response R to the change in the quantity or concentration C that is measured

$$S = \frac{dR}{dC} \quad \text{or} \quad \frac{\Delta R}{\Delta C} \tag{26-1}$$

where ΔR and ΔC represent small but finite differences. The sensitivity is likely to be dependent on experimental conditions. A parameter often used in preference to sensitivity is the *limit of detection*, defined as that quantity (or concentration) for which an analytical signal just disappears as the amount present approaches zero. In most cases, the signal, hence the concentration, must be considerably larger to permit unequivocal identification, and larger yet for a quantitative determination.

It is difficult to generalize about the relative ultimate detection limits for various methods, since the data differ widely from one element or type of compound to another. Karasek[1] has given typical figures for several methods (Table 26-1), and Morrison[2] has compiled a valuable comparison for several analytical methods as applied to all the elements for which data were then available. Figure 9-10 presents similar data for several spectroscopic techniques.

Table 26-1 Detection and identification limits for analytical methods† (g)

Method	Detection limits	Identification limits
Gas chromatography	10^{-6}–10^{-12}	
Infrared spectrophotometry	10^{-7}	10^{-6}
Ultraviolet spectrophotometry	10^{-7}	10^{-6}
NMR (time-averaged)	10^{-7}	10^{-5}
Mass spectrometry (batch inlet)	10^{-6}	10^{-5}
Mass spectrometry (direct probe)	10^{-12}	10^{-11}
GC-MS combination	10^{-11}	10^{-10}

† From F. W. Karasek.[1]

Such compilations can be taken as a general guide in the selection of an appropriate method, but exact detection limits may vary greatly with changes of experimental details, and often with the matrix. Preconcentration procedures will often permit marked extension of the limits.

The maximum span of concentrations over which reliable measurements can be made is known as the *dynamic range*. Its lower limit is established by random fluctuations (noise) in the instrumental response. The ratio of signal to noise (S/N) should be at least 2 for a measurement to be considered just barely observable, but a larger ratio is required for high precision. The upper limit of the dynamic range is imposed by some kind of saturation phenomenon, e.g., the extent of solubility of the analyte, or a limit in the ability of the detector to respond. Some methods have a dynamic range covering 4 or 5 orders of magnitude, while others are limited to 1 order.

PRECISION AND ACCURACY

The precision of a determination, defined in terms of the spread of replicate determinations, is measured inversely by the standard deviation. The smaller its value, the better the precision. Precision is intimately related to the accuracy, which is the closeness between the observed result and the known or "true" value. A highly precise result may be poor in accuracy as the result of some systematic source of error that affects all replicate determinations alike.

The precision of a determination can be improved by repetition of the analysis and suitable statistical treatment of the data. Titration, as a general procedure,

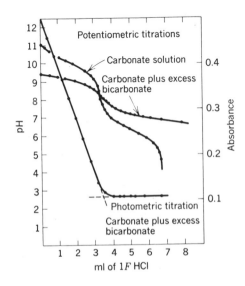

Figure 26-1 Potentiometric and photometric titrations of 3.4×10^{-2} M Na_2CO_3 containing 1 M $NaHCO_3$. (*Analytical Chemistry*.[3])

has a similar effect in that an extended series of measurements are taken to establish the titration curve that will determine the location of the equivalence point. Drawing a smooth curve through the points increases the overall precision in the same way that would be obtained by taking the same number of replicate readings on a solution without titrating. (It must be remembered, of course, that the information obtained may not be qualitatively the same, but may pertain to different equilibrium states.)

The precision obtainable from one method, as compared with another, is often affected by the form of the response curve, as well as by the inherent ability of the instrument to detect signals. Figure 26-1 shows two titration curves corresponding to the same reaction, the titration of carbonate in the presence of large concentrations of bicarbonate.[3] The potentiometric curve does not permit the precise determination of an equivalence point, whereas the photometric titration (at wavelength 235 nm, where carbonate absorbs but bicarbonate does not) shows an excellent end point, obtained by extrapolating two straight-line segments.

COMPARISON WITH STANDARDS

The majority of instrumental analytical methods involve the comparison of a physical property of the unknown with the corresponding property of a standard or series of standards containing the same material in known amounts. This may be achieved by means of a calibration curve, which is a plot of the magnitude of the physical property against the concentration of the desired constituent (or some simple function of the concentration, such as its logarithm or reciprocal). Sometimes the shape of the curve is predicted by theory (Beer's law, the Ilkovič equation, etc.), and it may be more convenient to perform a calculation based on the equation than to employ a calibration curve. This is the case, for example, in the determination of a cation by the measurement of a half-cell potential using the Nernst equation. The equation actually represents a curve that can be drawn for the graphical comparison of unknowns with the standard solution from which $E°$ was originally evaluated (cf. Fig. 14-1).

Another general procedure for comparison of unknowns and standards is to bracket the unknown between two suitably close standards, one slightly below and one slightly above it with respect to the quantity measured. This has the advantage that the system response can be considered linear over such a small range. This technique finds applications in optical comparators in which the intensity of color is matched directly by eye.

In all comparisons it is highly desirable that the standards duplicate the unknowns as closely as possible. This principle results in a substantial reduction of systematic errors that have the same effect on all solutions. In some cases the precision can be greatly increased, since the full-scale span of the instrument can be applied to measuring the difference between two rather similar values, rather than the distance of each value from zero. This has been mentioned in connection with photometric analysis in Chap. 3, but the principle is of wider applicability.

Closely related is the type of instrument in which the comparison between unknown and standard is made directly in a single operation. Examples include the potentiometric concentration cell, the thermal conductivity detector in GC, and photometers and spectrophotometers that employ a balanced system of two light beams passing through two samples. It must always be remembered that comparison with standards cannot improve the *precision* of an analysis, but only *its accuracy*. The accuracy of a determination can never exceed that with which the standard was prepared.

The preparation and preservation of standards for extremely dilute solutions (micromolar to nanomolar) can be quite difficult. The walls of a storage vessel tend to adsorb solutes, and may reduce the concentration significantly below the intended value; this can be overcome in favorable cases, by rinsing out the vessel with some of the solution to be stored.

An important aid in the direction of overall standardization is provided by the extensive series of standard materials made available by the National Bureau of Standards. Every sample is accompanied by a certificate bearing the concentration of each constituent, from the major elements down to those present in only a few thousandths of one percent. A great many determinations can be tested as to accuracy by means of these samples.

STANDARD ADDITION AND SUBTRACTION†

Undesirable matrix effects can be diminished or perhaps eliminated entirely by the application of the method of standard addition, in which a portion of standard is added directly to the sample. Consider first the case in which the instrument response R is directly proportional to concentration, after correction for any background. We can write, using subscript zero for the original solution,

$$R_0 = k \frac{M_0}{V_0} \qquad (26\text{-}2)$$

where concentration is represented by the number of moles M in volume V. Suppose now that we add a portion of a standard solution containing M_1 moles in volume V_1. Rewriting Eq. (26-2) for the resulting solution gives

$$R_1 = k\left[\frac{M_0 + M_1}{V_0 + V_1}\right] \qquad (26\text{-}3)$$

This can be simplified if V_1 is kept small with respect to V_0, easily accomplished by using a sufficiently concentrated standard, so that

$$R_1 = \frac{k}{V_0}(M_0 + M_1) \qquad (26\text{-}4)$$

† This section is adapted from Ref. 4, by permission.

Eliminating (k/V_0) between Eqs. (26-2) and (26-4), and solving for M_0, gives

$$M_0 = M_1 \left[\frac{R_0}{R_1 - R_0} \right] \qquad (26\text{-}5)$$

This procedure eliminates the majority of instrumental variables, represented by the constant k. A determination of M_1, and hence of the concentration, can then be made, given knowledge of the volume.

It can be shown[5] that best precision can be obtained when the added increment is somewhat larger than the amount of analyte initially present. A more complex treatment must be drawn upon in the presence of strong interferences with the desired analyte.[6]

It is essential that the measurements with and without the standard be made in the presence of identical amounts of all other components of the solution. It is not prudent to assume that the matrix effects are completely eliminated, however, so the procedure should be repeated with additional increments of standard to give readings R_2 and R_3. The results can be plotted as in Fig. 26-2, and M_0 evaluated graphically.

For the exponential case, where $R = R' + K \ln (M/V)$, a similar treatment, incrementing M, gives

$$M_0 = M_1 \left[\exp \left(\frac{R_1 - R_0}{k} \right) - 1 \right]^{-1} \qquad (26\text{-}6)$$

When applied to potentiometry, k becomes the factor RT/nF (where R is the gas constant).

Comparable expressions to Eqs. (26-5) and (26-6) can be derived for other functions of concentration.

Sometimes an analogous procedure called *standard subtraction* is applicable, in which one adds a known amount of a reagent that will effectively remove a

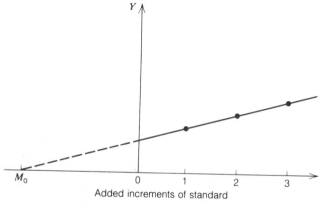

Figure 26-2 Graphical determination of M_0 from standard addition data. The plot can serve to check the linearity of response at concentrations greater than that of the analyte in the sample.

corresponding amount of the analyte from the sample by precipitation or complexation. The mathematical relations are the same as for standard addition, with appropriate changes of sign.

It is important to reiterate that, in any comparison with standards, all conditions must be held uniform. This is sometimes difficult or impossible to do, but is nevertheless required for highest precision. The ionic strength and the concentration of complexing agents, for example, should not be allowed to vary when a standard addition is made.

DATA PLOTTING

The precision with which data can be read from a graph can be greatly affected by the manner in which they are plotted. It will be instructive to consider a number

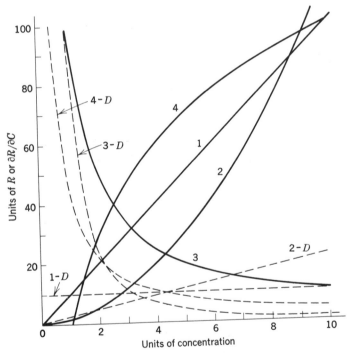

Figure 26-3 Various functions of concentration and their derivatives; the curves correspond to the following formulas:

(1) $R = k_1 C$	(1-D) $\partial R/\partial C = k_1$	$k_1 = 10$
(2) $R = k_2' C^2 + k_2 C$	(2-D) $\partial R/\partial C = 2k_2' C + k_2$	$k_2 = k_2' = 1$
(3) $R = k_3(1/C)$	(3-D) $\partial R/\partial C = -k_3(1/C^2)$†	$k_3 = 100$
(4) $R = k_4 \log C$	(4-D) $\partial R/\partial C = 0.434k_4(1/C)$	$k_4 = 100$

† The negative sign ignored for convenience in plotting.

of functions of the form $R = f(C)$, relating instrument response to a concentration term, which might describe the behavior of some analytical systems. In Fig. 26-3 curves are plotted for four such functions: (1) linear, $R = k_1 C$; (2) square-law or power series, $R = k_2' RC^2 + k_2 C$; (3) reciprocal, $R = k_3/C$; (4) logarithmic, $R = k_4 \log C$. The derivatives $\partial R/\partial C$ of these functions are also plotted. It is apparent from the figure that the reciprocal and logarithmic functions give very steep curves, hence greatest sensitivity, as defined above, at low concentrations, while the square function gives greater sensitivity at higher concentrations. For the linear function, as expected, the sensitivity is constant over the whole range.

The slopes in Fig. 26-3 are written as partial derivatives to emphasize the fact that there are likely to be other variables affecting the sensitivity. An example is spectrophotometric analysis, in which the sensitivity can be varied by a change in wavelength. The response curve will be of the same form, but the horizontal scale will be compressed or expanded.

It is often useful to plot data on log-log paper. There may be two reasons for doing this: (1) to compress data covering several orders of magnitude onto one set of coordinates, and (2) to determine the constants k and n in a relation of the form $y = kx^n$. The first of these objectives is attained, for example, when one plots an absorption spectrum as $\log A$ against wavelength (cf. Fig. 3-4); there is no theoretical reason for doing this, as there is in the plotting of A [$= \log(1/T)$] in place of T.

The second case is applicable only if the relation $y = kx^n$ actually describes the experimental system at hand. Data plotted in this manner in an attempt to discover a previously unknown mathematical relation may give the impression of a correlation more significant than is actually justified. Possible pitfalls and their avoidance have been vividly described by P. N. Rowe.[7]

PROBLEMS

26-1 Identify instrumental methods as corresponding to each of the functions plotted in Fig. 26-3, and show equations to justify your choices.

26-2 Beer's law can be expressed in the form $R = k_5 \cdot 10^C$. Plot this and its derivative on Fig. 26-3. (Select a value of k_5 such that $R = 10$ for $C = 4$ units.) Comment on the results.

26-3 How would you best determine water quantitatively in each of the following circumstances (outline a procedure where possible):

(a) Water vapor in tanks of compressed H_2 or O_2.
(b) Water dissolved in "pure" chloroform or ether.
(c) Water content of the atmosphere in a sealed space vehicle.
(d) Water collected in the bottom of a large gasoline storage tank.

26-4 Devise an instrumental method for the determination of TEL (tetraethyl lead) and TML (tetramethyl lead) when either or both may be present in a gasoline.

26-5 One of the most difficult chemical separations is between Zr and Hf. A result of the "lanthanide contraction" is that Zr and Hf atoms are almost precisely the same size, and this, together with their similar electronic structure, makes them nearly identical chemically. Suggest at least two tentative methods by which you might attack their separation. In each method, what data would you look for to evaluate success? What nonseparative analytical methods might be used to analyze mixtures of compounds of these elements?

26-6 Manganese and chromium can be determined in steel by oxidation to Mn(VII) and Cr(VI) followed by photometric determination. However, the color of Fe(III) will cause interference unless suitable precautions are taken. It is possible to remove the bulk of the iron by ether extraction in the presence of HCl, or by ion exchange following oxidation of the Mn and Cr, or the iron may be complexed with citrate, tartrate, or other reagents to destroy its color. Alternatively, the iron may be allowed to remain in the solution, and its absorbance corrected for by taking photometric readings before and after the oxidation of the Mn and Cr, or combinations of these methods could be employed. Compare these procedures critically. Why is mercury-cathode electrolysis inapplicable as a separation method?

26-7 Mention has been made of the use of NaI crystals "activated" by admixture of a trace of TlI, as a phosphor in scintillation counting. Devise a nondestructive method for determining the amount of TlI in NaI crystals. Estimate the expected precision.

REFERENCES

1. F. W. Karasek, *Anal. Chem.*, **1972**, *44(4)*; 32A.
2. G. H. Morrison and R. K. Skogerboe, in *Trace Analysis: Physical Methods*, G. H. Morrison (ed.), Wiley-Interscience, New York, **1965**.
3. A. L. Underwood and L. H. Howe, III, *Anal. Chem.*, **1962**, *34*, 692.
4. B. H. Vassos and G. W. Ewing, *Electroanalytical Chemistry*, Wiley-Interscience, New York, **1983**, pp. 207 ff.
5. K. L. Ratzlaff, *Anal. Chem.*, **1979**, *51*, 232.
6. B. E. H. Saxberg and B. R. Kowalski, *Anal. Chem.*, **1979**, *51*, 1031.
7. P. N. Rowe, *Chem. Tech.*, **1974**, *4*, 9.

TWENTY-SEVEN

ELECTRONIC CIRCUITRY FOR ANALYTICAL INSTRUMENTS

The great majority of instrumental methods treated in this book require electrical circuits, and this, in all but the simplest cases, implies the need for electronics. So for a full understanding of analytical instruments, their limitations and what can go wrong with them, some knowledge of electronics is essential. The account in this chapter and the next can only be considered a brief survey. No attempt is made to derive the fundamental mathematical relations; a more complete treatment can be found in Ref. 1 and other texts. Nevertheless, sufficient information should be found here to clarify most of the design problems encountered in the previous chapters.

The heart of any electronic device is one or more components that act directly on electrons. This includes a variety of solid state components, including semiconductor diodes, transistors, and photocells. These active elements can never stand alone; they always require supplementary circuits composed largely of resistors, capacitors, and inductors. A power supply is also required, which may be a selection of batteries, or may be rectified alternating current. In addition, there will frequently be included other components for convenience or safety, such as switches, fuses, and pilot lights.

Present-day electronic circuitry depends heavily on *integrated circuits* (ICs). Each IC contains the equivalent of many individual transistors and diodes, all fabricated as a unit on a single small piece ("chip") of silicon. ICs are packaged as plug-in units with up to 40 connecting pins.

There are many advantages to the use of ICs, as compared to the older discrete transistors and other components. The user does not need to master the intricacies of design of such units as logic gates or operational amplifiers; they have been designed for him by the manufacturer. An added advantage is that individual ICs are inexpensive and a supply of the common ones is easily kept on hand for replacement purposes or for building new devices.

SEMICONDUCTORS

A semiconductor is a solid substance that is intermediate between metallic conductors on the one hand and nonconductors (insulators) on the other. It is characterized by a relatively large negative temperature coefficient of resistance, whereas the coefficient is positive for metals; this provides a convenient criterion for distinguishing between the two types of conductors. By far the most used semiconductor material is elementary silicon. Germanium is used in place of silicon when its special properties are needed.

In a pure crystal of silicon (or germanium) each atom is bound covalently to each of four other atoms (the diamond structure) and, since each atom has just four valence electrons, it is fully satisfied by this structure. To make the crystal useful for electronic purposes, it must be *doped*, that is, a trace of impurity added. The foreign atoms must be of such nature that they can replace some of the host atoms in the crystal lattice.

If the impurity is a pentavalent element, such as arsenic or antimony, then each of its atoms possesses an extra valence electron beyond those needed for the covalent lattice bonds. The extra electrons are easily torn loose from their parent atoms by thermal energy, and then are free to wander at random throughout the lattice. The impurity atoms become unipositive ions imbedded in the crystal.

On the other hand, if the impurity is trivalent gallium, indium, or gold, then there will be a deficiency of one electron per atom. The spot where the electron is lacking is called a *hole*. Occasionally the thermal vibrations of an electron in a normal covalent bond will bring it so close to the hole that it will escape completely from its previous berth and move into the hole. The result of such a process is that the hole has moved from one spot to another within the lattice. In a piece of silicon doped in this way, the holes appear to wander freely through the crystal in a manner exactly analogous to the motion of the surplus electrons in a piece doped with arsenic or antimony. The mobility of the holes, however, is somewhat less than of the electrons.

Silicon in which the impurity is an electron donor is called *n*-type silicon, and that doped with electron-deficient atoms is *p*-type.† An electric field applied across a piece of doped silicon causes current to flow that is carried almost exclusively by the excess electrons or holes provided by the impurity. Thus the *majority carriers* in *n*-type silicon are electrons, and in *p*-type silicon are holes.

---

† It should be understood that silicon or germanium that is doped, even relatively heavily, is still from the *chemical* point of view extremely pure. A controlled impurity of the order of 1 ppm is usually adequate to impart the desired electrical properties.

DIODES

A crystal diode is a two-terminal semiconductor device that has the ability to pass current in one direction but to block it from flowing the other way. It is made from a chip of silicon or germanium that is partly p and partly n type, as indicated schematically in Fig. 27-1. When connected to a source of potential making the n region negative and the p region positive, the dominant carriers in both sections tend to move toward the pn junction. At the junction electrons from the n side fall into holes from the p side, and so current flows easily. In the reverse connection, with the n region positive and the p region negative, both holes and electrons are pulled away from the junction, leaving an intermediate region depleted of carriers, so current cannot flow (except for a brief transient when the potential is first applied).

The characteristic current-voltage curves for silicon and germanium diodes are shown in Fig. 27-2. For positive (i.e., forward) potentials, the current is an exponential function of the voltage. If a negative (reverse) potential is applied, the current, called the *leakage current*, is almost zero and nearly constant, until (for silicon) a critical value E_z is reached, at which the current increases (negatively) until limited by the series resistance in the circuit. This critical point, called the *zener*, or *breakdown*, voltage, corresponds to the potential necessary to tear electrons out of covalent bonds in the crystal, thus creating pairs of positive and negative carriers which are swept toward the respective circuit connections. By varying the manufacturing technique, silicon diodes can be prepared with zener voltages anywhere in the range of 2 to 200 V. Germanium diodes have a lower reverse resistance than silicon, and no well-defined zener breakdown potential.

Diodes have many areas of usefulness. In the larger sizes they are used as power rectifiers to convert alternating to direct current as a power source for other devices. Smaller diodes are applied to the rectification of ac signals; in this

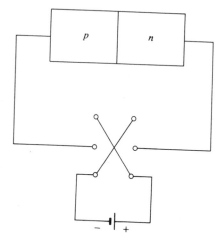

Figure 27-1 A *pn*-junction diode, schematic.

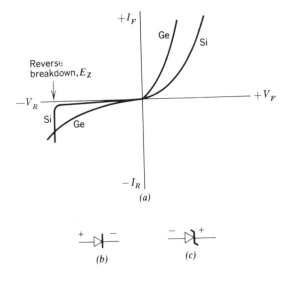

(a)

(b)   (c)

Figure 27-2 (a) Dc characteristics of germanium and silicon diodes. (b) symbol for a simple diode. (c) symbol for a zener diode. The current scale for the lower half of (a) is exaggerated relative to the top half.

service they can be called *detectors* or *demodulators*. Diodes optimized for sharp zener breakdown potential, called *zener diodes*, are used extensively to provide reference voltages.

TRANSISTORS

The basic amplifying semiconductor device is the transistor. It exists in many modifications, the most important for our purposes being classed as (1) bipolar, and (2) field-effect transistors.

The bipolar transistor (Fig. 27-3) consists of a wafer of silicon containing two p-type segments separated by a thin layer of n-type material, thus forming two junctions each of which has the properties described above for diodes. For transistor action, the junction between one p region, called the *emitter*, and the n material, called the *base*, is given a small forward bias, while the junction with the second p region, the *collector*, is reverse-biased. Current can flow easily across the

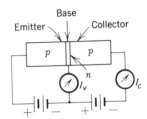

Figure 27-3 Schematic representation of a *pnp* transistor. The p-type regions are obtained by alloying a metal containing p-type impurities into an n-type silicon wafer, in one mode of fabrication.

emitter-base junction. The base region, being both thin and lightly doped, is poor in electrons, so that most of the holes from the emitter diffuse across it, as they have a greater probability of being "collected" by the large collector junction than of combining with electrons in the base. The ratio of collector current to I_C to base current I_B is determined solely by the geometry of the structure. The magnitudes of these currents, however, are determined by the voltage applied between the base and emitter, since an increased positive potential at the base makes it easier for holes to cross into the collector. This is the source of the amplifying ability of the transistor.

The transistor described above is of the *pnp* type, but it is equally possible to fabricate a unit with the opposite characteristics, an *npn* transistor. The two types can be used in the same circuits, except that the polarities of all voltages and currents must be reversed. Figure 27-4 shows the standard symbols for the two types. The arrowhead on the emitter indicates the direction of easy positive-current flow for the emitter-base junction.

The amplification factor, denoted by β, is the ratio of a small change in collector current I_c to the change in base current I_b responsible for it

$$\beta = \frac{dI_c}{dI_b} \tag{27-1}$$

For transistors intended for amplifying small signals, β usually lies between 50 and 200, but power transistors have much lower values (5 to 10).

A simple circuit that demonstrates the amplification possible with a single transistor is given in Fig. 27-5. The circuit is powered from a battery or rectifier at voltage V_{cc} relative to ground. Resistors R_1, R_2, and R_E, known as *bias resistors*, provide a suitable dc potential between base and emitter, so that when no signal is present the transistor will draw a small current, about the middle of its range. Suppose that an ac signal of 1-mV amplitude, originating in a source with a resistance of $R_S = 1$ kΩ, is fed into the base of the transistor through the coupling capacitor C_S. This produces an ac component of base current equal to the ratio E_S/R_S, namely 10^{-3} V$/10^{+3}$ $\Omega = 10^{-6}$ A or 1 μA. Multiplying by β (100) shows that the resulting ac component of the collector current will be 100 μA. This current, flowing through the *load* resistor R_L produces an ac potential drop of $(100 \times 10^{-6}$ A$)(15 \times 10^3$ $\Omega) = 1.50$ V. To summarize, 1 mV in gives 1.5 V out.

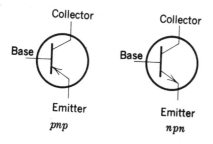

Base — Collector / Emitter

pnp

Base — Collector / Emitter

npn

Figure 27-4 Symbols for *pnp* and *npn* transistors.

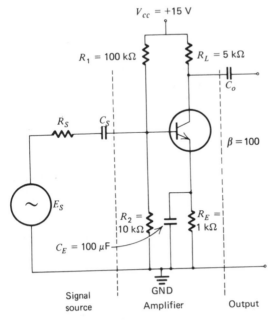

Figure 27-5 A single-stage transistor amplifier. The component values are illustrative only. For a *pnp* transistor, the only change necessary is the sign of V_{cc}.

The *gain* of this circuit (the ratio of the output to the input) can be calculated in terms of voltage, current, or power. These gains are:

$$\text{Voltage gain} = G_V = 1.50/(10^{-3}) = 1500$$

$$\text{Current gain} = G_I = \beta = 100$$

$$\text{Power gain}\dagger = G_P = G_V G_I = 150,000$$

THE FIELD-EFFECT TRANSISTOR (FET)

This device works on quite a different principle from that of the bipolar transistor discussed above. Consider the sketch in Fig. 27-6. A bar of *n*-type silicon, called the *channel*, is provided with connections at each end, the *source*, S, and *drain*, D. The channel is sandwiched between layers of *p*-material (connected together) called the *gate*, G. In some models the gate is all one piece, completely surrounding the channel. Both *n*- and *p*-channel FETs are available.

If no voltage is applied to the gate, current will flow unhindered through the channel, electrons passing from source to drain. In its normal mode, the gate-to-

---

† Since power is given by the product of potential and current, the power gain is

$$G_P = \frac{E_{\text{out}} \cdot I_{\text{out}}}{E_{\text{in}} \cdot I_{\text{in}}} = G_V \cdot G_I$$

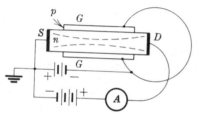

Figure 27-6 Schematic representation of an n-channel FET.

channel pn junction is reverse-biased. This has the effect of depleting the area between the gate and the dashed lines, with respect to electrons, compressing the channel and increasing its resistance, thus decreasing the flow of source-to-drain current. Voltage amplification can be achieved by placing a load resistor in series with the drain. A change in gate potential, by changing the current through the load resistor, can produce a much larger change in output voltage.

The reverse biasing also prevents the passage of appreciable current in the gate circuit. The voltage applied to the gate may be as great as several volts. Since no current can flow in this circuit, the gate characteristic is given in volts, rather than in current units as with bipolar transistors.

The principle advantage of the FET is its high input impedance, resulting from the reverse-bias condition; this impedance may be as high as tens or even hundreds of megohms.

The *insulated-gate FET*, often called MOSFET (for *metal oxide semiconductor* FET) is a modification wherein a thin film of insulating material, usually silicon dioxide, separates the gate from the channel. This eliminates the rectifying junction, so that the gate can be given either polarity without drawing current. The electrostatic field between gate and channel is still able to modify the distribution of holes or electrons in the channel, and so determine its resistance. The MOSFET has the highest input impedance of any transistor. Figure 27-7 gives the conventional symbols for the several types of FET.

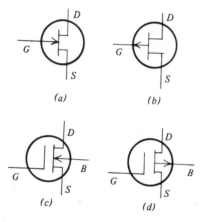

Figure 27-7 Standard symbols for FETs. (*a*) n-channel FET; (*b*) p-channel FET; (*c*) n-channel MOSFET; (*d*) p-channel MOSFET. *B* denotes connection to the bulk silicon substrate.

POWER SUPPLIES

Most modern laboratory instruments are powered from the ac lines (115 V, 60 Hz in the United States). Direct current is obtained by rectification with silicon diodes. There are several possible configurations for the rectifier diodes, each of which has merit for particular applications. The most common uses four diodes in a bridge connection, as in the circuit of Fig. 27-8, which operates as follows: On each half-cycle of the alternating current, two of the diodes conduct while the other two are reverse-biased, so that a pulsating dc potential appears across the output terminals of the diode bridge. On the next half-cycle, the functions of the diodes are interchanged, giving the same polarity of output. The large capacitor (C_1) acts as a filter to smooth out the pulsations. The component marked 7815 is a voltage regulating IC that converts the direct current from the rectifier (20–25 V) to exactly 15 V. The output capacitor (C_2) is optional, but increases the speed with which the regulator corrects for a change in load. Other regulators give other output voltages as indicated by the last two digits in their designation.

High voltage at low current (a few kilovolts at less than 1 mA) is required for such applications as ion-counters and photomultipliers. These requirements can be met by the use of an oscillator† producing alternating current at a few hundred kilohertz. The output can be stepped up in voltage by an air-core transformer, and rectified to give a very high potential. Filtering requirements are easily met at such a high frequency. Modern trend is toward an oscillator using two power transistors, combined with the transformer and rectifiers in a single package.

A source of *constant current* is required for coulometric applications and for excitation of certain light sources. This can most easily be obtained by connecting the regulator as in Fig. 27-9. The current delivered will be $I_{out} = (12/R) + I_0$, where I_0 is a constant for each regulator, about 1 or 2 mA. Thus if a current of

† Oscillators are discussed in a later paragraph.

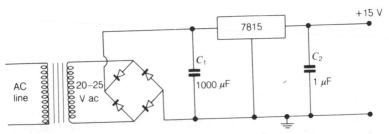

Figure 27-8 A regulated 15-V power supply. The rectifier bridge is available in a single package. For other voltages, substitute other items in the 7800 series of regulators.

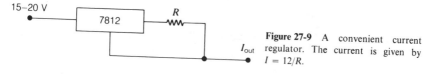

Figure 27-9 A convenient current regulator. The current is given by $I = 12/R$.

25 mA is desired, R should be $12/0.025 = 480 \ \Omega$, neglecting I_0. This can be trimmed to the exact value by a small variable resistor in series with R.

OPERATIONAL AMPLIFIERS

Discrete transistor circuits such as that in Fig. 27-5, and extensions of it with several transistors, are seldom used today because of the readily available, convenient and compact ICs known as *operational amplifiers* (op amps). The name derives from the ability of such an amplifier to perform mathematical operations on a signal presented to it. Appropriate external connections can establish conditions so that the output voltage will be (1) the algebraic sum of two or more input voltages, (2) the product of a voltage and a constant factor, (3) the time integral of the input, or (4) the time derivative of the input. Other mathematical functions, such as taking logarithms, squaring, or multiplying or dividing one variable quantity by another, can be implemented by the use of nonlinear components along with the amplifiers. Op amps can be used at any frequency from zero (i.e., direct current) up to about 10 kHz, and special models can go up into the megahertz region.

An op amp must have the following attributes: (1) it must have a large voltage gain, at least 10^4, with many commercial units well above 10^6; (2) it must have a large input impedance, not less than 10^5, often up to 10^{12};† (3) it must be capable of being nulled, that is to give zero output for zero input; and (4) it must have only minimal drift (i.e., a slow change in output even though the input is constant).

Most op amps have two input terminals, only one of which produces an inversion of sign. The terminals are conventionally marked + and −, as in Fig. 27-10. These designations do not mean that the terminals are to be connected only to potentials of the indicated sign, as would be true with similar markings on a voltmeter, but rather that the one marked − gives sign inversion whereas the other does not. In case the noninverting (+) input is not needed in a particular application, it should be connected to a point where the potential is zero, called the *ground* potential.

The basic connections are shown in Fig. 27-10b. Most circuits using op amps depend on negative feedback:‡ A connection is made through a suitable impedance

---

† Impedance in an electrical circuit is defined as the ratio of the potential across a circuit or component to the current flowing. In direct current circuitry, the impedance is identical to the resistance, but these often differ in ac circuits.

‡ An exception is the *comparator* circuit, mentioned later in this chapter.

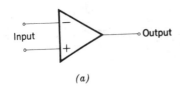

(a)

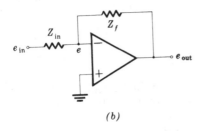

(b)

Figure 27-10 Operational amplifiers. (a) general symbol: (b) connected as an inverting amplifier, such that $e_{out} = -(Z_f/Z_{in})e_{in}$, provided that the internal gain $A \gg 1$. The triangular symbol implies that a suitable power supply is provided; all potentials are referred to ground.

Z_f from the output to the inverting input. If the signal to be sensed by the amplifier is a voltage, then it must be applied through an input impedance, Z_{in}. Since the input to the amplifier proper draws negligible current, the current flowing in Z_{in}, namely $(e_{in} - e)/Z_{in}$, must be equal to that in the feedback loop, given by $(e - e_{out})/Z_f$. This feedback current must come from the output of the amplifier. When an input signal is applied, the amplifier adjusts itself so that the feedback and input currents are precisely equal, or

$$\frac{e_{in} - e}{Z_{in}} = \frac{e - e_{out}}{Z_f} \qquad (27\text{-}2)$$

which can be rearranged to give

$$e_{out} = \frac{e(Z_f + Z_{in}) - e_{in}Z_f}{Z_{in}} \qquad (27\text{-}3)$$

This relation can be simplified by taking into consideration the high inherent gain of the amplifier (often called its *open-loop gain*). If the gain is 10^6, then an output of 10 V implies that the input to the amplifier will be at a potential only 10 μV removed from ground. This is so close to ground that the summing junction† is commonly said to be at *virtual ground* (provided that the noninverting input is grounded). Hence in Eq. (27-3) the term involving e can be neglected, giving

$$e_{out} = -e_{in} \cdot \frac{Z_f}{Z_{in}} \qquad (27\text{-}4)$$

---

† The *summing junction*, or *summing point*, is a designation given to the inverting input connection of an op amp, because it is here that the input and feedback currents are *summed* to zero.

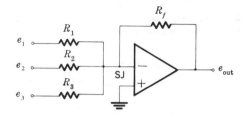

Figure 27-11 Operational amplifier connected as a summer. SJ denotes the summing junction. For $A \gg 1$,

$$e_{\text{out}} = -R_f\left(\frac{e_1}{R_1} + \frac{e_2}{R_2} + \frac{e_3}{R_3}\right)$$

which is the basic working equation of this op amp circuit. In practice, the ratio Z_f/Z_{in} is seldom made greater than 100 nor less than 0.01. If Z_f and Z_{in} are purely resistive, they can be replaced by corresponding R's.

Several inputs can be connected simultaneously to the summing junction, as in Fig. 27-11, in which case the output becomes the negative sum of the inputs, each multiplied by the appropriate ratio. Any of these multiple inputs can be given a negative signal, resulting in subtraction.

To perform integration, the feedback element must be a capacitor (Fig. 27-12). Since the input and feedback currents must be equal, and since the current flowing in a capacitor is given by the time derivative of the potential, it follows that

$$\frac{e_{\text{in}}}{R_{\text{in}}} = -C\frac{de_{\text{out}}}{dt} \tag{27-5}$$

which is equivalent to

$$e_{\text{out}} = -\frac{1}{R_{\text{in}}C}\int e_{\text{in}}\,dt + e_{(t=0)} \tag{27-6}$$

To differentiate, the locations of R and C in the circuit of Fig. 27-12 must be interchanged, and the relation is

$$e_{\text{out}} = -R_fC\frac{de_{\text{in}}}{dt} \tag{27-7}$$

This method of differentiation is little used in practice, as it overemphasizes the effect of random noise at the input.

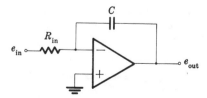

Figure 27-12 Operational amplifier connected as an integrator. For $A \gg 1$

$$e_{\text{out}} = -\frac{1}{R_{\text{in}}C}\int_0^t e_{\text{in}}\,dt$$

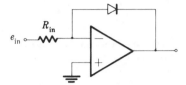

Figure 27-13 Op amp connected to give a logarithmic function. The diode is shown oriented for positive e_{in}. For $A \gg 1$,

$$e_{out} = k \log e_{in} - k'$$

in which k and k' are numerical constants.

The logarithm of a variable can be obtained by making use of the exponential characteristic of a forward-biased pn junction. Figure 27-13 shows the connections. The equation can be derived by setting equal the currents through the input and feedback portions of the circuit. The current-voltage relation of a diode is approximated by

$$\log I = k_1 V \qquad \text{or} \qquad I = k_2 \text{ antilog } V \qquad (27\text{-}8)$$

from which it follows that

$$e_{in}/R_{in} = k_2 \text{ antilog } e_{out}$$

or

$$e_{out} = k_3 \log e_{in} - k_4 \qquad (27\text{-}9)$$

Experiment shows that a silicon diode is more satisfactory for this purpose than one of germanium, but that a silicon transistor with grounded base (Fig. 27-13b) is better yet; it can give a linear-log relation over at least four logarithmic decades.

An exponential (antilogarithmic) function can be taken by interchanged connections, as in Fig. 27-14. It is possible to carry out multiplication or division of variables by taking logarithms, adding or subtracting them, then extracting the antilogarithm. All diodes or equivalent transistors must be at the same temperature (or compensated for temperature changes), to ensure precision results.

Errors in Operational Amplifiers

One major asset of op amps is that they follow closely these elementary mathematical relations. There are, however, several potential sources of error.

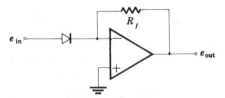

Figure 27-14 Op amp connected to give an exponential (antilogarithmic) function, shown for positive values of e_{in}. For $A \gg 1$

$$e_{out} = k \exp(-k'e_{in})$$

where k and k' are numerical constants.

Finite gain The formulas given earlier are all dependent on the assumption that the open-loop gain of the amplifier is large compared to the ratio Z_f/Z_{in}, which may be called the closed-loop gain. A detailed analysis shows that the equation for the performance of a simple inverter (Fig. 27-10b) is

$$e_{out} = -e_{in} \frac{Z_f}{Z_{in}} \left(\frac{A}{A - G} \right) \qquad (27\text{-}10)$$

where A is the open-loop gain and G is the closed-loop gain. This enables one to estimate the error resulting from too small a value of A: for example, if $A = 10^5$ and $G = 10^3$, then e_{out}/e_{in} becomes 1.01×10^3, an error of 1 percent. If greater precision is needed, one must either keep G below 1000 or use a better amplifier with $A > 10^5$.

Offset voltage Ideally an amplifier should give zero output for zero input, but slight asymmetries in the internal circuitry are likely to exist so that even with both inputs grounded a small voltage will often appear at the output. A variable trimming resistor can correct this condition. Slow drifts of the offset may arise even after the trimmer is adjusted, due to temperature changes, and this may well be the feature that limits the usefulness of the amplifier for use with slowly varying signals. Offset is especially detrimental when the amplifier is connected as an integrator, since the effect is cumulative.

Bias current Sometimes an op amp fails to behave ideally in that it draws some appreciable current at its inputs. This bias current can be compensated for, at least in part, by inserting a resistor of a few kilohms between the noninverting input and ground. The voltage drop developed in this resistor tends to compensate for the drop caused by similar bias currents in the input and feedback resistors. As with offset voltage, this fault is particularly objectionable in integrators.

TRANSDUCER APPLICATIONS OF OPERATIONAL AMPLIFIERS

Transducers in general are devices that can convert energy from one form to another, but in our context, the term can be limited to those devices that convert information about a chemical system into electrical signals. Transducers can be classified conveniently according to the electrical quantity that represents the signal. There are three major categories, in which the transducer can be considered to be (1) a variable resistor, (2) a source of potential, or (3) a current source.

The class of *resistive transducers* includes photoconductive cells, thermistors, metallic resistance thermometers, and cells for electrolytic conductivity. In

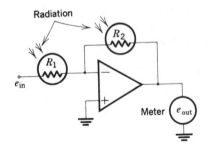

Figure 27-15 Resistance measurements with op amps.

The ratio of two resistances (shown as photoresistors): $E_{out} = -(R_2/R_1)E_{in}$.

principle, any of these can be used either as Z_{in} or Z_f in the op amp circuit of Fig. 27-10b. If the variable e_{in} is replaced by a constant potential E_{in}, then observations of e_{out} will allow the unambiguous determination of the resistance of the transducer. The reciprocal (a *conductance*) can be obtained directly by placing the transducer in the input circuit.

If the *ratio* of two resistances is desired, as it might be, for instance, in some dual-beam photometers, two identical transducers can be used in place of the two impedances in the op amp circuit, as in Fig. 27-15.

Transducers that produce *potentials* include the many potentiometric electrode combinations, photovoltaic cells, and thermocouples. The preferred circuit for this service is the *voltage follower*, shown in Fig. 27-16. The direct feedback from the output to the summing junction ensures that the input voltage will be exactly reproduced at the output. The direct connection of the transducer to an op amp input prevents current from being drawn from it, whereas moderate current, as may be needed to operate further equipment, *can* be taken from the output. The circuit of Fig. 27-10b is not suitable for potentiometric measurements because it requires current to flow from the source.

Current-producing transducers include vacuum (or gas-filled) phototubes and photomultipliers, flame-ionization GC detectors, and electrodes for voltammetry and amperometry. These current sources can be connected directly to the summing junction of an op amp, as in Fig. 27-17. In order to keep this junction at virtual ground, the amplifier forces an equal current through the feedback resistor, thereby building up a potential e_{out}. Examples of this current-to-voltage conversion appear in Figs. 3-20 and 3-21 in connection with photomultipliers and phototubes.

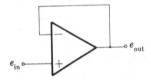

Figure 27-16 Potential measurement with an op amp, the voltage follower circuit. If $A \gg 1$, then $e_{out} = e_{in}$.

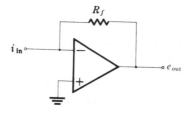

Figure 27-17 An op amp for current measurement. If $A \gg 1$, then $e_{\text{out}} = -R_f i_{\text{in}}$.

PHOTOCELLS

There are several types of semiconductor phototransducers. The most generally useful for light-measuring purposes is the *silicon pin photodiode*. This is fabricated on a thin wafer of *intrinsic* silicon (i.e., the pure, undoped element) with two heavily doped regions, *p* type on the front surface, where the radiation is incident, and *n* type on the back. Boron and phosphorus are appropriate dopants. The *pin* structure is preferable to the simpler *pn*, in that it permits high bias voltages to be applied without breakdown, and this favors a wide dynamic range.

The operation of a photocell of this type can be described by the family of characteristic curves of Fig. 27-18. In the area to the right of the origin (first quadrant) the cell acts as a photoconductive device. In this mode the photocurrent is a linear function of illumination. The second quadrant corresponds to operation in the photovoltaic mode, which means that the cell acts as a generator of electrical energy, and the output is no longer linear. The straight lines numbered 1, 2, and 3,

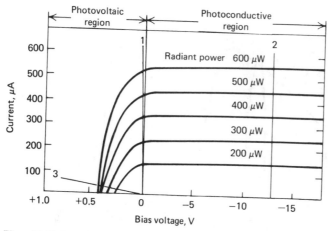

Figure 27-18 Current-voltage characteristic curves for a silicon photodiode; the load lines 1, 2, and 3, are discussed in the text. (*United Detector Technology.*)

correspond to three possible operating conditions: (1) with no bias voltage applied and with nearly zero series resistance in the measuring circuit, resulting in good linearity and zero dark current; (2) with a negative bias and a high resistance load, giving increased response speed; and (3) with zero bias and a high resistance load, producing a response proportional to the logarithm of the illumination.

Selenium cells, sometimes called *barrier-layer cells*, are limited to photovoltaic response. They were formerly employed extensively in filter photometers and fluorimeters, but have been displaced in newer designs by silicon diodes. Selenium cells have larger temperature coefficients and they suffer from "fatigue" effects, a lessening of sensitivity with time when exposed to light.

Photoconductive cells, showing no photovoltaic properties, are made of sulfides or selenides of lead or cadmium. CdS and CdSe cells are widely used for all sorts of applications in control and measurement where the greater sensitivity of silicon photodiodes is not required. PbS cells are the detectors of choice for the near IR, and are widely used in spectrophotometers in this region.

A number of combination semiconductor units are available, such as *photo-transistors* and *photo-FETs*, wherein the control function of the transistor is taken over by radiation. Their characteristics are similar to those of photodiodes with greater sensitivity, due to the built-in gain. A recent development is the fabrication of a linear array of a large number of photodiodes packed close together on a single substrate. This permits simultaneous observation of radiant intensity at successive points in the focal plane of a spectrometer. It can be used to simulate rapid scanning of a spectrum, or, in connection with a multichannel analyzer, to allow integration of a spectrum over a period of time.

Figure 27-19 gives the spectral response of several types of photosensitive devices. Vacuum phototubes and photomultipliers are described in Chap. 3.

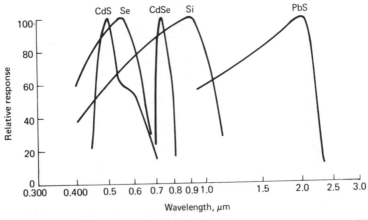

Figure 27-19 Wavelength response of typical photocells of various kinds. The CdS, CdSe, and PbS cells are photoconductive, whereas the Se and Si are photovoltaic.

MULTIPLE AMPLIFIER CIRCUITS

The polarographic circuit of Fig. 16-10 is an example of a complex instrument that can be easily assembled from standard op amps. A still more involved piece of electrochemical equipment is the controlled-potential coulometer shown in Fig. 27-20. In this instrument, three electrical quantities are of interest: the potential of the working electrode with respect to a reference, the current passing between working and auxiliary electrodes, and the number of coulombs required to carry out a chemical process. All these quantities can be controlled or observed with the circuitry shown.

Notice first that the working electrode is connected directly to a virtual ground point, the summing junction of amplifier 2. Therefore, to maintain a desired voltage between working and reference electrodes, the reference electrode must be held at a point away from ground. This is accomplished by amplifier 1, which forces the electrode to assume the manually selected potential E_{set}, which can be read from the panel voltmeter V. Amplifier 1 delivers as much current to the auxiliary electrode as it needs to maintain the desired condition through control of the electrochemical reaction at the working electrode. The current flowing

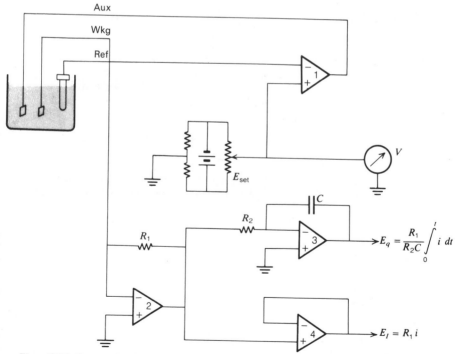

Figure 27-20 Op amp circuitry for controlled-potential coulometry. The reference potential, working current, and coulombs passed can be monitored simultaneously.

through the working electrode must successively pass through resistors R_1 and R_2, where it charges the integrating capacitor C in the feedback of amplifier 3. The output E_Q of this amplifier is thus proportional to the time-integral of the current, and hence to the quantity of charge passed. A voltage follower, amplifier 4, provides a measure of the electrode current.

SINE-WAVE OSCILLATORS

A source of alternating current, in addition to line frequency, is sometimes needed in laboratory instruments, and is most conveniently obtained by means of an electronic oscillator. In principle, any amplifier can be converted into an oscillator by providing a positive feedback path with a suitable frequency characteristic. This means returning part of the ac output to the input through a frequency-selective network, with such phase relations as to amplify signals at the desired frequency while attenuating all other frequencies.

Figure 27-21 shows one of many circuits that will do this, the Hartley oscillator. The feedback from output to input takes place through the mutual inductance of the inductor L. The frequency of oscillation is given, in hertz, by

$$f = \frac{1}{2\pi\sqrt{LC}} \tag{27-11}$$

where L is expressed in henries and C in farads. The frequency is conveniently altered by a change in the capacitance.

Another way in which the frequency can be fixed is by the use of an RC network such as the *twin-tee filter* shown in Fig. 27-22a. This filter will pass all frequencies *except* that given by the formula

$$f_0 = \frac{1}{2\pi RC} \tag{27-12}$$

A plot of impedance as a function of frequency shows a very sharp peak (Fig. 27-22b), the sharpness depending on how accurately the resistors and capacitors

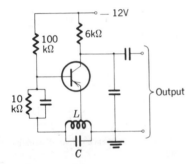

Figure 27-21 A Hartley oscillator circuit.

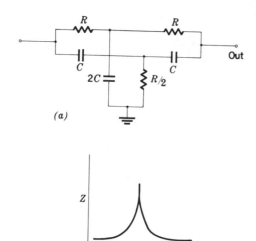

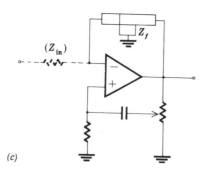

Figure 27-22 (*a*) A twin-tee rejection filter, for which the characteristic frequency is given by $f_0 = 1/(2\pi RC)$ Hz. (*b*) The impedance of the filter as a function of frequency. (*c*) An op amp oscillator with twin-tee feedback.

are matched. If this network is connected in the feedback loop of an op amp (Fig. 27-22*c*), then the net gain, $G = Z_f/Z_{in}$ will be low for all frequencies other than f_0, but high at this frequency. An unshielded summing junction will pick up enough noise at random frequencies to constitute an input (shown dashed in the figure), and this will cause oscillations to start at the filter frequency. To sustain oscillation, a small, untuned, positive feedback is injected at the noninverting input, via capacitor C_f. This oscillator is convenient for use at a fixed frequency, but is not readily made variable.

Highly accurate fixed-frequency oscillators are best built around a quartz crystal. A small wafer cut from a large crystal will vibrate at a characteristic frequency determined by its dimensions, when electrically energized through metallic electrodes mounted on opposite faces. Since the temperature coefficient of expansion of crystalline quartz is very small, the frequency of an oscillator using

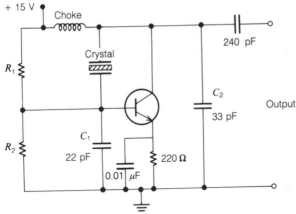

Figure 27-23 A circuit for a crystal-controlled oscillator. The resistors R_1 and R_2 establish the correct dc bias for the transistor. The capacitors C_1 and C_2 determine the feedback ratio. The ac produced is isolated from the power supply by a small inductor called a "choke."

a properly cut wafer is nearly independent of temperature. Frequencies attainable range from about 10 kHz to perhaps 50 MHz. Crystal oscillators are usually built with a single transistor (Fig. 27-23). Op amps are seldom suitable because of their limited high-frequency response.

SERVOMECHANISMS

An instrument servo system, in its most common form, consists of a small motor, either dc or two-phase ac, controlled in speed and direction by an amplifier. The system is provided with some sort of feedback, so that the turning of the motor produces a voltage which can be automatically compared with a standard or reference potential. The difference, called the *error signal*, is increased in power by the amplifier, and controls the motor in such a sense as to reduce the error to zero.

A servo may be included wherever a mechanical effect must be proportional to a varying signal. An example is its use in a recording spectrophotometer to control the slit width. The beam of radiation passing through the reference cuvet serves as the signal to maintain the transmitted energy constant as the spectrum is scanned. Another application is in the self-balancing strip-chart recorder, described in the next section.

AUTOMATIC RECORDERS[2]

Most electronic recorders for use with laboratory instruments operate on a null servo principle. An example is diagrammed in Fig. 27-24. The potential to be recorded, E_x, is connected in series opposition with a voltage E_p picked off from a

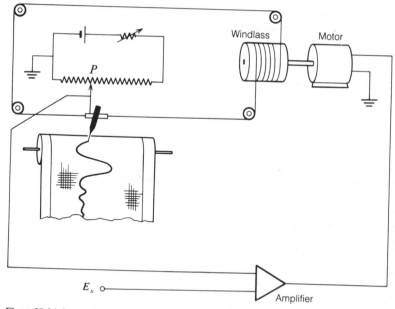

Figure 27-24 Servo system for a strip-chart recorder. The motor-driven carriage moves both the sliding contact on the voltage divider and the recording pen. (*From Ref. 1.*)

variable resistor P, called the *rebalance potentiometer*. With the polarities indicated in the figure, if $E_p > E_x$, the potential at point A will be negative, and if $E_p < E_x$, it will be positive. This voltage controls the direction of rotation of a small permanent-magnet dc servo motor. The motor has two functions: it drives the rebalance potentiometer to the point where $E_p = E_x$, and it moves the pen across the chart. The position of the pen will track accurately changes in E_x up to a limit set by the speed of response of the mechanical system. Most modern servo recorders can move the pen across the chart in as short a time as 1 s, many in half this time.

DIGITAL ELECTRONICS

The signals processed by the electronic circuits so far described are *analog* in nature, meaning that they are permitted to assume any values over a wide range, limited only by the properties of the electronic devices concerned. Computers, however, operate on *digital* signals, with values restricted to two levels, ON and OFF. In the systems of interest to us, these values are nominally 0 and $+5\,\mathrm{V}$, respectively. The computer is not able to respond to an intermediate level such as $+2\,\mathrm{V}$; a negative voltage, or a positive one much larger than $+5\,\mathrm{V}$ may well damage the computer. Hence to prepare the way for a study of computers in analytical instruments, we must look into some digital devices, and converters that bridge the gap between analog and digital domains.

Logic Gates

A "gate" is a device that controls the passage of a signal; those that we are presently concerned with do so as the result of logical commands. There are three basic types, called AND, OR, and INVERT. Their actions are conveniently described by means of *truth tables*. Figure 27-25 shows an AND gate with three inputs (A, B, and C) and one output. The accompanying truth table shows that for all inputs equal to 1, the output is also 1, but in all other cases it is zero. (The digits 1 and 0 are often used this way, as the equivalents of HIGH and LOW, respectively, but in manufacturers' literature the letters H and L are sometimes used instead; either 1 or H stands for a signal level of $+5$ V.

Figures 27-26 and 27-27 show in a similar manner the OR and INVERT gates. Both AND and OR gates can in principle have any number of inputs, but the inverter can have only one.

The function of the inverter can be combined with either AND or OR gates to give the logic functions called NAND and NOR, respectively (Figs. 27-28 and 27-29).

Each of these gates could be implemented with one or two discrete transistors (plus suitable ancillary components), but in practice are fabricated as ICs, usually with several gates in one module. The two series of gates most widely used are called TTL (for *t*ransistor-*t*ransistor *l*ogic) and CMOS (for *c*omplementary *m*etal *o*xide *s*emiconductor). CMOS gates use less power than TTL, but until recently have been slower in response because of their greater input capacitance.

Logic gates can be combined with each other by direct connection, to perform more complex functions. An example is given in Fig. 27-30, a circuit called the *exclusive-OR* (XOR) gate. The truth table is derived by listing the states at the

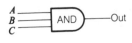

A	B	C	Out
0	0	0	0
0	0	1	0
0	1	0	0
0	1	1	0
1	0	0	0
1	0	1	0
1	1	0	0
1	1	1	1

Figure 27-25 A three-input logical AND gate and its truth table.

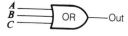

A	B	C	Out
0	0	0	0
0	0	1	1
0	1	0	1
0	1	1	1
1	0	0	1
1	0	1	1
1	1	0	1
1	1	1	1

Figure 27-26 A three-input logical OR gate and its truth table.

A	Out
1	0
0	1

Figure 27-27 A logical inverter and its truth table.

A	B	C	Out
0	0	0	1
0	0	1	1
0	1	0	1
0	1	1	1
1	0	0	1
1	0	1	1
1	1	0	1
1	1	1	0

Figure 27-28 A three-input logical NAND gate with its truth table.

A	B	C	Out
0	0	0	1
0	0	1	0
0	1	0	0
0	1	1	0
1	0	0	0
1	0	1	0
1	1	0	0
1	1	1	0

Figure 27-29 A three-input logical NOR gate with its truth table.

intermediate points P and Q, then combining these to give the output. The exclusive-OR is a particularly useful combination, giving a high output if either input is high, but not if *both* inputs are high.

Flip-Flops, Counters, and Registers

"Flip-flop" is the name given to a circuit that consists, in its simplest form, of two gates (either NAND or NOR), interconnected as in Fig. 27-31. The letters S and R (for *set* and *reset*) designate inputs, while Q and $\bar{Q}$ are outputs. (The bar notation is taken from boolean algebra; $\bar{Q}$ is read "Q-bar," or "not-Q," and means that in whatever state Q may be, $\bar{Q}$ is the opposite.)

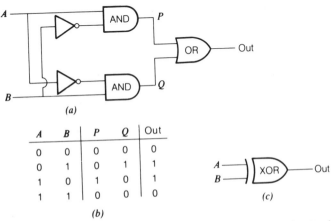

A	B	P	Q	Out
0	0	0	0	0
0	1	0	1	1
1	0	1	0	1
1	1	0	0	0

(b)

Figure 27-30 A logical EXCLUSIVE-OR gate (*a*) assembled from unit gates, (*b*) its truth table, and (*c*) its symbol.

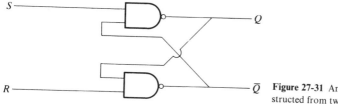

Figure 27-31 An RS-flip-flop constructed from two NAND gates.

In normal operation, both R and S inputs are kept at logic 1. Momentary transition to 0 at the S input produces $Q = 1$ and $\bar{Q} = 0$, whereas a momentary grounding of R produces $Q = 0$ and $\bar{Q} = 1$. Both states are stable. (Note that the Q output can be *set* to 1 or *reset* to 0.) After the circuit is set, subsequent changes in S are immaterial. The same holds true for the reset mode. If R and S are both made zero, then Q and $\bar{Q}$ will both become 1; on returning both inputs simultaneously to 1, the outputs will unpredictably go to either set or reset, hence this action must be avoided.

Another variety of flip-flop, the *D-flip-flop*, is shown in Fig. 27-32. This consists of an *RS*-flip-flop with the addition of two more NAND gates and an inverter at the input. The C input is connected to a *clock*, which gives a train of pulses to provide a timing signal. Analysis of the circuit demonstrates that a signal (1 or 0) presented to the D ("data") input will appear at the Q output as soon as a clock pulse is received. Q will then remain unchanged during the time that the clock is HIGH. This circuit is widely used as a *data latch*, to retain one bit of data in its memory long enough to be utilized by some other circuit.

Consider, for example, a digital voltmeter: it can respond almost instantly to a change in its input signal, but a second or more is necessary for an observer's eye to recognize the reading. An array of data latches clocked at one pulse per 2 or 3 s will freeze a particular value long enough to be read, before updating it.

Yet another related circuit is the *J-K master/slave flip-flop*. This unit actually contains two interconnected *D*-flip-flops (Fig. 27-33). The incoming bit of data at J or K is passed on to the first (the master) flip-flop (gates 3 and 4) only when the clock goes high. It is then transferred to the second (slave) flip-flop (gates 7 and 8) at the instant when the clock goes low. Signals can also be entered directly

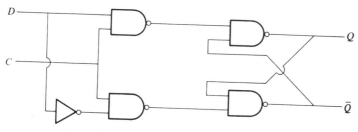

Figure 27-32 A D-type flip-flop constructed from gates.

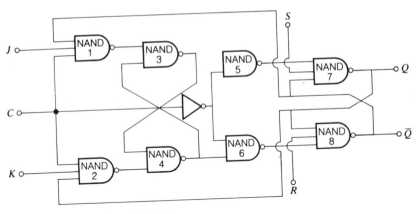

Figure 27-33 A master-slave JK-flip-flop.

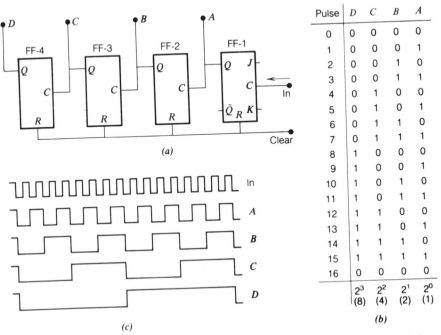

Pulse	D	C	B	A
0	0	0	0	0
1	0	0	0	1
2	0	0	1	0
3	0	0	1	1
4	0	1	0	0
5	0	1	0	1
6	0	1	1	0
7	0	1	1	1
8	1	0	0	0
9	1	0	0	1
10	1	0	1	0
11	1	0	1	1
12	1	1	0	0
13	1	1	0	1
14	1	1	1	0
15	1	1	1	1
16	0	0	0	0
	2^3	2^2	2^1	2^0
	(8)	(4)	(2)	(1)

(a)

(c)

(b)

Figure 27-34 (a) 4-bit binary counter made up of JK-flip-flops, (b) is truth table, and (c) its timing diagram.

to the slave unit by connections R and S. This versatile flip-flop has the advantage that because of the master–slave relation, signals stored temporarily in the master cannot be effected by nor have any effect upon data present in the slave.

Flip-flops can be cascaded in strings, called *registers*, that enable them to accomplish specific tasks. A *binary counter*, for example, can be constructed from a series of J-K flip-flops, as in Fig. 27-34. (The J and K inputs are not utilized but must be connected to $+5$ V.) Each clock pulse causes a transition of the Q output of FF-1, either $1 \to 0$ or $0 \to 1$. This signal is applied to the input of FF-2, and so along the chain, cutting the frequency in half for each step, as shown in b of the figure. The signal values at each output, A to D, are listed in the table (c). Output A corresponds to the *least significant bit* (LSB), and D to the *most significant bit* (MSB). This table provides an example of binary counting, as contrasted with the familiar decimal counting. Thus the table shows that decimal 6 is equivalent to

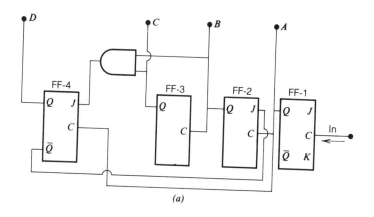

(a)

Pulses	D	C	B	A
0	0	0	0	0
1	0	0	0	1
2	0	0	1	0
3	0	0	1	1
4	0	1	0	0
5	0	1	0	1
6	0	1	1	0
7	0	1	1	1
8	1	0	0	0
9	1	0	0	1
(10)	0	0	0	0

(b)

Figure 27-35 (*a*) A 4-bit BCD decade counter constructed as a modification of the counter of Fig. 27-34. (*b*) Its truth table.

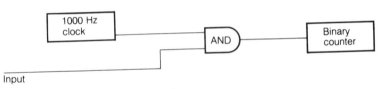

Figure 27-36 A binary counter used as a timer.

binary 0110 ($6_{10} = 0110_2$). The conversion of a binary number to its decimal equivalent can be carried out readily by reference to the powers-of-2 series shown below the table. The binary number 0110 can be expressed decimally as (0×2^3) + $(1 \times 2^2) + (1 \times 2^1) + (0 \times 2^0) = 0 + 4 + 2 + 0 = 6$. For numbers greater than 15 a fifth bit is needed with the value of 2^4, and one more flip-flop must be added to the register.

A binary counter can be converted to a decimal readout by a change in connections plus an added AND gate leading to the J-input of FF-4, as in Fig. 27-35. A property of the J-input is that when it is grounded (i.e., at level zero), it forces the Q output to zero and $\bar{Q}$ to 1, whereas if it is high, it permits counting to continue. Hence the connections shown in the figure will cause the count to return to 0000 following the ninth count. This type of counter is known as BCD, for binary coded decimal. The four outputs can be connected to a series of gates that produce seven parallel signals to energize the appropriate portions of a 7-segment luminous display, as found in many laboratory instruments.

A counting register can be used as a *timer*, either to measure the elapsed time between two events or to cause an event to occur at a predetermined time. The former function can be implemented with an AND gate, Fig. 27-36. The counter will display in milliseconds the time during which the input to the gate is high. For longer times a slower clock rate would be more convenient; a 1-Hz clock, for instance, would give a readout directly in seconds.

Establishing a precisely timed sequence of events can be done with a counting register and a series of AND gates wired to select various combinations of Q and $\bar{Q}$ outputs from successive stages. For detailed description, see pp. 222–225 of Ref. 1.

INTERDOMAIN CONVERSIONS

We will now examine the major components that perform the actual conversion of analog signals to their digital counterparts and the reverse. There are many different circuits for carrying out these conversions, and we will only describe one of each type. For more detailed discussions, see Refs. 3 and 4.

A common type of *digital-to-analog* (D/A) converter is diagrammed in Fig. 27-37. A series of electronic switches corresponding to the digits of a binary number connect a reference voltage to successive segments of a "ladder" resistor network

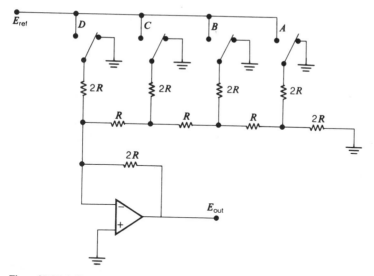

Figure 27-37 A digital-to-analog (D/A) converter using an $R/2R$ resistive ladder network.

leading to an op amp. Analysis shows that the output of the circuit of Fig. 27-37 is given by

$$E_{out} = -E_{ref}\left(D + \frac{C}{2^1} + \frac{B}{2^2} + \frac{A}{2^3}\right) \qquad (27\text{-}13)$$

where the letters A to D correspond to switch positions that are "0" when the resistor is grounded, or "1" with the resistor connected to E_{ref}. For this "4-bit" converter, it is convenient to use 8.000 V for E_{ref}, as this will give an output equal in volts to the decimal equivalent of the binary number. Thus 0110_2 gives $E_{out} = 8(0 + 0.5 + 0.25 + 0) = 6$ V. Additional segments in the ladder permit increased precision by accommodating more bits of digital information.

Figure 27-38 gives a circuit for an *analog-to-digital* (A/D) converter. It consists of a binary counter and a D/A converter, together with an R/S flip-flop and other control components. Momentarily grounding the "ready" line resets both the flip-flop and the counter. Upon release of the ready switch, Q goes high, permitting the clock pulses to propagate into the counter. The counter proceeds to increment its output to higher and higher count until the voltage $E_{feedback}$, produced by the D/A equals the analog input, as sensed by a *comparator*. This latter component is essentially an op amp lacking a negative feedback path; its output is always at its maximum value, either positive or negative. In the present case the output is bounded by the two diodes, which prevent it from going either negative or more positive than $+5$ V. When $E_{feedback}$ becomes great enough to exceed the input voltage, the output of the comparator abruptly changes from zero to $+5$ V. This sends Q low and freezes the action of the clock. The output of the counter is then

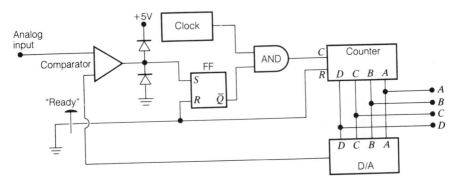

Figure 27-38 An analog-to-digital (A/D) converter.

the binary number that the D/A converter recognizes as being the equivalent of the input voltage.

We have now given some consideration to the principal components that are required to interface a laboratory instrument to a computer. The next chapter will suggest some ways in which this can be accomplished.

PROBLEMS

27-1 In the circuit of Fig. 27-11, let $e_1 = +200$ mV, $e_2 = +700$ mV, $e_3 = -500$ mV, $R_1 = 2$ kΩ, $R_2 = 1.4$ kΩ, $R_3 = 10$ kΩ, and $R_f = 10$ kΩ; calculate the value of the output voltage, e_{out}. What would be the result of changing R_f to 100 kΩ while keeping the other values unchanged?

27-2 The technique of biamperometric titration, discussed in Chap. 16, requires impressing a small constant voltage across a cell while monitoring the current. An analogous titration procedure calls for passing a small constant current through the cell while measuring the potential. Design op amp circuits to implement both of these techniques.

27-3 Design an op amp circuit for implementing the equation

$$e_{out} = kXY^n$$

where X and Y are two variable voltages, n is a variable parameter, and k is a numerical constant. The circuit can be based on Figs. 27-13 and 27-14.

27-4 An IR spectrophotometer has a rotating shutter that chops the radiation at 17 Hz. The signal amplifier system includes two twin-tee filters, tuned to frequencies of 17 and 60 Hz, arranged as in Fig. 27-39. In which positions should the two filters be placed? Explain their functions in the circuit.

27-5 Write truth tables for the two gate circuits of Fig. 27-40.

27-6 The circuit of Fig. 27-41 can act as a BCD counter, just as can that of Fig. 27-35 (though it may be slower acting). Explain how it works.

27-7 What is the difference in operation of flip-flops using the circuit of Fig. 27-31 and a similar one in which the NAND gates have been replaced by NOR gates?

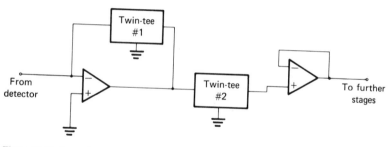

Figure 27-39 A tuned amplifier (see Prob. 27-4).

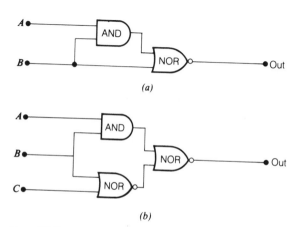

Figure 27-40 Logical networks for Prob. 27-5.

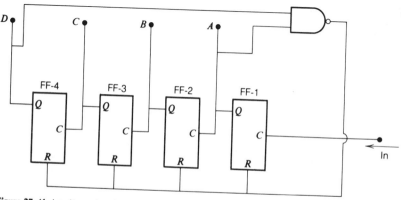

Figure 27-41 An alternative circuit for a BCD counter (see Prob. 27-6).

REFERENCES

1. B. H. Vassos and G. W. Ewing, *Analog and Digital Electronics for Scientists* (2d ed.), Wiley-Interscience, New York, **1980**.
2. G. W. Ewing and H. A. Ashworth, *The Laboratory Recorder*, Plenum Press, New York, **1974**.
3. E. L. Zuch (ed.), *Data Acquisition and Conversion Handbook*, Datel-Intersil, Inc., Mansfield, MA, **1980**.
4. D. H. Sheingold (ed.), *Analog-Digital Conversion Notes*, Analog Devices, Inc., Norwood, MA, **1977**.

TWENTY-EIGHT

COMPUTERS IN ANALYTICAL INSTRUMENTATION

One of the most significant advances in instrumentation has only been hinted at in previous chapters: the integration of a computing capability into the basic instrument. This is far too complex a matter to deal with exhaustively in this book. The most we can do here is to summarize some of the most important features.

The student in an instrumental analysis laboratory is likely to encounter computers in several different situations. Many, perhaps the majority, of modern analytical instruments have built-in microprocessors, together with as much memory as may be needed. The "program," or "software" required to operate the instrument has been provided by the manufacturer, and all the user must do is to introduce the specific parameters appropriate to the application at hand.

Another point of contact with computers involves interfacing instruments to a stand-alone unit of the type often referred to as a "personal computer." This situation is becoming more and more common, so we will discuss it in some detail. But first we will give some consideration to the fundamental nature of a computer.

COMPUTER ARCHITECTURE

Most digital computers are built on the same fundamental plan, as diagrammed in Fig. 28-1. The component designated by CPU, the *central processing unit*, is the heart of the computer, where the essential logical decisions are made. All other parts of the computer are attached to the CPU and subordinate to it. These include

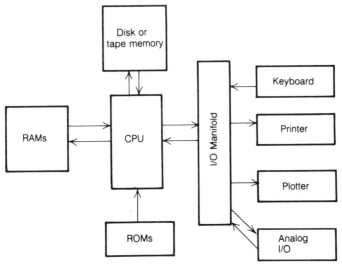

Figure 28-1 Architecture of a typical computer.

most of the storage area devoted to memory, and the input/output (I/O) peripheral devices.

Memory in a computer is of three different types. Every computer must have *random access* memory (RAM), which it uses for temporary storage of programs and data. "Random" in this context means that items of information can be placed in any vacant spot, and can be retrieved at will. A second kind of memory, *read-only* memory (ROM), is loaded with information during manufacture, and cannot be changed by the user. Simple, frequently used, programs are stored in ROMs. An example is the sequence of steps necessary to extract square roots. An important ROM is one that is programmed to initialize all parts of the computer when the power is first turned on, to make sure that all circuits are ready for operation.

A third type of memory is permanent *magnetic storage*, on disks or tape. This kind of memory requires mechanical drive mechanisms, and is usually considered to be part of the peripheral equipment rather than a part of the computer per se. Information stored in RAM is "volatile," which means that it is lost if the power is interrupted, which is not true of ROM or magnetic storage.

The I/O peripherals most often encountered are a keyboard for manual introduction of both commands and data, a printer for hard-copy presentation of results, and a plotter for producing a graphic record. Two or all three of these functions are sometimes combined in one device. A video screen may also be provided for convenience in programming, and for viewing results prior to printing. Of particular interest to laboratory instrumentation, a number of channels may be provided for accepting data directly from transducers and for sending commands to external instruments. It is this last class of I/O devices that we will treat next.

COMPUTER INTERFACING

The majority of transducers, as we have seen, give analog signals functionally related to the chemical quantity of interest. This can be translated into its digital equivalent by means of the A/D converters described in the previous chapter. Any one instrument will usually require several separate transducers. An ultra-violet spectrophotometer, for instance, would need not only the photomultiplier (perhaps two of them), but also devices to report to the computer the status of the slit-width control and the wavelength setting. The latter two might be digital in nature, rather than analog, but typically there will be several analog signals that must be converted to digital. This calls for a *multiplexer*, a unit that can accept several inputs and transmit them one at a time, in sequence, to the computer. Some multiplexers will control analog signals, while others are designed for digital signals.

The interface designer is presented with two options: he can use separate A/D converters for the analog channels and sort out the signals with a digital multi-plexer, or alternatively he can multiplex the analog signals and require only a single A/D converter. In principle, the results will be equally valid either way. In practice, if all units are physically close together (inside the same instrument case), it is more economical to use the analog multiplexer and one converter. However, if the transducers are at some distance from the computer, the system will function better if the cables connecting the instrument to the computer carry only digital signals (because the effect of noise pickup will be less), and so it may be worth the extra expense to install separate converters close to the transducers and to feed the digital outputs to a multiplexer in the computer.

The computer and its peripherals interchange information through a com-munications link called a *bus*. This is actually a set of conductors that can be connected to each module through a three-state buffer, a device that has the ability to transmit digital signals in one direction or the other or not at all, hence the designation "three-state." A command from the CPU will tell the buffer which mode it should assume at any point in an operation. An address code determines which of the many units connected to the bus should be activated.

As an example, a spectrophotometer might have four or more I/O units connected to the bus, besides the CPU, as in Fig. 28-2. In order to make the appropriate sensitivity settings, the CPU needs to acquire several items of in-formation from the instrument, and so it will command the buffers in sequence to transmit information to it. It might first turn ON the buffer connected to the wavelength indicator, enabling it to transmit in the incoming direction, while at the same time turning OFF the slit, PMT, and recorder buffers. The CPU will receive the information it needs about the wavelength setting, and will store this information in temporary RAM memory. It will then reset the buffers to obtain information from the slit indicator, and so on. As a result of using the information so received, the CPU may sense, on the basis of the instructions contained in its program, that the slit needs adjustment to bring the signal within reasonable limits; it will then open the "slit motor" buffer to allow a correction signal to

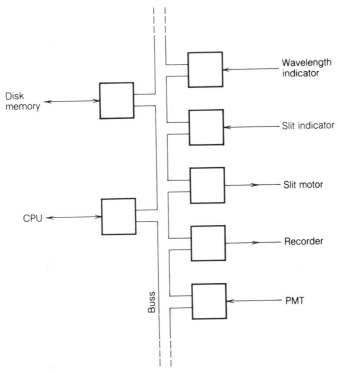

Figure 28-2 Buss structure of a computer-controlled spectrophotometer.

pass, and at the same time reverse the CPU buffer to allow a signal to flow in the outward direction. The next step might be to read the output of the PMT and pass it to the recorder.

Clearly, all signals must be carefully encoded to avoid ambiguity. Precise timing and sequencing of commands is essential.

COMPLETE INTERFACES

It is possible for the user to design and build his own interface. Several books are available that give detailed directions for doing this.[1,2,3] Interfacing to the inexpensive Sinclair ZX81 (or Timex Sinclair 1000) has been described recently, and might make a good place to start such a project.[4]

There are a number of complete interface units available commercially. One of these, the "Isaac," made by Cyborg Corporation, is dedicated to use with the Apple II computer, and can accept as many as 16 analog input channels and provide 4 analog output ports for controlling instrument parameters. Less expensive interfaces, that can be used with nearly any computers, are manufactured by a number of concerns; some of these lack the ability to control experiments.

PROGRAMMING

Once the interface connecting an instrument to the computer has been constructed, it is necessary to provide detailed operating instructions. This can be done by means of a program given to the computer in the form of software. Since the computer can only accept digital commands, and since people normally use only highly structured languages such as English, a method must be established for communication. This is done by means of a computer "language."

Few operators choose to learn the system of notation that comes naturally to the computer, namely *machine language*, to write programs. This would be economical in terms of the amount of computer memory required, but programming in machine language is a slow and tedious process. It is usually preferable to go to *assembly language*, which makes use of a series of three-letter mnemonics, each of which is translated into machine language by an internal program, called an "assembler," supplied by the computer manufacturer. This is easier on the programmer, although it uses more memory space.

For the computer user who is not a programming expert, neither machine nor assembly language is very practical. He should undertake to master one of the higher level languages such as BASIC, FORTRAN, or PASCAL. Probably BASIC is the best choice, at least as a start. Programs written in these languages are converted to machine codes by a "compiler." More memory is required than for assembly language.

These languages utilize commands that are structured more nearly like human languages, and hence are easier to learn and use. The scientist who does not know at least the rudiments of programming in one of these is working under a handicap. There are many excellent books available on programming in various languages, that will serve as a useful introduction.

CAVEAT

The microcomputer is undoubtedly a boon to instrument designers and users, but it carries with it a risk factor. The machine works so beautifully, and the numerical or printed results look so convincing, that there is a real temptation to accept the answers as valid without taking enough care to be sure that the underlying chemistry is equally correct. For example, in the majority of analyses, it is essential to run standards alternately with samples, but the computer may not tell you to do that. An excellent discussion of such factors, as applied to AA, has been published recently by Koirtyohann,[5] in a discussion that applies equally well to other analytical methods.

On the other hand, the computer should take care of the routines of data processing to such an extent that the analyst can devote his time and thought to the fundamental chemistry of the process that he is using.

REFERENCES

1. J. T. Arnold, *Simplified Digital Automation with Microprocessors*, Academic Press, New York, **1979**.
2. B. A. Artwick, *Microcomputer Interfacing*, Prentice-Hall, Englewood Cliffs, N. J., **1980**.
3. D. Barnaal, *Digital and Microprocessor Electronics for Scientific Application*, Breton Publishers, North Scituate, Mass., **1982**.
4. D. C. Webster, *Am. Lab.*, **1983**, *15*(2), 48.
5. S. R. Koirtyohann, *Anal. Chem.*, **1980**, *52*, 736A.

STANDARD REDUCTION POTENTIALS†

Electrode	Reaction	$E°, V$ versus SHE
F_2, F^-	$F_2 + 2e^- \rightarrow 2F^-$	+2.85
Co^{3+}, Co^{2+}, Pt	$Co^{3+} + e^- \rightarrow Co^{2+}$	+1.84
Au^+, Au	$Au^+ + e^- \rightarrow Au$	+1.68
Ce^{4+}, Ce^{3+}, Pt	$Ce^{4+} + e^- \rightarrow Ce^{3+}$	+1.46
MnO_4^-, Mn^{2+}, Pt	$MnO_4^- + 8H^+ + 5e^- \rightarrow Mn^{2+} + 4H_2O$	+1.49
Au^{3+}, Au	$Au^{3+} + 3e^- \rightarrow Au$	+1.42
Cl_2, Cl^-	$Cl_2 + 2e^- \rightarrow 2Cl^-$	+1.360
$Cr_2O_7^{2-}$, Cr^{3+}, Pt	$Cr_2O_7^{2-} + 14H^+ + 6e^- \rightarrow 2Cr^{3+} + 7H_2O$	+1.33
Tl^{3+}, Tl^+, Pt	$Tl^{3+} + 2e^- \rightarrow Tl^+$	+1.25
O_2, H_2O	$O_2 + 4H^+ + 4e^- \rightarrow 2H_2O$	+1.229
Pt^{2+}, Pt	$Pt^{2+} + 2e^- \rightarrow Pt$	+1.2
Br_2, Br^-	$Br_2(liq) + 2e^- \rightarrow 2Br^-$	+1.065
Hg^{2+}, Hg_2^{2+}, Pt	$2Hg^{2+} + 2e^- \rightarrow Hg_2^{2+}$	+0.905
Ag^+, Ag	$Ag^+ + e^- \rightarrow Ag$	+0.800
Hg_2^{2+}, Hg	$Hg_2^{2+} + 2e^- \rightarrow 2Hg$	+0.799
Fe^{3+}, Fe^{2+}, Pt	$Fe^{3+} + e^- \rightarrow Fe^{2+}$	+0.770
Ag_2SO_4, Ag	$Ag_2SO_4 + 2e^- \rightarrow Ag + SO_4^{2-}$	+0.653
		Continued

† From data compiled by J. F. Hunsberger, in *Handbook of Chemistry and Physics*, 58th ed., CRC Press, West Palm Beach, FL. p. D-141.

Electrode	Reaction	$E°$, V versus SHE
$AgC_2H_3O_2$, Ag	$AgC_2H_3O_2 + e^- \rightarrow Ag + C_2H_3O_2^-$	$+0.64$
I_2, I^-	$I_2 + 2e^- \rightarrow 2I^-$	$+0.535$
Cu^+, Cu	$Cu^+ + e^- \rightarrow Cu$	$+0.522$
Ag_2CrO_4, Ag	$Ag_2CrO_4 + 2e^- \rightarrow 2Ag + CrO_4^{2-}$	$+0.446$
VO^{2+}, V^{3+}, Pt	$VO^{2+} + 2H^+ + e^- \rightarrow V^{3+} + H_2O$	$+0.337$
$Fe(CN)_6^{3-}$, $Fe(CN)_6^{4-}$, Pt	$Fe(CN)_6^{3-} + e^- \rightarrow Fe(CN)_6^{4-}$	$+0.46$
Cu^{2+}, Cu	$Cu^{2+} + 2e^- \rightarrow Cu$	$+0.340$
UO_2^{2+}, U^{4+}, Pt	$UO_2^{2+} + 4H^+ + 2e^- \rightarrow U^{4+} + H_2O$	$+0.334$
Hg_2Cl_2, Hg	$Hg_2Cl_2 + 2e^- \rightarrow 2Hg + 2Cl^-$	$+0.268$
AgCl, Ag	$AgCl + e^- \rightarrow Ag + Cl^-$	$+0.222$
$HgBr_4^{2-}$, Hg	$HgBr_4^{2-} + 2e^- \rightarrow Hg + 4Br^-$	$+0.21$
Cu^{2+}, Cu^+, Pt	$Cu^{2+} + e^- \rightarrow Cu^+$	$+0.158$
Sn^{4+}, Sn^{2+}, Pt	$Sn^{4+} + 2e^- \rightarrow Sn^{2+}$	$+0.15$
Hg_2Br_2, Hg	$Hg_2Br_2 + 2e^- \rightarrow 2Hg + 2Br^-$	$+0.140$
CuCl, Cu	$CuCl + e^- \rightarrow Cu + Cl^-$	$+0.137$
TiO^{2+}, Ti^{3+}, Pt	$TiO^{2+} + 2H^+ + e^- \rightarrow Ti^{3+} + H_2O$	$+0.1$
AgBr, Ag	$AgBr + e^- \rightarrow Ag + Br^-$	$+0.071$
UO_2^{2+}, UO_2^+, Pt	$UO_2^{2+} + e^- \rightarrow UO_2^+$	$+0.062$
CuBr, Cu	$CuBr + e^- \rightarrow Cu + Br^-$	$+0.033$
H^+, H_2	$2H^+ + 2e^- \rightarrow H_2$	0.000
HgI_4^{2-}, Hg	$HgI_4^{2-} + 2e^- \rightarrow Hg + 4I^-$	-0.04
Pb^{2+}, Pb	$Pb^{2+} + 2e^- \rightarrow Pb$	-0.126
Sn^{2+}, Sn	$Sn^{2+} + 2e^- \rightarrow Sn$	-0.136
AgI, Ag	$AgI + e^- \rightarrow Ag + I^-$	-0.152
CuI, Cu	$CuI + e^- \rightarrow Cu + I^-$	-0.185
Mo^{3+}, Mo	$Mo^{3+} + 3e^- \rightarrow Mo$	-0.2
Ni^{2+}, Ni	$Ni^{2+} + 2e^- \rightarrow Ni$	-0.23
V^{3+}, V^{2+}, Pt	$V^{3+} + e^- \rightarrow V^{2+}$	-0.255
$PbCl_2$, Pb	$PbCl_2 + 2e^- \rightarrow Pb + 2Cl^-$	-0.268
Co^{2+}, Co	$Co^{2+} + 2e^- \rightarrow Co$	-0.28
$PbBr_2$, Pb	$PbBr_2 + 2e^- \rightarrow Pb + 2Br^-$	-0.280
Tl^+, Tl	$Tl^+ + e^- \rightarrow Tl$	-0.336
$PbSO_4$, Pb	$PbSO_4 + 2e^- \rightarrow Pb + SO_4^{2-}$	-0.356
PbI_2, Pb	$PbI_2 + 2e^- \rightarrow Pb + 2I^-$	-0.365
Ti^{3+}, Ti^{2+}, Pt	$Ti^{3+} + e^- \rightarrow Ti^{2+}$	-0.37
Cd^{2+}, Cd	$Cd^{2+} + 2e^- \rightarrow Cd$	-0.403
Cr^{3+}, Cr^{2+}, Pt	$Cr^{3+} + e^- \rightarrow Cr^{2+}$	-0.41
Fe^{2+}, Fe	$Fe^{2+} + 2e^- \rightarrow Fe$	-0.409
Ga^{3+}, Ga	$Ga^{3+} + 3e^- \rightarrow Ga$	-0.560
TlCl, Tl	$TlCl + e^- \rightarrow Tl + Cl^-$	-0.557
U^{4+}, U^{3+}, Pt	$U^{4+} + e^- \rightarrow U^{3+}$	-0.61
TlBr, Tl	$TlBr + e^- \rightarrow Tl + Br^-$	-0.658
Cr^{3+}, Cr	$Cr^{3+} + 3e^- \rightarrow Cr$	-0.74
TlI, Tl	$TlI + e^- \rightarrow Tl + I^-$	-0.753
Zn^{2+}, Zn	$Zn^{2+} + 2e^- \rightarrow Zn$	-0.763
TiO^{2+}, Ti	$TiO^{2+} + 2H^+ + 4e^- \rightarrow Ti + H_2O$	-0.89
Mn^{2+}, Mn	$Mn^{2+} + 2e^- \rightarrow Mn$	-1.029
V^{2+}, V	$V^{2+} + 2e^- \rightarrow V$	-1.12
Ti^{2+}, Ti	$Ti^{2+} + 2e^- \rightarrow Ti$	-1.63

Continued

Electrode	Reaction	$E°, V$ versus SHE
Al^{3+}, Al	$Al^{3+} + 3e^- \rightarrow Al$	-1.706
U^{3+}, U	$U^{3+} + 3e^- \rightarrow U$	-1.8
Be^{2+}, Be	$Be^{2+} + 2e^- \rightarrow Be$	-1.85
Np^{3+}, Np	$Np^{3+} + 3e^- \rightarrow Np$	-1.9
Th^{4+}, Th	$Th^{4+} + 4e^- \rightarrow Th$	-1.90
Pu^{3+}, Pu	$Pu^{3+} + 3e^- \rightarrow Pu$	-2.07
AlF_6^{3-}, Al	$AlF_6^{3-} + 3e^- \rightarrow Al + 6F^-$	-2.07
Mg^{2+}, Mg	$Mg^{2+} + 2e^- \rightarrow Mg$	-2.375
Ce^{3+}, Ce	$Ce^{3+} + 3e^- \rightarrow Ce$	-2.335
La^{3+}, La	$La^{3+} + 3e^- \rightarrow La$	-2.37
Na^+, Na	$Na^+ + e^- \rightarrow Na$	-2.711
Ca^{2+}, Ca	$Ca^{2+} + 2e^- \rightarrow Ca$	-2.76
Sr^{2+}, Sr	$Sr^{2+} + 2e^- \rightarrow Sr$	-2.89
Ba^{2+}, Ba	$Ba^{2+} + 2e^- \rightarrow Ba$	-2.90
K^+, K	$K^+ + e^- \rightarrow K$	-2.924
Li^+, Li	$Li^+ + e^- \rightarrow Li$	-3.045

B

NUMERICAL PREFIXES FOR UNITS

Factor	Prefix	Symbol	Factor	Prefix	Symbol
10^{18}	exa	E	10^{-1}	deci	d
10^{15}	peta	P	10^{-2}	centi	c
10^{12}	tera	T	10^{-3}	milli	m
10^{9}	giga	G	10^{-6}	micro	μ
10^{6}	mega	M	10^{-9}	nano	n
10^{3}	kilo	k	10^{-12}	pico	p
10^{2}	hecto	h	10^{-15}	femto	f
10^{1}	deka	da	10^{-18}	atto	a

NATURAL CONSTANTS

Speed of light in vacuo	c	$2.9979 \times 10^8 \text{ m} \cdot \text{s}^{-1}$
Electronvolt	eV	$1.6022 \times 10^{-19} \text{ J}$
Planck's constant	h	$6.6262 \times 10^{-34} \text{ J} \cdot \text{s}$
Boltzmann's constant	k	$1.3807 \times 10^{-23} \text{ J} \cdot \text{K}^{-1}$
Faraday's constant	F	$9.6485 \times 10^4 \text{ C} \cdot \text{mol}^{-1}$
Avogadro's number	N	$6.0220 \times 10^{23} \text{ mol}^{-1}$
Gas constant	R	$8.3144 \text{ J} \cdot \text{K}^{-1} \cdot \text{mol}^{-1}$
Electronic charge	e	$1.6022 \times 10^{-19} \text{ C}$
Base of natural logs	e	2.7183
log e		0.4343
ln 10		2.3026

D

GREEK ALPHABET

alpha	A	α		nu	N	ν
beta	B	β		xi	Ξ	ξ
gamma	Γ	γ		omicron	O	o
delta	Δ	δ	∂	pi	Π	π
epsilon	E	ε		rho	P	ρ
zeta	Z	ζ		sigma	Σ	σ
eta	H	η		tau	T	τ
theta	Θ	θ		upsilon	Υ	υ
iota	I	ι		phi	Φ	ϕ
kappa	K	κ		chi	X	χ
lambda	Λ	λ		psi	Ψ	ψ
mu	M	μ		omega	Ω	ω

INDEX